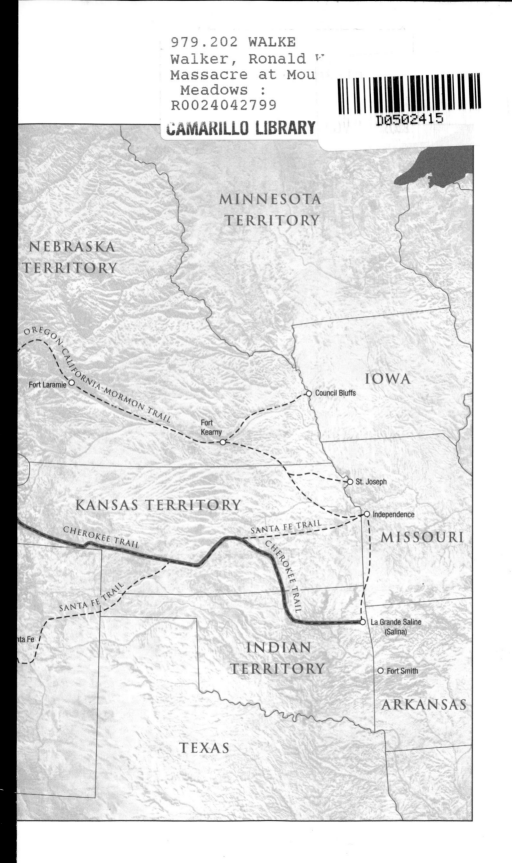

MINNESOTA
TERRITORY

NEBRASKA
TERRITORY

IOWA

OREGON-CALIFORNIA-MORMON TRAIL

Fort Laramie

Council Bluffs

Fort
Kearny

St. Joseph

KANSAS TERRITORY

SANTA FE TRAIL

Independence

CHEROKEE TRAIL

CHEROKEE TRAIL

MISSOURI

SANTA FE TRAIL

La Grande Saline
(Salina)

nta Fe

INDIAN
TERRITORY

Fort Smith

ARKANSAS

TEXAS

MASSACRE AT MOUNTAIN MEADOWS

RONALD W. WALKER

RICHARD E. TURLEY JR.

GLEN M. LEONARD

MASSACRE AT MOUNTAIN MEADOWS

OXFORD
UNIVERSITY PRESS

2008

OXFORD
UNIVERSITY PRESS

Oxford University Press, Inc., publishes works that further
Oxford University's objective of excellence
in research, scholarship, and education.

Oxford   New York
Auckland   Cape Town   Dar es Salaam   Hong Kong   Karachi
Kuala Lumpur   Madrid   Melbourne   Mexico City   Nairobi
New Delhi   Shanghai   Taipei   Toronto

With offices in
Argentina   Austria   Brazil   Chile   Czech Republic   France   Greece
Guatemala   Hungary   Italy   Japan   Poland   Portugal   Singapore
South Korea   Switzerland   Thailand   Turkey   Ukraine   Vietnam

Copyright © 2008 by Oxford University Press, Inc.

Published by Oxford University Press, Inc.
198 Madison Avenue, New York, NY 10016

www.oup.com

Library of Congress Cataloging-in-Publication Data
Walker, Ronald W. (Ronald Warren), 1939–.
Massacre at Mountain Meadows / by Ronald W. Walker,
Richard E. Turley Jr., Glen M. Leonard.
p.   cm.
Includes bibliographical references and index.
ISBN 978-0-19-516034-5
1. Mountain Meadows Massacre, Utah, 1857.
I. Turley, Richard E.   II. Leonard, Glen M.   III. Title.
F826.W23 2008
979.2'02—dc22   2008014451

5 7 9 8 6 4

Printed in the United States of America
on acid-free paper

TO THE VICTIMS

Contents

Preface

On September 11, 1857, Mormon settlers in southern Utah used a false flag of truce to lull a group of California-bound emigrants from their circled wagons and then slaughter them. When the killing was over, more than one hundred butchered bodies lay strewn across a half-mile stretch of an upland meadow. Most of the victims were women and children.

The perpetrators were members of the Church of Jesus Christ of Latter-day Saints, aided by Indians. What did the terrible atrocity say about the killers? What did it say about their church and its leaders? Did early Mormonism possess a violent strain so deep and volcanic that it erupted without warning? And what did the Mountain Meadows Massacre say about religion generally? A modern age wants to know whether people might be better off without their religious beliefs.

While these questions can only be partly answered by any book, they are the themes of our story. The massacre "is a ghost which will not be laid," said historian Juanita Brooks before publishing her pathbreaking study, *The Mountain Meadows Massacre*, in 1950. "Again and again, year after year, it stalks abroad to cast its shadow across some history, or to haunt the pages of some novel. Even books to which it is not natural, either from point of time or location, reach out a long arm and draw it in...until it has been made the most important episode in the history of the state [of Utah], eclipsing every achievement and staining every accomplishment."[1]

Brooks may have exaggerated to make her point, but the stream of articles and books goes on—recently expanded by television programs, films, and websites. The past fifteen years have seen a flood of new materials on the subject. And more are on their way. If Brooks thought her book would exorcize the demons, she was wrong.

Why then *our* book? During the past two decades, descendants of both emigrants and perpetrators have worked together at times to memorialize the victims. These efforts have had the support of leaders of the Church of Jesus Christ of Latter-day Saints, officials of the state of Utah, and other institutions and individuals. Among the products of this cooperation have been the construction of two memorials at the massacre site and the placing of plaques commemorating the Arkansas emigrants. In 1990, at dedication ceremonies for the first of the recent memorials, relatives of the victims joined hands with Brigham Young University president Rex E. Lee—a descendant of one of the most prominent participants in the massacre—in a gesture of forgiveness and conciliation.[2] He suggested that in the future the Meadows should symbolize for those now living "not only tragedy and grief, but also human dignity, mutual understanding, [and] a willingness to look forward and not back."[3]

One participant in this ceremony, Judge Roger V. Logan Jr. of Harrison, Arkansas—who could count some twenty victims and five survivors among his relatives—later reminded the public that there had to be some important looking back. "While great strides have been made in recent years," Logan said, "until the church shows more candor about what its historians actually know about the event, true reconciliation will be elusive."[4] That much seems sure: Only complete and honest evaluation of the tragedy can bring the trust necessary for lasting good will. Only then can there be catharsis.

Thoroughness and candor have been our ideals in writing this book, but with so many minds already made up about the role and guilt of participants, we are sure to disappoint some readers. We have done our best to go where the evidence led us, which meant changing some of our early opinions. We hope our readers will have the same spirit of discovery—even if our findings might run against their previously accepted ideas.

We began our book at the end of 2001 with the decision that ours would not be primarily a response to prior historical writing—to the arguments or conclusions of any previous author. Rather, we would take a fresh approach based upon every primary source we could find. That goal sent colleagues from the Family and Church History Department of the Church of Jesus Christ of Latter-day Saints and Brigham Young University to every promising archive in the country, at times as they went about other duties. It also resulted in a careful search for materials in the church's history library and archives, as well as in the archives of the First Presidency, the church's highest governing body. Church leaders supported our book by providing full and open disclosure.

The result of our searches has been a rich body of historical material. Local and genealogical sources yielded new information about the emigrants who were killed. Regional and national newspapers proved to be an important source on immigration, the Utah War, and conditions in Utah Territory during the summer of 1857. The extensive collections of church and militia records housed in the Family and Church History Department and elsewhere allowed us to reconstruct an almost daily record of events for the six weeks leading up to the massacre.

Among the most significant discoveries in the church's collections were the field notes of assistant church historian Andrew Jenson, who collected several reminiscent accounts of the massacre in 1892. This discovery, in turn, led to the full collection of Jenson materials in the First Presidency's archives. In this collection, massacre insiders told what happened, at times defensively but in some cases with self-incriminating honesty. The nineteenth-century historian Orson F. Whitney had used these materials in his *History of Utah*, but perhaps because he did not cite sources, his work did not get into the historical mainstream.[5] Scholars of the massacre were unaware of its importance or chose to ignore it.

When Jenson went to southern Utah to gather this material, the First Presidency gave him a letter asking church members to cooperate. "There is an opinion prevailing that all the light that can be obtained [on the massacre] has not been thrown upon it," the letter read. "We are anxious to learn all that we can upon this subject, not necessarily for publication, but that the Church may have the details in its possession for the vindication of innocent parties, and that the world may know, when the time comes, the true facts connected with it."[6] Today, more than a century later, we are the beneficiaries of this foresight, though Jenson did not enjoy his experience. "I...have been successful in getting the desired information for the First Presidency," he wrote in his diary, "but it has been an unpleasant business. The information that I received made me suffer mentally and deprived me of my sleep at nights; and I felt tired and fatigued, both mentally and physically when I returned home."[7] It was a reaction that we, as authors, have come to appreciate.

Our interest in primary sources led us to investigate one of the mainstays of previous writing. A close comparison of John D. Lee's journals, letters, and statements with his posthumously published *Mormonism Unveiled* convinced us that the book's account of the massacre could not always be depended upon. Almost certainly Lee's editor or publisher—perhaps both—introduced details into the memoir. We disregarded this source when the cumulative effect of other sources contradicted it.

We also sensed anomalies in the transcripts of John D. Lee's two trials. As we wrote, LaJean Purcell Carruth—a rare specialist in transcribing nineteenth-century shorthand—worked to complete a new transcript of the trials from original shorthand records in the church's archives and at the Huntington Library in San Marino, California. She found that many passages of the nineteenth-century transcripts did not accurately reflect the original shorthand record of the trials. Carruth also discovered important shorthand passages never previously transcribed.

The collection of material for our book became an embarrassment of riches. We concluded, reluctantly, that too much information existed for a single book. Besides, two narrative themes emerged. One dealt with the story of the massacre and the other with its aftermath—one with *crime* and the other with *punishment*. This first volume tells only the first half of the story, leaving the second half to another day. An exception is the epilogue, in which we touch briefly on the second half of the story to conclude this volume.

Some may find our book to be a quiet one. In keeping with our decision to rely on primary documents, we have avoided the temptation to argue with previous authors, except at critical points when we concluded readers might want to know the reasons for our interpretation—and these discussions are usually confined to the endnotes. We wanted the story itself to remain in the foreground.

Our choice of style or presentation entered into this decision. We believed the best way to present our information was by narrating it, largely forgoing topical or critical analysis. This decision, more than observing a current historical fashion, was meant to appeal to a larger audience than just scholars.

Broadly speaking, since historians and others began to tell the story of the massacre, they have followed three main approaches. The first two are poles apart. One approach portrays the perpetrators as good people and the victims as evil ones who committed outrages during their travel through central and southern Utah. Some descendants of the perpetrators and several Mormon historians have adopted this approach because it seems, on the surface, to excuse or soften what happened. The second approach looks at the innocence of the emigrants and the evil of their killers, who at best are described as followers of misguided religion. Some relatives of the emigrant families, church critics, and many non-Mormons have found this position attractive.

Readers of our book will find little sympathy for either of these two approaches. Each overlooks how complex human beings can be— good and evil, after all, are widely shared human traits. Nor do these approaches recognize how diverse the two groups were. Moreover, each of the two polarized explanations breaks down logically. Nothing that the emigrants purportedly did comes close to justifying their murder. Their wagon company was made up mostly of young families traveling through the territory in pursuit of their dreams. The leading men and women among them had been substantial citizens in their Arkansas communities and promised to make their mark in California. Likewise, most of the killers led exemplary lives before and after the massacre. Except for their experiences during a single, nightmarish week in September 1857, most of them were ordinary humans with little to distinguish them from other nineteenth-century frontiersmen. Some in fact would have been pillars in any community.

The third main approach to understanding the massacre attempts to navigate between the extremes of the other two. This approach is partly a commonsense recognition that both victims and perpetrators were decent but imperfect people whose paths crossed in a moment of history that resulted in a terrible tragedy. Brooks's 1950 book had this insight, and it is one reason we admire her work, though new information now permits a more complete and accurate telling of the massacre.

This third approach, however, leads to a troubling question: How could basically good people commit such a terrible atrocity? There are no easy answers, but the professional literature dealing with nineteenth-century American violence offers a starting point. In the early to mid-1800s, the United States could be a violent place, particularly for racial, ethnic, and religious minorities. The period from 1830 to 1860 has been called "The Turbulent Era," and indeed it was for many Mormons.[8] These men and women experienced violence in Missouri and Illinois, and when a U.S. army marched toward Utah Territory in 1857—the year of the massacre—they believed they were about to become victims again. One of the bitter ironies of Mormon history is that some of the people who had long deplored the injustice of extra-legal violence became its perpetrators. In carrying out the Mountain Meadows Massacre, they followed a familiar step-by-step pattern used by vigilantes elsewhere.

Scholars who have investigated violence in many cultures provide other insights based on group psychology. Episodes of violence often begin when one people classify another as "the other," stripping them of any humanity and mentally transforming them into enemies. Once this process of devaluing and demonizing occurs, stereotypes take over, rumors circulate, and pressure builds to conform to group action against the perceived threat. Those classified as the enemy are often seen as the transgressors, even as steps are being taken against them. When these tinderbox conditions exist, a single incident, small or ordinary in usual circumstances, may spark great violence ending in atrocity.[9]

The literature suggests other elements are often present when "good people" do terrible things. Usually there is an atmosphere of authority and obedience, which allows errant leaders to trump the moral instincts of their followers. Atrocities also occur when followers do not have clear messages about what is expected of them—when their culture or messages from headquarters leave local leaders wondering what they should do. Poverty increases the likelihood of problems by raising concerns about survival.[10] The conditions for mass killing—demonizing, authority, obedience, peer pressure, ambiguity, fear, and deprivation—all were present in southern Utah in 1857.

These concepts of American extralegal violence and the group psychology common in religious and ethnic violence color much of our thinking and writing. We are too much believers in institutional and personal responsibility, however, to leave the massacre to historical patterns or models. We believe errors were made by U.S. president James Buchanan, Brigham Young and other Mormon leaders, some of the Arkansas emigrants, some Paiutes, and most of all by settlers in southern Utah who set aside principles of their faith to commit an atrocity. At each point along the chain of acts and decisions—especially in Iron and Washington Counties—a single personal choice or policy might have brought a different result. Those who acted as they did bear a responsibility—some a great deal more than others—though we as authors know the presumption of judging past events without having lived in them.

We also acknowledge an element of the unknowable. A citizen who did not take part in the killing but lived in southern Utah in 1857 later told his son: "You would not understand if I told you. You know nothing about the spirit of the times. . . . You don't understand and you can't understand."[11]

For too long, writing about the massacre has been characterized by a spirit of charge and countercharge. These frames of reference usually center on personalities and conspiracies: What was the role of John D. Lee? Did church authorities unfairly magnify his crimes? Was Brigham Young guilty of secretly ordering the massacre? Which of the southern Utah leaders was most responsible? These questions, we believe, are best answered by telling the story and letting events speak for themselves.

It is for this reason that much of our book deals with the final days before the mass killing. We hope that readers will see not scapegoats but a complex event in which many people and forces had a role.

Readers should know our rules of navigation. One, we give priority to the documents closest in time, distance, and person to the events. Two, we believe that most testimony about the massacre—whether Mormon or non-Mormon—contains a great deal of truth, except at times when men and women speak of their own roles or those of close associates and family members. Generally, the problem is omission. Of the admonition to "tell the whole truth and nothing but the truth," many statements fail the first clause but honor the second. Three, for important points in our narrative, we have sought confirmation from multiple witnesses while also searching for witnesses with differing viewpoints. Four, chronology and sequence are keys to our understanding, another reason so much of our book is devoted to the telling of daily events. It is here that the causes of the massacre become most clear. Five, we think context is the historian's best friend. Readers of our book must expect passages about setting and personality—knowing, too, that for every paragraph in the text, three or four often ended up on the cutting-room floor. Finally, our method has been to compare relevant documents to seek consistent details and general patterns. Above all else, we look for the weight of evidence, understanding that, inevitably, some pieces of evidence will prove to be anomalous.

The institutions with which we have been professionally associated—Brigham Young University and the Family and Church History Department of the Church of Jesus Christ of Latter-day Saints—were generous in supporting this book, both in allowing us professional time to research and write, and in funding the work of colleagues and research assistants who helped with the project. Throughout, we were given the freedom to make our own judgments and have retained full editorial control over our manuscript—all the more remarkable given the sensitivity of our topic. To the institutions and the many men and women who have contributed to our book, we extend the usual disclaimer. As authors, we alone are responsible for the book's contents.

Ronald W. Walker

Richard E. Turley Jr.

Glen M. Leonard

MASSACRE AT MOUNTAIN MEADOWS

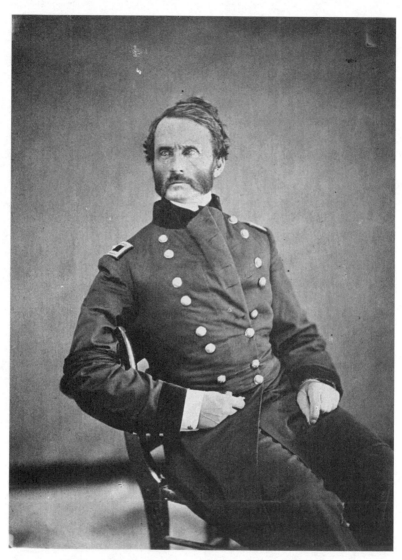

JAMES HENRY CARLETON. *Courtesy Library of Congress.*

A Picture of Human Suffering

Mountain Meadows, May 1859

IN APRIL 1859, Brevet Major James Henry Carleton received the orders that would mark his place in Utah history. He and his First Dragoons were to escort Maj. Henry Prince, U.S. Army paymaster, on the first leg of his journey from California's Fort Tejon to northern Utah's Camp Floyd.[1] But that was not all. "When I left Los Angeles," Carleton later explained, "General [N. S.] Clarke, commanding the department of California, directed me to bury the bones of the victims of that terrible massacre" at the Mountain Meadows in southern Utah.[2]

A three-week march through the Mojave Desert and up the lip of the Great Basin brought Carleton and his men to the Meadows in mid May. The necklike valley, about a mile and a half wide and six miles long, lay a cool mile above sea level, hedged on every side by low-rising hills. "Pathfinder" John C. Frémont had called it *"las Vegas de Santa Clara"*—the Meadows of Santa Clara—when heading east from California during his 1844 exploring expedition. The place was "rich in bunch grass, and fresh with numerous springs of clear water, all refreshing and delightful to look upon," Frémont reported.[3] Nearly a decade after Frémont's expedition, a California-bound emigrant wrote admiringly of rich, waving grass and numerous rills, adding, "These vegas are called by the Mormons, Mountain Meadows."[4] Just days before Carleton's arrival, U.S. Indian superintendent Jacob Forney called the Meadows "the most extraordinary formation west of the Rocky Mountains."[5]

Yet more striking to Carleton's eyes than the natural beauty of the place was the carnage that now defiled it. "The scene of the massacre, even at this late day," he wrote, "was horrible to look upon. Women's hair in detached locks, and in masses, hung to the sage bushes, and was strewn over the ground in many places. Parts of little children's dresses, and of female costume, dangled from the shrubbery, or lay scattered about. And among these, here and there, on every hand…there gleamed, bleached white by the weather, the skulls and other bones of those who had suffered."[6]

Despite repeated attempts to lay to rest the remains of the victims, their bones—like the truth—refused to stay buried.

Superintendent Forney and his company were the first of an influx of federal officers who toured the site in 1859, and each tried to do something about the remains. In April, Forney's men spent two or three hours burying—not much more than a gesture.[7] When troops from Camp Floyd arrived in early May to rendezvous with paymaster Prince, they too had buried bones.[8]

Still the work was not done. On May 20 Major Carleton and his men scoured the ground for fragments of bodies. Jacob Hamblin, a Mormon who lived at the north end of the Meadows, helped by showing troops where he had interred remains the previous summer. Hamblin had counted 120 victims then. From this spot and from ravines and clumps of sagebrush, Carleton reported, "I gathered many of the disjointed bones of thirty-two persons. The number could easily be told by the number of pairs of shoulder blades, and of lower jaws, skulls and parts of skulls."[9] A Mormon who witnessed the work said Carleton's "wagon was loaded with bones."[10] "A glance into the wagon," said Carleton, "revealed a sight which can never be forgotten."[11]

The wagon's grim load was taken to the slaughtered emigrants' old encampment on the south end of the Meadows, where two other bodies were found in a nearby ravine. Carleton put the bones in the earth and built a cone-shaped cairn of stones over the mass grave. The monument was some sixteen feet in diameter and twelve feet high. Rising another dozen feet from the stones was a heavy cross hewn from red cedarwood. On the horizontal plank of the cross, the troopers wrote the inscription:

VENGEANCE IS MINE: I WILL REPAY SAITH THE LORD.

On a slab of stone set against the northern side of the monument, the men cut the words,

HERE
120 MEN, WOMEN AND CHILDREN,
WERE MASSACRED IN COLD BLOOD,
IN SEPT., 1857.
THEY WERE FROM ARKANSAS.[12]

Finally, a monument marked the victims' final resting place. But Carleton meant the monument to be more than a mausoleum. He meant it to shame the Mormons.

Driven by what he had seen, Carleton "endeavored to learn the circumstances" surrounding the massacre. He began penning a report from his camp near the spot where twenty months earlier the emigrants battled for their lives from their wagon corral before filing out under a false promise of protection.[13]

"The idea," Carleton wrote, "of the melancholy procession of that great number of women and children—followed at a distance by their husbands and brothers—after all their suffering, their watching, their anxiety, and grief, for so many gloomy days and dismal nights at the *corral*, thus moving slowly and sadly on up to the point where the Mormons and Indians lay in wait to murder them; these doomed and unhappy people, literally going to their own funeral; the chill shadows of night closing darkly around them, sad precursors of the approaching shadows of a deeper night; brings to the mind a picture of human suffering and wretchedness on the one hand, and of human treachery and ferocity upon the other."[14]

Carleton's words stumbled over themselves in fury. "I would to God," he wrote to Clarke's assistant adjutant general after returning to California, "that General Clarke with an adequate force, and with his hands unfettered by red tape, could have the management of those *damned* Mormons just one summer, and that 'I could be there to see.' Major, it is no use to talk or split hairs about that accursed race. All fine spun nonsense about their rights as citizens, and all knotty questions about Constitutional Rights should be solved with the sword. Self preservation, the *first* law, demands that this set of ruffians *go out* from amongst us as a people.... Give them one year, no more; and if after that they pollute our soil by their presence make literally *Children of the Mist* of them."[15]

He was not the first or last to curse the Mormons.

CHAPTER ONE

Exiles from Freedom

New York to the Iowa Plains, 1830–1846

THE MORMONS KNEW they were "peculiar" people. They had no prepared liturgies, no starched clerical collars, and no purchased pews. They accepted new scripture, including the Book of Mormon, and considered their church "the only true and living church upon the face of the whole earth"—the only one with God's authority. They gathered themselves into their own communities, where their leaders preached that they should be one people—unified—and in those days that went for their politics, too. For them, social, political, and religious issues mingled as easily as they did for Puritans in seventeenth-century New England.[1]

The Mormons saw themselves as Christian, but in a different way. They rejected some popular concepts about God, such as Trinitarianism, and accepted living prophets and apostles like those in the Old and New Testaments. For a time, they also practiced polygamy, much to the scandal of other Americans. Just as Christianity emerged from Judaism as a new covenant with God, Mormons considered themselves part of a new dispensation—a "new and everlasting covenant." They were creating what one modern scholar has called "a new religious tradition."[2]

Their church was organized in upstate New York in 1830 by twenty-four-year-old prophet Joseph Smith, who translated old scriptural records and issued new revelations.[3] Smith also spoke of the "last days," which eventually became part of the church's formal name, the Church of Jesus Christ of Latter-day Saints. Its members called themselves Latter-day Saints, or just Saints, and outsiders began calling them Mormons. "We rejoice that the time is at hand when, the wicked who will not repent will be swept from the earth with the besom of destruction and the earth become an inheritance for the poor and the meek," Smith wrote. "And we are led to...mingle our prayers with those saints that have suffered the like treatment before us, whose souls are under the altar crying to the Lord for vengance upon those that dwell upon the earth."[4]

Smith's words showed how close the last days were to him, as well as God's justice, which often was about separating those who accepted the new message from those who did not.[5] This kind of thinking—believers versus nonbelievers or "gentiles," as the Mormons termed them—followed a pattern. The categories of "good–evil, pious–hypocrite, elect–damned" were part of the early history of Christianity, and indeed they exist among many religious groups.[6] Such categories, however, sometimes get believers into trouble since nonbelievers do not like being declared on the opposite side of truth.

The Mormons' unusual beliefs and practices brought them opposition beginning in New York and Pennsylvania and continuing during the church's sojourn in Ohio, Missouri, Illinois, and finally the Rocky Mountains.

The Mormons saw their troubles as religious persecution, but the violence they experienced was also a reflection of American culture at that time. The belief that citizens had the right to take the law into their own hands to protest unjust conditions existed in colonial America, where citizens violently defied British rule and finally overthrew it. By the time of Joseph Smith, the traditional "right of riot" was also being used against individuals and groups.[7] The people had so often heard "that all power, government, and authority of right belong to them," wrote a contemporary critic of American conditions, "that they occasionally mistake the true limit of that sovereignty, and undertake to exercise despotic powers."[8]

American cities had "labor riots, election riots, anti-abolitionist riots, anti-Negro riots, [and] anti-Catholic riots," wrote Richard Maxwell Brown, a leading historian of violence. Rural America likewise had its roughnecks, bushwhackers, and night riders, who put down anybody they strongly disliked. This "continuous and often intense violence" was frequently aimed at unpopular minorities, whether

RIOT IN PHILADELPHIA
JUNE 7 1844.

RIOT IN PHILADELPHIA. *Courtesy Library of Congress.*

racial, ethnic, or religious.[9] Some Americans reacted even to verbal slights with quick tempers, swift blows, and deadly duels that the law seemed unable to control.[10]

Contributing to the problem was poor law enforcement. During America's colonial era, sheriffs and constables did their best to uphold peace, aided by local militias. But by the mid-1800s this system could not keep pace with the rising violence that came with growing populations. Some cities reacted by establishing professional police forces, but other Americans simply chose to maintain order by taking the law into their own hands.[11]

In March 1832 an Ohio mob, led by what Joseph Smith described as religious rivals, kidnapped him and stretched him for castration. The vigilantes "concluded not to kill [or deform] me, but pound and scratch me well, tear of[f] my shirt and drawers and leave me naked," Smith said. The men smeared hot tar on Smith's skin and coated him in feathers before leaving him writhing on the frozen ground with injuries that afflicted him the rest of his life.[12]

The next year, Missourians who opposed Mormons moving into their state reflected their views in a formal document signed by hundreds of Jackson County citizens. They were determined "to rid our society" of the Mormons, "'peaceably if we can, forcibly if we must,'" the manifesto said.

It is more than two years since the first of these fanatics, or knaves...
made their first appearance amongst us,...pretending...to receive
communications and revelations direct from heaven; to heal the sick
by laying on hands; and in short, to perform all the wonder working
miracles wrought by the inspired apostles and prophets of old.

...They have been daily increasing in numbers, and...were of the
very dregs of that society from which they came,...for...they brought
into our county little or no property...their conduct here stamps their
characters in their true colors. More than a year since, it was ascertained that they had been tampering with our slaves...in a late number
of the Star, published in Independence by the leaders of the sect, there
is an article inviting free negroes and mulattoes from other States to
become mormons and remove and settle among us...

They declare openly that their God hath given them this county
of land, and that sooner or later they must and will have possession of
our lands for an inheritance...we believe it a duty we owe ourselves, to
our wives and children, to the cause of public morals, to remove them
from among us...

...We, therefore, agree, that [if] after timely warning, and receiving an adequate compensation for what little property they cannot take
with them, they refuse to leave us in peace, as they found us, we agree
to use such means as may be sufficient to remove them.[13]

Among the document's signers were several of the community's leading
men, including R. W. Cummins, a local Indian agent who earlier stopped
Mormon missionaries from preaching to native peoples across the border
in Indian territory—a man whose name would later raise fears among
those Saints who thought he had been appointed governor of Utah.[14]

The Jackson County manifesto embraced many of the cultural,
economic, religious, social, and psychological issues present when
two religious or cultural groups oppose each other. Most of the Saints
in western Missouri were northerners whose values clashed with the
southerners who made up much of the state's population. The Mormons' religious tenets, their belief that Jackson County was their promised land, and their growing political and economic power angered
many Missourians. Rising sectional tension over slavery was another
factor, though the Mormons' radical abolitionism and moral threats
to Missouri society were little more than wild rumors.[15] Claiming the
right of self-preservation, Missourians began driving the Saints from
their communities—beating them, destroying their homes, and threatening those who dared stay behind.[16]

During this period of violence, the Saints worried whether they should fight to defend themselves. In August 1833 Joseph Smith received a revelation telling his followers to "renounce war and proclaim peace." This document told them not to respond to their enemies till after the third or fourth provocation, and then after raising "a standard of peace." Even then, those who chose not to fight would be "rewarded for th[eir] righteousness."[17] Likewise, the Book of Mormon repeatedly cautioned that men should fight only defensive or just wars.[18] "So tenacious were they for the precepts of the gospel," wrote one man present during the Jackson County violence, that "up to this time the Mormons had not so much as lifted a finger, even in their own defence."[19]

Mormon apostle Parley P. Pratt summed up his experience when his people were driven from Jackson County in November 1833. "All my provisions for the winter were destroyed or stolen, and my grain left growing on the ground for my enemies to harvest. My house was afterwards burned, and my fruit trees and improvements destroyed or plundered." Other Mormons also suffered. "In short, every member of the society was driven from the county, and fields of corn were ravaged and destroyed; stacks of wheat burned, household goods plundered, and improvements and every kind of property destroyed," Pratt recounted. "One of this banditti afterwards boasted...that, according to their own account of the matter, the number of houses burned was two hundred and three."[20]

After being displaced yet again in 1836, the Saints relocated to a sparsely settled part of the state, where Caldwell County was created for them by state legislators. As they grew in number and spread beyond its borders, however, anti-Mormon violence broke out again.[21] In many cases, those who attacked the Mormons were aided by local militia and civil officers, who cited established tradition and even patriotism as their authority. It "was Cruel to fight a people who had not Broke the law," admitted one Missouri vigilante who took part. Still, he said, "altho we are trampling on our law and Constitution...we Cant Help it...while we possessed the Spirit of 76."[22]

The Saints appealed to Missouri governor Daniel Dunklin to protect their constitutional rights. "Public sentiment," he replied, "may become paramount law; and...it is useless to run counter to it....In this Republic, the *vox populi* is the *vox Dei*" (the voice of the people is the voice of God).[23]

The majority could take the law into its own hands with impunity, but when minorities employed the same approach or tried to fight back, it usually backfired. In 1836, after repeated acts of extralegal violence against the Saints, Smith decided it was time to take a stand. He proposed that his people covenant that "if any more of our brethren are slain or driven from their lands in Missouri by the mob that we will give ourselves no rest until we are avenged of our enimies to the uttermost." The congregation replied with a resounding "hosanna and Amen."[24]

Another Mormon leader, Sidney Rigdon, used the majority's concept of *vox populi* in telling dissenters to leave the Saints' communities. "When a county, or body of people have individuals among them with whom they do not wish to associate," said Rigdon, "and a public expression is taken against their remaining among them and such individuals do not remove, it is the principle of republicanism itself that gives that community a right to expel them forcibly."[25]

An Independence Day speech by Rigdon in 1838 set off the final storm. He spoke of the Mormons' patriotism and insisted they would "infringe on the rights of no people." But Missourians remembered only Rigdon's defiant final words to any "mob" that dared come against the Saints. "We take God and all the holy angels to witness this day, that we warn all men in the name of Jesus Christ, to come on us no more forever.... And that mob that comes on us to disturb us; it shall be between us and them a war of extermination, for we will follow them, till the last drop of their blood is spilled, or else they will have to exterminate us; for we will carry the seat of war to their own houses, and their own families, and one party or the other shall be utterly destroyed."[26]

About a month later, a riot broke out at a Daviess County polling place. Several Mormons, including recent convert John D. Lee, used sticks, boards, or whatever else they could find to fight off Missourians who attacked them when they tried to exercise their right to vote. Lee believed God was with him as he fought. "Like Sampson, when leaning against the pillar," he recounted, "I felt the power of God nerve my arm for the fray."[27]

Exaggerated reports of the riot and other skirmishes led to virtual civil war. Some of the Saints, including Lee, responded to Missouri vigilantes by forming bands called "Danites" that made preemptive strikes against vigilante targets, answering violence with violence.[28] Smith, who at first sanctioned the Mormon response, later recoiled at Danite excesses.[29] Even then, one historian concluded, "Mormon marauding against non-Mormon Missourians in 1838 was mild by comparison with the brutality of the anti-Mormon militias."[30]

After attempting to defend themselves or strike back, the Saints were soon overwhelmed by even greater anti-Mormon violence.[31] On October 27, 1838, Missouri governor Lilburn W. Boggs ordered that the Mormons be "exterminated or driven from the state." He called out thousands of state militiamen to enforce his order.[32] During this final wave of Missouri violence—and even before receiving Boggs's order—rogue militiamen attacked the Latter-day Saint settlement of Haun's Mill. The militia killed seventeen Mormon men and boys and wounded fourteen people, including a woman and a seven-year-old boy. One ten-year-old child was dragged from his hiding place and shot point blank in the head as he begged for his life.[33]

Soon Missouri militiamen arrested and imprisoned Smith, Rigdon, and other church leaders and forced Mormons to give up their arms and leave the state.[34] While the Saints never made a full accounting of their casualties, their various reports listed rape, gunshot wounds,

MASSACRE OF MORMONS AT HAUN'S MILL.

MASSACRE OF MORMONS AT HAUN'S MILL. *Charles Mackay*, The Mormons, or Latter-day Saints (*London, 1851.*)

beatings, exposure, and dozens of resulting deaths.[35] Before they could leave, some were forced at bayonet point to sign deeds surrendering their land. Their losses of real and personal property ran into the hundreds of thousands of dollars, which Missourians took as wages of war.[36] When the violence ended, as many as eight thousand Latter-day Saints fled to Illinois, some in the distress of winter.[37] For them, Missouri and Missourians became bywords.

As his people suffered, Smith languished for months in a Missouri prison dungeon. He felt the futility of the Saints' trying to seek justice on their own. "We can not do any thing only stand still and see the Salvation of God," he wrote. "He must do his own work or it must fall to the ground we must not take it in our hands to avenge our wrongs Vengeance is mine saith the Lord and I will repay." As for his own safety, Smith wrote, "I shall stand unto death God being my helper."[38]

After Smith fled captivity in Missouri, the Saints established their headquarters at Nauvoo, Illinois, where they experienced a few years of peace. But soon the same cycle began again: a cultural clash between themselves and their neighbors, rumors leading to attacks, vigilantes claiming the right of majority rule and self-preservation, and Mormons attempting to defend themselves or strike back before being overwhelmed in a still larger wave of violence.[39] Tensions grew after Smith and his followers organized their own state-sanctioned militia, the Nauvoo Legion, to defend themselves and also used the Nauvoo city council and courts to protect Smith from Missouri's repeated attempts to extradite him.[40]

Some Illinoisans felt the Mormon prophet was setting up a theocratic kingdom that would infringe upon their rights. "Let us stand by each other, and each others rights," declared one anti-Mormon newspaper. "Let us watch the Mormons, expose their usurpations, and oppressions, check their arrogance by determined resistance to their overbearing course, and if at last, we are driven to arms, let it be the result of an inevitable necessity."[41]

Emotions boiled over in June 1844 when Mormons, under color of law, destroyed the press of an opposition newspaper, the *Nauvoo Expositor*. "We have only to state, that this is sufficient!" proclaimed an editorial in the neighboring community of Warsaw. "War and extermination is inevitable! CITIZENS ARISE, ONE and ALL!!!—Can you *stand* by, and suffer such INFERNAL DEVILS! to ROB men of their property and RIGHTS, without avenging them. We have no time for comment, every man will make his own. LET IT BE MADE WITH POWDER AND BALL!"[42]

Before giving himself up for arrest on charges stemming from the paper's destruction, Smith acquiesced to his fate. "I am going like a lamb to the slaughter," he said, "but I am calm as a summer's morning."[43] Within days, a mob that included state militiamen, their faces blackened in disguise, murdered Joseph Smith and his brother Hyrum at Carthage Jail, about twenty miles from Nauvoo. To Mormons, the death of their beloved leaders shook heaven and earth. "Their *innocent blood*, with the innocent blood of all the martyrs under the altar that John [the Revelator] saw, will cry unto the Lord of Hosts, till he avenges that blood on the Earth," wrote John Taylor, a newspaperman and future church president. His eyewitness account of the murders would become a part of Mormon scripture.[44]

Immediately after the murders, many Carthage citizens fled, fearing a Mormon attack. "The people of the county are greatly excited, and fear the Mormons will come out and take vengeance," Mormon apostle Willard Richards wrote to Nauvoo from Carthage. "I have pledged my word the Mormons will stay at home...and no violence will be on their part, and say to my brethren in Nauvoo, in the name of the Lord—be still."[45]

Instead of retaliating, thousands of Latter-day Saints gathered in Nauvoo to await the arrival of their martyred prophets' bodies. "The day that [the bodies of] Joseph and Hyrum were brought from Carthage to Nauvoo it was judged by menny...that there was more then five barels of tears shead," Mormon apostle Brigham Young wrote. "I cannot bare to think enny thing about it."[46] The church's newspaper recorded that the "vast assemblage...with one united voice resolved to trust to the law for a remedy of such a high handed assassination, and when that failed to call upon God to avenge us of our wrongs!"[47]

When the trial of the Smiths' killers ended without convictions, the Saints contained their outrage, falling back on the moderation of their scriptures and their past experience. Instead of taking vengeance into their own hands, they began in their public meetings and temple assemblies to call on God to avenge the blood of the prophets.[48] In doing so, they echoed a passage in the New Testament book of Revelation. "I saw under the altar the souls of them that were slain for the word of God," the apostle John wrote. "How long, O Lord, holy and true, dost thou not judge and avenge our blood on them that dwell on the earth?"[49]

In the face of continued violence, the Saints just moved on. "We could fight our way clear," a Latter-day Saint editorial said at the

DEATH OF JOSEPH SMITH. *Charles Mackay,* The Mormons, or Latter-day Saints *(London, 1851).*

time. But "we will suffer wrong rather than do wrong... The Gospel whispers peace."[50]

Like Missouri governor Boggs, Illinois governor Thomas Ford wanted the Mormons out of his state, although his memoir, *History of Illinois*, was full of hand-wringing over how it was done. Ford said that even after the Mormons agreed to leave and most had crossed the Mississippi River, "the anti-Mormons were no less anxious" to expel those who remained behind. The final scene in Nauvoo began when vigilantes, again styling themselves as state militiamen, began a cannon assault on the city.[51]

The "siege of Nauvoo" lasted only a few days. When it was over, vigilantes forced the remaining Saints from their homes and across the Mississippi, violating earlier agreements. "Many of them were taken from sick beds, hurried into the boats, and driven away by the armed ruffians now exercising the power of government," Governor Ford said. "The best they could do was to erect their tents on the banks of the river and there remain to take their chance of perishing by hunger or by prevailing sickness. In this condition the sick, without shelter, food, nourishment, or medicines, died by scores."[52]

Even before the siege of Nauvoo, the Saints were looking to the West where they might have their own version of majority rule—where they could "live in peace and not be hunted down like the wild deer on the mountains."[53] They were believers in the "Manifest Destiny" thinking of their time—that Americans had the self-evident right to the American West.[54]

Brigham Young, the senior apostle at Joseph Smith's death, would lead the westward exodus. Young was born on June 1, 1801, at Whitingham, Vermont, the ninth of eleven children in a struggling household. Shortly before his third birthday, the Young family moved to upstate New York, where their economic challenges continued. Young remembered working in summer and winter, ill clad, "with insufficient food until my stomach would ache."[55] Chopped logs and planted fields became his curriculum. His most continuous days of formal schooling, by his own account, were eleven—and that did not come until after his twenty-second birthday. His mother died when he was fourteen, and his father, though having the virtues of integrity, work, and love for his children, was as stern as the Yankee countryside. With him it was "a word and a blow," Young remembered, "but the blow came first." Young was on his own at age sixteen, making his living as a laborer and craftsman.[56]

Young, like Smith, was a product of western New York's "burned-over district," where religious emotion flowed easily.[57] Although spending

"many anxious hours" studying the "Episcopalians, Presbyterians, New Lights, Baptists, Freewill Baptists, Wesleyan and Reformed Methodists," Young found little comfort.[58] His first religious profession was Methodism, but he joined the denomination without much conviction.[59] By his late twenties, he was, by his own admission, "cast down, gloomy," "everything wearing...a dreary aspect." During these years, he remembered despising the world and "the poor miserable devils" that ruled it. "I hated them with a perfect hatred," he said.[60]

His Mormon baptism gave him a cause and lifted him out of his depression. Within seven months after his conversion, Young had raised up a dozen Mormon congregations in New York and surrounding states. His religious feeling, like the hero in John Bunyan's *Pilgrim's Progress*, was "life, life, eternal life."[61]

Young's quick temper and pungent speech may have been the reason some church members shook their heads when he was called into the Quorum of the Twelve Apostles in 1835. Seeing only the unpolished exterior, one man compared him to a half-sweet, half-sour apple and called his selection a "disgrace to the House of Israel."[62] Yet Young's prayers and other devotions were as fervent as any man's. Visitors to his office later compared him to a retiring New England farmer or London alderman—so different from the strong-armed image that others fashioned upon him.[63] Thomas L. Kane, a Philadelphia lawyer and politician who became his lifelong friend, described him as "an eccentric great man."[64] He stood about five feet ten inches, had blue-grey eyes, a light complexion, and a strong mouth. "His lips came together like the jaws of a bear trap," remembered one man.[65]

When Young became the Mormons' leader, he already had a record of accomplishment. As Joseph Smith fled Ohio in 1838, Young helped raise funds to aid him in his journey. During the Missouri expulsion when Smith lay in prison, Young organized the Saints' evacuation and, despite heavy odds, kept the church together. From 1839 to 1841, he led the Latter-day Saint apostles in a proselyting mission to Great Britain. They and those who followed them had such success that for the rest of the nineteenth century, nearly half of church members were Britishers or their sons and daughters.[66]

After Smith's death, as Young looked for a future home for the Saints, everything seemed "pleasant ahead but dark to look back."[67] He wanted to find a place requiring enough hard labor to discourage too many outsiders from joining the Saints as co-settlers, but with enough resources for a hardscrabble "Zion"—as the Saints would call their home.[68] Mormon leaders looked at the semiarid region lying between the Sierra Nevadas and the Rocky Mountains that explorer John C. Frémont called the Great Basin. On the Basin's eastern border lay the Salt Lake Valley, which reportedly had fertile land requiring irrigation for small-plot agriculture. The mountains were another virtue. The high peaks and deep canyons would provide natural defenses if needed.[69]

The Mormons were still on the Iowa plains, the worst of their journey, when the U.S. government requested five hundred volunteers of them for the Mexican War. Young had hoped for such an opportunity and complied by recruiting the "Mormon Battalion."[70] Suddenly, the likely expansion of the American Republic into the Mexican-owned Great Basin forced the Saints to consider their future relations with American civil leaders and magistrates. Writing to U.S. president James K. Polk from the Omaha nation, Young explained that although the Saints respected the American Constitution and would regard their own U.S. territorial government "as one of the richest boons of earth," his people would "rather retreat to the deserts, Islands or mountain caves th[a]n consent to be ruled by governors & judges . . . who delight in injustices & oppressions."[71]

THE PIONEERS.

PIONEER WAGON TRAIN. *T. B. H. Stenhouse*, The Rocky Mountain Saints
(*London, 1874*).

In writing to Polk, Young was looking over his shoulder to the past tragedies of Ohio, Missouri, and Illinois, where state and local officers had often been his people's enemies. Would the future hold more of the past?

As the Saints were preparing to head west, they still tasted the bitterness of their American experience. "We owe the United States nothing," John Taylor wrote in an editorial. "We go out by force, as exiles from freedom. The government and people owe us millions for the destruction of life and property in Missouri and in Illinois. The blood of our best men stains the land, and the ashes of our property will preserve it till God comes out of his hiding place, and gives this nation a hotter portion than he did Sodom and Gomorrah. 'When they cease to spoil they shall be spoiled,' for the Lord hath spoken it."[72]

Taylor's quoted scripture came from Isaiah, used by the Jews many centuries before to create their own identity as exiles.[73]

CHAPTER TWO

Peals of Thunder

Utah, 1847–1857

T HE VANGUARD COMPANY of Mormon pioneers arrived in the
Salt Lake Valley in the latter part of July 1847. It was the
beginning of the largest mass migration by a single group
in nineteenth-century America.[1] But moving west did not end the
Mormons' troubles.

At first, the federal government met the Latter-day Saints half
way in their desire for self-government. In 1851 President Millard
Fillmore appointed Brigham Young governor and superintendent of
Indian affairs for Utah Territory. Washington split its other six territorial appointees among Mormons and non-Mormons, and the division
between wary partisans virtually assured a clash.[2] The outside appointees were hardly in Utah before they left, taking the territory's congressional appropriation of twenty-four thousand dollars with them. The
"runaways" announced the Mormons had not received them properly
and were guilty of "malicious sedition," which reflected the deeply held
feelings on both sides. The affair became a national cause célèbre.[3]

There were other incidents as well. In 1853 Pahvant Indians in
central Utah killed U.S. Army Capt. John W. Gunnison and seven
members of his party who were surveying a possible route for a railroad to the Pacific. The following year, Washington ordered Lt. Col.
Edward J. Steptoe and his command to aid Utah officials in bringing

the killers to justice. When the case came to trial, a local jury dismissed the charges against some of the Indians and found three others guilty only of manslaughter. The jury believed the main ringleaders were still at large and that the crime had been an act of retributive justice for the killing of a Pahvant leader by Missouri emigrants going to California. It was also true the settlers did not want to provoke the usually friendly Pahvants. But critics reacted strongly to the verdict. They believed the Mormons had not upheld the nation's military honor, and rumors spread that Mormons and Indians were conspiring behind the federal government's back.[4]

In December 1854 a soldier sparked a row between Steptoe's men, some Mormons, and local police. Two days later, on Christmas Day, tensions between soldiers and citizens erupted into a "regular melee" that injured men on both sides, including eighteen-year-old Brigham Young Jr. The soldiers' efforts to woo Mormon women also offended local sensibilities. One officer tried to seduce a daughter-in-law of Brigham Young whose husband was absent on a preaching mission. When the army left, perhaps as many as one hundred Mormon women went with them. "Everybody has got one except the Colonel and Major," boasted one soldier. "The Doctor has got three—mother and two daughters. The mother cooks for him and the daughters sleep with him."[5] The incident outraged and embarrassed the Mormons, hardening their resolve not to have troops stationed near their communities.[6]

The Mormons and the federally appointed judges had one running battle after another, which, if they had not been so serious, were almost comic in their tone. After a local man was acquitted in federal court, the presiding judge, W. W. Drummond, reportedly threatened him, and a Mormon-controlled grand jury in turn indicted Drummond and his servant for assault "with intent to kill." The purpose of the trial, according to one participant, was to show Drummond "in his proper light."[7] Later, rowdies broke into the law library of federal judge George P. Stiles, a Mormon who had been excommunicated for "immoral conduct." The vandals burned his law firm's books and papers in a privy.[8]

The local people also had conflicts with other U.S. appointees— surveyors and Indian agents—as well as with ex-Mormons and gentile merchants, a class of men Young would eventually dub "the Clique."[9] These men, whose power would grow during Utah's territorial years, were united by their strong opposition to Mormonism, by their ambitions for political and economic influence in the territory, and often by their Eastern ties. After the American Civil War, this breed of men would be recognized for their virtues and vices, and branded with the pejorative titles of "carpetbaggers" and "scalawags."[10]

The conflicts mocked Mormon hopes for a quiet society in Utah. "The United States Judges are not here as kings or Monarchs," Young protested, "but as servants of the people." Recalling how American society had treated the Saints in Missouri and Illinois, he added, "If I Come here & act the tyrant…you ought to kick me out and all officers ought to be served in the same way."[11] Young had similar anathemas for the federal surveyors, whose work, he believed, was sloppy and fraudulent.[12]

W. M. F. Magraw, who lived briefly in Utah, had another reason to be upset with the Mormons. Local settlers had outbid him and his partners for a federal contract to transport mail between Independence, Missouri, and Salt Lake City.[13] Writing to President Franklin Pierce in October 1856, Magraw claimed there was "no vestige of law and order" in the territory and that the "so-styled ecclesiastical organization" was "despotic, dangerous and damnable."[14]

Two reasons explain the strong words that passed on both sides—besides the obvious clash of self-interest and personalities. Two rival kingdoms or cultures were opposing each other. On one hand, the Mormons were still determined to create a religious commonwealth. During the first days of their settlement, they spoke of a "land of promise held in reserve by the hand of God" that fulfilled the promises of Isaiah.[15] Other sermons insisted on the need for a strict Christian purity—Sabbath-keeping, honesty, and the need for "order" and "righteousness." Outsiders willing to obey the new standard would be accepted, but others should go elsewhere.[16] As a symbol of their new society, members of the first pioneer party in the Salt Lake Valley were rebaptized and reconfirmed members of the church. "We had, as it were, entered a new world and wished to renew our covenants and commence in newness of life," explained one of the men.[17]

The settlers called their new community "Deseret," a Book of Mormon name that was also meant to set it apart as the Kingdom of God—a religious and political government, which, when fully established, might prepare for Christ's coming reign. "All other governments are illegal and unauthorized," said a Mormon theoretical tract. "Any people attempting to govern themselves by laws of their own making, and by officers of their own appointment, are in direct rebellion against the kingdom of God."[18]

The Saints felt the ideals of religious theocracy most strongly during the first years of their settlement or in times of uncertainty when they thought the millennial days were close by. Their on-and-off hopes were not well received, as most Americans in the mid-nineteenth century considered theocracy an already-turned page from John Winthrop's Massachusetts Bay colony two hundred years before.

Another reason for the clashes in Utah was the American territorial system. The famed Northwest Ordinance of 1787 required settlers to gain self-government and statehood through a step-by-step process that could be slow, particularly in the American Southwest. Territories were virtual colonies—not unlike the colonies under British rule before the American Revolution—and citizens were denied "the rights to self-government that most white males elsewhere took for granted." The result in one western territory after another was the same: squabbles between the local people and the men Washington sent west—and the feeling that the federal government was "an obtrusive presence."[19] Even the best appointees often lacked the one quality westerners demanded: Their loyalties must be focused on the local welfare, not on Washington or their own careers.[20]

Like others, the Saints latched on to a popular constitutional theory of the time. Hoping to quiet the rising storm in Washington over expanding slavery in the territories, politicians like presidential candidates Lewis Cass and Stephen A. Douglas took the idea of neighborhood majority rule and applied it to the western territories, calling their proposal "squatter" or "popular" sovereignty. They argued "that a community was ready for self-government from the moment it was first settled," and majorities in the territories—not the U.S. Congress—should have the final say about local conditions.[21]

The Saints had come west hoping for local control, and popular sovereignty fit their aspirations perfectly. If power lay with the local people in a territory, Utah had a right to establish its theocracy and polygamy.[22] Historian Howard Lamar remarked how ordinary so much of the Saints' behavior was. The doctrines of the church were "not at war with the optimistic, perfectionist, comfort-seeking society of Jacksonian America," he wrote. But Lamar also noticed something different was going on in Utah, too, at least in degree. "What was missing was a single voice of dissent, an opposition, an evidence of popular elections." And by 1857, some outsiders thought conditions in Utah were out of control. "A federal court had been disrupted," official records were rumored to have been seized and burned, "and public officials could honestly report that they had been unable to perform their duties. Every single function the federal government was responsible for in a territory, outside of tax collection and defense, had been defied."[23]

For Young, confident in his religious and political authority, the exodus of bothersome federal authorities was a virtue. "Their number & quality [are] diminishing & becoming beautifully less," he wrote.[24] During the 1850s, as many as sixteen federal officers left their positions in the territory in "frustration, fright, or both."[25] While each of the territories surrounding Utah had a history of conflicts with Washington's appointees, none rivaled Utah's in number or overall drama.[26]

The strong Mormon response may well have been a sign of inward distress. By the mid-1850s, Mormon leaders believed their kingdom was not going well. The harvest of converts in America and Great Britain had fallen off. The Saints faced bad weather, insect plagues, poor crops, and near famine. Young sensed a spiritual lethargy among his people, perhaps because of their decade-long focus on pioneering but also because of the growing number of apostates and dissenters. Many immigrants to Zion were proving to be indigestible chaff.[27] To Young, Mormons were not living up to the standard of their mission.[28]

Church leaders tried several cures, including an invitation for members to look inward and make token pledges of their property to the Lord. But less than half of Utah's families made "consecrations" to the church.[29] A "home missionary" program was established in the hope that systematic preaching might stir "the people to repentance and a remembrance of their first love"—the gospel.[30] When these programs failed to achieve full reform, Young called for sterner measures. "Instead of…smooth, beautiful, sweet…silk-velvet-lipped preaching," he said, the people needed "sermons like peals of thunder."[31]

Young had precedents for his preaching. "A revival of religion in New England meant a time when that deep spiritual undercurrent of thought and emotion with regard to the future life…exhaled and steamed up into the atmosphere which pervaded all things," wrote Harriet Beecher Stowe.[32] The Mormons, so much like the Puritans, had such a campaign when camped on the plains during their westward migration, and their Book of Mormon chronicled the many times when ancient American prophets were able to bring people back to their religious devotion by strong preaching.[33]

These earlier revivals became patterns for the famed Mormon Reformation of 1856–57. "There are sins that men commit," Young preached at the beginning, "for which they cannot receive forgiveness in this world, or in that which is to come, and if they had their eyes open to see their true condition, they would be perfectly willing to have their blood spilt upon the ground, that the smoke thereof might ascend to heaven as an offering for their sins."[34] Sometimes the reformation sermons about "blood atonement" threatened more than "peals of thunder." "The time has been in Israel under the law of God," Young said, "that if a man was found guilty of adultery, he must have his blood shed, and that [time] is near at hand."[35]

The reform shook mightily. For a time, church leaders suspended the sacrament of the Lord's Supper, and Young remained in seclusion—signs that it was no longer business as usual in Utah. "Teachers" were dispatched into homes to "catechize" members about their sins, and in one part of southern Utah, local church authorities told the teachers to search church members' private boxes and drawers to "see that every thing is clean and pure."[36] One member remembered that the teachers' intrusion could be a "fearful ordeal," resulting in embarrassment and false confessions.[37]

As the enthusiasm grew, the language of some church leaders became especially harsh, particularly beyond Salt Lake City where distance seemed to magnify the revival. In several communities, gangs of zealots—usually young men led both by a spirit of adventure and religious excess—engaged in acts of intimidation: "hellish murderous conduct," said one victim.[38] Their assaults were aimed at those considered of weak faith or apostate, or even those who might speak against their activity.[39] In Cedar City in the southern part of the territory, church leaders spoke of clear lines of judgment—of "blood sucking gentiles," pruning the "bitter branches" of disbelief, and the need to obey strictly "those who are over us."[40]

Perhaps a majority of the Saints, believing themselves in spiritual jeopardy, searched their souls and bettered their lives. Church meetings became more frequent and better attended. Items previously taken "in hours of darkness" were returned.[41] Tithing and other church donations increased, as did polygamous marriages, another measure of Mormon observance at the time. Every Saint wishing to be considered a Saint received the sin-washing ordinance of rebaptism, part of the reformation's mercy when Young and the church seemed willing to forgive the gravest sin if only men and women would try to do right.[42]

The reformation was extraordinary, and nothing in Mormon history had been like it—or would be. From Young's perspective, the reformation accomplished a great deal of good, though the tough talk about blood atonement and dissenters must have helped create a climate of violence in the territory, especially among those who chose to

QUESTIONS

LATTER DAY SAINTS.

Have you committed murder, by shedding innocent blood, or consenting thereto?

Have you betrayed your brethren or sisters in anything?

Have you committed adultery, by having any connection with a woman that was not your wife, or a man that was not your husband?

Have you taken and made use of property not your own, without the consent of the owner?

Have you cut hay where you had no right to, or turned your animals into another person's grain or field, without his knowledge and consent?

Have you lied about or maliciously misrepresented any person or thing?

Have you borrowed anything that you have not returned, or paid for?

Have you borne false witness against your neighbor?

Have you taken the name of the Deity in vain?

Have you coveted anything not your own?

Have you been intoxicated with strong drink?

Have you found lost property and not returned it to the owner, or used all diligence to do so?

Have you branded an animal that you did not know to be your own?

Have you taken another's horse or mule from the range and rode it, without the owner's consent?

Have you fulfilled your promises in paying your debts, or run into debt without prospect of paying?

Have you taken water to irrigate with, when it belonged to another person at the time you used it?

Do you pay your tithing promptly?

Do you teach your family the gospel of salvation?

Do you speak against your brethren, or against any principle taught us in the Bible, Book of Mormon, Book of Doctrine and Covenants, Revelations given through Joseph Smith the Prophet and the Presidency of the Church as now organized?

Do you pray in your family night and morning and attend to secret prayer?

Do you wash your body and have your family do so, as often as health and cleanliness require and circumstances will permit?

Do you labor six days and rest, or go to the house of worship, on the seventh?

Do you and your family attend Ward meetings?

Do you preside over your household as a servant of God, and is your family subject to you?

Have you labored diligently and earned faithfully the wages paid you by your employers?

Do you oppress the hireling in his wages?

Have you taken up and converted any stray animal to your own use, or in any manner appropriated one to your benefit, without accounting therefor to the proper authorities?

In answer to the above questions, let all men and women confess to the persons they have injured and make restitution, or satisfaction. And when catechising the people, the Bishops, Teachers, Missionaries and other officers in the Church are not at liberty to pry into sins that are between a person and his or her God, but let such persons confess to the proper authority, that the adversary may not have an opportunity to take advantage of human weaknesses, and thereby destroy souls.

REFORMATION CATECHISM. *Courtesy LDS Church History Library.*

take license from it. As the revival proceeded, church leaders in Salt Lake City began cautioning local leaders not to go beyond the preaching of righteousness.[43] Still later, word was sent to southern Utah to "keep things perfectly quiet and let all things be done peacefully but with firmness and let there be no excitement. Let the people be united in their feelings and faith as well as works and keep alive the spirit of the Reformation."[44]

In the summer of 1856—shortly before the reformation's crescendo—Young sent Mormon apostles John Taylor and George A. Smith to the nation's capital with petitions for statehood.[45] Becoming a state would mean Utah could end its squabbles with territorial appointees. But Sen. Stephen A. Douglas of Illinois, an old acquaintance and former legislative representative of the Saints, and Utah's territorial delegate, John M. Bernhisel, both advised that the political winds then blowing made it an unfavorable time to push for statehood.[46]

Irked at the prospect of continued colonial rule, in January 1857 the Utah legislature drafted strongly worded memorials asserting "the right to have a voice in the selection of our rulers."[47] Young told Smith and Bernhisel that a new batch of unfit federal appointees would be turned out "as fast as they come let the consequences be what they may." The Saints were "determined to claim the right of having a voice

JAMES BUCHANAN. *Matthew Brady, Courtesy Library of Congress.*

in the selection of our officers," Young said.[48] Following instructions, Bernhisel met with newly elected U.S. president James Buchanan and, a few days later, presented the memorials to Jacob Thompson, the secretary of interior. The last interview did not go well. Thompson called Utahns' demand for territorial officers of their own liking and their promise to send away any others a virtual "declaration of war." "When you tell a man that he *must* do a thing," Thompson lectured, "it excites in him a feeling to resist." If the Mormons "got into trouble with the General Government," Thompson believed, it would be their own fault.[49]

The Mormon memorials did not come close to the firebrand language of many Southern "states' righters" before the Civil War.[50] They did, however, come at a dangerous time. "These petitions and the cabinet's reaction to them were fateful," historian William P. MacKinnon wrote, pointing also to letters that came into the government's hands within two days of the memorials.[51] The first was from Judge Drummond, complaining that Brigham Young and the Mormons maintained a virtual reign of terror. Drawing on the Stiles incident, he claimed the Mormons had burned the papers, dockets, and law books of the Utah Territorial Supreme Court, a charge that later proved untrue. Drummond also reported that Young, "more traitorous than ever," was responsible for the Gunnison killings and the death of Territorial Secretary Almon W. Babbitt, recently slain by Cheyenne raiders in Nebraska Territory. Drummond's letter appeared in the *New York Herald* on March 20, the day after the administration received it.[52] On the day of its publication, Utah's chief justice, John F. Kinney—who was visiting Washington—presented the U.S. attorney general similar letters from himself and Utah surveyor general David H. Burr, both urging that a U.S. military force be sent to Utah. Thus "within two weeks of taking office, James Buchanan and his cabinet had a collection of stunning new inputs on Utah affairs from the territory's truculent legislative assembly, its chief justice, an associate supreme court justice, and the surveyor general," wrote MacKinnon.[53]

Soon many American newspapers were responding sharply to what was going on. A letter published under the name "Veratus" in the April 29, 1857, *American Journal* made the outlandish claim that one hundred thousand Mormons were poised to fight the U.S. government, aided by two hundred thousand "spies and emissaries" and three hundred thousand "savage" Indian allies. Veratus demanded that five thousand U.S. troops be sent to Utah to put down the supposed threat.[54] The *New York Tribune* told its readers that Utah was full of espionage, rape, robbery, and suicide. "Surely there never was a more atrocious and revolting tyranny," it said.[55] The *New York Times* demanded Young be replaced by a new territorial governor, backed by a military force "to tender the Constitution with one hand, while a drawn sword is held in the other."[56]

The anti-Mormon newspaper campaign assumed the worst about conditions in the territory and was more than just a response to the letters of Drummond and others. From the beginning of the United States as a nation, a strain of popular culture reacted against many minorities and outsiders with unusual virulence—"heated exaggeration, suspiciousness, and conspiratorial fantasy," said cultural historian Richard Hofstadter.[57] By the middle 1850s, this strain of culture was flowing against such widely different groups as Catholics, Jews, Masons, and Mormons, who were viewed as threats to "the very basis of American life—democracy, religion, and justice." The Anti-Masonic Party, the "Know Nothings" and their American Party, and eventually the fast-rising Republican Party voiced some of these nativist or traditionist concerns.[58]

"I regret to say that within the last few months prejudice against us as a people has greatly increased," Bernhisel warned Young, "not only at the seat of the Central Government, but throughout this extended Republic." While the letters and memorials had touched a nerve, Buchanan and Thompson in their talks with Bernhisel mentioned another complaint against the Mormons: polygamy. The Saints' "'peculiar institution' is looked upon with a holy horror," Bernhisel warned Young.[59] Buchanan had recently emerged from a presidential campaign against the Republicans, who had gained political ground with their platform denouncing the "twin relics of barbarism"—slavery and polygamy. Buchanan's Democrats, now in office, were in no mood to appear soft on the issue.

In addition, Buchanan had no wish to let the Mormons use popular sovereignty for their own purposes. If the unpopular Utahns were allowed to use the doctrine to defend theocracy and polygamy, the federal government would have less power to heal the slave controversy and preserve the Union, just at a time when the nation was at full pitch over the great North–South issues of the Fugitive Slave Act, the Supreme Court's Dred Scott decision, and growing bloodshed in Kansas Territory. "Public sentiment favoring both a firm assertion of federal authority in Utah and the curbing of Brigham Young's political power had made some kind of response on [Buchanan's] part almost mandatory," historian Kenneth Stampp concluded.[60] In the process, the new administration could send a message to would-be Southern secessionists that rebellion would not be tolerated.

George A. Smith asked the federal government to investigate conditions in the territory and see for itself what was going on. He later said he furnished the government "with sufficient testimony to satisfy any unprejudiced mind" that his people were innocent of wrongdoing, or at least enough to convince Washington "there were two sides to the question." But Washington officials were either not convinced or felt that sympathizing with Mormons was politically unwise. Despite his efforts, he did not gain the government's consent to investigate conditions in Utah.[61]

On May 28, 1857, two months after Bernhisel had his interviews, the Buchanan administration declared Utah "in a state of substantial rebellion" and issued military orders.[62] Buchanan's action went against the advice of the nation's chief military officer, Gen. Winfield Scott. Scott argued that there was not enough time to recruit, supply, and move an army safely to Utah before the winter of 1857.[63] But by now events had their own momentum and were beyond careful planning. Mormon demands for local control, the anti-Mormon clique's letters, and a growing national repugnance for plural marriage had come together during a time of rising nativism and sectional controversy.[64]

Without the instant news provided by a transcontinental telegraph (it would not be finished for another four years), Mormon leaders got word that things were coming to a head when Bernhisel and Smith arrived in Salt Lake City on May 29. They came with the spring mail coach, the first to get through the melting mountain snow, and the two men, along with the mails, brought with them the disturbing rumor that Washington might replace Young with a new governor, backed by thousands of troops. Young's four-year term had expired in 1854, and for two and a half years he had been serving on an interim basis.[65]

Young, hearing Bernhisel and Smith's news, wanted his people to be informed. At a time when few Utahns had access to national news, he arranged a public reading of the recently arrived anti-Mormon newspaper editorials and the published letters of Drummond and Magraw. The reading took four long hours. "Never did sat[a]n reign in the hearts of men as he does now," wrote one Saint who heard a summary of the session.[66] In a letter, Young tried to lighten the situation with humor. "Uncle Sams 'Puppies' do not appear particularly affectionate toward the 'poor Mormons,'" he told one of his correspondents.[67]

When the next mail coach arrived on June 23, the Saints got more bad news. Parley P. Pratt, a popular Mormon apostle, had been murdered in Arkansas. Church members called Pratt their "Archer of

Paradise" and admired him for his many roles, which included those of missionary, explorer, preacher, and writer. Pratt's most important book, *A Voice of Warning* (1837), had led to many baptisms, and its arguments helped shape Mormon historical and theological thinking for many years to come.[68]

In 1854 Parley Pratt had met Mormon convert Eleanor McLean in San Francisco during one of his missionary tours. Another missionary described her as "intelligent" and "energetic" but also "overzealous."[69] For several years, her marriage with Hector McLean had been unraveling, and her decision to become a Mormon and have her two young sons baptized ended any hope of a reconciliation. Hector, a hard drinker, put Eleanor "by violence" from their home one night and later planned to confine her to a mental asylum. Without her knowledge, he sent their children to Eleanor's parents in New Orleans. Eleanor followed and tried to reclaim the children. But her parents resisted—they, like Hector, did not want them to be Mormons. Finally, Eleanor made her way to Salt Lake City, where she became Pratt's plural wife.[70]

In the fall of 1856, Young asked Pratt to help direct church activities in the eastern United States—but with a caution. He pointedly told Parley to devote himself to his church duties. Eleanor was going east at the same time in another attempt to reclaim her children, and Young did not want the apostle to become involved. Parley obeyed—technically. While he did not go to New Orleans, he hoped to escort Eleanor and her children to Utah after learning she was successful in securing them from her parents. Eleanor and Parley planned to meet somewhere in the lower Midwest.[71]

By the spring of 1857, the custody battle had become a public sensation. Eleanor had gotten the children, but Hector was in hot pursuit. He had her arrested in Indian Territory, just west of Arkansas. Pratt also was arrested on his way to meet her, and they were both brought before a Van Buren, Arkansas, magistrate in mid-May.[72]

Five hundred men and women crowded the courtroom and nearby grounds. Most wanted summary justice against the Mormon apostle, who had committed no Arkansas crime but had violated the unwritten law of the day giving a husband strong control over a wife.

"Gentleman, I do not rely on weapons," Pratt said when a judge released him early in the morning and offered him a knife and pistol to protect himself. Soon Hector McLean and his supporters caught up with the defenseless and fleeing Pratt twelve miles north of Van Buren. Hector fired half a dozen bullets at his victim and stabbed him twice. He returned ten minutes later to fire another bullet into Pratt's neck. The Mormon apostle died of his wounds later that day.[73]

Hector boasted of his exploit. His accomplices included "the best men of the place and surrounding country," including fellow Masons "gathered from all parts of the territory," he said, as if the prevailing custom of vigilante action excused the killing. Because Hector was never charged with a crime and because Arkansans were involved, the public assumed the Mormons would have their revenge. The "seething and boiling" Mormons might attack Arkansas emigrants going through Utah, a California editor suggested on July 9, 1857.[74] The idea would later become a stock explanation for the Mountain Meadows Massacre.

Upon hearing news of Pratt's murder, Brigham Young said little publicly about it, and his letters belied the idea of vengeance. "The seeing of our faithful Elders slaughtered in cold blood," he wrote on July 4, is "at times almost to[o] grievous to be borne, but…the Spirit within me whispers, peace be still."[75] Another letter sent to Orson Pratt, Parley's brother, had the same plaintive quality. "I regret very much to learn of the assassination of Bro Parley by the villain McLane," Young wrote. "One more good man has gone to assist Bro. Joseph [and] Hiram [Smith]," the earlier Mormon martyrs.[76] A third letter simply invoked Providence: "the Lord's not my will be done," it said.[77] While deploring Pratt's death and mourning his passing, Young also believed that his fellow churchman had been unwise and disregarded counsel.[78] Other Mormons were less philosophical, and Pratt's murder undoubtedly increased Mormon anger and the growing division between Utahns and easterners.

One event after another had drawn borders between Utahns and their fellow citizens. Two rival kingdoms were struggling against each other. One was religious and local. The other was civil and national. The issue was not just law and order, but whose law and order. Resolving the issue would embroil Utah and the federal government in a conflict that would come to be called the Utah War—and create the atmosphere for a massacre.

CHAPTER THREE

No More Submit to Oppression

Silver Lake, July 24, 1857

TEN YEARS HAD passed since July 24, 1847—the day that Brigham Young and fellow Mormons first arrived in the Salt Lake Valley. They had been celebrating the anniversary of that "Pioneer Day" ever since.[1] By 1856 Young became aware of a crystal lake in the mountains near the top of Big Cottonwood Canyon southeast of Salt Lake City. That year he hosted 450 Pioneer Day guests at the site, which became known as Silver Lake. He enjoyed the celebration so well that at its close he proposed "that we do not dissolve" the party "but adjourn it until the 23d day of July, 1857...preparatory to celebrating the 24th."[2] Going ahead with his plans, Young sponsored the two-day picnic again, except that this year—the tenth anniversary of the Mormons' arrival—everything was on a grander scale.

The Pioneer Day celebration was the kind of event Brigham Young liked. He and his office staff created a lengthy guest list and sent out formal invitations. Even though Young invited two thousand guests and their families, he regretted he could not include more. "I never know where to stop in my feelings until every Latter-day Saint is invited," he told a Salt Lake City congregation a few days before the festivities. "If I were to satisfy my feelings, I would invite the whole of you." There was, however, one important condition. His guests must "go, tarry, and return in harmony and peace." He wanted order.[3]

PIC-NIC PARTY

AT THE

HEAD WATERS

OF

BIG COTTONWOOD.

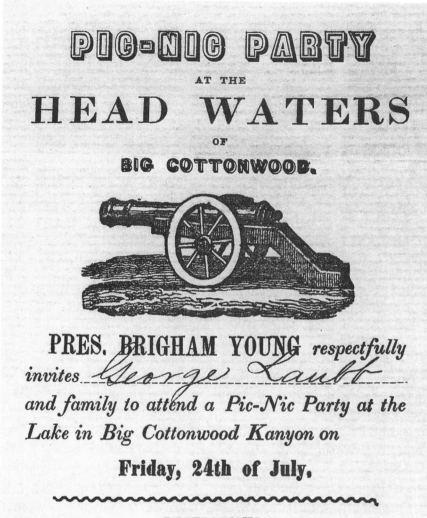

PRES. *BRIGHAM YOUNG* respectfully *invites* George Laubt *and family to attend a Pic-Nic Party at the Lake in Big Cottonwood Kanyon on*

Friday, 24th of July,

REGULATIONS.

You will be required to start so as to pass the first mill, about four miles up the Kanyon, before 12 o'clock, on Thursday, the 23rd, as no person will be allowed to pass that point after 2 o'clock, p.m. of that day.

All persons are forbidden to smoke cigars or pipes, or kindle fires, at any place in the Kanyon, except on the camp ground.

The Bishops are requested to accompany those invited from their respective Wards, and see that each person is well fitted for the trip, with good, substantial, steady teams, wagons, harness, hold-backs and locks, capable of completing the journey without repair, and a good driver, so as not to endanger the life of any individual.

Bishops will, before passing the first mill, furnish a full and complete list of all persons accompanying them from their respective Wards, and hand the same to the Guard at the gate.

GREAT SALT LAKE CITY, July 18, 1857.

BRIGHAM YOUNG PICNIC INVITATION. *Courtesy Special Collections, Marriott Library, University of Utah.*

By heritage, Young was a Puritan, but contrary to that people's modern image, he was not puritanical, if only to help his people get through their hardships.[4] Pioneering in the American West had been hard work, and the past two years harder still. Drought and a scourge of crop-devouring grasshoppers and worms had led to poor harvests and hunger.[5] Salt Lake City's bishops, charged with the public welfare, took stock of each neighborhood and fed the hungry, some of whom were found begging in the streets.[6] Fortunately, crop conditions had improved by the summer of '57, providing another reason for celebrating.[7]

On the afternoon of July 22, 1857, Young and his party left Salt Lake City for the Pioneer Day celebration, traveling some seventeen miles southeast to a mill a few miles up Big Cottonwood Canyon. Early the next morning, they continued through the canyon toward a campsite along Silver Lake.[8] Young passed hundreds of his waiting guests, who then followed for the final fourteen miles in some 460 carriages and wagons of various kinds and descriptions.[9] The people were equally diverse, with varied languages, dialects, and clothes of faded American and European fashion—the fruits of Mormon missionary efforts at home and abroad.[10]

By that night, the Latter-day Saints were dancing, fishing, and enjoying the alpine beauty.[11] At twilight, Young spoke to his guests. He said "he had things on his mind" that he had never told them. "These are the secret chambers of the mountains...calculated to ward off the traveller on the outside from coming down in here."[12] If only the Mormon people "would do right," he promised, their enemies would never drive them from their mountain valleys.[13] At the end of the program, Heber C. Kimball, one of Young's counselors, "offered a prayer of thanksgiving unto God for his goodness to his people, prayed for Israel and Israel's enemies, and renewedly dedicated and consecrated unto God the ground" where the Saints were camped.[14]

The next day, July 24, the Saints' celebration included patriotic speeches and three cannon salutes in honor of the people's rights, their independence, and their leaders. Repeatedly, the partygoers also offered "three groans" for the state of Missouri.[15] The Mormons had not lost their sense of humor, but neither had they lost their memory of the suffering they experienced in that state. Still later the territorial militia drilled, including a cohort of teenagers. Militia drills were a common part of public celebrations in mid nineteenth-century America.

About noon, the idyllic charm was broken by an unexpected visit. Five horsemen rode into camp, including Salt Lake City mayor

PICNIC AT BIG COTTONWOOD CANYON. *T. B. H. Stenhouse*, The Rocky Mountain Saints (*London, 1874*).

Abraham O. Smoot. Several weeks earlier Smoot had been carrying mail and looking after church business in the East. Arriving in Kansas Territory, he saw streams of heavy freight wagons heading west. They belonged to the Russell, Majors & Waddell freighting company. When Smoot asked the company's captains and teamsters where they were going and why, he got only vague answers.[16]

Smoot hurried to the Kansas City office of William H. Russell, one of the freighting company's owners. Russell confirmed Smoot's fears. The wagons, Smoot learned, were carrying supplies for as many as twenty-five hundred government troops just ordered to Utah. They were to serve under a newly appointed governor and other new federal appointees to enforce U.S. law and put down a reported Mormon rebellion.[17]

Besides confirming the army's long-rumored approach, the Mormon travelers learned another unsettling fact. When one of Smoot's associates tried to pick up the mail at nearby Independence, Missouri, the postmaster waved him off. The government did not intend to deliver "more mail for Salt Lake City at present," he said with no more explanation. This news meant the federal mail contract with Utahns had been cancelled. For nervous Mormons, the cancellation raised an unsettling question: Was Washington cutting Utah off from the rest of the nation, the kind of action nations take before launching a war?[18]

With news of the oncoming army and the cancelled contract, Smoot and his associates gathered their mail station outfits and stock and headed for home. East of Fort Laramie in present-day Wyoming, Smoot's party ran into fellow mail courier and frontiersman Porter Rockwell. Rockwell, Smoot, and another courier decided to leave the slower-moving stock for others to bring, while they made a run for Salt Lake City. They hitched two spans of their "best animals to a small spring wagon" and traveled the final 513 miles from Fort Laramie in five days, arriving in Salt Lake City on July 23.[19]

Eleanor McLean Pratt returned to Salt Lake City with them, still fleeing from Hector McLean, who remained intent on locking her in an insane asylum.[20] Eleanor was eager to provide vivid details of Parley's assassination, but the accounts of the Silver Lake picnic would not mention her, perhaps because she didn't attend or because Parley's death had been known in Utah for more than a month. It was old news.[21]

When Smoot and his fellow horsemen reached the camping grounds near Silver Lake on July 24, they were ushered into Lt. Gen. Daniel H. Wells's tent, where they reported to church leaders the information they had learned. Since spring the leaders had known an army might come, but Smoot brought new, disturbing details that rekindled old Mormon fears.[22]

The army was to be led by Gen. William S. Harney, a two-fisted Jacksonian Indian fighter. For Mormons unsure of the army's purpose, the news of Harney's appointment raised concerns of renewed violence against them. Utah had seen soldiers before, but Harney's leadership suggested severe measures. "I said if General Harney came here, I should then know the intention of [the] goverment," wrote Brigham Young in his journal.[23]

Harney was a skilled commander, but one with a reputation for violence. He had earned the title "Squaw Killer" for the massacre of eighty-six Sioux, including women and children, at Ash Hollow, Nebraska Territory, in 1855.[24] Known for his "quick temper" and "violent nature," he had been court-martialed four times by the army. A civil court had also tried him for the torture death of one of his female slaves, who he believed had taken his keys. According to one newspaper report, "She was lacerated and mangled in so horrid a manner that the Jury of inquest was unable to determine whether it was done with whips or hot irons. The general opinion was that it was done with both."[25] The trial jury acquitted Harney, though his biographer did not believe justice had been done. "White society in the 1830s cared little about the death of a slave," he wrote, "and the murderer proceeded with his life and military career."[26]

Besides Harney's approach, Smoot announced the suspended mail contract, which meant the end of one of Young's most ambitious ventures, the Brigham Young Express or "Y.X." Company—a forerunner of the Pony Express and the Ben Holladay Stagecoach line, and a potential competitor of the Russell, Majors & Waddell freight trains. Young had hoped the company would improve the postal service, lower the cost of Utah's imported goods, and aid Mormon immigration.[27]

Along with this news, Smoot may have reported that the likely new governor was named Cumming. At least one Mormon leader mistook the name for "Cummins"—an old Missouri persecutor of the Saints who had signed the Jackson County manifesto. The idea that R. W. Cummins would command Utah's civil government produced "utter horror and detestation," George A. Smith later said.[28] As the church leaders listened to each of Smoot's discoveries, the gravity of the situation settled on them. Perhaps worst of all, Washington had made key decisions affecting Utah but explained nothing to the people of the territory—a foreboding silence.[29]

The men who met in Wells's tent tried coming to grips with everything Smoot told them. At the end of the meeting, the leaders agreed on a general policy. First, the Mormons would accept the new territorial appointees—but only if they "would behave themselves," Young said. This willingness apparently included accepting the illusory "Cummins." However, Harney and the army were different. If he crossed South Pass—the main route into Utah and roughly the territory's eastern border—there would be a fight, and "the *buzards* Should *pick his bones,*" Young said. The Saints would "no more…submit to oppression either to individuals towns Counties states or Nation."[30]

That evening Daniel H. Wells spoke at the canyon celebration's final prayer service. Years earlier, Wells had been a politician, militia officer, and land dealer in the Mississippi River bottoms when the Latter-day Saints arrived in Illinois and established their headquarters at Nauvoo. Sympathetic to the Saints, he played a major role in the city's final defense against local vigilantes, and he later accepted the Mormon faith. Once in Utah, Wells was given command of the territorial militia, which Utahns called the Nauvoo Legion in memory of bygone years. In January 1857, Young chose the forty-two-year-old Wells to be his second counselor in the church's ruling First Presidency.[31]

Although Wells had many talents, he was seldom easy or impressive before a crowd. He looked much like fellow Illinoisan Abraham

Lincoln, and one of his critics described him as "a lantern-jawed, long-faced, raw-boned, loose boned, loose-jointed, shambling-gated man."[32] But on this occasion, Wells seemed transformed. Lifted up on a large boulder to speak and pray, he spoke of liberty and rights and the need sometimes to defend them.[33] An observer that night wrote, "Our Independence was declared as a free people by Brigham and his counselors and…all…said Amen."[34] One man wrote a song on the spot:

> Powder Bullet Sword and Gun
> Boys arouse we'll have some fun
> As sure as fate the time has come
> So fix your Guns for shooting.[35]

Ironically, while some Mormons talked about fighting the United States and gaining their independence, American flags flew on the peaks on each side of Silver Lake.[36]

From its earliest years, Mormonism had been poised on the millennial cusp. Its people believed they were preparing for the end of times, and with an army marching against them, the final years never seemed so close.[37] In the next few months, they might fight a war and witness the inauguration of the long-promised latter-day kingdom of heaven.

DANIEL H. WELLS. *Courtesy Nelson B. Wadsworth.*

That, too, might bring Mormon political independence. Was Zion, as the Saints called their home, about to make its own way in the world?

When the evening closed, the partygoers determined not to let the news ruin their holiday. One record of the canyon picnic said that after the evening's prayer service, the people resumed their "former cheerfulnes," and "amusements & sports... continued with redoubled interest."[38] Young, who liked being a contrarian, believed that Smoot's visit had in fact "helped the people to enjoy themselves."[39] Some of the revelers continued until the early hours of the morning, and then, at 5:00 a.m., Young called them together to give instructions about breaking their camp and to wish them a good journey back to their homes and their ordinary lives.[40]

But the coming months would be anything but ordinary in Utah.

CHAPTER FOUR

Avoid All Excitement, But Be Ready

Salt Lake City to Parowan, July 24–August 8, 1857

SMOOT'S NEWS AT the Big Cottonwood Canyon picnic changed everything. Earlier when Young had heard of the newspaper outcry against the Saints in the East, he was not ruffled. "We have become like the little boy that got so in the habit of being whip[p]ed every night that he could not go to sleep without a whipping," he said.[1] Throughout the summer he had predicted that once easterners got a close look at the Mormons' chief accuser, Judge W. W. Drummond, they would see that they had been "effectually humbugged."[2] In a private aside, Young described Drummond as "vi[c]ious and brutal, whining and snappish, vain as a peacock and ignorant as a jack-ass."[3] Nothing serious could come from such a man, he believed. In June, Young had suggested that if an army came to Utah, it would "find nothing to fight," for the Mormons would not resist. "I trust in the Lord of hosts to rule and overrule all for the good of his Saints," he said.[4]

Twelve days before Smoot's arrival, George A. Smith expressed hope that despite the rumors, no army would be sent. Speaking before one congregation, he reasoned, "Any wise Statesman will see that if they [U. S. government officials] interfered with one Territory, they would have plenty of Business in others." Besides, the government had enough to do without worrying about Utah.[5]

But Smoot's July 24 news suddenly made the rumored prospect of a coming army real. From the moment Young and other Mormon leaders gathered together in Wells's tent that day, their world changed. By the time the Saints broke camp and started down the canyon, hard words were rolling off the tongue, as only fresh anger can do: "Squaw Killer" Harney, twenty-five hundred troops, the cancelled Mormon mail contract, the end of the Y.X. Company, the replacement of Young as governor, and most remarkable of all, Washington's utter failure to explain its intentions.[6] While the church had endured many things in its twenty-seven-year history, the Saints saw the government's sending an army against its own citizens as an abuse of power. For the next several months, Utahns referred to the approaching "Utah Expedition" as an armed "mob" and Harney as the chief mobber.[7]

The Saints were hardly back in their homes after the canyon picnic when trouble broke out. Some of the returning partygoers and other Mormons turned their anger on members of the U.S. surveyor's office, whom they saw as partly responsible for Washington's decision to dispatch troops. On Saturday afternoon, July 25, two Mormons in Salt Lake City used stones and clubs to give Cornelius G. Landon, a clerk in the surveyor's office, a "tremendous thrashing." Landon had been overheard telling overland emigrants what "damned rascals" the Saints were. The emigrants, standing nearby, were horrified by the attack but resisted their instinct to get involved.[8] Landon was an excommunicated Mormon who had been fined a month earlier for public "drunkeness & breaking the Peace."[9] Meanwhile, he had been investigating the Saints' military capacity, or as he put it, "prying into Mormon secrets rather minutely."[10] On the afternoon of Landon's thrashing, surveyor Charles Mogo ran into a store to avoid being pelted by stones. He left the territory within the week without waiting for his family to go with him.[11]

Two days later, Landon met with more trouble. During the evening of July 27 two or three dozen men surrounded the surveyor's office looking for Landon and another clerk, W. H. Wilson. Landon escaped by jumping from a second-story window and hiding in a warehouse. He later fled to California in disguise.[12] Wilson was less fortunate. The vigilantes hauled him to the Jordan River west of the city. There, according to Wilson, his interrogators put a rope around his neck and pressured him at gun- and knife-point "to make statements against" the surveyor general of Utah, David H. Burr. Wilson was released the next day unharmed.[13] The identities of the men who planned and took part in the incident never became public. Like their own tormentors in Missouri and Illinois, the Mormons had taken action against those who were not in *their* mainstream, men deemed to be enemies.

For two years the local people and the surveyors had complained about each other. In reports sent east, the surveyors said the settlers were meddling with Indians by cultivating a close friendship with them. They also struck against local Mormon power by saying Utahns obstructed their work and made "extensive depredations upon the public lands," including taking land for church purposes.[14] "The inhuman cruelty of this [Mormon] people is equal to their sensuality," charged one surveyor's letter published in the *New York Herald*.[15]

Such accusations nettled Young. The surveyors believed "every body except themselves were trespassers" on the domain, Young protested. They "throw down fences, and even houses...graze their animals upon the grain field, and use fence poles for fuel," he said. If anyone complained, the surveyors abused and insulted them, as though "no person has any right to say a word, or make any complaint about it."[16] Young had not forgotten the double-dealing of surveyors and magistrates in Missouri that cost some of the Saints their land titles there.[17] He also believed—probably correctly—that the Utah surveyors had been sloppy in their work and had submitted fraudulent accounts to Washington.[18] The Mormons especially suspected Wilson—the man who said he was taken to the Jordan River and threatened—and they demanded he account for the government property in the surveyor's office.[19]

Young's first sermon after the canyon celebration made clear that the contention between the Mormon settlers and the surveyors was part of a larger battle. By "whining, bickering, howling, grovelling, squalling, and scratching,...many are striving to most egregiously befool our Government and squander its revenue," Young said of the territorial officers and their allies. He also had a word for anyone who opposed his people, including Christian ministers who, he believed, had a role in leading or influencing some of the Missouri and Illinois mobs. "Woe, woe to those men who come here to unlawfully meddle with me and this people," he warned.[20]

Young cited the second chapter of Daniel, a favorite Old Testament passage for the Saints. It told of a stone, cut without hands from the mountain, that was destined to roll forth and "never be destroyed," though it would be "a stone of offence to the nations of the earth." To Young and many Mormons, the scripture foretold their church's role in ushering in Christ's latter-day kingdom.[21]

Yet much of Young's speech suggested that the suddenness of the current crisis also had him seeking secure footing. He wondered how a serious-minded government could put soldiers on the plains in the middle of the summer—too late to make a successful march into Utah unless the Mormons helped them in. Was the crisis some kind of show to satisfy eastern public opinion? Facing this uncertainty, Young relied on his strong sense of providence. Would not God protect the Saints? he asked.[22]

On the same day as Young's sermon, Heber C. Kimball, his plain-spoken first counselor, framed the dilemma that faced the Mormons. "If we will not yield to [the government's] meanness," he said, "they will say we have mutinized against the President of the United States, and then they will put us under martial law and massacre this people." It was a case of being damned *regardless*, just as had happened under state officials in the Mormon past. Kimball ended his remarks in his typical earthy style. "Send 2,500 troops here...to make a desolation of this people!" he exclaimed. "I have wives enough to whip out the United States for they will whip themselves."[23]

The following Sunday when the Saints met again to worship, a week's worries seemed to have overtaken any slender hope for a peaceful settlement. Kimball warned that the army wanted to take Mormon women back to the States. Although he did not cite the Steptoe incident, it had to be on his mind, chapter and verse. Kimball also condemned the United States to a "mildew" of destruction, like one of the Mosaic plagues of Egypt.[24]

When Young took the pulpit, the Final Days seemed to be closing in. "The Lord is...bringing to pass the sayings of the Prophets faster than the people are prepared to receive them," he said. "The time must come when there will be a separation between this kingdom and the kingdoms of this world...The time must come when this kingdom must be free and independent from all other kingdoms." He asked the congregation, "Are you prepared to have the thread cut to-day?"[25]

On many Sunday evenings, Young gathered church leaders in his private office for a prayer meeting. Young used these occasions to build consensus and smooth policy. When Mormon leaders met on August 2, the same evening that Young and Kimball preached, the men were bracing for the coming conflict. The prayer meeting became a virtual council of war, and over the succeeding weeks Young decided how to face the emergency.[26]

First, Young announced that he wanted the Saints outside of Utah to join the main settlements in the territory. The war would put them at great risk, and, once in Utah, they would strengthen Mormon numbers. During the coming months, the Mormons abandoned their missions in California and present-day Nevada. Scattered Saints in the East were also urged to hurry to Utah.[27]

Second, Young spoke of his military strategy. The Mormons would use hit-and-run, scorched-earth, and guerrilla tactics, attacking the army's thousand-mile line of supply. Every mile on the Great Plains and every barrier and fissure of the Rocky Mountains would become an ally to the mountain-toughened Mormons.[28] "The US are fools to come upon this people & so are those men who are bringing great quantities of Goods unto us this season," Young said, referring to the army's freighters. If the United States wanted to fight a war, Young intended that "they shall furnish [us] with arms and aminition."[29] Mormon raiders would simply take them from the army.

Third, Young had a plan if Gen. Harney made it to Utah. He promised that the general would find Salt Lake City in ashes, like Moscow after Napoleon's invasion of Russia. Perhaps the Saints would scatter in the mountains or find a new place to gather in some remote region of the West. It was better to destroy their cities than to leave them for outsiders, as had happened with Mormon towns and villages in Missouri and Illinois. Young wanted the army to be without any kind of succor if it got to the Great Basin—no buildings to house soldiers and no food from village gardens—nothing but the semidesert the Saints had found when they arrived a decade earlier.[30]

The last part of Young's plan included Indians. "We shall have the Lamanites with us," he declared, applying a Book of Mormon term to native people.[31] Young came to believe that no successful guerrilla war could be fought without the aid of surrounding Indian tribes. They could gather information about the army's movements and perhaps help harass the troops. At all costs, they must not ally with the government against the Mormons: that would be fatal for the kind of operation Young was planning.[32]

Employing Indians for warfare was not a concept unique to Young. As historian Martin Ridge observed, "The English, the French, and the Spanish all used Indians as allies when they waged war against each other."[33] American military leaders also relied on Indians to help fight their battles, as did Andrew Jackson at the Battle of Horseshoe Bend in 1814.[34]

Young's reliance on Indians, however, had a theological basis. From the first days of their church, the Mormons believed the Indians would have a special role to perform before the Second Coming of Christ. They were part of the House of Israel, like the Mormons themselves, descended from the Old Testament prophet Jacob or Israel. Mormon scripture said that this branch or "remnant" of the chosen people would accept the latter-day gospel, "blossom as the rose," and perhaps even cleanse the land of the ungodly.[35] "Ye shall be among them as a lion among the beasts of the forest, and as a young lion among the flocks of sheep, who, if he goeth through both treadeth down and teareth in pieces, and none can deliver," the Book of Mormon promised.[36]

The Saints' thinking in this regard was extraordinary, although they saw themselves as defenders, not rebels. Their viewpoint took on a sharper edge as they learned more about the makeup of the army. They sent spies into the army camps, hoping to "see and count" what they could.[37] The soldiers, who may have seen through these disguises, replied with stories to make the Mormons nervous. They wanted to "scalp old Brigham," they said, and spoke of the good times they would have in Utah, especially with the women.[38] Another rumor said the officers were deciding whether they should hang Young "with or without a trial."[39] A variant said Harney would "capture Brigham Young and the twelve apostles, execute them in a summary manner, and winter in the Temple of the Latter-day Saints."[40] To the Saints, these threats had credibility because of their previous experiences, especially in Illinois. There militiamen helped murder Mormon leaders at Carthage, expel the Saints from Nauvoo, and desecrate the Nauvoo temple.[41]

Harney was, in fact, living up to his tough reputation and hoping to subdue the Mormons. After receiving his military command, he made the request that he be appointed Utah's governor "with full powers to declare martial law." As long as Brigham Young lived, he told his superiors, the Mormons would recognize no other authority, "unless that other has the *power* to *compel* them to do so."[42]

The quality of some of the troops sent to Utah also made rumors of army violence believable. Reports circulating in the East claimed that the "Utah Expedition" had soldiers drawn from the "wildest and most rebellious men of the community," as well as foreign-born mercenaries.[43] Captain John Wolcott Phelps, a West Pointer with a distinguished military career ahead of him, said some of the men he commanded in the Utah Expedition would not meet even the low standards of army life in their native countries. Seven of Phelps's eight noncommissioned officers were foreigners, and other companies had a similar ratio. The rank-and-file soldiers "would sell their best article of clothing for liquor, though they have reflection enough to know that they will suffer from bitter cold in consequence," Phelps complained to his diary.[44]

The Mormons also believed the army's camp followers posed a threat. Almost five hundred privately owned wagons accompanied the army, each with its own teamsters or wagon masters. Other men rode horses or walked, many of them strung along for adventure and quick money. Contemporary non-Mormon accounts described these men as "unruly," "hot-headed Southerners," or even the "scum of the great Western Cities."[45] Included were legends or legends-in-making: grizzled mountain men Jim Bridger, Jim Baker, and Tim Goodale, and famous raiders or gunslingers of the post–Civil War era William Quantrill and George Shepard.[46] Even if the Mormons "managed to live in peace" with the army, concluded one Utah War historian, they "still r[a]n the risk of collision with the civilians who accompanied it."[47]

During the first week in August, convinced that war was closing upon him, Young wrote a series of important orders. He told the Mormons in San Bernardino, the largest Mormon settlement outside of Salt Lake City, to come home.[48] Elsewhere he asked his men to cultivate relations with Sioux and Cheyenne of the plains and to learn their languages quietly but quickly, "for the prospect is *that all Israel* will be needed to *carry on the work* of the *last days*."[49] On the day these letters were written, Young asked Jacob Hamblin to head the church's Indian mission in southern Utah. "Continue the conciliatory policy toward the Indians, which I have ever recommended," he told Hamblin, "and seek by works of righteousness to obtain their love and confidence, for they must learn that they have either got to help us, or the United States will kill us both."[50] Hamblin's appointment began a legendary career for the rugged but soft-spoken frontiersman, who became his church's leading "Indian apostle" on its southern frontier.[51]

Mormon leaders took other steps to ready their people for war. On August 1, Nauvoo Legion General Daniel H. Wells signed his "General Orders," directed to all military district commanders throughout the territory. Drawing on principles of the American Revolution in which his forefathers had served, Wells wrote, "When anarchy takes the place of orderly government, and mobocratic tyranny usurps the power to rule: [the people] are left to their inalienable right to defend themselves against all aggression upon their constitutional privileges."[52]

Wells wanted each military district ready on a moment's notice to march anywhere in the territory with arms, ammunition, transportation, and clothing for a winter campaign. Just as important was the matter of grain, one of the few foodstuffs that stored well. Grain had been the focus of Mormon leaders' admonitions for years. Isolated in the Great Basin, the Saints had been at times on the edge of starvation, something that might be avoided, leaders said, if the people would save their excess for times of need. The recent drought added to the worry. Now with the army approaching, they reemphasized those admonitions. "Report without delay any person in your district that disposes of a kernel of grain to any Gentile merchant or temporary sojourner or suffers it to go to waste," the orders read. With the policy came a caution: "Avoid all excitement, but Be ready."[53]

Territorial Utah with its theocracy easily mixed military, civic, and church departments, but Young, in the crisis, wanted the spiritual voice to be heard. The day after Wells wrote his military orders, Young signed a circular letter directed to presiding elders, bishops, and stake presidents in southern Utah. Generally speaking, in the Mormon church structure of the 1850s, presiding elders headed small "branch" congregations, bishops oversaw larger ones called "wards," and stake presidents supervised areas called "stakes" that might include several congregations. Young's letter was similar to Wells's orders, though it had a spiritual dimension. He counseled the Saints, "Prepare yourselves in all things—particularly by liveing your religion."[54]

Young directed the people to prepare everything necessary for survival if they came under siege. "Every pound of wool" was to be used to make warm clothing, ammunition was to be saved and firearms kept in working order, every kernel of grain was to be saved. "Those who persist in selling grain to the gentiles, or suffer their stock to trample it into the earth," he wrote, "I wish you to *note* as such."[55]

The flurry of orders put Utah on a war footing. The U.S. troops of the Utah Expedition were moving slowly, but to the Saints their progress was relentless, like a distant drumbeat growing louder. Utahns would not learn the full details of the approaching army's military orders until February 1858, and then only through government back channels. As it turned out, the instructions were similar to those previously issued to soldiers in "Bleeding Kansas," torn by sectional unrest. The army, the orders said, was to subordinate itself to the executive and judicial territorial officers appointed by the U.S. government. "In no case will you, your officers or men, attack any body of citizens whatever, except on such requisition or summons, or in sheer self-defense," read the instructions.[56] But without this information, Utah's people poured their fears into the uncertainty caused by reports of an opposing army and a government that seemed to accept the word of anyone but the local citizens themselves.

By the first week of August, leaders in Salt Lake City sent couriers throughout the territory with the militia orders, including communities situated in the north, west, and south.[57] Militia brigadier general Franklin D. Richards, a Latter-day Saint apostle, put his officers in northern Utah on notice. "We have experienced the repeated desolation of our homes," Richards wrote. "Our prophets and brethren have been imprisoned and murdered, & the people *en masse* have been exterminated from their midst." It was not just the suffering but the lack of due process that upset Richards. "We have appealed to Judges and Governors of those States for redress of our wrongs in vain, and when we applied to the President of the United States for our rights we were told '*your cause is just but we can do nothing for you*'"—words of U.S. President Martin Van Buren when Joseph Smith had asked for his help. "We now appeal to the God of our Fathers & Prophets for protection against the hostilities of any Mob that shall invade our Territory, and invoke aid of the heavens to strengthen us in defending ourselves against further aggressions." Richards's letter concluded by urging the preserving of grain. Any person giving "a Kernel of grain to any Gentile merchant and temporary sojourner, or suffers it to go to waste" was to be reported.[58] George A. Smith would deliver a similar message to the communities of southern Utah.

Smith was one of those Mormon leaders who had been so outspoken during the Sabbath preaching on August 2. "If I did not talk strong," he later said of his remarks, "it was not because I did not feel strong."[59] He told the Saints that he believed the community was facing another Missouri or Illinois—"the [old] constant annoyance of an approaching enemy," followed by persecution. Months afterward, he said the government seemed to be saying, "Damn you, submit to my will or I will pierce your vitals."[60]

During the prayer meeting in Young's office when Young laid out the Mormons' war policy, Smith had made an important point. If the Mormons actually defeated Harney and the federal army, Washington would send even more soldiers. On that occasion, Young rejected his opinion, predicting the public would turn against President Buchanan by that time.[61]

With Salt Lake City preparing for the advancing army, Smith started on a journey south early in the morning of August 3. Since returning to Utah from his year-long trip to the East, Smith had planned to visit a wife and child living in Parowan in southern Utah.[62] But his trip had another purpose. He was carrying the two documents that put Utahns on military alert: Young's letter and Wells's general orders

GEORGE A. SMITH. *Edward Martin, Courtesy LDS Church History Library.*

telling church and military leaders in the settlements to conserve grain and ammunition and prepare for a possible war. Smith delivered the directives to church leaders as he went.[63]

He took the road that went through Provo, Springville, Nephi, Fillmore, and Beaver.[64] Parts of the route had been in use for longer than anyone could remember, first as an Indian trace and later as a white man's pack trail. Mormons used it as they moved up and down their string of settlements at the foot of the Wasatch Mountains, and as the road to southern California. For them it was the main thoroughfare for travel and news, their *Camino Real* or "King's highway" made famous in California and other parts of the old Spanish domain. The settlers called part of the highway the "State Road," later "State Street." Some overland emigrants also used it to travel to California, though emigrant traffic on this southern route never came close to equaling the heavy traffic of its northern counterpart, the main transcontinental road. The latter provided the most direct route to California's gold fields and to the attractive San Joaquin and Sacramento River valleys, not to mention the rising cities of Sacramento and San Francisco.[65]

George A. Smith was an unusual personality. Cautiously estimated at 250 pounds on a five-foot, ten-inch frame, he was a jolly-looking man with a sense of humor to match. Some Paiute Indians called him *Non-choko-wicher*—"takes himself apart"—after they saw him remove his glasses, his false teeth, and, most stunningly, the wig that rested uneasily on his head. At times when preaching from the pulpit, he would "remove his wig and mop his brow to the great amusement of the audience." "When my wig is off," he quipped, "there is scarcely a hair between me and Heaven."[66]

Smith had been a Mormon apostle since 1839—at twenty-one, the youngest man ever to occupy that office. He liked to read, especially history, and had a prodigious memory, which may have been reasons for his 1854 appointment as church historian and recorder at his faith's headquarters in Salt Lake City.[67]

Brigham Young often asked Smith to receive important visitors, who usually warmed to "George A.," as he was often called. An Irish traveler described him as "a huge, burly man, with a Friar Tuck joviality of paunch and visage, and a roll in his bright eye which, in some odd, undefined sort of way, suggested cakes and ale."[68] American journalist and writer George Alfred Townsend wrote after meeting him, "Smith is one of us literary folks, a man of the stamp of Thackeray, Peter Force and Washington Irving…a *collaborateur*, lover of traditions and family reminiscences, and a pleasing, dignified *raconteur* and politician. He has no avarice, no love of war, no vindictiveness, and he is yet a sincere, hale, immovable Mormon."[69]

A first cousin of church founder Joseph Smith and an early convert himself, George A. Smith experienced many of Mormonism's early difficulties: Ohio, Missouri, Illinois, and the trek west.[70] In Utah he quickly became a leading man. In the early 1850s he led a colony of settlers to the area that would become Parowan, the first Latter-day Saint settlement on the southern Utah frontier. He "sowed the first wheat" there, "built the first saw and grist mill," and during the winter taught the first school in the open air next to a large, crackling bonfire.[71] His next assignment was Provo, where settlers needed George A.'s common sense and steadying leadership.[72] Soon he had the job of overseeing all points south of the Salt Lake Valley, with the assignment of getting families to settle these semiparched lands. During the 1853/54 Indian skirmishes known as the Walker War—after Ute leader Wakara (Walker)—Brigham Young and Daniel H. Wells made Smith, then a colonel in the territorial militia, the military commander over all militia units in southern Utah. During these months

Smith pushed himself to restore order, at times approaching physical collapse.[73]

Now he was returning to Parowan, no longer as commander of the local militia but as a man much loved by his friends and with a great deal of influence as the "father" of southern Utah.[74] When he arrived on Saturday evening, August 8, he found the militia drilling. Like other military districts in the territory, the Iron Military District, headquartered at Parowan, had been reorganizing under orders previously received from Wells—a sign that the Mormons may have been preparing for conflict as early as the winter of 1856/57.[75] A few days before Smith arrived, news of the coming U.S. Army had reached the southern settlement. These reports relayed all the details being discussed up north, including the news of Harney's 2,500-man force.[76] It was a "mob," southern Utah resident John M. Higbee later said, picking up on the familiar refrain.[77]

According to the rumors, the troops intended to kill Brigham Young and anyone else with "more than one wife," meaning most of Utah's prominent men. The local people believed their most basic institutions—their prophet, country, and religion—were in danger. To modern ears, such talk might seem wild, something no U.S. Army would do. But the Saints had been conditioned by their past experiences, and the southern Utah militia was on alert.[78]

"Delighted to behold" Smith, militia members in Parowan asked their former district commander to make a speech.[79] Hoisting himself onto a wagon, Smith said he was pleased the settlers had caught the "spirit of the times." Their instructions were "to be prepared for the worst," including, "if necessary, to lay down our lives in defense of the Kingdom of God."[80]

On Sunday, August 9—the day after he arrived—Smith preached twice in Parowan. He repeated the rumors circulating in Salt Lake City when he left. The soldiers "intend to hang about 300 of the most obnoxious Mormons," some quickly without due process and the rest after sham trials, he said. "More to be dreaded than the soldiers," however, were the civilian teamsters accompanying them, "the worst description of men, picked up on the frontiers" and "making great calculations for 'booty and beauty.' "[81]

Smith also wanted local Saints to understand Young's plans for defeating the army. If Harney and his troops forced their way into Utah, Smith explained, the Saints would flee to the mountains with their provisions, fighting from there using guerrilla tactics. "We will haunt them as long as they live," Smith roared, adding with characteristic humor, "unless they live longer than we do." But there was no humor about those who might try to sell goods to the invading troops. "Will we sell them grain or forage?" Smith queried. "I say damn the man who feeds them; I say damn the man who sympathizes with them: I say curse the man who pours oil and water on their heads." Smith also preached quieter and more reassuring doctrines, proclaiming, "We must trust in God, for if we trust in any one else, we shall find ourselves the losers."[82] All in all, however, one local settler described his remarks as "a regular war sermon."[83]

CHAPTER FIVE

Preaching a Military Discourse

Southern Utah, August 9–21, 1857

EXCEPT FOR GIVING a sermon in nearby Paragonah, Smith spent the week after his arrival in Parowan resting, building a fence around his garden, and visiting with family and "scores of friends."[1] It had been nearly seven years since he first led a company of pioneers to southern Utah.

From the time that Spanish and Mexican explorers of the Dominguez-Escalante expedition went through the region in 1776, people had talked of the region's rich resources.[2] Parley P. Pratt and a party of Mormon explorers dispatched by Young in 1849 reported "a hill of the richest Iron ore," though iron, according to Pratt, was only one advantage. He also described acres of cedar that might provide "inexhaustible" fuel for smelting.[3]

Pratt's report delighted Young. "Iron we need, and iron we must have," he said, recognizing the commodity's key role in nineteenth-century life.[4] "Nails, wire, shovels, hoes, hammers, bits, horseshoes, stirrups, axes, chisels, blades and hundreds of other items were costly to buy and impossible to replace without easy access to iron," explained one local history of the region.[5]

In late 1850, Young sent Smith and his party south to found Parowan, the first of three main settlements in what became known as the church's "Iron Mission."[6] The second settlement was Cedar City,

RUINS OF FORT HARMONY. *Wally Barrus (2005).*

about twenty miles south of Parowan and closer to ore and coal deposits. The new community was situated along the banks of hard-rushing Coal Creek, which provided water for the iron-manufacturing process. The new town's name suggested yet another advantage: It was near rich cedar forests necessary for fueling machinery and making charcoal, another vital commodity. By 1853 Cedar City had outstripped Parowan in population.[7]

By the fall of 1852 John D. Lee and more than a dozen other men began to build the third settlement—Fort Harmony—roughly twenty miles southwest of Cedar City on Ash Creek. With "excellent grazing land" and nearby water, the site was deemed a good location to pasture the settlers' cattle. The fort could serve as a military outpost, and its men would protect the livestock.[8] The location may also have been chosen for its view of the stunning, red-fingered cliffs to the east. Lee had an eye for such things.

Each of the three main communities had its leading man. At Parowan, it was William H. Dame, a town founder who had accepted one leadership role after another. In 1852 church leaders asked him to serve as a member of the high council—the twelve men who help the stake president coordinate policy in every Mormon stake. The year before, Parowan's citizens elected him to serve as the town's first mayor. He was also chosen as a representative to the territorial assembly and at various times held the offices of county recorder and surveyor.[9] When George A. Smith was asked to serve as church historian, Dame took his place as commander of the militia district, which included southern Utah's Iron and Washington counties.[10] Finally, in 1856 Young appointed Dame to serve as the president of the Parowan Stake.[11]

Church leaders in Salt Lake City seemed to like Dame, although many of his neighbors were less sure. Critics saw him as roundabout in his dealing and uncomfortable with hard decisions. He "wished to push off all the responsible things that were not agreeable for him to shoulder" and would always look for and find a "loop hole."[12] Still others passed him off as vain. "Every pulsation of his vitality" was to preside—the kind of man who came to meetings early just to show himself off, one man said.[13]

Perhaps Dame's problem was nothing more serious than his personality. Though enjoying praise and capable of agreeable conversation, he was by nature timid and quiet. Flinty as the New Hampshire countryside where he was born in 1819, he had neither the time nor interest in the open ways that were so much a part of western life. The result was that Dame had few close friends. Adding to his unusual profile, he was a polygamist with no children.[14]

Still, many people credited him with honesty, kindness, and hard work, and these good qualities became more apparent as he lived out his life. Toward the end of his career, the *Salt Lake Tribune*—no friend of the Mormons at the time—called him "a well-to-do farmer" who had the look of a "well disposed and inoffensive" gentleman.[15] A photograph taken of him at middle age confirmed this judgment. It showed him, square-set and stately, sitting outdoors with three of his wives, a book on his lap and a hint on his face of an impassive quality.

Details of his youth are sketchy, but one document written by Thomas Edgerly, chairman of the Farmington, New Hampshire, Board of Selection, says a great deal. "This may certify that I have been acquainted with the bearer Mr. William H. Dame of this town from his childhood," it said. "His reputation has ever stood fair so far as has ever come to my knowledge—I believe him to be a person of sober life and conversation, and of good moral character. He is considered a good scholar, and well qualified to teach a common English School." At the time, Dame was eighteen years old.[16] Three years later, at Nauvoo, he joined the Latter-day Saints and never seemed to look back. When his mother pled for him to come home after his brother and father died of typhoid fever, he chose to keep his hand steady on the gospel plough—just as Jesus required.[17]

WILLIAM H. DAME AND WIVES. *Courtesy Special Collections, Sherratt Library, Southern Utah University.*

Dame's counterpart at Cedar City was Isaac C. Haight, perhaps the most able man in southern Utah. Born at Windham, Greene County, New York, in 1813, he flirted with a "rigid close communion Baptist" type of Protestantism when he was a young man. He even thought about a future mission to the "heathen" people of the world.[18] When that enthusiasm cooled, no church interested him until he met Mormonism. His baptism was as dramatic as any convert's. "Although the cold was severe so much so that our clothes froze stiff the moment we came out of the water yet our hearts were warm with the Spirit of God," he wrote.[19] Feeling a growing confidence in himself and his faith, he began to serve Latter-day Saint missionary tours.[20]

At Nauvoo, Haight served as a policeman, protecting the city as well as its leader, Joseph Smith. These assignments made him a member of the city posse that destroyed the press of the anti-Smith *Nauvoo Expositor*; and he was a part of the guard that went with Joseph and Hyrum Smith to Carthage, Illinois. Several days later, Haight had returned and was doing sentry duty at the Nauvoo Temple when he heard of the brothers' murders. "My Heart Sunnk within me," he wrote in his diary, "and I felt to curse the purpetrators of that dark and diabolical deed."[21]

A sense of persecution took hold of him. "My mind is filled with great anxiety about getting away," he said as the Saints' wagons left the city during the evacuation. Sick with the pleurisy and unable to sell his property, Haight had to remain for a time in Nauvoo. "My trust is in the Lord that he will open the way for us to get away from this wicked nation stained with the blood of the Prophets," he said. Haight had more troubled words once his family joined the Saints in their journey. "We are even like the Saints of old having no abiding city," he wrote, "but are wanderers and Pilgrims on the Earth." Another diary entry was still more poignant. "Many have laid down their bodies in the grave[,] among them...my little son two weeks old."[22]

Once in the West, Haight was asked to go with Parley Pratt's 1849/50 southern exploring expedition. He felt a tug when passing through the site that later became Parowan, calling it "one of the most lovely places in the Great Basin."[23] With such feelings, Haight might easily have enrolled with the first settlement parties to southern Utah. But Young wanted him for a proselyting mission to England. During his twenty-eight-month tour, Haight experienced English culture firsthand. He visited such sites as Regent Park's Zoological Gardens and the Tower of London, and watched some Yeomanry Hussars drill. He also viewed the pomp of the Duke of Wellington's funeral.[24]

But it was his labor in the vineyard that shaped him most. He preached to "many thousands" and took on important leadership roles. When leaving England, he mourned the people's poverty and the grasp of the "power of the Tyrant." He was given the heavy responsibility of leading the season's emigration from England and carrying almost $37,000 in church tithing and emigration funds. By August 1853 he was back in Salt Lake City, reporting his success in Brigham Young's office and enjoying his leader's welcome. Five weeks later, Haight went south to Cedar City to take charge of the Deseret Iron Company.[25]

A family biographer gave Haight the virtues of a brilliant mind and a fair-spoken way that easily made him friends.[26] Haight described himself as a person with "a light and boyant spirit" who relished amusements.[27] These included music, especially hymns, and he was known to offer his devotions with an impromptu rendition.[28] John D. Lee, his neighbor and sometime adversary, was more critical, pointing to

Haight's pride and ambition—common enough human emotions. But during the reformation it was Haight's zeal that stood out. The Cedar City leader had "almost become a terror to evil doers," Lee wrote admiringly in 1856.[29]

Haight was forty-four years old in 1857, stood five feet eleven inches tall, and weighed around 170 pounds—a "well built man, one who carried himself with great dignity." Piercing eyes shown out from his dark complexion and black hair.[30] After living in southern Utah only four years, he had a heavy concentration of titles and authority. In addition to leading the iron company and the Cedar City Stake, he was also mayor, legislator, and militia battalion major.[31] Few men in Utah seemed to have a brighter future.

John D. Lee—the leading man at Fort Harmony—was, like Dame and Haight, middle-aged in 1857. He was born at Kaskaskia, Illinois, on September 6, 1812. His father was supposedly linked to the famous Lees of Virginia, a family tradition too thin to prove. More definite

ISAAC C. HAIGHT, CA. 1858. *Courtesy LDS Church History Library.*

were Lee's early years, which were filled with the social distress of a Dickens novel. An intruder beat his mother senseless, leaving her impaired. Lee remembered his father as "a kind-hearted, generous, noble man" when sober, though he drank heavily and provided poorly.[32]

John's mother died when he was three, and five years later his father "went to Texas."[33] The boy was sent to his mother's sister—"a regular spit-fire" of a woman who believed in not sparing the rod. "I have been knocked down and beaten...until I was senseless, many times," Lee said of her usage.[34]

The conditions were so harsh that young Lee even considered suicide. But at the age of sixteen, he left his aunt's home and went to work successively as a mail courier, stage driver, Mississippi River roustabout, farmer, store clerk, and bartender. He briefly dealt cards and gambled professionally. But this last activity, he came to realize, had too much chance and cheating for any long-term profit. In 1832 Lee served in the Black Hawk War and fought at the final Battle of Bad Axe in Wisconsin Territory. After his marriage to Agatha Ann Woolsey, Lee established a small store and farmed in Fayette County, Illinois. Still in his twenties, he had acquired 160 acres, good buildings, two hundred cattle, and a thousand sheep. "I...had good success in all that I undertook," Lee said confidently.[35] He found he could easily outtalk, outtrade, and outwork almost anyone.

Born a Roman Catholic, Lee listened to Methodist, Baptist, and Campbellite preachers but was not impressed. His feelings about religion changed, however, after he rescued two frost-bitten Mormon missionaries from "a dreadful snowstorm," which "set him to thinking and searching the scriptures." "I believed the Book of Mormon was true," he said, "and if so, everything but my soul's salvation was a matter of secondary consideration." In 1838 he and Agatha Ann gave up their comfortable situation in Illinois to join the main body of Saints then located in northwestern Missouri.[36]

During missionary tours to Illinois, Kentucky, and Tennessee, Lee said he beheld heavenly visions, contested with evil spirits, and defeated other Christian ministers with strong, inspired words. Although at first timid and inexperienced before a congregation, he soon believed he was transformed by a higher power. "My tongue was like the pen of a ready writer. I scarcely knew what I was saying," he reflected, after speaking to a congregation for an hour and a half.[37] "I grew in grace from day to day," he said, "and I have never seen the day that I regretted taking up my cross and giving up all other things to follow and obey Christ, my Redeemer and Friend."[38]

Lee thrived in Nauvoo, building a large home and serving as the city's wharfmaster and as librarian of the Masonic lodge.³⁹ He also served as a bodyguard to Joseph Smith and, upon Smith's death, Brigham Young. "I became very popular among the Saints," Lee recalled without a blush. "I was young, strong and athletic. I could drive ahead and work all day and stand guard half of the night, through all kinds of weather."⁴⁰

On becoming better acquainted with Lee, Young liked what he saw. "They are all workers," he said of Lee and his family.⁴¹ Young agreed to adopt Lee in a spiritual father-son relationship through a ritual common to Mormons of the time. When the practice was first introduced, Lee rushed to join Young's spiritual family. "I was adopted by Brigham Young," he explained, "and was [therefore] to seek his *temporal* interests here [on earth], and in return he was to seek my *spiritual* salvation."⁴² Although just one of many men adopted to Young, Lee took the matter more seriously than some, perhaps because it set him apart from other church members or gave him the father figure he missed in his youth—even though Young was just nine years his senior.⁴³

Lee reached Utah in 1848, and two years later Young asked him to help settle southern Utah, where his whirlwind energy might do some good. Young may have had another reason for sending Lee south. Both before and during the Saints' westward migration, Lee had trouble getting along with people and found himself called before church tribunals for offenses that included bickering, lewd talk, boasting of a sexual orgy with one of his wives, and domestic violence. "He threatened to cut my throat," said wife Nancy Bean in a December 4, 1847, statement that detailed instances of Lee's physical and emotional abuse. "I have heard him often say that if he managed to keep his actions secreted from Brigham and the Twelve [Apostles]," Bean said, "he did not care for any other persons—as nobody else had a right to say anything about him." Lee often denied the stories others told about him, casting them as outlandish charges aimed to destroy his public character. But Young and others came to believe that Lee had been guilty of some misconduct. In one tribunal, after Lee was "reproved...vary sharply for trying to cover his faults & Justify himself in his errors," Young "backed up" the "reproof & reproved Br Lee himself."⁴⁴

The incident caused a minor stir; Lee's reputation had been damaged and possibly his career in the church as well. For his part, Young was willing to leave the matter to "eternal oblivion" and never raised the issue again, even after the two men later became estranged.⁴⁵

JOHN D. LEE. *Courtesy LDS Church History Library*.

Young's hope that Lee might have a second chance was probably one reason he sent Lee south as a member of the Iron Mission—and a reason that Lee accepted the assignment, despite preferring to stay in the Salt Lake Valley. He went, he said, "to redeem my standing."[46]

Lee soon was reporting that his new assignment had been for the best. Earlier in life, he told Young, he "had Zeal but not acording to knowledge" and failed "to bear with the people & would gain their Ill will by my own folly." But pioneering, Lee said, had smoothed things and "placed me in circumstances where of necessity I had to Rub up my Tallent."[47]

July 1853 saw the outbreak of the Walker War, skirmishing between Mormon settlers and some of the territory's Indians who chafed because white men were taking their land and resources. Young, acting as the territory's governor and superintendent of Indian affairs, decided on a policy unusual for the American frontier. Instead of fighting the Indians, he sent general orders requiring settlers in outlying areas to move within the forts of larger and stronger settlements while he tried to negotiate peace. Young also ordered the settlers to send their surplus livestock to Salt Lake City for safekeeping.[48]

This policy of "defense and conciliation," while eventually quieting the frontier, caused problems among the settlers, who were forced to live in crowded forts for months. Some were malleable, like William Dame, who abandoned his new $3,000 house in Paragonah and moved back to the Parowan fort.[49] Others bristled at the new restrictions. Some settlers in the Cedar City fort rebelled against the order to send their cattle north. A few "brought out their Guns" and "threatened to shoot the man who would touch their cattle."[50] In cash-starved pioneer Utah, cattle were as close to a circulating medium as most people had, and despite the territory's reputation as a submissive society, these men were unwilling to trust Young when it came to their pocketbooks. Some preferred the old American way of fighting Indians instead of seeking peace with them, or thought Young had greatly exaggerated the danger.[51]

When Matthew Carruthers, a Scottish convert and Cedar City's militia major, resigned his commission rather than comply with the order to send cattle north, he was replaced by Lee, who had been militia captain at Harmony and would soon be promoted to major.[52] By Lee's own account, he forced the citizenry to toe the line. He later told Young that he girded on his sword, "called the people togeather" and said that "by the help of god & the Faithful of my Brethren, I was determined to carry out the instructions & requirements contained in the general orders, if it need be by the shedding of the Blood, of those cursed wicked apostate fault[-]finding wretches."[53]

The men who rebelled were put in chains, and local military authorities even talked of the death penalty for their mutiny in a time of war.[54] When the matter ended, no men lost their lives, but militia records had a dozen or more pages devoted to courts-martial—some for minor offenses—and there was a great deal of bitterness.[55] Thirty-one men and women who found "the presiding Officers tyranical in their rule" left the Iron Mission for California, and for their desertion they were quickly excommunicated.[56] The lesson was clear: There were unpleasant penalties for disobeying militia leaders.

In May 1854 the Walker War ended just as Young hoped—with a meeting and negotiation between himself and Ute leader Wakara.[57] But the conflict led Young to conclude that he and his church were not doing enough for the territory's native people. Months before the war's end, he decided to establish a mission for them, just as Mormon missions had been created in other parts of the world. Young called missionaries to live among the Indians, to learn their language and customs, and to teach, feed, clothe, and convert them.[58]

While the Walker War prompted Young to found the Southern Indian Mission, his interest in the Indians of the region went back almost to the beginning of the Mormons' settlement of Utah. During these first years, Wakara himself had asked Young to establish a colony in the area to teach his people how to farm.[59] During Parley Pratt's exploring expedition, a local headman had also welcomed the Mormons and "invited and strong[ly] urged our people to settle with them and raise cornee," Pratt reported.[60] These requests agreed with the Saints' hope to bring the Christian message to local Indians and spiritually "redeem" them.[61]

The hope for a great Indian destiny was one thing; reality was another. The northerly Utes maintained several camps in the south, mainly one near Beaver led by Wakara's kinsman Ammon. Ammon's borderland band included southern Utah Indians the white men called "Paiutes," or sometimes "Piedes." The usually passive Paiutes had a rich culture of their own based on agriculture and harmony with the land, which met most of their basic needs until white incursions depleted the game and native plants.[62] One Mormon called the impoverished Paiutes "the most destitute People I ever Saw."[63] Young believed that work among Utah's Indians, like "other works of great philanthropy," would probably be "gradual in its operation."[64]

During the Walker War, the Paiutes sided with the Mormons for good reason. The settlers buffered them from Ute raiders who had often taken Paiute children and women to sell as slaves in New Mexico and California. The Paiutes had neither the horses nor rifles of the Utes with which to resist. Their loose family groups were better suited to food-gathering and small-scale farming than fighting. In the 1850s Paiutes ranged from Beaver Creek on the north to the Colorado River on the south, reaching west across what is now southern Nevada into California.[65]

The Mormon Indian missionaries provided the Paiutes clothing, established schools for them, and sought to learn their language while teaching them English.[66] Though the Paiutes had a long history of irrigated farming, the missionaries introduced them to the white man's plow and large-scale irrigation techniques.[67] They also taught their religion to the Indians, baptized converts, gave them new names from scripture, and tried to convince local bands to follow Paiute leaders who were pliable to white man's ways. Like many humanitarians of the time, the Mormons believed the Indians would be best off if they abandoned their own culture and became a part of the white man's developing world.[68]

At the time of the establishment of the Southern Indian Mission, John D. Lee's fort at Harmony was the Mormon settlement deepest within Paiute territory. From this hub, the missionaries spread outward.[69] In 1854 Santa Clara, thirty-three miles southwest of Harmony, became the Indian mission's next major post, near where many Paiutes lived. There missionaries and Indians worked together to build two cabins—one for the whites and one for the Paiutes. The next year, the two groups worked together to erect a fort at Santa Clara—most Mormon frontier communities began with a fort.[70] To expand farmable Paiute land, the Mormons built canals and at least one new dam.[71] Tutsegavits, an influential Paiute, wanted the best of this new acreage, citing an ancestral claim that the missionaries did not question. "We have ever kept in mind not to rob the Indians of their rights but rather sought to help them in every way that we could," said one missionary, though over succeeding years, the whites would not live up to this ideal.[72]

While relations between the missionaries and the Paiutes at first thrived, relations between the missionaries and Lee were troubled from the start. Shortly after the missionaries' arrival in Harmony, Lee met with their leaders, who had been appointed in Salt Lake City, and told them there should be only one "head" in Harmony, and "this was his place." The missionaries agreed to cooperate for the time being but would appeal to Young when he came on a visit a few weeks later.[73]

When Young and his traveling party arrived in late spring of 1854, he sought to resolve the tension in Harmony by maintaining the missionaries' leadership over the Indian mission but allowing Lee to lead the local congregation as its presiding elder. "Be united and seek to know the mind of the Spirit of the Lord," Young told the group.[74]

Young apparently felt he had solved the problem. But Harmony had little peace, and by early 1855 conditions were at a breaking point. One of the missionaries, Thomas D. Brown, wrote an extended passage in his diary that accused Lee of having an "abundance of dreams, visions and revelations" that he used for his own purposes. Brown believed the actual source of Lee's information was more ordinary. "He listened behind a fence to Bros. P[eter] Shirts and W[illia]m Young who were talking of his immeasurable selfishness, and he repeated it next meeting as having read it from a sheet let down from the heavens before his eyes," Brown claimed. In another incident, "when another Bro. was exhorting to meekness, humility, and against theft, Bro. Lee followed and all but accused said brother of hypocrisy, blackness of heart and evil speaking, and said he himself would not hesitate to steal from the Gentiles who had so often robbed the Saints."[75]

Another complaint accused Lee of staging a tantrum over a small dispute, throwing his hat and shoe to the floor, "spoiling both, and cursing in wrath." More easily confirmed was the missionaries' complaint that Lee was writing to Young behind their backs. Lee admitted writing a letter but denied sending it.[76] Yet two such letters arrived at church headquarters. Lee did not wish to be "finding fault" with the missionaries, one of the letters said. He was only keeping Young informed.[77]

A year later, Lee again wrote Young, this time about some veiled misconduct on his part. He implied that local church leaders were making him the target of "religious opposition," and he feared for his position in the church. He also worried that he had lost Young's favor. Addressing Young as "beloved Father," Lee explained, "I say Father because a Father you have been to me…To know that my course of conduct is aproved of by you is to me more than all the riches positions and honors in this world." It would be a privilege, he said, to step between Young and the "cannons Mouth." Lee said that without Young's approval, he felt "wretched."[78]

As it turned out, Young was not angry with Lee and probably did not know of the charges being made against him by church authorities in the south. Before receiving Lee's letter, Young had already sent his own to Lee, appointing him as a U.S. Indian farmer to the Paiute people. When Lee learned of his appointment, he wept—not because it satisfied his ambition, he said, but because it allowed him to continue to serve. He later said that several days before Young's letter arrived, "an angel of the Lord…stood by [his] bedside and talked…about these and many other things."[79]

Unfortunately, neither angelic interview nor Young's letter helped Lee understand his new assignment, which he wrongly assumed gave him control of Indian mission affairs in the south. He began a flurry of activity that brushed aside anything and anyone in his way, including the Indian missionaries.[80] Young had to correct him; he had only wanted Lee to assist the Indians with their farming and distribute government farming supplies to them. The Indian mission was off limits.[81]

Lee apologized to Young but blamed others for his misunderstanding. The damage had been done, however, and a petition against Lee—which included the signatures of Indian missionaries and settlers—circulated at Harmony. Haight, who had ecclesiastical jurisdiction, heard about the matter and came to Harmony to hold a hearing. When it was over, Lee was voted out of his church office as presiding elder of Harmony. He said that the margin was five votes and later complained that "7 women voted on the negative," as if the voters' gender called into question the final result.[82] Haight, reporting to Salt Lake City, said the vote against Lee was a more decisive twenty-six to six.[83]

Lee was retained as Indian farmer and kept his rank as major over the Harmony battalion of the Iron militia. That was still too much authority for the Indian missionaries, who moved their headquarters from Harmony to the small settlement of Pinto, sixteen miles to the northwest, where summers were cooler and they had easier access to Santa Clara and the Indians who lived near there. This new location also put a mountain range between them and the volatile Lee.[84] A year later when George A. Smith made his tour through southern Utah to sound the war cry against the federal army, Lee was still a divisive figure in the region.

After Smith's week of respite with his family in Parowan, he joined William Dame and several other militia leaders on a wide, circular sweep of local settlements. Smith asked Dame's adjutant, James H. Martineau, to keep a detailed record of the journey, and Martineau recorded that the trip's purpose was "completing the organization [of] our regiment, ... inspecting the troops in their various localities and giving them such injunctions as should seem necessary."[85] The itinerary included stops at Cedar City, Harmony, and Washington to the south, and Santa Clara, Mountain Meadows, and Pinto to the southwest. "The spirit seemed to burn in my bones to visit all these settlements," Smith said.[86]

Though Smith said his tour was "a mission of peace to preach to the people," his sermons continued to blaze. Preaching in Sunday services in Cedar City, he said that "in spite of all I could do I found myself preaching a military discourse" that left the people full of "enthusiasm." Haight showed the traveling party the iron works, improvements to the city, and the imposing new home he was building of burned brick—"the only one in [the] Territory," Smith's office journal recorded.[87]

Young had earlier sent word to Haight that Smith was coming south with general news of "things transpiring in the lower world"—the

United States—as well as bearing vital dispatches. "I wish you to pay the strictest attention to the instructions which I forwarded to you by him," Young wrote, referring to the letters about conserving grain and putting the militia on alert. Young's letter also praised Haight's work in trying to make iron and announced Young's intention to put new leaders in charge of the Indian mission. The letter was dated August 4, the day after Smith left Salt Lake City, and was meant to leave no doubt in Haight's mind about how important the war policy was.[88]

When Dame's party reached Harmony, Smith's sermon to the local congregation "partook of the military more than the religious," Smith later reflected. "It seemed that I was perfectly running over with it."[89] One listener recorded, "President G A Smith delivered a discourse on the Spirit that actuated the United States towards this people—full of hostility and virulence."[90] Following the same pattern as in Cedar City, Dame drilled the battalion at Harmony, and the local militia leader, Lee, joined the traveling party, as did Haight.[91] By this time the party had a dozen and a half members, some on horseback and others riding in wagons. Several of the men's wives were also along.[92] Dame, Haight, and Lee—a triad of future massacre leaders—soaked up the apostle's message of coming war.

Because of the warm temperature of the region and its prospect for growing cotton, the Mormons called the land south of Harmony their "Dixie," but it was more formidable than anything found in the American South.[93] "I think if the Lord had got up all the rough, rocky and the broken fragments of the earth in one he might have dropped it down there," Smith said of the landscape.[94] He described the trail they traveled, which would be called the Black Ridge Road, as "the most desperate" he had ever seen, full of "stones, volcanic rock, cobble heads…and in places deep sand."[95] At the memorable "Peter's Leap," wagons had to be eased down a precipice, two or three feet at a time, by men holding ropes.[96]

Two days into this strenuous leg of their journey, an event took place that gave it a sense of urgency. The party was overtaken by a rider from Parowan carrying a military express for Col. Dame from Gen. Daniel H. Wells in Salt Lake City.[97] Before Smith left for the south, it was believed the federal army would be unable to reach Utah before winter. But word had come that Col. Edwin V. Sumner's First U.S. Cavalry, reported to be chasing Cheyenne Indians, had been spotted on the Sweetwater River just a few hundred miles northeast of Salt Lake City.[98] Mormons suspected that Sumner's pursuit of the Indians was a ruse to get him closer to Salt Lake City before the populace learned of his movements. Later, Mormons remembered variants of these rumors. One said that a group of soldiers planned to attack from the south, "travel North to meet the main body of the U.S. forces, and clean out the inhabitants as they went along."[99] Still another said that an army captain had gone to Texas to gather volunteers to make a southern attack.[100]

In Salt Lake City, leaders began to worry that U.S. troops might enter Utah anywhere along its eastern borders and perhaps from California as well, though the northeast Echo Canyon road remained the likely route for the main assault.[101] Not wanting the Saints to "be taken at any point by surprise," Wells sent an express to military commanders throughout Utah, especially in the south, to guard the mountain approaches into the territory. He wanted this duty performed by the local militias and, where possible, by Indians, who Mormon leaders continued to hope would side with them in the approaching war. The Indians, Wells said, should be told they were in as much danger as the Mormons were.

Besides stressing the need for Indian cooperation, Wells's express reemphasized the importance of grain. Not a kernel was to be lost, he urged. "Drop other business" to get the crops in, "thrash out the grain," and find "good safe places in the mountains where grain can be cached and where women and children can be safe in case we have to take to the mountains."[102] Wells's dispatch gave George A. Smith's words an even harder edge. Within days, Utah's southern militia began to watch the mountain passes, east and west, while Smith and Dame and their party continued their tour, preaching of the coming crisis and drilling the militia.[103]

Wells's instructions to secure Indian help was nothing new—Young had suggested this policy during his August 2 prayer meeting with Mormon leaders—but the new orders put the southern leaders on notice of its importance as they entered a country heavily inhabited by Paiutes. At the new community of Washington, after Smith and Dame once more did their preaching and drilling, they parleyed with local Indians. As the party turned west and made its next camp, Paiutes cared for the Mormons' horses, and the Indians and Mormons probably had more talks.[104] The next day Dame and Smith's party arrived at the Santa Clara fort, where a large number of Paiutes gathered to "see the 'Mormon Captain.'" When the interview was over, Smith described it as "glorious."[105]

The good feeling continued as the party turned north to return to Cedar City, having reached the most distant point of their trip. Now they were on the California road, which branched southwest from Cedar City. The group headed up the Santa Clara River canyon with its occasional steep walls and underbrush. Several years before, a wife of one of the Indian missionaries shuddered as she traveled through the area—"a very favorable place for the Indians to attack travelers," she said of its reputation.[106] Yet the dominant Paiute leader in the area, Jackson, despite his later reputation for robbery and mayhem, offered Smith and his party hospitality, which they declined.[107]

After passing through the Santa Clara canyon, the Mormons traveled to the Indian camp of another local headman, Kahbeets, where hundreds of Paiutes gathered around the travelers and gave them roasted corn and melons. "We stopped over night with them, and not one of them asked me for a thing," Smith said. "I was treated as well as if I had been among the Saints, and I never enjoyed a treat better."[108]

Leaving the camp, the party passed north through the Mountain Meadows. In the middle 1850s, Indian missionary Jacob Hamblin and a few other Mormons had established an outpost at its northern springs, calling the tiny settlement Hamblin's Ranch. The Meadows' southern springs, four miles below, were used by California-bound travelers before they dropped into the canyon of the Santa Clara and out onto the deserts of what became southern Nevada. Smith's party stopped at the Meadows for "toast & cheese."[109]

The last settlement on the tour was Pinto, home to missionaries who had broken off from Harmony. Smith preached and Dame drilled the militia. Then, after a week of travel, the party returned to Cedar City, having completed a 186-mile circuit through "the most barren, desolate and miserable country I ever saw inhabited," Smith said.[110]

IN AFTER YEARS SMITH'S JOURNEY to southern Utah became a matter of controversy, with some interpreting his sermons and even the places he stopped as a deliberate prelude to the Mountain Meadows Massacre less than a month later. John D. Lee's several posthumously published "confessions"—which appeared two decades after the tour—said that while the party was passing through the Santa Clara canyon, Smith asked, "Brother Lee, what do you think the brethren would do if a company of emigrants should come down through here making threats? Don't you think they would pitch into them?"[111]

"They certainly would," Lee replied, to which Smith said, "I asked Isaac (meaning Haight) the same question, and he answered me just as you do."[112]

Several months after the first publication of this conversation, another version of Lee's confessions appeared under the title *Mormonism Unveiled*. It made the charge against Smith even stronger. "I have always believed, since that day, that General George A. Smith was then visiting Southern Utah to prepare the people for the work of exterminating Captain Fancher's train of emigrants," the book said, "and I now believe that he was sent for that purpose by the direct command of Brigham Young."[113] The passage would be used by some writers as key evidence for saying that Smith and Young had planned the massacre.[114]

These statements, however, would have required remarkable prescience on Smith's part. Even if he knew which trains would take the northern or the southern routes to California, it is doubtful that he knew their behavior on the road would include making threats against southern Utah people. Moreover, Lee's attorney and editor, William W. Bishop, almost certainly reworked Lee's "confessions" in *Mormonism Unveiled* after Lee died to make the book more sensational and to improve its sales, including the charges against Smith and Young. Bishop had a motive for making these changes as his legal fees were tied to the book's royalties.[115]

Just moments before Lee's execution—and after he had supposedly written the words in *Mormonism Unveiled*—Lee talked with a reporter from the then unabashedly anti-Mormon *Salt Lake Tribune*. The reporter pressed Lee to know what Smith had said to him before the massacre.

"Did he preach hostile to the emigrants?" the reporter asked.

"He was visiting all the settlements and preaching against the emigrants," Lee said. Then referring to the people killed at Mountain Meadows, he added, "I don't know that he meant those particular emigrants."[116] This—Lee's final statement on the subject—makes it unlikely that he made the statement attributed to him in *Mormonism Unveiled*, especially since he had been offered his life by prosecutors if he would just charge Smith and Young with ordering the massacre. He went to his death instead.[117]

Jacob Hamblin, who traveled with Smith during part of his August 1857 journey, confirmed this overall judgment. "George A.'s instructions to the people were that our enemies were going to make us more trouble, and that the people should be careful to save every spoonful of grain," Hamblin later said. "I never heard from George A. an idea of a hint that we should molest or mistreat an emigrant."[118]

Yet *something* may have happened at the Santa Clara. Wells's recent dispatch had ordered the settlers to guard all the mountain passes into

Utah, and during the next several weeks southern Utahns would closely watch the approaches to the east and west.[119] Smith understood, as did everyone, that if troops came from California in a surprise attack, they would likely come on the well-traveled California road, and that the strategic and difficult Santa Clara canyon would be the best place to stop them.[120]

Smith may well have asked Lee if he thought the local people could stop a threatening company traveling up the canyon.[121] While passing through Cedar City after completing his circle tour in Washington and Santa Clara, Smith asked Maj. Haight what he would to do if six hundred dragoons descended upon the city as rumored. The decisive Haight replied that there would be "no time to wait for any instruction." He would "take his battalion and use them up before they could get down through the kanyons, for said he, if they are coming here they are coming for no good."[122]

Smith returned to his home in Parowan on August 21, where he spoke once more before heading back to Salt Lake City.[123] Reflecting on his tour, he said, "In all the course of my trip south I have not yet seen any one alarmed as yet." He counseled the Parowan settlers to "prepare for the worst and hope for the best." Noting some fault-finding in the town, he counseled the settlers "not to pick flaws" with their leader, Dame.[124]

Dame himself seemed to be taking a careful course. On August 23 he wrote a letter to Wells giving a progress report: "Every inlet of the District south of Beaver is now guarded," he wrote. "If a hostile force is found to be approaching us, we shall immediately express to you, and await your further orders; unless attacked, in which case we shall act on the defensive, and communicate immediately with you."[125] While Smith saw no panic in the south and Dame was acting deliberately, tensions and emotions were nevertheless rising, some caused by Smith's preaching but primarily due to the rumored invasion. "Men were stationed in all the dangerous places, women were excited, and the people as a whole were ready for any emergancy," remembered one of the local settlers.[126]

Farther up the road outside of Beaver, Smith heard that Indians discovered tracks from shod horses, at first thought to belong to army scouts. The Beaver militia immediately investigated, only to find that the trail led to Parowan and belonged to that city's own militia. Still, everyone was on alert, and at Fillmore and other points south, Smith thought that a single "word" would be enough "to set in motion every man, or set a torch to every building, where the safety of this people is jeopardized."[127]

Some of his Fillmore impressions may have come from Emily Hoyt, Smith's cousin, with whom he often stopped when traveling up or down the southern road. On August 19 Hoyt wrote in her diary that she felt "considerable excitement in [con]sequence of the express which came on [the previous] Sunday"—probably Wells's message about guarding the passes. A week later, she heard "more startling reports." She wrote anxiously, "What the [U.S.] troops want or want to do we do not know."[128]

The rising feeling Smith found during his journey south had an element of relish for some, which troubled him. Some Mormons, hating "to owe a debt and not be able to pay it" were eager to get on with the fight with the U.S. Army, which the Mormons continued to call a mob. At Provo, Charles Jameson, who had been wounded in the Haun's Mill Massacre in Missouri nearly twenty years before, was praying for the troops to come quickly, "for he wanted to have a chance at them."[129] Old hatreds were being easily transferred to new opponents.

When Smith preached to the Saints in Salt Lake City after returning from his trip, he seemed to have two minds about preparing for war. If a defense of the Saints was required, he wanted no faltering. "No one will ever get to heaven unless he is willing to die," he said.[130] Yet he looked with trepidation at the coming conflict. "I do not know but it is on account of my extreme timidity," he said, but "I would a great deal rather that the Lord would fight the battles than me, and I feel to pray that he will punish [the army] with that hell which is to want to and can't."[131]

CHAPTER SIX

A Splendid Train

Arkansas to Utah, Emigration Season, 1857

THE THREAT OF WAR in Utah did little to slow the flood of emigrants who would pass through on the way to California— though for a time the weather did. After two years of drought, the winter of 1856/57 had brought ten feet of snow to some Utah communities. The snow pack in the mountains averaged twenty feet. At first winter refused to give up. Prairie grass east of South Pass was "six weeks later than ever known," and some emigrant cattle died for the lack of feed.[1] Then, suddenly, spring came, unleashing the pent-up emigration.

People crowded the Missouri River loading docks. "Every boat to this place comes crowded with emigrants, and we scarcely ever have less than one and sometimes as many as three or four [boats] each day," reported a Leavenworth, Kansas, newspaper editor.[2] Emigrants poured onto the trails, and when the tide began to ebb in late summer, the register at a "Mormon mail station" in present-day Wyoming showed that 12,500 emigrants, 950 wagons, 67,000 head of cattle, 2,500 horses and mules, and 10,000 sheep had passed Devil's Gate during the season. These totals omitted the Mormon trains. They also did not include emigrants from southwestern Missouri and northwestern Arkansas who took the Cherokee Trail, following the Arkansas River before turning north to join the more celebrated Oregon-California Trail

PIONEERS IN THE ROCKY MOUNTAINS. *Frances F. Palmer, Currier and Ives, Courtesy Library of Congress.*

west of Fort Laramie.[3] The Cherokee Trail lay near the cattle markets of Texas, Arkansas, and Missouri, and was the likely choice of citizens traveling from those areas and taking their cattle to California.[4]

Whatever the actual scope of the '57 migration, it left observers marveling. One San Francisco newspaper called the traffic coming in from western Utah Territory "one uninterrupted chain" of wagons and cattle. "The wagons are in sight of each other the whole way," it reported.[5] This last observation had to be newspaper hyperbole, but it captured the excitement of the day. America was moving west, and the emigration of 1857 had its own personality. Some emigrants were desperate. "I'll be dog-gone if I'll stay in a country where the cold weather freezes the shucks off the cattle's feet," chewed one Missourian.[6] He was reflecting the bad times brought on by the recent unusual weather that reached from California to midcontinent. For others, the decision to go to California had to do with the "pull" of profits and not the "push" of hardship. They believed fortunes could still be made in California—not from gold but from livestock.

Before the legendary cattle drives of the Abilene, Chisholm, or Bozeman trails, there was the livestock traffic on the California trail— "the first of the great cattle drives."[7] It owed its origin to the California gold camps, where miners grew weary of their usual diet of salt bacon and pork or the sinewy beef of the old California herds, bred for tallow and hides. Tender beef from across the plains was the answer, and a California butcher might pay top dollar for a steer from Arkansas or Missouri, especially if the animal had been fattened at the end of the trail on the rich grasses of California's Central Valley.[8] To get the herds west, some men used the English system of drovers—not the later, more familiar techniques of the Spanish-Mexican cowboys. These drovers—sometimes called "bullwhackers"—walked or rode near the herds and controlled the animals with great snapping whips capable of killing a large steer if the aim were bad and the whip's end hit a vulnerable part of the beast.[9]

During the early 1850s, enterprising cattlemen drove herds westward and returned with tales of riches from the cattle trade. A rush followed that glutted California with beef, and by early 1856 the cattle market was beginning to falter.[10] With grass scarce and feed costly, some cattlemen began selling their herds in California for whatever they could get. "I am getting down on this country," one of them wrote back home. Still, herders kept driving stock to California, chasing the mirage of quick riches.[11] Others went to build homes and grow rich from patient ranching.

By 1857 many herds on the road west were accompanied not just by drovers but by whole families relocating to California.[12] Men who earlier had gone to California for gold or cattle-profit were now going back with their wives and children, convinced of the state's long-range potential. Their enthusiasm rubbed off on extended family members and neighbors who joined them. The family wagon trains included " 'a right smart sprinkling' of young ladies," promising to brighten "the dreary home of some old bachelors there," according to one traveler.[13]

The enthusiastic emigrants headed west in 1857 did not know of the sagging market, ignored it, or focused on long-term prospects. The late spring forced the emigrants into the middle and late stages of the migrating season, further snarling trail traffic and creating anxiety. Would there be enough grass along the way? Would so many people produce more than the usual number of disputes among emigrants? And what about Indians? The more emigrants, the more trouble there often was between them and native peoples as they competed for dwindling grass and game.[14] This year's heavy traffic increased the odds.

John Twitty Baker, "generally known by the name of 'Jack,' or 'Captain Jack Baker,' " was among the emigrants of '57.[15] Born to parents who settled in Madison County, Alabama, in about 1807, he knew firsthand the relationship of hard work and rising fortunes. Jack's parents had done well by buying hundreds of acres of property and building them up by shrewd planning and industry. Soon they had a large home of cedar logs and an estate that included sixteen slaves.[16] Toward the end of their lives, their assets were impressive for the time: ten thousand dollars in real property and another thirty-seven thousand in personal wealth.[17] But there was not much pretense. Jack's mother, part-Cherokee, "smoked a corncob pipe and walked with a cane with a crook on the end, with which she grabbed a grandchild if they misbehaved."[18]

Jack followed his parents' examples. Moving to nearby Jackson County, Alabama—just across the county line from their home—he settled down with his wife, Mary, and began his own patient pursuit of wealth by farming with slave labor. Like his mother and father, he had a hardy, rough quality. Neither he nor Mary picked up book learning. Moreover, Jack "did not, always, get along with some of their neighbors," said a family member, diplomatically.[19]

One dustup involving Jack came when a public gathering ended in drink and argument. Before long, "the fighting got to be a general thing." One of the men in the brawl attacked another with "a good rock," knocking him down before running off "so fast you could have played cards on his shirt tail as it floated out behind him."[20]

But not every one of these encounters was viewed in good humor. Jack Baker, known to "regularly imbibe," once went to buy supplies in town, where he met three men who "were not his best friends." A fight broke out and, according to family tradition, Baker killed his three attackers. It was probably one of those blood feuds that were so much a part of Appalachia and the southwestern frontier. Although Baker was badly hurt, he got himself home. Mary dressed his wounds and sent him to the sanctuary of his parents' home across the county line to protect him from angry relatives of the three slain men. When he finally returned to his own property, he found his barn burned down, many of his cattle gone, and the threat of more depredations looming constantly before him. He put up with the retaliation for years before finally selling out in October 1848.[21]

His new address was Crooked Creek Township, Carroll County, Arkansas, in the half-wild northwest frontier, south of present-day Harrison.[22] Almost immediately, Jack Baker became a presence. The 1850 U.S. Census put his real estate at forty-five hundred dollars— higher than anyone else's in the township.[23] He also was a prominent slaveholder in the region.[24] His dominance rubbed people either right or wrong. A neighbor said, after his death, that he was one of "our best citizens…a warm friend and a bitter enemy."[25]

In the early 1850s, the Baker family heard the siren call of California. Some said Jack himself visited the state and liked what he saw.[26] More likely, the reconnaissance was done by Jack's sons; George W. Baker lived for a time in Stockton, Sonora, and Columbia, California, and younger brother John Henry lived in California from 1852 to 1854. (John Henry did not join the Baker family train of 1857).[27] According to George's daughter Sarah, "my father and some of the other men from our neighborhood went out to California to look over the lay of the land and they came back with stories about gold that would just about make your eyes pop out. There wasn't anything to do but for everybody in the family to pack up, bag and baggage, and light out for the coast."[28] The Bakers sought gold not by mining but by selling their beef to hungry miners.

Basil Parker, who lived several miles from Jack Baker on the Buffalo Fork of the White River, later claimed a role in getting him to go west. Parker, like the Baker sons, had already been to California and now prepared for a second trip. "My doing so," said Parker, "had a tendency to stimulate a man of the energy of Captain Baker, so he fitted out a splendid train and had about six hundred head of cattle, mules and horses."[29]

Jack's share of the cattle was 138 head, described by Mary as "all good stock…three years old and upwards…picked cattle." Jack also had nine yoke of work oxen, two mules, a mare, a large ox wagon, and as Mary would put it, "provisions, cloathing, and camp Equ[i]page for him self and five hands." The equipment included a tent, saddles and bridles, and firearms, including one of Samuel Colt's famous repeating pistols. The family believed Baker's trail property and cattle were worth over $4,000 in Arkansas, and even more in California.[30]

Three of Jack and Mary's children were part of the gathering train. Nineteen-year-old Abel was single and probably went along to help herd the stock.[31] George, by now twenty-seven and independent in his own right, had about as many beef cattle, wagons, and work oxen as his father.[32] He and his wife, Manerva Beller Baker, had four small children going with them, as well as Manerva's younger brother and sister and two hired hands.[33]

Yet another child of Jack and Mary who joined the company was twenty-one-year-old Sarah Baker Mitchell, married to Charles Mitchell. The couple brought their infant son. Charles Mitchell and his brother Joel were the sons of William C. Mitchell, one of their neighborhood's most prominent citizens.[34] The Mitchell boys started out with $275 in cash, thirteen yoke of oxen, and sixty-two head of cattle. According to a later inventory, there were a lot of miscellaneous items as well: "one large ox wag[on], log chains... wearing apparel, beds, and beding and cooking utencils... guns, Pistols and Bowie knives," as well as "one horse, saddle and bridle" and "camp equ[i]page."[35] The brothers bought more stock in nearby Washington County after leaving home, giving them about a hundred head, including their oxen, by the time they reached the Arkansas border.[36]

Overlanders typically started their journey in April, when the winter mire began to firm and spring offered new grass. The Baker family, prepared and resolute, began to assemble near Beller's Stand, a store once owned by George Baker's late father-in-law, William Beller.[37] Here last-minute provisions could be secured, and a spring—later called Caravan Spring—provided fresh water. The surrounding, gentle prairie was ideal for camping, grazing, and outfitting.[38] When the party finally rolled out, neighbors, relatives, and friends turned out to see them off. Some went along for a few miles, helping with cattle and delaying their final goodbyes. The Baker train took the military road west, while the Parker train went southwest. Like other emigrants, they would meet again later in the Cherokee Nation, a region just across the Arkansas border.[39]

Comfortable Mary Baker decided to stay behind, at least for the present. She had borne a dozen children and had enough of pioneering.[40] "Arkansas is plenty good enough for me," she told her husband, "and Arkansas is where I'm going to stay." Others said, despite her protesting, she planned on coming out later and that her reluctance had to do with an uneasy premonition.[41] Before leaving Arkansas, Jack authorized a will, "knowing the uncertainty of life and the certainty of death and not knowing the time of my dissolution." Besides providing for Mary and their heirs, he hoped that his body might receive "a decent burial in the bosom of it[s] mother Earth" and that his spirit would return "to the God who gave it."[42]

Somewhere along the line, perhaps at Crooked Creek, two large Dunlap families joined the Baker train. Jesse Dunlap Jr., a merchant, had reportedly been in business with William Mitchell. The 1855 tax records for Marion County showed Jesse to be worth $570 in taxable property. Jesse and his wife, Mary, had ten children. His older brother, Lorenzo Dow Dunlap, a tenant farmer, and his wife, Nancy, had eight.[43]

Finally, of necessity, the party had its drovers to herd stock. One man who traveled with the Bakers said that "a large number of hired men accompanied the train as 'bullwhackers' and stockherders."[44] Jack Baker alone had "five hands," which might have included his son Abel.[45] Other stock herders in the company were young men from the neighborhood or perhaps farther away who looked forward to the adventure of the West.[46] Some black men may have done this duty, too. The Baker family census enumerations of 1850 and 1860 suggested the possibility, as did the Dunlap family tradition that black slaves served in the train as laborers.[47] No contemporary observer confirmed this, although a few black men or women in a company of southern emigrants probably would not have elicited much comment.[48]

The makeup of most emigrant companies changed during the course of their journey, and the Bakers were no different. At some point, the party met up with another family grouping led by Alexander Fancher. Like the Baker sons and Basil Parker, Fancher had been to California before. Born in northern Tennessee in 1812, Fancher and his wife, Eliza Ingram, lived in Illinois and Missouri before settling in Arkansas in the 1840s and raising their nine children.[49] The Fancher family had been cattle people for generations, and Alexander's relatives were among the land and slave owners of the Ozark hill country west of Crooked Creek.[50]

In 1849 Alexander served as a private in the state militia during the Tutt-Everett War, a "dark and bloody chapter of contention and crime" growing out of one of the feuds of Ozark clans. He served under the command of Capt. William C. Mitchell, whose sons were tied to Jack Baker's family as well as to Baker's emigrant train. Mitchell's contingent marched from William Beller's farm on Crooked Creek and experienced "open war in all its pomp."[51]

A year later Alexander and his elder brother John traveled to California, likely taking the southern route through Utah and stopping at the Mountain Meadows before reaching San Diego, where Alexander and his family appear in census records.[52] For these farmers and cattlemen, southern California did not have the same charm as the fertile grassland of California's central San Joaquin Valley, nor the nearby market of the hungry gold seekers. Soon John went north, where he registered the first cattle brand in Tulare County in late 1852. He was in Mariposa County three months later, still closer to the miners.[53]

Sometime in the early to mid 1850s, Alexander Fancher and his family returned to Arkansas to drive more cattle to California. The timing of this trip was again right for making money in California's cattle boom.[54] In 1854 and 1855 Fancher was back in Arkansas, where he purchased land in Benton County, on the northwest edge of the state, perhaps as a staging ground for acquiring cattle for his third trip.[55] According to a local historian, Fancher "related stories of the wonderful land of opportunity [California]...and succeeded in interesting much of the cream of the citizenship in his westward journey."[56]

In April 1857 Fancher was forty-five years old and seasoned in the ways of the frontier. He also had talent and charisma. A family history described him as "a farmer, tall, slim, erect, of dark complexion, a singer, and a born leader and organizer of men," with "great common sense."[57] A newspaper reporter who interviewed his neighbors years later painted a similar portrait of "superior intelligence, integrity and courage."[58]

According to close family members, Fancher had four wagons with teams of oxen and mules. He may also have had as many as two hundred head of cattle, although that figure was less certain. He carried "considerable money," up to $2,000 in cash.[59] When the Fancher company left Benton County in 1857, it was—like the Baker company—an extended family. With Alexander was Eliza, then thirty-three, and nine Fancher children, twenty-two months to nineteen years. His party or Baker's also included two of Alexander's cousins, James Matthew Fancher and his brother Robert.[60]

The growing stream of Arkansas emigrants had many small tributaries. Also from Benton County came the Peter Huff and Saladia Ann Brown Huff family. Peter, a forty-one-year-old Tennessee farmer, had settled in Missouri before getting to Arkansas.[61]

Nearby Johnson County, Arkansas, in turn furnished several more families. These included John Milum Jones and Eloah Angeline Tackitt Jones. They brought their two small children; John's brother, Newton Jones; and Eloah's forty-nine-year-old widowed mother, Cyntha Tackitt. Widow Tackitt had eight children, including a son Pleasant Tackitt, who joined the train with his wife, Armilda Miller Tackitt, and their two sons. Historical records suggest that the Joneses and the Tackitts were tenant farmers who probably struggled to get by.[62]

Others went in the Jones-Tackitt group, making almost a small caravan to themselves. When friends met them on the trail, they reported seeing three men named Poteet with the group and also a man named Basham. One of the Poteets had his wife and children with him. The members of the group "left the state of Arkansas for California together," a neighbor said, "sometime in the month of April 1857."[63]

William and Martha Cameron were also part of the Arkansas migration. They were natives of Tennessee who lived in Alabama before moving west to Arkansas and establishing themselves at Crooked Creek

Township in the early 1840s.[64] They were likely in the neighborhood when Jack Baker first arrived, though later they moved farther south, around Clarksville, Johnson County. The couple had nine children, six of whom started the journey in Arkansas, including their daughter Matilda, married to Josiah Miller, along with their four children. Two other adult Cameron children joined the family along the way. Malinda Cameron, the oldest of the children, was married to Henry D. Scott, had three small children, and was pregnant with a fourth. Tillman Cameron owned a racehorse named One-Eye Blaze and was in business at Fort Smith, near where Mormon apostle Parley Pratt would be killed on May 13, 1857.[65]

At some point along the trail, a small company from Ohio may have joined the Arkansas travelers; the Ohio contingent, under the leadership of W. B. Duck, later claimed they had "set out with the [Baker] train from the Arkansas line."[66] Pioneers like those in Duck's company often took the river route from Ohio to Arkansas because Fort Smith had a reputation as a good place to gather and buy provisions—"the best point for emigrants...to assemble, and make preparations," one local booster said. Fort Smith was a gateway to the Cherokee Trail for those headed west.[67]

As the emigrants began their journey, these groups—Baker, Fancher, Jones-Tackitt-Poteet, Mitchell, Cameron, Parker, Duck, and others—were often in flux, camping together occasionally and then separating with plans to rendezvous later on the trail. That may also have been the case with Peter Campbell's family. Nancy Ann Campbell, at the time only four years old, recalled the family's train moving slowly to present-day Oklahoma—and then waiting a month for fifty wagons from Missouri.[68]

Little Nancy Ann Campbell's memory of Missourians being in the party remains one of the unsolved mysteries of the emigrant company. Rumors about Missouri wagons traveling near the Baker, Parker, and Fancher parties would also surface along the trail and in Utah. A member of the Duck group said that a Reed family from Missouri, along with the Bakers, "were the principal owners of the [live]stock," with enough money to make some land investments in southern California.[69]

The point where the predominantly Arkansas parties may have first camped together for their overland trip was near present-day Salina, Oklahoma—then known by its French-trapper name of La Grande Saline (from La Grande River and nearby salt springs). This village was in Indian Territory, land where the U.S. government relocated the Cherokee and other Indians in the 1830s.[70]

Some gave Alexander Fancher the credit for leading the forming company. He "was well fitted for the leadership in the expedition which his followers by a unanimous choice assigned him," they said. Utah and Western historians followed suit for most of the next century, calling the Arkansans "the Fancher company." However, a public meeting at Carroll County, Arkansas, less than a year after the emigrants left, put Jack Baker's name at the top of a list of pioneers and Fancher's near the end.[71] Basil Parker, who knew and saw both men en route to California, described Baker as the most influential but said Fancher was "one of the leading men."[72] More likely, with so many groups semi-allied but loosely organized on the trail, the Fancher and Baker companies each had their own leaders, at least until they reorganized in Utah.

According to Parker, sometimes his own "train was in the lead," sometimes Baker's. But the two were close enough together that "folks visited back and forth." They were also close enough for Parker to see that some members of Baker's party were "wasteful" with their gunpowder and lead. Like many overlanders, the Baker people "could not resist" shooting at whatever fancied them along the trail, he said. The behavior was especially understandable for Ozark hunters, who measured manhood by how well they used their Kentucky long rifles.[73] It probably also reflected their expectation of being able to buy more ammunition once they reached Salt Lake City.

Target shooting was a way of staying sharp and relieving monotony. For Nancy Campbell, ever anxious to get there, the travel seemed beyond patience; at least she described one delay after another as her train lumbered along.[74] Malinda Cameron Scott also recalled the slow, mile-after-mile travel. "There was no such a thing as a [settlement] from the time we left Cherokee Nation," she remembered, "but just the bare ground and we never saw a place where you could buy a thing from there to Salt Lake. . . . It was just one long traveling road." When asked by a questioner, "Do you know where you crossed the Rocky Mountains?" she replied that "it all seemed to be Rocky Mountains all the way."[75] Of course, trading posts and small settlements were on the trail, and the Rocky Mountains were not so ever-present as she said. But many years later, it was the rough, solitary loneliness of her travel that stuck in her memory.

Successful overland caravans started early in the morning, nooned for several hours in the heat of the day to relieve the oxen, and traveled again in the late afternoon and early evening. On a good day, work animals might go sixteen or eighteen miles—much more might cause them injury. Campsites were naturally fixed by the need for water and good grass.[76] The Arkansas trains observed another general rule of overland travel—they rotated the wagons in the lead. As one participant remembered: "The man driving the leading wagon in the train, should be responsible to aid in choosing the camp site for the night. The following day that wagon would become the last in line, and the one behind it would be first...each wagon thus having a day in each position in line." The process meant the travelers took turns enduring the dust and manure of the forward wagon teams. There were other routines, too, including much-needed wash days and delays caused by broken-down wagons.[77] On these occasions, members of the party might split apart for a time until the stragglers, scurrying, caught up.

Parker remembered disagreements. "We got along fine until we came to the first small desert," he said, perhaps in what became eastern Colorado. Then "some of the train said I was too strict, so several persons concluded to travel by themselves, but they were glad to get back to us before we met any indians."[78] This last fear, which gripped many overlanders, offset any fractious feeling, as men and women traveling in small parties could hardly defend themselves against a serious attack. "Many a night we sat up and watched all night," said one of the emigrants, because of fear that "Indians would break in at any time."[79]

Emigrants often exaggerated the Indian danger, especially for the first half of the California road. Their primal fears of the plains Indians usually outweighed reality.[80] But there were in fact conflicts along the trail in 1857.[81] Native peoples were angry about the damaging traffic on their lands; U.S. troopers, reacting to Indian unrest, swept through the area, raising native emotions still more.[82] Many overlanders added to the trouble by having what one historian called a "callous attitude of cultural and racial superiority." Their airs and fears led to one depredation after another against Indians.[83]

Once Parker was catching up with the rest of his party after stopping for repairs. He saw what he described as five hundred Indians arrayed before the emigrants' cattle; they wanted "pay for the grass the cattle ate"—a request the frontiersman refused. "I determined to make a big bluff," Parker's later account said, "and dashed up at one of the indians who was getting ready to shoot a calf, then coming to a sudden stop I leveled my pistol at him and yelled for him to 'vamos' or I would kill him....The indians drew off and I gave the signal to my wife for the train to move on and move on it did although the indians threatened us as we went by. I never got away with a bluff so easy."[84]

Later, some of the emigrants' horses were stolen, perhaps as payback for Parker's imperativeness. The frontiersman then seized a nearby

Indian leader until the animals were returned.[85] It was Parker's way of doing business. Earlier in his career, during a confrontation between whites and Indians, he had shot a fleeing Indian. In still another incident, he had approved the vigilante-like killing of an Indian accused of cattle-stealing.[86]

But such actions often came with a price. When Nancy Campbell's family fell a quarter mile behind the next wagon in line, Indians dashed up on horses and reached for the Campbells' three children, who were sitting on the wagon bed. The riders rode off empty-handed "as quickly as they had come" but startled the children and scared their mother.[87] Perhaps the incident was nothing more than an act of bravery by the young Indians or an attempt to frighten the travelers. Or perhaps the native youth were expressing how they felt about the emigrants.

On another occasion, an Indian came into the Baker party's camp and asked to stay the night. The emigrants gave their permission but put their guest under heavy guard. The night passed without incident, though native campfires dotted the hills and Indians appeared to be everywhere—at least to the emigrants. The next morning the Indian was sent off with gifts of sugar and milk. "Nothing was again seen or heard of him or his friends," said Nancy Campbell. "If he had planned some sort of signaling, his plans were thwarted."[88]

Three times the herds of the Arkansas emigrants were stampeded—twice from unknown causes and once by Indians.[89] According to one emigrant, this last attempt was stopped by a "noted plainsman from Missouri," who led a several-day chase to get the animals back. During the chase, "the party captured an Indian and pressed him into their service as a guide."[90]

In July after some three months of travel, the Arkansas emigrants began arriving at Fort Bridger, then a part of Utah Territory. Most of their cattle apparently made it through, too, although at least one party behind them was not so fortunate; "Captain Henry of Texas" lost 151 head to Arapaho raids.[91] By late July there was a fresh uncertainty at the fort. The Mormon outpost buzzed about how the U.S. mail had been suspended because of troubles in the territory, and the Mormons talked excitedly of a coming fight with the U.S. government.[92]

The emigrants had their own problems. According to one account, some of them quarreled, and a few families split off from the main party and took the Fort Hall route to California. In addition, Peter Huff, "one of the leaders from Arkansas," developed a sore on his hand. No one saw what caused it, but the emigrants assumed "a tarantula, or some

CATTLE ON THE RANGE. *F. M. Steele, C.R.I. & P. Railway System, Courtesy Library of Congress.*

other venomous creature" struck him in his sleep. He suffered for days before he died, "leaving a widow and a large family of young children." The Huffs had been traveling in the train that included the Bakers, and Peter's illness and death "delayed the party for some days."[93] Other emigrant trains moved ahead, gradually making their way through the canyons that led into the Salt Lake Valley. Frank King, an emigrant who later converted to Mormonism, reported traveling with the Fancher group for two weeks from Pacific Springs back near South Pass to Emigration Canyon east of Salt Lake City. According to King, the Arkansas party was traveling in tandem with a train "called the Illinois company." The Fancher emigrants camped for some time in the canyon or moved down it slowly; King said, "I went out to Emigration can[y]on three times to see them." He remembered several families in the group, including Fanchers, Dunlaps, and Hamiltons.[94]

While the Fancher group lingered in the canyon, the Illinois company may have pressed forward on its own. On Monday, July 20, clerks in the Church Historian's Office in Salt Lake City recorded, "About noon a company of emigrants for Cal arrived mostly from Illinois." That Saturday, the clerks noted the arrival of another company of

California-bound emigrants, who camped at Townsend's, a public house in the heart of Salt Lake City where some of Col. Steptoe's men had boarded nearly three years earlier. On Monday, July 27, the clerks wrote, "More Emigrants arrived."[95] Other Arkansas travelers passing through the Salt Lake Valley on or before August 3 saw the Fancher, Cameron, and Dunlap companies "encamped six miles from Salt Lake City," where they had been "for some time." The passing travelers reported that "Baker had not arrived."[96]

About July 26 Eli Kelsey, a Mormon Indian missionary just released from his post south of Fort Bridger, joined some well-to-do Arkansas emigrants traveling through the mountain passes—probably the Baker group. "They were moral in language and conduct, and united regularly in morning and evening prayers," Kelsey reported years later, after becoming disaffected from Mormonism. They had "peace of domestic bliss and conscious rectitude" and were "an exceedingly fine company of emigrants, such as was seldom seen on the plains." Kelsey said he had "never travelled with more pleasant companions."[97]

But Kelsey spoke harshly of a rough set of men who joined the Arkansas people in the leap-frog manner of the overland trail. He called these men "Wild-cats" from Missouri and said their camp rang with "vulgar song, boisterous roaring, and 'tall swearing.'" And they spoke of the need to wipe out the Mormons. Kelsey said that when traveling with the Arkansans, he warned them to separate themselves from the rowdy group as much as possible as "at that time it was easy to provoke a difficulty" with the Saints and perhaps the Indians as well. Still later, he visited their Salt Lake City camp to warn them again. The emigrants reportedly thanked him and said they would heed his advice.[98]

The identity of these Missouri "Wild-cats" would become a matter of controversy. Some writers concluded that they traveled with the Arkansas companies all the way to the Mountain Meadows and perished there.[99] Missourians were probably among those killed at Mountain Meadows, but the "Wild-cats" Kelsey described may have taken the northern route to California. Parker, who lagged behind the Bakers and other emigrants at Fort Bridger, later caught up with the Thomas D. Harp train, which stopped to recover cattle taken by Indians on the headwaters of the Humboldt in present-day Nevada. A party of "mostly Missourians" helped retake the cattle and, according to emigrant Helen Carpenter, "some of them were disposed to treat the squaws as the Border Ruffians did the women of Kansas," and "some were for having the squaws killed." She felt relieved that "there were enough real men" in the party to save the native women.[100]

The Baker train—and presumably the "Wild-cats"—pulled into Salt Lake City on August 3.[101] If the "Wild-cats" parted with the Bakers and went north out of the city, however, other Missourians were already camped with the south-bound Fanchers, Camerons, and Dunlaps before the Bakers arrived to join them. These Missourians "fell in with" the three advance Arkansas companies, according to California-bound emigrants passing through the valley at the time.[102]

The passers-by said the members of the camped Arkansas trains planned to rest for weeks until the hot weather moderated for their trip across the southwestern deserts. A long stay in the valley would also fatten the cattle for the remainder of the trip. If in fact those were their plans, they soon changed. Few emigrants driving large herds of cattle had any desire to linger in Utah in 1857; range was limited and tempers were rising.[103]

CHAPTER SEVEN

Restless and Excited Beings

Northern Utah, July–August 1857

W EST OF SOUTH PASS in what became the state of Wyoming, most California-bound overlanders turned toward what is now Idaho, avoiding all but the northwest corner of present-day Utah. Others drove southwest into Salt Lake City—and thereby added miles, trail time, and the worry of mingling with the reputedly fanatical Mormons.[1] Despite the rumors, those who braved the Mormon capital found a bit of frontier civilization.

The city of several thousand citizens was carefully laid out. Wide streets on a grid crossed each other at right angles. Neat adobe-brick and log homes sat on one-and-a-quarter-acre lots in checkerboard fashion, bordered by vegetable and flower gardens, orchards, and shade trees. Water from the canyons to the east and northeast flowed in refreshing rivulets along the streets.[2] For trail-worn travelers seeing the city for the first time, it seemed a "paradise," as one overlander put it, "the most lovely place I ever saw."[3]

"These Mormons look and act like human beings," marveled one 1853 emigrant.[4] They could also be the source of benefits. The emigrants who took the road from Fort Bridger to Salt Lake wanted produce, flour, grain, and the chance to rest and repair their outfits. Worn stock might be exchanged for fresh animals. The arrangement also worked well for the Saints. It gave them the chance to make some

WAGONS ON MAIN STREET, SALT LAKE CITY, CA. 1869. *Baron de Joseph Alexander Hubner*, Passeggiata intorno al mondo (*Milano, 1879*).

money and secure hard-to-get goods that filled—and often slowed—the emigrants' wagons. The local people might complain of damage done by passing livestock or entertain fears of disease that trains brought. But overall, Utahns counted the advantages.[5]

Beginning in late July each year, overlanders flooded Salt Lake City's streets, and the tide was especially high in 1857. Church clerks sometimes noted the arrival of emigrants, but the Mormons did not formally record the names of non-Mormon companies nor keep a running tally of visitors. Other sources, however, suggest the number of persons traveling through northern Utah in 1857 may have approached a thousand, perhaps even more. "Our streets are daily thronged with emigrants from the States for California," reported Mormon apostle Wilford Woodruff in early August.[6] That season, dozens of emigrant groups arrived in, departed from, or formed in the Salt Lake Valley—the large majority of them being non-Mormon. A dozen of these emigrant parties drove a total of nearly eight thousand head of cattle.[7]

The great number of people and animals was one reason for the tension in 1857. Years earlier, Salt Lakers had grown tired of emigrants who "turn their teams loose in our streets, and near our city," causing "much destruction of crops and grass." Emigrant cattle had overgrazed land near the city, forcing local citizens to go as far as twenty miles to cut hay and even farther to winter their herds. To solve these problems, in 1851 animals were forbidden from roaming inside the municipality of Salt Lake, "which extends to some six or eight miles square."[8] Instead, emigrants and their stock might be met at the city limits and piloted through town to herd grounds outside the city.[9]

Normally, the system worked reasonably well, but by 1857 two years of drought had left the Mormons' animals weak and underfed, which made locals not only in Salt Lake but throughout the territory especially protective of pasture lands. While the grass had improved because of heavy snow the prior winter, large emigrant herds still taxed the natural resources.[10]

But an even greater problem was the threat of war—and everything that flowed from it. As the Saints prepared for the army's arrival, one of the main reasons for emigrants taking the road from Fort Bridger to Salt Lake City—trading—became a matter of exasperation and friction. The stiffly toned orders from Daniel H. Wells and Brigham Young during the first week of August forbade selling grain to outsiders.[11] The policy was another setback for the travelers. This season's late and overgrazed grasses, occasional stampedes, and the usual disease and weariness of overland travel had already taken a toll on the cattle. A little Mormon grain could have helped them a great deal, though cattle could get by with feeding on the range. More critical were the emigrants' mules and horses. They needed grain.[12]

Also scarce in Salt Lake City were powder and lead, which must have made the members of the Baker train regret their target practice on the plains. "I know they were una[b]le to buy any from the Mormons," their occasional traveling companion Basil Parker said, for the Mormons "had offered me almost any price" for such supplies.[13] Gunsmiths were busy fixing Mormon guns, and one correspondent wrote, "The question is asked hundreds of times during the day, Where can I buy a rifle? Where can I purchase some amunition?"[14] One traveler reported that Mormon women followed the wagons of overlanders pleading for guns and ammunition.[15]

The emigrants did not leave Salt Lake City entirely empty-handed. Local citizens sold them fresh produce that would not store, and likely a limited amount of grain and flour.[16] When one of the 1857 trains passed through Spanish Fork, south of Salt Lake City, its members declined to buy potatoes and flour offered for sale, saying "they did not need any supplies"—a sign that they had replenished their stores in Salt Lake.[17] The Baker and Fancher companies may have bought equipment and sundries from the firm Gilbert & Gerrish, one of the principal merchant establishments in the city.[18] The threat of war and pressure to have unsympathetic gentiles leave town eventually persuaded these merchants to sell out to Mormons for whatever they could get.[19]

The Mormons' grudging policy toward the range and trade were symptoms of growing tension in the territory. Emigrants passing the trading post of Fort Bridger near Utah's northeast border met Mormons going east to watch for U.S. troops. These scouts vented their feelings, speaking of the old torment of Missouri and Illinois and of "the unjustness and tyranny of the people of the United States." If Gen. Harney "was coming peaceably, we will let him come," they said, "but if not, we will drive him back." As these emigrants got closer to Salt Lake City, they met a Mormon named John Killian who lived on the main road through Emigration Canyon. He complained about territorial officers and the Buchanan administration. He unabashedly "rejoiced that the time had come when the saints would be avenged on their enemies."[20]

The sixty-one-year-old Killian was an example of how close and personal these encounters could be. He had joined the Saints in 1831, and his new religion soon made him the target of violence in Missouri. Killian served as an officer in the Mormon-controlled Caldwell County militia, and he and his family had been driven from the state.[21] In Utah he worked for Daniel H. Wells in levying tolls for lumber taken from the canyon.[22] Killian's nearby home allowed him to watch incoming emigrants, one of whom was Nicholas Turner, a Missourian who arrived in the Salt Lake Valley not long after the Fanchers and Bakers and would follow them south with his own train. Killian's first wife, Lydia Ann Hopper, was a cousin of Turner's wife, Keziah McClure. When Lydia Ann died, Killian married Keziah's sister, making him Turner's brother-in-law. More than family ties connected the two men. Turner had commanded the Johnson County militia during the 1838 Missouri conflict with the Mormons in Caldwell County.[23]

But an emigrant did not have to be a known Mormon fighter to be a target of the locals' ire. "There did not seem to be much love between the Mormons and Missourians," said one 1857 overlander generally.[24] The Mormons were preparing for war, and all outsiders—whether from Missouri, Arkansas, or elsewhere—were seen as potential enemies. For their part, the emigrants saw the Mormons as expatriates and even traitors. During August and September, local militia units were busy drilling to defend their homeland.[25] For the outsiders, every military maneuver was evidence the local people were on the wrong side in what might be a coming civil war. These people were "the most restless and excited beings on earth," one emigrant said after traveling through Salt Lake City.[26]

The brewing animosities played themselves out in various ways. When William Cureton's emigrant party entered the Salt Lake Valley, a quiet couple that had traveled with it immediately left the train without notice. They were Mormons who apparently felt they had to keep their religion to themselves. Later, after Cureton passed through the city and camped, a dozen "villainous looking" Indians seemed to be peering at his wagons as if getting ready for a future raid, he said. He was in the area, too, when Richard Pettit and Joseph Thompson thrashed lapsed Mormon C. G. Landon of the surveyors office—and outraged emigrants came dangerously close to getting involved in the scuffle. With so much uncertainty in the air, Cureton was probably relieved to leave the Mormon capital after only two or three days.[27]

According to Hamilton G. Park, Brigham Young's property manager, the tension in Salt Lake City almost turned into general fisticuffs when a few emigrants who had been drinking boasted that they had helped drive the Saints out of Missouri and that they were "among the mob at Carthage when Joseph and Hyrum Smith were murdered." Some Mormons took the bait and made plans to give the emigrants "such a drubbing that if the[y] survived the[y] would not forget." Park said Young learned of the plan and summoned the Mormons to his office, where he dressed them down "as only Brigham Young could do." He did not want "a finger" raised against any of the emigrants, some of whom, Park believed, were later killed at Mountain Meadows.[28]

Others also spoke of emigrant-settler conflicts in Salt Lake City. According to Basil Parker, who arrived in the city the day after the Bakers left, Mormons claimed that members of the Baker party had "insulted" Mormon women—probably references to polygamy. The Mormons also told Parker that Baker's group "accused the Mormons of poisoning the water that had killed some of the emigrants' cattle"— a charge that other Latter-day Saints would later make against the emigrants themselves. One Mormon, sitting in Parker's tent, was so agitated at the emigrants' remarks that he "almost threatened" Baker's train—at least that was how Parker remembered the event.[29]

In later years, southern Utah settler and judge John Steele left behind notes that were probably meant as a draft for a formal statement. Steele, who did not participate in the massacre but had an interest in explaining it, apparently interviewed a few Salt Lake City citizens about their interactions with 1857 emigrants. One witness he interviewed claimed that emigrants let down a fence and turned their animals into a local hay field. When Mormons "told [them] to get on to where there was more room and not damage the Setlars," the emigrants used "terrible oaths" and taunted settlers about having the firearm that killed Joseph and Hyrum Smith.[30]

Because the statements of Park, Parker, and Steele were written so many years later, they may have been tainted by retrospective myths and rumors about the emigrants. Yet it is difficult to dismiss them entirely. Park had a reputation for reliability, while Parker—a non-Mormon and fellow Arkansan—would seem to have no motive for saying Baker's company had insulted Mormon women. As for Steele's account, two of his informants, William Strong and Lyman Leonard, were known to have ties to the Salt Lake City neighborhood through which the emigrant companies probably passed.[31]

The accounts had also the broad truth of the tension that was building between local settlers and emigrants, which erupted on the road that ran north out of Salt Lake City. This road eventually veered northwest to join the main overland trail at the landmark called "The City of Rocks" in present-day southern Idaho. Most emigrants leaving Salt Lake City took it.

Apostle Lorenzo Snow, presiding at Brigham City, about sixty miles north of Salt Lake City, and Verulam Dive, a Mormon bishop in a settlement between those two cities, were the first to sound an alarm. Snow's and Dive's letters to Young reported that during late July and early August, emigrants and Indians were quarreling, and the Mormons, because they lived nearby and needed Indian allies, were in the middle of it.[32] Such troubles would continue into September.[33]

On July 30 Indians stole six horses from an emigrant company at Blue Springs, forty miles north of the Mormon settlement of North Willow Creek (present-day Willard, Utah). While pursuing the thieves south toward the settlement, the emigrants hired a Mormon to pay two Indians to recover the animals. The Indians drove five of the horses from a hiding place in the nearby mountains to a place where the emigrants could retrieve them. Another Mormon offered to locate the last missing horse if the emigrants "would be peaceable and not Kill the Indians." The emigrants spurned the offer, saying that "if they Killed any their Scalps should pay the debt." Before the emigrants reached the recovered horses, two Indians rushed in to steal them again. According to Dive, the emigrants and Indians arrived at the horses "about the same time when the Emigrants firing their Revolvers killed one" Indian and "the other escaped."[34]

The emigrants, with their recovered horses, then traveled to a camp-site about four miles north of Willow Creek, where they were soon surrounded by twenty-five Indians upset by the shooting. The confrontation ended only after the emigrants gave the Indians "one Horse some Blankets & shirts." The next morning, not distinguishing one emigrant party from another and still angry over the killing of one of their men, the Indians "poured out their spite" on a small group of emigrants camped within the local Mormon fort. Again, gifts staved off an attack.[35]

A few days later emigrants killed another Indian near the Bear River's estuary into the Great Salt Lake. "Much excitement prevailed," Snow wrote Young on August 7, "and we had much difficulty in protecting [an]other company of emigrants from being massacred by the fury of the Indians."[36]

Emigrant trains continued to experience trouble. D. C. Hail, an emigrant who passed through Salt Lake City in August, reported that as his train moved north from Salt Lake City, Mormons treated the emigrants like "highway robbers or murderers," and at one point two dozen Indians and perhaps ten Mormons had confronted the train. "The Indians attempted to drive off our stock," he said, "the Mormons, at the same time, cursing us, and telling us 'to give up our blankets and some of our cattle, or they [the Indians] would murder us!' We then succeeded in driving them [the Indians] back, but they followed on in pursuit of us."[37]

For years the Saints had mediated disputes between overland travelers and Indians. This season alone, Young said, the Mormons had helped nearly twenty parties, small and large, get through the territory, usually by providing gifts to Indians from the church or federal government.[38] Yet it was a thankless job. Lorenzo Snow grumbled that if the season's "emigrants would...have one tenth part of the forbearance with the ignorant people of the forest that we have they would find it for their interest."[39]

Many of the emigrants could not understand why the Saints wanted to maintain the Indians' friendship, unless for some sinister reason. Emigrants in Brigham City saw Indians, supposedly so angry and out of control, "chating and laughing" with Mormons. The result was damning, as Snow well knew. "I have acted as prudently as I knew how between the Indians and emegrants," he wrote Young on August 13, "and yet I am certain they will tell an *awful* tale of Brigham City being in league with the Indians & we are in for it most posatively." The travelers were "humble as kittens while here," Snow said, but he predicted that once beyond the settlements they would have "the spirit of the damned."[40] Sure enough, on reaching California the emigrants denounced the Saints for not being more on their side.[41]

After the conflicts near Brigham City, Snow could report, "The Indians feel well at present."[42] But the Mormons' role as mediator risked putting them between Indians whose friendship they needed in the coming war and travelers who treated native peoples harshly. Early in the season, a group of eastbound Californians coming across present-day Nevada reportedly "shot at every Indian that they saw."[43] Some westbound overlanders did the same, including M. W. Buster's train. Buster, from Greenfield in southwest Missouri, began "killing Indians indiscriminately" as early as Fort Laramie and later wiped out eighteen more near Gravelly Ford on the Humboldt River after the Indians supposedly "bantered the boys to fight."[44] These were notorious examples, but other emigrants displayed what one leading historian of the overland migration, John D. Unruh Jr., described as "blatant superiority" and "reckless actions" with regard to native people, even "shooting at Indians on sight."[45]

By the second week in August, the large herds on the trail, the brutal acts of some emigrants, and the unsettling possibility of war made some Indians restive. When an emigrant told Little Soldier's band of Indians at the East Weber, about twenty miles east of the Willow Creek episode, that Brigham Young was going to cut their throats and take their women as his wives, they appeared to believe the worst.[46] Some Indians may have believed that Mormon help had been too little and too late. Reports reaching Salt Lake City suggested "great commotion" among the Indians and the possibility of a "general outbreak"—just at the time the Saints anxiously wanted them as allies.[47]

Young acted swiftly to restore calm. Still serving officially as U.S. superintendent of Indian affairs for the territory, he dispatched gifts—flour, potatoes, corn, cattle, and ammunition worth $1,700—to such native leaders as Little Soldier (at Ogden Hole, present-day Huntsville), Pi-bi-gand (Box Elder), and Ke-tant-mah (East Weber). His action was in keeping with his belief that it was easier to feed Indians than to fight them, though the incident could not have come at a worse time for the Mormons. They needed the goods to supply their own militia if it came to war.[48]

To handle the negotiations and the distribution of gifts to the Indians, Young sent his chief Indian scout and brother-in-law Dimick B. Huntington. Huntington was a stoutly built native of Jefferson County, New York, and an early Latter-day Saint convert who considered his work with the Indians to be a religious mission conferred upon him by Joseph Smith. "God has shown to me that you have got to go among the Lamanites," Smith told him in 1839. Arriving in Utah eight years later, Huntington began to trade with Indians and soon was able to make himself understood in the Ute and Shoshone dialects. In the years that followed, Young used him as his right-hand man in one Indian matter after another. In 1853 he received the grisly task to recover and bury the bodies of the Gunnison massacre victims and to retrieve the slain party's papers and property. In sending Huntington to help ease the tension along the northern road, Young had someone who had influence with the Indians of Utah Territory, partly because the Indians understood his close ties with Young.[49]

Huntington kept a record of the negotiation that went along with the gifts. Meeting with northern Indians in August—first with four hundred and later with a thousand—Huntington urged Little Soldier, whose relations with the Mormons had been mixed, to convert to the Saints' beliefs and adopt white man's farming. He warned of a Last Days' siege and famine that might go on for seven years.[50] In addition, there may have been a show of force; according to William Bell,

DIMICK HUNTINGTON. *Courtesy LDS Church History Library.*

a non-Mormon Salt Lake City merchant, conditions did not completely cool until a militia company entered the area.[51]

These Mormon countermeasures persuaded the Indians not to oppose the local settlers. But it was at best an arm's-length relationship, not the close alliance for which Young had hoped. Little Soldier, saying he feared the approach of U.S. soldiers, told Huntington that he planned to retreat to the mountains and see how the struggle between the Mormons and the government turned out; he was satisfied to be a bystander. Over the next several weeks, other Indians said the same thing.[52]

When offering a public prayer on August 13, Young still hoped the Indians might rise to what he believed was their prophesied destiny, pleading that they might yet "do thy will & be as a wall of defense around about us."[53] On the same day, Gen. Wells sent out his important dispatch telling the Saints to watch the mountain passes and cultivate Indian friendship.[54] But it was not until the following Sunday, August 16, that Young gave his clearest reaction to the events that had taken place in northern Utah.

His address began with the emotional kindling of the Mormons' past persecution and the threat of war. He also spoke publicly for the first time of his military strategy of guerrilla fighting. He then announced a new Indian policy. If the army comes and commences war on the Saints, he declared, "I will tell you honestly, and plainly, and in all good feeling that I will not hold the Indians still while the emigrants shoot them, as they have hitherto done, but I will say to them [the Indians], go and do as you please."[55] The old policy of mediating between emigrants and Indians had almost led to an Indian war just at the time when Young was trying to curry favor with native peoples for the coming conflict.[56] Something else may also have kindled Young's anger. He had been a federal Indian superintendent for years, and yet Washington had failed to reimburse him and his people fully for keeping peace with the Indians; the arrears by 1857 had reached more than $30,000—a large sum for the time.[57]

One extended passage in the August 16 sermon was clearly meant for Washington, possibly in hopes of bringing about a settlement. "I...wish to say to all Gentiles," Young told non-Mormons in the congregation, to "send word to your friends that they must stop crossing this continent to Calafornia for the indians will kill them." He wanted Washington to know what it would lose by alienating the Mormons. The Mormon leader was raising the stakes by threatening the flow of goods and people across the middle of the continent. But there was also the practical reality that if the Saints fled to the mountains to fight a guerrilla war, they could no longer mediate between emigrants and Indians. "This people have always done good to the travelers," Young insisted. "They have kept the Indians from injuring them and have done all in their power to save the lives of men, women and children, but all this will cease to be, if our enemies commence war on us."[58]

For three weeks, the emotions of the Saints had been building. During his speech when Young asked if they were willing to "lay wast[e] and desolate every thing behind you" and flee to the mountains, there was an emotional outburst.[59] Members of the congregation raised both hands in the air and waved and clapped their assent. "We declared with uplifted hands that we would from this time fourth defend ourselves from any further oppression from the Gentiles[,] God being our helper," said one of the settlers who was present.[60] One of the clerks, unsure a mere transcript could capture the moment, penned into his record, "The feeling that prevailed in the meeting cannot be discribed."[61]

Young's sermon also chastened non-Mormon merchants in the audience who, Young believed, were part of the clique working against his people in Washington. Several days later, keying off Young's remarks, local zealots forced their way into gentile stores to seize lead, clothes, and other items. When Young learned what had been done, he rebuked the men and took steps to safeguard the merchants' property. "A mean course of conduct to the Gentiles would result in fighting [against] the Saints," he said. Two of the men involved in the raid were Richard Pettit and Joseph Thompson, who had earlier participated in the beating of C. G. Landon.[62]

Young's August 16 address had softer themes, too, as he urged his people to build up God's kingdom and fill the earth with peace. Some passages were heartfelt soliloquy. "How my soul has longed to see the time when the sufferings of the people will cease," he said. "How my soul has been pained while I have been in the world, to see the people poor, bound down and suffering for food and raiment, to see them imprisoned innocently and bound down by priestcraft. How my soul has desired to see the fetters broken asunder." The Mormon mission of "revolutionising" the world must go forward, he said.[63]

But it was Young's wartime preaching that stood out. The raids on the gentile merchants showed how his pulpit language—and the threat of war—could have unexpected consequences. Perhaps Young accepted these risks as a necessary part of war, but he seemed uneasy by the decisions he was making. "I wish to meet *all men* at the judgment Bar of God without any to fear me or accuse me of a wrong action," he told his diary several days after his August 16 address. Before any fighting was to be done, he wanted to give his "enemies fair warning."[64] A week later, Young reportedly sent a letter to Harney telling the U.S. commander that he and the Mormons did "not wish to fight anybody"—but if the army continued its advance the soldiers should expect resistance.[65]

Neither Harney nor Washington were interested in Young's pleas and protests—if they saw Young's letter at all. The war had its own momentum. As the U.S. soldiers continued to march to Utah, the Mormons, as inexorably, continued to get ready to fight.

‘

CHAPTER EIGHT

We Have Better Claim

Salt Lake to Fillmore, August 1857

T HOUGH MOST TRAINS took the northern trail out of Salt Lake
City in 1857, a few took the southern route. Among them was
the large train later massacred at Mountain Meadows. About
two weeks before the atrocity, these emigrants camped near the north-
bound Jacob Hamblin in central Utah, where they told Hamblin that
their "one train was made up near Salt Lake City of several trains that
had crossed the plains separately; and being southern people had pre-
ferred to take the southern route."[1]

Arkansas emigrants who took the northern route remembered seeing parts of the train before it headed south. Camped together near
Salt Lake City were Fanchers, Camerons, and Dunlaps—"three, and
perhaps four companies from Arkansas, while the balance...was made
up from Missourians."[2] Farther back on the road they saw other emigrants who would join the southbound group, emigrants they also knew
by name: the Bakers, the Mitchells, Milum Jones, and Cyntha Tackitt.[3]
When all of these emigrants joined together to form a new company
in Salt Lake, they may have chosen Alexander Fancher as their overall
leader.[4] While the Baker group had most of the property and people,
Fancher had Utah experience. Because of the predominance of Arkansans in the train, it would come to be called "the Arkansas company."[5]

The Missourians seen encamped with the Fanchers, Camerons,
and Dunlaps were never identified by name. They may have traveled

SOUTHERN ROAD TO CALIFORNIA

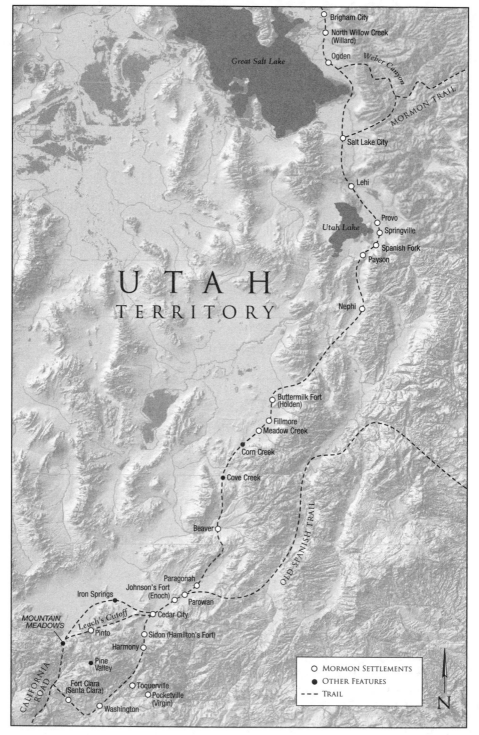

Map by Sheryl Dickert Smith and Tom Child

with the Arkansans to Mountain Meadows—relatives of the Arkansas victims and historians have been able to account with certainty for only about three-fourths of the approximately 120 killed in the massacre. Members of the company who met Hamblin told him their group was "mostly from Arkansas," and Hamblin said there were "outsiders" traveling with the train who were "rude and rough," though he failed to say who they were.[6] Brigham Young later spoke of a group of emigrants who had lingered in Salt Lake City for six weeks before leaving. "It was very noticeable that they did not hurry along like other emigrants," he said. None of the companies identified as going south in 1857 stayed in the city more than a couple of weeks.[7]

The Mormons may have urged these loiterers and the Arkansas emigrants out of town. The Camerons, Dunlaps, and Fanchers had been camping in the Salt Lake Valley "for some time" and, according to other emigrants who had seen them there, wanted to stay for several weeks to spare themselves the summer heat on the southern road.[8] But with an army marching toward the territory, the local people did not want hosts of strangers milling behind the lines of a possible battle. The Saints made the same point when ridding themselves of the surveyors and, still later, the gentile merchants.[9]

While Young heard something from apostle Charles Rich about the company that stayed six weeks, he said little about the Arkansas company that went south. In a sworn deposition eighteen years later, Young denied hearing anything much about it, except by rumor.[10] His statement, made under the advice of legal counsel, may have minimized what he knew. It made no mention of the near-brawl in Salt Lake City between emigrants and Mormons that Young's manager Hamilton Park later reported, nor Young's intervention to stop local rowdies from carrying out their plans.[11]

Peyton Welch, a member of Nicholas Turner's company, said two trains started south before his—the broadly construed Fancher and Baker portions of the Arkansas company.[12] They were a typically fluid group that probably broke apart and came together as it traveled south, depending on circumstances like the availability of good grass, good water, and good company. Often, there was another reason for joining together—anxiety. Usually this meant fear of Indians, and native people could be seen about Salt Lake City in the late summer of '57. But for the southbound emigrants, the perceived threat of the Mormons must have been greater. The sullen mood of a territory on the eve of war warned emigrants to be on guard.[13]

When all its members traveled together, the Arkansas train had about 140 people.[14] At times there may have been more. After the massacre, other emigrants or their families told stories of parting with the company just before its destruction, though some of the stories lack credibility and others deal with emigrants who probably took the northern road.[15]

One emigrant who took the northern route was Malinda Cameron Scott. She and her husband went north, while her parents and other family members went south and would be murdered at Mountain Meadows. Not long after starting north, Malinda's husband was killed by a member of his own train following a dispute. Adding to her trials, Malinda soon gave birth to a child on the trail. Yet she eventually reached the San Joaquin Valley in California.[16]

The Arkansas company as it headed south was a bustling village on the move, made up largely of young families. The senior citizens of the group included Jack Baker, as well as William and Martha Cameron—all in their fifties. The widow Cyntha Tackitt was forty-nine; Alexander Fancher, forty-five. The two Dunlap brothers, Jesse and Lorenzo, and their wives, Mary and Nancy, were all about forty. A few others in the company were known to be in their thirties.[17]

Beyond these, young people were the norm, making up as much as two-thirds of the train. Of those known to have been in the company, more than two dozen were in their twenties, just starting out their adult lives, some bringing with them small families. About the same number were in their teens, three out of four of them boys. The teens must have filled the camp with youthful life—and in the case of the young men, muscle and sinew to help with the cattle. Finally, three dozen or more of the children—two-thirds of them girls—were age twelve and younger, half of them below the age of seven.[18]

The Arkansas company pulled out of Salt Lake City sometime during the "hot and sultry" first week of August. Midway through the week, the thermometer read 97 degrees at early evening.[19] The heat-soaked train had around twenty wagons, perhaps more.[20] These carried blankets and bedding, chains and tools, knives and cooking utensils, clothing, firearms, and what the pioneers simply called camp "fix-ins"—the staples required for travel and some things for a new life in California. Near the wagons lumbered hundreds of head of loose cattle that had survived disease, stampedes, and other hazards of the trail. The cattle were among the first Texas longhorns seen in southern Utah. In addition to these were the draft animals and riding horses, which swelled the count even more.[21]

The total worth of the emigrants' property is difficult to calculate, but a good guess at 1857 prices would be about fifty thousand dollars. Adjusting for inflation, that amount would be more than a million dollars in 2007, a century and a half later.[22] William Carey, who later prosecuted John D. Lee, described the train as reputedly "the best equipped and richest that had ever crossed the Rocky Mountains," an overstatement even for the emigration of 1857.[23] Still, the emigrants' property made the train "exceptionally well to do."[24] The poor people in southern Utah, struggling to carve out an existence in their frontier settlements, must have looked upon the train with wonder, and some even with envy.

As the party worked its way south, the summer sun bore down on boys and men snapping their bullwhips and on children and sunbonneted women walking through clouds of dust kicked up by animals and wagons. No records from the train itself survived, making it difficult to describe the journey south from the emigrants' perspective. But accounts of earlier travelers give a feel for the terrain they experienced.

An 1855 freighter reported that between Salt Lake and Cedar City, "the road is excellent, with water, grass and wood, at short intervals, the entire distance."[25] A year later, German emigrant Hans Hoth, once a Mormon but now eager for a new life in California, left a diary of his travel. North of Fillmore, about 150 miles south of Salt Lake City, he remembered going all day without a drink of fresh water; that was a difficult stretch of the road. But in the places where water was found, it brought forth life in abundance. Along one stream, Hoth saw wild scrubs—saffron and peppermint, he thought—as well as twenty varieties of cactus, some in bloom.[26]

The trail had other hazards besides thirst. Once wolves stole meat that Hoth and his companions had put under one of their wagons. Another night, the company's livestock bellowed because a bear and her cub roamed nearby. Some emigrants feared Indians. Two days after Hoth's train had left Corn Creek, south of Fillmore, its members herded their livestock together and put the herd under the watch of a double crew. "Cattle are often stolen in these parts," Hoth explained. But in most respects, the southern road was like other emigrant trails in the West—one tiring footstep after another.[27]

The Arkansas company was not the only large train on the southern road in '57. Leaving Salt Lake City twelve or fourteen days behind the combined Arkansas company was Nicholas Turner's train of emigrants. Near it traveled William Dukes's and Wilson Collins's wagons.

CALIFORNIA-BOUND WAGON TRAIN. *M. Le Baron De Hubner (Paris, 1862).*

The Turner, Dukes, and Collins trains—whose members came from Missouri, Arkansas, and Texas—came together at some point to form a single unit, which became known as "the Missouri company."[28] In between these main parties or following them were smaller ones, some probably anonymous and lost to history.[29] To Volney King, who was ten years old in 1857 and living in Fillmore, companies seemed to travel past all season long.[30]

By the end of the third week of August, more than 250 emigrants were on the southern road with more than 1,200 head of cattle.[31] Because the Arkansas and Missouri companies traveled so close together, their identities and actions were later blurred. "I saw the Dukes company pass through Spanish Fork city on its way to California," remembered settler George Armstrong Hicks. "They were quiet and orderly as far as I know.... They were that same that was so cruely murdered at Mountain Meadows."[32]

Hicks's confusion—he was wrong about the fate of the Dukes group and perhaps also about the identity of the party he saw in Spanish Fork—was not unusual. Non-Mormons traveling behind the trains may also have confused them. After reaching California, these travelers associated the massacred train with all the conflicts they heard about

as they journeyed south. Whether their identification was correct in every instance remains unclear. Yet it is certain that a series of conflicts took place between settlers, emigrants, and Indians that mirrored the atmosphere in northern Utah.

Mormon militiamen east of Salt Lake City "showed us no favors," said a member of the Turner party, "as they considered us Americans," referring to the anger that was being expressed on both sides.[33] Eight days after the July 24 picnic and less than a week before the Arkansas train reached his community, Provo stake president James C. Snow called Haun's Mill massacre survivor Charles Jameson to the pulpit during that town's Sunday services. "I feel like fighting," Jameson said, "& if any Mob comes here I feel like giving them the best I have got in the locker."[34]

Compounding the problem was the way Utah had changed in the seven years since Alexander Fancher first may have traveled through the region. In 1850 few Mormons lived south of the Salt Lake Valley. But by 1857 Mormon colonization had expanded dramatically along the southern road to California, with new residents claiming land along most of the main rivers and streams that flowed from the mountains and the springs that seeped out or bubbled up near the trail. They had also claimed the best grassland as pasture for their animals.

The wartime atmosphere and competition for grass and water combined to create disputes. One took place before the second week of August in Provo, some fifty miles south of Salt Lake City. When local lawman Lyman Woods found emigrant cattle grazing on the red top and timothy grass that were the town's winter range, he asked the emigrants to move and offered to guide them to another campsite. According to Woods the company's captain retorted, "This is Uncle Sam's grass. We are his boys. We have better claim on it than a bunch of rebel Mormons."[35]

The U.S. government had not yet established a land office in Utah, which meant that technically the settlers did not have title to the range. But everyone understood squatters rights—including the government, which typically came down on the side of residents in land disputes.[36] Both sides felt justified in their positions. The emigrants depended on grass to feed their cattle, and if the cattle suffered, so might dreams of profit in California. The grass was also vital to the Mormons, whose thin herds were just beginning to thrive after the drought.[37]

Woods gave the emigrants one hour to move and called out the local "minute men." Whether the Mormons entrenched and barricaded themselves into a firing line, as Woods later claimed, or merely conducted a militia muster nearby, the show of force had its intended effect. Five minutes before Woods's deadline expired, the emigrants began packing up. "They wisely concluded that even if they won the battle," Woods later boasted, "the survivors would never be able to move to the north, or run the gauntlet of a Lexington line of riflemen stretching 200 miles to the southern border."[38] Stake president Snow said in August 9 church services, "I was pleased with the Military yesterday. It was the greatest turn out that I ever s[aw]."[39]

Provo leaders' minds were fixed on the approaching army. Failing to distinguish between the army and outsiders in general, one told his congregation "that the Gentiles are coming here to hang all our leaders & to make Eunichs of the rest." If the Saints ever did "come in contact with Uncle Sam," he predicted, they would discover "that the Lord has got a Battle axe that the Gentiles does not dream o[f]"—a reference to Indians whose favor the Mormons were trying to gain. Snow concluded, "Uncle Sam is determined to make us gain our independence as did the people of the U.S. from Great Briton."[40]

War fever or not, some local people could not resist trading with the emigrants. On Sunday, August 16, after the Arkansas company had passed through, Provo bishop E. H. Blackburn chided his congregation, "Men went last week & sold their flour to our enemies right against the counsel of Prest B. Young." Earlier that day, Snow had reiterated Young's directive to preserve "every kernal of Grain" and prepare warm clothing against the coming siege. Snow later added, "You know that I said this forenoon that I did not want you [to] render any aid or comfort to any person that is not for us." Anyone that did, he now said, was a traitor.[41]

Emotions were also running high in other settlements in Utah Valley. Snow's jurisdiction included Springville, just six miles south of Provo. Some settlers at Springville had been a law unto themselves, most seriously in March, when they killed two disaffected Mormons and a third man died in the cross fire.[42] The Parrish-Potter murders were apparently a part of reformation excitement that was still simmering in the area when the emigrants passed through the town in mid August. Later that month, the same Springville vigilantes would threaten still another dissenter, telling him not to talk about the local violence and exclaiming, "We have declared war against the whole world."[43]

Some ten miles south of Springville lay Payson. Eighteen-year-old James Pearce saw the Arkansas company as it went through town. He later passed it as he traveled to southern Utah to join his family there. Pearce remembered that the emigrants had "pretty good teams," though "they was pretty well drilled down" by then. "They was going very slow," he said. Pearce said he saw "mostly men" in the train, with only "a few women and children."[44]

Decades after the massacre, Payson bishop Charles B. Hancock said that some men in the town "marshalled" themselves at "unusual h[o]urs" against a company of emigrants, but he was able to hold the vigilantes back. Hancock wrote that "the emigrant company was part of those, when joined by others and on the way to California," that were "used up by John D. Lee and Company in 1857."[45] Hancock did not say what incited the local men or how he knew these emigrants were among those killed at Mountain Meadows.

Two other accounts offer possible explanations, though both, like Hancock's story, came years after the massacre. Ann Eliza Webb, who married and divorced Brigham Young and became a strong anti-Mormon lecturer, said that when the train passed through her town of Payson, she was almost thirteen years old. That was old enough, she insisted, to remember that "three apostate women" joined the emigrant group, which angered the local people.[46] Another of stake president Snow's sermons showed that he believed the rumor. Snow claimed that Abagail Parrish, sister-in-law to the murdered William R. Parrish, "apostatized & said she would go to California or die a trying." At the time Snow made these last remarks, he believed Abagail had been killed at the Meadows, though in fact she had traveled south behind the Arkansas company and survived.[47]

George Nebeker, nine years old in 1857, later told his daughter that while he and other boys tended the town herd outside of Payson, they "got acquainted with a bunch of people from the East" camped there. "Some of the party were ill," Nebeker remembered, "and they were waiting for them to get well before moving on" toward California. The train had several children Nebeker's age who offered the herd boys candy and "nick-nacks," leading to a friendship between the young-sters. Before long, some men of the company began target shooting toward Payson. A local man asked them not to, saying that "if some one would happen to be coming over the hill they might kill them." According to Nebeker, one of the emigrants responded, "I hope to God old Brigham Young himsel[f] would come over the hill. I'd like to put a bullet through his heart. I helped to drive the mormons out of m[iss]o[uri]." The incident "frightened the little boys and they never like[d] to play there so well again."[48]

Although it is not clear who the emigrants at Payson were, it is clear that the Arkansas company stopped about twenty-eight miles south of there near Nephi, a settlement sometimes called Salt Creek. Some of the company made their camp on land claimed by local citizens and named after the mayor, Josiah Miller. "There is a company of Gen-tiles at Millers Springs who have 300 head of Cattle," Mormon settler Samuel Pitchforth wrote in his diary on August 15, 1857. "The Bishop sent out to them requesting them to move for they were distroying our winter feed. They answered that they [w]ere American Citizens and should not move."[49] Two days later, Pitchforth recorded that "the company of Gentiles passed through [Nephi] this morning—they wanted to purchase flour."[50] He mentioned no conflicts or disturbances in town.

John Pierce Hawley, who later left Utah and its leading church, spent three days traveling with the Arkansas emigrants south of Nephi and recalled a conversation with the train's leader that confirmed Woods's and Pitchforth's accounts: "The captain of the company told me that they had had some trouble with the Mormons in two of their settlements. Salt Creek being one and Provo being the other." The captain downplayed the incidents. "We have a Dutchman with us, a single man, and he has given us all the trouble we have had. He would not obey orders but was sassy with officers in these places and it all originated by our cattle being grazed on there herd grounds, but we intend to observe the laws and rules of the territory." After spending time with the emigrants, Hawley believed that the "Saints gave them more trouble than they ought."[51]

Though Hawley did not identify him by name, the captain was probably the trail veteran Alexander Fancher, and other evidence would corroborate his statement about the troublesome Dutchman in the company. When the massacre was over and Mormons gave their account of what had happened, they remembered one man among the emigrants whose "greater height and strength warranted him in almost any kind of domineering." They also remembered a "Dutchman." Perhaps they were the same man.[52]

In the 1850s, the term *Dutchman* referred to people who spoke Dutch and others with northern European roots, especially those who spoke German (*Deutsch*) or had a Germanic accent. The United States had hundreds of thousands of such men and women living within its borders, many of them recent immigrants who had arrived in a great tide of mid-century migration. Longtime U.S. citizens sometimes treated them with derision, using the phrase, "D—d Dutchman."[53] Such sentiment gave rise to the rapidly growing nativist "Know Nothing" or "American Party," aimed against the German and Irish.[54]

The "Dutchman" traveling with the emigrants may have been John Gresly, whose family had emigrated from Germany and settled in York, Pennsylvania, becoming "Pennsylvania Dutch." John's brother, Henry J. Gresly, said he had a brother who died at Mountain Meadows. The 1850 U.S. Census for York listed fourteen-year-old John Gresly as a member of the Andrew and Rosanna Gresly family, but John's name would not appear on later national counts, suggesting an untimely death.[55]

Members of the Gresly family were known for combative behavior. In 1842 John's father, Andrew, was charged with assault and battery; in 1851 young John was found guilty of malicious mischief. Years later, another son, George, was arraigned on two charges—assault with intent to commit murder and carrying deadly weapons—for chasing down and shooting a man. Yet another son, Anthony, was convicted of assault and battery.[56] In 1857 John Gresly would have been twenty-one-years old and because of his young age was likely single, matching the description of the Dutchman in the Arkansas train. Whoever the mysterious man was, he was by both emigrant and Mormon accounts a troublemaker.[57]

After Hawley traveled with them, the Arkansas company came to the settlement of Buttermilk Fort (present-day Holden) and then the territorial capitol of Fillmore just below. The Arkansas company and possibly the Missouri company passed through these settlements shortly before non-Mormon emigrant George Powers of Little Rock, Arkansas. When Powers reached Buttermilk Fort, he and his three-wagon train "found the inhabitants greatly enraged at the train which had just passed, declaring that they had abused the Mormon women, calling them w—s, &c., and letting on about the men." Powers reported that the locals "had refused to sell that train any provisions, and told us they were sorry they had not killed them there; but they knew it would be done before they got in."[58]

Powers said the settlers did not plan to attack the train themselves, but "were holding the Indians in check until the arrival of their chief, when he would follow the train and cut it in pieces." Powers's company was close enough to the offending train that some men of the settlement confused the two. When his group tried to buy butter from local women, "the men came running and charging, and swore we should not have it, nor anything else, as we had misused them. They appeared to be bitterly hostile," said Powers.[59]

George W. Davis, another Arkansan traveling near or with Powers, described a similar episode, though he put it at Fillmore. The stories told by Davis and Powers were so much alike that they were likely describing the same event, with one of the men mistaking the location. According to Davis, the bishop at Fillmore—Lewis Brunson— "said that he could scarcely withhold the brethren from following after the train (which was afterwards massacred) and cutting it into pieces; because parties of that train cursed the Mormons for not selling them provisions." The bishop explained "that they had instructions from Brigham Young not to sell any provisions to emigrants unless they could get guns, revolvers, or ammunition for pay." This response had "very much enraged a Dutchman, who threatened, or said, that if he had a good riding horse, he would go back to Salt Lake and kill Brigham." The threat to kill Young so aroused local passion that, according to Davis's account, "the Bishop said that the only way that he could control his men was, that he promised them to set the Indians on the doomed train."[60] Though Davis believed the massacred train caused the uproar, the evidence is not conclusive. The Turner train or other elements of the Missouri company, traveling somewhere behind the Arkansas company, may also have passed through Fillmore before Davis's arrival.

Thomas Cropper was just fourteen years old when the emigrants passed through Fillmore. His recollections aligned with an element of Davis's contemporary account. Cropper remembered one emigrant saying, "I would like to go back and take a pop at Old Brig, before I leave the territory." Cropper added that "there appeared to be two companies of them joined together for safety from the Indians," one of them being mostly men. Cropper claimed they "called themselves the Missouri Wild Cats....I heard one of them make the brag that he helped to mob and kill Joe Smith." Cropper's account, given many decades later, was probably influenced by other Utah stories about the wagon train that proliferated after the massacre.[61]

Not all in Cropper's account, however, was negative. He said he and other boys were herding cattle on nearby mountain benches when they saw "the unusual sight of an immigrant train." Eager for excitement, the boys rushed down to meet the emigrants and went with them the next "two miles into Fillmore." Cropper mentioned no problems during this leg of the trip, only good-natured fun. "They dares us to ride one of their wild steers," Cropper recalled. He mounted the animal "and it dashed into Cattelin's Mill pond which caused them a lot of merriment."[62]

John A. Ray, a Mormon who was away from home as a missionary at the time, wrote in 1859 what he heard about the passage of one group of emigrants through Fillmore. When the travelers stopped in the center of town, some of them hailed passing citizens and "inquired how far it was to any houses"—an insult aimed at the settlers' log cabins or their new state house, both in clear view. "Angry feelings arose between the parties," said Ray, and "the emigrants then in a crowing & insulting manner inquired whether there were any men in the place." Ray said the taunting emigrants next mocked the Mormons, "connecting the name of Deity with all their oaths," and "stated that [the] Government had sent Troops to kill every G—damed Mormon in Utah...& that they should like to help them do the job."[63]

Philetus Warn left another report. He arrived in Salt Lake City on August 7 and spent two-and-a-half weeks visiting friends, helping with chores, and listening to Mormon preaching. He left the city on August 26 with the fast-moving freighting company owned by half-brothers Sidney Tanner and William Mathews, Mormons headed to California in hopes of acquiring arms and ammunition for the coming confrontation with the approaching army. Traveling for days behind all the companies on the road—the Fanchers, Bakers, Turners, Dukes, and the smaller parties—Warn said "he everywhere heard" the settlers' "threats of vengeance" against the emigrants ahead because of their "boisterousness and abuse of Mormons and Mormonism." Whatever good feeling Warn may have had for the Mormons would dissipate by the time he passed through the Meadows two days after the massacre. Just a few weeks later, a newspaper recounting the stories of Warn and Powers opined on what sparked the atrocity. Besides owning "considerable valuable property," which "excited the cupidity of the Mormons," it said, "the [emigrant] men were very free in speaking of the Mormons; their conduct was said to have been reckless, and they would commit little acts of annoyance. . . . Feeling perfectly safe in their arms and numbers, they seemed to set at defiance all the powers that could be brought against them."[64]

The conflicts on the road had been two-sided. There was "profanity and ribaldry arrayed against each other," Daniel Wells said in an interview that he and Brigham Young gave twenty years after the massacre—the only time either of them spoke to the eastern press about the massacre and one of the few times they spoke publicly about it at all. Wells explained why he believed the settlers had been so ready to fight, citing "our previous history [of persecution], the condition of our people and their crops at the time, our relations with the Indians and the extraordinary news and rumors which accompanied the simultaneous advance on Utah of Harney's United States army and Arkansas emigrants." The result was "a combination of circumstances such as will probably never exist again," in which the "desperate" Mormons came to believe the emigrants were somehow "leagued with the soldiers."[65]

It is also true that the Saints later exaggerated the emigrants' acts. The wrangling over pasture was viewed as serious in its day—more serious on the southern road than the northern one because the Mormons and their animals were concentrated there. But most of the emigrants' acts were nothing more than taunting words or, at the very worst, small acts of vandalism. These annoyances caused momentary excitement, but according to Wells, in many settlements were "forgotten almost as soon as reported."[66] Wells's claim was borne out by reports coming from Fillmore, where some of the tension occurred. After the Arkansas company passed through the settlement, militia and church leaders sent messages to Salt Lake City on August 27 and August 29 that failed to mention any local problem.[67] Another possibility is that the Fillmore problems may have been caused by the party led by the Saints' old Missouri nemesis, Nicholas Turner. Turner's train did not get to central Utah until two or three days after the dispatches were sent north, which might explain why the letters did not mention any trouble.

PEOPLE IN EVERY SOCIETY build a memory or reconstruction of the past—the way in which past events are seen or interpreted by new generations.[68] This tendency was certainly true with many of the Mormons and their view of the events leading to the Mountain Meadows Massacre. The terrible tragedy was hardly over before a version of events began to form that downplayed the settlers' wrongs and built up the emigrants'. This retelling made the incidents at settlements along the southern route into an explanation that gave the atrocity a sense of grim inevitability.[69] While some perpetrators of the massacre encouraged this interpretation by making false or misleading statements, for most Mormons the process was an attempt to make sense out of the unfathomable and to defend their society from assaults being made against it. The result was a version of history that smoothed Mormon guilt by suggesting that the emigrants somehow got what they deserved. An already troubled tale became still more confusing.

There were conflicts on the southern road. But the emigrants did not deserve what eventually happened to them at Mountain Meadows. The massacre was not inevitable. No easy absolution for the perpetrators is possible. Their later posturing and rationalization could never overcome one irrefutable fact: All the purported wrongs of the emigrants—even if true—did not justify the killing of a single person. The best that could be argued was that during a time of uncertainty and possible war, some of the Mormons, like other men and women throughout history, did not match their behavior with their ideals.

CHAPTER NINE

Men Have Magnified a Natural Circumstance

Corn Creek to Parowan, Late August–Early September 1857

ORN CREEK, TWELVE miles south of Fillmore, ran thirteen feet wide and two feet deep during heavy runoff, though in late August when the Arkansas company arrived, much of the force was spent. Still, there was water enough to supply people and animals, both from the creek and nearby springs and sloughs. In good seasons, there was also enough moisture in the soil to nourish "immense quantities of grass"—a feature that made Corn Creek a fine resting place for cattle companies on the southern road.[1]

The Pahvant Indians, a band that mixed the cultures of the Utes and Paiutes, had occupied the Corn Creek region for centuries. The Pahvants had wide contacts with other Indians, especially those in the Paiute heartland farther south.[2] The Pahvants had a history of simple agriculture—growing "corn, beans, pumpkins, squashes, and potatoes"—but they also relied heavily on native plants and animals for their support.[3]

One tradition claimed that Kanosh, a leading Pahvant, was born on Shoshone land near the eastern mountains of California and spent time as a youth learning white man's ways at a Franciscan mission.[4] "He was

CORN CREEK. *Courtesy LDS Church History Library (2002).*

not fond of roaming and wished to be instructed in tilling the soil," Kanosh told Brigham Young when the two first met in 1851. Kanosh looked as though he could be the ally Mormons were seeking—an Indian who might show other Great Basin bands the value of Anglo-American farming.[5] In 1855 federal Indian agent Garland Hurt—a vigorous advocate of Indian farming—reported that sixty acres had been plowed at the Indian farm on Corn Creek, mainly in wheat, as the Pahvants "embraced farming more extensively than any of the Indians in the Territory."[6] Two years later, the cultivated fields had more than doubled.[7]

Early trappers saw the Pahvants as desperately poor, and despite the recent expansions of the Pahvants' tilled fields, loss of game and natural plants meant that their food supply had not improved much.[8] Like other native peoples, they expected outsiders to recognize their rights in the land and to compensate them for any trespass. The Pahvants' requests for a fee from outsiders using their lands sometimes led to conflicts, the most notable of which ended in the 1853 Gunnison massacre.[9]

The Arkansas company reached Corn Creek by August 25. Late that evening, a small party of white men and Indians in two wagons drove into the Corn Creek grasslands from the south, passed the emigrants, and set up their own camp about fifty yards north across the creek.[10] It was George A. Smith, returning from his tour of the southern settlements, along with several other men. Southern settlers Silas Smith, Elisha Hoopes, and Philo Farnsworth would continue north with the Mormon apostle a day or two more. Jacob Hamblin, the Paiute leader Tutsegavits, Ammon, and other Indians would accompany him to Salt Lake City, where they would meet with Brigham Young.[11]

For a moment the two groups eyed each other. The Mormons thought the emigrants appeared "excited," doubling the eight-man guard over their cattle as Smith's group pulled in. Three of the emigrants, including "the Captain," soon visited the Mormons' camp and introduced themselves. The emigrants asked if the Indians camped nearby posed a threat. George A. replied that as long as they "had not committed any outrage upon the Indians," there was no danger. "They assured us," Smith said, "that there had been no interruption whatsoever."[12]

George A. Smith later described the three emigrants as "gentlemen," though the Mormons found the "blasphemous language" in their "common conversation" a little rough. Silas remembered the emigrants calling their captain "Mr. Fancher."[13]

JACOB HAMBLIN. *Courtesy LDS Church History Library.*

The emigrants asked about road conditions, the disposition of Indians, and where "they could get good grass and water" as they traveled south. Hamblin described "the camping places clear to the Muddy," remembered Hoopes, referring to the Muddy River, whose waters met the southern route in the desert southwest of Mountain Meadows. Hamblin also told the emigrants that the "Meadows was the best point to recruit their animals before they entered upon the desert."[14]

Hamblin's advice could not have been a surprise. Travelers had camped and grazed their animals at the same sites for years, and Fancher had likely used them before.[15] After conflicts over their choice of pasture at Provo and Nephi, the emigrants were probably trying to determine which range lands they could use without running into more trouble with settlers. As for Indian concerns, when the emigrants told Hamblin they had forty or fifty men who could bear arms, he judged them and their cattle safe with "half that number."[16]

To Hamblin, the emigrants "seemed to be ordinary frontier 'homespun' people" in general, most traveling as families. But he also said "some of the outsiders were rude and rough, and calculated to get the ill-will of the inhabitants." He did not say whether this was his own impression or part of the "information [he] got in conversation with one of the men of the train." The train's captain had made a similar comment to John Hawley just days before.[17]

As Smith and his group hitched up their teams the next morning, the emigrants came to them with a final question. Would the Indians accept as a gift an ox that had died in the night? George A. replied that they probably would; Silas remarked that he thought the Indians "were better fed" than to eat a dead ox. The Mormons thought the emigrants' question a bit odd, and "it created suspicion, that they would play foul games, by some means." The group left Corn Creek feeling some unease about the emigrants, and Hamblin remembered George A. Smith saying "he belie[ve]d some evle would be fall them."[18]

As the Mormons pulled away, they could see the dead ox, the captain standing over it with a bottle in his hand. The suspicious Hoopes asked Smith what the man was doing. Smith replied "that he was probably taking a drink." Hoopes would later say he saw the man stab the carcass a few times and pour something from the bottle into the cuts. Silas Smith refuted his story. "I saw nothing of this throwing anything from a vial into [the ox]," he testified.[19]

The next emigrants to reach Corn Creek noticed nothing unusual there. George Powers and George Davis, traveling behind the Arkansas company, said they found plenty of Indians at the place, "all peaceable and friendly."[20] But the mood changed by the time members of the Missouri company reached the site. The Turner and Dukes divisions of the company were now journeying separately "on account of scarcity of grass" and internal strife.[21]

Peyton Welch of the Turner division found the Indians at Corn Creek "very ill disposed toward us."[22] Stephen B. Honea, traveling with the Dukes train, learned more from a man "who represented himself as the Indian agent"—undoubtedly Peter Boyce, a government employee at the Indian farm a few miles southeast of the Corn Creek campsite. Boyce told Honea that "a short time before" his train arrived, another train passed that had "poisoned an ox." Boyce "spoke in abusive terms of the men of that train, for having acted in an improper manner."[23]

Boyce had tried to stop the men from trading the Pahvants powder and lead for food from the Indian farm. It was "contrary to law" to give the Indians ammunition, Boyce told them, trying to get them to move on. The men said they "had the law with them, 'seventeen rounds.'" The territory's no-trade policy had made it difficult for them to replenish their food supplies, and they would not let Boyce stand between them and this opportunity. They stayed long enough to have the Pahvants "thrash out wheat" for them and "dig up potatoes" that "were not half grown." Concerned about the Pahvants' winter food supply, Boyce kept trying to stop the exchange, but the emigrants "cared not for me or what I said," he complained. He called the emigrant men "the roughest set that ever passed by that place."[24]

When Philetus Warn and the Tanner-Mathews freight train reached Corn Creek on September 5, Boyce told Warn that "six Indians had died" from the "poisoned" ox and that "others were sick and would die." With "one of them, the poison had worked out all over his breast, and he was dead next morning," Boyce said.[25] Over the next month, more cattle in the area died, and people who handled carcasses became ill or perished.[26]

To Boyce and his neighbors, the conclusion seemed obvious that the Arkansas emigrants poisoned the ox and nearby water. Overlanders, after all, could be highhanded and harsh toward Indians. Emigrant Eleanor F. Knowlton recalled an incident in her 1857 train near the Humboldt River on the northern road. After an Indian shot one of the emigrants' oxen with an arrow, the men of the company "put poisen in the ox" in order "to kill the Indians if they ate of it." Knowlton was indignant, calling the episode "very inhuman." The Mormons who lived near Corn Creek thought the same thing had happened there.[27]

Elisha Hoopes fueled the rumors. No one told the story of the supposed poisoning with more enthusiasm than Hoopes, whom Brigham Young had called "a kind of perpetual Telegraph" the year before. After seeing the emigrant standing over the dead ox when he was with George A. Smith at Corn Creek, Hoopes had continued north with Smith's party to Fillmore, where he worked several days. At Fillmore or passing through Corn Creek again as he returned south to Beaver, Hoopes must have learned about the dead or dying Indians. He and others concluded that the emigrants had poisoned the ox carcass before giving it away. Hoopes repeated the story at Beaver, where he arrived in early September.[28] Later when he heard about the massacre, he expressed his satisfaction, saying the emigrants "carried poison with them, and had only got their just reward."[29]

In 1859 federal Indian superintendent Jacob Forney commenced an investigation that brushed aside the poisoning charges. "That an emigrant company, as respectable as I believe this was, would carry along several pounds of arsenic and strichnine, apparently for no other purpose than to poison cattle and Indians, is too improbable to be true," he concluded.[30] Forney's companion, U.S. deputy marshal William Rogers, debunked the poisoning story by looking at the volume and force of water at Corn Creek. "A barrel of arsenic would not poison it," he said.[31]

In retrospect, the best guess is that microbes, not poison, caused the reported sickness—a disease borne by cattle and passed to humans. Arsenic and strychnine, the typical poisons of the time, caused symptoms different from those described in the Corn Creek area, and only large doses could account for the reported loss of people and livestock over a several-week period. Moreover, poison would have taken effect quickly, and Powers and Davis saw nothing amiss in the immediate wake of the Arkansas company's passing.

Many livestock died on overland trails due to disease and other problems.[32] One common disease was so-called "Texas Fever" or "Spanish Fever," notoriously carried by Texas longhorns, like those present in the Arkansas herds. An infected animal might appear healthy but still spread contagion to local breeds.[33] By the mid-1850s, Missouri farmers were so outraged by "Texas Fever" that they "declared war" on the longhorns.[34]

Though humans can contract Texas Fever, the most plausible explanation for what happened at Corn Creek is anthrax.[35] In 1975 cattle pastured along a pioneer-era cattle trail in northern Utah died within twelve to forty-eight hours after becoming inexplicably ill. Medical researchers first investigated arsenic poisoning as the cause but soon tied the outbreak to disturbed anthrax spores that may have lain dormant since the 1850s. The researchers concluded that "the geographic spread of anthrax in the western United States seems coupled unquestionably with the cattle drives of the Texas Longhorn stock."[36] During the mid-to late 1850s along the trail from Utah to southern California, people died or became seriously ill after handling cattle carcasses.[37] Medical doctors reviewing these documented cases 150 years after the massacre concluded that anthrax was the likely cause of the recorded symptoms.[38]

Anthrax can pass from animals to humans as victims breath its spores, eat diseased meat, or take in spores through a cut or sore in the skin. In rare cases, the result can be massive swelling of the abdomen, a limb, or even the face.[39] More often, there is an inflamed pustule, with a black or ash-gray ulcer at the center. Before modern penicillin was available for treatment, the disease could bring high fever, discomfort and disorientation, and, in its most serious form, death.[40]

The emigration of 1857 had several hints of anthrax. "Quite a number of horned cattle have died this fall from some complaint that is not understood by stock-owners," a California newspaper reported in November 1857. One man "lost an ox, which he afterwards skinned and came near losing his own life from the effect of the blood of the animal, which became inoculated in a sore in his left hand."[41] Some of the Arkansas company's cattle may have contracted the disease along the trail. The mysterious bite to the hand that killed Arkansas emigrant Peter Huff near Fort Bridger may actually have been a pustule of skin anthrax.[42]

Within a week after the first Arkansas parties arrived in Utah with their cattle, Salt Lake City resident Elias Smith wrote in his diary about the sudden death of "the only cow I had." His was not alone. "Many cattle are said to be dying in the same way in the city and country," he wrote.[43] A few days later the Baker train arrived in the city and members of the company complained that Mormons had poisoned their cattle.[44] When the Arkansas company got to Corn Creek, the emigrants told Hamblin "they had from four hundred to five hundred head of horned cattle," a count significantly lower than before they left Arkansas.[45] Perhaps the hazards of the trail—including disease—had taken a toll.

The symptoms of anthrax in the Corn Creek area in 1857 might have been taken from a modern medical handbook. One of Fillmore resident John Ray's wives, cutting up a dead cow for its tallow, picked up an infection through a cut on her hand. It swelled and turned black, and she became ill.[46] In another case, fifteen-year-old Proctor Robison of Fillmore scratched a small sore on his nose while skinning a dead animal. He was dead within days. "He was so swollen and bloated," a friend said, "I would not have recognized him."[47] A twentieth-century family historian, after consulting medical experts, concluded that Robison "probably died of anthrax."[48] These incidents took place weeks after the Arkansas emigrants had passed through the area and long after any poison they might have left could have had an effect. The dead cattle were primarily found around the Corn Creek sinks—exactly where one might expect to find the spores.[49]

No one in America at the time understood germ theory, spores, bacteria, or viruses—and they certainly did not understand anthrax. With no other way to explain the Corn Creek illnesses, the local people assumed the worst about the emigrants and saw poison as the cause. Their reaction fit the times, as poison in America had become a popular catchall. One group of 1852 overlanders, seeing many of their cattle die, blamed the deaths on Indian poisoning.[50] Antebellum Texans accused abolitionists and slaves of "wholesale poisoning," which, like the overlanders' charges, seemed "to have been the product almost entirely of fertile imaginations."[51] Capitalizing on the public's fixation, popular detective novels made poisoning—and its discovery—a major plot theme.[52] In short, poison was full of mystery and seemed everywhere, including at Corn Creek. It explained the unexplainable.

Anthrax's multiday incubation period explains the delay in the appearance of the disease's effects at Corn Creek. Silas Smith, who traveled north with George A. Smith after meeting the emigrants there, reported no problems when he headed back south through the area a couple of days later. The Indians had been friendly to Davis and Powers when they arrived at Corn Creek "several days" behind the Arkansas company. But by the time members of the Turner party arrived, they found the situation changed dramatically, with the local Indians "hostile" and seeking "the blood of the Americans."[53]

Oblivious to the turmoil and confusion that would follow in their wake, the Arkansas emigrants pushed on from Corn Creek to Indian Creek, a few miles north of Beaver. There Silas Smith, returning to his home near Parowan, "took supper" with the emigrants and watered his horses before going on to Beaver.[54]

When Beaver resident Robert Kershaw heard that the Arkansas wagons were approaching his village, there seemed no cause for alarm. Stories of Corn Creek had not yet reached the town. All Kershaw reported was that the emigrants were stymied again as they tried to purchase food in town. When the company stopped in front of Kershaw's garden, they "wanted to buy peas, potatoes, melons and onions," but "I told them I had none to spare," he said. "I had been forbid to trade." Kershaw and others from Beaver later ventured outside the town to the emigrants' camp—but so did a local "policeman," who "intimidated people from trading there."[55]

By the time Powers and Warn reached Beaver in the first week of September, the locals were "incensed against the train." The story Powers heard there seemed to be Hoopes's: An emigrant had opened the carcass of an ox with his knife and poured "some liquid into the cut from a phial." Indians ate the meat and died; "several more were sick and would die."[56] Suspicious of the Mormons, Powers and Warn tried to confirm the reports. Powers found an English-speaking Indian in the area, who answered "that he did not know" if there was any truth to the poisoned meat story, but he did know "that several of the Indians had died, and several were sick." The Indian thought watermelons had brought on the scourge and that Mormons had somehow poisoned them. Warn may have spoken with the same Indian, whom he identified as the Ute leader Ammon. Back south after meeting with Brigham Young, Ammon told Warn several Indians were sick, though he did not know why.[57]

Word of the purported poisoning would continue to spread, eventually reaching the southern Utah communities with closest ties to the massacre. Local settlers remembered that rumors of poison reached their communities in the first week of September, some carried by Indian runners. As a result, the "excitement had got to be pretty large," said one citizen of Cedar City.[58] But the extant evidence does not confirm that the rumors reached these settlements before the initial attack on the Arkansas company at Mountain Meadows.[59] Nevertheless, in the wake of the mass killing, the poisoning story quickly became the perpetrators' main explanation for their crime. Angry Indians, they claimed, took vengeance on the company for poisoned comrades.[60] No other supposed provocation by the emigrants could measure up to poisoning.

Jacob Forney suggested there was a difference between perception and reality. "Those persons in Fillmore, and further south, who believe that a spring was poisoned with arsenic, and the meat of a dead ox with strichnine, by said company, may be honest in their belief, and attribute the cause of the massacre to the alleged poisoning," he said. But it was not true. "*In my opinion*," he concluded, "*bad men*, for a bad purpose, have magnified a natural circumstance for the perpetration of a crime that has no parallel in American history for atrocity."[61]

Though contemporary accounts confirm there were conflicts on the southern route in 1857, complaints about the emigrants proliferated after the massacre. "The Missouri company acted all right in passing through Beaver but the part[y] o[f] Arkansas Company had acted very wicked both to Mormons and Indians," said Willson Gates Nowers, who was in the area shortly after both trains—and the rumors—passed through.[62] Another settler claimed he met some of the Arkansas emigrants on the road ten miles south of Beaver. "I see that you have not been killed yet by any of those Mormons," he said to an emigrant, probably tongue-in-cheek. "No," the man replied, they "dare not tack[le] us or they would have done so before this."[63] Outside of Parowan, the next town after Beaver, the emigrants reportedly made "terribl[e] oaths." One said he was present when Joseph Smith was killed. Another man called his ox "Brigham."[64] But such charges were written down many years after the massacre, some by men who played key roles in the crime, making the claims suspect.

Just before the emigrants got to Parowan, a torrent of rain forced the company to pull up. William Dame, writing to George A. Smith, reported that water flushed down the canyon east of the village, "bringing with it all the bridges for 7 miles up" and a dam. The water "ran north outside the [fort] wall to the bastion by the East gate tore it all to flinders, [and] buried some of our fields."[65] After the massacre, rumors circulated that the Parowan city gates had been closed to the emigrants. The problem may have been nothing more than muck and water.[66]

But more than floods made the city inhospitable. Even before 1857, leaders in southern Utah had tried to ban trading with outsiders because of the poverty in the settlements and the need to conserve food.[67] Despite such counsel, some settlers continued to trade with passersby in hopes of profiting or because they felt local leaders interpreted policies too tightly.[68] One man who traded was Jesse N. Smith, a cousin of George A. Smith and one of Dame's two counselors in the Parowan stake presidency. He sold flour and salt to the Arkansas company when it came to his home in Paragonah northeast of Parowan but did not provide them grain—Young's policy from the beginning. His brother Silas Smith said the Arkansas emigrants found where he lived in Paragonah and "camped near that." Silas went to their camp and, for the third time, visited with the emigrants. Jesse's retrospective diary gave no hint that he or any of his neighbors had bad feelings for the emigrants.[69]

But William Dame, at Parowan, strongly opposed trade with emigrants. He sent enforcers to William Leany's house after it was reported that Leany had sold produce to William Aden, a young man thought to be part of the company.[70] Aden would have a hapless and tragic role in the events at the Meadows.

The episode involving Leany and Aden provides a glimpse into the strong feelings then existing in southern Utah. Aden's father, Dr. S. B. Aden, described nineteen-year-old William as being "well grown, quite sprightly, a good *Sign Painter*," someone who "writes *Poetry* & sometimes Prose pretty well, makes a pretty good speach" and "picks the *Banjo* tolerably well." The father also considered his son "pretty good looking" and "one of the most injenius men of his age." The description had an element of pathos; it was written eighteen months after the massacre by a father hoping his missing son had escaped death.[71]

Leany's connection to Aden began many years earlier in Paris, Tennessee. Leany at the time was a Mormon missionary, preaching at the courthouse when mischievous lads fired a cannon as a prank. Thinking himself under assault, Leany ran from the building and was on the outskirts of the village when S. B. Aden calmed him down and invited him to his home. His son William had been one of the pranksters.[72]

William left home in 1857 intending a California adventure. He was at the Y. X. mail station at the last crossing of the Sweetwater River in present-day Wyoming when he met a kindred spirit, twenty-one-year-old William Roberts from Provo, Utah. Roberts, a musician and member of Provo's first dramatic association, had gone to the station to trade with passing emigrants in company with Daniel W. Jones.[73]

Aden wrote to his father on July 23 from the station on the Sweetwater, explaining "that he expected to spend the winter in *Provo*, as he had undertaken a good job of painting scenery for a *Theater* there, and would likely go on to Cal[ifornia] in the spring." Presumably, Aden traveled to Salt Lake with the returning Roberts and Jones, arriving on August 15. After reaching Provo about August 17, he changed his plans and decided to "overtake a party of emigrants, who were then some fifty miles ahead of him," promising Roberts a letter "as soon as he got through."[74] The party was the Arkansas company.

Aden eventually reached Parowan, where he stopped to visit William Leany. As a parting gift, the Parowan settler gave the youth some vegetables, which local authorities took as a violation of the trading ban. "Dame sent a crowd of his dogs to kill Me in my own door yard," Leany later charged. During the assault, Leany was hit on the head, some said with a fence post, leaving him impaired for life. When Leany later tried to write an account of the attack, it was rambling and sometimes unclear.[75]

Besides emotions, war rumors continued to stir. According to local church records, on August 28 "Br. Hawley arrived from G. S. L. City" with news that Brigham Young "had caught some of the enemies spies" in Salt Lake City. Hawley—who had traveled for a time with the Arkansas company on his way south—said the Mormon leader had dispatched a thousand "men to meet the Gentile Army in the mountains." More startling, a Ute Indian visiting Paragonah reported Americans had been seen "coming in at or near San Pete valley," about a hundred miles northeast.[76] This last rumor seemed to confirm Wells's warning that U.S. troops might enter Utah in the south—and soon.

Hawley must have brought word about the approaching emigrants, as undoubtedly others did too. Aden had traveled south with a small Mormon company that included Joseph Adair and James Pearce. Pearce had seen the emigrants in Payson and passed them on his journey south. Adair surely saw them, too.[77]

Even as late as Parowan, however, the situation seemed manageable. The Leany episode was about trading; no one in Parowan spoke of fights or near-fights between the villagers and outsiders. One later attestant remembered the emigrants' decency and peace. From the outset, each individual, with his or her own history and emotions, saw what they chose to see in the emigrants.[78]

At Cedar City, twenty miles south, it was the dangerous perceptions that would play themselves out. "So the wind grew into the whirlwind," Juanita Brooks wrote in memorable prose. "Exaggeration, misrepresentation, ungrounded fears, unreasoning hate, desire for revenge, yes, even the lust for the property of the emigrants, all combined to give justification which, once the crime was done, looked inadequate and flimsy indeed."[79]

Since the time Brooks wrote these words, scholars of religious or ethnic violence have described the step-by-step process that leads to mass killing. "Violence is not only what we do to the Other," Regina M. Schwartz wrote. "It is prior to that. Violence is the very construction of the Other."[80] As emotions build, the perpetrators become convinced that their opponents are a threat to their people and values. They claim to act defensively, even while they are the aggressors. Rumors are everywhere, and perception becomes reality. The final cataclysm is sudden and almost inexplicable.[81]

Certain social factors must be in place, and often there are three. "Most ordinary people readily allow the dictates of 'authorities' to trump their own moral instincts," one scholar wrote, summarizing a half century of experimental and historical experience. "The second [factor] is conformity. Few people have the courage to go against the crowd." The third is the "dehumanization of the victims." Ordinarily, there is no conspiracy. "Orders, peer expectations and dehumanization need not be explicit to have a powerful effect. In adversarial settings...subtle cues and omissions—the simple failure of authorities to send frequent, clear and consistent messages about appropriate behavior, for instance—can be as powerful as direct orders."[82]

The southern road in late summer 1857 was not just about miles traveled or events along the way. It was also about that complex web of fear, misunderstanding, and retribution that prepares normally decent people to kill. Most everything fit the scholarly pattern: The settlers began to see the emigrants as the "other" or enemy, believing the outsiders somehow threatened the values and well-being of the Mormon community. Rumors circulated that were untrue or enlarged beyond proportion, and southern Utah society was vulnerable to this excitement. The region was isolated from Salt Lake City. Mixed signals floated down the trail about Indian and emigrant policy. Civil, religious, and military power was dangerously held in the hands of a few. Impoverished settlers knew the virtues of obeying. Even in hierarchical, theocratic Utah, there were few places like Iron County.

For the most part, the men who committed the atrocity at Mountain Meadows were neither fanatics nor sociopaths, but normal and in many respects decent people. The modern age, confronted with mass violence and killings, has rediscovered a fundamental aspect of old theology. "If only there were evil people somewhere insidiously committing evil deeds and it were necessary only to separate them from the rest of us and destroy them," wrote Russian Nobel Prize winner Alexander Solzhenitsyn. "But the line dividing good and evil cuts through the heart of every human being. And who wants to destroy a piece of his own heart."[83]

CHAPTER TEN

Make It an Indian Massacre

Cedar City, July 24–September 5, 1857

A LONG THE CALIFORNIA ROAD some 250 miles south of Salt Lake City and 20 miles south of Parowan lay Cedar City, the heart of the Mormons' Iron Mission. To Brigham Young and his people, iron making was almost a religious sacrament, as worthy a Saint's consideration as preaching the gospel.[1] Iron making even became a Mormon metaphor. "We found a Scotch party, a Welch party, an English party, and an American party," reported Mormon apostle Erastus Snow after touring the area in 1852, "and we...put all these parties through the furnace, and run out a party of Saints for building up the Kingdom of God."[2]

By the middle 1850s, however, Cedar City's iron idealism gave way to slag. Without adequate financing, good technology, or experienced managers, the iron business floundered and most of the local people "lived in isolation and dire poverty, often going without shoes and warm clothing."[3] "Kisses without the bread and cheese," quipped one of the settlers, mocking the hard times with an expression of the day.[4]

Hans Hoth had nothing good to say about Cedar City when he passed through in 1856. He described poorly built homes lying haphazard on the land and people whose condition was no better. "Never before had I seen such dirty and ragged people among the Mormons as here," he wrote. Nor did Hoth like the residents. Told by their leaders

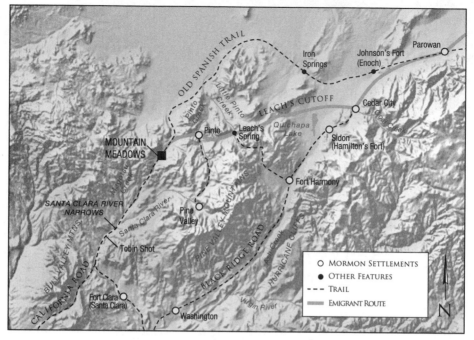

Map by Sheryl Dickert Smith and Tom Child

for years not to trade with outsiders, many residents refused to trade openly with Hoth's party, though Hoth learned that the cover of night brought possibilities. Prices for this secret trading ran high, as did his suspicions. "I have become acquainted with many bad people among the Mormons," he said, "and here at this place I did not meet with one good and sincere person."[5] A Mormon apostate fleeing Utah, Hoth was bitter toward its people, but he was right about Cedar City's dire condition.

When iron production seemed most hopeful, the village had a boomtown population of almost a thousand men, women, and children, making it one of Utah's largest communities at the time. By 1857 most of the people still lived in "Old Town," an expansion of the makeshift pioneer fort built four years before, during the Walker War. An adobe wall enclosed much of the place, and at the center was a large area used as a public square. Some of the citizens, however, had begun moving to more permanent and less flood-prone quarters on the bench land to the southeast, putting up cabins or digging dugouts. At least two fine buildings anchored this "New Town": Isaac Haight's new home, still under construction, and the "tithing office." The latter, a place to bring the offerings and donations of the people, served also as the main public building in the city, "a meeting house, school, theater, and everything."[6]

On July 24, 1857, Cedar City had its own Pioneer Day celebration, just as Brigham Young was holding his in Big Cottonwood Canyon. Haight—Cedar City's leading citizen—delivered an oration on the scenes "the Church has passed through," and in a parade, residents carried banners celebrating virtue, unity, and industry. Two of the banners had more of an edge. Twelve uniformed young men carried the inscription, "A terror to evil doers"—a biblical term sometimes given those who enforced law and loyalty in England and America. It was the phrase recently applied to Haight by John D. Lee. In addition, two dozen young boys carried the title "Zion's Avengers."[7]

In early August, when news reached Cedar of the approaching U.S. Army, it flew from house to house, and the "people gathered at the public square." "I am prepared to feed the enemy the bread he fed to me and mine," Haight reportedly said.[8] When George A. Smith arrived several days later on his southern Utah tour, his speeches further roused the people's enthusiasm. Dispatches from Daniel H. Wells, the territorial militia commander, warned of a possible attack on the southern settlements and stressed the need to shore up alliances with local Indians.[9] "You will never know how black the clouds were over our people," one Cedar City citizen later told his son.[10]

Like other Utah communities, Cedar City had recently revitalized its militia in response to legislation passed early in the year. But the rumors of war had accelerated preparations for military action. Haight seemed ready, if not anxious, to defend the city.[11]

"The 'Nauvoo Legion' was fully organized and drilled,... spying out the passes in the mountains, discussing the best means for defending ourselves and families against the approaching army, looking out places of security for our families in case we had to burn our towns and flee to the mountains," recalled John M. Higbee, a Cedar City militia major, town marshal, and one of Haight's two church counselors.[12]

By the end of August other news was making its way to Cedar City, not of an approaching army but of a coming emigrant train. Exactly what the local people heard about the train before its arrival is difficult to determine. What can be established with some certainty is that the people of Cedar City knew a non-Mormon company was approaching and that its members had many cattle. Cedar City bishop Philip Klingensmith said he heard the company had been ordered out from

Salt Lake City, and John Hawley may have told what he heard about the problems over grazing lands at Provo and Nephi.[13] Rumors of the supposed poisoning at Corn Creek reached Beaver by the first week of September and then Cedar City, though it is not clear exactly when.[14] A few reminiscent accounts place its arrival ahead of the emigrant company, perhaps reflecting stories told in the massacre's wake.[15]

After the massacre, its perpetrators and their neighbors—trying to explain or even justify why it happened—recounted what they heard about the company before it reached Cedar City and what happened on its arrival. Local resident Mary Campbell claimed that before the emigrants reached Cedar, Haight gave an impassioned speech that rehearsed rumored wrongs of the emigrants. "The rumors raised the ire…of people," she said. Campbell recalled Haight saying that "the people in southern Utah needed some stock just then, as if he was giving the citizens a hint to get the stock away from the company."[16]

If Campbell's reminiscence was accurate, Haight may have been thinking of his people's welfare. If the Saints came under siege by approaching troops, they would need cattle, in addition to grain, to survive in the mountains. Haight's comment also fit one later explanation of the massacre. As Philetus Warn later put it, the train "was known to be in possession of considerable valuable property, and this fact excited the cupidity of the Mormons."[17] Even Brigham Young eventually came to a similar conclusion. Some men had taken advantage of "the disturbed state of the country to accomplish their desires for plunder," he said in 1877.[18]

The members of the Arkansas company reached Cedar City around noon on Thursday, September 3, staying only "a little over one hour."[19] The company's loose stock—one local citizen estimated five hundred head—stayed outside the walls, but between twelve and twenty wagons with oxen and horse teams drove through Old Town en route to Klingensmith's mill just east of the fort.[20] Samuel Jackson Sr., who farmed southwest of Cedar, had ignored orders not to part with grain to outsiders and sold the Arkansas people about fifty bushels of wheat, along with some corn.[21] Waiting for the grain to be ground at the mill, some emigrant men sampled the Mormon "Sage Brush Whiskey" sold at the nearby distillery. "Getting a little more of this than they should," one settler said, "they talked very freely."[22]

Trouble broke out when the miller, following "the counsel of I C Haight," demanded a cow in trade for grinding the grain—an exorbitant price, though isolated trading posts along western trails often charged whatever they could get for goods.[23]

The high price charged at the last mill before California "caused some to curse and swear and say hard things about the Mormons," one Cedar City resident recorded. Another settler, Charles Willden, claimed that fifteen to twenty emigrant men began "talking in a loud excited and boisterous manner profaning and threatening to do bodily harm and Kill some of the citizens"—including Bishop Klingensmith. Willden said these men affirmed "that they had helped to Kill Joseph Smith...and other Mormons at Nauvoo & Missouri, and that By___ G___ they would Kill some more yet. That the United States troops were on the plains enroute to Utah, that they the said Company would go on to the Mountain Meadows, and wait there until the arrival of the said troops into the Territory and would then return to Cedar...and carry out their threats."[24]

Willden's testimony, recorded in 1882, summarizes the animosity and fear engendered by the emigrant train, and the link the Saints made between the emigrants and the army. His memory was likely influenced by justifications some Mormons gave for the massacre after the fact, but he was not the only settler who remembered it that way. Nephi Johnson, who was visiting Cedar City that day, said "the company was of a mixed class, some being perfect gentlemen, while others were very boastful, and insulting, as they said that they were coming back, and assist the [U.S.] army to exterminate the Mormons." Alexander Fancher tried to calm the men. Johnson reported, "I did hear Capt. F[a]ncher, who was the leader of the emigrants, rebuke the boastful ones of the company, for making these threats."[25]

Another run-in took place at the Deseret Iron Company store near the center of the fort. Store clerk Christopher J. Arthur, Haight's son-in-law, remembered that some of the emigrants "came in to buy several articles that was not in the store which caused them to act mean." With profanity, they vented their anger when they were again unable to buy badly needed supplies, a problem they had faced repeatedly up the trail.[26]

Some of the emigrants went looking for Haight at his nearby house in Old Town, perhaps wanting to complain about what happened at the mill and store. Haight was, after all, town mayor and manager of the Deseret Iron Company. One account said that "cursing" and "drunk" men went to Haight's house and demanded that he come out "if he was a man." The men also yelled threats about sending an army from California to seize Young, Haight, Dame, and "every other damn Mormon in the country."[27]

Haight slipped out the back door and ordered Higbee, as town marshal, to arrest the men.[28] The emigrants had not physically harmed anyone, but Haight had sufficient legal cause to arrest and fine them. Territorial ordinances declared that anyone "publicly intoxicated, so as to endanger the peace and quiet of the community, shall be liable to arrest" and fined. "Profaning the name of God" was also subject to a fine.[29]

By now a pattern was emerging. At various points through the territory, the emigrants had a hard time getting the food and other supplies needed for their survival and comfort. Some vented their frustration in ways that made the Mormons—already apprehensive about the approaching army—feel even more threatened. At Cedar City the cycle reached a crescendo. As the emigrants were leaving town, one reportedly said that if "old Brigham, and his priests would not sell their provisions, by G–d they would take what they wanted any way they could get it." With that, he "killed two chickens, and threw them into his wagon."[30] They may have been Barbara Morris's. When the sixty-three-year-old woman crossed the street from her home to the central corral, a loudmouthed "tall fellow" on horseback "addressed her in a very insulting manner," her son later claimed. The man "brandished his pistol in her face" and "made use of the most insinuating and abusive language."[31] The "man on a grey horse was the most loud mouthed of the lot," said Mary Campbell, perhaps speaking of the same emigrant.[32]

Some men in Cedar City, like men elsewhere in America, followed a code of honor that required anyone who insulted a "wife, mother, or sister" to apologize or "be punished."[33] Barbara Morris was the mother of Elias Morris—a militia captain and Haight's second counselor—and the wife of John Morris, one of Bishop Klingensmith's counselors. When Marshal Higbee tried to arrest the horseman for profanity and disorderly conduct, he "refused to be taken, and his companions stood by him." Higbee was forced to back down.[34]

Some of the emigrants went farther south to Hamilton's Fort, where they were able to trade. No troubles were reported in this tiny settlement. Most of the train then camped a few miles southwest of town near Quichapa Lake.[35]

News of the Cedar City disturbance traveled up the road. Nephi diarist Samuel Pitchforth recorded that on September 8 he heard "the emegrants who went through a short time since was acting very mean—Threatening the Bishops life."[36]

Minutes of Cedar City's Female Benevolent Society also provide contemporary evidence that residents believed the emigrants were a threat. Later in the week, two women whose husbands followed the emigrants to Mountain Meadows counseled the other women in their group "to attend strictly to secret prayer in behalf of the brethren that are out acting in our defence." Another woman, "Sister Haight," told the women not to be fearful and "to teach their sons & daughters the principles of righteousness, and to implant a desire in their hearts to avenge the blood of the Prophets"—referring to the murders of Joseph and Hyrum Smith.[37]

A persistent element in the stories told against the emigrants was that one boasted of having a gun that killed Joseph Smith. The Benevolent Society minutes suggest that vengeance for Smith's death was a current topic during the week of the massacre. If an emigrant in fact made such a boast, it was probably just part of the venting that went on in Cedar City. None of the identified victims of the massacre is known to have had anything to do with the Smith brothers' deaths.

Even if local Saints believed they had identified a killer of Joseph Smith, however, that would not have justified a massacre. Mormon doctrine strongly held that men should be punished for their own sins and not for the sins of others, and Latter-day Saint scripture declared the shedding of innocent blood to be unforgivable.[38] A year and a half before the massacre, Brigham Young and Wilford Woodruff were discussing a scripture on the topic, and Young observed that it "was a vary nice point to distinguish between innocent Blood & that which is not innocent." He observed that if the Saints were commanded of God "to go & avenge the Blood of the prophets," they would not know "what to do in such a case" because they wouldn't be able to tell who was innocent and who was not. "There is one thing that is a consolation to me," Young concluded, "and that is I am satisfied that the Lord will not require it of this people until they become sanctifyed & are led by the spirit of God so as not to shed inocent Blood."[39]

After the Arkansas company left town, Cedar City leaders discussed what to do. As often happens in times of conflict, they focused not on the peaceful emigrants, who made up the vast majority of the company, but on a minority whose actions colored their view of the whole. From the Cedar City leaders' point of view, outsiders had defied the law, faced them down in front of their own people, and resisted arrest. They had threatened townspeople, mocked the values of the community, and announced themselves ready to support the army that seemed at southern Utah's doors.

The men of the train would not live to tell their side of the story. But the fact that not one Utah citizen was physically harmed by the

Arkansas company speaks for itself. Any menacing words from the emigrants were probably just idle threats and boasts made out of frustration and in the heat of the moment. But in the charged environment of 1857, Cedar City's leaders took the men at their word.[40]

Not willing simply to let the matter go, the leaders sent a message that day to military district commander William Dame in Parowan, "stating they could hardly keep people from collisions with them [the emigrants] on account of their violent language and threats, and asking what to do." Haight needed Dame's permission before he could use the Cedar City militia to aid Higbee's embarrassed sixteen-member police force.[41]

Twenty-two-year-old John Chatterley carried the message to Parowan. Chatterley waited until early the next morning for a reply to carry back to Haight. Inside Dame's home, he could hear the voices of some of Parowan's leading citizens, including Edward Dalton, John Steele, Samuel H. Rogers, and Jesse Smith, as well as Dame.[42] The council saw the Cedar City turmoil for what it was—disturbing, but hardly a threat that called for harsh measures. The council decided that "all possible means should be used to keep the peace until the emigrants should leave and proceed upon their journey." Dame's adjutant, James Martineau, said, "Dame sent a letter in answer counselling peace, and for them not to regard their threats, as 'words are but wind.'" In a later account, Martineau said the words of the letter read, "Do not notice their threats, words are but wind—they injure no one; but if they (the emigrants) commit acts of violence against citizens inform me by express, and such measures will be adopted as will insure tranquility."[43]

Haight could not have been pleased by Dame's response. After all, his community—not Dame's—had experienced the conflict. Haight may have believed that Dame, never known for meeting matters head on, did not understand the situation. George A. Smith later said Dame had an aversion to bloodshed and Haight felt "contempt for him on this account."[44] Whatever the reasons, Haight did not accept Dame's direction. Instead he and others moved ahead with a plan to take action against the emigrants.

No record of the decision-making survived, but everything about 1857 must have been part of the calculation: the reformation, the war, the rumors, and the nerves. Yet it is still difficult to fathom how the Cedar City conflicts, so minor in retrospect, turned into an atrocity. The literature of modern behavioral science, whose scholars describe the conditions leading to mass riots and killings in many cultures, provides enlightenment.

By the first week in September, the typical components for group violence existed in Cedar City, including the demonizing of opponents, a concentration of authority, and a lack of clear orders from headquarters. The final spark that ignites violence may be small but seem large in the eyes of perpetrators. "Fear of the victims...may have a realistic component," wrote violence expert Ervin Staub, "but the victims' power or evil intentions are usually exaggerated."[45] "Great evil can come from small, unremarkable, seemingly innocent beginnings," agreed Roy Baumeister in his study of violence. "One does not have to be at all evil to cross the line. [But] once one has done so, there are powerful forces that sweep one along into greater acts of cruelty, violence, or oppression."[46]

Brigham Young's new Indian policy, announced August 16, may have confused some local leaders. Young had said that "if the United States send their army here and war commences" then emigrant "trains must not cross this continent." If a war began, Young said, "I will say no more to the Indians, let them alone, but do as you please."[47] Word of the policy traveled by mouth, with each hearer interpreting it individually. On August 30 Bishop Blackburn in Provo reported that Indians near the Malad River on the northern route had stampeded some six hundred head of emigrant cattle and horses. "Our Prophet says he had held the Indians back for 10 years past but shall do it no longer," Blackburn said.[48] News of Young's speech had probably reached Cedar City by late August.[49]

Haight's interpretation of the policy may have influenced his next decision. Without mustering out the militia, Haight could try using local Indians, the Paiutes, to do what he thought needed to be done. After receiving Dame's message, Haight and other leaders in Cedar City decided "to arm the Indians, give them provisions and ammunition, and send them after the emigrants" to "give them a *brush*" and take their cattle.[50] Haight asked Cedar City resident William Willis, a Mexican War veteran, "the best way to make an attack on the train." Willis offered advice that now seems ordinary: The attack should come when the emigrants were traveling. If the attack came while the emigrants were in camp, he told Haight, "the emigrants would whip his Indians."[51]

Haight and other leaders thought they knew just the place for an ambush. The California road went west from Cedar City along Leach's Cutoff to Pinto and then southwest through the Mountain Meadows. A dozen miles farther south, the road descended "a very steep incline" into a canyon created by the merging Magotsu Creek and Santa Clara

River.[52] The road wound through groves of trees and below cliffs that provided ideal hiding places for attackers.

Hans Hoth, traveling the Santa Clara River route in 1856, described the "many Indians" living there. Hoth also wrote of its reputation among non-Indians. "Several travelers have already been attacked, murdered, plundered or crippled by the tribe that lives closest to the trail," he recorded nervously before descending into the canyon. Two days later, as his company passed along the river, Paiutes armed with guns, bows, and arrows swarmed his company, stripping the men of their outer clothing and demanding gunpowder and blankets but not killing anyone.[53]

Troubles on the road had started long before Mormon settlement of the region. Traders and emigrants going to and from California drove stock through the area, depleting fragile native food sources and trampling or grazing Indian gardens and fields. Slavers captured Paiute women and children for sale in New Mexico and California, and travelers sometimes shot Paiute men. Santa Clara canyon provided Paiutes who survived with terrain in which they could defend themselves from depredations and at times, as Hoth learned, try to even the balance with outsiders.[54]

Whites also recognized the canyon's advantages as an ambush site. In February 1857, California-bound John Tobin and three other horsemen camping in the canyon came under fire as they slept. Tobin and two

SANTA CLARA NARROWS OVERVIEW VISTA. *John W. Telford, Courtesy LDS Church History Library.*

Massacre at Mountain Meadows

others were wounded. The next morning, the men saw "boot prints and the tracks of eight shod horses." Shortly before the attack, the four men had parted company with "seven or eight" fellow-travelers, among whom were two ex-convicts. Blame for the attack, however, was soon laid on Mormons reacting to a circular letter from Brigham Young. The letter instructed southern leaders to be on alert for the two recently released convicts, who might attempt a horse or cattle raid. Horse thieves and cattle rustlers often received summary justice on the frontier, and Young's circular expected that if a crime were committed, there would not "be any prosecutions for false imprisonment or tale bearers left for witnesses."[55]

Though the ex-convicts committed no crimes as they went south, one historian later suggested that when Dame got Young's letter, he may have overreacted. The writer concluded that either Dame or Haight might have assigned others to attack the travelers, and they simply shot the wrong men.[56] Others who have studied the incident suggest the victims may have been attacked by the seven or eight horsemen from whom they had just splintered, including the ex-convicts.[57]

Whether he had a role in the Tobin shooting or not, Haight—with his fellow leaders in Cedar City—clearly identified Santa Clara canyon as the place to ambush the Arkansas company. To them, it offered "opportun[itie]s for such an attack" that were "more evident" than elsewhere.[58] They planned to have Paiutes "follow the emigrant train" along the Santa Clara River. Then, "at some opportune point on that stream, while the company was strung out along the road, traveling, the Indians should attack it, kill as many of the men as they could, and get away with as much cattle and spoil as possible, but not to harm the women and children."[59]

For the plan to work, Haight had to convince Paiutes to participate. He turned for help to the energetic John D. Lee, a fellow major in the Iron Military District who was still serving as government-appointed farmer to the Paiutes. Lee recalled a rider coming to Harmony with a message that "Haight wanted me to be at Cedar City that evening without fail."[60] Years later, Lee's wife Rachel described her husband and Haight as "bitter" enemies at the time.[61] Contemporaneous evidence, however, shows they were on good terms when Haight summoned Lee to Cedar City that day.[62]

Haight's experience told him he could depend on Lee. The year before, the two were camped at Cove Creek in the mountains north of Beaver when Haight's horses disappeared. Haight, with his pleurisy-scarred lungs, remained in camp alone while Lee braved deep snow

SANTA CLARA NARROWS. *John W. Telford, Courtesy LDS Church History Library.*

to hunt for them. All day and into the next, Haight waited. Then Lee reappeared with the horses in tow. Somehow he had managed the two- to six-foot drifts and difficult terrain to find the animals and rescue Haight.[63]

As Lee traveled from Harmony to Cedar City, Haight sent several riders west along the trail taken by the Arkansas company. They would get ahead of the emigrants and set the attack plan in motion. Working through Higbee, Haight first asked Ellott Willden, Josiah Reeves, and possibly Benjamin Arthur to go to Mountain Meadows, where the emigrants were expected to camp eventually.[64] The three young men were told that the "plan was to...have the Indians ne[a]r to attack on [the] Santa Clara, instead of the civil authorities arresting the offenders in Cedar."[65] Part of the men's assignment was "to find occasion or something that would justify the Indians being let loose upon the emigrants."[66] They were also to get the company "to move on"—an effort to hurry the emigrants into the trap.[67]

Someone carried an order to twenty-four-year-old Samuel Knight, who lived at the north end of Mountain Meadows and helped work the ranch. With Indian mission president Jacob Hamblin away, Knight, as his counselor, was next in line. Knight was ordered to go south near Washington and Santa Clara "and instruct the Indians to arm themselves and prepare to attack the emigrant train." The attack was to occur "at the junction of the Santa Clara and Magotsu."[68]

The Paiutes, who generally lived in small groups spread across the landscape, had never attacked nor killed on anywhere near the scale that the Cedar City plan required. For the scheme to succeed they would have to be convinced to participate and then gathered en masse to the attack site.[69]

Besides Willden, Arthur, and Reeves, two more riders headed west from Cedar City. One was Joel White, who served as captain of one of Cedar's militia companies. The other was Klingensmith, one of the most ardent supporters of the plan to attack the train. White and Klingensmith were on their way before twilight Friday evening.[70]

The two afterwards claimed their mission to Pinto was "to passify the Indians there if possible and to let the emigrants pass."[71] According to their story, they rode a couple of miles out of town, where they met Lee, who was driving a wagon into Cedar City. "He asked us what the calculation of the people was in regard to those emigrant people—in regard to letting tham pass," White recalled. They told Lee "the conclusion was...to have the Indians passified as much as possible to let them pass." The news seemed to annoy Lee. "I have something to say in that matter and I will see to it," he reportedly said.[72] He then shook the reins and resumed his journey toward Cedar City.

Lee denied the incident ever took place.[73] He said White and Klingensmith went "by way of Pinto, to raise the Indians in that direction."[74] Lee was probably right. Klingensmith and White could hardly have been going to pacify Indians who did not know of Cedar City's plans.

White and Klingensmith drove hard, traveling at night. They took Leach's Cutoff, working their way through the low mountains west of Cedar City and onto the sloping, grassy area near Leach's Spring. In the darkness they passed the emigrants camped at the spring "just off from the road"—the Arkansas company's last overnight stop before Mountain Meadows. A half dozen more miles brought White and Klingensmith to Pinto.[75] White claimed they awoke one of the Indian missionaries, perhaps Richard Robinson, to give him the sealed order.[76] Robinson said he could not "remember such a circumstance."[77]

Soon White and Klingensmith were back on the road toward Cedar City.[78] Riding east on Saturday morning, September 5, they saw the emigrants pulling up a hill a few miles east of Pinto. As they passed the train, Klingensmith discreetly pointed out to White the "principal ones" in the company, particularly the man who "had made these threats, that he had helped kill Joe Smith."[79] White had not seen the emigrants before, being absent when the company passed through Cedar City.[80]

Klingensmith said he and White met Cedar City high councilman Ira Allen as they neared town. Allen purportedly told them a "decree had passed" countermanding their efforts at peace. "He said that the doom of the emigrants…was sealed, that the die was cast," Klingensmith claimed.[81] But White testified he could not "recollect of meeting any body on the road." If such an incident had taken place, White maintained, he would have remembered it.[82] Klingensmith's stories of meeting Lee when they left Cedar City and Allen when they returned may have been a later effort to clear his name: his alibi was that he had gone toward the Meadows to stop an attack, and the countermanding decision to destroy the emigrants was made while he was gone.

While Klingensmith and White were riding west on Friday night, Lee arrived from Harmony and met Haight at the public square in Cedar City shortly after nightfall. Haight said he wanted to have "a

PHILIP KLINGENSMITH.
Courtesy Anna Jean Backus.

long talk on…private and particular business." The two men retired to Haight's new, partially built, brick home near the iron works in New Town.[83] "We spent the night in an open house on some blankets," Lee said, "where we talked most all night." Lee claimed Haight told him terrible things about the emigrants, that they "were a rough and abusive set of men" who "had insulted, outraged, and ravished many of the Mormon women." They had heaped abuses on the people "from Provo to Cedar City" and had poisoned water along the road. "These vile Gentiles" had "publicly proclaimed that they had the very pistol" that killed Joseph Smith, and wanted "to kill Brigham Young and all of the Apostles." They had threatened "to return from California with soldiers…and kill every d—d Mormon man, woman and child." Finally, they had broken Cedar City ordinances and resisted arrest "by armed force." Because Haight never left an account, there is no way of knowing how much of the barrage was his—and how much later came from Lee. But whatever complaints Haight made that night, Lee said he "believed all that he said."[84]

According to Lee, Haight thought that "unless something was done to prevent it, the emigrants would carry out their threats." The Cedar City leaders had decided to provision Indians and send them to kill the men of the company and take their cattle. But Lee told Haight that in such a large-scale attack, others would die, too. "You know what the Indians are," Lee said he told Haight, reflecting a nineteenth-century stereotype of Indians. "They will kill all the party, women and children, as well as the men."[85]

The Cedar City plan—which began as a harsh response to a minor conflict—was morphing into a massacre of men, women, and children.

"Perpetrators make many small and great decisions as they progress along the continuum of destruction," Ervin Staub observed, and "extreme destructiveness…is usually the last of many steps along [the] continuum." According to Staub, "There is usually a progression of actions. Earlier, less harmful acts cause changes in individual perpetrators, bystanders, and the whole group that make more harmful acts possible. The victims are further devalued. The self-concept of the perpetrators changes and allows them to inflict greater harm—for 'justifiable' reasons. Ultimately, there is a commitment to…mass killing."[86]

In the end, who got killed didn't seem to matter to the planners, so long as they could blame the casualties on Paiutes. "It was then intended that the Indians should kill the emigrants," Lee explained, "and make it *an Indian massacre*, and not have any whites interfere with them." According to the plan, "no whites were to be known in the matter, it was to be all done by the Indians, so that it could be laid to them, if any questions were ever asked about it."[87] After the massacre, the story of an attack solely by Indians would be told as a coverup again and again, long after it had any kind of credibility.[88]

For Lee and Haight, their all-night meeting was full of fervor—terrible and, in their minds at the time, necessary. Later, when emotions cooled and the crime was apparent, a controversy began over which of the men was most responsible for their decisions. Haight's friends blamed Lee. Lee had "seemed very determined that the company should be made to suffer severely for their impudence and lawlessness," said Elias Morris, who claimed he saw Lee "counseling with Isaac C. Haight." Speaking of the emigrants, Lee had assured Haight "he had Indians enough around him to wipe the whole of them out of existence." Haight, "more moderate in his feelings," had at last agreed.[89]

Lee had his own excuses. He claimed Haight forced him to obey by placing him under orders, and that these had come from Dame, the chief military officer in southern Utah. "I knew I had to obey or die," Lee said.[90] But Dame had not ordered a militia attack, and Lee probably knew it. Haight and Lee both held the rank of militia major, though Haight, as major of the second battalion, was by law technically superior to Lee, major of the fourth.[91] Haight, as stake president, was also Lee's church leader. But Lee was bold enough to challenge Haight's authority if he disagreed. Headstrong, black-and-white in personality, and speaking his mind to a fault, Lee would have been the first to object if he had felt Haight's plans were wrong—and then dare Haight to do something about it.[92]

The most likely scenario was that when the two men breakfasted at Haight's house on Saturday after their meeting, they were partners—but with some differences.[93] Lee, the religious zealot, wanted to play a meaningful role in what he supposed to be God's purpose. The emigrants "were enemies to us, &...this was the beginning of great and important events," he said shortly after the massacre.[94] Haight was caught up by the threat he perceived in the emigrants and wanted "to put them out of the way before they done any more harm."[95] Both men also felt the need to settle old scores with the "gentiles," and the idea of taking some cattle and other spoils could not have been too far from the surface.[96]

In retrospect their motives made little sense, but the continuum that leads to mass murder is not a rational process. Both men were being swept by "powerful forces" into "greater acts of cruelty, violence,...[and] oppression."[97] Both Haight and Lee were quick to make judgments and to execute on those decisions—hallmarks of extralegal justice and unchecked power. During the Walker War, Lee had strapped on his sword, "called the people together," and declared that "by the help of god & the Faithful of my Brethren" he would, if necessary, shed the blood of the "cursed wicked apostate fault finding wretches" in their midst.[98] More recently, Haight had told George A. Smith that if troops threatened his community, he would not wait for instruction, but "take his battalion and use them up before they could get down through the kanyons."[99]

Before the meeting ended, Lee said he asked Haight if it wouldn't "be well to hold a council of the brethren before making a move." Haight replied, "We can't now delay for a council of the brethren." He would bring the matter before a council on Sunday; in the meantime, Lee was to send Paiute interpreter Carl Shirts to gather Indians in the south, and Haight would ask interpreter Nephi Johnson to do the same in the north.[100]

Haight and Lee soon began to execute on the plan. On Saturday, Mary Campbell, whose cabin was at the northwest corner of Old Town, saw four men going to the cottonwoods west of Cedar City, where members of the Coal Creek band of Paiutes often camped. The four men were Haight, Lee, Higbee, and Klingensmith, who had just returned from his overnight trip west. The men persuaded Paiutes there "to follow up the emigrants and kill them all, and take their property as the spoil of their enemies." That evening, Paiute women visited Old Town and told Campbell that Indian men had left the camp and were on their way "to kill the 'Mericates'" (Americans)—the Paiute term for non-Mormons.[101]

The white leaders' inciting of the generally peaceful Paiutes to participate in the attack is one of the most disturbing aspects of the entire story. The Southern Indian Mission had established close ties between the settlers and the Paiutes, which in cases created a sense of trust, and even dependence, that made them willing to comply. Wells's letter warning of possible U.S. troops in the area, which was received in southern Utah about a fortnight earlier, had urged Mormon leaders to tell the Indians of their peril—"that our enemies are also their enemies."[102]

One theory used to explain Paiute participation had to do with a meeting that Brigham Young, Jacob Hamblin, and Dimick Huntington held in Young's Salt Lake City office during the evening of

September 1. Pahvant leader Kanosh from Corn Creek was present, along with eleven other Indian leaders, including Ute leader Ammon from Beaver and two leading Paiutes: Tutsegavits, a headman from the Santa Clara and Virgin River region, and Youngwuds from the Ash Creek area near Harmony.[103] These men, along with Ammon's wife and Jacob Hamblin, had traveled to Salt Lake City when George A. Smith returned from his southern Utah tour because they wanted to "find out about the soldiers."[104]

As part of his developing war policy, Young wanted Indian leaders to ally themselves with the Saints against the approaching troops and prepare for a long siege. The day before the meeting, Huntington had met with Indians camped near Ogden north of Salt Lake. In the meeting, he "gave them all the Beef cattle & horses that was on the Road to Cal Afornia the North Rout," telling them that "they must put them into the mountains & not kill any thing as Long as they can help it but when they do kill take the old ones & not kill the cows or young ones."[105]

Running off cattle and saving them in the mountains would help assure food for the Indians—and perhaps the white settlers—in the event of an anticipated siege. Having horses to ride during the coming war would also prove an advantage.

Similarly, in the September 1 meeting, the native leaders from central and southern Utah were told, apparently by Young himself, that they might take "all the cattle that had gone to Cal the southe rout."[106] Some historians have linked this meeting to the subsequent massacre at Mountain Meadows. "The conflicts the Arkansas train encountered on the trail mattered not at all in the final balance," wrote Will Bagley, because as the company "struggled southward, its fate was being sealed in a meeting in Great Salt Lake City between the leaders of the southern Paiute bands and the man they called 'Big Um'—Brigham Young.... After their meeting with the Mormon prophet on September 1, the Paiute chiefs slept in Great Salt Lake City and left precipitously the next morning."[107] Bagley concluded that when Young "'gave' the Paiute chiefs the emigrants' cattle on the southern road to California," he "encouraged his Indian allies to attack the Fancher party."[108]

But neither chronology nor unfolding events confirm such a charge. Young's invitation for Indians to take cattle was a generalized war policy, not an order to massacre the Arkansas company. As the conflict continued, Young directed members of the territorial militia to take cattle and destroy supplies owned not only by the federal government but also by its private contractors. Despite the wartime atmosphere, this was done successfully with very few casualties.[109]

Haight and his associates were recruiting Paiutes before word of the September 1 meeting reached southern Utah. In addition, the Indians attending the September 1 meeting in Salt Lake were reluctant to take part in the crisis. According to Huntington's account, when the meeting ended, the Indians declared themselves "afraid to fight the Americans & so would raise grain & we [the Mormons] might fight."[110]

The Indians did not rush south. United States government vouchers recorded payment for entertaining "Kanosh & 14 of the band, Ammon & wife, four days," in Salt Lake City from September 1 through September 4. The total number of Indians was identical to the number in the Hamblin entourage and probably included the Paiutes Young-wuds and Tutsegavits.[111] Kanosh and three men of his band received hats and shoes in Salt Lake City on September 2.[112] Tutsegavits, in turn, was ordained a Mormon elder in the city on September 13.[113] According to the Jacob Hamblin journal, "the Chiefs was treted with mutch respect [They] was taken to the work Shops gardens orchards and other plases to Sho them the advantages of industry and incourag...them to labor for a living."[114] Before Tutsegavits left town, he and Hamblin stopped for another visit with Brigham Young. Wilford Woodruff demonstrated the advantages of horticulture by showing the Indian leader through his garden. He gave him peaches to eat and peach pits to plant.[115]

Indian recruitment for the massacre was local, not influenced by the September 1 meeting, and it built on trust that southern Utah leaders had already developed with Paiutes. One Indian account told of a mild protest. "I have not guns or powder enough," said Moquetas, one of the Paiute leaders, when asked to help with the attack. John D. Lee promised him both. Moquetas next asked about plunder, and Lee offered "clothing, all the guns and horses [of the emigrants], and some of the cattle to eat."[116]

Less than two weeks after the massacre, an Indian from northern Utah reported meeting a large band of Paiutes who acknowledged their role in the killings and said the Mormons had "persuaded them into it." According to their account, "John D. Lee came to their village and told them that Americans were very bad people, and always made a rule to kill Indians whenever they had a chance. He said, also, that they had often killed the Mormons, who were friends to the Indians. He then prevailed on them to attack the emigrants...and promised them that if they were not strong enough to whip them, the Mormons would help them."[117]

Despite their promise to help, white leaders wanted to gather enough Indians together so that white participation would be minimal. "My orders were to go home to Harmony," Lee remembered, "and see Carl Shirts, my son-in-law, an Indian interpreter, and send him to the Indians in the South, to notify them that the Mormons and Indians were at war with the '*Mericats*'...and bring all the Southern Indians up and have them join with those from the North, so that their force would be sufficient to make a successful attack on the emigrants."[118] While his son-in-law roused Indians in the south, Lee was to gather Paiutes living around Harmony.

Lee said that on his way back to Harmony from Cedar City, he met "a large band of Indians under Moquetas and Big Bill, two Cedar City Chiefs," probably the Paiutes that he, Haight, Higbee, and Klingensmith had recruited at the cottonwoods. "They were in their war paint, and fully equipped for battle." The Paiutes asked Lee "to go with them and command their forces."[119] Despite Lee's earlier promises to them, they remained hesitant.

"I told them," Lee recalled, "that I could not go with them that evening, that I had orders from Haight, the *big Captain*, to send other Indians on the war-path to help them kill the emigrants, and that I must attend to that first." Lee told them "to go on near where the emigrants were and camp until the other Indians joined them." He would then "meet them the next day and lead them." The Paiutes wanted to take with them Lee's adopted Indian son, Lemuel or "Clem," perhaps as security that Lee would show up. "After some time I consented," Lee said.[120]

There would be no backing out now.

CHAPTER ELEVEN

A Fearful Responsibility

Cedar City and Southwest, September 5–7, 1857

U NAWARE OF THE Cedar City plans, the Arkansas emigrants
drove on to their next camp. Leaving Leach's Spring on Saturday morning, they continued along Leach's Cutoff past
Pinto, through the scrub oak and cedar and below the sturdier tim-
ber of the highlands to emerge at the northern neck of the Mountain Meadows. For centuries, Paiute bands had lived in and near the
Meadows, and just the year before, a county court had granted Jacob
Hamblin herding rights there "for the benefit of the Indians Stationed
on the Santa Clara."[1]

The emigrant scouts on horseback reached Hamblin's ranch at
the north end of the Meadows late Saturday morning or early in the
afternoon. The slower wagons with their lumbering teams pulled into
the valley a few hours later. Both were expected. David Tullis, who
worked at the ranch, remembered Mormon messengers Ellott Willden,
Benjamin Arthur, and Josiah Reeves arriving there shortly before the
emigrants with a warning of their "sauciness."[2] As ordered, the three
young men had come to watch the emigrants for reasons to justify the
planned Indian attack in Santa Clara canyon and to hurry them toward
the ambush site.[3]

Tullis, who was building a house and corral for the absent Hamblin,
eyed the emigrants cautiously but found them "respectable-looking"

MOUNTAIN MEADOWS CAMP AND SIEGE SITE. *John W. Telford, Courtesy LDS Church History Library.*

despite Cedar City's forebodings. "One of the men rode up to where I was working, and asked if there was water ahead," he remembered. Tullis gave them the same answer Hamblin had at Corn Creek, pointing to the springs at the south end of the Meadows. Tullis had no complaints about the emigrants, who he said treated him "civilly."[4]

Hamblin's wife, Rachel, also watched. She displayed reserve, also wary because of the rumors. When the wagons drove past her home without incident, she must have felt relieved.[5] Her husband was still in Salt Lake City and had left Samuel Knight in charge.[6]

Knight was caring for his Danish-born wife, Caroline, who had given birth to a daughter a short time before. The delivery had not gone well, and Caroline lay "nearly at the point of death." To spare her the heat of their home in Santa Clara, Samuel had recently moved his family to the Meadows, where their temporary dwelling was a wagon box. Samuel's life had not been easy. His mother, Sally, one of Joseph Smith's earliest and staunchest converts, died in childbirth during the Missouri troubles; after the Saints' expulsion from Nauvoo, Samuel's father, Newel, made it only to the winter camp in present-day Nebraska before he too died. Samuel struggled to Utah in 1847, just fourteen years old.[7]

Samuel and Caroline were at Hamblin's when the emigrants approached. The men who visited the ranch asked Samuel where they could pasture their animals and rest "for a few days before starting out on the deserts to the west." Just as Tullis had, Samuel "directed them to the south end of the valley where grass and water were abundant." Knight's job was to care for the cattle, and like Hamblin, he wanted the emigrant cattle away from the Mormon herds ranging the foothills near the ranch.[8]

"I saw the train encamp at [a] spring from a high point of land where I was cutting wood," remembered Albert Hamblin, a Shoshone in his mid-teens whom the Hamblins had taken into their family several years earlier.[9] Normally the practice of emigrants was to park their wagons in a rough circle and cluster themselves inside in family groups.[10] But at the Meadows the members of the Arkansas company camped with their wagons only loosely grouped—evidence that they felt no danger. They pitched tents near the wagons and probably herded their cattle into a grassy draw just over a small ridge northwest of their camp.[11]

They posted herdsmen at strategic points to look after the grazing stock, concerned more about wolves and other animal predators than about human raiders. By now the emigrants had passed through the last Utah settlement on the trail, and the Mormons were far less numerous. The Paiutes seemed no threat. Besides, the undulating plain, sweet grass, and gurgling spring had a beguiling peace.[12] With milk cows and prized horses staked nearby and the loose cattle lowing in the distance, the emigrants settled down for the night.

The bucolic scene continued the next morning, Sunday, September 6, with men managing livestock, women and children gathering firewood and filling pails from the spring, and fires dotting the campsite. Tradition suggests that after breakfast, the people gathered under a large tent to commemorate the Lord's day, guided by a "white haired, old, Methodist pastor" and perhaps other clergymen in the group. If the tradition is true, the clergy may have been lay ministers, for no known members of the group were men of the cloth.[13] That morning one of the emigrants visited Rachel Hamblin to see if he could buy butter and cheese. "I had none," she said, "and he stayed but a short time, saying his people had camped at the spring, where they would stay awhile to recruit their stock."[14]

Doing reconnaissance duty, Ellott Willden and another man visited the emigrants twice. When John Higbee sent them to the Meadows to find something to justify an Indian attack, he also instructed them to tell the emigrants "to move on, on the pretense that the Meadows belonged to them." When Willden and his companion visited the camp, the emigrants "acted civil," saying they were on their way to "Lower California, but that some of them might return if they did not like the country."[15] They also planned "to send some of their men back" to hunt for cattle they had lost while camped at Quichapa Lake. Other men from their train had already gone southeast of the Meadows "into the mountains toward Pine Valley to make tar...to grease their wagons, as wagon grease could not be obtained in the settlements." The emigrants said that when all their men returned, "the company expected to continue the journey to California."[16]

After talking with the emigrants, the two Mormons returned to Hamblin's ranch and helped Tullis make adobe bricks. Later that morning, William Aden and another emigrant "rode up to the ranch and watered their horses." They told the men at Hamblin's that they were headed back along the trail to hunt for lost cattle. Soon they headed back east through Leach's Cutoff toward Quichapa.[17]

Sometime during the emigrants' stay at the Meadows, Amos Thornton of Pinto also paid a visit to their campground, accompanied by two other Mormons.[18] Thornton may have wanted to see for himself if the emigrants were really as threatening as the Cedar City leaders represented.

Confident in their strength or unaware that their hour in Cedar City had lasting repercussions, the emigrants had no reason to believe they were in danger. But side by side with the emigrants' feelings of security were the deadly plans of Cedar City's leaders, which were going forward at several places. At the Meadows, Samuel Knight was an unwilling tool. Before noon on Sunday he went south from the Meadows with orders from "the authorities in Cedar City" to rouse the Paiutes on the Santa Clara and Virgin Rivers. Knight's instructions were to have them "arm themselves and prepare to attack the emigrant train...at the junction of the Santa Clara and Magotsu" in Santa Clara canyon.[19]

Knight did not welcome the assignment. He did not want to leave his bedridden wife and their newborn daughter, and more importantly he was aware of the gravity of the message—and the responsibility he assumed by carrying it. But it was "an order that could not be disobeyed without imperiling [my] own life," he later tried to explain. Knight could not remember whether his orders came from Cedar City's military or religious leaders, but Isaac Haight wore both hats, and the two were often indistinguishable.[20]

Meanwhile at Harmony, John D. Lee was a whirlwind of activity. Returning from Cedar City on Saturday evening, he sent messages to local Paiutes to gather at the fort. He also held a Saturday night meeting at his woodpile with men of the settlement, including Lee's future brother-in-law, Gilbert Morse. "The subject under discussion was the extermination of the emigrant train," Morse recalled, and "the best way to get at them." When Morse protested the attack, Lee told him to leave the group, threatening that "if he did not carry himself straight, he would get his tail cut off just below the ears."[21]

Lee got enough of the other men to agree with the Cedar City plan that he felt confident speaking about it at a general meeting the next day—Sunday, September 6—his forty-fifth birthday. The meeting took place in lieu of worship services, which normally began at 10:00 a.m. Lee stood at the speaker's stand, full of outrage, conducting a war rally. Gentiles had driven the Saints from Nauvoo, causing some to perish, he reminded his audience. Now, he said, gentile emigrants had stirred trouble in Cedar City, including at Haight's home, threatening an attack not only on the leaders but also "every other damn Mormon in the country." Faced with this danger, Lee said Haight and Dame "thought it was best to put them out of the way."[22] Haight had either lied to Lee about Dame's approval, or Lee was using the district commander's name to gain support for the plan.

Lee asked his listeners to show agreement by raising their hands. Harmony was off the main road, and, like those in Parowan, its citizens did not have the same strong feelings as leaders at Cedar City. But Lee had said Haight and Dame were behind the plan, and, in the end, the decision for many may have come down to what they thought their leaders wanted. "So of course they lifted up their hands as that was law," remembered Annie Elizabeth Hoag. The supporting vote carried by a large majority, though some like Hoag hesitated. She started to vote her opposition but dropped her hand. Only two or three in the congregation opposed Lee; probably Annie's then-husband, Peter Shirts, and one of the Shirts sons.[23]

Later that day Lee made an attempt at flourish. He "fixed up as much like a military officer as he could with the clothes he had," tying "a red sash around his waist." Then with "a sword in his right hand," he "marched around the inside of the Fort...at the head of about 40 or 50 Indians," said John Chatterley, visiting from Cedar City.[24] Another witness put the number of Paiutes at seventy-five.[25] During the swagger Lee asked those present to express their support for "success to Israel," and two or three responded with lukewarm "amens." A second try brought a little more enthusiasm.[26]

The Indians who marched around the fort included a group from Cedar City. Sometime Sunday morning, more than a dozen of them arrived to escort Lee on the expedition. An Indian known as Comanche had second thoughts about the "program of slaughter" but was persuaded to rejoin the ranks.[27] At least one important Harmony Indian did not go. Youngwuds, a leading headmen of the Ash Creek bands, had left Harmony two weeks earlier to visit Salt Lake City and was still at the Mormon headquarters.[28]

From Harmony, "Bro. J. D. Lee went on an expedition South," said the cryptic and partially incomplete historical record of the community.[29] The Santa Clara narrows—southwest of Harmony—remained his final destination. After soliciting ten days' provisions from the people at Harmony and asking them to pray aloud in their families three times daily for his success, "Lee, at the head of the Indians with Carlos Schurz [Carl Shirts] as his interpreter, set out on the expedition against the emigrants."[30] The group left the fort about noon on Sunday.[31]

Shirts, Lee's new son-in-law, headed south to gather more Indians near Washington and lead them up Santa Clara canyon from the south.[32] Lee and his entourage took a route that would arch northwest to Leach's Cutoff, pass through Pinto, and then sweep southwest through the Mountain Meadows and into Santa Clara canyon from the north. Lee's party stopped three miles above Pinto to eat roasted potatoes from a patch grown by some of the Indian missionaries. The potato patch was a rendezvous point for the gathering Paiutes and not far from Mountain Meadows and the unsuspecting emigrants.[33]

Another drama played out at Carl Shirts's destination, the small settlement of Washington, about thirty miles below Harmony. A few days before, Washington's citizens may have heard about the train from James Pearce and Joseph Adair, men coming down from Utah County who passed it on their way.[34] If Washington resident William Young was at Lee's woodpile meeting on Saturday night as later reported, he may have brought news of the Haight-Lee plan. William Young and Shirts probably arrived in Washington late Sunday or early Monday—though perhaps not together. Shirts went to work recruiting Paiutes. "The Indians about Washington became very excited running to and fro," Young testified, without hinting at who stirred them up.[35]

"John D. Lee and other officials was having their interpreters sti[r] up the Indians to commit hostilities on this camp of emigrants," said John Hawley, the Mormon who had traveled with the Arkansas company for three days before reaching his home in Washington. Hawley knew of the Dutchman's taunts and the trouble between settlers and emigrants over grazing land in Provo and Nephi. But he thought the men in Washington were overreacting.[36]

No instructions had come for them to mobilize; the plan at that point was still to have the Paiutes do the dirty work. But some of the whites decided to go along anyway. "When the Indians had become very excited…We come to the conclusion at last that we would call upon our military," said William Young, laying the blame to the Indians. A group of Washington militiamen—less than one-fourth of their total number—took their guns and headed toward Santa Clara canyon.[37]

While the plan was unfolding everywhere else, it began to unravel in Cedar City. At 4:00 p.m. on Sundays, after the regular worship service, the local leaders sometimes convened a council meeting to discuss and coordinate policy. At the September 6 meeting, Haight sought the council's support for the plan to attack the emigrant train as he had earlier promised Lee to do. The meeting included members of the Cedar City stake presidency—Haight and his two counselors, John Higbee and Elias Morris; the Cedar City bishopric—Klingensmith and his counselors, James Whitaker Sr. and Morris's father, John; and members of the stake high council. Other leading citizens were also present.[38]

One member of the high council, Laban Morrill, was a resident of Fort Johnson, a half dozen miles north of Cedar City. He was a blacksmith—a six-foot, 200-pound block of a man with a rugged and determined manner to match. "His fine head, strong, yet kindly features and dignified bearing marked him as an altogether superior man," said an admirer.[39] But he had an irritating pattern of speech, that of constantly repeating phrases in staccato fashion.[40] Morrill entered the meeting late and immediately sensed "confusion" and some "little excitement."[41]

When Morrill asked "what was up," he heard the Cedar City concerns. "I was told there was an emigrant train that had passed down along to near Mountain Meadows, and that they made their threats in regard to us as a people—signifying they would stay there and destroy every damn Mormon," Morrill said. The leaders took the threat seriously because they believed "there was an army coming on the south and one on the north," and were debating "what method we ought to take in regard to preserving the lives of the citizens."[42]

Elias Morris recalled that "the more radical members present, suggested harsh measures," though he claimed none favored "any wholesale killing." Klingensmith later acknowledged that some in the meeting advocated killing, though he did not put himself among them. Morrill remembered, however, that Klingensmith, Haight, "and one or two" others thought it best to destroy the emigrants. "Some had heard the statement that they had helped to kill Old Joe Smith out of this emigrant train and [it] made a little excitement."[43]

Morrill was stunned by what he heard. "Do not our principles of right teach us to return good for evil and do good to those who despitefully use us?" he later remembered countering. "To fall upon them and destroy them was the work of savage monsters rather than that of civilized beings of our own enlightened time."[44]

Morrill wanted to know "by what authority" Haight and the others were planning such drastic measures. Had something come from Col. Dame? If so, Morrill demanded to see the documents. In response, Haight and his supporters had to admit they were acting on their own. Nothing had come from Parowan, they said.[45] The full truth went further: Dame had actually told Haight to let the emigrants alone.[46] Still more damning, Haight did not tell the council about Lee and the forces that were already gathering near the Meadows. At least no one present recorded such an admission.

Morrill said others joined his opposition, although he did not list them by name.[47] Years later, Elias Morris and Klingensmith claimed they spoke against the plan, though their claims lack credibility.[48] Both Morris and Klingensmith had been with Haight and Lee in the early stages of the planning, and their subsequent behavior showed they were not opposed to killing.[49] Morrill said Klingensmith was "the hardest man I had to contend with."[50] At one point during the heated discussion, according to Klingensmith, Haight "jumped up and broke up the meeting and went out doors."[51]

The debate continued until Morrill finally got the men to agree "that all should keep still [and] quiet and that there should be a dispatch to Governor Young to know what would be the best course." Brigham Young's views far outweighed anyone else's in the territory, and consulting him was one way to bring the badly divided men together. The motion, however, may have been more than an attempt at consensus. Morrill and others likely believed that Young's answer would end the matter quickly and stop the local conspiracy.[52]

Who in pioneer Utah could oppose such a motion? The vote was unanimous, but Morrill took pains to have Haight assure him he would send the dispatch the next morning.[53] Utah did not yet have a telegraph system, and an express dispatch from Cedar to Salt Lake City and back would require a week of hard riding.[54]

Morrill saw two of Haight's supporters, William Stewart and Daniel Macfarlane, leave the meeting early, a move that roused his suspicions. When it came time to go home, Morrill thought Macfarlane and Stewart—good men in normal times—were waiting to "waylay" him. He gave his horses "the reins" and hurried back to Fort Johnson by an alternate route.[55]

Morrill returned home safely "feeling that all was well."[56] He had stood up to the extremists and prevailed. The Sunday afternoon meeting had worked the way the Mormon system of councils was intended. There had been a thorough discussion that checked extremism.

At some point during or after the meeting, Haight decided to send messengers to Lee. Later that evening, Stewart and Joel White headed west toward Pinto, where Lee was supposed to be rendezvousing with Indians. Macfarlane, who served as White's adjutant, had probably been excused from the meeting to tell White to prepare for his mission.[57]

No one ever explained why Haight sent the two men. If he wanted the attack to go forward in spite of the council's objections, he may have sent Stewart and White to spur Lee on. More likely, given the council's decision to seek Brigham Young's advice, he hoped to back Lee off.

There seemed to be enough time to call off the planned attack in Santa Clara canyon. As far as Haight knew, the emigrants might spend days resting themselves and their cattle at the Meadows, even though he had sent Willden and his companions to prod them on. When the slow-moving cattle company did begin to leave, the journey to the Santa Clara narrows would require two more days of travel.

But Haight also knew Lee. Something lingered in Lee's personality that warned against giving him too much power or trusting his decisions. "Lee was an aspiring Glory Seeking man, who ran before he was sent," Higbee later complained, trying to explain what happened.[58]

Whatever the reason, sometime Sunday evening Lee decided to make an attack at Mountain Meadows instead of Santa Clara canyon. According to Ellott Willden, the change in plans took place at the potato patch near Pinto where Lee and the Paiutes intended to camp that night. One of the Paiute "chiefs" dozed off "while the corn and potatoes were roasting for the evening meal," said one later account. In his sleep, he "dreamed that his double-hands were filled with blood." The Indian leader purportedly regarded "this as a favorable omen, and rousing his braves," they began "the hot and furious march for the emigrant camp...the untasted supper being left in the embers."[59] Placing the blame on the Paiutes, Willden said that "Lee could not hold the Indians back."[60]

Or perhaps he urged them on. According to one source, it was "Lee who interpreted the 'double handful of blood' as a victory for the red-men...that they would secure the blood of the emigrants." This statement fit Lee's belief that he himself was an interpreter of dreams, a modern-day Joseph of Egypt. If Lee had wanted to restrain the Indians he could have sought help at nearby Pinto or Hamblin's ranch.[61]

The notion that bloodthirsty "savages" were primarily to blame for the attack on the emigrants, forcing white settlers to participate, would become a persistent part of massacre lore.[62] No one was more active in promoting it than Lee, whose manufactured stories put him anywhere but at the Meadows when the first attack took place.[63] The truth was that Paiutes would not have attacked the company unless local settlers had stirred them up. And at the final and decisive moment, Lee led them—and any white men who may have participated.[64]

The impromptu plan that emerged Sunday night and early Monday morning required surprise—"to attack the emigrant party before daylight when they would be in the most profound slumber, and to massacre them before they could awake and arm themselves."[65] Before daybreak, which was about 5:30 a.m., the attackers, their faces painted, moved into place. The position most dangerous to the emigrants was the gully southeast of the emigrant camp. This ravine drained the Meadows' southern spring, forming the headwaters of Magotsu Creek. By creeping through the gully, the assailants could be within twenty-five yards of the main camp, near enough to rush the emigrants and kill them at close range.[66]

But things went wrong from the beginning. Instead of immediately rushing the sleeping emigrants, the Paiutes waited for daylight, which gave the emigrants a chance to start campfires for breakfast. Their dogs, sensing strangers nearby, "got to barking."[67]

Lee planned to take out the emigrant herdsmen, "not wishing to appear, if possible to avoid it, at the slaughter of the main party." But this plan, too, faltered—if an account recorded years later had any truth to it. According to its narrative, when Lee came across a sleeping emigrant and tried to shoot him, "the cap burst without exploding the pistol." The man woke and Lee chased him toward the main party, shooting him "just as he stooped to go" into one of the tents.[68] Claiming he was not really present that morning, Lee later told a reporter that "one fool Indian off on the hill fired his gun, and spoilt the whole plan." The gunshot shattered any hope of surprise, and the Paiutes, according to Lee, "fired and killed" several of the emigrants.[69]

At first the surprised emigrants made easy targets. Lee claimed seven of them died, and another sixteen had wounds, although Indians put the total number of dead and wounded at fifteen.[70] Despite the heavy casualties, the Ozark pioneers quickly regrouped and soon were firing back. One child who survived the massacre remembered the "distinct picture" of his twenty-six-year-old aunt, Eloah Angeline Tackitt Jones, fighting along "with the men...using the gun of one of the fallen emigrants."[71]

Most of the Paiutes were stationed in the ravine and at some point made a confused rush toward the wagons, only to be repulsed by emigrant gunfire that killed one Paiute and wounded two others. The wounded men, according to Lee, were "two of the chiefs from Cedar," Moquetas and Bill, who were "shot through the legs, breaking a leg for each of them."[72] Martha Elizabeth Baker, another child survivor, was just five years old at the time. She remembered that after the main assault failed, "the Indians...retreated to the brush-covered hillside and sought safety behind the huge rocks there." From these positions, "a desultory fire pelted our camp."[73] The emigrants fired upon the Indians "every time they showed themselves," said one report, their bullets nicking the stones where the attackers lay concealed.[74]

Four miles north, the people at the ranch house heard the firing, which Rachel Hamblin said went on for half an hour.[75] "The boys at Hamblin's wer astonished," Ellott Willden said of himself and his companions. "The attack on Monday was not...a part of the plan." As soon as it was light enough to see, Willden and two of the others rode south to learn what had happened. They traveled just far enough to see "Indians running to and fro,...the emigrants' cattle running about and several head of stock lying dead." Thinking it dangerous to go farther, they retreated to the ranch.[76] Most Mormon accounts insisted that Lee was the only white man involved in the attack, though it was to their advantage to insist on this version of events.[77]

By the time Willden and the others got back, two Cedar City militia leaders had arrived at the ranch house—William Stewart and Joel White, the two men Haight sent out Sunday evening. If they had planned to call off Lee, they were too late. Someone at the ranch told them several emigrant men were outside the Meadows searching for stray cattle and making pine tar. Stewart asked to borrow Willden's pistols, saying he would "fix" the two emigrants who had gone back to Quichapa for cattle. If the emigrants returned to camp and saw what was happening, they might ride off to report the attack and get help.[78]

Stewart and White backtracked toward Cedar City and eventually found their quarry. The two emigrants were on horseback returning to camp and had paused to let their mounts drink from Little Pinto Creek near Leach's Spring. Stewart and White approached the unsuspecting men and struck up a conversation. The Mormons learned that one of the emigrants was William Aden, the other the much-talked-of "Dutchman." Seeing a tin cup attached to the back of Aden's saddle, Stewart asked to borrow it to get himself a drink. When Aden turned to reach for it, Stewart "shot him through the head, killing him instantly." The Dutchman "put spurs to his horse and fled," dodging the bullets fired after him, one of which apparently wounded him. The men at Hamblin's ranch saw him speed past. So did the besieging Indians, who tried unsuccessfully to bring him down before he entered the corrall.[79]

After the initial attack that morning, the emigrants had circled their wagons, easing the wheels into quickly dug pits so the wagon beds were flush with the ground. For added security they chained the wheels together and filled the gaps with dirt. Inside their makeshift fort, they dug a semicircular ditch, twenty feet long and four or five feet deep. Here, most of the emigrants huddled like cordwood.[80]

The wagon corral was only slightly less congested—about a hundred feet across. Within this space, the emigrants had to bury bodies,

LEACH'S SPRING. *John W. Telford, Courtesy LDS Church History Library.*

nurse the wounded, and comfort terrified infants and children. More than 120 men, women, and children survived the initial onslaught, and as the siege wore on, these had to cope with the necessities of eating, sleeping, and sanitation. There were other problems. Ammunition was running low.[81] Just as critical was the lack of water. The Meadows' rippling springs and brook mocked just out of safe reach.[82]

While the emigrants fortified their corral, Lee and the Paiutes took charge of the spoils, although some of the cattle scattered and ran.[83] Other cattle were killed by the Paiutes for food or as debt-payment for dead or wounded comrades. Still others would be taken by Paiutes who left for home.[84]

Soon after Monday's initial attack and the start of the siege, Lee knew he was in trouble. The plan to wipe out the emigrants in one quick assault failed, and the Paiutes were angry because of the casualties they suffered and the failure to achieve the easy victory they had been promised.[85] Lee himself had a close call. According to one report, he was on a knoll near the emigrants' camp when they opened fire on him. One bullet passed through his hat, another through his left sleeve. During the next several days and later in his life, Lee told the story of his narrow escape many times and with various details, almost always denying his role in the first attack. Once he said he had been grazed just above his belt, "cutting through my clothes to the skin some six inches across."[86]

Lee realized he needed reinforcements. On Monday morning, he sent one Indian runner to Zadok Judd, the acting bishop of Santa Clara, explaining "that Indians had surround[ed] [the] emigran[t] camp, and help was wanted."[87] After waiting some time for a response, Lee grew desperate. The Paiutes were becoming unsettled, and there seemed no way to end the siege without more men. Lee finally set out to get the needed reinforcements himself, promising the Indians he would "go and bring other friends to their aid."[88]

Lee had nearly reached the junction of the Santa Clara River and Magotsu Creek when he heard someone coming and hid himself in the brush. It proved to be Samuel Knight, returning from his mission to alert Paiutes downstream, along with Dudley Leavitt, his fellow counselor to Jacob Hamblin in the Southern Indian Mission presidency.[89] Lee was "disappointed at not seeing Indians with K[night] & L[eavitt], for he had expec[t]ed [a] force with which to renew the attack the next morning."[90]

Lee caught Knight and Leavitt up on the news: the attack, the siege, and the bullet holes in his clothing, which he saw as tokens of his courage and God's protection. Lee also had a request. He wanted Knight and Leavitt to ambush the emigrants who had gone to Pine Valley to make pine tar. "If any killing was to be done," Leavitt replied tartly, it had to be done "fair and square." Lee backed down. Neither Knight nor Leavitt liked what was going on, and after their conversation with Lee they continued to Hamblin's ranch, which for Knight meant reunion with his wife and daughter.[91]

Lee continued south until he met Shirts, the men who were coming up from Washington, and about 150 Indians. For Lee, the dozen or so Washington men were a welcome surprise—no orders from Cedar City had requested them. Seeing them together with the Indian force, he now felt resupplied. "The whites camped there that night with me," Lee claimed, "but most of the Indians rushed on to their friends at the camp on the Meadows."[92]

Meanwhile on Monday morning in Cedar City, Haight was trying to manage his own difficulties. Sunday's council meeting had rejected his plan to attack the emigrants and instead required an express rider be sent to Brigham Young. Around noon, Haight learned more upsetting news, probably from an Indian runner arriving from the Meadows.[93] For the first time, he became aware of Lee's failed attack, and with this information, the Cedar City leader understood that everything had changed. He now had to explain and manage a situation that was rapidly getting out of control. How much should Brigham Young be told? And how should the situation at the Meadows be resolved?

Each of these two questions required an express rider, one for Salt Lake City and another for the Meadows. Finding riders would not be easy; it was harvest time, and the trips would be grueling. By midmorning, Klingensmith had asked Joseph Clewes, a twenty-five-year-old stone mason, who grimaced. Klingensmith tried to be reassuring. "Do not be afraid, it is a good cause you are going to ride in," he said. He told Clewes to get a horse and meet Haight at the iron company store at noon.[94] Although Klingensmith did not reveal Clewes's destination, at the time it was probably Salt Lake City as news from the Meadows had not yet reached town.

After that news arrived, Cedar City leaders also recruited James Haslam, a thirty-one-year-old carpenter and plasterer who served as a musician in the militia.[95] Haslam was "a big, husky fellow"—not the usual profile for an express rider but willing and available.[96] Within fifteen minutes of agreeing to go, Haslam was home, in his riding clothes, and back at the iron company store waiting for his dispatch.[97] By the middle or late afternoon, the two riders received their assignments. Haslam was asked to carry Haight's letter to Young—a letter that was later lost or destroyed, though several people remembered its contents. The emigrants had been acting "verry mean," the letter reportedly said, and it rehearsed their threats. The letter also claimed the emigrants had gotten into trouble with Paiutes, who had surrounded them and forced them "to seek shelter behind their wagons." Finally, it sought counsel from Young on "what they must do with the *Americans*," suggesting that Haight had heard about Young's changed Indian policy and was uncertain about it. Haslam read the letter, which he later summarized as saying, "The Indians had got the emigrants corralled at the Mountain Meadows, and Lee wanted to know what should be done." Carefully folding and putting the letter away, Haslam "put spurs to his horse" and galloped north toward Parowan, the first stop on his long ride to Salt Lake City.[98]

Express riders seeking Young's advice were not uncommon in pioneer Utah. But Haslam's ride probably had few parallels. He was given one hundred hours—about four days—to make the roughly five-hundred-mile round trip.[99] Later, his ride was so highly celebrated that it became chronicled by exact riding times and the settlements passed through.[100] At Parowan, the startled Dame gave Haslam a letter telling up-road bishops and militia commanders to furnish "horses and supplies, to forward [this] Express [without delay] to Gov or Prest Young."[101]

Within five minutes after Haslam galloped out of Cedar City, Clewes received his dispatch telling Lee to back off, with instructions to take it to Pinto and "get there as quick as I could." His only weapon was "an old rusty horse pistol," borrowed from a friend. To Clewes, it looked as if it had not been used in twenty years. Clewes hurried west across the valley. At the mouth of Leach's Canyon, he met Stewart and White, who were returning to Cedar City after killing Aden. They asked Clewes where he was going, and he told them of the message he carried from Haight. "Your letter is of no use," they frowned. "Lee with the Indians jumped on the emigrant camp this morning and got a lot of Indians wounded." After a moment's reflection, however, they changed their minds. "No, go on," one of them said, thinking of Haight. "I cannot interfere with his orders."[102]

Seeing Clewes's rusty pistol, they traded with him. "Here," one of them said, "give me that old pistol and take these," handing Clewes the pistols Stewart borrowed from Willden that morning—the weapons used in Aden's murder. He probably asked Clewes to return the pistols to Willden, Clewes's brother-in-law, still at Hamblin's ranch.[103]

When Clewes arrived at Pinto, he handed Haight's dispatch to Amos Thornton and then, looking over Thornton's shoulder, got a glimpse of its contents. "Take this dispatch to John D. Lee as quick as you can get it to him," said one sentence. Clewes also remembered the main message: "Major John D. Lee: You will use your best endeavors to keep the Indians off the emigrants and protect them from harm until further orders." Thornton later showed the message to the presiding militia and religious leader at Pinto, Richard S. Robinson, who remembered about the same. "Word had been sent to Salt Lake City," Robinson said, "and Lee was to draw the Indians off and satisfy them with beef if necessary but not to kill the emigrants."[104]

While Clewes was reaching Pinto, Stewart and White returned to Cedar City with their news, and none of it was good. They must have reported more details on the failed attack at the Meadows, as well as the killing of Aden and the escape of the Dutchman, who could testify that white men—not just Indians—were killing emigrants. What if the people of California learned these facts? And how could Haight explain to his own people that his assurances during the Sunday night council meeting meant nothing? When Haight sent Haslam to Salt Lake City, his letter had omitted key details—a first effort at cover-up. The same impulse would lead to still greater crimes in the coming four days.[105]

Sometime on Monday, Haight sent for Nephi Johnson at Johnson Springs, a few miles north of Cedar City. The twenty-three-year-old Johnson had learned the Paiute language while a teenager, and perhaps no Mormon understood or spoke it better. Johnson had a further asset: the Paiutes trusted him. Such credentials, Haight knew, were invaluable. But he also knew that the neighboring Johnson and Morrill families were so closely connected that Johnson might share Laban Morrill's opposition to the anti-emigrant activity. Haight's message to Johnson was suitably vague and probably misleading: "Prest Haight Wanted me to Come to Cedar to talk with the Indians as the Squaws Were Stealing Wheat Out of the Field," Johnson later said of the express.[106]

When Johnson arrived in Cedar City, Haight rehearsed recent developments. He told Johnson of his overnight meeting at his home near the iron works, though he put most of the responsibility on Lee. "Lee had proposed to Him to gather up the Indians And Distroy the train of emigrants," Johnson remembered Haight saying. Haight had merely "consented to it." Haight also told Johnson he had sent a message to Brigham Young, but he now seemed reluctant to wait for Young's reply and hinted of quick action. Johnson responded, "It Would Be a Fearful Responsibility for a Man to take upon Himself to Distroy that train of Emigrants...I Would Wait until I Rec[eived] word from President Young." Johnson did not know that the emigrants had already been attacked, and Haight did not disabuse him. To delay matters, Johnson suggested putting off any action until the Santa Clara narrows. "I was in Hopes He Would put off the Distruction of the Train until He Rec[eived] Word from President Young," Johnson explained, "for I was satisfied What His Answer Would Be."[107]

By this time, Haight must have realized that Johnson was in Morrill's camp and, for the moment, told him to go home. But it would not be the last time he would call upon the young man.[108]

CHAPTER TWELVE

Finish His Dirty Job

Parowan to Mountain Meadows,
September 7–10, 1857

JAMES HASLAM'S RIDE north through Parowan late Monday afternoon brought Dame word that the emigrants had gotten into a difficulty with Indians at Mountain Meadows. Whether Dame believed the message or read between the lines is unclear.[1] But he heard enough to summon a council for advice that evening. The Parowan men "decided to render aid and protection to the emigrants, should they call for assistance," remembered one of the council participants. "Otherwise it was considered just, in view of the threats and insults the company had offered to the Saints in passing through the settlements, to let them fight it out with the Indians as best they could."[2]

The council's decision reflected rumors circulating about the emigrants. It may also have reflected its members' understanding of Brigham Young's Indian policy, announced August 16, that Mormons not jump into disputes between emigrants and Indians. In any case, Dame knew of the need for an Indian alliance in the coming war. Salt Lake City headquarters had made that point emphatically with the southern commander.[3]

At two o'clock Tuesday morning, September 8, an Indian runner reached Parowan with new details. "The Indians had attacked the emigrant company at Mountain Meadows" and had killed two or three of its members, said the runner, who had come to recruit Paiutes around Parowan. The news, of course, was of Monday's attack, but the reported killings and plea for reinforcements made the situation more serious. Dame told local Paiutes not to go but wanted more information about exactly what was happening at the Meadows.[4]

He called on one of his counselors, twenty-three-year-old Jesse N. Smith, to get answers. An express rider found Smith harvesting wheat on his farm at Paragonah, four-and-a-half miles north. Smith hurried to Parowan, where Dame told him to go "to Cedar City and ascertain the truth about the matter." Smith traveled with Edward Dalton, a Parowan man with a well-deserved reputation for moderation and good judgment.[5]

When the pair reached Cedar City on Tuesday, Haight waved them off. When they asked about the reported attack at Mountain Meadows, he told them, vaguely, that he too "had heard the same rumor" but offered nothing more.[6] In fact, Haight knew of the attack, and even the killing of Aden, but was unwilling to share this information with Dame's emissaries.[7] Haight also held back that he had just sent a group of men to the Meadows under Higbee's command, including Stewart, White, Klingensmith, high councilman Charles Hopkins, and former British army officer William Tait.[8]

Lee later said these men came to the Meadows "merely to see how things were."[9] Haight needed more details about the situation at Mountain Meadows, but the men he dispatched on Tuesday were on more than just a reconnaissance mission. From what Stewart and White must have told him when they reached Cedar the night before, Haight knew that at least a few emigrant men were outside the besieged corral. Unless something was done to stop them, they might spread word of the attack to other California-bound companies.

Some fourteen miles west of Cedar, Higbee's westbound group met Joseph Clewes, the courier Haight had sent to the Meadows the day before. After delivering Haight's message to Amos Thornton, Clewes had spent the night at Hamblin's ranch and started for home Tuesday morning. When they met, however, Higbee ordered Clewes to turn around and go with him; he might need the courier. "I had to obey," Clewes said. "There was no other alternative." It would be the great regret of his life.[10]

Higbee and his party continued west along Leach's Cutoff toward the Meadows. After nightfall in the cedars near Leach's Spring, some—if not all—of the men dispatched that day from Cedar City "met two other men coming from the emigrant camp and going to Cedar to obtain help," Ellott Willden later learned. Thinking the Cedar men would be their saviors, the two emigrants excitedly told them that Indians had surrounded their "camp on the previous Monday, that the camp was still surrounded by the savages, and that they had been sent to obtain help from the settlements." In response to the plea for aid, some of the Cedar men "immediately commenced firing," killing the two emigrants. Willden said Klingensmith was one of the killers. The Cedar City men then went on to Hamblin's ranch to spend the night.[11]

If Clewes witnessed the killings, they must have left him badly shaken. When he delivered Haight's message to Pinto the day before, he had "felt relieved," believing it would put an end to the violence.[12] He could not have been more wrong.

Besides sending Higbee's group west on Tuesday, Haight sent out at least one other man. Isaac Riddle was an Indian missionary who lived in Pine Valley, where a few emigrants had gone to make pine tar before Monday's attack. Riddle was at the Cedar City mill on Tuesday "to get a grist of flour." As he later put it, Haight approached him and said "that there was a fuss in the country" where Riddle lived and that he should go home and attend to his "affairs." Riddle left his wagon, wife, and grist in Cedar and "shucked out for home." He overtook Higbee and the others on the trail, and rode with them as far as Pinto before turning south toward Pine Valley.[13] The record is silent on what Riddle's "affairs" were—and what part Higbee's men may have played—but nothing more was ever heard of the pine tar gatherers.[14]

Hours before Riddle and Higbee's men left Cedar City, more violence had erupted at the besieged emigrant camp four miles south of Hamblin's. As Lee and the Washington men traveled north from their camp in Santa Clara canyon to the Meadows on Tuesday morning, they "met a small band of Indians returning with some eighteen or twenty head of cattle." The Paiutes were upset. One had been shot in the shoulder and appeared to have broken ribs. "He had no shirt on" and was "bleading very bad," reported William Young.[15]

Arriving at the Meadows, Lee said he "found about two hundred Indians…in a high state of excitement," including the "two wounded chiefs, Moqueetus and Bill," from Cedar City. The Paiutes, their numbers strengthened Monday night by Indian reinforcements from the south, had "attacked the emigrants again, about sunrise…Tuesday, and had one of their number killed and several wounded."[16] One Paiute leader from the Santa Clara—Jackson—said "that a brother of his was killed by a shot from the corral at a distance of two hundred yards, as he was running across the meadow."[17] Things were not going as Lee had promised when he lured the Paiutes to the Meadows and, not surprisingly, they were upset.[18]

The Paiutes had killed dozens of cattle and wanted to kill more, either out of anger or just to collect their promised reward. Lee, Carl Shirts, and Indian missionary Oscar Hamblin "succeeded in getting the Indians to desist from killing any more stock that night."[19] Lee had his own designs on the emigrants' livestock and would eventually get control over most of the herd as farmer to the Indians.[20]

One of Lee's sons later said that his father "traded the Indians out of some very fine work horses which the Indians did not prefer because of their weight, and an excellent race horse."[21] The racehorse may have been Tillman Cameron's "One-Eye Blaze."[22] Interpreter Nephi Johnson gave a slightly different story. During the week of the massacre, some Paiutes told Johnson that Lee had promised them "all the horses, and now Lee had sent some of the best to Harmony, and they were going to kill Lee if he did not return them."[23]

That was not all that bothered the Paiutes. After Tuesday morning's attack Lee received Haight's message via Thornton "to keep the Indians off the emigrants and protect them from harm until further orders."[24] Following Haight's direction, Lee at first reversed his earlier course and with his companions from the south told the Paiutes to hold off on further attacks. But the white men's vacillation may have seemed nonsensical—if not two-faced—to the Paiutes, and "the attack was renewed that night by the Indians, in spite of all we could do to prevent it," Lee said.[25]

In an account that seemed to borrow from his close call on Monday, Lee later claimed he was miraculously spared again as he and two other white men ran toward the Indians to stop Tuesday night's attack. "The bullets came around us like a shower of hail," Lee said. While others "threw themselves flat on the ground to protect themselves from the bullets I stood erect and asked my Father in Heaven to protect me from the missiles of death and enable me to reach the Indians. One ball passed through my hat and the hair of my head, and another through my shirt, grazing my arm near the shoulder.... The cries and shrieks of the women and children so overcame me that I forgot my danger and rushed through the fire to the Indians."[26] That was Lee's later version of events.

The Indians saw it differently. Paiutes told Nephi Johnson about "three different attacks, in the third of which"—on Tuesday evening—"Lee led the attack in person, and received one bullet through his hat, and one on each side of his body through his shirt, but his skin was not broke."[27] In one of the earliest records of the massacre, Paiutes reported that Lee "prevailed on them to attack the emigrants," which they did, being "repulsed on three different occasions."[28] Lee's earliest accounts align more closely with the Paiute version. Just days after the massacre, Lee said he was forced to lead Tuesday night's attack "to save his life," because the Paiutes "was very mad" at him "for getting them into the scrape" and "wanted him to help to use up that company."[29] The Paiutes said "they was not going to do the dirty work alone," reminding him that "he had taken them there."[30]

Whatever the case, Lee said he broke down in tears and begged the Paiutes to desist, evoking their contempt.[31] That, Lee claimed, was the origin of his Paiute nickname "Yauguts," or "crying man," which he would never lose. Tears flowed freely for him throughout his life—both before and after the massacre.[32]

Some of the Santa Clara Paiutes threatened to kill Lee and his companions, calling Lee "a squaw" who "did not have the heart of a brave." According to Lee's account, Jacob Hamblin's brother stepped in to rescue him. "I owe my life on that occasion to Oscar Hamblin, who was a missionary with the Indians....Hamblin shamed them and called them dogs and wolves for wanting to shed the blood of their father (myself), who had fed and clothed them."[33] James Mangum, an interpreter from Washington, said it was Lee's adopted Paiute son, Lemuel, who saved them. "Had it not been for an Indian boy that John D. Lee raised, the Indians would have killed John D. Lee, Oscar Hamblin and myself," he said.[34] Whatever Lemuel said to spare the men's lives apparently cost him his trust with those Paiutes. The next day an Indian runner would plead with Nephi Johnson to come interpret for them at the Meadows because "they were tired of Lees Indian Boy Interpeter [as] He Lied to Them so Much."[35]

According to Lee, he and the interpreters were finally able to convince the Paiutes at the Meadows "to suspend hostilities" on Tuesday evening and return to their camp, promising they "would hold a council" and "send for big Captains to come and talk." They said Dame and Haight might come and "give them part of the cattle and let the company go." They told the Paiutes "they had punished the emigrants enough, and may be they had killed nearly all of them."[36]

The Tuesday night incident gave Lee the excuse he would use the rest of his life. Denying he participated in the first attack on Monday, Lee would claim he did not arrive at the Meadows until Tuesday, when he did everything in his power to save the emigrants from angry Indians. It was a self-serving story built on half-truths and a persistent effort to make the Paiutes responsible for what Lee and the Cedar City leaders started.

Before anyone from Higbee's party reached them, Lee and the men at the south end of the Meadows "held a council and decided to send a messenger to Haight." Lee later claimed a tenderhearted reluctance. "Tell Haight, for my sake, for the people's sake, for God's sake, send me help to protect and save these emigrants, and pacify the Indians." The message, without its later varnish, recommended the offensive be called off for good and asked for "further instructions." The courier was probably George Adair, whose regular work included carrying mail between Washington and Parowan.[37]

When the massacre was over, firebrands like Lee said they tried to stop things, and at this point it appears Lee really did.[38] But crime has its own momentum. Once begun, its perpetrators find it hard to draw back, if only to hide what has already taken place.

At noon on Wednesday, with nothing to do but await Haight's decision, Lee slipped across the valley toward the ridge northwest of the corral to reconnoiter. On his way, he said, "the company recognized me as a white man and sent two little boys about 4 years old to meet me." Lee quickly hid himself and the boys turned back, but the emigrants persisted in their attempts at communication, hoisting "a *white flag* in the middle of their corral."[39]

From the ridge, Lee could easily see the emigrants' chained wagons and the pit they had dug inside. "The only show for the Indians was to starve them out, or shoot them as they went for water," he later said, as though the Paiutes were solely responsible for what was happening.[40] The best the emigrants could do was to wait for someone to rescue them—or for their attackers to grow weary and leave. Trapped inside their wagon fort, the survivors had little or no kindling for cooking, no fresh water, and no milk for the children. A rumor later reached Cedar City that when one emigrant woman slipped from the fort to milk a cow, a sharpshooter killed her.[41] Though the concerted attacks had stopped, fitful "shooting between the emigrants and Indians was continually going on."[42]

From his hidden perch northwest of the corral, Lee may have noticed a commotion east of him on the low-lying hill that concealed the Indian camp. Paiutes were crowded "pretty thick" around two white men, "pull[ing] and push[ing]" them to the top of the ridge. The two were Ellott Willden and Joseph Clewes.[43]

Wednesday morning at Hamblin's ranch, Higbee had sent the two brothers-in-law to the south end of the Meadows "to find out how the Indians were acting and how many there were." Obediently, Willden and Clewes found the Indian camp, which was concealed between "two low ridges" northeast of the emigrant corral. They saw Paiutes "lying around on every side," wounded among them. The Indians were still upset with Lee. They had not seen him all day and resented that he "had left them with their dead and wounded," Willden said.[44]

At one point—perhaps after getting bullet holes in his clothing—Lee had told the Paiutes "that the bullets of the emigrants would not hurt the 'Mormons' the same as the Indians." Seeing Willden and Clewes, the Paiutes decided to test Lee's claim. They "demanded that Willden and Clewes should put on Indian attire and run unarmed past the emigrant camp within easy range of their rifles, to a neighboring point about a hundred yards distant." It may have been the same route Jackson's brother took when he was shot. The two white men concluded they would have to "take their chances" in doing what the Indians demanded "or risk being killed by them. So they ran, amid a shower of bullets from the emigrant camp and reached the opposite point in safety." The men then returned to the Paiute camp, where they "were heartily cheered for their bravery after their perilous run."[45] Soon, said Clewes, "we were hailed from a ridge on our left; we looked around and there stood John D. Lee."[46]

Lee told the Indians to return to their camp—"pacif[ying] their feelings by making explanations to them"—then sat down to talk with Clewes and Willden. "Willden asked Lee if he had received the express taken out by Clewes and Thornton," the one in which Haight told Lee to back off. Lee said he had, but that "it was too late, the break on the Indian camp having already been made." Willden chided Lee for angering the Paiutes, nearly costing him and Clewes their lives as they were forced to run through emigrant gunfire. Lee told the young men they "were getting some valuable experience, and besides it was no worse for them than for him." He then showed them the bullet holes in his clothing.[47]

After their talk, Lee "went over the ridge," and Willden and Clewes met up again with Higbee and his men.[48] Higbee looked the situation over and later used it to advantage in trying to blame the massacre on Paiutes. Higbee's account bristled with danger. It was "bedlam or hell," he said of what he found Wednesday at the Meadows. Dead horses and cattle were scattered about, a scene from the "Infernal regions," as "deamon like as Could be imagined." Higbee inflated the number of

Indians to between three and six hundred, calling them "blood thirsty and crazy" savages "determined…to accomplish the destruction of the Company if they had to fight all the Mormons in the Southern Country." The Paiutes were in war paint, he recalled, as were a couple of unnamed white men in disguise—Willden and Clewes. "Lee was trying to Pasify [the Indians] and have them Scatter and go away and let the Emigrants go," Higbee wrote.[49]

Although Higbee exaggerated the pandemonium at the Meadows, there was debate in the Mormon ranks about what to do. Young James Pearce from Washington remembered the emotions. Some of the leaders "talked as though they [the emigrants] must be put out of the way," Pearce later testified. Others said "it never would do."[50]

The leaders from Cedar City on the field met to decide "what Should be done," and their decision was far-reaching. The Haight-Lee plan had been designed to be an Indian and not formally a militia affair. Now, "after a good deal of deliberation," the Cedar men agreed that calling out the militia under Col. Dame's orders to assist was the only way to end the standoff quickly. Higbee, Klingensmith, and Hopkins returned to Cedar City to report to Haight.[51]

Now there was nothing for the men who remained at the Meadows to do but wait. Some of them spoke of the humdrum routine, seemingly oblivious to the suffering of the corralled emigrants. The Mormon settlers and Indians "were engaged in broiling beef and making their hides up into lassoes," Lee recalled. Other men shot at targets. Joel White said he slept and lounged after his arrival. Pearce described a diet heavy in meat that led White and some others to Hamblin's ranch for buttermilk and salt.[52] Three Cedar City men killed time pitching quoits near Hamblin's house.[53]

With the lull, some Paiutes took their spoil of cattle and left, though many remained. Pearce remembered Indians "pow-wowing around," mixing with the whites.[54] White recalled a "good many Indians" milling around the Mormon wagons and resting in the brush and shade. He thought "they were friendly."[55] Like the Mormon settlers, many of the Paiutes were reluctant to get too close to the wagon fort. "The emigrants had long guns and were good shots," they said.[56] At night, the valley was quiet, except for "the Indians whooping and yelling—maybe hollering around," racket perhaps aimed at keeping the emigrants on edge. "Nothing more than that," White said.[57]

Higbee arrived at Cedar City by Wednesday evening and consulted with Haight. The situation had become more tangled than anyone imagined at the outset. People had been murdered and survivors would talk. The emigrants had seen Lee and recognized him as a white man in spite of any disguise he might have worn. Even if they hadn't, the man who witnessed Aden's murder and returned to the wagon corral "of course would give the alarm in camp."[58] If the emigrants were allowed to go on to California, Cedar City residents would pay a price. And where would it stop? With anti-Mormon feeling already running strong in the country and an army marching on the territory, the lives of the entire community might be at risk.

The Cedar City leaders believed they had to do something to bring events to a conclusion—fast.[59] It was emigration season, and they knew more travelers on the California road were bound to reach southern Utah and the Mountain Meadows soon. They had also been told that U.S. soldiers might enter the region at any moment. James Haslam was expected to return eventually with Brigham Young's response, but could the matter wait that long? And although Haight had convinced himself he was acting in behalf of the Saints, what if Young disagreed?

Events were coming to a head, and the conspirators saw just two chilling options. They could lift the siege and let the emigrants carry word of the attack to California, which they feared would unleash aggression on the southern Mormon settlements. Or they could leave no emigrants alive who were old enough to "tell tales."[60] The Paiutes could not kill the remaining emigrants on their own, and the militia could not be ordered to commit such an act without the consent of their commanding officer, Dame.

Late Wednesday evening Haight left for Parowan in a light wagon, taking his counselor Elias Morris with him. "His face and countenance indicated that something weighed heavily on his mind, and he desired to go and talk with Col. Dame, his superior in military command," Morris later said circumspectly.[61] In truth Morris knew what was going on. The two men had to get Dame to give the order that would bring the Mountain Meadows matter to what they thought was its inexorable conclusion.

Haight must have also been worrying about Smith and Dalton, the men Dame sent to investigate the Indian report of an attack at the Meadows. Unable to get the information they needed from Haight in Cedar on Tuesday, the two men had gone to Pinto, where they learned that the "emigrants were undoubtedly attacked." Smith said he and Dalton were advised to go no farther because Mountain Meadows "was filled with Indians." The two men returned to Cedar City on Wednesday and, after resting from their hard riding, took off for home.[62] By the time Haight and Morris reached Parowan, Dame would know that Cedar City leaders had blatantly disobeyed his directive to let the emigrants pass unharmed.

But Smith and Dalton's report was not Dame's only headache on Wednesday. Dame had been busy that day trying to calm another emigrant crisis. According to Turner company member Peyton Welch, the Pahvants were upset when his group of emigrants reached Corn Creek several days before. Perhaps the "poisoning" was beginning to take its toll in the area: anthrax spores would have had enough time by then to start doing damage. Or perhaps members of Turner's company were responsible, after all, for reported insults and threats in the Fillmore area, and Fillmore bishop Lewis Brunson had made good on his promise "to set the Indians" on them. If so, like Haight at Cedar, Brunson may have taken advantage of what he saw as Young's new Indian policy. At stake were the safety of "twenty-three wagons, 450 head of loose cattle, and 107 men, women and children."[63]

Tuesday evening, Philo T. Farnsworth, Beaver's bishop and militia captain, learned from a local Indian that Pahvants were preparing to attack the Turner company near Beaver. Farnsworth sprang into action, first visiting Dukes's party, which had pushed ahead to a camp just below Beaver earlier in the day, leaving Turner about six miles back at Indian Creek.[64]

Farnsworth urged Dukes to turn back to help protect Turner's group, but he refused. Members of his company "were so demoralized he could do nothing with them," he said.[65] Farnsworth offered to detach some of his own men to rescue the Turner company if Dukes would do likewise, and Dukes finally agreed. By the time the combined rescue party got to Indian Creek, Pahvants had tried to run off the emigrants' cattle, and Turner's men had shot an Indian.[66]

As the rescuers escorted Turner's group south to the Dukes camp, the Pahvants kept firing on the company's cattle—they could then use the abandoned carcasses for food.[67] Turner's men wanted to return fire, but the Mormon rescuers stopped them, positioning themselves between the two groups. "From this," one of the emigrants complained, "we became more apprehensive of the [Mormons] than of the Indians."[68] Their position in the middle epitomized the Mormons' dilemma. In rescuing Turner and his men, they pleased neither the distrustful emigrants nor the Pahvants whose friendship they needed in the coming war. Young's new Indian policy had warned about avoiding just such a situation.

Soon the Turner company was camped with the Dukes party just outside of Beaver, but the fighting was not over—and the Mormons at Beaver remained in the middle. When emigrant leaders Turner, Dukes, and Wilson Collins visited the town Wednesday morning, an Indian named Sissix shot Turner, hitting him "just above the hip."[69] Collins ran for the safety of the blacksmith shop, only to be pushed back into the open by an occupant who either had no sympathy for the outsider or felt threatened by the sudden intrusion. Collins then sustained a serious gunshot wound to the arm, while Dukes, also in the open, was "grazed by two or three bullets."[70] Farnsworth, who was eating breakfast when the shooting began, ran out into the street between the emigrants and the Indians, telling Sissix to get out of town.[71]

Farnsworth quickly sent word of the attack to Col. Dame at Parowan, thirty-five miles south, and Turner, Dukes, and Collins returned to their combined train. Soon they had "corralled their wagons and made rifle pits and were in self defense," their cattle scattered on the plains— a scene eerily similar to the one at the Meadows.[72]

Farnsworth's express reached Parowan as Dame was meeting with Mormon freighters Sidney Tanner and William Mathews. Traveling with them since Beaver was George Powers's three-wagon company. Powers had been traveling with the Dukes party but was hopping wagon trains, hoping to catch up with his fellow Arkansans in the Fancher company.[73]

The Tanner-Mathews train had already passed through Parowan, but Dame had sent an express after it, requesting the train "not...proceed any further that day" and that Tanner, Mathews, and Powers come back and meet with him. When the three spoke with Dame in Parowan on Wednesday, the southern commander talked of the Tuesday morning message about an Indian attack at the Meadows and advised Powers to return to the Dukes company further north. Though he made no mention of it, Dame had sent Smith and Dalton to investigate what was going on at the Meadows, and if Mormons were involved in the attack, he didn't want any California-bound outsiders stumbling into the situation.[74]

"I asked him" said Powers of Dame, "if he could not raise a company, and go out and relieve the besieged train. He replied, that he could go out and take them away in safety, but he dared not, he dared not disobey counsel.[75] Dame was unwilling to oppose the Monday night decision of the Parowan council, which had voted to help the emigrants "should they call for assistance." Otherwise, given the "threats and insults the company had offered to the Saints," they would simply "let them fight it out with the Indians as best they could."[76]

Before Tanner, Mathews, Powers, and Dame could finish their conversation, Farnsworth's express came in, requesting help and "stating that the Indians had attacked my train in the streets of that place," said Powers. Dame hastily convened another council of leaders to discuss this latest crisis. The council did not change its policy on the situation at the Meadows—Smith and Dalton had not yet returned from their fact-finding mission. But it responded to Farnsworth's express by sending ten militiamen north "to assist in the protection of the emigrants and settlers in Beaver from the hostility of the Indians." They arrived at Beaver "very late in the night."[77]

The crisis at Beaver was soon peacefully resolved. The influential Ute leader Ammon, who attended the important Indian meeting in Brigham Young's office on September 1, had returned to the area late Wednesday afternoon. Ammon told the Pahvants "they must not touch another man." He and Farnsworth went together to the emigrants' corral and "assured them they should not be molested."[78]

Ammon's good offices came at a price. He wanted the emigrants to give up "six head of cattle" and a horse they had received in trade with the Indians. The emigrants complied.[79] Ammon was well positioned to work a deal. He had influence not only with his camp at Beaver but also with the Pahvants. He "had great control over the Indians," said Farnsworth.[80]

After the council meeting at Parowan, Dame met again with Powers, Tanner, and Mathews and reversed his earlier advice that Powers return to the Dukes company. Because of the attack on Powers's former train, he could continue on with Tanner and Mathews—but only under certain conditions. When "passing through the Indian country," Powers reported, "it might be necessary for me to be laid flat in the wagon and covered with blankets, for two or three days, as the Indians were deadly hostile to all Americans." Powers agreed to the terms.[81]

Late Wednesday, Smith and Dalton reached Parowan, where they "expressed much disgust over what they had seen and learned, as John D. Lee and other white men were assuming a very hostile attitude toward the emigrants in connection with the Indians." In addition, Smith and Dalton probably reported Haight's stonewalling. The Pinto missionaries would have told them of the couriers coming and going from Cedar City.[82]

Dame finally retired to his home on Wednesday night, but his long day was not over. Just before midnight, Haight and Morris knocked on his door. For the second time in several hours, Dame convened a council. Calvin Pendleton and Jesse Smith, Dame's two counselors, were present, as were Parowan resident William Barton and other "leading men in the settlement."[83]

"The subject discussed," read Morris's carefully phrased account, "was concerning the Arkansas company, who had been attacked by Indians at Mountain Meadows"—nothing about the role of Haight and Lee, which must have been the quiet subtext for everything said. Morris's words hardly hinted at the crosscurrents present.[84] The meeting was the first between Haight and Dame since the crisis began, and everything smacked of insubordination. If the point needed to be made, Smith, just back from Pinto, was in the room and could make it.

Although the Monday night Parowan council had decided to let the emigrants handle the Indian troubles on their own, based on what its members had since learned, the council now reversed its decision. "A propos[i]tion made by Pendleton was adopted," said Barton, "to the effect, that a company should be sent out from Parowan...to call the Indians off, gather up the stock for the company, and let them continue their journey in peace."[85]

Haight later admitted to Barton, "I would give a world if I had it, if we had abided by the deci[s]ion of the council." Instead, Haight asked Dame for a private session immediately after the meeting. If he could get the district commander on his own, away from his council, Haight knew Dame might relent. The two men, along with Morris, walked to a pile of tanning bark lying near Dame's barn by Parowan's east gate. Barton, who attended the just-ended council, watched from a distance. He could not hear the words, but he later learned their significance. It was "right there and then" that the "whole programme and plan was changed," Barton said.[86]

What would become known as the "tan bark council" lasted about half an hour. While Dame and Haight later argued bitterly about what was agreed upon, the gist of their talk was more certain. Haight probably shared with Dame details he was unwilling to mention at the earlier council: the emigrants' recognition of Lee as a white man, the wounded man making it into the corral after witnessing Stewart's murder of Aden, perhaps even the killing of the two emigrant messengers who asked for help. Mostly the conversation was about covering up the white men's role in the killing in order to protect their people from what they feared would be harsh retribution. Haight also implied that most of the fighting was over, sharing Lee's assertion that the Indians had killed nearly all the emigrants.[87]

Dame must have shared some new information of his own. The Missouri company—Turner, Dukes, and Collins—was at Beaver and would soon be heading south. Sidney Tanner and William Mathews's freighters, traveling with Powers's small train of outsiders, were even nearer the Meadows, waiting at Summit south of Parowan. How long would it be before any of these California-bound parties reached the Meadows and discovered the truth?[88]

"It seemed to become necessary to kill all [the Arkansas emigrants] to silence the rest," Ellott Willden summed it up. "Hence the tan Bark Council and other councils."[89] In a rare account of his meeting with Haight, Dame later told Jacob Hamblin that the final decision was about consequences. "L[ee] & the Indians had commenced it and it had to be done," he said. "For if it should come to the ears of President Bucanann, it would endanger the lives of the Bretheren."[90] When their talk ended early Thursday morning, Haight, anxious for a resolution, took what he wanted from the discussion. Whether he really believed it or was just protecting himself, he told his stepson, Daniel Macfarlane, that Dame gave him "the final order to destroy the entire company."[91]

Later on Thursday, Dame left for Beaver to see if the problems there were resolved, only to learn along the way that the Missouri company crisis had been settled. Because of Ammon's and Farnsworth's mediation and the arrival of the Parowan militia, the emigrants at Beaver were out of immediate danger and ready to move on.[92] "Had J. D. Lee taken this course," Farnsworth later wrote, laying the blame to only one conspirator, "the Mountain Meadows Massacre would never have been."[93]

Haight, meanwhile, reached Cedar City early Thursday morning feeling he had authority to call out the militia and move ahead with the killing, not waiting for Haslam to return with Young's reply.[94] He would make the most of his agreement with Dame. "Returning to Cedar City Haight called the brethren of that place together," said Macfarlane.[95]

Several of the men who mustered at Cedar later claimed they were called to the Meadows to "burry the dead." They did "not know that they must first make the dead," Haight said privately.[96] Yet only a fraction of the men took shovels or spades with them, and most took guns.[97] When private John Bradshaw, a thirty-eight-year-old English brick maker, showed up at the mustering grounds with just a spade, Haight wanted to know why he was not carrying a gun. Where was his ammunition? "I told him I didn't know that it required a gun to bury dead people," Bradshaw replied. "He…called me a fool; told me I didn't know anything about it, didn't understand things." Haight dismissed Bradshaw, sending him home.[98]

Many of the men who went to the Meadows were militia officers or had attended Sunday's council in which the emigrants' destruction was proposed. Most likely these men saw the euphemisms and untruths for what they were and only later claimed to be unaware of their true meaning. In crime, the first casualty is often truth.

Nephi Johnson certainly knew what was going on. Haight still needed Johnson and his Paiute language skills. After Haight sent Johnson home on Monday, the young interpreter hoped to avoid getting involved. When an Indian came asking for his help interpreting at the Meadows on Wednesday, Johnson refused. "I Did Not Want Anything to Do with killing the Emigrants," he said, "for I was Determined in my Own Mind that I would Keep Away from them." But on Thursday Haight gave him no choice. Two express riders arrived at Johnson's home with written orders, telling him Haight required him to go to Cedar City whether he "wanted to or Not."[99]

During Johnson's second meeting with Haight, he was told the recent details. Haight said Lee had gone to the Meadows to kill the emigrants. There had been three attacks, but "the emigrants were better fighters than…expected," and some Indians had been killed or wounded. Haight said "the indians were getting tired of the job" and threatened Lee, and "Lee had suggested letting the emigrants go." Now Haight wanted the situation to come to an end. Haight told Johnson that he "had sent word for [Lee] to finish his dirty job, as he had started it." Johnson was to help him. He wanted the Indian interpreter to go to the Meadows with the militia to help end the siege.[100] Both men understood what that meant.

The situation in which Johnson found himself became a common theme after the massacre. One man after another said he had gone to the Meadows because of military orders—they had been coerced. For some it was probably true; but it was also true that many men did not go, giving rise to a healthy store of folklore—proud families telling stories of how their ancestors refused to participate in the crime. "Old Joseph Walker…when told to go to the Meadows, put his fist in Haights face and told him to go to hell and do his own dirty work," said one account.[101] Another man claimed that his stepbrothers "hid in the furrows of a potato patch until the Cedar party went on."[102] Peter Nelson reportedly concealed himself in a bin of grain and escaped the soldiers' detection by breathing through a straw.[103] Yet another man supposedly dodged service by claiming to be ill, first lying in a pile of hot bricks to simulate a fever.[104] Legend had it that the men who refused to go felt that the emigrants "had gone on"—they were old history—"and that their threats about returning with an armed force was all wind."[105] While there may have been some conscientious objectors, the operation did not require most of the militia to go. All told, less than one-fifth of Cedar City's militiamen went to the Meadows.[106]

The men mustered out on Thursday left for their grim task at the Meadows around midday, led by Major Higbee.[107] At 2:00 that afternoon, leaders of the Cedar City Female Benevolent Society held their regular meeting. "Sister Haight" reported she had been visiting some of the Cedar women and "taught them the necessity of being obedient to their husbands" and not to be fearful in these "troublesome" and "squally times." "We ought to attend to secret prayer in behalf of our husbands, sons, fathers, & brothers," she said. She instructed the women to teach their children "the principles of righteousness, and to implant a desire in their hearts to avenge the blood of the Prophets." Additionally, "Sister Hopkins" and "Sister White," whose husbands had gone to the Meadows on Tuesday, said they had advised the women they visited "to attend strictly to secret prayer in behalf of the brethren that are out acting in our defence."[108]

As THE WOMEN HELD THEIR MEETING and the militiamen set their sights on the Meadows, James Haslam was barreling south through the Salt Lake Valley, carrying Brigham Young's response to Haight. The last three days since he left Cedar City had been grueling. After passing north through Beaver on Monday night, Haslam faced delay in Fillmore. Bishop Brunson was off hunting, and Haslam had to wait hours for him to return, only to receive a horse that did not make it far. Returning to Fillmore for a better horse, Haslam pushed on to Payson and the home of Charles Hancock, the local bishop. Could he sleep on the porch? Haslam asked. "I made a bed for him and he fell asleep quick," Hancock remembered. A short hour later, Hancock got some cold water to wake and brace him, and after downing coffee and "vituals," the express rider was once again on his way. Hancock had a fresh horse saddled and waiting by the gate.[109]

At Provo and American Fork, Haslam again found fresh mounts. Traveling through the night, the exhausted rider finally arrived in Salt Lake City about noon on Thursday. He had ridden hard but calculated that a third of his sixty-hour trip had been spent getting horses.[110] Despite the letter he carried from Dame asking bishops and militia commanders to furnish him horses, some were not eager to lend their best animals to a hard-riding expressman.[111]

In Salt Lake City, Haslam turned left off the upward slope of State Road onto South Temple Street, stopping at the Lion House, one of Brigham Young's homes.[112] Soon Haslam was ushered into an office where Young and a dozen other church leaders were meeting with Jacob Hamblin, who had been asked to instruct them on how Indians stored food. The subject was important. The Mormons were still thinking of fleeing to the mountains, where they would cache provisions for their survival if the army got through.[113]

While they were still preparing for the worst, their fears had been somewhat assuaged two days before by the arrival of Capt. Stewart Van Vliet—the first representative from the U.S. government to explain the army's intentions. Although Mormon leaders remained wary, Van Vliet had assured them the army meant no harm to the Saints, that Gen. Harney had been retained for duties in Kansas, and that the troops were not likely to reach Utah settlements before winter.[114]

Hamblin gave the fullest account of what happened when Haslam entered Thursday's meeting, important because the text of Haight's incoming express did not survive. "While in S. L. City an express came from Iron Co, asking what should be done with a certain Company of Emigrants, that had behaved verry mean while passing through the differant Towns," Hamblin said. "The spirit of the Express rather asked the privilege to chastize them....President Young answered them rather haistily, saying No, when I want Marshal Law proclaimed, I will let you know."[115]

Young's comment suggested that Haight proposed using the militia against the emigrants—just as he had proposed earlier to Dame. Martial law—often proclaimed by governments in times of war—would have allowed the militia to take the law into its own hands in an emergency. Young had been considering a martial law proclamation for some time but would not issue it until September 15, after discussions with Van Vliet convinced him that army leaders were intent on reaching Utah regardless of how its citizens felt.[116]

Young asked Haslam, who had spent most of the last sixty hours in the saddle, if he "could stand the trip back" to Cedar City. When Haslam replied that he could, Young told him to get a little sleep and be back in the office in an hour for his written reply.[117]

Copies of Young's letter would survive both in rough and final draft form, the latter preserved in sequential order in Young's bound letterpress copybooks—clear evidence the letter was a contemporary document. The express, addressed to Haight and dated September 10, began with news that was apparently intended to relieve Haight's fear of imminent attack:[118]

> Dear Brother,
>
> Your note of the 7th inst is to hand. Capt Van Vliet acting Commissary is here having come in advance of the army to procure necessaries for them, We do not expect that any part of the army will be able to reach here this fall. There is only about 850 men coming, they are now at or near Laramie. A few of the freight trains are this side of that place, the advance of which are now on Green River. They will not be able to come much if any farther on account of their poor stock. They cannot get here this season without we help them, so you see that the Lord has answered our prayers and again averted the blow designed for our heads.[119]

The letter's next two sentences addressed Young's concerns about fairness in times of conflict. Although determined to resist the approaching army, Young had pondered deeply the morality of war. "[If] I have to fight," he wrote in his journal three weeks earlier, "I wish to give my enemies fair warning, and then if the[y] will not take it they must abide the consequences." His concern was not just earthly ethics. "I wish to meet *all men* at the judgment Bar of God without any to fear me or accuse me of a wrong action," he wrote.[120] Now he gave similar advice to Haight:

In regard to emigration trains passing through our settlements we must not interfere with them untill they are first notified to keep away. You must not meddle with them.[121]

Haight's letter said the emigrants had gotten into a scrape with Indians, and Young had emphasized the importance of not alienating native tribes since their help was wanted to resist the army. His instruction to Haight reflected his new policy of letting Indians and emigrants resolve their own problems without Mormon interference:

BRIGHAM YOUNG LETTER TO ISAAC C. HAIGHT, SEPTEMBER 10, 1857. *Courtesy LDS Church History Library.*

The Indians we expect will do as they please but you should try and preserve good feelings with them.[122]

With Hamblin nearby to advise him, Young must have known the Paiutes posed little threat on their own to the well-armed wagon company. At Corn Creek, when the emigrants asked Hamblin's opinion, he had told them they could handle the Indians with half the number of men in their party.[123]

828

be on the alert on hand and always ready we should also possess ourselves in patience, preserving ourselves and property, ever remembering that God rules. He has overruled for our deliverance this once again and he will always do so if we live our religion, be united in our faith and good works. All is well with us. May the Lord bless you and all saints forever

I remain as ever your Brother in the Gospel of Christ.

Brigham Young

Young concluded his letter by preaching to Haight the need for peace, patience, and reliance on God:

> There are no other trains going south that I know of if those who are there will leave let them go in peace. While we should be on the alert, on hand and always ready we should also possess ourselves in patience, preserving ourselves and property ever remembering that God rules. He has overruled for our deliverance this once again and he will always do so if we live our religion, be united in our faith and good works. All is well with us.
>
> May the Lord bless you and all saints forever.
>
> I remain as ever your Brother in the Gospel of Christ.[124]

When Haslam returned to the office after his brief rest, the letter was ready for him. Young wanted the message to reach Cedar City as soon as possible. He walked the rider to the hitching post near the outer gate and repeated his instruction several times as Haslam mounted his horse and adjusted the saddle girth. "Brother Haslam," Young instructed, "I want you to ride for dear life; ride day and night; spare no horse flesh."[125]

Haslam "shot off like an arrow down Theatre Hill and was soon out of sight."[126]

CHAPTER THIRTEEN

Decoyed Out and Destroyed

Mountain Meadows, September 10–11, 1857

Hours after nightfall on Thursday, the new detachments from Cedar City reached Hamblin's ranch house at the north end of the Meadows and set up camp. A few key men "found Lee and others, and found how matters stood."[1] Lee "and some of the principal chiefs of the Indians were gathered" at Hamblin's, awaiting word from Cedar.[2] Higbee relayed the orders, saying they had come from Haight and Dame. The emigrants were "to be decoyed out and destroyed with the exception of the small children" who were "too young to tell tales," Higbee said, "and if the Indians cannot do it without help, we must help them."[3]

Through interpreter Nephi Johnson, Lee suggested to the Paiute leaders "that he would try and get the emigrants out of their camp as well as giving up their arms after which they would kill them."[4] At first, Johnson hesitated to interpret the awful message. Lee "wanted me to talk to the Indians in a way I didn't want to," Johnson later recalled. Despite his initial reluctance, Johnson repeated the plan in Paiute, "and the Indians agreed to assist in killing the emigrants."[5]

Higbee, Lee, Klingensmith, and other militiamen then traveled south to the main Mormon camp, where they met with Ira Allen, Charles Hopkins, Robert Wiley, William Bateman, and a few other leaders. The men sat in a circle off by themselves and began by praying

MOUNTAIN MEADOWS

Map by Sheryl Dickert Smith and Tom Child; photo by Wally Barrus

for "Divine guidance," a sacrilege that only the passions of the time could explain.[6] Then the serious discussion began. When Higbee shared the orders he had brought, objections arose. Lee later claimed to be the one who raised them.[7]

Responding to the dissent, Higbee spoke of the killing of William Aden and his companion's escape to the emigrant camp. "White men have interposed and the emigrants know it," he said, "and there lies the danger in letting them go." Someone reasoned, "If we let them go,…they will raise hell in California, and the result will be that our wives and children will have to be butchered and ourselves too, and they are no better to die than ours."[8] No one knew for sure what would happen if they let the besieged emigrants go. But in the twisted rationalization that leads to mass killing, sometimes "murder becomes a service to humanity."[9]

Having reached a consensus, the men then discussed how to implement the orders. They "decided to send a man with a flag of truce and request that the emigrants send out a delagation to arrange terms upon which they would leave their camp." Once the emigrants had left the protection of their wagon fort and were strung out on the road, the militia and Indians would destroy them.[10]

The most common word used by the plotters to describe the plan was "decoy." But "deceive" and "double-cross" would have been better choices. The new plan carried the fewest risks for the militia, and the planners justified the treachery in a hollow defense of faith and hearth, a necessary cover-up of what already had taken place that week.[11]

The first traces of light filled the pleasant valley when the council put the matter to a vote. "Every man now had to show his colors," Lee said. "It was not safe to have a Judas in camp." Lee had every man in the council "express himself." Again no one dared go against the group. "All said they were willing to carry out the counsel of their leaders; that the leaders had the Spirit of God and knew better what was right than they did." Each passed the moral buck up the line.[12]

Although Lee said all the men in the meeting consented to the plan, their support probably ranged from fervent to begrudging.[13] Whatever their ardor, the men had deluded themselves into thinking they were justified in what they were about to do. When Lee told of these events in later years, he blamed others but credited them with good intentions. "They were enthusiastic," he said, "but their motives were pure."[14] Even on more frank occasions, when he spoke of his own role, Lee clung to his self-deception, insisting he did "nothing designedly wrong."[15]

After the council meeting, interpreters Nephi Johnson and Carl Shirts were sent down toward the Paiute camp "to inform the Indians of the plan of operations, and to place the Indians in ambush, so that they could not be seen by the emigrants." Lee had doubts about the interpreters. "So suspicious was Lee of me," said Johnson, "that he sent an Indian boy who could talk English"—probably Lemuel—"to see that I carried the right message."[16]

After breakfast at the white encampment, the militiamen were called together to receive instructions from their leaders.[17] Klingensmith said the men were organized into a "hollow square"—a common military formation of the day—with about fifty men facing inwards, a dozen or so on each side. Majors Lee and Higbee stood in the center.[18] Mountain Meadows was in Washington County—Lee's jurisdiction—but the two majors shared leadership on the field. Daniel Macfarlane served as adjutant, while Klingensmith, only a militia private, exercised informal leadership because he was Cedar City's bishop and because he supported strong action against the emigrants.[19]

In the excuse-making that followed the massacre, some participants crafted alibis that put them elsewhere at the time of the killing. Still enough accounts survived to assemble nearly a full roster of those present that day. Cedar City furnished roughly thirty of the militiamen, about a dozen came from Washington, and a few, including those working at Hamblin's ranch in September 1857, were from Santa Clara. Lee and Carl Shirts hailed from Harmony, and Nephi Johnson was called out from Fort Johnson. But none of the Indian missionaries from Pinto—the nearest settlement to the Meadows—were identified by anyone as joining in Friday's massacre. Nor had Dame sent out any of the Parowan militia.[20]

Although by law every state and territory in America had a militia, Utah had its own peculiar organization in 1857. The Iron Military District had four battalions—one in Parowan, two in Cedar City, and one headquartered in Harmony. Haight and Higbee were majors over the two Cedar City battalions, and Lee was battalion major at Harmony. Captains commanded the battalions' companies, which in turn were divided into platoons, each led by a second lieutenant and sergeant who oversaw at most eight privates. This organization, because of its top-heavy officer corps and small squads, was an "extreme alteration" of normal procedure "never known to the Army before," wrote one modern military specialist.[21]

The militiamen at the "hollow square" were mostly officers and represented only about 15 percent of the Iron Military District.[22] The low turnout suggests that Haight had difficulty finding men to go to the Mountain Meadows—or recruited only the men he needed.

When it came time to explain their acts, some of the militiamen excused themselves by saying they were acting under orders; others cited their youth and inexperience.[23] Three were teenagers: William Edwards was fifteen, James Pearce eighteen, and Columbus Freeman nineteen. A dozen or so were in their early twenties. More than two-thirds of them, however, were a mature twenty-five years or older. The average age was thirty-one. More than 80 percent of the men were married, and about a third of those married had entered polygamy. All told, this was a seasoned group of men.[24]

When the militia meeting began, Higbee and Lee gave the men detailed instructions. All the emigrants except the small children were to be killed. The emigrants would be lured from their camp by "a flag of truce." They would be told that "the Indians were determined on their destruction" and that the Mormons "dare not oppose the Indians, for we were at their mercy." Instead, if the emigrants would "trust them-selves in our hands," then "the best we could do for them" would be to place a few of their belongings—including their guns—in two wag-ons and escort the emigrants to the settlements. The wagons would also carry "the small children and wounded," and the emigrant women would "follow the wagons and the men next, the troops to stand in readiness on the east side of the road ready to receive them." When Higbee finally gave the signal "Halt," the militiamen were to kill the emigrant men and older boys, while the Indians were to "dispatch the women and larger children."[25] Higbee ordered most of the militiamen to put their horses out on the range. He wanted them walking next to their victims, ready to fire at close range.[26]

Until they heard the plan announced, some of the men remained uncertain how the scene would wind up. Some had gone to the Mead-ows without a clear understanding of what was taking place there, and speculation had continued in the ranks about just what they might be expected to do.[27] When the plan was finally explained, some were stunned. "A good many objected," Johnson said years later, "but they didn't dare to say anything."[28] Some of the men's later claims, of course, were posturing—attempts to convince others and even themselves that they were not responsible for what happened. Though "a good many" may have inwardly objected, Johnson conceded that "most of the men who took part in the killing, also considered them [the emigrants] as their common enemies, and under the excitement caused by the advent of the [approaching] Army they felt partly justified in distroying them."[29]

When the militia meeting dissolved and the men began to move off, Higbee saw Joseph Clewes. The unarmed courier stood "riveted to the ground," as perplexed and nervous as when Haight had called him into service on Monday afternoon. "Clewes, we have no further use for you here," Higbee barked. "Get on that mule and ride back to Haight, and tell him how things are up to this time; and," he added, shaking his finger, "not a word of this…to any one." Clewes left immediately, this time all too happy to obey.[30]

During the hollow square meeting, Johnson and Shirts had been at the Paiute encampment telling "the Indians what they were expected to do." The Paiutes were to hide in the sagebrush, scrub oak, and rocks on the north side of a low ridge that extended from the eastern foothills near the Mormon camp to a point just east of the California road. The ridge formed part of the Rim of the Basin, which divides waters that flow into the Pacific from those that remain in the Great Basin. From this location, more than a mile northeast of the emigrants' camp, Johnson and Shirts "were to rally the Indians, and rush upon and dispatch the women and larger children."[31]

The role assigned to the Paiutes was a feeble attempt on the militia leaders' part to salve their own consciences. Though reconciled to killing the emigrant men, they wanted to limit the number of women and children they would have to kill themselves—as if planning and directing the crime were not enough.[32] After placing the Indians in ambush, Johnson turned his horse east and rode up the ridge, from where he "could see it all."[33] For the next sixty years, his role in the plot would rack him. Memories of the massacre would haunt him in the delirium of his deathbed.[34]

In the highly democratic culture of the Paiutes, each man decided for himself whether to participate.[35] Since the attack on Monday morning, the number of Paiutes at the Meadows had fluctuated as some came and went. How many Paiutes participated in Friday's massacre would become a highly disputed matter. Some Paiutes later said that none of their people participated in the killings. If they were present, they merely watched from the surrounding hills. Others acknowledged Paiute participation but portrayed it as minimal. Understandably, none relished the odium that white leaders from the beginning had planned to fix on them.[36] One contemporary Paiute who knew massacre participants concluded, "All the Indians there were not more than one hundred."[37]

The white participants, not surprisingly, described the Paiute participants as plentiful. Higbee's accounts put the number as high as six hundred, while Joel White put it as low as forty with perhaps "a good many more."[38] Nephi Johnson said that on the day of the massacre, "There were about 150 Indians present."[39] On "Thursday…the Indians had been largely reinforced during the day," Clewes wrote.[40] "They was there for to help finish the massacre," remembered Klingensmith. "The hills were pretty full around there, and they done the massacre-ing of the women generally."[41]

U.S. Army Brevet Maj. James Henry Carleton, investigating the massacre in May 1859, concluded that "fifty or sixty Mormons" partic-ipated in attacking the train. "They had, also," he wrote, "all the Indi-ans which they could collect at Cedar City, Harmony, and Washington City, to help them; a good many in number." Carleton cited Paiute leader Jackson as saying that a "combined force of Mormons and Indi-ans" carried out not only "the first attack" but also "the last massa-cre."[42] Non-Mormon Indian agent Garland Hurt sent a young Indian man south to investigate the massacre just days after it happened. He returned saying he had "met a large band of the Piedes" coming from Iron County who "acknowledged having participated in the massacre of the emigrants, but said that the Mormons persuaded them into it."[43] A modern Paiute history would conclude "that although local Nuwuvi [Paiutes] were involved, they played a secondary role to the local set-tlers in the actual murders."[44]

AT ABOUT 10:00 A.M., some four dozen militiamen began moving toward the emigrant corral in an unstructured fashion, "like a lot of men would go to a meeting house," someone said. Allen, Higbee, and adjutant Daniel Macfarlane were on horseback. With the men were wagons driven by Samuel McMurdy and Samuel Knight.[45] McMurdy had brought his wagon from Cedar on Thursday evening, and a reluc-tant Knight had been recruited to bring his from Hamblin's ranch on Friday morning.[46] The militiamen were a motley bunch, armed with assorted weapons, including revolvers, jaeger rifles, "shotguns, Kentucky rifles, flint locks and every imaginable firearm."[47]

Cedar City sergeant Samuel Pollock and Washington privates William Young and James Pearce stayed in or near camp, perhaps to help guard the militiamen's property. At age fifty-two, Young was the old man of the group, and eighteen-year-old Pearce was sick with "the botts" after eating too much "fresh beef."[48]

After a dusty mile or so, the militia stopped two hundred yards northeast of the corral near a three-way intersection in the roughly defined road. By that time they had formed a line. The emigrants and militia were now "within a rifle shot" of each other. To the southwest the soldiers saw a small, white swag hung from a pole visible above the wagons. The emigrants had raised the cloth above their camp on Wednesday when they saw Lee, a white man, cross the valley.[49] It signaled both hope and despair.

With the approach of the militia, the emigrants' hopes of deliverance seemed about to be realized. After four days of siege, the Indians had disappeared, replaced by citizen soldiers carrying a white flag. Yet there were warning signs. Instead of flocking to the emigrant camp as rescuers might be expected to do, the militiamen had stopped short, positioning themselves at the strategic junction that led from the campground.[50]

Higbee called William Bateman to carry the militia's white flag and make the first contact with the emigrants. Bateman, who had participated in that morning's council of leaders, served as a constable in Cedar City and as sergeant in one of the platoons. As he crossed the open land between the two groups, a man left the wagon corral and met him halfway with his own "white rag on a stick."[51] The two men talked briefly. "The emigrant was told we had come to rescue them if they were willing to trust us," Lee later said. The man agreed to a second meeting, and Lee, glib and smooth, walked out next.[52]

The name of the emigrant representative would be obscured by time and the massacre. Alexander Fancher was dead, and Jack and George Baker were wounded.[53] Lee said the man's name was "Hamilton," a surname that appears in later lists of emigrants.[54] A Fancher family tradition would hold that the primary negotiator was James Mathew Fancher, Alexander's twenty-five-year-old cousin.[55] Whoever the man was, he met Lee outside the corral and talked. After about fifteen minutes, Lee motioned for Knight and McMurdy to follow him in their wagons to the corral, where the emigrant negotiator unhitched some of the chains that held the makeshift barricade together and moved one of the emigrant wagons to open a channel.[56]

It was now around noon, and the September sun stood high in the sky.[57]

Lee's senses absorbed the details as he entered the emigrants' enclosure. He saw and smelled the signs of close quarters and paid particular attention to the defenses. The defenders' guns were "mostly Kentucky rifles of the muzzle-loading style," he noted. Inside the circle of chained wagons was a "rifle-pit" large enough for the entire company. "I found that the emigrants were strongly fortified," he said.[58]

Men, women, and children crowded around Lee. "Some felt that the time of their happy deliverance had come," he said, "while others, though in deep distress, and all in tears, looked upon me with doubt, distrust and terror." Seeing the emigrant families up close for the first time jolted Lee. "My position was painful, trying and awful…as I thought of the cruel, unmanly part that I was acting," Lee remembered. "My tongue refused its office"—but not for long. "I delivered my message."[59]

Word of the rescue terms, each of them false or misleading, spread within the corral. The emigrants were promised safe conduct to Pinto and then Cedar City, but they must first lay down their weapons. The Indians had "gone off over the hills" but would be watching. If the emigrants displayed their arms it would be seen "as an unfriendly act" that might renew the attacks.[60] Second, the emigrants must leave behind their cattle and other belongings as payment to the Indians for ending the siege.[61] Third, Lee promised to carry the wounded, a few children, and whatever other belongings could fit in the two militiamen's wagons. Lee told them to hide their firearms under the bedding and baggage in the wagons, with the wounded on top.[62]

The most extraordinary demand was that the emigrants leave the compound in a specific order. Knight's and McMurdy's wagons would lead, followed by the women and children. The men and older boys would then file out in the rear, each escorted by an armed militiaman. No one explained how Lee was able to sell the emigrants on the contrived proposal. Perhaps he argued that the main target of Indian anger was the Arkansas sharpshooters who had wounded and killed Paiute men. By having the men and older boys march together, he could assure the safety of the women and children. Then by putting an armed militiaman next to each emigrant man, he could assure their protection, too.[63]

The emigrants feared a trap. The orchestrated attack on their train earlier in the week suggested that more than Indian forces were at work. The emigrants' raising of a white flag two days before signaled that they may have seen Lee or other white men during the assaults. Even if they hadn't, Aden's wounded companion had made it back to the wagon corral, bearing word that white men had fired on the two.[64]

Because of the emigrants' suspicions, Lee faced tough questions from them. They "were afraid they would be killed," he reported. In response, Lee asked a question of his own. Did he look like the kind of man that might betray them?[65] "No," the emigrants replied, but "they were sure that white men had been with the Indians when the attacks had been made" earlier in the week.[66] Despite Lee's assurances, some of his listeners remained suspicious. One emigrant man warned that any agreement with the militia would make them all dead men. He called their companion who conferred with Lee a "fool" for considering the Mormons' proposals.[67]

In the end, it didn't matter much. The talk was less negotiation than dictation. Four days of death, suffering, squalor, and thirst left the emigrants with only desperate options.[68] While they now had access to fresh water to slake their thirst—a welcome relief after days of baking in the sun—they had nearly run out of ammunition. Lee thought the entire camp was down to twenty remaining shots. "If the emigrants had had a good supply of ammunition they never would have surrendered," he mused. "I do not think we could have captured them without great loss, for they were brave men and very resolute and determined."[69] Despite the long odds, the suspicion, and the unusual terms Lee presented to them, the emigrants finally gave in. Lee offered them hope—the only hope they had.[70]

As the emigrants prepared to leave their wagon fortress, Lee sat for a time on the ground "near where some young men were engaged in paying the last respects to some person who had just died." In another account, Lee spoke of seeing the emigrants wrapping buffalo robes around the corpses of "two men of note" and laying them in a grave. From various emigrants, Lee learned the inside details of the four-day standoff—including the number of dead and wounded—things he earlier could only guess about.[71]

A woman described by Lee as "a large, fleshy old lady" told and retold him about the emigrants' recent troubles. Was Lee an Indian agent? she asked, seeking assurance. "In one sense I am," Lee replied, "as [the] Government has appointed me Farmer to the Indians." Lee later said, "I told her this to satisfy her."[72]

The wagons and teams Lee had motioned into the camp became the center of activity as he and the emigrants began loading them.[73] Knight's wagon bed was "loaded to its utmost capacity" with people and possessions, including firearms.[74] McMurdy's wagon had similar cargo—bedding, clothing, luggage, and miscellaneous "truck," he remembered. The blankets in one wagon were bright red with black borders, one surviving child said. Some of the emigrants carried their belongings "as if they were going on a journey."[75] They did not know how short their trip would be.

Knight thought he had "two men, one woman and I think some children" sitting on top of the baggage, but his memory was unsure.[76] McMurdy recalled having half a dozen in his wagon.[77] The priority went to those who were wounded. Loaded next were the small children, though some babies and other youngsters stayed with their walking mothers. A few older women were given the wagon space that was left.[78]

By now Lee had been in the corral for an hour or more. The negotiation and loading took longer than the impatient militia leaders expected.[79] Would their plan hold together? The Paiutes, about a mile up the road in their sage-and-cedar hideout, were growing uneasy.[80] Nor was time on the militiamen's side. They stood on the road east of the corral, jaws set and minds racing for what lay ahead. Killing is best done quickly, without time to think.[81]

Higbee, waiting outside the corral with the men, ordered his twenty-year-old aide, Daniel Macfarlane, to hurry the emigrants. In better times Macfarlane sang the bass part in the church choir and took Shakespearean roles in the Cedar City theater. His widowed mother had become one of Haight's plural wives, and Macfarlane himself would later marry one of Haight's daughters. Macfarlane rode to the emigrants' camp to hurry things up "for fear that the Indians would come back and be upon them." It was another in a string of deceits.[82]

Finally, the two heavily laden wagons led out through the corral and soon turned north towards Hamblin's ranch. Lee had told McMurdy to take this route—"steer north, across the valley," he said. The wagons' route lay a little west of the road where the militia stood. From their position a short distance away, the militiamen could see the bobbing heads of the wounded, the elderly, and some of the children as the wagons passed by.[83]

Lee walked along between the two wagons, and behind them rode Macfarlane on horseback, leading the way for dozens of women and children—and two men, wounded but walking.[84] Macfarlane led the women northeastward, "right up to the troops," where they then turned north, following some distance behind the wagons.[85] The women's full dresses brushed against the dust of the road. It was their first exercise away from the stench of the corral for days and must have been bracing.

The emigrant men and older boys followed next. By now their ranks were heavily depleted. Seven men had died in Monday's attack, and a few more had since perished from wounds.[86] Another five or so were killed outside of the Meadows—Aden, the two men shot near Leach's Spring on Tuesday, and presumably the men sent to make pine tar before the first attack. In addition, sometime during the week three men had slipped from the corral in a last desperate attempt to reach

California to summon help—or at least report the emigrants' sad fate. With a half dozen or more men riding in the wagons or walking with the women, the column of emigrant men and older boys totaled about two dozen, perhaps a few more.[87]

The militiamen had numbers heavily on their side. McMurdy, Lee, Knight, and Macfarlane were with the forward party; Johnson and Shirts waited with the Indians; Pollock, Young, and Pearce remained at the militia camp; and Clewes, the courier, was on his way back to Cedar City. Still, the militiamen waiting on the road outnumbered the men and boys from the corral by as much as two to one.[88] As the emigrant men approached, the militiamen slung their guns across their arms, preparing to walk alongside them.[89]

According to Macfarlane, "One of the emigrants, a boy or young man, returned to the camp again, after leaving it, declaring that he believed there was treachery connected with the move, and his comrades had all they could do to persuade him to follow them."[90]

When the emigrant men reached the militia, they "halted a little while" as the children and women were "hurried ahead."[91] A few of the emigrants raised a mild cheer, "as if they believed that [the militiamen] were acting honestly."[92] Higbee ordered "his men to form in single file and take their places" four or five feet to "the right of the emigrants."[93] The parallel columns of men then followed some distance behind the wagons and women.[94] The march had no rhythm; most walked haphazardly.[95]

Farther north at the head of the procession, McMurdy's horses, "a very fast walking team," easily outpaced Knight's newly broken pair. Lee walked behind McMurdy and sometimes alongside of Knight.[96] Lee wanted a fast pace to put distance between the wagons and the walking emigrants when the killing began.[97] But he also wanted the two wagons to stay together, and at times McMurdy moved too fast— Lee had to tell him to slow down "several times."[98]

Albert Hamblin, Jacob's adopted Indian son, and his friend John, a young Indian who lived with Samuel Knight, reported watching the procession from a distance. "The women were on ahead with the children," Albert said of what they saw. He did not mention the lead wagons, now well beyond most of the women and children. Lastly, about a quarter mile behind the middle group were the older boys and men. "It was a big crowd," Albert said, claiming also to have seen Indians hiding in the scrub oak and sage brush. "I said to John, I would like to know what the emigrants left their wagons for, as they were going into a 'worse fix than ever they saw.'"[99]

It was now midafternoon.[100]

So far, everything was going according to the militia leaders' plan. In front, the wagons carried the emigrants' firearms, now well beyond the men accustomed to using them and difficult, if not impossible, for the injured in the wagons to reach because of the bedding and passengers set over them. The middle group—the women and children—were easy targets. From their nearby hiding places, the Indians could descend on them. Finally, the emigrant men were unarmed, outnumbered, and within the dead-on range of the militiamen's arms. The militia leaders used the landscape in their plan. The women and children soon reached the Rim of the Basin, beyond which the Indians were hiding.[101]

The plan was succeeding because it was so calculated, because the emigrants had no real options, and because it was so improbably sinister. Even many of the tough and practical emigrants, used to surprises on the trail, could not have imagined anything happening to them that was so premeditated, evil, and cunning.

Some of the Mormons could not believe it either. Despite all their uncertainties and fears, their feelings of anger or hatred, and their willingness to obey leaders, they struggled when faced with the reality of what they were about to do. Maj. Higbee, on horseback in the middle of the long train, was to start the slaughter with the simple command of "Halt." But when he reached the point where he was supposed to give the signal, he said nothing and allowed his horse to saunter. Higbee reportedly hoped for a reprieving stay—some last minute, impossible order from Haight that would spare the emigrants.[102] Perhaps it was the sight before him that made him waver. Up ahead on the trail, dozens of defenseless women and children were walking toward the deadly ambush he would unleash.

As Higbee hesitated, the women and children walked past the hiding Indians toward the open valley where surprise would be more difficult. The Paiutes scurried to keep up, moving from one concealing object to another. As the trail began to open up, they were running out of places to hide and "though[t] they were going to be deceived" by the militiamen. According to Ellott Willden, "Lee afterwards scolded Higbee for this delay."[103]

The women and children were now a quarter mile past the planned site of the ambush.[104] Higbee, realizing the plan was unraveling, turned his horse across the road and looked back. Finally he shouted, "Halt!"[105]

The first volley was like "one loud shot," said one of the militia-men, and the firing went on for a minute or two.[106] When the heavy smoke lifted, blood and horror were everywhere where the emigrant men once stood. The militia had killed at close quarters, sometimes face-to-face. Many of the bullets hit their victims in the front or back of the head.[107] Several of the Mormon men "shed tears at the sight of the dead lying before them, and only in obedience to what they considered legitimate military authority would they have done what they did," reported one. Not all of the militia took part, refusing to fire or shooting into the ground or air. Under duress, they failed to kill quickly and efficiently, if at all.[108]

Others made up for it, out of duty or conviction or because once the killing began, they lost control of themselves. William "Bill" Stewart—the man who killed Aden—and Joel White, his accomplice, took out after the few emigrant men spared in the fusillade, who were now running for their lives. The two Mormons nearly got themselves killed by running into the line of fire.[109] Their act helped earn them the repu-tation for being the "most bloodthirsty" men on the field.[110]

The leaders had planned for possible runaways. Higbee and Allen, each on horseback, were at opposite ends of the line of emigrant men, and Macfarlane rode at the front of the women. Their duty was to "round in those who might try to escape."[111] The fleeing emigrant men did not get far. Some were dead within twenty steps, although one emigrant almost got to the mountains, a half mile off.[112]

When later asked if he killed his man, obeying orders to his "fullest capacity," Klingensmith acknowledged that he had.[113] Then he said he watched Higbee do one of the follow-up killings. His account made it sound as if Higbee and his victim knew each other. "That man was wounded, a little" and "lying on the ground," Klingensmith said. "John M. Higbee went up to him and dr[ew] his knife out and cut his throat. This man begged for his life....He said, Higbee, I wouldn't do this to you." Higbee replied, "You have done something just as bad."[114] Klingensmith gave no explanation of what Higbee meant.

As the emigrant men were being killed, another horrific scene played out a few hundred yards up the trail. Moments after Higbee gave his order, Johnson, who was still on the hill overlooking the militia and the Paiutes, "gave the word to the Indians to fire."[115] They rose up from their hiding places "yelling and whooping," some rushing toward the front of the group of women and children and others toward the back. At first the terrified women and children ran back toward their men "until the Indians cut them off; headed them off," said William Young, who watched the slaughter from the ridge, near the militia camp. The Indians hurled "rocks at them and I saw them fall from the rocks and laid on the ground as though they was dead."[116] Carl Shirts's father said "the women and children were knocked down with stones, clubs, and gun barrels, struck in the neck and butchered like hogs."[117]

Young saw one Indian use a large rock to crush life from a teenage boy who had fallen. Two or three times, the man raised the rock and crushed it into the boy's chest.[118]

One large woman, "hollowing for her husband and children," somehow made it through to the white men, only to be shot in the back by one of them. When she fell, Klingensmith remembered, there was no quiver.[119]

Other women and children who weren't initially struck down "wheeled" and ran toward the brush or the two wagons on the north. One blood-covered girl, perhaps ten or eleven years old, got within about sixty yards of the wagons before an Indian shot her.[120] Another girl was fleeing for her life when an Indian "plunged his knife through her."[121]

NEPHI JOHNSON. *Frank Esshom,* Pioneers and Prominent Men of Utah (*Salt Lake City, 1913*).

Some of the victims simply "clung together" in terror.[122] Others fought for their lives. "I saw the women fight," said Young, "and then I saw the Indians kill as many as three women; I saw them strike at them." Young also saw "an Indian kill an infant child, that a woman had in her arms before she fell, with a knife."[123]

Rebecca Dunlap, six years old at the time, remembered the terror. She ran and hid in a cluster of sagebrush near the road. From her hiding place she saw two of her older sisters killed, their bodies falling nearby. She also heard her one-year-old sister, Sarah, crying. She found the infant "entwined" in their dead mother's arms. Sarah "had been shot through her right arm, below the elbow, by a large ball, breaking both bones and cutting her arm half off." Rebecca pulled Sarah free and took her back into the sagebrush to hide. She stayed there until she saw a white man and begged him for help.[124] She was spared only because of her young age.

Six-year-old John Calvin Miller "was near his mother when she was killed." He desperately "pulled arrows from her back" as she lay dying.[125] When the massacre was over, a militiaman said he saw arrows "scattered here and there around among the bodies."[126]

Another surviving child recalled, "I remember standing by my mother, holding onto her skirt, while my mother stood with my baby brother in her arms, and when the white man, not an Indian, raised his gun to take the life of my mother, she said: 'God, have mercy on my children!' "[127]

Four-year-old Nancy Saphrona Huff, whose father had died on the plains, remembered that Jack Baker was carrying her when he was shot.[128] Baker may have been one of the two wounded men seen walking with the women and children. Or perhaps he was among the wounded riding in the wagons, holding little Nancy in his arms.

A third killing site was at the wagons, where, as elsewhere, the later claims and counterclaims would make it difficult to find the precise truth. When McMurdy heard Lee order him to "halt," he pulled on the reins and brought his team to a stop. "At that instant," he said, "I heard the sound of a gun." Turning to look, McMurdy saw a woman falling backward and Lee standing with a long-barreled gun to his shoulder.[129]

The sharp clap of the firearm spooked McMurdy's and Knight's animals.[130] As McMurdy turned back to his horses, he heard behind him a dull thud such as "a heavy instrument, something like a gun would make" hitting a human head. From the second wagon, Knight saw Lee striking a woman with "a club or gun." When McMurdy looked back again, he saw Lee firing his pistol, close-up, at two or three of the wagon riders. According to Lee, one of his pistols accidentally went off, sending a bullet at McMurdy, cutting his buckskins "below the crotch" and probably catching some flesh. Then Lee's gun jammed.[131]

Sarah Frances Baker remembered sitting on her wounded father George's lap in one of the wagons when the same bullet that snuffed out his life took a nick out of her left ear. Sarah wasn't quite three years old. "But even when you're that young," she maintained more than eighty years later, "you don't forget the horror of having your father gasp for breath and grow limp, while you have your arms around his neck, screaming with terror." She recalled "the blood-curdling war-whoops," "the banging of guns," and "the screaming of the other children and the agonized shrieks of women" being killed. "And you wouldn't forget it, either," she said, "if you saw your own mother topple over in the wagon beside you, with a big red splotch getting bigger and bigger on the front of her calico dress."[132]

Nephi Johnson, watching from the hill, said he saw Lee and an Indian pull at least one man from a wagon. The motion of Lee's arm made Johnson think "that he was cutting a man's throat," although he could not see for sure.[133]

In the first two weeks after the massacre, Lee would tell others of his killings. Then, for the next twenty years, he repeatedly denied taking any life. Shortly before his death, however, he privately acknowledged having "killed five emigrants and possibly six."[134]

Both Knight and McMurdy claimed Lee did all the killing at the wagons, saying they had their hands full with their teams. But Lee was not the only man at the wagons who was taking human life. "The drivers with me killed the sick and the wounded," Lee wrote in his confessions.[135] Lee said McMurdy, armed with a double-barreled shotgun, "shot a man who was lying with his head on another man's breast; the ball killed both men." Lee also claimed Knight "shot a man with his rifle" and then clubbed a fourteen-year-old boy, crushing his head.[136] McMurdy denied killing anyone, although he wavered during cross-examination at Lee's trial. "I believe I am not upon trial, sir," he finally told a defense attorney who questioned him on the subject. "I don't wish to answer."[137] Knight persistently claimed that he did no killing—even in a private interview with a Mormon leader near the end of his life. Rather than do any shooting, he insisted, he had jumped from the wagon to hold his fractious animals.[138]

Nineteen years later, Lee accused Knight and McMurdy of witnessing falsely against him. They "swore that I committed the awful deeds, that they did with their own wicked hands."[139]

Knight testified that another Mormon participated in the killings at the wagons, and Johnson agreed, although neither witness identified the killer. "Who he was I do not know," Johnson said when testifying at the Lee trial. "I can't tell and I never enquired to find out."[140]

One or two Paiutes were at the wagons as well. Because they had run some distance from their hiding places, they arrived after the carnage started, but "took some part of the killing," said Johnson.[141] According to Lee, one of the Paiutes at the wagons was "an Indian...called Joe," from Cedar City. After the massacre, a Joe worked for Elisha Groves at Harmony and dressed himself in pants and a coat taken from the emigrants, though he may not have been the man Lee mentioned.[142]

For the most part, the massacre of the emigrants was over in a few minutes—Johnson said no more than five.[143] In the years following the mass killing, the white participants persisted in blaming the tragedy primarily on Paiutes. Even Johnson, who saw most of what happened from his position on the hill, at times joined in the finger-pointing.[144] But during a conversation with a senior Mormon leader from Salt Lake City in 1895, Johnson said that "white men did most of the killing."[145]

The carnage was astonishing. "I saw the bodies of men, women, and children, butchered in the most horrible manner," Samuel Pollock said.

"Some of the children with their heads mashed in by rocks, I suppose."[146] Klingensmith gave a similar description. "I found [the bodies] in almost every condition," he said, "some with their throats cut, some heads smashed, some shot."[147] Few if any scalps were taken.[148] When Jacob Hamblin examined the victims' skeletons in 1858, he "observed that about one-third of the skulls were shot through with bullets, and about one-third seemed to be broken in with stones."[149] Although the militia leaders had planned to spare those "too young to tell tales," at least a half dozen of these young children became part of the terrible harvest, too.[150]

Though the main slaughter was "quick," the follow-up killings took longer.[151] Jimmie Pete, the son of Tau-gu ("Coal Creek John"), a Cedar City Paiute who was at the killing fields, confirmed that the militia and Indians were careful and systematic. In an oral interview, Pete said his father told him that after the first wave of killing was over, "they was going over them [the bodies] again. My father was, I guess, about third place. Some white man was ahead of him and trying to stir them up, to see [if]...they was alive." All that showed signs of life, said Lee, were immediately shot through the head. As the men checking the bodies approached them, two emigrants pretending to be dead sprang up and made an impossible dash for freedom. "My father chased them clear up the mountain and got them up there," said Pete.[152]

Some emigrants—like little Rebecca and Sarah Dunlap—were found in hiding. The "Dutchman" or "German," whose role figured so prominently in Mormon accounts about the emigrants, was one of "several that was hid out that they didn't get." The "German" was probably one of the men seen walking with the women and children and was holding an infant when he was found. A single bullet killed both of them, and the double killing became one of the infamous stories told about the massacre.[153]

Later, when Lee received the brunt of blame for the butchery, he was accused of this double murder. Lee reportedly talked about the killing in a public meeting immediately after he returned to Harmony, casting it as a dream in which he, dressed like an Indian, led Paiutes in the attack. Harmony resident Annie Elizabeth Hoag remembered Lee saying that

> when they came to one man that had his child in his arms an infant babe, he says give up that child. No, Lee, says the man, I know you, I recognise you [even] if you are painted[,] and you know the penalty of shedding innocent blood. If you kill me you kill my child, I will part

with the last drop of blood there is in my body before I give up my child. Lee asked him again, if he would give up his child and he said no; then John D. Lee said it was his turn to assist and he shot him through the heart and killed the child at the same time. He said he didn't consider himself under the penalty of shedding innocent blood, he could not help it, because the man would not give up his child.[154]

Soon after, Lee told Peter Shirts, who attended the Harmony meeting, that the events he related were no dream.[155]

Even though Lee may have been disguised with paint during the initial attacks earlier in the week, he could not have been painted during Friday's massacre because he was with the emigrants and won their trust immediately before the massacre began. But Ellott Willden confirmed Hoag's testimony that Lee shot a man and baby, clarifying that the murdered German carried not his own but "somebody elses child."[156]

Two Dunlap sisters, probably twelve-year-old twins Lucinda and Susannah, were among the last emigrants to be killed. During the

TAU-GU AND JOHN
WESLEY POWELL,
1873. *John K. Hillers,
Courtesy National
Anthropological Archives,
Smithsonian Institution.*

slaughter, the girls tried to escape by climbing into the eastern hills and hiding "in some bushes." Albert and John, the two young Indian wards of the Mormons, saw them go. Albert said he and John "ran down and tried to save them....A man, who is an Indian doctor, also told the Indians not to kill them."[157]

From his perch on the hill, William Young "saw an Indian leading two girls one in each hand." The Indian "led them up in sight of me," said Young. He "led them up in among the balance of the Indians and I saw no more of the two little girls."[158] When Lee came down the road after the killing at the wagons, a Cedar City "chief" brought the girls out and asked him "what he should do with them." The Paiute did not want the girls killed because they were "pretty," Lee later told Jacob Hamblin. But Lee insisted. "They was too big and too old to let live," he said. Lee claimed he told the Indian to shoot one of them and he cut the other's throat. When Hamblin returned from Salt Lake City some days after the massacre, however, he saw the girls' bodies, both with slit throats, lying together "some ways off" from the other emigrants' remains.[159]

Some stories about the killing of the girls had even more lurid details. One account said one of the girls begged for life and offered to marry Lee, who took her into the brush for half an hour before killing her.[160] "My name's heralded all over the country as the biggest villain in America," Lee told journalist John H. Beadle in 1872. "It is published for a sworn fact that I violated two girls as [they] were kneeling and begging to me for life, and so help me God, it is an infernal lie!"[161]

When the killing ended, the looting began. Militiaman George Adair said Higbee told the men that if they took property off the bodies, "it would burn them." Apparently that curse didn't apply to everyone. Adair claimed that when he found "a long purse filled with gold" and held it away from himself "as a thing accursed," Higbee "grabbed the purse, and pushed it in his pocket," threatening to slit Adair's throat if he ever told anyone. At least that was Adair's version of the incident.[162]

Lee said he found Higbee, Klingensmith, and Stewart searching bodies for money, watches, and jewelry, and that they asked him to hold a hat for them to collect the valuables. Lee said that only a little money was found, although several rumors contradicted the claim.[163] Gilbert Morse said that after the massacre, Lee "sported a handsome gold watch and chain." Holding it up for Morse to see, Lee said he had eight more like it.[164]

According to Paiute oral traditions, the militiamen told the Indians "that if they saw any round gold pieces (coins) lying on the ground the Indians were not to pick them up because they were poison and would kill them." Instead, "the Mormons picked up all the coins and put them in a sack and kept them."[165] Not all of the Paiutes heeded the admonishment. Tau-gu said, "Don't tell us no, cause what we want to do, we want to do." Ignoring the white men, some "kept on feeling in the shirts."[166] By morning most of the bodies would be "stripped of all the clothing," as well.[167]

Nephi Johnson said Lee ordered him to the emigrant corral "to keep the Indians from taking things out [of] the wagons."[168] By the time Johnson got to the wagons, several Paiutes were gathering blankets, bedding, clothes, cooking utensils, saddles, and most anything else that they could quickly pack or hide in the hills and rocks around them. Johnson told them to stop, and "some of them would and some of them would not," he said. Johnson, perhaps recalling Lee's earlier failure to reward Paiutes as promised, did not press the matter too strongly.[169]

By late evening, the militia leaders gained control over most of the property. Over the next several weeks, they would distribute it largely among themselves. Some of the Paiutes drawn to Mountain Meadows by promises of gain felt the massacre leaders had cheated them.[170]

Before the looting, Klingensmith had moved up the road to pick up the surviving boys and girls. "I immediately put the little children in baggage-wagons belonging to the regiment and took them to Hamlin's Ranch," he said.[171] Klingensmith left out grisly details. While many of the children were in the wagons of McMurdy and Knight during the slaughter, others were scattered on the ground near their dead mothers or were walking numbly about. Klingensmith chose which ones would live. "I was told at the time," said Johnson, that "Klingin Smith, selected seventeen of the smallest children together, and handed the older ones over to the Indians who killed them."[172] Nancy Saphrona Huff remembered, "At the close of the massacre there was 18 children still alive, one girl, some ten or twelve years old they said was to big and could tell so they killed her, leaving 17....I saw them shoot the girl after we were gathered up."[173]

When the wagons with the crying and blood-stained children reached Hamblin's ranch, Rachel Hamblin took them into her shanty and surrounding yard. She did her best, one woman caring for seventeen children, in addition to her own. Some babies were still nursing and wailed for the comfort of their mothers' breasts. Two of the young survivors showed outward wounds. Sarah Frances Baker's ear was bleeding, and little Sarah Dunlap's arm still oozed near the elbow, "the bone being entirely severed."[174] The inner damage was still worse—young hearts and minds in terrible trauma. Though they had not had peaceful rest in days, "the children cried all night."[175]

The scent of human blood in the Meadows brought coyotes from their dens, and their howls mingled with the crying of the children and the bawling of the emigrants' cattle.[176] That night campfires flickered here and there in the Meadows, although the militia leaders, including Lee, went to Hamblin's ranch house in time for supper at sundown. Despite the din and the fresh memories of the slaughter, Lee rolled out his saddle blanket and slept soundly.[177] Exhausted from the week's action, he also had the facility to shield his mind from self-inspection. He had done his duty; that was all he allowed himself to think.[178]

Like Lee, some militiamen may have rested well, but the sleep of others must have been more fitful. However much they sought solace thereafter, memories of the massacre at Mountain Meadows would lurk in their minds and haunt them to their deaths. Some sought refuge in excuses or denial. Others fled the land in a vain hope of escaping the recurring visions of that day. None was ever the same again.[179]

THE TRAGEDY AT MOUNTAIN MEADOWS played out on several levels. The murdered emigrants lost their hopes, their dreams, their property, and their lives. Some lost their very identity, their names forever effaced from human memory. The surviving children were robbed of the warmth and support of parents, brothers, and sisters. Their first sobbing night at Hamblin's was just the start of their ordeal. The Paiute participants would bear the brunt of blame for the massacre, shamelessly used by the white men who lured them to the Meadows. For the militiamen who carried out the crime—as well as their families, descendants, and fellow church members—there was another kind of tragedy. It was the gnawing, long anguish that flows from betrayed ideals. The burdens of the massacre would linger far beyond what anyone imagined on the night of September 11, 1857.

CHAPTER FOURTEEN

Too Late to Back Water

Mountain Meadows to Cedar City, September 11–13, 1857

A S THE HORROR of the massacre unfolded on that Friday after-noon, militia courier Joseph Clewes hurried his mule from the Meadows to Cedar City. While Clewes sped east, two westbound horsemen rode toward him—Elias Morris, a militia cap-tain and one of Haight's two counselors in the stake presidency, and Christopher J. Arthur, Haight's son-in-law. Morris and Arthur had left Cedar for the Meadows that morning, purportedly to check out the "many conflicting and terrible reports" about events there. According to Morris, before they left town Haight encouraged him "to use his influence in the interest of peace, and do everything possible to avert the shedding of blood."[1]

The statement was corroborated by Clewes, who met Morris and Arthur midway between Cedar City and the Meadows. Morris told Clewes that he had "an order to save the emigrants and render them all the assistance that could be given." Clewes blurted, "Go! go! as fast as your horses can take you. You may be in time to save them." But even as Morris and Arthur spurred their horses on, Clewes's heart sank, "for," he said, "I could not see how they could be in time."[2]

Haight left no record of sending such a message. Did he have last-minute regrets? Or was he trying to create an alibi to hide his own role in the plan? Still another possibility is that Morris and Arthur invented the story about their purpose to protect themselves. Morris had been present in early discussions of killing the emigrants, including the Sunday council meeting in Cedar City on September 6. More men had gone to the Meadows from Morris's militia company than from any other Cedar City company, and he had accompanied Haight to Parowan on Wednesday night, September 9, and took part in the tan bark council early the next morning. Arthur had a run-in with some of the emigrants in Cedar City when they came into the town store. It seems unlikely that Haight, so set in his policy for days, had made a startling about-face on Friday morning. Nor were Morris and Arthur so unaware of what was going on as they implied.[3]

After his encounter with Morris and Arthur, Clewes continued on to Cedar City. The nine heavy freight wagons of Sidney Tanner and William Mathews beat him there by two hours, rolling in from the north at 1:00 p.m. Following their meeting with William Dame on Wednesday, the members of the Tanner-Mathews company had stayed in camp six miles south of Parowan for two more nights, then started out for Cedar City on Friday morning.[4] After the train pulled into the old fort at Cedar, Mathews went to see Haight, arriving at his home just ahead of William Dame.[5]

Like the Tanner-Mathews train, Dame had left for Cedar City on Friday morning. After seeing that the Turner-Dukes-Collins stand-off with Pahvants ended peacefully, Dame decided to hurry "to the Meadows, for the purpose of putting a stop to the massacre…having repented of what th[ey] had agreed to do."[6] Three other Parowan men went with Dame, one of whom was James Lewis, the Iron County probate judge and major of Parowan's militia battalion.[7]

When Dame saw Mathews in Cedar City, he told him he needed fresh animals to get him to the Meadows. Mathews replied that his partner, Tanner, might spare him some mules. Dame and Haight then met at Haight's house.[8] That afternoon, two messengers came into Cedar City from the Meadows. The first was an Indian who left the Meadows early that morning. He reported that a close-up reconnaissance of the emigrants' corral showed that "only five or six" of them "were killed." The message understated the week's casualties but also belied statements of Lee and Haight that the killing of the emigrants was all but finished by Tuesday night.[9]

The next messenger was Clewes, who arrived at Haight's home about 3:00 p.m. He reported that barring some unexpected event, it was already too late to stop the mass killing. The report sparked tension between the two senior leaders who heard it. Though Dame and Haight said nothing in Clewes's presence, "They were angry at each other," Clewes remembered. "I could see it in them." The courier then returned home, carrying with him "a horrible remembrance of those five days."[10] Clewes would eventually leave Utah and Mormonism.[11]

While Dame, Haight, and Clewes met behind closed doors, a curious Mathews made coffee, perhaps hoping the refreshments would get him admitted into their chamber. When Mathews knocked on the door, announcing that the coffee was ready, Dame and Haight refused to let him in. Mathews grew impatient. "Do you want the mules?" he called from the threshold. "Yes," Dame replied bitterly, "I want to go to see to the burying of the dead."[12]

Dame and Haight left with a party for the Meadows sometime Friday evening.[13] They stopped at the Tanner-Mathews camp to eat supper and borrow the mules. According to Philetus Warn, a non-Mormon traveling with the train, as the men rode away, someone in the camp called out, "Be careful, and don't get shot, Mr. Haight." Haight replied, "We shall have no shooting," with emphasis on *we* "as if he meant to imply that the shooting would be all over before he arrived."[14] E. C. Mathews, William's son, remembered the mission differently. He testified that Dame told the camp, "he was going on out to try and call the Indians off."[15] Was Dame hoping against hope that something had intervened to stop the massacre, or was he posturing for outsiders in the train? Word was already spreading through Cedar City that "the job had been done."[16]

In the early morning hours of Saturday, September 12, Haight and Dame rode up to Hamblin's shack.[17] When they found the seventeen surviving children, huddled and crying, Dame's last hopes were dashed, reigniting the rancor that had been smoldering between him and Haight. Klingensmith witnessed an argument between the two men over who was responsible for the killings. Haight told Dame that if he were going to report the massacre to the authorities then he, Dame, should never have ordered it in the first place.[18]

Their quarrel roused Lee from his slumber. Lying outside on his saddle blanket, he recognized the familiar voices arguing. "I heard some very angry words pass between them," Lee later wrote. "Dame said that he would have to report the destruction of the emigrant camp and the company."

"How," Haight replied, "as an Indian massacre?"

Dame said he was not so sure he would put the blame on Indians.

"How the h—l can you report it any other way without implicating yourself?" Haight exclaimed.

"Dame lowered his voice almost to a whisper," and Lee could not make out the rest of the conversation.[19]

Haight and Dame went to the makeshift home of Samuel Knight for something to eat. Years later, Knight confided that while listening to their conversation, he learned that none of the church leaders in Salt Lake City "had sanctioned or encouraged in any way the dastardly deed of which these fanatics were guilty." Instead, the two leaders worried over how to report to Salt Lake what they had done.[20]

Through the night a few miles south, Nephi Johnson and Cedar City militiaman John Urie had remained at their posts in the wagon corral, watching over the emigrant property now claimed by the white participants.[21] Indians had already removed much of the bedding, taken off the wagon covers, and ripped open feather beds, scattering the contents in a search for valuables. As the sun rose, other militia members returned from their camps to the massacre scene, drawn by a mixture of duty, curiosity, and disbelief. Lee, Dame, Haight, and others from Hamblin's "rode up to that part of the field where the women were lying dead." As they stopped among the naked, mutilated bodies, Dame, seeing the carnage for the first time, "seemed terror-stricken."[22]

Another argument ignited between him and Haight. Dame "spoke low, as if careful to avoid being heard," and he again insisted that the attack would have to be reported. Incensed, Haight blustered, "You know that you counseled it, and ordered me to have them used up."

"I did not think that there were so many women and children," Dame replied. "I thought they were nearly all killed by the Indians."

Sensing Dame might try to evade all responsibility for the massacre, Haight seethed, "It is too late in the day for you to back water. You know you ordered and counseled it, and now you want to back out."

Dame asked Haight if he had any written orders to prove his assertion, then walked away, with Haight screaming after him: "You throw the blame of this thing on me and I will be revenged on you if I have to meet you in hell to get it."[23] In truth, there was fault enough to go around for both men—and for Lee, who walked beside them.

Chided by Lee for their public display of disunity, Dame and Haight stopped bickering and rode down into the southern part of the Meadows. The twisted bodies of the dead, some already torn open by wolves and coyotes, mocked the armchair planning that had led to the deaths of so many men, women, and children. Both men gave vent to the emotion welling up in them. William Young, walking among the bullet-pocked emigrant wagons that morning, recalled that "Haight made quite a lamentation." John Higbee later described Dame's "consternation" at the eerie spectacle.[24]

If the leaders' growing regrets did not give them decency enough to bury the victims' remains, their desire to keep the massacre a secret did. Bodies on the landscape would testify of the crime that had occurred there. The men from Washington hurried home that morning, leaving only part of the militia to inter the bodies, and the picks and shovels brought to the Meadows supplied just a fraction of the remaining men. Despite later claims that the Cedar City men went to the Meadows just to bury the dead and "took their shovels along," most had brought only their guns. Some of the burial detail used the emigrants' own shovels, pulled from their wagons, to dig graves.[25]

Samuel Pollock described how the burial detail worked. The men found the ground "was very hard; it was impossible for us to dig it." They looked for natural cavities and soft places such as washes where holes could be more easily dug. Most of the bodies were buried close to where they fell, in graves about three or four feet deep. Some graves contained three or four bodies. Visitors to the Meadows in coming months described three major burial areas: one within the emigrants' wagon corral, another where the men were shot by the militia, and a third where the women and children were killed.[26] Interring the bodies was a grim task, and now ironic. Putting picks and shovels to work finally fulfilled Haight's original propaganda that the men were going to the Meadows to "bury the dead." As the men beheld the corpses in the light of the new day, they faced the stark realization of what they had done—adding to feelings of guilt that would haunt many of them the rest of their lives.[27]

Lee later claimed not all in the burial detail expressed remorse as they worked. Some laughed and talked as if to free themselves from any second thoughts.[28] In general, the men were anxious to work quickly and get out of the Meadows. They felt like Samuel McMurdy, who, when he was later asked, "Did you go back at all?" responded "No, sir." "Never wanted to go back?" "No, sir, never."[29] Pinto missionary Amos Thornton, according to his stepson, "helped bury the dead" and "wished he had not, as the memory of that terrible sight he could not forget."[30]

The bodies did not stay buried for long. The scent of rotting flesh in the shallow graves attracted wolves, coyotes, and other scavengers.

MOUNTAIN MEADOWS MASSACRE SCENE. Harper's Weekly, *August 13, 1859.*

Within a day or two, many of the bodies had been pulled to the surface, torn into pieces, and scattered across the Meadows. Samuel Knight later reported that "the wolves…uncovered the remains and picked the bones." This disinterring of victims gave rise to a widespread belief that no effort at all was made to bury them.[31]

The militia leaders tried to cover not only the bodies but also their own tracks. Knowing they could not suppress news of the emigrants' deaths, they stuck to their original plan to portray the massacre as an Indian atrocity. On Saturday, September 12, as some of the men prepared to leave the Meadows, Haight and Klingensmith told them to keep what had happened secret. "The leaders in it didn't want it to get out," Nephi Johnson later explained. Despite their wishes, the truth about the massacre, like the victims' bones, would not stay buried.[32]

After the corpses were covered, most of the remaining militiamen trailed uncceremoniously home. "We went back promiscuously [randomly] just about as it happened," Joel White said. He passed by Hamblin's ranch but did not stop.[33]

The leaders, meanwhile, turned their attention to the emigrants' livestock, wagons, and surviving children. When Haight visited the corral where Johnson still watched over the property, he asked what he thought should be done with it. Johnson replied, "You have made a sacrifice of the people, and I would burn the property and turn the cattle loose upon the range, where the Indians could kill them if they wanted to, and go home like men."[34] Johnson's statement—if he made it—was a bold one.[35] Yet the poverty of the southern settlements and the possibility of a long war made the suggestion unattractive. To some degree a desire for the emigrants' property had been a motive leading to the attacks. Instead of abandoning the property, the leaders took charge of it.[36]

Not all of the emigrants' stock had stayed in the Meadows during the week of the siege. Some cattle may have fled over the nearby hills and mountains, frightened by the noise and confusion of the attacks. Stories would persist for decades after the massacre about wild cattle thought to have originated with the massacred company. Other animals had died during early assaults on the train, been eaten by the attackers, or been driven off by Indians who left after the first attacks.[37]

The day after the massacre, the emigrants' "loose stock...were left at the Meadows for the time being," though Klingensmith and Higbee "ordered some oxen to be brought up, and the herders drove in enough to haul the [emigrants'] wagons" away.[38] The men did not know "how the oxen had been mated before, and consequently when they happened to get a [left] ox on the [right] side or vice-versa they would not pull together."[39] Johnson went with the wagons as they moved north out of Mountain Meadows. They went to Iron Springs along the Old Spanish Trail, the route that had been superseded by Leach's Cutoff between Cedar City and the Meadows. Off the beaten path, Iron Springs had water and grass for the cattle, and a place to park the dozen or more wagons close to Cedar City but beyond travelers' eyes.[40]

Finally, there was the question of what to do with the seventeen surviving children, who had been delivered on the night of the massacre to Hamblin's ranch, where Rachel Hamblin did her best to care for them.[41] Lee claimed "to act as an agent for the Indians" in bartering the children to the whites who gathered at Hamblin's. Mormon families sometimes bartered for Indian children to provide what they considered a better life.[42] Albert and John, the two young Indians at the ranch, were examples of such adoptions.

Less than two years later, Rachel Hamblin told a federal investigator that Lee's pretense of acting for the Indians "was a mere sham."[43] Hamblin entreated Lee to let her keep three Dunlap sisters. Wounded one-year-old Sarah, she insisted, could not be moved. When six-year-old Rebecca and four-year-old Louisa begged not to be parted from their baby sister, "I persuaded Lee not to separate them," Hamblin said, "but to let me have all three of them. This he finally agreed to."[44] Klingensmith, bishop of Cedar City and caretaker of the local needy, took responsibility for transporting the other children to Cedar City.[45]

And so the three daughters of Jesse and Mary Dunlap said goodbye to the other surviving children: their first cousins Prudence Angeline and Georgia Ann, daughters of Lorenzo and Nancy Dunlap; Martha Elizabeth, Sarah Frances, and William Twitty, children of George and Manerva Baker; Christopher "Kit" Carson and Triphenia, children of Alexander and Eliza Fancher; Nancy Saphrona, daughter of Peter and Saladia Huff; Felix Marion, son of John and Eloah Jones; John Calvin, Mary, and Joseph, children of Josiah and Matilda Miller; and Emberson Milum and William Henry, sons of Pleasant and Armilda Tackitt.[46]

After leaving Hamblin's ranch, Klingensmith stopped in Pinto to leave "one little child there," five-year-old Martha Elizabeth Baker. When the wagonload of children rolled on, she remained behind with the Amos Thornton family.[47]

After word of the massacre reached Cedar City, many of the local women gathered to ask one of Isaac Haight's wives, Eliza Ann Snyder Haight, what she knew. She told them that Indians had spared some of the children and sold them to the whites. "They are our children now to be cared for and loved as our own," she said, asking the women to open their homes to the orphans. "These children will be afraid, afraid of everything, afraid of us," she said, the last phrase perhaps hinting that she knew what really happened at the Meadows. Klingensmith brought the children to the Haights' next-door neighbor, Lydia Hopkins, a midwife and the president of Cedar City's Female Benevolent Society.[48] Lydia was the wife of massacre participant Charles Hopkins.

When the wagons bearing the orphans arrived, the women gathered around to offer temporary shelter for the children. On Sunday, Lydia Hopkins would begin finding families to adopt them, but the important task for the night was to feed the children and provide them a place to sleep. Many of the Cedar City children had stayed up waiting for the new arrivals. Hearing that the orphans might be frightened, one local boy had suggested that he and other children be on hand to greet the newcomers. "They wouldn't be afraid of us," he said, and the mothers agreed.[49]

Seven-year-old Mary Ann Haight, Isaac and Eliza Ann's daughter, watched as her mother helped the children from the wagon, speaking to them and introducing them to the families with whom they would stay that night. As Mary Ann observed the children being taken off the wagon to different homes, she worried that "there won't be one for us." Then she heard Klingensmith announce, "There is just one more, a little girl who is ill." The sick child was asleep, and Klingensmith offered to carry her into the house. Eliza Ann turned to her daughter, saying, "Mary Ann will show you the way to her bed, and I will come up in a few minutes." Klingensmith carried the child and set her on Mary Ann's bed.[50]

"She was still asleep," Mary Ann would remember, "and I was left alone with her. She was about my size, she lay there so still I was afraid she was dead, her hair was tangled and her clothes were very soiled." Soon Mary Ann's mother appeared with milk and bread and woke the new arrival. The girl opened her eyes and said, "Mama."[51]

But her "Mama" was not there, and she began to cry. The family did their best to comfort her, and when the child relaxed, they bathed her and put her to bed. "Presently Mother came back," Mary Ann said, "tucked us down, said a prayer, kissed us good night and assured our new sister we would love her and take good care of her."[52] The Haights, including little Mary Ann, called the girl Maria or Anne Marie.[53] She was probably four-year-old Mary Miller.[54]

Nancy Saphrona Huff, who was also four at the time of the massacre, went to live with Frances and John Willis, who did not yet have children of their own. Huff later charged, "I saw Willis during the massacre, he carried me off from the spot, I could not be mistaken, living with him made me know him beyond a doubt."[55]

With one child in Pinto, three at Hamblin's ranch, and Nancy Huff going to live with John Willis, twelve of the surviving seventeen children still needed homes. The Haight family kept the girl who spent the first night with them, and Lydia Hopkins "rustled around" to get the remaining children more permanently settled.[56]

Most of the children settled into their Utah homes within weeks after the massacre, some going to live with massacre participants. Lydia Hopkins and her husband, Charles, took in two-year-old Sarah Frances Baker, sister of Martha Elizabeth, who had been left in Pinto.[57] The girls' nine-month-old brother, William Twitty Baker, went to live with Cedar City residents Sarah and David Williams.[58] Higbee took the two Tackitt brothers, four-year-old Emberson Milum, who appeared older than his age, and nineteen-month-old William Henry.[59] Higbee later gave the younger brother to Elias Morris.[60]

Mary Ann and William Stewart took into their home eighteen-month-old Felix Marion Jones.[61] Elenor and Joseph H. Smith of Cedar City took charge of twenty-two-month-old Triphenia Fancher.[62] Prudence Angeline Dunlap, five-year-old cousin of the three girls left at Hamblin's ranch, went to the Samuel Jewkes family.[63] Her one-and-a-half-year-old sister, Georgia Ann, who was still nursing, went first to Klingensmith and one of his wives who had her own nursing baby. When Georgia Ann was weaned, the Klingensmiths gave her to Jane and Richard Birkbeck, a couple that had no children of their own.[64] Cedar City resident George Bowering recorded that some of the "babes was taken by our sisters...and allowed to share the comforts of the breast with their own natural babes."[65]

SARAH C. BAKER MITCHELL.
Courtesy Utah State Historical Society.

Other children were settled at Harmony. Christopher "Kit" Carson Fancher, age five, joined the household of John D. Lee, who called him Charley.[66] The Elisha Groves family from Harmony took in six-year-old John Calvin Miller, elder brother of Mary, the girl the Haights kept.[67]

The last of the seventeen children was the Miller children's one-year-old brother, Joseph, adopted by Harmony residents Alexander and Agnes Ingram, who later moved to Pocketville, about twenty miles south.[68] The childless couple dearly wanted a baby and traveled "a good ways" to retrieve him.[69] Eight-year-old Elizabeth Ann Shirts, a younger sister of Carl Shirts, remembered the child arriving at Harmony and the group that surrounded him. "I kept pushin' in till I got up close to where they was," she recalled. The baby was hungry, crying, and meant for "a barren woman" who was "happy to death to get this child." The child wanted nothing to do with Agnes but warmed up to the eight-year-old. "I kept gettin' up closer and closer and it saw me and stopped cryin' a little and held out its arms," Elizabeth Ann recalled. She took baby Joseph in her arms. "I can feel the little thing's flesh on mine now, jist like it was yesterday," she said eighty years later. For a while, she stayed with the Ingrams until the child bonded with Agnes.[70]

CHRISTOPHER "KIT" CARSON FANCHER. *Courtesy Utah State Historical Society.*

Some of the surviving children were moved from one location to another. These transfers were one reason for later rumors of children being "put out of the way." Neighbors saw them disappear from their old surroundings and assumed the worst.[71] One story said an emigrant boy identified a Paiute as "his father's murderer" and was never seen again. It concluded, "Perhaps he too, joined the caravan of souls that winged their flight from the red sod of Mountain Meadows."[72] A similar story told of a girl who recognized her father's killer and then supposedly disappeared.[73]

None of these stories had numbers on their side. A Mormon source shortly after the massacre recorded that seventeen children had been saved.[74] The same number of children were later turned over to federal authorities in 1859, including John Calvin Miller, the boy supposedly killed for knowing too much.[75]

After getting control of the property and sending the children off, the remaining militiamen at the Meadows drifted back to their homes.[76] Annie Hoag remembered seeing Lee coming back into Fort Harmony on Sunday, September 13. "I looked out...to see John D. Lee...at the head of the Indians," she said. The Indians "gathered about us there," and Lee gave them "mellons, squashes, punkins and pies...blankets shoes and one thing and another and so on."[77] Elizabeth Ann Shirts remembered, "John D. Lee feasted the Indians in town...and they had the most outlandish garbs on. They had the clothes off the dead people, their hats and all, and the women had the womens things on them."[78]

On the same Sunday morning, John Hamilton Sr. of Hamilton's Fort discovered people and stock in his field. Investigating, he saw dozens of painted Indians, some with "blankets, quilts, cooking utensils, and women's saddles and men's saddles, horses and an amount of cattle." While he stared, they shot down two head of cattle for food. Hamilton kept his distance but made mental notes. He saw "bloody clothes, both men's and women's garments in a pile" three feet high.[79]

Thomas T. Willis, a teenager in Cedar City at the time of the massacre, remembered Coal Creek Paiutes returning from the Meadows with clothing from the massacre victims. "It was generally covered with blood," he remembered, and had "bullet holes shot through it. And the Indians said it came from there, that they had taken it off the dead bodies." He watched these Paiutes wash the blood-stained clothes in a Cedar City water ditch. They also had horses and other property. "I saw the horses the Indians had," Willis testified. "They didn't have any horses before that. When they came back they was riding horses and saddles, some of them was dressed up in red topped boots and high crowned hats sailing around with clothing that they didn't have before."[80]

Non-Mormon traveler George Powers reported seeing a similar scene on the previous day. Powers and the Tanner-Matthews train, traveling toward the Meadows en route to California on Saturday afternoon, September 12, met some militiamen coming in the opposite direction. Powers said Tanner and Mathews spoke privately with the militiamen and then reported back to their group that the entire Arkansas company had been massacred. "And, as it was still dangerous to travel the road, they had concluded it was better for us to pass the spot in the night," said Powers.[81] The Mormons, of course, did not want Powers and Warn to spot any evidence of what had happened.

The Tanner-Mathews train moved on "without much conversation." Near dusk, in the canyon a mile east of Leach's Spring, the train next met Dame, Haight, and other white men "in company with a band of some twenty Indian warriors," Powers said. He reported:

> These Indians had a two-horse wagon, filled with something I could not see, as blankets were carefully spread over the top. The wagon was driven by a white man, and beside him, there were two or three Indians in it! Many of them had shawls, and bundles of women's clothes were tied to their saddles. They were also all supplied with guns or pistols, besides bows and arrows. The hindmost Indians were driving several head of the emigrants' cattle. Mr. Dame and Mr. Haight, and their men, seemed to be on the best of terms with the Indians, and they were all in high spirits, as if they were mutually pleased with the accomplishment of some desired object. They thronged around us, and greeted us with noisy cordiality.[82]

Dame returned to Tanner the mules he had borrowed the previous day. He and the others "had been out to see to the burying of the dead," Dame said, explaining only part of what happened. "We did not learn much from them," Powers said. "They passed on, and we drove all night in silence." He found it suspicious that the Mormons had come from the Meadows with Indians. Nor did he sense much regret over the emigrants' death.[83]

Somewhere along the road that evening the Tanner-Mathews train also passed Klingensmith and the wagons full of orphaned children. Klingensmith had ordered the wagons to pull off the road, where he "pacified" the children "and gave them something to eat and drink," he said. The freighting train passed silently at a distance, but close enough that the watchful Klingensmith could identify "old Billey Mathews" and other men he knew among the San Bernardino freighters.[84]

The Tanner-Mathews wagons pushed to get beyond the Meadows before daylight, and they barely made their goal. With dawn about to break, E. C. Mathews, son of William Mathews, was driving the third or fourth wagon in the train when it went through the valley. He noticed that the teams ahead of him made a slight turn. When he reached the spot, he did the same and then saw the reason—dead bodies near the road. "They were just laying on the ground without clothes on," he testified.[85] Either the burial detail had missed them or animals had already pulled them from their graves.

Seventeen-year-old Francis Marion Lyman, son of Mormon apostle Amasa Lyman, was traveling with the Tanner-Mathews company to his home in San Bernardino. He later wrote that a herd of cattle, which he assumed belonged to the massacred train, "came rushing around our wagons, making the night hideous with their bawling, and that, mingling with the unearthly stench from the decaying bodies of the human beings, made it the most terrific night of my life. I felt great relief as we put distance between us and the fatal spot."[86]

The train continued on three miles beyond the Meadows to some springs, where for the first time since leaving Cedar City, the teamsters took the harnesses off their mules. It had been a long drive. After resting for two or three hours on Sunday morning, September 13, they pushed on, driving another twenty miles and camping that night on the Santa Clara River near the Indian village that was home to the Paiute leader Jackson. He and members of his band had reached the Meadows on Monday night or Tuesday morning near the start of the emigrant siege, and some had probably stayed on to the end.[87]

Jackson seemed angry. One of his relatives had been killed in the fight, and he may have supposed Warn and Powers were friends of the emigrants who shot him. Or perhaps things he had been told about the approaching U.S. Army made him suspicious of all Americans. He and members of his band approached Powers and Warn. Powers said Jackson "accused me of being an American; appeared mad; stepped round; shook his head; and pulled his bowstring."[88]

Into the tense situation rode Ira Hatch, a Mormon from nearby Santa Clara. The teamsters importuned him to stay with them and placate the Indians. "It was a fortunate circumstance for us that this Mr. Hatch arrived at our camp at the very moment that we were wishing for him most," Powers recalled. "Mr. Mathews told me [Hatch] was an Indian Missionary, and of great influence among them. He could do more with them than anybody else; and if he could not get me over the road, nobody could. Mr. Tanner had declared that he would not go on without Mr. Hatch, and pretended to be afraid of the dangers of the road." The next morning, however, Hatch left the train and headed toward the Muddy River. Mathews, feeling nervous without Hatch, told his company they must leave the area as soon as possible.[89]

More was afoot than Powers knew. Before the final massacre at the Meadows, three of the emigrants' "best scouts" had crept out of the wagon corral and scrambled toward California.[90] They carried with them "a petition…addressed to any friend of humanity" describing the siege—a last desperate plea for help. The letter reportedly hinted "that white men were with the Indians, as the latter were well supplied with powder and weapons." It listed the names, ages, birthplaces, and homes of all the emigrants, as well as their material possessions, occupations, and affiliations with churches and fraternal groups in Arkansas and Missouri.[91]

One of the three messengers was "young Baker," probably Jack Baker's son Abel.[92] The identity of the other two messengers would remain uncertain.[93] Accounts about the fate of the three messengers differ in detail. Just sixteen days after the final massacre, John D. Lee spoke openly about "three that got away in the night," of which "one was overtaken the next day."[94] Seventeen years after the massacre, investigative journalist C. F. McGlashan, relying on knowledgeable local informants like Jacob Hamblin, reported that Jackson himself had killed the emigrant. McGlashan's dramatic account claimed Jackson "crept stealthily up to the sleeping man, placed the flinty arrow-point just above the collar bone, drew back the bow-string, and sent the shaft down into the sleeper's breast." Waking aghast, the victim leaped to his feet and "ran nearly forty yards before he fell, faint and dying."[95] If Lee was right about the timing, the killing took place shortly before Jackson's run-in with Warn and Powers.

Sometime later, Jackson took an informant—apparently Hamblin—to the victim's remains. They had been burned, leading McGlashan to surmise that the victim had "lived long enough to be tortured," though Paiutes at times cremated even their own dead. Near the spot where the messenger was killed, Jackson reportedly found the emigrants' petition, "a sad, despairing cry of distress."[96] An Indian reputedly gave the document to Hamblin, "who kept it many years" until "Lee learned of its existence, took it from him and destroyed it after administering a sharp reproof."[97]

The dead man's two companions got as far as the Virgin Hills in present-day Nevada, but accounts differ as to their fate. According to McGlashan's sensational details, Paiutes surrounded them, stripped them of their clothes, and told them to run for their lives. Wounded by an arrow in the capture, one of the two men did not get far. His captors "tied him to a stake," and "faggots were soon blazing around his quivering body...amid all the excruciating agony known to savage torture." The third messenger—Baker—fled naked from the scene "with the swiftness of a deer," though an arrow pierced his arm, "inflicting a severe wound."[98]

The wounded man propelled himself another fifty miles, aided by friendly Paiutes along the way who gave him pants, moccasins, and mesquite bread.[99] Continuing west to Cottonwood Spring, he met two Mormon brothers, Henry and McCan Young, who were en route from California to Utah. One of the Young brothers said that when they met Baker, "he seemed to be terror-stricken; his mind was wandering." He babbled "incoherently about the massacre, and of his purposes." Knowing nothing about the manhunt for Baker, the Young brothers gave him a horse to ride and persuaded him to turn back, believing he would die if he tried to cross the blazing deserts ahead. Although accounts of Baker's fate vary, the three men apparently ran into a search party of Paiutes led by Ira Hatch, who told the Youngs that Baker had to die. "No sooner had he said the word," McGlashan's account explained, "than the Indians discharged a shower of arrows at the poor fellow." One Indian "put an end to the torture by striking the man on the head with a stone, crushing his skull."[100]

As the last of the emigrants were being tracked and killed on the California road, Isaac Haight waited nervously back in Cedar City for Brigham Young's response to the letter he had sent north with Haslam on Monday. Haslam left Salt Lake City at 1:00 p.m. on September 10—the day before the Friday bloodbath—with carte blanche orders from Brigham Young for fresh horses at every settlement. He reached American Fork inside of four hours and Provo by 8:00 p.m. On Friday morning outside of Nephi, he was "sailing out again on a fresh Mustang" and was in Fillmore for supper. At Beaver he pushed his animal "as fast as he could stand it." He used "bronchos, Mustangs, and work animals" to cover the 250 miles to Cedar City in about seventy hours. Even then, he had trouble finding fresh mounts. The trip south took a few hours longer than his journey north.[101]

Haight and Haslam lived a quarter mile apart in Cedar. After attending church, where he offered a prayer on Sunday morning, Haight left for Haslam's to see if his express rider had returned. Haslam arrived home a short time earlier and started toward Haight's house. They met halfway.

Haslam handed Haight the unsealed letter from Young directing him to let the emigrants "go in peace."

Haight took the letter, read through it, and broke down. For half an hour, he sobbed "like a child" and could manage only the words, "Too late, too late."[102]

Under Sentence of Death

Beaver to Mountain Meadows,
March 20–23, 1877

THE ORDERS CAME down on Tuesday afternoon, March 20, 1877. They directed U.S. Army 2nd Lt. George T. T. Patterson and a detachment from his company to proceed with "utmost secrecy" to the "appointed place." There the soldiers, each fortified by "forty...rounds of ammunition and six days rations," were "to prevent any interference...with the proper execution...of John D. Lee, a convict under sentence of death."[1] A posse with Lee in its charge would follow Patterson's company the next day.[2] At 7:30 Tuesday evening, after the last glow of twilight had faded, Patterson and his twenty-three men slipped quietly from southern Utah's Fort Cameron, two miles east of Beaver.[3]

Patterson and his party rode west, skirting Beaver before turning south and following the road to California that the ill-fated Arkansas company emigrants took nearly twenty years earlier just before they were massacred. During their trip, Patterson's party passed Paragonah, Parowan, and finally Cedar City, where they took the road west for Leach's Cutoff and then Mountain Meadows.[4]

Almost twenty-four hours after Patterson's entourage left Fort Cameron, U.S. Marshal William Nelson drove to the fort to tell prisoner John D. Lee to prepare for a "journey." Lee, knowing this to be his death march, was surprised only by the timing. The court had decreed that he die on Friday between 10:00 a.m. and 3:00 p.m., and it was just Wednesday evening. With little emotion, the prisoner asked for a bath and fresh clothes. He "wanted to die clean."[5]

The nation had watched closely as Lee's first trial, in 1875, ended in a hung jury, and his second, the following year, saw him convicted for his role in the massacre.[6] Now in March 1877, reporters for newspapers from coast to coast were again in town to witness and report his execution. Tipped by Nelson that Lee was about to be moved a day earlier than planned, the journalists hurried to join the sizable caravan, which soon strung out on the road. Inside Nelson's carriage, Lee sat facing a deputy holding a "double barrelled gun."[7]

The suspense made good newspaper copy for a nation that seemed riveted on Lee and the massacre.

During the ride to the Meadows, Methodist minister George Stokes, father of the deputy who arrested Lee, accompanied him. According to a reporter, Lee ventured a confession of sorts, telling Reverend Stokes "that he killed five emigrants and possibly six."[8] That was the one thing Lee kept to the last.

For years, he maintained that he rushed to the Meadows as a peacemaker and had done all in his power to stop the killing. In a written "confession" drafted in the last months of his life, he had even mixed up dates to conceal his role in the first attack. That same "confession" also claimed he made a full disclosure to Young two weeks after the massacre.[9] But he had omitted important details then, including those he now gave Stokes.[10]

Officials never explained their unusual decision—kept secret until the final hours—to end Lee's life at the Meadows. Seldom in U.S. jurisprudence had a criminal been taken to the scene of crime for execution.[11] In this case, the effort required great expense and inconvenience; Mountain Meadows was almost one hundred bone-shaking miles from Beaver. Part of the reason may have been rooted in moral example. Could a more appropriate place be found? Crime *and* punishment would go together, a perfect stage for any moralist or tragedian.

Hope also lingered that Lee might implicate Brigham Young, the big game for post-massacre hunters who hoped to destroy Young and Mormonism. For many Americans, it had become almost an article of faith that Young had a hand in virtually everything going on in "hierarchical, tyrannical" Utah. It seemed to follow then, logically, that Young had a role in the massacre, too.[12]

Lee himself affirmed just the opposite. He repeatedly denied that Young ordered the massacre, but that was not enough for some.[13]

Young must be guilty, they insisted, and this truth must be pried from Lee. That hope was almost certainly a reason for taking Lee to the Meadows. Facing death and the horrid visage of the place, Lee might at last implicate his adoptive father.

The party conducting Lee arrived at the Meadows on Thursday, and soldiers and guards set up camp partway down the valley. Later in the evening as the men gathered by a campfire, Lee was placed in a wagon with Reverend Stokes. Seclusion with the minister may have been yet another attempt to get Lee to connect Young to the crime. Instead, Lee talked mostly about religion, defending his Mormon faith with a torrent of scripture.[14]

Brigham Young was attending a church conference in St. George, less than forty miles away by the roads of the day, and he too wanted to know how the final scene would play out. Young was aging; he would be dead within six months. On rare occasions over the last twenty years, he had spoken publicly about the massacre, condemning it and offering help to government officials in prosecuting the perpetrators.[15] But for the most part, he held his tongue on the subject, for policy and personal peace, and now said nothing about his preaching and war policies that formed part of the backdrop for events in 1857. He asked some men to ride through the night to witness the execution and give him a report.[16] Josiah Rogerson, a stenographer and telegrapher who had reported Lee's first trial, hurried from Beaver. He would provide a record of Lee's last words.[17]

Though estimates would vary widely, by midmorning as many as three hundred onlookers were at the Meadows, many of them Mormons from nearby settlements. Patterson's men kept most people at a distance—some climbed surrounding hills for a better view.[18] The official party, closer in and new to the area, seemed surprised by what they saw. Instead of the legendary lush grasses of the Meadows, they saw deep gullies, scrub oak, and sage. Near the old springs—or perhaps just its remains—was a "sunken pool of slimy, filthy water." The rivulet that once ran through the southern end of the valley had been replaced by an ugly wash 20 feet deep and about 150 feet wide. Some said the change was from natural erosion. Others said it was the "cu[r]se of God."[19]

Lee's life was now measured by minutes. U.S. Attorney Sumner Howard, Marshal Nelson, and Reverend Stokes took him aside for one last interview—and one last attempt to have him accuse Young. In the end, Lee signed a document implicating "two or three others" in the massacre—but not the man they wanted most. Lee probably pointed to John Higbee, William Stewart, or the man most responsible, Isaac

Haight, who were all fugitives from the law. Several times during the morning, Lee was again asked about George A. Smith's statement at the Santa Clara narrows. He had said all he wished on the subject and now cut off any further questioning. "Let it pass," he said.[20] Smith had died eighteen months earlier.

A grand jury had indicted nine men for their roles in the massacre: William Dame, Haight, Higbee, Philip Klingensmith, Lee, and Stewart—all of whom played key parts in the tragedy—as well as three lesser known figures, George W. Adair, Samuel Jewkes, and Ellott Willden. Most had been arrested. Klingensmith turned state's evidence; Adair, Dame, Jewkes, and Willden were released for lack of evidence.[21] Haight, Higbee, and Stewart spent most of their lives running from deputies and, like their fellow perpetrators, from their own consciences.[22] Only Lee was tried by a jury and asked to pay with his life.[23]

On the way back to the main party, Lee rested on the arm of Reverend Stokes and "faltered just perceptibly" right before reaching his coffin, which had been set in front of three government wagons cloaked with blankets. Lee sat down on the coffin's lid, resting briefly before arising to make his final speech.[24]

He began deliberately, with few gestures, "then rushed off into a humid style."[25] "I have done nothing designedly wrong," he said, repeating the phrase that had been his salve for nearly twenty years. "My Conscience is clear before God and man. I am ready to meet my Redeemer." When he spoke of his family, his eyes moistened.[26] He had married nineteen wives and fathered more than sixty children, the youngest being three years old.[27] His wives had mostly deserted him; he named just three as he spoke.[28]

Lee was conscious that reporters were writing down each word, and he paused at times to allow them to catch up or to check himself from saying too much. Toward the end, his voice became stronger. "I do not believe everything that is now taught and practised by Brigham Young. I do not care who hears it, it is so. I believe he is leading the people astray, downward to distruction, but I believe in the gospel that was taught in its purity and introduced by Joseph Smith in former days." The speech lasted five minutes.[29]

Lee said nothing about the fears, the rumors, the mistaken beliefs, the bad timing, the poor communication, the leadership failures, the violent times, the perversion of religion, the concentration of authority, the unintended consequences of the Utah War—and the simple bad luck—that led to the massacre. He said nothing about such things as guilt, crime, and redemption—how he and others in the massacre represented the human struggle in a large and horrible way. And he said nothing of how the Meadows became an obscenity to all the good things Mormonism stood for.

When Lee last met Young, seven months before Lee's arrest, they were friendly. Four years before the meeting, after learning details of the massacre that were new to him, Young had excommunicated Lee from the church for "extreem wickedness."[30] Even earlier, Young condemned Lee for his role in the massacre, but as his adoptive father and spiritual leader, encouraged him to live the best he could in the remaining years of his life.[31] Before their final meeting, Young heard Lee was keeping bad company, playing cards, and using foul language. "John," he chastened, "you Must be careful & stand to your integrity." He then blessed Lee and drove on.[32] They would not meet again.

In the final moments of his life, unable to undo the atrocity that played out on his execution site two decades before or to face fully the reality of what he had done, Lee clung to a last vestige of integrity. He had grown bitter toward Young for abandoning him in his final years. But even as he faced the firing squad, Lee refused to accuse Young of the massacre.

Lee sat erect on his coffin, hands on his head, his chest thrust out. "Don't let them mangle my body," he said to the marshal.[33]

At exactly 11:00 a.m., five balls tore through Lee and left a skipping pattern on the grass behind.[34]

EXECUTION OF JOHN D. LEE.

JOHN D. LEE EXECUTION. *Jacob Piatt Dunn*, Massacres of the Mountains (*New York*, *Harper & Brothers*, *1886*.)

Acknowledgments

W<small>E EXPRESS APPRECIATION</small> to the many men and women across the United States whose assistance made this book possible.

Colleagues in the Family and Church History Department and other departments of the Church of Jesus Christ of Latter-day Saints and Brigham Young University traveled to many libraries, archives, and other historical institutions, prepared hundreds of research memos, read our manuscript, offered helpful suggestions, and engaged us in scholarly debate that left our manuscript improved. We extend special thanks to Grant Anderson, Ronald O. Barney, Melvin L. Bashore, Jay G. Burrup, Craig L. Foster, Chad Foulger, Janiece Johnson, Jeffery O. Johnson, Michael N. Landon, Chad M. Orton, Brent Reber, Jennifer Reeder, Brian D. Reeves, Glenn N. Rowe, and Michael L. Shamo.

We benefited from the professionalism of several editors, including Amanda Midgley Borneman, Rachel Evans, Edward A. Geary, Daryl Gibson, Marny K. Parkin, and Heather Seferovich. Alison Kitchen Gainer—a relative of massacre victims—led the cite-checking effort. As content editor, Barbara Jones Brown became a colleague in the writing task, helping not only with diction but with narrative suggestions and organization. We also express thanks to Cynthia Read, our editor at Oxford University Press, production editor Joellyn Ausanka, and copy editor Mary Sutherland.

With her expertise in reading nineteenth-century Pitman short-hand, LaJean Purcell Carruth made a modern transcript of John D. Lee's two trials, as well as other manuscripts of shorthand records held in the Church History Library and other institutions. Likewise, Amy Carruth's skill in reading "Deseret Alphabet," the short-lived Latter-day Saint pioneer phonetic spelling system, also gave first-time access to several other historical records.

William W. Slaughter helped with historical images; Micheal Richards created our original cover design; Tom Child and Sheryl Dickert Smith laid out maps; and Wally Barrus, John W. Telford, and James W. and Marlene C. Walker took present-day photographs.

Others at church headquarters or Brigham Young University who gave countless hours of assistance with their various skills and knowledge include Jeff Anderson, Mary Teresa Anderson, Stephanie Anderson, Loren G. Ashcraft, Christy Best, Tim Bingaman, Ada-lia Bollschweiler, Karen S. Bolzendahl, Aaron M. Chomjak, Scott R. Christensen, Christine Cox, Ted Cox, Richard H. Davis, W. Randall Dixon, Larry W. Draper, Patrick C. Dunshee, Terrence Durham, Marie Hyatt Erickson, Mary K. Gifford, Carolyn Gull, Michael J. Hall, Elaine E. Hasleton, Sharalyn D. Howcroft, Dean C. Jessee, Dawn C. Martindale, Robbie McArthur, Marie McBride, Pauline K. Musig, Veneese Nelson, Jerry A. Niederhauser, Steven L. Olsen, Richard Oman, Kathryn Phillips, Sidney H. Price, David F. Putnam, David E. Rencher, Shirley Rogers, Bonnie Shuler, Marianne Skinner, T. Michael Smith, Brian W. Sokolowsky, Sarah Sorenson, Mark Staker, Vicki Standing, John D. Stemmons, Russell Taylor, F. Michael Watson, Ronald G. Watt, Vivian Wellman, David J. Whittaker, and April Williamsen. We also appreciate the contribution of numerous church service missionaries. In order to understand mid-nineteenth-century cattle diseases and deaths near Corn Creek, Utah, we asked medical specialists for advice: Paul V. Christofferson, DVM; Edmund C. Evans, MD; DeVon C. Hale, MD; Quinton S. Harris, MD; John H. Holbrook, MD; Robert K. Maddock Jr., MD; John M. Matsen, MD; and George F. Snell, MD. Fritjof F. Langeland, MD, and Larry J. Wright, MD, along with Shannon A. Novak, helped debunk the old myth that victims of the massacre showed signs of venereal disease. Ugo A. Perego and Scott Woodward offered advice on DNA and other laboratory questions. We acknowledge the forensic and archeological advice of Shane Baker, Shannon A. Novak, and George J. Throckmorton.

We have endeavored to listen to the various voices of people and groups represented in the Mountain Meadows story. The following men and women have helped us understand the viewpoint of relatives of massacre victims and perpetrators: Don Baker, Phil Bolinger, Robert H. Briggs, Lucile Wilcock Brubaker, Sharon Chambers, Diana Dowden, Renee Durfee, Bob Fancher, Diann and Harley Fancher, J. K. Fancher, Karen and Scott Fancher, Lynn-Marie Fancher, Terry Fancher, Brian W. Higbee, Talana S. Hooper, Kyle Kennedy, LeRoy Lee, Richard and Rosemary Lee, Verne R. Lee, Roger V. Logan Jr., Ronald E. Loving, Gerald Lynch, Karen Maxwell, Patty Norris, Randall Paul, Shirley H. Pyron, Betty Ramsey, James Sanders, Stella Lee Shamo, Susan Skinner, Carmen R. Smith, Jared O. Smith, Jim W. Tackitt, Eric Wadsworth, Cheri Baker Walker, David L. and Sharon Willden, and Richard Wilson.

We actively sought the perspective of Southern Paiutes, including Annette "Nikki" Borchardt, Jeanine Borchardt, Barbara Chavez, Darlene Pete Harrington, Marilyn Virginia Rice Jake, Shirley Jake, Vivienne C. Jake, Wilford Moroni Jake, Clarence John, Earnestine Lehi, Dorena Martineau, Willard G. Pete, Arthur Richards, Glenn Rogers, Alex Shepherd, Eleanor Bushhead Tom, Gary Tom, Lora Tom, Gloria Vincent, and Rita Pete Garcia Walker. We also wish to recognize Logan Hebner, who has spent much of his free time capturing Paiute oral histories.

Our research has been aided by the skills and knowledge of archivists, librarians, historians (including local and family historians), trail experts, collectors, and others with technical and subject specialties, some of whom responded to our newspaper solicitation for information. These include but are not be limited to Ann Rogerson Adams, Curtis R. Allen, Ron Andersen, Lavina Fielding Anderson, Richard L. Anderson, Sharon Avery, Anna Jean Backus, Russell Baker, Philip L. Barlow, Daniel R. Bartholomew, Lowell C. Bennion, Gary James Bergera, LaMar C. Berrett, Peter J. Blodgett, Lee Bracken, Newell G. Bringhurst, Spencer and Lavelle Brinkerhoff, Ann Buttars, McClain Bybee, Kent Bylund, Raydene Cluff, John L. Cooper III, Robert D. Crockett, Kevin Cromar, Forrest S. Cuch, Charles H. Cureton, Dennis "C" Davis, Paul R. DeBry, Peter H. DeLafosse, Terry Del Bene, Jonathan A. Dibble, Dixie Dillon, Maurianne Dunn, Christine M. and George H. Durham, John Eldredge, Ed Firmage, Jack Earl Fletcher, Patricia K. A. Fletcher, Annewhite T. Fuller, John S. Gardner, Tina Gillman, Kenneth W. Godfrey, John R. Gonzales, Jean and John H. Groberg, Jo Lynne Harline, Howard Hatch, Julie Held, Wayne K. Hinton, Mark W. Holden, Dennis B. Horne, John C. Houston, George Hurt, Larry Hutchings, Lisa Irle, Marian "Omar" Jacklin,

Suzanne Scott Jennings, Laura R. Jolley, Christopher Jones, Rhonda Larkin, Nicholas S. Literski, Clint Lytle, Allen J. Malmquist, Jeffrey Mann, Michele Margetts, Paul S. Martineau, Shirley L. McFadzean, Brandon J. Metcalf, Tom Milner, Paula Mitchell, Dorothy O'Brien, Nathan B. Oman, Dennis Osmond, Carolyn and James C. Pace, Ardis E. Parshall, Michael Harold Paulos, Richard Peuser, Merle Prince, Stephen J. Pyne, W. Paul Reeve, Richard L. Rieck, Brent and Lynette Robinson, Stephen D. Robison, Merle Romer, Ronald E. Romig, Rod Ross, Vicki Rounsavall, William J. Sawaya, Janet Burton Seegmiller, Lyle E. and Tracy Shamo, Edwina Jo Snow, G. Murray Snow, James LeVoy Sorenson, E. Diane Stemmons, Dell Stout, Stephen C. Sturgeon, Jennifer M. Thomas, Morris A. Thurston, Paul Tinker, Ernest Carl Turley, John Wadsworth, Nathaniel Wadsworth, Jeffrey Walker, John W. Welch, Sharon White, Gary Williams, Camille Woodland, and Fred E. Woods.

The administrative assistants at church headquarters and at Brigham Young University provided invaluable assistance: Melissa Cantwell, Marjean Crowther, Jo Lyn Curtis, Dorsalle G. Ford, Joan S. Harding, Viola Knecht, Laura Korth, Valerie Lindeman, Andrea H. Maxfield, Kiersten Olson, Marilyn R. Parks, Renee Powell, JaNell H. Riley, Gina Sconiers, Karen Lee Westenskow, and Kally Whittle.

Although we sought to work from primary sources wherever possible, we also consulted many works already written about the massacre and acknowledge the contributions of their authors through our source notes.

As our manuscript was coming into focus, we asked more than three dozen friends and scholars to read it and offer feedback. These men and women, who represented a cross section of disciplines and viewpoints, greatly improved our manuscript, confirming again that scholarship is a joint effort and that many of its best practitioners are generous contributors. We acknowledge Douglas D. Alder, Brent F. Ashworth, R. Davis Bitton, Annette "Nikki" Borchardt, Robert H. Briggs, Karl F. Brooks, Lucile Wilcock Brubaker, Richard L. Bushman, John K. Carmack, Sharon Chambers, Lawrence G. Coates, Todd M. Compton, Peter H. DeLafosse, Sheri L. Dew, Ronald K. Esplin, Kathleen Flake, Sarah Barringer Gordon, Leo A. Jardine, Richard L. Jensen, Verne R. Lee, Patricia H. MacKinnon, Patrick Q. Mason, Armand L. Mauss, Cory H. and Karen Maxwell, Louis A. Moench, Reid L. Neilson, Patty Norris, Eric C. Olson, Ardis E. Parshall, Gene A. Sessions, Jan Shipps, Paul H. Smith, John Thomas, Lora Tom, Shirley S. Turley, John Turner, and Eric Wadsworth. We express special thanks to Thomas G. Alexander and William P. MacKinnon. In addition to reading the manuscript, the former joined our weekly discussions for several months and gave invaluable input, while the latter sometimes suggested language which, with his permission, we adopted. We also express appreciation for the support and feedback of Russell M. Nelson and Dallin H. Oaks, advisors to the Family and Church History Department, and of Marlin K. Jensen, Church Historian.

One of the goals of our book was exhaustive research. We thank the following institutions and their staffs for their help:

Alabama: Huntsville–Madison County Public Library, Huntsville; M. Louis Salmon Library, University of Alabama, Huntsville.

Arizona: Arizona Historical Society, Tucson; Cline Library, Northern Arizona University, Flagstaff; Hayden Library, Arizona State University, Tempe; University of Arizona Library, Tucson.

Arkansas: Alma Public Library, Alma; Arkansas History Commission, Little Rock; Benton County Historical Society, Bentonville; Boone County Heritage Museum, Harrison; Boone County Library, Harrison; Carroll County Clerk-Recorder, Berryville; Carroll County Historical and Genealogical Society, Berryville; Crawford County Genealogical Society, Alma; Fort Smith Public Library, Fort Smith; Franklin County Library, Ozark; Grace Keith Genealogical Collection, Fayetteville Public Library, Fayetteville; Grand Lodge Masonic Library of Arkansas, Little Rock; Johnson County Public Library, Clarksville; L. S. and Hazel C. Robson Library, University of the Ozarks, Clarksville; Marion County Arkansas Heritage Society, Yellville; Madison County Library, Huntsville; Newton County Historical Society, Jasper; Newton County Library, Jasper; Northwest Arkansas Genealogical Society, Rogers; Pope County Library, Russellville; Van Buren Public Library, Van Buren.

California: Bancroft Library, University of California, Berkeley; Beale Memorial Library, Bakersfield; Calaveras County Historical Society, San Andreas; California State Library, Sacramento; Cecil H. Green Library, Stanford University, Stanford; Charles E. Young Research Library, University of California, Los Angeles; College of the Sequoias Library, Visalia; Columbia State Historic Park, Columbia; Colusa County Free Library, Colusa; Doris Foley Library for Historical Research, Nevada City; Fresno City and County Historical Society Archives, Fresno; Fresno County Public Library, Fresno; George and Verda Armacost Library, University of California, Redlands; Gerald D. Kennedy Reference Library, San Joaquin County Historical Society & Museum, Lodi; Haggin Museum, Stockton; Henry Wilson

Coil Masonic Library and Museum, Grand Lodge of the Free and Accepted Masons of California, San Francisco; Humboldt County Historical Society, Eureka; Huntington Library, San Marino; John M. Pfau Library, California State University, San Bernardino; Lake County Historic Courthouse Museum, Lakeport; Mariposa County Assessor and Recorder's Office, Mariposa; Mariposa County Library, Mariposa; Merced County Historical Society, Merced; Merced County Library, Merced; Merced County Recorder's Office, Merced; Meriam Library, California State University, Chico; Modesto Public Library, Modesto; Mojave River Valley Museum, Barstow; Napa City-County Library, Napa; North Baker Research Library, California Historical Society, San Francisco; Northern Mariposa County History Center, Coulterville; Oviatt Library, California State University, Northridge; Porterville Public Library, Porterville; San Joaquin Recorder/County Clerk's Office, Stockton; Stanislaus County Clerk-Recorder Office, Modesto; Stockton-San Joaquin County Public Library, Stockton; California State Library-Sutro, San Francisco; Sutter's Fort State Historic Park, Sacramento; Tulare County Museum, Visalia; Tulare County Library, Visalia; Tulare Public Library, Tulare; Tulare County Clerk-Recorder's Office, Visalia; Tuolumne County Museum and History Center, Sonora; Tuolumne County Library, Sonora; Tuolumne County Recorder's Office, Sonora; University Library, California State University, Sacramento; University Library, California State University, Stanislaus, at Turlock; University Library, University of California, Davis; University of California, San Diego; William Knox Holt Memorial Library, University of the Pacific, Stockton; Workman and Temple Family Homestead Museum, City of Industry.

Colorado: Denver Public Library; National Archives and Records Administration, Rocky Mountain Region, Denver; Stephen H. Hart Library, Colorado Historical Society, Denver; University Libraries, University of Colorado, Boulder.

Connecticut: Beinecke Rare Book and Manuscript Library, Yale University, New Haven.

Georgia: Columbus Public Library, Columbus; Georgia Historical Society, Savannah; Troup County Historical Society Archives, LaGrange.

Idaho: Eli M. Oboler Library, Idaho State University, Pocatello.

Illinois: Abraham Lincoln Presidential Library, Springfield; Charleston Carnegie Public Library, Charleston; Coles County Historical Society, Mattoon; Mattoon Public Library, Mattoon; Research Center, Chicago History Museum, Chicago.

Indiana: Allen County Public Library, Fort Wayne; Indiana Historical Society, Indianapolis.

Iowa: Grand Lodge of Iowa, A.F. and A.M., Masonic Library and Museum, Cedar Rapids; State Historical Society of Iowa Library, Des Moines.

Kansas: Kenneth Spencer Research Library, University of Kansas, Lawrence; Leavenworth Public Library, Leavenworth; State Archives and Library, Kansas State Historical Society, Topeka.

Maryland: National Archives and Records Administration, College Park.

Michigan: Alfred P. Sloan Museum, Flint; Archives of Michigan, Lansing; Bentley Historical Library, University of Michigan, Ann Arbor; Detroit Public Library, Detroit; Flint Public Library, Flint; Genesee County Genealogical Society, Flint; Genesee County Probate Court, Flint; Library of Michigan, Lansing.

Mississippi: J. D. Williams Library, University of Mississippi, University.

Missouri: Barry-Lawrence Regional Library, Cassville; B. D. Owens Library, Northwest Missouri State University, Maryville; Boonslick Regional Library, Warsaw; Clay County Archives and Historical Library, Liberty; Community of Christ Archives, Independence; Duane G. Meyer Library, Missouri State University, Springfield; F. W. Olin Library, Drury University, Springfield; George A. Spiva Library, Missouri Southern State University, Joplin; Henry County Museum, Clinton; James C. Kirkpatrick Library, Central Missouri State University, Warrensburg; Johnson County Clerk, Warrensburg; Joplin Public Library, Joplin; Joseph R. Palmer Family Memorial Library, Elsberry; Kansas City Public Library, Kansas City; Lincoln County Recorder of Deeds, Troy; Mid-Continent Public Library, North Independence Branch, Independence; Mid-Continent Public Library, Platte City Branch, Platte City; Miller Nichols Library, University of Missouri–Kansas City; Missouri State Archives, Jefferson City; National Frontier Trails Museum, Independence; Northwest Missouri Genealogical Society, St. Joseph; Ozarks Genealogical Society, Springfield; Powell Memorial Library, Troy; Springfield-Greene County Library, Springfield; State Historical Society of Missouri, Columbia; Trails Regional Library, Lexington Branch, Lexington; Trails Regional Library, Warrensburg Branch, Warrensburg.

Montana: Montana Historical Society, Helena.

Nebraska: Nebraska State Historical Society, Lincoln.

Nevada: Lied Library, University of Nevada, Las Vegas; Lincoln County Recorder's Office, Pioche; Nevada Historical Society, Reno; Nevada State Library and Archives, Carson City; Noble H. Getchell Library, University of Nevada, Reno.

New Jersey: Firestone Library, Princeton University, Princeton.

New Mexico: Center for Southwest Research, University of New Mexico, Albuquerque.

New York: New-York Historical Society, New York.

North Carolina: Danbury Public Library, Danbury; Dobson Community Library, Dobson; Greensboro Public Library, Greensboro; Louis Round Wilson Library, University of North Carolina, Chapel Hill; North Carolina State Archives, Raleigh; Olivia Raney Local History Library, Raleigh; Orange County Public Library, Hillsborough; Rare Book, Manuscript, and Special Collections Library, Duke University, Durham; Rockingham County Public Library, Eden Branch, Eden; Rockingham County Public Library, Madison Branch, Madison; State Library of North Carolina, Raleigh.

Oklahoma: Oklahoma Department of Libraries, Oklahoma City; Oklahoma Historical Society, Oklahoma City; Oklahoma State University Library, Stillwater; Western History Collection, University of Oklahoma, Norman.

Oregon: Oregon Historical Society, Portland; Southern Oregon Historical Society, Research Library, Medford.

Pennsylvania: Historical Society of Pennsylvania, Philadelphia; Lancaster County Historical Society, Lancaster; United States Army Military History Institute, Carlisle; York County Archives, York; York County Heritage Trust Library and Archives, York.

Tennessee: Charles C. Sherrod Library, East Tennessee State University, Johnson City; Chattanooga–Hamilton County Bicentennial Library, Chattanooga; Clyde W. Roddy Library, Dayton; East Tennessee Historical Society, Knoxville; Fentress County Library, Jamestown; Fort Loudoun Regional Library, Athens; Greeneville/Greene County Public Library, Greeneville; Jean and Alexander Heard Library, Vanderbilt University, Nashville; Meigs-Decatur Public Library, Decatur; Millard Oakley Library, Livingston; Overton County Archives, Livingston; T. Elmer Cox Library, Greeneville; Tennessee State Library and Archives, Nashville.

Texas: Center for American History, University of Texas, Austin; University Library, University of Texas El Paso.

Utah: Beaver County Offices, Beaver; Church History Library, The Church of Jesus Christ of Latter-day Saints, Salt Lake City; Family

History Library, The Church of Jesus Christ of Latter-day Saints, Salt Lake City; Gerald R. Sherratt Library, Southern Utah University, Cedar City; Harold B. Lee Library, Brigham Young University, Provo; Howard W. Hunter Law Library, Brigham Young University, Provo; J. Willard Marriott Library, University of Utah, Salt Lake City; Merrill-Cazier Library, Utah State University, Logan; Pioneer Memorial Museum, International Society-Daughters of the Utah Pioneers, Salt Lake City; S. J. Quinney Law Library, University of Utah, Salt Lake City; Spencer S. Eccles Health Sciences Library, University of Utah, Salt Lake City; Stewart Library, Weber State University, Ogden; St. George Regional Family History Training Center, St. George; Utah State Archives, Salt Lake City; Utah State Historical Society, Salt Lake City; Utah Territorial Statehouse State Park Museum, Fillmore; Val A. Browning Library, Dixie State College of Utah, St. George; Washington County Library, St. George.

Virginia: Loudoun Circuit Court, Leesburg; Thomas Balch Library, Leesburg; Wythe-Grayson Regional Library, Independence.

Washington, D.C.: Daughters of the American Revolution Library; Library of Congress; National Archives and Records Administration; Smithsonian Institution.

Wyoming: American Heritage Center, University of Wyoming, Laramie.

Finally, we express gratitude to our families, without whose support we could never have completed this book.

Appendix A

The Emigrants

THE FOLLOWING IS a list of emigrants known or strongly believed to have perished in the Mountain Meadows Massacre, along with the seventeen children who survived. The emigrants are listed alphabetically by family name, then by age within each family group. The names of unmarried children are indented after the names of their parents; the surviving children's names appear in italics. After each name is the person's approximate age at the time of the massacre.[1] Subscript notes indicate that a person was memorialized as a massacre victim on the 1955 monument in Harrison, Arkansas (designated by *H*); on the 1990 monument at Mountain Meadows (designated by *M*); or on the program published for the September 10, 1999, memorial service at Mountain Meadows (designated by *MS*). Some names that follow do not appear on any of these three lists. Some persons identified in the past as massacre victims, like Charles Stallcup and Alf Smith, do not appear. Though originally thought to have perished in the massacre, these persons, in fact, left the wagon train sometime before the massacre and thus survived.

For additional information about the emigrants, including other possible victims and lists of emigrants who traveled with or near the victims during their journey west, see mountainmeadowsmassacre.org.

Aden, William Allen, 19. He crossed the plains with another train but joined the Arkansas company around Parowan, where he visited William Leany, who had been befriended by his father in Tennessee. Shot on Monday, September 7, at Leach's Spring by William C. Stewart.[2] H, M, MS

Baker, George W., 27. A son of John Twitty Baker, he had previously spent time in Stockton, Sonora, and Columbia, California, during the gold rush.[3] H, M, MS

Baker, Manerva Ann Beller, 25. Older sister of David W. and Melissa Ann Beller. H, M, MS

> **Mary Lovina, 7.** During the massacre, her sister Martha saw her being led by a couple of men over a ridge.[4] H, M, MS
>
> *Martha Elizabeth*, **5.** She later married James William Terry of Harrison, Arkansas, and resided there until her death in 1940.[5] H, M, MS
>
> *Sarah Frances*, **2.** She eventually married Joseph A. Gladden and moved to Muskogee, Oklahoma. After Gladden's death, she married Manley C. Mitchell. Died in Muskogee in 1947.[6] H, M, MS
>
> *William Twitty*, **9 months.** Later worked as a mail carrier. Married twice and was the father of fourteen children. Died in Searcy County, Arkansas, in 1937.[7] H, M, MS

Baker, John Twitty, 52. Captain of one of the trains that made up the Arkansas company, he left his wife and some grown children back in Carroll County, planning to meet up with them again after his trip across the plains.[8] H, M, MS

> **Baker, Abel, 19.** Probably one of three men who left the wagon corral during the week of the massacre to seek help in California and were killed before reaching their destination.[9] H, M, MS

Beach, John, 21. Stood four feet six inches and was known for being very dexterous. He was probably hired as a drover for the cattle.[10] M, MS

Beller, David W., 12. An orphan, he was a ward of George W. Baker.[11] H, M, MS

Beller, Melissa Ann, 14. An orphan, she was a ward of George W. Baker.[12] H, M,

Cameron, William, 51. Lived in Carroll County before moving to Johnson County, Arkansas, his home previous to his journey west.[13] H, M, MS

Cameron, Martha, 51. H, M, MS

Tillman, 24. He owned the racehorse called One-Eye Blaze. He had been in business at Fort Smith, Arkansas, before joining his family on the trip west.[14] M, MS

Isom, 18. M, MS

Henry, 16. M, MS

James, 14. M, MS

Martha, 11. M, MS

Larkin, 8. M, MS

Cameron, Nancy, 12. Niece of William Cameron. M, MS

Coker, Edward, 27. Tried ranching in Texas before joining the emigration to California.[15]

Coker, Charity Porter, 37. The Cokers were reported to have **two children** traveling with them.

Cooper, William E., 29. A carriage maker by trade, he and his wife were living in Dubuque, Scott County, Iowa, in 1856.[16]

Cooper, Abbey, 29.

Deshazo, Allen P., 22. Brother-in-law of John H. Baker and son-in-law of John Twitty Baker. He may have worked as a cattle drover during the trip.[17] H, M, MS

Dunlap, Jesse, Jr., 39. Brother of Lorenzo D. Dunlap, brother-in-law and mercantile partner of William C. Mitchell, a former Arkansas state senator.[18] H, M, MS

Dunlap, Mary Wharton, 39. Sister of Nancy Wharton Dunlap. H, M, MS

Ellender, 18. M, MS

Nancy M., 16. M, MS

James D., 14. M, MS

Lucinda, 12. Twin sisters Lucinda and Susannah were reportedly murdered after most of the other emigrants were already dead.[19] M, MS

Susannah, 12. M, MS

Margarette, 11. M, MS

Mary Ann, 9. M, MS

Rebecca Jane, **6.** She and her two surviving sisters lived with Jacob Hamblin until she was returned to Arkansas. She married John Wesley Evins and resided in Calhoun and then Drew County, Arkansas. She died in 1914.[20] H, M, MS

Louisa, **4.** She eventually married James M. Linton and settled first in Pope County, Arkansas, and then in Oklahoma, where she died in 1926.[21] H, M, MS

Sarah Elizabeth, 1. She was "shot through one of her arms, below the elbow, by a large ball, breaking both bones and cutting the arm off." While living with the Hamblins, she developed an eye infection and eventually went blind. She later married James Lynch, who assisted in rescuing the surviving children. She died in 1901.[22] H, M, MS

Dunlap, Lorenzo Dow, 42. Brother of Jesse Dunlap and brother-in-law of William C. Mitchell.[23] H, M, MS

Dunlap, Nancy Wharton, 42. Sister of Mary Wharton Dunlap. M, MS

    Thomas J., 18. M, MS

    John H., 16. M, MS

    Mary Ann, 13. M, MS

    Talitha Emaline, 11. M, MS

    Nancy, 9. M, MS

    America Jane, 7. M, MS

    Prudence Angeline, 5. She married Claiborne Hobbs Koen and settled in Texas, where she raised eight children. She died in 1918.[24] H, M, MS

    Georgia Ann, 18 months. Eventually married George Marshall McWhirter and settled in Dallas, Texas. She died in 1920.[25] H, M, MS

Eaton, William M., adult, age unknown. Originally from Indiana, he appears to have been farming in Illinois when he decided to go west. He sent his wife and children back to Indiana to await his return.[26] H, M, MS

Edwards, Silas, age unknown. According to Baker descendants, he was a younger brother of John Twitty Baker's mother, Hannah.[27] M, MS

Fancher, Alexander, 45. Described as "tall, slim, erect, of dark complexion, a singer, and a born leader and organizer of men." He served in the Carroll County militia to end the Tutt-Everett War in neighboring Marion County, Arkansas. Led his own company west. Probably captained the Arkansas company that formed in Salt Lake City before heading south.[28] H, M, MS

Fancher, Eliza Ingram, 33. H, M, MS

    Hampton, 19. H, M, MS

    William, 17. H, M, MS

    Mary, 15. H, M, MS

    Thomas, 14. H, M, MS

    Martha, 10. H, M, MS

    Margaret A., 8. H, M, MS

    Sarah G., 8. H, M, MS

Christopher "Kit" Carson, **5.** He died in 1873 at the home of his cousin Hampton Bynum Fancher.[29] H, M, MS

Triphenia, **22 months.** Married James Chaney Wilson and had eleven children. She died in Osage, Carroll County, Arkansas, in 1897.[30] H, M, MS

Fancher, James Mathew, 25. Cousin of Alexander Fancher and brother of Robert Fancher.[31] H, M, MS

Fancher, Frances "Fanny" Fulfer, age unknown.[32] M, MS

Fancher, Robert, 19. Cousin of Alexander Fancher and brother of James Fancher. H, M, MS

Gresly, John, 21. Possibly the man identified as the troublesome "German" or "Dutchman." Born in Pennsylvania to German parents.[33]

Hamilton. Frank King identified a Hamilton with the company; John D. Lee said a man named Hamilton met him outside of the emigrants' corral before the final massacre and acted as the emigrants' spokesman.[34] H, M, MS

Huff, Saladia Ann Brown, 38. Saladia's husband, Peter Huff, died on the plains before reaching Salt Lake City. Her daughter Nancy Saphrona remembered seeing her shot in the forehead and fall dead during the massacre.[35] H, M, MS

> **John, 14.** Likely one of the unidentified Huff sons listed on the monument. M, MS
> **William C., 13.** M, MS
> **Mary E., 11.**
> **James K., 8.** Likely one of the unidentified Huff sons listed on the monument. M, MS
> *Nancy Saphrona,* **4.** She remembered being held in the arms of John Twitty Baker at the time he was killed. She later married George Dallas Cates and died in Yell County, Arkansas, in 1878 at the young age of twenty-five.[36] H, M, MS
> **son, age unknown.**[37]

Jones, John Milum, 32. Brother of Newton Jones and son-in-law of Cyntha Tackitt. Left from Johnson County with the Tackitts and planned to start a ranch with his brother, Newton.[38] H, M, MS

Jones, Eloah Angeline Tackitt, 26. Daughter of Cyntha Tackitt. H, M, MS
> **child, age unknown.**[39] H, M, MS

Felix Marion, 18 months. Government officials initially misidentified the recovered child as "Elisha Huff" and, later, "Ephraim Huff." Eventually, as a young man, he moved to Texas, where he married Martha Ann Reed and fathered five children. He died in 1932.[40] H, M, MS

Jones, Newton, 23. Brother of John M. Jones.[41] M, MS

McEntire, Lawson A., 21. His older brother, John, had gone west several years earlier but died of tuberculosis in Salt Lake City. Lawson probably worked as a drover for the wagon train.[42] H, M, MS

Miller, Josiah (Joseph), 30. The uncle of Armilda Miller Tackitt, he and his family left from Crawford County, Arkansas.[43] H, M, MS
Miller, Matilda Cameron, 26. Daughter of William and Martha Cameron. Her son, John Calvin, told how he pulled arrows from his mother's body during the massacre.[44] H, M, MS

> **James William, 9.** M, MS
> *John Calvin*, 6. Government officials originally misidentified the recovered Miller children as having the surname of "Sorel." He accompanied Jacob Forney to Washington, D.C., to testify about the massacre and by 1860 was back in Carroll County, Arkansas. H, M, MS
> *Mary*, 4. She may have been the girl the Haight family called Ann Marie and is thought to have eventually settled in Tennessee.[45] H, M, MS
> *Joseph*, 1. As an adult, he went by the name of William Tillman Miller. Married Brancey Ann Reese Boyd or Boyed in Navarro County, Texas, and fathered six children. He later moved to California and died in Turlock, Stanislaus, California, in 1940.[46] H, M, MS

Mitchell, Charles R., 25. Son of prominent Arkansan William C. Mitchell and nephew of Jesse and Lorenzo Dunlap, he planned to start a cattle ranch with his brother Joel.[47] H, M, MS
Mitchell, Sarah C. Baker, 21. Daughter of John Twitty Baker. H, M, MS
> **John, infant.** H, M, MS

Mitchell, Joel D., 23. Brother of Charles R. Mitchell, son of William C. Mitchell, and nephew of Jesse and Lorenzo Dunlap. H, M, MS

Prewit, John, 20. From Marion County, Arkansas, he was probably hired as a drover.[48] H, M, MS

Prewit, William, 18. Brother of John Prewit, he too was probably a drover. H, M, MS

Rush, Milum Lafayette, 29. When he traveled west, his wife and two young children remained behind to wait for his return.[49] H, M, MS

Tackitt, Cyntha, 49. Commonly known as "Widow Tackitt" because her husband, Martin Tackitt, had died several years before she traveled west. She and her family left from Johnson County, Arkansas, and were traveling to Tuolumne County, California, where a son resided.[50] H, M, MS
    William H., 23. H
    Marion, 20. H, M, MS
    Sebron, 18. M, MS
    Matilda, 16. M, MS
    James M., 14. M, MS
    Jones M., 12. M, MS

Tackitt, Pleasant, 25. A son of Cyntha Tackitt, he left from Johnson County.[51] H, M, MS

Tackitt, Armilda Miller, 22. Niece of Josiah (Joseph) Miller and first cousin to John Calvin, Mary, and Joseph Miller.[52] H, M, MS
    Emberson Milum, **4.** He accompanied Jacob Forney to Washington, D.C., to testify about the massacre. He married Mary Bilinda Snow of Carroll County, Arkansas. He later settled in Texas and then Prescott, Yavapai County, Arizona, where he served as a deputy sheriff. He died in 1912.[53] H, M, MS
    William Henry, **19 months.** He eventually married Viney Harris and settled on Shoal Creek above Protem, Taney County, Missouri. He died in 1891.[54] H, M, MS

Wilson, Richard, 27. According to family tradition, he was from Marion County, Arkansas, married Elizabeth Coker, and fathered one son.[55] H, M, MS

Wood, Solomon R., 20. Brother of William Wood and brother-in-law to Charles Stallcup and James Larramore, two men sometimes associated with the company. He was probably hired as a drover.[56] H, M, MS

Wood, William Edward, 26. Brother of Solomon Wood. H, M, MS

Appendix B

The Emigrants' Property

THE FOLLOWING TABLE lists the known property of the emigrants slain at Mountain Meadows. The amount and estimated value of property is taken from statements given by surviving friends and family members, as well as tax records from 1855 through 1857.

The table does not include all of the emigrants' property for two reasons. First, no property records exist for some of those known to have been killed in the massacre. Second, some of the victims have never been identified by name, making it impossible to account for property they may have owned. Witnesses in Utah gave several accounts of the emigrant property they saw, ranging from twelve to forty wagons and three hundred to eight hundred head of cattle to a variety of horses and mules, camp supplies, and provisions.[1]

The sources for the property values appear in the notes next to each emigrant's name. Discrepancies in values appear in the original source documents. For example, George W. Baker's oxen are estimated at $55 per yoke, while his father's are estimated at $50 to $70. Some of the sources provide numbers of items (such as wagons) but give no value. In such cases, endnotes are used to explain how the value was estimated. (See, for example, entry for value of Silas Edwards's horse.)

Name	Wagons	Wagon Value	Oxen	Oxen Value	Loose Cattle
Baker, George W.[2]	2	$250–75	16	$440[3]	134–44
Baker, John Twitty[7] Cameron, Tillman[11]	1	$100–$125	18	$450–$630[8]	130–40
Cameron, William[13]	2–3[14]	$500–$1,250[15]	16–24	$1,200–$3,000[16]	25–35[17]
Deshazo, Allen P.[21]					16–17
Dunlap, Jesse Jr.[23]	3	$300	18	$540[24]	30
Dunlap, Lorenzo Dow[27]	1	$100	8	$240[28]	12
Edwards, Silas[30]					
Fancher, Alexander[33]	4	$400–$550[34]	12	$300–$900[35]	200
Fancher, James Mathew[38]					
Huff, Peter & Saladia Ann[39]					20
Jones, John Milum & Newton[43]	1	$125	2–8	$65–$260[44]	6–8
Mitchell, Charles R. & Joel D.[46]	1	$120	26	$780[47]	72–74[48]
Rush, Milum Lafayette[52]					10–12
Poteets, & Basham[54]	0–2[55]	$0–$275[56]	*		0–60
Tackitt, Pleasant[59]	1	$100–$137.50[60]	*		
Totals	16–19	$1,995–$3,257.50	116–30	$4,015–$6,790	655–752

Francis Rowan remembered, "The Peteats and Pleasant Tackett had oxen and other property but I can not say how many." Fielding Wilburn recalled, "The Peteats, Basham, and Tacketts had three waggons several yoke of good oxen to each waggon and had one horse—had apparently plenty of provisions, cloathing and a general outfit to make the trip comfortable." Francis Marion Poteet and his family, and perhaps Basham, broke away from the group at some point

Loose Cattle Value	Horses	Mules	Horse & Mule Value	Cash	Misc. Personal Property	Total Value
$2,010–880[4]	3	0	$300–$375[5]	$400–$1,200[6]	$550–$685	$3,950–$5,855
$2,600–800[9]	1	2	$350–$400[10]	$98	$350–$500	$3,948–$4,553
	1[12]		$2,000–$6,000			$2,000–$6,000
$1,875–$3,150[18]	2–5	0–2	$160–$1,150[19]	$0–$3,000[20]		$3,735–$11,550
$240–55[22]					$60	$300–$315
$360[25]	2		$200[26]	$320	$450	$2,170
$180[29]					$400	$920
	1[31]		$40–$150[32]			$40–$150
$2,400–$4,000[36]	3	8	$730–$1,730[37]	$1,000–$2,000		$4,830–$9,180
	3		$120			$120
$250[40]	3	1	$225[41]	$1,200[42]		$1,675
$120–60[45]				$20–30	$515–$640	$845–$1,215
$864–88[49]	1		$100	$131–55[50]	$350	$2,369[51]
$150–80[53]				$25	$63	$238–68
$0–$1,200[57]	0–1		$0–$150[58]			$0–$1,625
						$100–$137.50
$11,049–$16,303	20–24	11–13	$4,225–$10,600	$3,194–$8,028	$2,738–$3,148	$27,240–$48,102.50

in their journey and arrived safely in California. It is not known how much of the listed property the Poteets took with them when they separated. Francis M. Rowan and Fielding Wilburn, depositions, October 24, 1860, PPU; Douglas McEuen, The Legend of Francis Marion Poteet and the Mountain Meadows Massacre *(Pleasanton, TX: Zabava Printing, 1996), 58, 122, 135; California, Los Angeles County, Los Angeles, 1860 U.S. Census, population schedule, 377.*

The documented property figures for the slain emigrants show they were a well-equipped group and that the bulk of the train's wealth was in its livestock. William C. Mitchell, a relative and acquaintance of many of the slain emigrants, estimated that the entire group leaving Arkansas had about nine hundred head of cattle, a number that may have included the work oxen as well as the loose cattle.[61] Many of the emigrants undoubtedly hoped to profit through the eventual sale of their cattle in the California market. Members of the Baker and Fancher families had been to California in the early 1850s when the cattle market reached its peak.[62] During that period, the price of cattle was as high as $75 per head in San Francisco and $40 in southern California.[63] By 1857, California prices had fallen to between $15 and $28 per head but still offered a potential profit for some, depending on the type and quality of stock. For example, milk cows ranged in price from $38 to $45.[64]

The property taken from the massacred emigrants also had considerable value in frontier Utah. In southern Utah in the fall of 1857, a wagon was valued between $75 and $100, a yoke of work oxen from $100 to $150, mules up to $150, milk cows around $50, and loose cattle between $35 and $60 per head.[65] Some of the emigrants' property was taken back to Cedar City and sold at a public auction held at the tithing office.[66] Some of the massacre participants ended up with much of the property. John D. Lee's total property value increased from $2,500 in 1850 to $49,500 in 1860, in part because of his industry but also because of the emigrants' property.[67] An acquaintance of slain emigrant Silas Edwards believed he saw Isaac Haight riding Edwards's horse a few days after the massacre.[68] Though he did not explain whether they bought them at the auction or took them at the Meadows, Lee said that Haight and Philip Klingensmith each got a span of mules, John Higbee got one mule, Samuel Knight and Joel White each got a mare, and Haight, Higbee, Richard Harrison, and Ira Allen each had a wagon.[69] Other sources said Harrison had a yoke of oxen and that two of the wagons were at Klingensmith's.[70] Paiutes were also seen with some of the cattle, horses, clothing, and other property.[71]

Appendix C
The Militiamen

THE FOLLOWING IS a list of men in the Iron Military District of Utah Territory's Nauvoo Legion militia whose names have been associated with the Mountain Meadows Massacre. The names have been gathered from a variety of sources including eyewitness accounts, arrest warrants and criminal indictments, and newspaper articles.

A completely accurate list of those who participated in or witnessed the murders of the California-bound emigrants may be impossible to compile. Many of the participants kept silent about their roles. The testimonies of many witnesses were given fifteen years or more after the massacre. Those who admitted being at the massacre were usually careful not to incriminate themselves and their closest associates.

The names are organized in alphabetical order. Each entry includes life span, as well as age, militia rank, and residence at the time of the massacre.[1] Because of the varying credibility of evidence, a note of *[A]* or *[B]* has been placed after each individual's name and age; *[A]* indicates there is strong evidence the individual planned, authorized, participated in, or witnessed the killing of emigrants, and *[B]* indicates that the evidence is inconclusive. Men whose names have been associated with the massacre are not listed if there is little or no evidence to support that association.[2]

For additional information on the militiamen, see mountain meadowsmassacre.org.

Adair, George Washington, Jr. (1837–1909), 20. [A] Private, Company I, Fifth Platoon, Washington City. One of the nine men indicted for the massacre. Adair admitted going to Mountain Meadows and was present for the massacre. He may have also been used as a messenger between the Meadows and Cedar City.[3]

Allen, Ira (1814–1900), 43. [A] Second Lieutenant, Company E, Fifth Platoon, Cedar City. At the September 6 council meeting, he sided with Isaac Haight's plan to destroy the emigrant company. He was one of the men on horseback during the final massacre whose orders were to catch and kill emigrants who attempted to escape the slaughter.[4]

Arthur, Benjamin A. (1834–83), 23. [A] Sergeant, Company D, Fourth Platoon, Cedar City. He was one of three men John M. Higbee sent to the Meadows to watch the emigrants. John D. Lee reported Arthur present when William Stewart and Joel White killed emigrant William Aden. Arthur was at the Meadows for the final massacre, though Ellott Willden claimed he was unarmed.[5]

Arthur, Christopher Jones (1832–1918), 25. [B] Adjutant, Company G, Cedar City. The son-in-law of Isaac C. Haight, he arrived at the Meadows with Elias Morris shortly after the massacre ended.[6]

Bateman, William (1824–69), 33. [A] Sergeant, Company G, Fourth Platoon, Cedar City. Prior to the massacre, he carried the white flag to the emigrants' corral.[7]

Cartwright, Thomas Henry (1814–73), 42. [A] Private, Company D, Fourth Platoon, Cedar City. Samuel Pollock recalled traveling with him to the Meadows.[8]

Clark, John Wesley (1818–69), 39. [A] Private, Company I, Third Platoon, Washington City. He was part of the Washington group that arrived at the Meadows on Tuesday morning.[9]

Clewes, Joseph (1831–94), 25. [B] Private, Company F, First Platoon, Cedar City. He served as a messenger between the Meadows and Cedar City. He left the Meadows before the final massacre but may have witnessed the killing of two emigrants near Leach's Spring on Tuesday.[10]

Coleman, Prime Thornton (1831–1905), 25. [B] Private, Company H, First Platoon, Fort Clara. Coleman admitted to massacre investigator James H. Carleton that he went with Ira Hatch toward the Muddy River and saw the footprints of three emigrants who escaped from Mountain Meadows. His statement led Carleton to believe that he assisted Hatch in tracking and killing those men.[11]

Curtis, Ezra Houghton (1822–1915), 35. [A] Second Lieutenant, Company E, First Platoon, Cedar City. Samuel Pollock said Curtis ordered him to go to Mountain Meadows. Curtis was seen by Lee at the Meadows with other militia officers before the massacre.[12]

Dame, William Horne (1819–84), 38. [A] Colonel, Iron Military District, Parowan. One of the nine men indicted for the massacre. As the senior militia officer in southern Utah, he originally directed Haight not to attack the emigrants. During the early morning hours of Thursday, September 10, however, he consented to their death. He argued with Haight after the massacre over how the killings would be reported to authorities.[13]

Dickson, Robert (b. 1807), 50. [B] Private, Company H, Third Platoon, Pinto. Albert Hamblin recalled seeing Dickson with other Pinto men at Hamblin's ranch during the week of the massacre.[14]

Durfee, Jabez (1828–83), 29. [B] Private, Company E, First Platoon, Cedar City. Only Lee's memoirs place Durfee at Mountain Meadows before the massacre.[15]

Edwards, William (1841–1925), 15. [A] Cedar City. Too young to serve officially in the militia, Edwards admitted he was at the massacre, though he claimed he was drawn there under false pretense to bury the dead from an Indian massacre. Edwards also claimed that he "with many of the other white men refused to discharge his weapon."[16]

Freeman, Columbus Reed (1838–1907), 19. [A] Private, Company C, Fifth Platoon, Parowan. Though listed on Parowan militia rolls in June 1857, Freeman may have gone to the Meadows from Washington, where his parents and siblings were living at the time of the massacre.[17]

Haight, Isaac Chauncey (1813–86), 44. [A] Major, Second Battalion, Cedar City. One of the nine men indicted for the massacre. Even though he was not at the massacre itself, he was a chief leader in its planning and execution. He sent the militiamen to the Meadows and obtained approval from Colonel William Dame for the emigrants' destruction.[18]

Hamblin, Oscar (1833–62), 24. [B] Second Lieutenant, Company H, Second Platoon, Fort Clara. He apparently recruited Paiutes along the Santa Clara River and acted as an interpreter at the Meadows, at least until Tuesday, September 8. Oscar's brother, Jacob, maintained that Oscar brought Indians to Mountain Meadows and then left.[19]

Harrison, Richard (1808–82), 49. [A] Second Lieutenant, Company E, Third Platoon, Cedar City. Frank Jorden, a stepson of Harrison, recalled him leaving Cedar City with other militiamen. Lee saw Harrison at Mountain Meadows on Thursday, September 10.[20]

Hatch, Ira (1835–1909), 22. [A] Private, Company H, First Platoon, Fort Clara. Hatch was not at the massacre, but he reportedly led Indians in tracking and killing three emigrants who escaped the siege site before the main slaughter on Friday.[21]

Hawley, George (1824–1905), 32. [B] Sergeant, Company I, Fourth Platoon, Washington City. Although Hawley's brothers John and William are often named as massacre participants, only one list, attributed to Lee, identified George at the massacre.[22]

Hawley, John Pierce (1826–1909), 31. [B] Sergeant, Company I, Fifth Platoon, Washington City. Lee said John Hawley was with the group of men from Washington. Hawley denied Lee's assertion and later claimed to have spoken publicly to Lee and others against the massacre after it was over.[23]

Hawley, William Schroeder (1829–93), 27. [A] Sergeant, Company I, Second Platoon, Washington City. Lee claimed he was with the Washington group that arrived at the Meadows on Tuesday, September 8.[24]

Higbee, John Mount (1827–1904), 30. [A] Major, Third Battalion, Cedar City. One of the nine men indicted for the massacre. Higbee led two groups of massacre participants to the Meadows from Cedar City. On Thursday night he carried the orders for the emigrants' destruction, and on Friday he gave the signal for the massacre to begin.[25]

Hopkins, Charles (1810–63), 47. [A] Private, Company D, First Platoon, Cedar City. Despite his rank, Hopkins was considered one of the leaders at the massacre, probably because of his relatively senior age, prominence in the community, and military experience.[26]

Humphries, John Samuel (1825–1903), 31. [A] Musician, Company F, Cedar City. Although several lists of massacre participants identify Humphries, they give no specifics about his role.[27]

Hunter, George (1828–82), 29. [A] Sergeant, Company D, First Platoon, Cedar City. He was seen at the Meadows by witnesses before and after the massacre.[28]

Jacobs, John (1825–1919), 31. [B] Private, Company E, Fourth Platoon, Cedar City. Although Lee claimed John Jacobs was at Mountain Meadows shortly before the massacre, Jacobs wrote to the *Salt Lake Daily Herald,* "I was not there at all, nor indeed within thirty-five miles of the place at the time."[29]

Jacobs, Swen (1823–91), 33. [A] Second Lieutenant, Company E, Fourth Platoon, Cedar City. He was identified as being at the Meadows by John D. Lee and Philip Klingensmith.[30]

Jewkes, Samuel (1823–1900), 34. [B] Musician, Company E, Cedar City. One of the nine men indicted for the massacre, Jewkes was identified in Lee's memoirs as being at the massacre. Other information, however, casts some doubt on the claim.[31]

Johnson, Nephi (1833–1919), 23. [A] Second Lieutenant, Company D, Second Platoon, Fort Johnson. He acted as a Paiute language interpreter at the Meadows and gave the orders on Friday for Indians to attack.[32]

Klingensmith, Philip (1815–81?), 42. [A] Private, Company D, First Platoon, Cedar City. One of the nine men indicted for the massacre. Though only a private, he was considered a key supporter of the massacre and used his role as local bishop to exert his influence. Traveling to the Meadows late Tuesday, September 8, he killed one of two emigrants found in the cedars near Leach's Spring. He admitted shooting one of the emigrant men on Friday. He also reportedly had at least one of the children killed. Klingensmith turned state's evidence and thereby avoided prosecution.[33]

Knight, Samuel (1832–1910), 24. [A] Private, Company H, Second Platoon, Fort Clara. He drove one of the wagons that carried the wounded and small children. Although Lee said Knight helped kill those in the wagons, Knight and Nephi Johnson claimed he was busy calming his horses, which were startled by gunshots.[34]

Leavitt, Dudley (1830–1908), 27. [B] Private, Company H, First Platoon, Fort Clara. Leavitt's son Henry said of his father's role in the massacre, "It was always my understanding that father was one of the scouts who rode horseback with messages back and forth," though no other sources confirm it. Historian Juanita Brooks recalled that Leavitt, her grandfather, said, "I thank God that these old hands have never been stained by human blood."[35]

Lee, John Doyle (1812–77), 45. [A] Major, Fourth Battalion, Harmony. Lee was the only person tried and executed for his role in the massacre. He led the first attack on the emigrants. He negotiated the emigrants' surrender and helped kill those in the two lead wagons. Although he reportedly admitted killing five or six emigrants, his confessions, published posthumously by prosecuting attorney Sumner Howard and Lee's defense attorney William Bishop, maintained that he objected to what was done and did not kill anyone.[36]

Loveridge, Alexander Hamilton (1828–1905), 29. [A] Sergeant, Company F, Third Platoon, Cedar City. He was seen leaving Cedar City with other militiamen bound for the Meadows.[37]

Macfarlane, Daniel Sinclair (1837–1914), 20. [A] Adjutant, Company D, Cedar City. He rode at the head of the women and children and behind the lead wagons just before the Friday slaughter. As one of the few horsemen, Macfarlane was to round in any emigrants who tried to escape.[38]

Macfarlane, John Menzies (1833–92), 23. [B] Adjutant, Second Battalion, Cedar City. There is debate about whether John Macfarlane was at the massacre. Judge John Cradlebaugh issued a warrant for his arrest in 1859. Lee's confession in *Mormonism Unveiled* asserts Macfarlane's presence, but with some uncertainty.[39] Macfarlane served as an attorney on the defense team for Dame and Lee in 1875, and there is speculation that Lee's attorney and editor, William Bishop, added Macfarlane's name to Lee's original manuscript because of a personal dislike for him.

McMurdy, Samuel (1830–1922), 26. [A] Private, Company E, First Platoon, Cedar City. During the final massacre, he drove the lead wagon and may have assisted Lee in killing those in it.[40]

Mangum, James Mitchell (1820–88), 37. [A] Private, Company I, Fourth Platoon, Washington City. James Mangum claimed he was recruited to go to Mountain Meadows by Carl Shirts to help with Indians but returned home after the Indians threatened his life. William Young, however, recalled returning to Washington with Mangum after the massacre.[41]

Mangum, John (1817–85), 40. [B] Private, Company I, Fourth Platoon, Washington City. Lee's memoirs say that John Mangum helped him talk to Paiutes at Mountain Meadows before the massacre but may have mistaken James for John.[42]

Mathews, James Nicholas (1827–71), 30. [B] Second Lieutenant, Company I, Second Platoon, Washington City. Lee was the only witness who identified Mathews, saying he saw him with the other men from Washington on Monday night.[43]

Morris, Elias (1825–98), 32. [A] Captain, Company E, Cedar City. Though he did not go to the Meadows until after the massacre was over, he was with Haight at key planning meetings, including the "tan bark council" in which Dame approved destroying the emigrants.[44]

Pearce, Harrison (1818–89), 38. [A] Captain, Company I, Washington City. Pearce led militiamen from Washington toward Mountain Meadows on Monday, arriving the next day. John Hawley recalled Harrison Pearce making inflammatory speeches against non-Mormons in a public meeting after the massacre.[45]

Pearce, James (1839–1922), 18. [A] Private, Company I, Fifth Platoon, Washington City. Though Pearce was at the Meadows during the week of the massacre, he remained at the militia encampment due to illness during Friday's final slaughter.[46]

Pollock, Samuel (1824–91), 33. [A] Sergeant, Company E, First Platoon, Cedar City. Pollock witnessed the massacre from in or near the militia campsite, where he may have been on guard duty.[47]

Reeves, Josiah (1835–1914), 21. [B] Private, Company G, First Platoon, Cedar City. One of three men sent by Higbee to the Meadows to watch the emigrants. When his brother-in-law Samuel Pollock passed Hamblin's ranch, he noticed Reeves keeping Mormon stock apart from the emigrants' scattered stock.[48] It is unclear where Reeves was during Friday's massacre.

Riddle, Isaac (1830–1906), 27. [B] Private, Company H, Fourth Platoon, Harmony. He was in Cedar City on Tuesday when Haight suddenly sent him back to his home in Pine Valley. While traveling home, he overtook Higbee's detachment headed for the Meadows and may have witnessed the murder of two emigrants who had gone to seek help.[49]

Robinson, Richard Smith (1830–1902), 26. [B] Second Lieutenant, Company H, Third Platoon, Pinto. Since he was considered the leader of the Pinto settlement, he received messages from Cedar City during the days leading to the massacre. Albert Hamblin saw him at Mountain Meadows during the week of the massacre.[50]

Shirts, Don Carlos (Carl) (1836–1922), 21. [A] Second Lieutenant, Company H, Fourth Platoon, Harmony. At the time a son-in-law of Lee, Shirts was sent by him to recruit Paiutes as part of the original plan to attack the emigrants. Shirts also played a role in instructing Paiutes for the final massacre.[51]

Slade, William Rufus, Sr. (1811–72), 46. [A] Private, Company I, Third Platoon, Washington City. Klingensmith remembered talking to William Slade Sr. at the Meadows just before the final massacre.[52]

Slade, William, Jr. (1834–1902), 23. [A] Sergeant, Company I, Third Platoon, Washington City. William Slade Jr. was seen by Lee and Klingensmith at the Meadows before the massacre.[53]

Smith, Joseph Hodgetts (1819–90), 38. [B] Private, Company F, First Platoon, Cedar City. A list of massacre participants attributed to Lee and released to the public by his attorney William Bishop identified "Joseph Smith, of Cedar City." However, Lee makes no mention of Smith in his published confessions, nor is there mention of Smith in any other eyewitness accounts.[54]

Spencer, George (1829–72), 27. [A] Adjutant, Company I, Washington City. In 1867 Spencer wrote to Mormon apostle Erastus Snow confessing that he was "in that horrid 'Mountain Meadow affair.'" An 1875 article called Spencer a "mono-maniac" about the massacre, explaining that "he talked constantly of the part he had enacted in the frightful tragedy."[55]

Stewart, William Cameron (1827–95), 30. [A] Second Lieutenant, Company F, First Platoon, Cedar City. One of nine men indicted for the massacre. Stewart killed emigrant William Aden on Monday and during the final massacre on Friday broke from the ranks to chase and kill emigrants who survived the initial volley of bullets.[56]

Stoddard, David Kerr (1830–1913), 27. [B] Musician, Company F, Cedar City. Although no eyewitnesses saw him at the Mountain Meadows, Stoddard's neighbor John Bradshaw recalled seeing him at Cedar City with other men mustered to go to the Meadows.[57]

Stratton, Anthony Johnson (1824–87), 33. [A] Second Lieutenant, Company E, Second Platoon, Cedar City. John D. Lee identified Anthony Stratton with other militia recruits from Cedar City at the Meadows the night before the final massacre.[58]

Tait, William (1818–96), 38. [A] Captain, Company F, Cedar City. A former drill master in the British Army, Tait was one of the few men in the Iron Military District with formal military training. Tait admitted being at the massacre on Friday but claimed that he and his men didn't kill anyone.[59]

Thornton, Amos Griswold (1832–1902), 24. [B] Sergeant, Company H, Third Platoon, Pinto. Albert Hamblin recalled seeing him at Hamblin's ranch during the week of the massacre, likely to deliver the message Joseph Clewes gave him at Pinto.[60]

Tullis, David Wilson (1833–1902), 24. [A] Private, Company H, First Platoon, Fort Clara. One of the surviving children, six-year-old Rebecca Dunlap, reportedly identified an "Englishman named Tullis" as having killed one of her parents. According to Albert Hamblin, after the massacre Tullis transported the surviving children from the massacre site to Hamblin's ranch.[61]

Urie, John Main (1835–1921), 22. [A] Adjutant, Third Battalion, Cedar City. Lee said Urie was at the Meadows on the night before the massacre. After the massacre, Urie guarded the emigrants' property and later helped transport it to Cedar City.[62]

Western, John (1807–65), 49. [B] Sergeant, Company F, First Platoon, Cedar City. Some accounts name "John Weston" as a massacre participant.[63] Although the name is difficult to decipher in the shorthand of the second Lee trial, Nephi Johnson recalled a John "Weyson," "Weeson," or "Reeson" taking a wagon to Mountain Meadows the night before the massacre. In longhand transcriptions of the trial, the name was recorded as "Weston" or "Western," an inaccurate reflection of the original shorthand.[64] No one named Weston is known to have lived in southern Utah in 1857. "John Western" is the closest name, but evidence of Western's participation is inconclusive.[65] Johnson may have been referring to John Willis.[66]

White, Joel William (1831–1914), 26. [A] Captain, Company D, Cedar City. White wounded another emigrant when William Aden was murdered on Monday, September 7. Although White claimed he did not have a gun for Friday's massacre, Ellott Willden claimed he broke ranks to chase after and kill emigrants who survived the initial gunshots.[67]

White, Samuel Dennis (1818–68), 39. [B] Private, Company F, Fifth Platoon, Fort Sidon [Hamilton's Fort]. Although Samuel White was identified as a massacre participant in lists released to the public by Lee's attorney William Bishop, Lee made no mention of Samuel White in his published confessions.[68]

Wiley, Robert (1809–72), 47. [A] Sergeant, Company E, Third Platoon, Cedar City. Shortly before the massacre, Wiley met with Lee, Klingensmith, and other leaders at Hamblin's ranch.[69]

Willden, Ellott (1833–1920), 23. [A] Private, Company F, Fourth Platoon, Cedar City. One of the nine men indicted for the massacre. Willden and two others were sent by Higbee to the Meadows to watch the emigrants. Willden claimed to be unarmed at the Friday massacre, though Lee said that earlier in the week Willden fired his gun toward the emigrant camp. Willden owned the pistols William Stewart borrowed to kill William Aden.[70]

Williamson, James (1813–69), 44. [A] Private, Company D, First Platoon, Cedar City. Joel White said Williamson traveled to Mountain Meadows with him.[71]

Willis, John Henry (1835–88), 22. [B] Second Lieutenant, Company G, First Platoon, Cedar City. Though Willis insisted he did not go to the Meadows until after the massacre, Klingensmith said he took his wagon and team to the Meadows the night before.[72] Klingensmith could not remember if Willis joined the militiamen at the massacre or remained at Hamblin's ranch.[73] Massacre survivor Nancy Saphrona Huff lived with Willis's family until 1859 and remembered him taking her from the massacre site.[74]

Young, William (1805–75), 52. [A] Private, Company I, Fourth Platoon, Washington City. The eldest militiaman at Mountain Meadows, he remained at the militia encampment and witnessed the massacre from a nearby hill.[75]

Appendix D

The Indians

THE PRINCIPAL AGGRESSORS in the Mountain Meadows Massacre were white Mormon settlers in southern Utah communities.[1] They persuaded, armed, and directed some Southern Paiutes to participate.[2] The various groupings of native peoples designated in modern times as Southern Paiutes were not a monolithic, homogeneous group in 1857, the year of the massacre.[3] They consisted of numerous bands and camps scattered principally over a wide swath of what is now Utah, Nevada, Arizona, and California. Most of these people did not participate in the massacre.[4]

Paiutes who participated under white direction in the Monday morning attack were from Coal Creek and Ash Creek bands. They were recruited by Isaac Haight, John M. Higbee, Philip Klingensmith, and John D. Lee.[5] Beginning Monday night or Tuesday morning, they were joined by some Paiutes living along the Santa Clara and Virgin rivers who were recruited principally by Samuel Knight, Oscar Hamblin, and Carl Shirts.[6] According to Jackson, a Paiute headman living near the Santa Clara River, whites "directed the combined force of Mormons and Indians in the first attack, throughout the siege, and at the last massacre."[7]

Two major lines of Paiute oral history have developed about participation in the massacre. One line says that no Paiutes participated in the massacre. Although this line may in part be a reaction to white efforts to pin all blame for the massacre on Indians, it also reflects the fact that the vast majority of Paiutes had nothing whatsoever to do with the killings.[8] The second line of Paiute oral history recognizes some Paiute participation.[9]

The following is a list of Indians—primarily but not exclusively Paiutes—whose names have been associated with the massacre in various sources. The names are spelled the way they appear in the sources, most being Anglo nicknames or anglicized versions of Paiute names. Where both Paiute and Anglo names are known, preference is given to the Paiute names, with the Anglo or other names in parentheses. Because of the varying credibility of evidence, a note of *[A]* or *[B]* has been placed after each individual's name; *[A]* indicates there is strong evidence the individual participated in or witnessed the killing of emigrants, and *[B]* indicates that the evidence is inconclusive.

Some of the names on the list appear at the top of a November 20, 1857, report written to Brigham Young, territorial superintendent of Indians affairs, by John D. Lee as Indian farmer. Lee's letter served two purposes: (1) to provide a written report of the massacre (albeit a false one), and (2) to itemize third-quarter 1857 Indian expenses claimed by white residents of southern Utah. Young's clerk David O. Calder subsequently added to the top of the document the names of several Paiutes—"Tat-se-gobbitts, Non-co-p-in, Mo-quee-tus, Chick-eroo, Quo-narah, Young-quick, Jackson, Agra-pootes"—and the date range "between 21st to 26th Sept."[10] These names do not correspond directly to Lee's letter but instead are copied from a voucher submitted for reimbursement by Salt Lake City merchant Levi Stewart for "articles furnished sundry bands of Indians, near Mountain Meadows."[11]

Some historians have assumed that all of the Indian leaders listed in this note and their bands participated in the massacre.[12] Though these historians place these Paiute leaders in the vicinity of the Meadows in the weeks after the massacre, there is no conclusive evidence that most participated in or witnessed the killings. Evidence also suggests that two of the Paiute leaders named in these sources, Tutsegavits and Youngwuds, were in Salt Lake City during the massacre and played no role in it at all. Their names, along with others who have been wrongly accused, appear in a separate list at the end of this appendix.

For additional information on the Indians, see mountain meadowsmassacre.org.

Agarapoots [B]. Though his name appears in Calder's notation on top of Lee's account to Brigham Young, evidence of his participation is inconclusive. Jacob Hamblin's reminiscent account even suggests he might have died months before the massacre.[13]

Bill [A]. Isaac Haight and other leaders at Cedar City persuaded him to attack the emigrants. Bill was wounded during the first attack on Monday, September 7.[14]

Buck [A]. One of the Paiutes wounded at the Meadows during the week of the massacre.[15]

Comanche [A]. Harmony resident Benjamin Platt recalled fourteen Cedar City Paiutes leaving for the Mountain Meadows with Lee on Sunday, September 6. Platt said Comanche "objected to the program of slaughter, but was finally induced to accompany the expedition."[16]

Chick-eroo [B]. His name appeared in Calder's notation at the top of Lee's account to Brigham Young, the only link that connects him to the massacre.[17]

George [B]. He was reportedly one of the Paiute leaders who traveled to Salt Lake City in early September and may have been Youngwuds, who stayed in Salt Lake City until after the massacre. Other sources identify a Paiute named George as a massacre participant, though they may be referring to someone other than Youngwuds.[18]

Hamblin, Albert [A]. The adopted Shoshone son of Jacob Hamblin who, together with John Knight, witnessed much of the massacre from a hill. He either witnessed or participated in the murder of the Dunlap twins.[19]

Hunkup, Isaac [A]. Some oral histories of the massacre originate with the Paiute elder Isaac Hunkup, who resided for a long time in the Cedar City area and died in the mid-twentieth century. These oral histories differ as to whether Hunkup participated in the massacre or just witnessed it from a nearby hill.[20]

Jackson [A]. A notable Paiute leader who lived along the Santa Clara River and was at the Meadows on Tuesday, September 8. He said his "brother"—a broad term in Paiute culture—was killed by emigrant gunfire. He reportedly left the Meadows and assisted Ira Hatch in tracking down and killing three emigrants who escaped the wagon corral before the final massacre.[21]

Joseph (Joe) [A]. John D. Lee reported that "an Indian from Cedar City, called Joe" killed one of the wounded men in the lead wagons. Harmony resident Annie Elizabeth Hoag testified that a boy living with Elisha Groves, massacre survivor John Calvin Miller, identified an Indian named Joe, who worked for Groves, as wearing the clothes of his slain father.[22]

Kahbeets [B]. He and his band were known to be living in the vicinity of Mountain Meadows just a few weeks before the massacre, though no known sources confirm that they participated in or witnessed it.[23]

Kanarra [B]. He and his band lived near Harmony, and his name is in the notation above Lee's report. Thomas Kane, who spent time investigating the massacre in Utah in 1858, reported that Kanarra's band participated in the massacre.[24]

Knight, John [A]. A Paiute who lived with Samuel Knight, John Knight watched the massacre with Albert Hamblin from a nearby hill. John Knight may be the same person as John Seaman.[25]

Kwi-toos [B]. A Paiute who lived in the vicinity of the Virgin River. Historian Juanita Brooks claimed that he and his men, carrying spoils from the massacre, accompanied Lee to Harmony after the massacre.[26]

Lee, Lemuel (Clem) [A]. The adopted Indian son of Lee, he accompanied Cedar City Paiutes to the Mountain Meadows and was used by Lee as an interpreter during the week of the massacre.[27]

Moquetas [A]. A leader among the Coal Creek Paiutes in the Cedar City area, he agreed to join the attacking party after Lee promised to furnish sufficient guns and ammunition and to give his band the emigrants' "clothing, all the guns and horses, and some of the cattle." He was shot in his left thigh during the initial attack and never fully recovered from his wound.[28]

Myack [B]. Some newspapers reported that Philip Klingensmith testified about seeing "one Indian, Myack, cut a little boy's throat." The *Steubenville Daily Herald*, however, reported that Klingensmith said he "saw one Indian myself cut a little boy's throat," raising questions about whether the Indian Klingensmith identified was named Myack.[29]

Non-cap-in [B]. He was listed in the notation above Lee's account of the massacre, the only link that connects him to it.[30]

Seaman, John [A]. According to Paiute oral tradition, John Seaman witnessed the massacre from a mountain top. The account states, "he got scared but three guys went…he watched all those people die off." This account of Indians witnessing the massacre from a high vantage point is similar to Albert Hamblin's account and suggests that Seaman may have been John Knight.[31]

Tau-gu (Coal Creek John) [A]. Later an influential headman among Paiutes in southern Utah, he told his son that before the massacre, a white man gave Indians guns to use against the emigrants. He also said he and other Indians, along with white perpetrators, killed emigrants and looted bodies.[32]

Toanob [A]. Wounded at Mountain Meadows during the week of the massacre.[33]

Tom [A]. Identified by Philip Klingensmith as one of the Paiute "chiefs" wounded at Mountain Meadows. Possibly Tom Whitney, whom Mormon leaders blessed ("set apart") as chief of the Paiutes in Iron County in 1855.[34]

Tonche [B]. According to James H. Carleton, a Paiute "chief" named Tonche, who lived along the Virgin River, claimed that "a man named Huntington" delivered a letter from Brigham Young ordering the emigrants to be killed. Indian interpreter Dimick Huntington could not have delivered such a letter at that time, since he did not arrive in southern Utah until weeks after the massacre.[35]

Toshob [B]. In 1869, U.S. Army surveyor George Wheeler implicated Toshob, a Paiute then living in the Moapa Valley in present-day Nevada, as being a leader in the massacre.[36]

Tunanita'a [A]. According to Paiute oral tradition, he and another Paiute were picked up by John D. Lee's group en route to Mountain Meadows but were not allowed to participate in the killing.[37]

Indian Leaders Not Involved with the Massacre

The following list includes the names of Indians who have been incorrectly associated with the massacre.

Ammon. One of the Indian leaders who met with Brigham Young in Salt Lake City on September 1, he returned to Beaver on Wednesday, September 9, in time to negotiate a truce between Indians and the Turner, Dukes, and Collins companies.[38]

Awanap. Awanap and his band were reportedly invited "to join the foray against the emigrants," but he and others from his band in Parowan were persuaded not to go by William Dame.[39]

Kanosh. As a leader of the Corn Creek Pahvants, he visited Brigham Young in Salt Lake City on September 1. Although many massacre accounts claimed that Pahvants followed and killed members of the Arkansas company in retaliation for a supposed poisoning at Corn Creek, neither Kanosh nor any of his band was involved in the massacre, though some Pahvants attacked the Turner company near Beaver.[40]

Tutsegavits. Considered by Mormons to be the principal leader over the Santa Clara Paiutes, he accompanied Jacob Hamblin to meet Brigham Young on September 1 and remained in Salt Lake City until after the massacre's conclusion. While there he toured shops, agricultural gardens, and orchards, and was ordained a Mormon elder. Though Tutsegavits had no role in the massacre, Thomas Kane reported that his band did participate.[41]

Youngwuds. From Harmony, he was one of the Paiute leaders who met with Young in Salt Lake City on September 1 and remained there until at least September 10. Though Youngwuds himself had no role in the massacre, Thomas Kane reported that his band participated.[42]

Abbreviations Used in Notes

The following abbreviations have been used to reduce the bulk of the notes for each chapter. For a complete bibliography, see mountainmeadowsmassacre.org.

Adams   George Rollie Adams, *General William S. Harney: Prince of Dragoons* (Lincoln: University of Nebraska Press, 2001).

AJ1   Andrew Jenson interviews, Jan. and Feb. 1892, Mountain Meadows file, Andrew Jenson, Collection, CHL.

AJ2   Andrew Jenson interviews, Jan. and Feb. 1892, Archives of the First Presidency, The Church of Jesus Christ of Latter-day Saints, Salt Lake City, UT.

Arrington1   Leonard J. Arrington, *Brigham Young: American Moses* (New York: Alfred A. Knopf, 1985).

Arrington2   Leonard J. Arrington, *Great Basin Kingdom: An Economic History of the Latter-day Saints, 1830–1900* (Urbana: University of Illinois Press, 2005).

Bagley   Will Bagley, *Blood of the Prophets: Brigham Young and the Massacre at Mountain Meadows* (Norman: University of Oklahoma Press, 2002).

Baumeister   Roy F. Baumeister, *Evil: Inside Human Cruelty and Violence* (New York: W. H. Freeman, 1997).

Beadle1   J. H. Beadle, "Interview with Jno. D. Lee of Mountain Meadows Notoriety," *Salt Lake Daily Tribune*, July 29, 1872.

Beadle2   J. H. Beadle, *Western Wilds, and The Men Who Redeem Them* (Cincinnati: Jones Brothers, 1878).

Beckwith   Frank A. Beckwith, *Indian Joe: In Person and In Background* (Delta, UT: DuWil Publishing, n.d.).

Bowering   George Kirkman Bowering, Journal, 1842–75, CHL.

Brooks1   Juanita Brooks, *John Doyle Lee: Zealot, Pioneer Builder, Scapegoat* (Logan: Utah State University Press, 1992).

Brooks2	Juanita Brooks, *The Mountain Meadows Massacre*, 2d ed. (Norman: University of Oklahoma Press, 1991).
Brown	Thomas Dunlop Brown, Diary, 1854–57, CHL. Conveniently published in *Journal of the Southern Indian Mission: Diary of Thomas D. Brown*, ed. Juanita Brooks (Logan: Utah State University Press, 1972).
"Butchery"	"Mountain Meadow Massacre: The Butchery of a Train of Arkansans by Mormons and Indians While on Their Way to California, Related By One of the Survivors," *Fort Smith (AR) Elevator*, Aug. 20, 1897.
"BY"	"Brigham Young: Remarkable Interview with the Salt Lake Prophet," *New York Herald*, May 6, 1877. Reprinted in "Interview with Brigham Young," *Deseret Evening News*, May 12, 1877.
BYU	L. Tom Perry Special Collections, Harold B. Lee Library, Brigham Young University, Provo, UT.
Cannon	Abraham Hoagland Cannon, Diary, 1879–95, Typescript, BYU. Copy located at CHL.
Carleton	James Henry Carleton, *Report on the Subject of the Massacre at the Mountain Meadows, in Utah Territory, in September, 1857, of One Hundred and Twenty Men, Women and Children, Who Were from Arkansas* (Little Rock, AR: True Democrat Steam Press, 1860).
"Cates"	"The Mountain Meadow Mas[s]acre: Statement of Mrs. G. D. Cates, One of the Children Spared At the Time," *Dardanelle Arkansas Independent*, Aug. 27, 1875. Reprinted in "The Mountain Meadow Massacre: Statement of One of the Few Survivors," *Daily Arkansas Gazette*, Sep. 1, 1875.
CCF	Utah Second District Court, Criminal Case Files, 1874–77, Series 24291, Utah State Archives, Salt Lake City, UT. Copy located at CHL. The number following the abbreviation is the case file number.
Chandless	William Chandless, *A Visit to Salt Lake; Being a Journey Across the Plains and a Residence in the Mormon Settlements at Utah* (London: Smith, Elder, and Co., 1857).
Chatterley	John Chatterley to Andrew Jens[o]n, Sept. 18, 1919, Mountain Meadows file, Andrew Jenson, Collection, CHL.
CHC	B. H. Roberts, *A Comprehensive History of The Church of Jesus Christ of Latter-day Saints*, 6 vols. (Salt Lake City: Deseret News Press, 1930).
"Children"	"'Children of the Massacre' May Meet in Reunion," *Arkansas Sunday Post Dispatch*, 1895. Also found in JH, 1857, Supplement, pp. 5–8.
CHL	Church History Library, The Church of Jesus Christ of Latter-day Saints, Salt Lake City, UT.
Clewes	Joseph Clewes, in "Mountain Meadows Massacre: Joe Clewes' Statement concerning It," *Salt Lake Daily Herald*, Apr. 5, 1877.

Clew/Will	Ellott Willden's corrections of Clewes account, made during interview with Andrew Jenson, Jan. 28, 1892, AJ2.
CM	Collected Material concerning the Mountain Meadows Massacre, CHL.
Corr1	Andrew Jenson, corrections to Hubert H. Bancroft, *History of Utah*, ca. Jan. 1892, AJ1.
Corr2	Ellott Willden, corrections to H. H. Bancroft, *History of Utah*, given to Andrew Jenson, Jan. 28, 1892, AJ2.
Cradlebaugh	*Utah and the Mormons: Speech of Hon. John Cradlebaugh, of Nevada, on the Admission of Utah as a State* (Washington, D.C.: L. Towers, 1863).
CSM	Cedar Stake, Minutes, William R. Palmer Collection, Special Collections, Gerald R. Sherratt Library, Southern Utah University, Cedar City, UT.
DBY	Brigham Young, *Diary of Brigham Young, 1857*, ed. Everett L. Cooley (Salt Lake City: Tanner Trust Fund/University of Utah Library, 1980).
"Extract"	"Extract from a Letter to the Editor, Dated Carroll Co., Jan. 5, 1858," *Little Rock Arkansas State Gazette and Democrat*, Feb. 13, 1858.
Fancher	Burr Fancher, *Captain Alexander Fancher: Adventurer, Drover, Wagon Master and Victim of the Mountain Meadows Massacre* (Portland, OR: Inkwater Press, 2006).
Farnsworth	Philo Taylor Farnsworth, Dictation, ca. 1886, Bancroft Library, University of California, Berkeley. Microfilm copy located at CHL.
FHL	Family History Library, The Church of Jesus Christ of Latter-day Saints, Salt Lake City, UT.
Fish	Joseph Fish, *The Life and Times of Joseph Fish, Mormon Pioneer*, ed. John H. Krenkel (Danville, IL: Interstate Printers & Publishers, 1970).
Forney	J. Forney to A. B. Greenwood, Sep. 29, 1859, in *Report of the Commissioner of Indian Affairs, Accompanying the Annual Report of the Secretary of the Interior, for the Year 1859* (Washington: George W. Bowman, 1860).
Furniss	Norman F. Furniss, *The Mormon Conflict, 1850–1859* (New Haven: Yale University Press, 1960).
Gardner	Hamilton Gardner, "The Utah Territorial Militia," ca. 1929, Typescript, CHL.
Gibbs	Josiah F. Gibbs, *The Mountain Meadows Massacre* (Salt Lake City: Salt Lake Tribune, 1910).
Greenhaw	Clyde R. Greenhaw, "Survivor of a Massacre: Mrs. Betty Terry of Harrison Vividly Recalls Massacre of Westbound Arkansas Caravan in Utah More Than 80 Years Ago," *Arkansas Gazette*, Sunday Section, Sep. 4, 1938.
Haslam	James Haslam, interview by S. A. Kenner, reported by Josiah Rogerson, Dec. 4, 1884, typescript, in Josiah Rogerson, Transcripts and Notes of John D. Lee Trials, CHL.

Hawley	John Pierce Hawley, Autobiography, 1885, Community of Christ Archives, Independence, MO. Published as John Pierce Hawley, *Autobiography* (Hamilton, MO: Robert Hawley, 1981).
HBM	Harmony Branch, Minutes, Henry E. Huntington Library, San Marino, CA, sometimes misidentified as Rachel Lee's journal.
HC	*History of the Church of Jesus Christ of Latter-day Saints, Period 1: History of Joseph Smith, the Prophet, by Himself*, ed. B. H. Roberts, 6 vols. (Salt Lake City: Deseret Book, 1953).
Hill	William Carroll Hill, *The Fancher Family*, ed. William Hoyt Fancher (Milford, NH: Cabinet Press, 1947).
HOGCM	Historian's Office, General Church Minutes, 1839–77, CHL.
HOJ	Historian's Office, Journal, 1844–1997, CHL.
Holt	Ronald L. Holt, *Beneath These Red Cliffs: An Ethnohistory of the Utah Paiutes* (Logan: Utah State University Press, 2006).
"Horrible"	"The Late Horrible Massacre," *Los Angeles Star*, Oct. 17, 1857.
Hoth	Hans Peter Emanuel Hoth, Diary, Typescript, trans. Peter Gulbrandsen, Bancroft Library, University of California, Berkeley.
Huntington	Dimick Baker Huntington, Journal, 1857–59, CHL.
Hurt	Garland Hurt to Jacob Forney, Dec. 4, 1857, in *Executive Documents Printed by Order of the House of Representatives during the First Session of the Thirty-Fifth Congress, 1857–58*, 14 vols. (Washington: James B. Steedman, 1858), Doc. 71, 10:199–205.
JD	*Journal of Discourses*, 26 vols. (Liverpool: F. D. Richards, etc., 1854–86).
JDL1-BT	*United States v. John D. Lee*, First Trial, Jacob S. Boreman Transcript, Jacob S. Boreman, Collection, Huntington Library, San Marino, CA. The numbers that follow this abbreviation stand for the book and page number, which are separated from each other by a colon.
JDL1-PS	*United States v. John D. Lee*, First Trial, Adam Patterson Shorthand Notes, Jacob S. Boreman, Collection, Huntington Library, San Marino, CA, transcription by LaJean Carruth located in CHL. The numbers that follow this abbreviation stand for the book and page number, which are separated from each other by a colon.
JDL1-RS	*United States v. John D. Lee*, First Trial, Josiah Rogerson Shorthand Notes, Josiah Rogerson, Transcripts and Notes of John D. Lee trials, 1875–85, CHL, transcription by LaJean Carruth located in CHL. The numbers that follow this abbreviation stand for the book and page number, which are separated from each other by a colon.
JDL1-RT	*United States v. John D. Lee*, First Trial, Josiah Rogerson Transcript, Josiah Rogerson, Transcripts and Notes of John D. Lee trials, 1875–85, CHL. The numbers that follow this abbreviation stand for the book and page number, which are separated from each other by a colon.
JDL2-BT	*United States v. John D. Lee*, Second Trial, Jacob S. Boreman Transcript, Jacob S. Boreman, Collection, Huntington Library, San Marino, CA. The numbers that follow this abbreviation stand for

	the book and page number, which are separated from each other by a colon.
JDL2-PS	*United States v. John D. Lee*, Second Trial, Adam Patterson Shorthand Notes, Jacob S. Boreman, Collection, Huntington Library, San Marino, CA, transcription by LaJean Carruth located in CHL. The numbers that follow this abbreviation stand for the book and page number, which are separated from each other by a colon.
JDLC	John D. Lee, Collection, Henry E. Huntington Library, San Marino, CA.
Jenson	Andrew Jenson, *Latter-day Saint Biographical Encyclopedia*, 4 vols. (Salt Lake City: Andrew Jenson History Company, 1901–36).
JH	Journal History of the Church of Jesus Christ of Latter-day Saints, CHL.
JHM	James Henry Martineau, Autobiography and Journal, photocopy of manuscript, CHL.
JHM1907	James Henry Martineau to F. E. Eldredge, July 23, 1907, "The Mountain Meadow Catastroph[e]," CHL, also located at BYU.
Journals	John D. Lee, *Journals of John D. Lee, 1846–47 and 1859*, ed. Charles Kelly (Salt Lake City: Western Printing, 1938).
JPDC	Jacob Piatt Dunn, Collection, Indiana Historical Society, Indianapolis, IN.
Kaibab	Richard W. Stoffle and Michael J. Evans, *Kaibab Paiute History: The Early Years* (Fredonia, AZ: Kaibab Paiute Tribe, 1978).
Kearny	[Lt. Kearny], "List of the Children Saved from the Mountain Meadows Massacre," *Los Angeles Southern Vineyard*, June 3, 1859. Also reprinted in "The Mountain Meadows Massacre—List of the Children Saved," *San Francisco Daily Evening Bulletin*, June 11, 1859, copy located in Historian's Office, Newspaper Scrapbook, 12:70, CHL.
Knack	Martha C. Knack, *Boundaries Between: The Southern Paiutes* (Lincoln: University of Nebraska Press, 2001).
Knight	Samuel Knight, affidavit, Aug. 11, 1904, First Presidency, Cumulative Correspondence, 1900–49, CHL.
Lair	Jim Lair, "Fancher: 'A History of a Remarkable Family,'" *Carroll County Historical Quarterly* 27, no. 1 (Spring 1982): 12–14.
"LC"	"Lee's Confession," *Sacramento Daily Record-Union*, Mar. 24, 1877.
LeCheminant	Wilford Hill LeCheminant, "A Crisis Averted? General Harney and the Change in Command of the Utah Expedition," *Utah Historical Quarterly* 51, no. 1 (Winter 1983): 30–45.
"Lee Trial"	"The Lee Trial: What the Chief [of] the Beaver Indians Has To Say About It," *Los Angeles Star*, Aug. 4, 1875.
"Letter"	P., Oct. 29, 1857, in "Letter from Angel's Camp," *San Francisco Daily Alta California*, Nov. 1, 1857.
"LLC"	"Lee's Last Confession," *San Francisco Daily Bulletin Supplement*, Mar. 24, 1877.

Logan1	Roger V. Logan Jr., "The Mountain Meadows Massacre," in *Mountain Heritage: Some Glimpses into Boone County's Past After One Hundred Years*, ed. Roger V. Logan Jr. (Harrison, AR.: Times Publishing, 1969), 25–31.
Logan2	"Wagon Train Kinships," Broadside of familial relationships of the Baker-Fancher emigrant party, Sep. 9, 2001. Copy located in MMMRF.
Lyman	Francis M. Lyman, Diary Excerpts of Francis M. Lyman, 1892–96, Typescript, in *New Mormon Studies CD-ROM: A Comprehensive Resource Library* (Salt Lake City: Smith Research Associates, [1998]).
M1877–10	Malinda Cameron Scott Thurston, affidavit in support of H.R. 1459, Oct. 15, 1877, 45th Cong., 1st sess., National Archives, Washington, D.C. Copy of transcript in CHL.
M1877–12	Malinda Cameron Scott Thurston, affidavit in support of H.R. 3945, Dec. 18, 1877, 45th Cong., 2nd sess., National Archives, Washington, D.C. Copy of transcript in CHL.
M1911	Malinda Cameron Scott Thurston, deposition, May 2, 1911, *Malinda Thurston v. United States*, U.S. Court of Claims, no. 8479, Selected Documents Relating to the Mountain Meadows Massacre, National Archives, Washington, D.C. Copy of transcript at CHL.
Marcy	Randolph B. Marcy, *The Prairie Traveler: A Hand-Book for Overland Expeditions* (New York: Harper & Brothers, 1859).
Martineau	LaVan Martineau, *The Southern Paiutes: Legends, Lore, Language, and Lineage* (Las Vegas: KC Publications, 1992).
"Massacre"	P., Oct. 14, 1857, in "The Immigrant Massacre," *San Francisco Daily Alta California*, Oct. 17, 1857. Also reprinted in "The Late Immigrant Massacre," *Weaverville (CA) Trinity Journal*, Oct. 24, 1857.
MBB	Minute Book B, 1869–81, Utah, Second District Court (Beaver County), Court Records, 1865–81, Film 485241, FHL. Original located at Southern Utah University, microfilm copy located at Utah State Archives, and photocopy located at CHL.
MC	John D. Lee, *A Mormon Chronicle: The Diaries of John D. Lee, 1848–1876*, ed. Robert Glass Cleland and Juanita Brooks, 2 vols. (San Marino, CA: Huntington Library, 2003).
McGlashan	C. F. McGlashan, "The Mountain Meadow Massacre," *Sacramento Daily Record*, Jan. 1, 1875.
"Meeting"	"Public Meeting of the People of Carroll County," *Arkansas State Gazette and Democrat*, Feb. 27, 1858.
Mitchell	Sallie Baker Mitchell, "The Mountain Meadows Massacre—An Episode on the Road to Zion," *American Weekly* (Aug. 25, 1940): 10–11, 15, 18.
MMMRF	Mountain Meadows Massacre Research Files, CHL.

MRIMD	Muster Rolls for Iron Military District, Oct. 10, 1857, U.S. War Department, Utah Territorial Militia Records, 1849–77, Utah State Archives, Salt Lake City, UT. Microfilm copy located at FHL.
MU	William W. Bishop, ed., *Mormonism Unveiled; or The Life and Confessions of the Late Mormon Bishop, John D. Lee; (Written by Himself)* (St. Louis: Bryan, Brand & Co., 1877).
NJ1908	Nephi Johnson, affidavit, July 22, 1908, First Presidency, Cumulative Correspondence, 1900–1949, CHL.
NJ1909	Nephi Johnson, affidavit, Nov. 30, 1909, CM.
NJ1910	Nephi Johnson to Anthon H. Lund, Mar. 1910, CM.
NJ1917	Nephi Johnson, conversation with Anthony W. Ivins, Sept. 2, 1917, typescript, Anthony W. Ivins, Collection, USHS.
Nuwuvi	*Nuwuvi: A Southern Paiute History* (Salt Lake City: Intertribal Council of Nevada, 1976).
"OBF"	Jack Baker Holt, "One of the Baker Families of Carroll (Boone) County Arkansas," transcript of tape, in *Boone County Historian* 5, no. 3 (Fall 1982): 160–66.
OIMD	William H. Dame, "Organization of the Iron Military District," June 1857, BYU.
"Outrages"	"More Outrages on the Plains!" *Los Angeles Star*, Oct. 24, 1857.
"Paiute"	Gary Tom and Ronald Holt, "The Paiute Tribe of Utah," in *A History of Utah's American Indians*, ed. Forrest S. Cuch (Salt Lake City: Utah State Division of Indian Affairs and Utah State Division of History, 2000), 123–65.
Palmer	William R. Palmer, "The Mountain Meadows Massacre," 1958, in William R. Palmer Material, First Presidency, General Administration Files, 1923, 1932, 1937–67, CHL.
Parker1	Basil G. Parker, *The Life and Adventures of Basil G. Parker* (Plano, CA: Fred W. Reed, 1902).
Parker2	Basil G. Parker, *Recollections of the Mountain Meadow Massacre: Being an Account of That Awful Atrocity and Revealing Some Facts Never Before Made Public* (Plano, CA: Fred W. Reed, 1901).
Peck	M. Scott Peck, *People of the Lie: The Hope for Healing Human Evil* (New York: Simon & Schuster, 1983).
PGM	Provo Utah Central Stake, General Minutes, CHL.
Pitchforth	Samuel Pitchforth, Diary, 1857–61, Photocopy of typescript, CHL.
PKS	Philip Klingon Smith, affidavit, Apr. 10, 1871, in "A Massacre by Mormons," *New York Times*, Sept. 14, 1872, also in "Mormon Monstrosity," *New York Herald*, Sept. 14, 1872.
PPU	Papers Pertaining to the Territory of Utah, 1849–70, 36th Cong., Records of the Senate, RG 46, National Archives, Washington, D.C.
PSHR	Parowan Stake, Historical Record, 1855–60, CHL.
Ray	John A. Ray to Editors of the *Mountaineer*, Dec. 4, 1859, Historian's Office, Collected Historical Documents, ca. 1854–60, CHL.

Rea	Ralph R. Rea, "The Mountain Meadows Massacre and Its Completion as a Historic Episode," *Arkansas Historical Quarterly* 16 (Spring 1957): 28–45.
Rogers	Wm. H. Rogers, "The Mountain Me[a]dows Massacre," *Salt Lake City Valley Tan*, Feb. 29, 1860.
SAJ	Jesse Nathaniel Smith, Autobiography and Journal, 1855–1906, CHL.
SDoc42	U.S. Congress, Senate, *Message of the President of the United States, Communicating, in Compliance with a Resolution of the Senate, Information in Relation to the Massacre at Mountain Meadows, and Other Massacres in Utah Territory*, 36th Cong., 1st sess., 1860, S. Doc. 42.
Shirts	[Peter Shirts], statement, ca. 1876, manuscript 3141, Smithsonian Institution, National Anthropological Archives, Suitland, MD.
SLDS	James B. Allen and Glen M. Leonard, *The Story of the Latter-day Saints* (Salt Lake City: Deseret Book, 1992).
Staub	Ervin Staub, *The Roots of Evil: The Origins of Genocide and Other Group Violence* (Cambridge: Cambridge University Press, 1989).
Stenhouse	T. B. H. Stenhouse, *The Rocky Mountain Saints: A Full and Complete History of the Mormons, from the First Vision of Joseph Smith to the Last Courtship of Brigham Young* (New York: D. Appleton, 1873).
Stout	Hosea Stout, *On the Mormon Frontier: The Diary of Hosea Stout*, ed. Juanita Brooks, 2 vols. (Salt Lake City: University of Utah Press/ Utah State Historical Society, 1964).
Tambiah	Stanley J. Tambiah, *Leveling Crowds: Ethnonationalist Conflicts and Collective Violence in South Asia* (Berkeley: University of California Press, 1996).
Terry	Elizabeth Baker Terry, in "I Survived the Mountain Meadow Massacre," *True Story Magazine*, n.d. Copy located at BYU.
TF	Morris A. Shirts and Kathryn H. Shirts, *A Trial Furnace: Southern Utah's Iron Mission* (Provo, UT: Brigham Young University Press, [2001]).
Thurston	*Malinda Thurston v. United States and Ute Indians*, U.S. Court of Claims, no. 8479, Selected Documents relating to the Mountain Meadows Massacre, National Archives, Washington, D.C. Copy of transcript at CHL.
Tullidge	Edward W. Tullidge, *History of Salt Lake City* (Salt Lake City: Star Printing, 1886).
Unruh	John D. Unruh Jr., *The Plains Across: The Overland Emigrants and the Trans-Mississippi West, 1840–60* (Urbana: University of Illinois Press, 1979).
UofU	Special Collections, Marriott Library, University of Utah, Salt Lake City, UT.
USBIA	U.S. Bureau of Indian Affairs, Letters Received by the Office of Indian Affairs, Utah Superintendency Papers, National Archives

Microfilm Publications #234, National Archives, Washington, D.C. Microfilm copy located at CHL.

USHS Utah State Historical Society, Salt Lake City, UT.

"Victims" "Lee's Victims," *San Francisco Chronicle*, Mar. 23, 1877. Also reprinted in "The Slaughtered Emigrants," *New York Herald*, Mar. 25, 1877, and *Daily Memphis Avalanche*, Mar. 31, 1877.

Welch Peyton Y. Welch, Oct. 26, 1857, in "More Trains Destroyed by the Mormons and Indians," *Hornellsville (NY) Tribune*, Jan. 21, 1858. Reprinted from the *Missouri Expositor*, Jan. 5, 1858.

Whitney Orson F. Whitney, *History of Utah*, 4 vols. (Salt Lake City: George Q. Cannon & Sons, 1892–1904).

Woodruff Wilford Woodruff, Journals, 1833–98, CHL.

YOF Brigham Young, Office Files, CHL.

Notes

All quoted matter preserves the spelling of the original sources, except where noted. Spelling corrections in square brackets [ ] have occasionally been made to enhance readability. Italics are as in original sources unless otherwise noted. Sources that have not been abbreviated appear with full citations at first mention in each chapter; all following citations of these sources within that chapter are shortened.

Preface

1. Juanita Brooks, "Side-Lights on the Mountain Meadows Massacre," type-script, 1940, copy at BYU; Juanita Brooks, *The Mountain Meadows Massacre* (Stanford, CA: Stanford University Press, 1950).
2. Anne Marie Gardner, "Forgiveness Highlights Meadow Dedication," *Salt Lake Tribune*, Sept. 16, 1990; Loren Webb, "Time for Healing, LDS Leader Says about Massacre," *St. George (UT) Daily Spectrum*, southern ed., Sept. 16, 1990; Art Challis, "Mountain Meadows Now Can Symbolize Willingness to Look Ahead, BYU Chief Says," *Deseret News*, Sept. 16, 1990; Cynthia Gorney, "Epilogue to a Massacre," *Washington Post*, Sept. 17, 1990.
3. Quoted by Gordon B. Hinckley at funeral services for Rex E. Lee, in Greg Hill, "Funeral Speakers Laud Life of Rex E. Lee," *Church News*, Mar. 23, 1996.
4. Roger V. Logan Jr., quoted in John Magsam, "Utah Massacre Memorial Dedicated," *Little Rock Arkansas Democrat-Gazette*, Sept. 12, 1999.
5. AJ2; Whitney, 1:692–709; AJ1.
6. First Presidency, letter, Jan. 21, 1892, in *Autobiography of Andrew Jenson* (Salt Lake City: Deseret News Press, 1938), 197–98.
7. Andrew Jenson, Journal, Jan. 31, 1892, CHL.
8. Michael Feldberg, *The Turbulent Era* (New York: Oxford University Press, 1980).
9. Regina M. Schwartz, *The Curse of Cain: The Violent Legacy of Monotheism* (Chicago: University of Chicago Press, 1997).

10. Staub; Peck, 212–53; Rosa Brooks, "Good People, Evil Deeds," *Los Angeles Times*, June 9, 2006, also reprinted in "Killings in Iraq by 'Bad Apples'? Probably Not," *Deseret Morning News*, June 18, 2006.

11. William R. Palmer to Joseph Anderson, Oct. 16, 1959, William R. Palmer, Material, First Presidency, General Administration Files, 1923, 1932, 1937–67, CHL.

Prologue

1. Aurora Hunt, *Major General James Henry Carleton (1814–1873): Western Frontier Dragoon* (Glendale, CA: Arthur H. Clark, 1958), 171; Rogers.

2. Carleton, 3.

3. Ibid., 28; Donald Jackson and Mary Lee Spence, eds., *The Expeditions of John Charles Frémont*, vol. 1, *Travels from 1838 to 1844* (Urbana: University of Illinois Press, 1970), 692–93.

4. LeRoy R. Hafen and Ann W. Hafen, eds., *Central Route to the Pacific, by Gwinn Harris Heap*, The Far West and the Rockies Historical Series, 1820–1875, vol. 7 (Glendale, CA: Arthur H. Clark, 1957), 231.

5. Jacob Forney to Elias Smith, May 5, 1859, in "Visit of the Superintendent of Indian Affairs to Southern Utah," *Deseret News*, May 11, 1859; Jacob Forney to Kirk Anderson, May 5, 1859, in *Salt Lake City Valley Tan*, May 10, 1859; Rogers.

6. Carleton, 29.

7. [James] Lynch, statement, in "The Mountain Meadows Massacre: Surviving Children of the Murdered Fix the Crime upon the Mormons," *San Francisco Daily Evening Bulletin*, May 31, 1859; Rogers; Forney to Smith, May 5, 1859, in "Visit of the Superintendent"; Forney to Anderson, May 5, 1859, in *Valley Tan*, May 10, 1859.

8. Charles Brewer to R. P. Campbell, May 6, 1859, in SDoc42, 16–17; Carleton, 28; John W. Phelps to Dear General, June 12, 1859, John W. Phelps Papers, New York Public Library.

9. Carleton, 28; Jacob Hamblin, in Carleton, 8; Jacob Hamblin, JDL2-BT 1:86; Marion Jackson Shelton, Diary, October 11, 1858, CHL, transcription of Pitman shorthand by LaJean Carruth, copy in MMMRF.

10. Shelton Diary, May 20, 1859.

11. Carleton, 29.

12. Ibid., 28–29; HOJ, July 19, 1860; Shannon A. Novak and Derinna Kopp, "To Feed a Tree in Zion: Osteological Analysis of the 1857 Mountain Meadows Massacre," *Historical Archaeology* 37, no. 2 (2003): 100.

13. Carleton, 3, 28.

14. Ibid., 29–30.

15. J. H. Carleton to W. W. Mackall, June 24, 1859, RG 393, Department of the Pacific, Letters Received, National Archives, Washington, D.C. See also Carleton, 30–31. Carleton's later actions demonstrated he was serious in advocating retributive violence. His reputation was later stained by "brutally

harsh" Indian campaigns and the ruthless internment of Navajos at Bosque Redondo. Arrell Morgan Gibson, "James H. Carleton," *Soldiers West: Biographies from the Military Frontier*, ed. Paul Andrew Hutton (Lincoln: University of Nebraska Press, 1987), 68–69; Dennis B. Casebier, *Carleton's Pah-Ute Campaign* (Norco, CA: By the author, 1972), 11, 18, 26, 44.

Chapter 1

1. See *SLDS*, 1–305.
2. Jan Shipps, *Mormonism: The Story of a New Religious Tradition* (Urbana: University of Illinois Press, 1985), ix–x; *SLDS*, 1–220, 224, 286–300, 349–474.
3. Richard Lyman Bushman, *Joseph Smith: Rough Stone Rolling* (New York: Alfred A. Knopf, 2005), xx.
4. Ohio Journal, Dec. 2, 1835, in Dean C. Jesse, ed., *The Papers of Joseph Smith*, vol. 2 (Salt Lake City: Deseret Book, 1992), 93; *HC*, 2:323–24.
5. For other examples of such thinking, see editorial comments in a church-run newspaper, *Times and Seasons* 4, no. 7 (1843): 98; *Times and Seasons* 6, no. 3 (1845): 811. For reviews of millennial studies, see Leonard I. Sweet, "Millennialism in America: Recent Studies," *Theological Studies* 40 (Sept. 1979): 510–31; Hillel Schwartz, "The End of the Beginning: Millenarian Studies, 1969–1975," *Religious Studies Review* 2 (July 1976): 1–15. Grant Underwood, *The Millenarian World of Early Mormonism* (Urbana: University of Illinois Press, 1993), examines how last days perspectives influenced early Mormonism.
6. Grant Underwood, "Millenarianism and the Early Mormon Mind," *Journal of Mormon History* 9 (1982): 43, citing John G. Gager, *Kingdom and Community: The Social World of Early Christianity* (Englewood Cliffs, NJ: Prentice-Hall, 1975), 25; Kenelm Burridge, *New Heaven, New Earth: A Study of Millenarian Activities* (New York: Schocken Books, 1969); Thomas S. Kuhn, *The Structure of Scientific Revolutions*, 2nd ed. (Chicago: University of Chicago Press, 1970).
7. Paul Gilje, *Rioting in America* (Bloomington: Indiana University Press, 1996), 1–86.
8. Jeremiah Hughes, *Niles' Register* 66 (July 27, 1844): 344–45, cited in David Grimstead, "Rioting in Its Jacksonian Setting," *American Historical Review* 77 (Apr. 1972): 392–93.
9. Richard Maxwell Brown, *Strain of Violence: Historical Studies of American Violence and Vigilantism* (New York: Oxford University Press, 1975), 30–33, 35. See also David T. Courtwright, *Violent Land: Single Men and Social Disorder from the Frontier to the Inner City* (Cambridge, MA: Harvard University Press, 1996), 1. Western historian Patricia Limerick maintains that political, religious, and economic differences could be as inflammatory as racial differences in the nineteenth-century American West, the violence against Mormons being one example. *The Legacy of Conquest: The Unbroken Past of the American West* (New York: Norton, 1987), 280–88.

10. Robert Wadman and William Thomas Allison, *To Protect and to Serve: A History of Police in America* (Upper Saddle, NJ: Pearson Prentice Hall, 2004); Richard Maxwell Brown, *No Duty to Retreat: Violence and Values in American History and Society* (New York: Oxford University Press, 1991), 157; Boyd W. Johnson, *The Arkansas Frontier* (St. Charles, AR: Perdue Printing, 1957), 129; Kenneth S. Greenberg, "The Nose, the Lie, and the Duel in the Antebellum South," *American Historical Review* 95 (Feb. 1990): 57–74.

11. Wadman and Allison, *To Protect and to Serve.*

12. Dean C. Jessee, ed., *The Papers of Joseph Smith*, vol. 1 (Salt Lake City: Deseret Book, 1989), 374–77; Historian's Office, History of the Church, 1:205–7, CHL; *HC*, 1:261–64; Luke Johnson, "History of Luke Johnson," *Latter-day Saints' Millennial Star* 26, no. 53 (1864): 834–35; George A. Smith, Nov. 15, 1864, in *JD*, 11:5–6; *CHC*, 1:280–82.

13. *Evening and Morning Star* (Dec. 1833): 226–28.

14. Ibid.; Max H. Parkin, "Lamanite Mission of 1830–1831," in *Encyclopedia of Mormonism*, ed. Daniel H. Ludlow (New York: Macmillan, 1992), 2:803.

15. Stephen C. LeSueur, *The 1838 Mormon War in Missouri* (Columbia: University of Missouri Press, 1987), 16–18; Warren A. Jennings, "Zion Is Fled: The Expulsion of the Mormons from Jackson County, Missouri" (PhD diss., University of Florida, 1962), 1–81, 129; Max H. Parkin, "A History of the Latter-day Saints in Clay County, Missouri, from 1833 to 1847" (PhD diss., Brigham Young University, 1976), 56–90; *Evening and Morning Star* (Dec. 1833): 226–28; Richard Bushman, "Mormon Persecutions in Missouri, 1833," *BYU Studies* 3 (Autumn 1960): 1–20.

16. Lyman Wight, testimony, in "Trial of Joseph Smith," *Times and Seasons* 4, no. 17 (1843): 264; Jennings, "Zion is Fled," 137–201; *Evening and Morning Star* (Dec. 1833): 226–28.

17. *Doctrine and Covenants of the Church of the Latter Day Saints* (Kirtland, OH: F. G. Williams, 1835), 217–19 (current D&C 98:16, 23–48).

18. *The Book of Mormon* (Palmyra, NY: E. B. Grandin, 1830), 344, 358, 459 (current Alma 43:46; 48:14; 3 Nephi 3:21).

19. John Corrill, *A Brief History of the Church of Christ of Latter Day Saints...* (St. Louis: Printed for the Author, 1839), 19. See also Alexander W. Doniphan, interview, "Mormon History," *Saints' Herald*, Aug. 1, 1881, citing *Kansas City Journal*; Jennings, "Zion is Fled," 137–201.

20. *Autobiography of Parley P. Pratt*, 3rd ed. (Salt Lake City: Deseret Book, 1938), 103.

21. LeSueur, *1838 Mormon War*, 19–27; Alexander L. Baugh, *A Call to Arms: The 1838 Mormon Defense of Northern Missouri* (Provo, UT: Joseph Fielding Smith Institute/BYU Studies, 2000), 13–14.

22. Thomas Wilson to Samuel Turrentine, July 4, 1836, in Durward T. Stokes, ed., "The Wilson Letters, 1835–1849," *Missouri Historical Review* 60 (July 1966): 505, 508; Marie H. Nelson, "Anti-Mormon Mob Violence and the Rhetoric of Law and Order in Early Mormon History," *Legal Studies Forum* 21 (1997): 353–88; William R. Hutchison, *Religious Pluralism in America: The*

Contentious History of a Founding Ideal (New Haven: Yale University Press, 2003), 30–58.

23. Daniel Dunklin to W. W. Phelps, July 18, 1836, in William Wines Phelps, Collection of Missouri Documents, 1833–37, CHL; Nelson, "Anti-Mormon Mob Violence," 371. See also Peter Crawley and Richard L. Anderson, "The Political and Social Realities of Zion's Camp," *BYU Studies* 14 (Summer 1974): 415–20; Jenson, 3:694.

24. Joseph Smith, Journal, Mar. 30, 1836, Joseph Smith, Collection, CHL; Jessee, *Papers of Joseph Smith*, 2:206.

25. Reed Peck, "Manuscript," 8, cited in LeSueur, *1838 Mormon War*, 39–40.

26. Peter Crawley, "Two Rare Missouri Documents," *BYU Studies* 14 (Summer 1974): 527.

27. *MU*, 56–60. See also Reed C. Durham Jr., "The Election Day Battle at Gallatin," *BYU Studies* 13 (Autumn 1972): 36–61; Brooks1, 32–33; William G. Hartley, *My Best for the Kingdom: History and Autobiography of John Lowe Butler, a Mormon Frontiersman* (Salt Lake City: Aspen Books, 1993), 51–61. On the Mormons' fighting back in Jackson County, see Warren A. Jennings, "The Expulsion of the Mormons from Jackson County, Missouri," *Missouri Historical Review* 64 (Oct. 1969–July 1970): 47–51.

28. Baugh, *Call to Arms*, 36–43; LeSueur, *1838 Mormon War*, 64, 112–28.

29. See, e.g., Dean C. Jessee, ed., *The Personal Writings of Joseph Smith*, rev. ed. (Salt Lake City: Deseret Book; Provo: Brigham Young University Press, 2002), 420–21.

30. D. Michael Quinn, *The Mormon Hierarchy: Origins of Power* (Salt Lake City: Signature Books, 1994), 99.

31. Gilje, *Rioting in America*, 77; Richard Maxwell Brown, "Violence," in Clyde A. Milner II, Carol A. O'Connor, and Martha A. Sandweiss, eds., *The Oxford History of the American West* (New York: Oxford University Press, 1994), 416; LeSueur, *1838 Mormon War*, 3–4; Donald L. Horowitz, *The Deadly Ethnic Riot* (Berkeley: University of California Press, 2001), 74–75.

32. L. W. Boggs to John B. Clark, Oct. 27, 1838, in Executive Orders, 1838, Missouri State Archives, photocopy at CHL; L. W. Boggs to John B. Clark, Oct. 27, 1838, in *Document Containing the Correspondence, Orders, &c. in Relation to the Disturbances with the Mormons* (Fayette, MO: Boon's Lick Democrat, 1841), 61; LeSueur, *1838 Mormon War*, 152; Richard Lloyd Anderson, "Clarifications of Bogg's 'Order' and Joseph Smith's Constitutionalism," in Arnold K. Garr and Clark V. Johnson, eds., *Regional Studies in Latter-day Saint Church History: Missouri* (Provo, UT: Brigham Young University, 1994), 27–83; Baugh, *Call to Arms*, 121, 140, 146n48.

33. Baugh, *Call to Arms*, 115–27; LeSueur, *1838 Mormon War*, 162–68.

34. LeSueur, *1838 Mormon War*, 161–244; Baugh, *Call to Arms*, 149–53.

35. Grant Anderson, "Research on Missouri Persecutions," Nov. 8, 2006, MMMRF.

36. For figures on Mormon property losses, see Clark V. Johnson, ed., *Mormon Redress Petitions: Documents of the 1833–1838 Missouri Conflict* (Provo, UT: Religious Studies Center, Brigham Young University, 1992), xxviii–xxix.

37. For figures on the number of Saints driven from Missouri, see Eliza R. Snow to [Isaac] Streator, February 22, 1839, copy at CHL, original at Western Reserve Historical Society, Cleveland, OH; B. H. Roberts, *The Missouri Persecutions* (Salt Lake City: Bookcraft, 1965), 264; William G. Hartley, "'Almost Too Intolerable a Burthen': The Winter Exodus from Missouri, 1838–39," *Journal of Mormon History* 18 (Fall 1992): 7; Alexander L. Baugh, "From High Hopes to Despair: The Missouri Period, 1831–39," *Ensign* (July 2001): 44.

38. Joseph Smith Jr. to Presendia Huntington Buell, Mar. 15, 1839, in Jessee, *Personal Writings of Joseph Smith*, 428.

39. Gilje, *Rioting in America*, 77; Brown, "Violence," 416; Horowitz, *Deadly Ethnic Riot*, 74–75; LeSueur, *1838 Mormon War*, 3–4; Glen M. Leonard, *Nauvoo: A Place of Peace, a People of Promise* (Salt Lake City: Deseret Book/Brigham Young University Press, 2002), 525–36.

40. Leonard, *Nauvoo*, 103–4, 280–81.

41. Thomas Sharp, *Warsaw (IL) Signal*, Feb. 21, 1844.

42. "Unparalleled Outrage at Nau[v]oo," *Warsaw Signal*, June 12, 1844.

43. *The Doctrine and Covenants of the Church of Jesus Christ of Latter Day Saints*, 2nd ed. (Nauvoo, IL: John Taylor, 1844), 444–45 (current D&C 135:4); Bushman, *Joseph Smith*, 541–47.

44. *Doctrine and Covenants* (1844), 445 (current D&C 135:7); Rev. 6:9–10, King James Version (hereafter KJV).

45. Willard Richards, John Taylor, and Samuel H. Smith to Emma Smith and [Jonathan] Dunham, June 27, 1844, in *Nauvoo (IL) Neighbor Extra*, June 30, 1844. On the Saints' restraint during this period, see M. R. Deming to the Citizens of Carthage and Hancock County, June 28, 1844, and Deming to Fellow Citizens of Hancock County, June 29, 1844, in *Nauvoo Neighbor Extra*, June 30, 1844.

46. Brigham Young to Vilate Young, Aug. 11, 1844, CHL; Arrington1, 112.

47. "Awful Assassination of Joseph and Hyrum Smith!" *Times and Seasons* 5, no. 12 (1844): 561.

48. Dallin H. Oaks and Marvin S. Hill, *Carthage Conspiracy: The Trial of the Accused Assassins of Joseph Smith* (Urbana: University of Illinois Press, 1975); "Centennial of Nauvoo Temple Dedication," *Improvement Era* 49 (May 1946): 294; Elden J. Watson, comp., *Manuscript History of Brigham Young, 1846–1847* (Salt Lake City: Elden J. Watson, 1971), 148; "Joseph Smith," *Times and Seasons* 5, no. 14 (1844): 607; Woodruff, Aug. 27, 1844. Historical evidence on an "Oath of Vengeance" is mixed. For a compilation and analysis of the sources, see Van Hale, "Mountain Meadows Massacre and the Oath of Vengeance," Supplement, Sunstone Symposium Paper, Salt Lake City, 2007.

49. Rev. 6:9–10 (KJV).

50. Editorial, *Nauvoo Neighbor*, Oct. 29, 1845. On the Nauvoo Legion, see Leonard, *Nauvoo*, 112–19.

51. Thomas Ford, *A History of Illinois, from Its Commencement as a State in 1818 to 1847* (1854; repr., Chicago: R. R. Donnelley & Sons, 1946), 2:306–8, 312–13, 322.

52. Ford, *History of Illinois*, 2:322–27; Richard E. Bennett, *Mormons at the Missouri, 1846–1852: "And Should We Die..."* (Norman: University of Oklahoma Press, 1987), 82–84.

53. Brigham Young, remarks, in Heber C. Kimball, Journal, Jan. 2, 1846, CHL; Brigham Young to E. L. Barnard, Dec. 26, 1845, Outgoing Correspondence, YOF; Brigham Young to William L. Marcy, Dec. 17, 1845, Outgoing Correspondence, YOF; Brigham Young, sermon, Jan. 2, 1846, Historian's Office, History of the Church.

54. "A Circular of the [Nauvoo] High Council," Jan. 20, 1846, in *Times and Seasons* 6, no. 21 (1846): 1096–97; Brigham Young to Daniel E. Morrison, Sept. 15, 1875, Letterpress Copybook 13:861, YOF; Brigham Young to Thomas L. Kane, Jan. 31, 1854, Letterpress Copybook 1:409, YOF; Brigham Young, remarks, July 27, 1850, HOGCM; Brigham Young to James Guthrie, July 31, 1854, Governor's Letterpress Copybook 1:119–24, YOF; Brigham Young to S. A. Douglas, Apr. 29, 1854, Letterpress Copybook 1:517, YOF.

55. Brigham Young, Oct. 8, 1868, *JD*, 12:287. For an account of Young's early New York years, see Rebecca Cornwall and Richard F. Palmer, "The Religious and Family Background of Brigham Young," *BYU Studies* 18 (Spring 1978): 286–310. The most complete Young biography is Arrington1.

56. Brigham Young, Oct. 5, 1856, in *JD*, 4:112; Brigham Young, sermon, Oct. 3, 1852, in "Discourse," *Deseret News*, May 11, 1854; Ronald W. Walker and Ronald K. Esplin, "Brigham Himself: An Autobiographical Recollection," *Journal of Mormon History* 4 (1977): 19–34.

57. On the burned-over district, see Whitney R. Cross, *The Burned-Over District: The Social and Intellectual History of Enthusiastic Religion in Western New York, 1800–1850* (Ithaca, NY: Cornell University Press, 1950).

58. Brigham Young, Aug. 9, 1857, in *JD*, 5:127; Brigham Young, Apr. 6, 1860, in *JD*, 8:38.

59. Brigham Young, June 3, 1871, in *JD*, 14:197; Brigham Young, remarks, Jan. 8, 1845, in *Utah Genealogical and Historical Magazine* 11 (1920): 109–10.

60. Brigham Young, Apr. 20, 1856, in *JD*, 3:320–21; Brigham Young, sermon, June 21, 1857, Historian's Office, Reports of Speeches, CHL. See also Brigham Young, sermon, Aug. 24, 1867, Historian's Office, Reports of Speeches.

61. Young, remarks, Jan. 8, 1845, in *Utah Genealogical and Historical Magazine*, 11 (1920): 109–13; Brigham Young, sermon, Feb. 3, 1867, Historian's Office, Reports of Speeches; Brigham Young, Apr. 20, 1856, in *JD*, 3:321; John Bunyan, *The Pilgrim's Progress from This World, to That Which is to Come* (New York: American Tract Society, n.d.), 24. See also Brigham Young, sermon, Oct. 3, 1852, in "Discourse," *Deseret News*, May 11, 1854.

62. HOJ, Oct. 23, 1859; Brigham Young, remarks, Mar. [9], 1856, HOGCM. On Young's temper and speech, see Arrington1, 196–98, 300.

63. Ronald W. Walker, "Raining Pitchforks: Brigham Young as Preacher," *Sunstone* 8 (May–June 1983): 8; Chandless, 189.

64. Thomas L. Kane to James Buchanan, ca. Mar. 15, 1858, draft, Utah War Correspondence, Thomas L. and Elizabeth W. Kane, Collection, BYU.

65. Sketch by S. A. Kenner, in *History of the Bench and Bar of Utah*, ed. and comp. C. C. Goodwin (Salt Lake City: Interstate Press Association, 1913), 12; *Chicago Times*, report filed Feb. 22, 1871, in Preston Nibley, *Brigham Young, The Man and His Work* (Salt Lake City: Deseret News Press, 1936), 469; LeRoy R. and Ann W. Hafen, eds., *Journals of Forty-Niners; Salt Lake to Los Angeles*, Far West and the Rockies Historical Series, 1820–1875, vol. 2 (Glendale, CA: Arthur R. Clark, 1954), 276n.

66. *HC*, 3:2; Arrington1, 62; James B. Allen, Ronald K. Esplin, and David J. Whittaker, *Men with a Mission: The Quorum of the Twelve Apostles in the British Isles, 1837–1841* (Salt Lake City: Deseret Book, 1992), xvi, 55; Wayne L. Wahlquist, "Population Growth in the Mormon Core Area, 1847–90," in *The Mormon Role in the Settlement in the West*, ed. Richard H. Jackson (Provo, UT: Brigham Young University Press, 1978), 129.

67. Brigham Young, remarks, in Kimball Journal, Jan. 2, 1846; Brigham Young to "Brother Joseph," Mar. 9, 1846, Outgoing Correspondence, YOF.

68. Brigham Young to James K. Polk, Aug. 8, 1846, Outgoing Correspondence, YOF; Thomas L. Kane to Polk, letter, n.d., *The Private Papers and Diary of Thomas Leiper Kane: A Friend of the Mormons*, ed. and intro. Oscar Osburn Winther (San Francisco: Gelber-Lilienthal, 1937), 51–53. Kane's identification of this land was specific: The anticipated Mormon lands were "about midway between the Missouri and the Pacific and may be loosely described as lying between the E. shore of Lake Tampanogos [Utah Lake], and the 111th. degree of W Longitude and extending at least from the 40th. parallel of Latitude to the 42° which lately formed the Northern boundary of the U. States."

69. Ray Allen Billington, *The Far Western Frontier, 1830–1860* (New York: Harper & Brothers, 1956), 196; Ray Allen Billington, "Best Prepared Pioneers in the West," *American Heritage* 7 (Oct. 1956): 20–25, 116–17; Kane to Polk, letter, n.d., *Private Papers and Diary of Thomas Leiper Kane*, 51–53; Lewis Clark Christian, "Mormon Foreknowledge of the West," *BYU Studies* 21 (Fall 1981): 403–15.

70. Brigham Young to the High Council at Council Point, Aug. 14, 1846, Outgoing Correspondence, YOF; *Manuscript History of Brigham Young*, 203–5, 236–37. For a survey of the recruitment and history of the Mormon Battalion, John F. Yurtinus, "A Ram in the Thicket: The Mormon Battalion in the Mexican War" (PhD diss., Brigham Young University, 1975); Norma Baldwin Ricketts, *The Mormon Battalion: U.S. Army of the West, 1846–1848* (Logan: Utah State University Press, 1996); David L. Bigler and Will Bagley, eds., *Army of Israel: Mormon Battalion Narratives* (Spokane, WA: Arthur H. Clark, 2000).

71. Young to Polk, Aug. 8, 1846, Outgoing Correspondence, YOF.

72. "To Our Patrons," *Nauvoo Neighbor,* Oct. 29, 1845.

73. See Isa. 33:1. Part of the passage was repeated in one of Smith's revelations, *Doctrine and Covenants of the Church of Jesus Christ of Latter-day Saints* (Salt Lake City: Deseret News, 1876), 365 (current D&C 109:50). Taylor's comments fit the millennial pattern. "Men cleave to hopes of imminent worldly salvation only when the hammerblows of disaster destroy the world they have known," observed Michael Barkun's, *Disaster and the Millennium* (New Haven: Yale University Press, 1974), 1. See also Underwood, "Millenarianism and the Early Mormon Mind," 46.

Chapter 2

1. Ray Allen Billington, *The Far Western Frontier, 1830–1860* (New York: Harper & Brothers, 1956), 196; Ray Allen Billington, "Best Prepared Pioneers in the West," *American Heritage* 7 (Oct. 1956): 20–25, 116–17; Thomas L. Kane to Polk, letter, n.d., *The Private Papers and Diary of Thomas Leiper Kane: A Friend of the Mormons,* ed. and intro. Oscar Osburn Winther (San Francisco: Gelber-Lilienthal, 1937), 51–53; Lewis Clark Christian, "Mormon Foreknowledge of the West," *BYU Studies* 21 (Fall 1981): 403–15.

2. Richard D. Poll, Thomas G. Alexander et al., eds., *Utah's History* (Provo, UT: Brigham Young University Press, 1978), 160; Arrington1, 227.

3. Lemuel G. Brandeburg, Perry [E.] Brocchus, and B. D. Harris to Millard Fillmore, December 10, 1851, in *The Spiritual Wife Doctrine of the Mormons Proved* (Cheltenham, UK: R. Edwards, [1852]), 1–11; Perry E. Brocchus, *Letter of Judge Brocchus, of Alabama, to the Public, upon the Difficulties in the Territory of Utah* (Washington, D.C.: Henry Polkinhorn, 1859), 18–31; Poll, Alexander, *Utah's History,* 160–63; Arrington1, 228; *SLDS,* 269–70.

4. See U.S. Congress, House of Representatives, *Reports of Explorations and Surveys, to Ascertain the Most Practicable and Economical Route for a Railroad from the Mississippi River to the Pacific Ocean,* 33rd cong., 2nd sess., Doc. 91, 10; U.S. Congress, House of Representatives, *Central Pacific Railroad,* 33rd cong., 1st sess., Doc. 18, 1–10; David Henry Miller, "The Impact of the Gunnison Massacre on Mormon-Federal Relations: Colonel Edward Jenner Steptoe's Command in Utah Territory, 1854–1855" (master's thesis, University of Utah, 1968); Ronald W. Walker, "President Young Writes Jefferson Davis about the Gunnison Massacre Affair," *BYU Studies* 35, no. 1 (1995): 146–70. Cf. Robert Kent Fielding, *The Unsolicited Chronicler: An Account of the Gunnison Massacre* (Brookline, MA: Paradigm Publications, 1993).

5. Stout, 2:536, Dec. 23, 25, 1854; Sylvester Mowry to Edward Joshua Bicknall, Dec. 31, 1854, Apr. 27, 1855, Mowry Letters, Beinecke Library, Yale University, New Haven, CT, cited in William P. MacKinnon, "Sex, Subalterns, and Steptoe: A Civil Affairs Nightmare Impacts 1850s Mormon-Federal Relations" (paper delivered at the Mormon History Association annual meeting, Casper, WY, May 2006), 12, 15–16, to be published as "Sex, Subalterns, and Steptoe: Army Behavior, Mormon Rage, and Utah War Anxieties," *Utah*

Historical Quarterly 76 (Summer 2008); Miller, "Impact of the Gunnison Massacre," 214–17; Mosiah Hancock, "The Life Story of Mosiah Lyman Hancock," 33, typescript, copies available at BYU and CHL.

6. See Edwin Woolley, Mar. 4, 1855, HOGCM.

7. Bill Hickman, *Brigham's Destroying Angel: Being the Life, Confession, and Startling Disclosures of the Notorious Bill Hickman, the Danite Chief of Utah*, ed. J. H. Beadle (New York: George A. Crofutt, 1872), 112; Stout, 2:583–84, Jan. 5–9, 1856.

8. Stout, 2:613, 622, Dec. 30, 1856, Feb. 13, 1857; Furniss, 58. On Stiles's excommunication, see *CHC*, 4:199; Woodruff, Dec. 22, 1856.

9. Brigham Young to Horace S. Eldredge, Dec. 30, 1858, Letterpress Copybook 5:21, YOF; Brigham Young to John M. Bernhisel, Jan. 2, 1859, Letterpress Copybook 5:19, YOF.

10. See Everett L. Cooley, "Carpetbag Rule: Territorial Government in Utah," *Utah Historical Quarterly* 26 (Apr. 1958): 107–29; Duane A. Smith, *Rocky Mountain West: Colorado, Wyoming, and Montana, 1859–1915*, Histories of the American Frontier (Albuquerque: University of New Mexico Press, 1992), 66–67; Odie B. Faulk, *Arizona: A Short History* (Norman: University of Oklahoma Press, 1970), 128; Ted Tunnell, "Creating 'the Propaganda of History': Southern Editors and the Origins of Carpetbagger and Scalawag," *Journal of Southern History* 72 (Nov. 2006): 789–822.

11. Woodruff, Jan. 13, 1856. See also ibid., Feb. 24, 1856.

12. Brigham Young to John M. Bernhisel, Aug. 30, 1856, Letterpress Copybook 3:39–41, YOF; Brigham Young to George A. Smith and John M. Bernhisel, Jan. 3, 1857, Letterpress Copybook 3:355, YOF. In a further inflammatory charge, Young claimed that the surveyors were "ready to take my life and the lives of this people." "Items of Interview between Prest B. Young & Messrs Livingston & Bell," July 6, 1858, Memorandums and notes, 1852–75, General Office Files, YOF. For a review of the controversy and an assessment of mismanagement and even fraud, see C. Albert White, *Initial Points of the Rectangular Survey System* (Westminster, CO: Professional Land Surveyors of Colorado, 1996), 310–30. See also Charles W. Moeller, affidavit, June 26, 1857, in *St. Louis Daily Missouri Republican*, July 23, 1857, reprinted in White, *Initial Points of the Rectangular Survey System*, 320–21; Lawrence L. Linford, "Establishing and Maintaining Land Ownership in Utah Prior to 1869," *Utah Historical Quarterly* 42 (Spring 1974): 136.

13. William P. MacKinnon, "The Buchanan Spoils System and the Utah Expedition: Careers of W. M. F. Magraw and John M. Hockaday," *Utah Historical Quarterly* 31 (Spring 1963): 132–35.

14. W. M. F. Magraw to Mr. President, Oct. 3, 1856, in U.S. Congress, House, *The Utah Expedition*, 35th Cong., 1st sess., 1858, Doc. 71, 2; LeRoy R. Hafen and Ann W. Hafen, *The Utah Expedition, 1857–1858: A Documentary Account of the United States Military Movement under Colonel Albert Sidney Johnston, and the Resistance by Brigham Young and the Mormon Nauvoo Legion*, The Far West

and the Rockies Historical Series, 1820–1875, vol. 8 (Glendale, CA: Arthur H. Clark, 1958), 361–63.

15. Woodruff, July 24, 1847. For references to Isaiah, see *The Orson Pratt Journals*, comp. Elden J. Watson (Salt Lake City: Elden J. Watson, 1975), 461–63, Aug. 1, 1847; July 25, 1847, HOGCM.

16. Woodruff, July 25, 28, 1847; Howard R. Egan, *Pioneering the West, 1846 to 1878* (Richmond, UT: Howard R. Egan Estate, 1917), 108; Minutes, July 25, 1847, HOGCM.

17. "Journey to Zion, From the Journal of Erastus Snow," Aug. 8, 1847, *Utah Humanities Review* 2 (July 1948): 281.

18. Orson Pratt, *The Kingdom of God* (Liverpool: S. W. Richards, [1852]), 1; Klaus J. Hansen, *Quest for Empire: The Political Kingdom of God and the Council of Fifty in Mormon History* (East Lansing: Michigan State University Press, 1967), 184–85. On Deseret, see Heber C. Kimball, Aug. 30, 1857, in *JD*, 5:164.

19. Richard White, *"It's Your Misfortune and None of My Own": A History of the American West* (Norman: University of Oklahoma Press, 1991), 155.

20. Howard Roberts Lamar, *The Far Southwest, 1846–1912: A Territorial History* (New Haven: Yale University Press, 1966), 13–14. For evaluations that the appointees were more than the "political hacks" that many westerners made them out to be, see Smith, *Rocky Mountain West*, 65–66; Kermit L. Hall, "Hacks and Derelicts Revisited: American Territorial Judiciary, 1789–1959," *Western Historical Quarterly* 12 (July 1981): 273–89.

21. Lamar, *Far Southwest*, 11–12. See also Julienne L. Wood, "Popular Sovereignty," *Dictionary of American History*, ed. Stanley I. Kutler et al., 3rd ed. (New York: Charles Scribner's Sons and Thomson Gale, 2003) 6:415–16; Paul K. Conkin, *Self-Evident Truths: Being a Discourse on the Origins & Development of the First Principles of American Government—Popular Sovereignty, Natural Rights, and Balance & Separation of Powers* (Bloomington: Indiana University Press, 1974), 2, 24–25.

22. On popular sovereignty and polygamy, see Sarah Barringer Gordon, *The Mormon Question: Polygamy and Constitutional Conflict in Nineteenth-Century America* (Chapel Hill: University of North Carolina Press, 2002), 8–10, 51, 54–83.

23. Lamar, *Far Southwest*, 308, 320–21, 338.

24. Brigham Young to William I. Appleby, Mar. 1, 1857, Letterpress Copybook 3:404, YOF.

25. David L. Bigler, *Forgotten Kingdom: The Mormon Theocracy in the American West, 1847–1896* (Spokane, WA: Arthur H. Clark, 1998), 59.

26. See Earl S. Pomeroy, *The Territories and the United States, 1861–1890: Studies in Territorial Administration* (Philadelphia: University of Pennsylvania Press, 1947); Lamar, *Far Southwest;* Thomas G. Alexander, *A Clash of Interests: Interior Department and Mountain West, 1863–1896* (Provo, UT: Brigham Young University Press, 1977).

27. Paul H. Peterson, "The Mormon Reformation of 1856–1857: The Rhetoric and the Reality," *Journal of Mormon History* 15 (1989): 60–65; Gustive O. Larson, "The Mormon Reformation," *Utah Historical Quarterly* 26 (Jan. 1958): 46, 48. On British converts, see Richard L. Evans, *A Century of "Mormonism" in Great Britain* (Salt Lake City: Deseret News Press, 1937), 244.

28. David O. Calder to William H. Miles, Feb. 28, 1857, in *Mormon*, May 9, 1857.

29. Leonard J. Arrington, Feramorz Y. Fox, and Dean L. May, *Building the City of God: Community and Cooperation among the Mormons* (Salt Lake City: Deseret Book, 1976), 15–40, 75.

30. William Gibson, Journal, Oct. 8, 1855, CHL; Brigham Young to William Gibson, Mar. 1, 1856, in Gibson Journal.

31. Brigham Young, Mar. 2, 1856, in *JD*, 3:222, 226.

32. Harrriet Beecher Stowe, *Old Town Folks* (1889; repr., Cambridge, MA: Belknap Press of Harvard University Press, 1966), 475.

33. Brigham Young, Dec. 20, 1846, in Historian's Office, History of the Church, 518–19, CHL; Brigham Young to Charles C. Rich, Jan. 4, 1847, Outgoing Correspondence, YOF; Brigham Young, remarks, Nov. 15, 1847, HOGCM; "Bishop Higbee," remarks, Nov. 25, 1847, HOGCM; *The Book of Mormon* (Palmyra, NY: E. B. Grandin, 1830), 230–32, 238–39, 266–73, 282–89, 303–4, 310–23, 340–45, 417–22 (current Mosiah 25; Alma 4, 6, 16–17, 21–22, 29, 31–35, 43; Helaman 5). "The New England leaders of the church, while playing the role of frontiersmen, were still Puritan at heart, and the Reformation reflected a clash between deep-rooted traditional convictions and the compromises and expediencies of frontier living." See Larson, "Mormon Reformation," 48.

34. Brigham Young, Sept. 21, 1856, in *JD*, 4:52–54.

35. Brigham Young, Feb. 8, 1857, in *JD*, 4:219.

36. PSHR, Oct. 17, 1856, 2nd section, 21; Hannah Tapfield King, Autobiography, 142–43, typescript, CHL.

37. King Autobiography, 142–43.

38. Chatterley.

39. See N. B. Baldwin to Brigham Young, Nov. 15, 1857, Incoming Correspondence, YOF.

40. Cedar Stake Journal, Dec. 19, 1856, Jan. 18, 29, Feb. 22, 1857, Special Collections, William R. Palmer Collection, Gerald R. Sherratt Library, Southern Utah University, Cedar City, UT.

41. Brigham Young to John Steele, Mar. 18, 1857, Letterpress Copybook 3:488, YOF; Brigham Young to George A. Smith and John M. Bernhisel, Jan. 3, 1857, Letterpress Copybook 3:355, YOF; John Ward Christian, Dictation, [1886], H. H. Bancroft Manuscript Collection, Bancroft Library, Berkeley, CA, microfilm copy located at CHL.

42. Peterson, "Mormon Reformation," 74–76. Peterson argues that one of the hallmarks of the reformation was its spirit of forgiveness and mercy. See also Brigham Young to Philo Farnsworth, Apr. 4, 1857, Letterpress Copybook 3:540, YOF.

43. See Wilford Woodruff, Nov. 23, 1856, in Historian's Office, History of the Church; Heber C. Kimball to James Snow, Mar. 6, 1857, Letterpress Copybook 3:468, YOF. In Aug. 1857 when Snow made harsh remarks in a public meeting, he paused and urged the members of the congregation "to not run off" and report what he had said to Brigham Young. PGM, Aug. 2, 1857.

44. Brigham Young and Daniel Wells to William H. Dame, Sept. 14, 1857, Letterpress Copybook 3:859, YOF.

45. Application for Statehood, Mar. 27, 1856, Governor's Letterpress Copybook 1:456–60, YOF; Stout, 2:595, Mar. 27, 1856; Edward Leo Lyman, *Political Deliverance: The Mormon Quest for Utah Statehood* (Urbana: University of Illinois Press, 1986), 8.

46. William P. MacKinnon, *At Sword's Point, Part I: A Documentary History of the Utah War to 1858*, Kingdom in the West: The Mormons and the American Frontier 10 (Norman, OK: Arthur H. Clark, 2008), 55.

47. "Expedition against Utah," *Deseret News*, Oct. 7, 1857; Memorial, Executive Files, Governor's Office Files, YOF.

48. Brigham Young to George A. Smith and John M. Bernhisel, Jan. 3, 1857, Letterpress Copybook 3:259, YOF.

49. John M. Bernhisel to Brigham Young, Mar. 17, Apr. 2, 1857, Utah Delegate Files, YOF.

50. See "Southern Secession," in *The Annals of America*, vol. 9, *1858–1865: The Crisis of the Union* (Chicago: Encyclopædia Britannica, 1968), 204–9.

51. MacKinnon, *At Sword's Point*, 67, 100–102, 107.

52. W. W. Drummond, letter, in "Dreadful State of Affairs in Utah," *New York Herald*, Mar. 20, 1857; W. W. Drummond to Jeremiah S. Black, Mar. 30, 1857, in *Executive Documents Printed by Order of the House of Representatives During the First Session of the Thirty-Fifth Congress, 1857–58* (Washington: James B. Steedman, 1858), Doc 71, 10:213. For a summary of Drummond's charges, see *CHC*, 4:202–5. See also Stout, 2:613, 622, Dec. 30, 1856, Feb. 13, 1857. Though the Mormons destroyed some of Judge George P. Stiles's law firm records, the federal records were not destroyed and were returned after Governor Alfred Cumming's 1858 arrival in Utah. See Curtis E. Bolton to Jeremiah S. Black, June 26, 1857, in *Executive Documents*, 10:214; Stout, 2:613, Dec. 30, 1856; Furniss, 57–59; Andrew Jenson, comp., *Church Chronology*, 2nd ed. (Salt Lake City: Deseret News, 1914), 61. The U.S. military investigated Babbitt's death and concluded he was killed by Cheyenne. U.S. Congress, House, *Almon W. Babbit—Administrator Of*, 35th Cong. 2nd sess., Jan. 21, 1859, H. Report 131, Serial 1018; U.S. Congress, House, *Almon W. Babbit—Administrator Of*, 36th Cong. 1st sess., Apr. 6, 1860, H. Report 346, Serial 1069. See also Stout, 2:601, 601–2n75, Oct. 4, 1856.

53. MacKinnon, *At Sword's Point*, 108–9.

54. "The Mormon Horde," *American Journal*, Apr. 29, 1857, in Historian's Office, Historical Scrapbooks, 6:33, CHL.

55. Editorial, *New York Daily Tribune*, May 18, 1857; "Highly Important from Utah," *New York Daily Tribune*, May 18, 1857.

56. "The Mormon Rebellion," *New York Times*, May 11, 1857. See also Drummond to Black, Mar. 30, 1857, in *Executive Documents*, 10:214.

57. Richard Hofstadter, "The Paranoid Style in American Politics," in Hofstadter, *The Paranoid Style in American Politics and Other Essays* (Cambridge, MA: Harvard University Press, 1964), 3; Peter Knight, *Conspiracy Culture: From the Kennedy Assassination to* The X-Files (New York: Routledge, 2000), 3; Mark Fenster, *Conspiracy Theories: Secrecy and Power in American Culture* (Minneapolis: University of Minnesota Press, 1999), xii–xiii.

58. Enoch Baker, "Mormonism," in Peter Knight, ed., *Conspiracy Theories in American History: An Encyclopedia* (Santa Barbara, CA: ABC-CLIO, 2003) 2:509; David Brion Davis, "Some Themes of Counter-Subversion: An Analysis of Anti-Masonic, Anti-Catholic, and Anti-Mormon Literature," *Mississippi Valley Historical Review* 47 (Sept. 1960): 205–24; Peter Knight, *Conspiracy Nation: The Politics of Paranoia in Postwar America* (New York: New York University Press, 2002), 4; Leo P. Ribuffo, "Religious Prejudice and Nativism," in Charles H. Lippy and Peter W. Williams, eds., *Encyclopedia of the American Religious Experience* (New York: Charles Scribner's Sons, 1988), 3:1525–35.

59. Bernhisel to Young, Mar. 17 and Apr. 2, 1857, Utah Delegate Files, YOF.

60. Kenneth M. Stampp, *America in 1857: A Nation on the Brink* (New York: Oxford University Press, 1990), 200; "Republican Platform of 1856," in Donald Bruce Johnson, comp., *National Party Platforms, 1840–1956* (Urbana: University of Illinois Press, 1978), 27; "To the Latter-Day Saints," *Circleville Ohio Herald*, Nov. 21, 1856.

61. "Remarks of Geo. A. Smith at the Peace Conference," June 12, 1858, Historian's Office, Letterpress Copybook 1:630, CHL.

62. George W. Lay to W. S. Harney, June 29, 1857, in House, *Utah Expedition*, Doc. 71, 7; Hafen and Hafen, *Utah Expedition*, 30–34.

63. Furniss, 95.

64. See Jean H. Baker, *James Buchanan* (New York: Times Books/Henry Holt, 2004); Stampp, *America in 1857*; Elbert B. Smith, *The Presidency of James Buchanan* (Lawrence: University Press of Kansas, 1975).

65. Joseph W. Young, Journal, May 19, 1857, in JH; George Laub, Journal, May 30, 1857, CHL; Bernhisel to Young, Mar. 17, 1857, Utah Delegate Files, YOF; Thomas L. Kane to Brigham Young, May 21, 1857, Incoming Correspondence, YOF; Bernhisel to Young, Apr. 2, 1857, Utah Delegate Files, YOF; HOJ, May 29, 1857; Woodruff, May 29, 1857; Brigham Young, July 5, 1857, in "Remarks," *Deseret News*, July 15, 1857; "Arrivals," *Deseret News*, June 3, 1857. On Young's serving on an interim basis, see Bigler, *Forgotten Kingdom*, 92n18.

66. Pitchforth, June 19, 1857; Wilford Woodruff to the editor of the *Millennial Star*, July 1, 1857, Historian's Office, Letterpress Copybook 1:472, YOF.

67. Brigham Young to Henry G. Boyle, July 4, 1857, Letterpress Copybook 3:694, YOF.

68. HOJ, June 23, 1857. A sampling and introduction to Pratt's prose is provided in Peter Crawley, ed., *The Essential Parley P. Pratt* (Salt Lake City: Signature Books, 1990).

69. John R. Young, *Memoirs of John R. Young: Utah Pioneer, 1847* (Salt Lake City: Deseret News, 1920), 70; Steven Pratt, "Eleanor McLean and the Murder of Parley P. Pratt," *BYU Studies* 15 (Winter 1975): 228.

70. Pratt, "Eleanor McLean," 225–34; *Memoirs of John R. Young*, 71. When a newspaper reporter asked Eleanor if she divorced McLean before marrying Pratt, she answered: "No, the sectarian priests have no power from God to marry; and as a so-called marriage ceremony performed by them is no marriage at all, no divorce was needed." Eleanor McLean Pratt, interview, in *New York World*, Nov. 23, 1869, in Pratt, "Eleanor McLean," 233n28.

71. John R. Young to William G. Black, Mar. 1930, typescript, CHL; Woodruff, Sept. 7, 1856; Pratt, "Eleanor McLean," 231–36, 238–39n43. See also Woodruff, Jan. 3, 1858.

72. Pratt, "Eleanor McLean," 234–39.

73. Ibid., 244–48; Eleanor Pratt to "Ye loved ones in Utah," May 14, 1857, in Parley P. Pratt, Collection, CHL; Hector McLean, statement, in "The Killing of Pratt—Letter from Mr. McLean," *San Francisco Daily Alta California*, July 9, 1857; Hendrick Hartog, "Lawyering, Husbands' Rights, and 'The Unwritten Law' in Nineteenth-Century America," *Journal of American History* 84 (June 1997): 67–96.

74. For the California editor's comment, see "Killing of Pratt." On the role of Masons in assisting McLean, see "An Unwritten Leaf of History," *Boonville (MO) Weekly Advertiser*, Feb. 14, 1890.

75. Brigham Young to Silas Smith and the Brethren on the Sandwich Islands, July 4, 1857, Letterpress Copybook 3:698–99, YOF.

76. Brigham Young to Orson Pratt and Ezra T. Benson, July 30, 1857, Letterpress Copybook 3:658, YOF; Young to Boyle, July 4, 1857, Letterpress Copybook 3:694, YOF.

77. Brigham Young to George Q. Cannon, July 4, 1857, Letterpress Copybook 3:691, YOF.

78. Brigham Young, remarks, May 1, 1865, in HOGCM; Woodruff, May 1, 1865.

Chapter 3

1. See Steven L. Olsen, "Celebrating Cultural Identity: Pioneer Day in Nineteeth-Century Mormonism," *BYU Studies* 36 (1996–97): 159–77; Thomas Bullock, "Report of Proceedings," July 24, 1849, HOGCM; Historian's Office, History of the Church, July 24, 1849, CHL. Young actually entered the Salt Lake Valley shortly after most members of his 1847 company, but the date for Pioneer Day was based on his July 24 arrival. *The Pioneer Camp of the Saints: The 1846 and 1847 Mormon Trail Journals of Thomas Bullock*, ed. Will Bagley (Spokane, WA: Arthur H. Clark, 1997), 237, 237n5.

2. "Celebration of the Twenty Fourth of July, 1856 in the Tops of the Mountains," *Deseret News*, July 30, 1856; Charles C. Keller, *The Lady in the Ore Bucket* (Salt Lake City: University of Utah Press, 2001), 58–59; Brigham Young, Office Journal, July 23–25, 1856, YOF.

3. Brigham Young, July 19, 1857, in *JD*, 5:56; *DBY*, 45–47, July 16–18, 1857; "Names of Persons Invited to Spend the 24 July 1857 at the Head Waters of Big Cotton Wood," General Office Files, President's Office Files, YOF; G. D. Watt, "The 24th of July in the Tops of the Mountains," *Deseret News*, July 29, 1857.

4. Brigham Young, Remarks, Jan. 17, 1848, in HOGCM.

5. See Heber C. Kimball to Franklin D. Richards, Aug. 31, 1855, Heber C. Kimball, Papers, 1837–66, CHL; Wilford Woodruff to Asa Fitch, July 31, 1856, Historian's Office, Letterpress Copybook 1:342–44, CHL.

6. Presiding Bishopric, Bishops Meeting Minutes, Mar. 11, 1856, CHL.

7. See Brigham Young to Silas Smith and the Brethren on the Sandwich Islands, July 4, 1857, Letterpress Copybook 3:698, YOF.

8. *DBY*, 48, July 22, 23, 1857; Woodruff, July 22, 23, 1857.

9. Stout, 2:633, July 22–23, 1857; Watt, "24th of July."

10. See Rex Thomas Price Jr., "The Mormon Missionary of the Nineteenth Century" (PhD diss., University of Wisconsin, 1991), 58–59, 265–76; Wayne L. Wahlquist, "Population Growth in the Mormon Core Area: 1847–90," in *The Mormon Role in the Settlement of the West*, ed. Richard H. Jackson (Provo, UT: Brigham Young University Press, 1978), 107–30; William E. Hughes, "A Profile of the Missionaries of the Church of Jesus Christ of Latter-day Saints, 1849–1900" (master's thesis, Brigham Young University, 1986), 7–14, 104–7, 182–91; Historian's Office, Missionaries of the Church of Jesus Christ of Latter-day Saints, ca. 1925, vol. 1, CHL.

11. Watt, "24th of July"; *DBY*, 48, July 23, 1857; *The Journal of Lorenzo Brown* (n.p.: Heritage Press, n.d.), 86, July 23, 1857; John H. Evans, "Grandmother's Stories of Early Days," *Juvenile Instructor* 40, no. 19 (Oct. 1, 1905): 577; Joshua Midgley, Diary, July 23, 1857, microfilm, CHL; Keller, *Lady in the Ore Bucket*, 65; Andrew Jackson Allen, Reminiscences and Journal, July 24, 1857, typescript, CHL; Woodruff, July 24, 1857.

12. Ira Ames, Autobiography and Journal, July 24, 25, 1857, CHL; Watt, "24th of July." Ames incorrectly puts the speech on July 24; other sources confirm it occurred July 23.

13. Allen, Reminiscences and Journal, July 24, 1857.

14. Watt, "24th of July"; Evans, "Grandmother's Stories of Early Days," 577; John Adams Wakeham, Autobiography, 8, CHL.

15. *DBY*, 49, July 24, 1857; Watt, "24th of July"; HOJ, July 24, 1857; Tullidge, 158; Woodruff, July 24, 1857.

16. A. O. Smoot, Letter, Feb. 14, 1884, in Tullidge, 156; *DBY*, 49, July 24, 1857.

17. Smoot, Letter, Feb. 14, 1884, in Tullidge, 156–57; Woodruff, July 24, 1857; *DBY*, 49, July 24, 1857; HOJ, July 23, 1857; Elias Smith, Journal, July 23, 1857, CHL.

18. Smoot, Letter, Feb. 14, 1884, in Tullidge, 156; *DBY*, 49, July 24, 1857.

19. Smoot, Letter, Feb. 14, 1884, in Tullidge, 157; Smith Journal, July 23–24, 1857; HOJ, July 23, 24, 1857. Rockwell would become a controversial and legendary lawman and gunslinger. See Harold Schindler, *Orrin Porter Rockwell: Man of God, Son of Thunder,* 2nd ed. (Salt Lake City: University of Utah Press, 1983).

20. Smith Journal, July 23, 1857; "Mrs. McLean," *Mormon,* June 27, 1857; Eleanor J. McComb Pratt, Account of the Death of Parley P. Pratt, ca. 1857, CHL; "The Utah Question," *San Francisco Daily Evening Bulletin,* July 1, 1857.

21. See Woodruff, June 23, 1857.

22. *DBY,* 49, July 24, 1857.

23. Ibid.

24. Adams, 128–34; LeCheminant, 31.

25. "Gen. Harney," *Circleville (OH) Herald,* June 20, 1856; Adams, 46–51, 286; William P. MacKinnon, ed., *At Sword's Point, Part I: A Documentary History of the Utah War to 1858,* Kingdom in the West: The Mormons and the American Frontier 10 (Norman, OK: Arthur H. Clark, 2008), 168.

26. Adams, 50–51.

27. Arrington2, 161–63; Smoot, Letter, Feb. 14, 1884, in Tullidge, 56; Smith Journal, July 23, 1857; HOJ, July 23, 1857.

28. "Remarks of Geo. A. Smith at the Peace Conference," June 12, 1848, Historian's Office, Letterpress Copybook 1:635–36. A clerk in Salt Lake City noted Smoot's July arrival in the city the day before the canyon celebration and recorded that the new governor was to be "Cumming of St. Louis." HOJ, July 23, 1857. Although Alfred Cumming, the new governor, did not actually accept his appointment until July 11 of that year, newspapers had been discussing his potential appointment for weeks." The confusion of Cumming with Cummins was understandable. Besides having a similar name, Cumming also had a Missouri connection, having most recently served as superintendent of Indian affairs for the Upper Missouri, headquartered in St. Louis. MacKinnon, *At Sword's Point,* 180–81; "Latest Intelligence," *New York Daily Times,* June 6, 1857; Charles S. Peterson, "A Historical Analysis of Territorial Government in Utah under Alfred Cumming, 1857–1861" (master's thesis, Brigham Young University, 1958), 8–9.

29. *DBY,* 48–49, July 24, 1857; Smith Journal, July 23, 1857; Smoot, Letter, Feb. 14, 1884, in Tullidge, 156–57; Arrington1, 250–52.

30. Woodruff, July 24, 1857; *DBY,* 49, July 24, 1857, emphasis in original.

31. Jenson, 1:63–64; Gardner, 319–21; Whitney, 4:175–77.

32. "Daniel," *Salt Lake Daily Tribune,* Dec. 4, 1874. On Wells's ability as an orator, see Bryant S. Hinckley, *Daniel Hanmer Wells and Events of His Time* (Salt Lake City: Deseret News Press, 1942), 23, 235, 418, 428.

33. Ames, Autobiography and Journal, July 24, 25, 1857; Allen, Reminiscences and Journal, July 24, 1857; Watt, "24th of July."

34. Henry Ballard, Journal, July 24, 1857, typescript, Joel E. Ricks Collection of Transcriptions, vol. 1, Utah State University Library, copy also located at the CHL.

35. Clarence Merrill, Autobiography, 9, CHL.

36. Allen, Reminiscences and Journal, July 24, 1857; Watt, "24th of July"; Woodruff, July 24, 1857; Wakeham, Autobiography, 8; *Journal of Lorenzo Brown*, 87, July 24, 1857; Ames, Autobiography and Journal, July 24, 25, 1857; Evans, "Grandmother's Stories of Early Days," 578.

37. See Louis G. Reinwand, "An Interpretive Study of Mormon Millennialism During the Nineteenth Century with Emphasis on Millennial Developments in Utah" (master's thesis, Brigham Young University, 1971).

38. *Journal of Lorenzo Brown*, 87, July 24, 1857. See also Ames, Autobiography and Journal, July 24, 25, 1857; Watt, "24th of July"; Midgley Diary, July 24, 1857.

39. *DBY*, 49, July 24, 1857.

40. Ames, Autobiography and Journal, July 24–25, 1857; Watt, "24th of July"; *Journal of Lorenzo Brown*, 87, July 24, 1857.

Chapter 4

1. Brigham Young, discourse, June 21, 1857, in Historian's Office, Reports of Speeches, CHL.

2. Brigham Young to Thomas L. Kane, June 29, 1857, Letterpress Copybook 3:667, YOF; "Judge Drummond of Utah," *San Francisco Western Standard*, July 3, 1857.

3. Brigham Young to John M. Bernhisel, Oct. 29, 1856, Letterpress Copybook 3:152, YOF; John M. Bernhisel to Brigham Young, Jan. 17, 1857, Incoming Correspondence, YOF. Mormons charged that before coming to Utah, Drummond had deserted his family and once in the territory displayed another woman, reportedly a prostitute, in his courtroom. John M. Bernhisel to Brigham Young, Jan. 17, 1857, Utah Delegate Files, YOF; W. I. Appleby, letter to the editor of *New York Daily Times*, Aug. 24, 1857, in "Mormon Affairs—Mr. Appleby in Reply to Judge Drummond," *Mormon*, Aug. 29, 1857. W. M. F. Magraw, the other main accuser, had led a Jackson County "band of ruffians" that threatened a Mormon with hanging. Later, his petty fights and delays associated with the nation's new Pacific Wagon Road would offend many of the people he worked with. See John Taylor to Bro. Appleby, July 9, 1857, in "Editorial Correspondence from the Plains," *Mormon*, Aug. 8, 1857; W. Turrentine Jackson, *Wagon Roads West: A Study of Federal Road Surveys and Construction in the Trans-Mississippi West, 1846–1869* (Berkeley: University of California Press, 1952), 175, 192–97, 200, 211–12; William P. MacKinnon, "The Buchanan Spoils System and the Utah Expedition: Careers of W. M. F. Magraw and John M. Hockaday," *Utah Historical Quarterly* 31 (Spring 1963): 134–43; John Wolcott Phelps, Diary, Sept., 3, 1857, in LeRoy R. Hafen and Ann W. Hafen, *The Utah Expedition, 1857–1858: A Documentary Account of the United States Military Movement under Colonel Albert Sidney Johnston, and the Resistance by Brigham Young and the Mormon Nauvoo Legion*, The Far West and the Rockies Historical Series, 1820–1875, vol. 8 (Glendale, CA: Arthur H. Clark, 1958), 122, original located in the New York Public Library.

4. Brigham Young to Thomas L. Kane, June 29, 1857, Letterpress Copybook 3:668, 670, YOF. For evidence the Saints heard rumors of the troops coming

before July 24, see George Laub, Journal, July 5, 1857, CHL; George
A. Smith, July 12, 1857, in PGM; Jens Christian Nielsen, "History of Jens
Christian Nielsen," 63, July 15, 1857, FHL. For other statements reflecting
Young's sense of providence, see Brigham Young, July 5, 1857, in "Remarks,"
Deseret News, July 15, 1857. Several years earlier when rumors spread that
Washington would replace him as governor, Young had said the govern-
ment "can do as they please, or rather as the Lord pleases…If no one else
acknowledges the hand of the Lord in such things, we do." Brigham Young to
Erastus Snow, Feb. 28, 1855, Letterpress Copybook 2:3, YOF.

5. Smith, July 12, 1857, in PGM.

6. See A. O. Smoot, Letter, Feb. 14, 1884, in Tullidge, 156; *DBY*, July 24, 1857.

7. See Lorenzo Snow to Brigham Young, Aug. [13], 1857, Incoming Correspondence, YOF. See also "From Salt Lake City," *Los Angeles Star*, Dec.
12, 1857; Susan Tate Laing, *Andrew Hunter Scott: Builder in the Kingdom*
(Provo, UT: The Andrew Hunter Scott Genealogical Association, 2001), 530,
Sept. 25, 1857.

8. HOJ, July 25, 1857; C. G. Landon, letter to the editor, Nov. 13, 1857, in
"Incidents of Mormon Life and Practices," *Sacramento Daily Union*, copy in
Historian's Office, Historical Scrapbooks, 1857, 267, CHL; C. G. Landon to
D. H. Burr, Sept. 18, 1857, General Land Office Correspondence, National
Archives and Records Administration, Rocky Mountain Region, Denver, CO
[hereafter GLOC]; William Bell to D. H. Burr, Mar. 1, 1858, GLOC.

9. Salt Lake City 6th Ward, Report of Excommunicated, 1857–59, Historian's
Office, Excommunication Lists, 1858–68, CHL, copy located in MMMRF;
Alonzo Hazelton Raleigh, Journal, June 13 1857, CHL.

10. Landon, letter to the editor, Nov. 13, 1857, in "Incidents of Mormon Life
and Practices."

11. Landon to Burr, Sept. 18, 1857, GLOC; David H. Burr to Thomas A. Hendricks, Oct. 19, 1857, GLOC; David H. Burr to Thomas A. Hendricks, Mar.
15, 1858, GLOC; A. B. Hoy, statement, in "Later from the Plains," *Memphis
Daily Appeal*, Sept. 18, 1857.

12. Landon to Burr, Sept. 18, 1857, GLOC; [C. G.] Landon, Sept. 18, 1857, in
"Mormon Outrages," *Weekly Richmond (VA) Enquirer*, Oct. 28, 1857, citing the
Washington Union; Burr to Hendricks, Oct. 19, 1857, GLOC; Landon, letter
to the editor, Nov. 13, 1857, "Incidents of Mormon Life and Practices"; Bell
to Burr, Mar. 1, 1858, GLOC; Burr to Hendricks, Mar. 15, 1858, GLOC.

13. W. H. Wilson, affidavit, Nov. 29, 1858, GLOC; Bell to Burr, Mar. 1, 1858,
GLOC.

14. C. L. Craig to David H. Burr, Aug. 1, 1856, GLOC; David H. Burr to
Thomas A. Hendricks, Mar. 28, 1857, GLOC; David H. Burr to Thomas
A. Hendricks, June 11, 1857, GLOC; C. G. Landon to David H. Burr, Sept.
18, 1857, GLOC.

15. Joseph Troskolaw[s]ki, May 19, 1857, in "Affairs among the Mormons," *New
York Herald*, May 24, 1857. For correspondence of the Utah surveyors sent

to headquarters, see Craig to Burr, Aug. 1, 1856, GLOC; David H. Burr to Thomas A. Hendricks, Aug. 30, 1856, GLOC; Burr to Hendricks, Mar. 28, 1857, GLOC; Burr to Hendricks, June 11, 1857, GLOC; Landon to Burr, Sept. 18, 1857, GLOC.

16. Brigham Young to John M. Bernhisel, Aug. 30, 1856, Letterpress Copybook 3:40, YOF. In a further inflammatory charge, Young claimed that Burr and others were "ready to take my life and the lives of this people." "Items of Interview between Prest B. Young and Messrs Livingston & Bell," July 6, 1858, Memorandums and Notes, 1852–75, General Office Files, YOF.

17. Jeff Walker, "Mormon Land Rights in Caldwell and Daviess Counties and the Mormon Conflict of 1838: New Findings and New Understandings," unpublished paper in possession of authors.

18. See Brigham Young to John M. Bernhisel, Aug. 30, 1856, Letterpress Copybook 3:39–41, YOF; Brigham Young to George A. Smith and John M. Bernhisel, Jan. 3, 1857, Letterpress Copybook 3:355, YOF; C. Albert White, *Initial Points of the Rectangular Survey System* (Westminster, CO: Professional Land Surveyors of Colorado, 1996), 310–30; Charles W. Moeller, affidavit, June 26, 1857, in *St. Louis Daily Missouri Republican*, July 23, 1857, reprinted in White, *Initial Points of the Rectangular Survey System*, 320–21; Lawrence L. Linford, "Establishing and Maintaining Land Ownership in Utah Prior to 1869," *Utah Historical Quarterly* 42 (Spring 1974): 136.

19. Brigham Young to Thomas A. Hendricks, Apr. 5, 1858, Governor's Office Files, YOF; HOJ, Sept. 22, 1857; Thomas L. Kane, Diary, Apr. 1858, Thomas L. Kane, Papers, Special Collections and University Archives, Stanford University Libraries, Stanford, California, copy at CHL.

20. Brigham Young, July 26, 1857, in *JD*, 5:75, 78. One outsider in the congregation even claimed that Young, to make his point, reached beneath his coat as if to put his hand on a concealed weapon. Hoy, statement, in "Later from the Plains."

21. Young, July 26, 1857, in *JD*, 5:75.

22. Young, July 26, 1857, in *JD*, 5:77–78.

23. Heber C. Kimball, July 26, 1857, in *JD*, 5:88, 95.

24. Heber C. Kimball, Aug. 2, 1857, in *JD*, 5:132, 138.

25. Brigham Young, Aug. 2, 1857, in *JD*, 5:98–99.

26. Woodruff, Aug. 2, 1857.

27. Woodruff, Aug. 2, 1857; *DBY*, 56, Aug. 4, 1857; Brigham Young to George Q. Cannon, Aug. 4, 1857, Letterpress Copybook 3:735, YOF; Brigham Young to C. W. Wandell, Aug. 4, 1857, Letterpress Copybook 3:740, YOF; Brigham Young to Silas Smith, H. P. Richards, Edward Partridge, Aug. 4, 1857, Letterpress Copybook 3:749–50, YOF; Brigham Young to William Crosby and W. J. Cox, Aug. 4, 1857, Letterpress Copybook 3:751, YOF; Brigham Young to H. S. Eldredge, Aug. 8, 1857, Letterpress Copybook 3:773, YOF; Brigham Young to William J. Cox and William J. Crosby, Oct. 1, 1857, Letterpress Copybook 3:882–83, YOF; Brigham Young to H. G. Whitlock, Oct. 1, 1857, Letterpress Copybook 3:885, YOF; Brigham Young to W. J. Cox, Nov. 5, 1857, Letterpress

Copybook 3:921, YOF; Brigham Young to William Matthews, Nov. 5, 1857, Letterpress Copybook 3:924, YOF; Arnold K. Garr, Donald Q. Cannon, and Richard O. Cowan, eds., *Encyclopedia of Latter-day Saint History* (Salt Lake City: Deseret Book, 2000), 190–92; James W. Hulse, *The Silver State: Nevada's Heritage Reinterpreted* (Reno: University of Nevada Press, 1991), 58–60.

28. See Furniss, 106–7, 114, 183.

29. Woodruff, Aug. 2, 1857.

30. See Brigham Young, Discourse, Aug. 16, 1857, reported by George D. Watt, in Historian's Office Reports of Speeches; David L. Bigler, *Fort Limhi: The Mormon Adventure in Oregon Territory, 1855–1858* (Spokane, WA: Arthur H. Clark, 2003), 175–80; Richard Bennett and Arran Jewsbury, "The Lion and the Emperor: The Mormons, the Hudson's Bay Company, and Vancouver Island, 1846–1858," *BC Studies* 128 (Winter 2000/2001): 57–62; Clifford L. Stott, *Search for Sanctuary: Brigham Young and the White Mountain Expedition*, University of Utah Publications in the American West, vol. 19 (Salt Lake City: University of Utah Press, 1984), 28–30.

31. Woodruff, Aug. 2, 1857.

32. See Brigham Young to Jacob Hamblin, Aug. 4, 1857, Letterpress Copybook 3:737, YOF; Brigham Young to William Felshaw, Aug. 4, 1857, Letterpress Copybook 3:759–60, YOF; Daniel H. Wells to William H. Dame, Aug. 13, 1857, William R. Palmer, Collection, Special Collections, Gerald R. Sherratt Library, Southern Utah University, Cedar City, UT; [Daniel H. Wells] to William B. Pace, Provo, Aug. 13, 1857, Utah Territorial Militia records, Utah State Archives, Salt Lake City, UT.

33. Martin Ridge, "Mormon 'Deliverance' and the Closing of the Frontier," *Journal of Mormon History* 18 (Spring 1992): 146.

34. http://www.nps.gov/hobe/historyculture/index.htm (accessed February 29, 2008).

35. *A Book of Commandments for the Government of the Church of Christ* ([Independence, MO]: W. W. Phelps, 1833), 116 (current D&C 49:24–28); *The Book of Mormon* (Palmyra, NY: E. B. Grandin, 1830), 488, 500, 528 (current 3 Nephi 16:15; 3 Nephi 21:11–21; Mormon 5:22–24).

36. *Book of Mormon* (1830), 497 (current 3 Nephi 20:14–17).

37. Phelps Diary, Sept., 15, 18, 1857, in Hafen and Hafen, *Utah Expedition*, 128, 130.

38. HOJ, Sept. 18, 1857; Stout, 2:638, Sept. 19, 1857; Arrington2, 175, 464n59.

39. Brigham Young to Jacob Hamblin, Aug. 4, 1857, Letterpress Copybook 3:738, YOF; Brigham Young to Silas Smith, H. P. Richards, and Edward Partridge, Aug. 4, 1857, Letterpress Copybook 3:748, YOF; Brigham Young to William Crosby and W. J. Cox, Aug. 4, 1857, Letterpress Copybook 3:752–53, YOF.

40. L. U. Reavis, *The Life and Military Services of Gen. William Selby Harney* (St. Louis: Bryan, Brand & Co., 1878), 276–79; Furniss, 121; LeCheminant, 30. Though the Salt Lake Temple would not be completed until 1893, outsiders used the term "temple" loosely to include other Mormon edifices on Temple Square, such as the Old Tabernacle.

41. See Glen M. Leonard, *Nauvoo: A Place of Peace, a People of Promise* (Salt Lake City: Deseret Book/Brigham Young University Press, 2002), 380–98, 595–621.

42. Adams, 166.

43. "The Mormon Exodus," *New York Times*, June 17, 1858; Furniss, 121.

44. Phelps Diary, Aug. 24, 1857, in Hafen and Hafen, *Utah Expedition*, 115.

45. Furniss, 122.

46. William P. MacKinnon, "Epilogue to the Utah War: Impact and Legacy," *Journal of Mormon History* 29 (Fall 2003): 221–22, 235.

47. Furniss, 122.

48. *DBY*, 56, Aug. 4, 1857; Young to Crosby and Cox, Aug. 4, 1857, Letterpress Copybook 3:751–54, YOF; Edward Leo Lyman, *San Bernardino: The Rise and Fall of a California Community* (Salt Lake City: Signature Books, 1996), 197–98, 371–83, 414–15.

49. Brigham Young to William Felshaw, Aug. 4, 1857, Letterpress Copybook 3:759–60, YOF; Brigham Young to Nathaniel V. Jones, Aug. 4, 1857, Letterpress Copybook 3:763–64, YOF.

50. Brigham Young to Jacob Hamblin, Aug. 4, 1857, Letterpress Copybook 3:737, YOF. See also Brigham Young to Philo T. Farnsworth, Aug. 4, 1857, Letterpress Copybook 3:739, YOF.

51. Juanita Brooks, *Jacob Hamblin: Mormon Apostle to the Indians* (Salt Lake City: Westwater Press, 1980); Pearson H. Corbett, *Jacob Hamblin, The Peacemaker* (Salt Lake City: Deseret Book, 1952).

52. Daniel H. Wells, General Orders, Aug. 1, 1857, Letter Book, 93, Nauvoo Legion (Utah) Adj. Gen. Records, 1851–70, CHL; Daniel H. Wells to F. D. Richards, Aug. 1, 1857, Daniel H. Wells, Letters, Beinecke Library, Yale University, New Haven, CT; Daniel H. Wells to Wm. H. Dame, Aug. 1, 1857, Palmer Collection; Whitney, 1:620–21. On Wells's forefathers, see Bryant S. Hinckley, *Daniel Hanmer Wells and Events of His Time* (Salt Lake City: Deseret News Press, 1942), 19–20.

53. Wells, General Orders, Aug. 1, 1857, Letter Book, 93, Nauvoo Legion (Utah) Adj. Gen. Records. On the admonitions regarding grain, see Brigham Young, sermon, July 14, 1850, in *Deseret News*, July 20, 1850; Brigham Young, sermon, Oct. 7, 1852, in George D. Watt, Papers, CHL, transcription by LaJean Carruth; Heber C. Kimball, sermon, Oct. 7, 1852, in Watt Papers, transcription by LaJean Carruth; Heber C. Kimball, sermon, circa May 8, 1853, in Watt Papers, transcription by LaJean Carruth; Brigham Young, June 5, 1853, in *JD*, 1:250; Orson Hyde, Sept. 24, 1853, in *JD*, 2:117–18; Brigham Young, Oct. 8, 1855, in *JD*, 3:117–19, 122; Brigham Young, Jan. 27, 1856, in *JD*, 3:196; Jedediah M. Grant, Jan. 27, 1856, in *JD*, 3:200; Heber C. Kimball, June 29, 1856, in *JD*, 4:3–4; Brigham Young, Aug. 17, 1856, in *JD*, 4:25, 30–31; Raleigh Journal, June 10, Aug. 6, 1857.

54. Brigham Young to Bishop Br[u]nson, Aug. 2, 1857, Letterpress Copybook 3:732, YOF, copy of which was "sent to president I. C. Haight for the Bishops and presiding Elders in and south of, Iron County."

55. Young to Br[u]nson, Aug. 2, 1857, Letterpress Copybook 3:732, YOF.

56. George W. Lay to W. S. Harney, June 29, 1857, in Hafen and Hafen, *Utah Expedition*, 30–31. On receiving the details of the orders in Feb. 1858, see Richard D. Poll, *Quixotic Mediator: Thomas L. Kane and the Utah War* (Ogden, UT: Weber State College Press, 1985), 16. On the orders being similar to those given in Kansas, see George W. Lay to W. S. Harney, June 29, 1857, in Hafen and Hafen, *Utah Expedition*, 30–31; Adams, 162–63.

57. Copies of the orders were sent to military leaders in Iron, Fillmore, Nephi, San Pete, Peteetneet, Provo, Box Elder, Weber, Davis, Lehi, Cedar Valley, and Tooele. Wells, General Orders, Aug. 1, 1857, Letter Book, 93, Nauvoo Legion (Utah) Adj. Gen. Records. See also Wells to Richards, Aug. 1, 1857, Wells Letters.

58. Franklin D. Richards, letter, Aug. 6, 1857, Utah Territorial Militia Records, series 2210, Utah State Archives, Salt Lake City, UT, also cited in Brooks2, 20–21. On Martin Van Buren's comment to Joseph Smith, see Joseph Smith and Elias Higbee to Hyrum Smith, Dec. 5, 1839, Letter Book 2:85, Joseph Smith, Papers, CHL; *HC*, 4:40, 80.

59. George A. Smith, Sept. 13, 1857, in "Remarks," *Deseret News*, Sept. 23, 1857.

60. Smith, Sept. 13, 1857, in "Remarks"; "Remarks of Geo. A. Smith at the Peace Conference," June 12, 1858, Historian's Office, Letterpress Copybook 1:636, CHL.

61. Woodruff, Aug. 2, 1857.

62. Woodruff to Editor of the *Western Standard*, Aug. 4, 1857, Historian's Office, Letterpress Copybook 1:476; HOJ, Aug. 3–8, 1857; Whitney, 1:696; Application for Statehood, Mar. 27, 1856, Governor's Letterpress Copybook 1:456–60, YOF.

63. George A. Smith, deposition, July 30, 1875, CCF 31.

64. HOJ, Aug. 3–8, 1857.

65. Lyman, *San Bernardino*, 28–30, 38, 243, 248–50; Unruh, 319. "State Road" and "State Street" information confirmed by Ezra C. Knowlton, *History of Highway Development in Utah* (Salt Lake City: Utah State Dept. of Highways, [1967]), 15; "Big Field," *Deseret News*, Apr. 3, 1852.

66. William Palmer, "Pioneers of Southern Utah," *Instructor* 79 (Jan. 1944): 24; George A. Smith to Hanah Buttler, Dec. 13, 1868, Historian's Office, Letterpress Copybook 2:732; C. Kent Dunford, "The Contributions of George A. Smith to the Establishment of the Mormon Society in the Territory of Utah" (PhD diss., Brigham Young University, 1970), 18–19; William R. Palmer, "Geo. A. Smith," William R. Palmer, Papers, CHL; Merlo J. Pusey, *Builders of the Kingdom: George A. Smith, John Henry Smith, George Albert Smith* (Provo, UT: Brigham Young University Press, 1981), 113.

67. Jenson, 1:37, 39, 41; Dunford, "Contributions of George A. Smith," 27–28; Garr, Cannon, and Cowan, *Encyclopedia of Latter-day Saint History*, 1114; Davis Bitton and Leonard J. Arrington, *Mormons and Their Historians* (Salt Lake City: University of Utah Press, 1988), 20.

68. Justin McCarthy, *Reminiscences* (New York: Harper & Brothers Publishers, 1899), 1:258.

69. George Alfred Townsend, *The Mormon Trials at Salt Lake City* (New York: American News, 1871), 47–48.

70. See Pusey, *Builders of the Kingdom*, 3–123; Dunford, "Contributions of George A. Smith," 23; Ray B. West Jr., *Kingdom of the Saints* (New York: Viking Press, 1957), 116; Whitney, 4:37.

71. George A. Smith to John Codman, Nov. 14, 1874, in John Codman, *Through Utah* (New York: 1875), 625; George A. Smith, letter, Jan. 17, 1851, in *Deseret News*, Feb. 8, 1851.

72. Jenson, 1:41; Whitney, 4:37; Isaac Higbee to Brigham Young, May 26, 1852, Incoming Correspondence, YOF. For Young's misgivings about the conduct of the people in Provo, see Brigham Young to William H. Hooper, Feb. 4, 1868, Letterpress Copybook 10:631–34, YOF.

73. Whitney, 4:37. During the so-called Walker War, Smith's headaches were so severe as to bring on temporary blindness. See George A. Smith to Brigham Young, Aug. 27, 1853, Nauvoo Legion (Utah) Records, ca. 1852–58, Utah State Archives, Salt Lake City, UT, microfilm copy at FHL.

74. In May 1854 Smith was replaced by William H. Dame as commander of the Iron County Militia. Daniel H. Wells, Special Orders, May 21, 1854, Nauvoo Legion (Utah) Records; William H. Dame, Journal, May 27, 1854, microfilm, CHL. On George A. Smith being the "father" of southern Utah, see William R. Palmer, "Geo. A. Smith," Palmer Papers.

75. JHM, Aug. 8, 1857, 131; PSHR, Aug. 8, 1857, 2nd sec., 32; James H. Martineau, letter to the editor, Aug. 22, 1857, in "Trip to the Santa Clara," *Deseret News*, Sept. 23, 1857; HOJ, Aug. 8, 1857. On the reorganization of the militia, see Gardner, 305–6, 316.

76. JHM, Aug. 2, 6, 1857, 130–31.

77. John M. Higbee, affidavit, June 15, 1896, in CM.

78. JHM, Aug. 2, 1857, 130; PSHR, Aug. 8, 1857, 2nd sec., 32.

79. Martineau, letter to the editor, Aug. 22, 1857, in "Trip to the Santa Clara"; HOJ, Aug. 8, 1875.

80. JHM, Aug. 8, 1857, 131; PSHR, Aug. 8, 1857, 2nd sec., 32; HOJ, Aug. 8, 1857.

81. George A. Smith, in PSHR, Aug. 9, 1857, 1st sec., 21–24; PSHR, Aug. 9, 1857, 2nd sec., 32–33; HOJ, Aug. 9, 1857.

82. Smith, in PSHR, Aug. 9, 1857, 1st sec., 23.

83. JHM, Aug. 9, 1857, 131.

Chapter 5

1. HOJ, Aug. 9–14, 1857; Zora Smith Jarvis, *Ancestry, Biography, and Family of George A. Smith* (Provo, UT: Brigham Young University Press, 1962), 215.

2. *TF*, 3.

3. "Pratt's Report to the Legislative Council," Feb. 5, 1850, in William B. Smart and Donna T. Smart, eds., *Over the Rim: The Parley P. Pratt Exploring Expedi-*

tion to Southern Utah, 1849–1850 (Logan: Utah State University Press, 1999), 179, 181–82.

4. Brigham Young, May 27, 1855, in *JD*, 2:282.

5. *TF*, 8, 193.

6. George A. Smith to John Codman, Nov. 14, 1874, in John Codman, *Through Utah* (New York: 1875), 625; George A. Smith, letter, Jan. 17, 1851, in *Deseret News*, Feb. 8, 1851; *TF*.

7. Smith to Codman, Nov. 14, 1874, in Codman, *Through Utah*, 625; Smith, letter, Jan. 17, 1851, in *Deseret News*, Feb. 8, 1851; Whitney, 4:37; Parowan Ward, Manuscript History and Historical Reports, 1847–1926, Aug. 4, Nov. 3, 5, 10, 1851, June 26, Nov. 5, 1852, Sept. 11, 1853, CHL; Woodruff, May 19, 21, 1855.

8. George A. Smith, letter to the editor, Dec. 8, 1852, in *Deseret News*, Dec. 11, 1852; Smith, letter to the editor, Oct. 24, 1852, in *Deseret News*, Nov. 27, 1852; Smith to Samuel W. Richards, Nov. 7, 1852, in "Prosperity of Iron County, Deseret," *Latter-Day Saints' Millennial Star* 15, no. 12 (Mar. 19, 1853): 188.

9. George A. Smith, Journal, May 16, 1851, George A. Smith, Papers, CHL; *TF*, 123, 216; John Steele, Reminiscences and Journal, June 18, 1853, CHL; William T. Davenport, "Life History of William H. Dame," 1–2, 1966, transcript, copy in CHL; William H. Dame, Journal, May 16, 1851, microfilm, CHL.

10. Daniel H. Wells, Special Orders, May 21, 1854, Nauvoo Legion (UT), Records, ca. 1852–58, Utah State Archives, Salt Lake City, UT, microfilm copy at FHL; Dame Journal, May 27, 1854; PSHR, Aug. 8, 1857, 2nd sec., 32; OIMD.

11. PSHR, Jan. 20, 1856, 2nd sec., 11.

12. Fish, 69; Minos, Nov. 24, 1874, in "Col. William H. Dame," *Salt Lake Daily Tribune*, Nov. 28, 1874; [Josiah Rogerson], untitled typescript, 4, CM.

13. [Rogerson], untitled typescript, 3, CM.

14. [Rogerson], untitled typescript, 3, 6, CM; Harold W. Pease, "The Life and Works of William Horne Dame" (master's thesis, Brigham Young University, 1971), 1, 148–49; Davenport, "Life History of William H. Dame," 1.

15. Minos, Nov. 24, 1874, in "Col. William H. Dame"; Davenport, "Life History of William H. Dame," 3; [Rogerson], untitled typescript, 3, CM.

16. Thomas F. Edgerly, Letter of Recommendation, Apr. 9, 1838, in William H. Dame, Papers, CHL.

17. S. S. Barton, "Death of W. H. Dame. A Brief Biographical Sketch," *Deseret Evening News*, Aug. 26, 1884; Jeremiah Gates Dame to William H. Dame, Oct. 1, 1855, Sarah M. Winn to William H. Dame, Oct. 17, 1855, Dame Papers; Pease, "Life and Works of William Horne Dame," 46–47. The scriptural allusion is to Luke 9:62.

18. Isaac Chauncey Haight, Journal, 1842–50, 1, 2, 4, CHL.

19. Haight Journal, 1842–50, 4–6.

20. See Ibid., 7.

21. Haight Journal, 1842–50, June 1844; Robert A. Slack, "A Biographical Study of Isaac Chauncey Haight, Early Religious and Civic Leader of Southern Utah" (master's thesis, Brigham Young University, 1966), 16. On the

destruction of the *Nauvoo Expositor*, see Dallin H. Oaks and Marvin S. Hill, *Carthage Conspiracy: The Trial of the Accused Assassins of Joseph Smith* (Urbana: University of Illinois Press, 1975), 14–16, 33, 46–51, 80, 197; Leonard J. Arrington and Davis Bitton, *The Mormon Experience: A History of the Latter-day Saints*, 2nd ed. (Urbana: University of Illinois Press, 1992), 77–78.

22. Haight Journal, 1842–50, Apr. 11, Sept. 16, 1846, Jan. 1, 1847. On Haight's illness, see Slack, "Biographical Study of Isaac Chauncey Haight," 4, 23–24.

23. Haight Journal, 1842–50, Jan. 9, 1850; Slack, "Biographical Study of Isaac Chauncey Haight," 40–42; Milton Hunter, *Brigham Young, the Colonizer*, 4th ed. (Santa Barbara: Peregrine Smith, 1973), 48.

24. Haight Journal, 1852–62, Aug. 25, 26, Oct. 5, Nov. 18, 1852, photocopy of manuscript, CHL.

25. Ibid., Jan. 8, 24, Aug. 29, Oct. 8, 1853.

26. Slack, "Biographical Study of Isaac Chauncey Haight," 5.

27. Haight Journal, 1842–50, 1.

28. See, for example, Frederick S. Dellenbaugh, *A Canyon Voyage: The Narrative of the Second Powell Expedition down the Green-Colorado River from Wyoming, and the Explorations on Land, in the Years 1871 and 1872* (New York: Knickerbocker Press, 1908), 157.

29. John D. Lee to Brigham Young, Nov. 4, 1856, Incoming Correspondence, YOF. See also *MC*, 2:299, Sept. 21, 1873.

30. Slack, "Biographical Study of Isaac Chauncey Haight," 5, 88.

31. *TF*, 416.

32. *MU*, 36–38; Spicer, Nov. 22, 1874, in "John D. Lee," *Salt Lake Daily Herald*, Nov. 26, 1874.

33. *MU*, 37–38, 40; Spicer, Nov. 22, 1874, in "John D. Lee"; Ancestral File v4.19. Spicer said Lee was only eighteen months old when his mother died.

34. Shorthand manuscript apparently written from dictation by Waddington L. Cook in 1888 on verso of Rogerson's shorthand record of R. N. Baskin, JDL1-RS; *MU*, 38–39; Spicer, Nov. 22, 1874, in "John D. Lee."

35. *MU*, 38–40, 43–50; Spicer, Nov. 22, 1874, in "John D. Lee."

36. *MU*, 37, 50–53; Spicer, Nov. 22, 1874, in "John D. Lee"; "The Lee Execution," *New York Herald*, Mar. 25, 1877.

37. John D. Lee, Journals, Apr. [13], 23, Nov. 27–28, 1842, Jan. 6, June 25, ca. July 25, Aug. 6, 1843, ca. June 29, July 6, 14–15, Aug. 3, 11, 1844, CHL; *MU*, 97–108, 112, 121–28, 139–40.

38. *MU*, 101; Brooks1, 45–53.

39. Lee Journal, 1844–46, 56–57; *MU*, 144, 156–57; Spicer, Nov. 22, 1874, in "John D. Lee."

40. *MU*, 132, 156–57; Lee Journal, 1844–46, 56.

41. *MU*, 201.

42. *MU*, 170, 197. On the adoption ritual, see Gordon Irving, "The Law of Adoption: One Phase of the Development of the Mormon Concept of Salvation, 1830–1900," *BYU Studies* 14, no. 3 (Spring 1974): 291–314.

43. That was the conclusion of editors Robert Glass Cleland and Juanita Brooks, eds., *A Mormon Chronicle: The Diaries of John D. Lee, 1848–1876*, 2 vols. (Salt Lake City: University of Utah Press, 1983), 1:xiii. On the men adopted to Young, see Brooks1, 73.

44. Nancy Bean, statement, December 4, 1847, copy in MMMRF; Woodruff, Dec. 9, 1847; *MU*, 180–81, 203, 205–10, 216–17; HOGCM, Dec. 9, 1847, CHL.

45. Brigham Young, Remarks, Dec. 9, 1847, copy in MMMRF.

46. John D. Lee to Brigham Young, May 2, 1856, Incoming Correspondence, YOF; Brigham Young, remarks, Dec. 9, 1847, in HOGCM; Lee Journal, Dec. 2, 1850.

47. John D. Lee to Brigham Young, Mar. 17, 1852, Incoming Correspondence, YOF; Brooks1, 172–73.

48. Howard A. Christy, "The Walker War: Defense and Conciliation as Strategy," *Utah Historical Quarterly* 47, no. 4 (Fall 1979): 395–96, 400–405; Brigham Young and Daniel H. Wells, General Orders Nos. 1, 2, July 21, 25, 1853, in *Deseret News*, July 30, 1853.

49. JHM, Aug. 10, 1853, 44.

50. Bowering, Aug. 8, 1853.

51. See Christy, "Walker War," 395–96, 405–8.

52. Bowering, Aug. 16, 1853; *TF*, 324.

53. John D. Lee to Brigham Young, Sept. 24, 1853, Incoming Correspondence, YOF.

54. Brown, June 25, 1854; Bowering, Aug. 8–9, 1853.

55. See Utah Territorial Militia Correspondence, Nauvoo Legion (Utah) Records, particularly for the months of Aug.–Oct., 1853.

56. Bowering, Oct. 8, 1853; Gardner, 267–69.

57. Thomas G. Alexander, *Utah: the Right Place*, rev. ed. (Salt Lake City: Gibbs Smith, 2003), 116; Christy, "Walker War," 395–420.

58. Brigham Young, remarks, in Brown, May 19, 1854; Brigham Young, Oct. 9, 1853, in "Synopsis," *Deseret News*, Nov. 24, 1853; Erastus Snow, Nov. 21, 1853, in "Minutes," *Deseret News*, Mar. 2, 1854; James G. Bleak, Annals of the Southern Utah Mission, May 1854, 22, CHL.

59. Meeting with Wakara and others, June 14, 1849, HOGCM; Parley P. Pratt to Orson Pratt, Sept. 5, 1848, in *Latter-day Saints' Millennial Star* 11 (Jan. 1849): 23; Ronald W. Walker, "Wakara Meets the Mormons, 1848–52: A Case Study in Native American Accommodation," *Utah Historical Quarterly* 70, no. 2 (Summer 2002): 215–37.

60. "Pratt's Report to the Legislative Council," Feb. 5, 1850, in Smart and Smart, *Over the Rim*, 182.

61. Ronald W. Walker, "Seeking the 'Remnant': The Native American During the Joseph Smith Period," *Journal of Mormon History* 19, no. 1 (Spring 1993): 1–33.

62. Hurt, 200, 203; "Paiute," 123–31; Knack, 1–94; Holt, 1–31; John D. Lee to [Willard] Richards, Feb. 5, 1853, in *Deseret News*, Mar. 19, 1853; Erastus

Snow to J. E. Tourtellotte, July 4, 1870, Record of the Utah Superinten-
dency of Indian Affairs, 1853–70, Bureau of Indian Affairs, National Archives
Microfilm Publications M834, Washington, D.C., copy located at CHL.

63. Hamblin Journal, 1854–58, 8.

64. Brigham Young, Dec. 11, 1854, in "Message of his Excellency Brigham
Young to the Legislative Assembly of the Territory of Utah," *Millennial Star*
17 (Apr. 28, 1855): 261.

65. Holt, 2, 5–11, 19–26; Knack, 1–4, 10–17, 20–21, 26, 36, 54–58. On Ute
slaving, see Ned Blackhawk, *Violence over the Land: Indian Empires in the Early
American West* (Cambridge, MA: Harvard University Press, 2006).

66. T. D. Brown, letter to the editor, May 19, 1854, in "Indian Mission,"
Deseret News, June 22, 1854; Richard L. Jensen, "Forgotten Relief Societies,
1844–67," *Dialogue* 16, no. 1 (Spring 1983): 108–18; Brigham Young to Rufus
C. Allen, Sept. 13, 1854, Letterpress Copybook 1:674–75, YOF.

67. George A. Smith, "History of the Settling of Southern Utah," Oct. 17,
1861, Smith Papers. See also *An Enduring Legacy*, comp. Daughters of Utah
Pioneers Lesson Committee, 12 vols. (Salt Lake City: Daughters of the Utah
Pioneers, 1978–90), 12:247–48.

68. "Paiute" 130–31, 139–40; Holt, 22–29; Knack, 48–78.

69. Brigham Young to Rufus C. Allen, Aug. 29, 1855, Letterpress Copybook
2:317, YOF.

70. Thomas D. Brown to Brigham Young, Dec. 22, 1854, Incoming Correspondence, YOF; George A. Smith, "History of the Settling of Southern Utah,"
Oct. 17, 1861, Smith Papers; *Enduring Legacy*, 12:247. "There has never been
a settlement in this territory but what word [has] been given to make a strong
fort before tak[ing] a woman and child to it." Brigham Young, discourse,
May 20, 1866, George D. Watt, Papers, CHL, transcription of Pitman
shorthand by LaJean Carruth.

71. Smith, "History of the Settling of Southern Utah," Oct. 17, 1861, Smith
Papers; *Enduring Legacy*, 12:247–48.

72. Rufus C. Allen to Brigham Young, June 13, 1856, Incoming Correspondence, YOF.

73. Brown, May 2, 1854.

74. Ibid., May 19, 1854; Bleak, Annals of the Southern Utah Mission, May 1854,
23–24.

75. Brown, Mar. 18, 1855.

76. Ibid.

77. Lee to Young, Feb. 1855, Feb. 19, 1855, Incoming Correspondence, YOF.

78. Lee to Young, May 2, 1856, Membership and Court Files, MMMRF.

79. Lee to Young, May 23, 1856, Incoming Correspondence, YOF.

80. Ibid.

81. Young to Lee, Aug. 4, 1856, Letterpress Copybook 2:927–30, YOF.

82. Lee to Young, Aug. 22, 1856, Incoming Correspondence, YOF.

83. Haight to Heber C. Kimball, Aug. 20, 1856, Incoming Correspondence, YOF.

84. See Rufus Allen to Brigham Young, Dec. 22, 1856, Jan. 29, 1857, Incoming Correspondence, YOF; Brigham Young to Rufus Allen, Jan. 15, 1857, Letterpress Copybook 3:283–84, YOF.

85. James H. Martineau, letter to the editor, Aug. 22, 1857, in "Trip to the Santa Clara," *Deseret News*, Sept. 23, 1857; George A. Smith, Sept. 13, 1857, in "Remarks," *Deseret News*, Sept. 23, 1857; HOJ, Aug. 9–15, 1857; JHM, Aug. 14, 1857, 131.

86. Smith, Sept. 13, 1857, in "Remarks"; JHM, Aug. 14–20, 1857, 131–33; PSHR, Aug. 15, 1857, 2nd sec., 33.

87. Smith, Sept. 13, 1857, in "Remarks"; HOJ, Aug. 15, 1857; JHM, Aug. 15, 1857, 132; PSHR, Aug. 15, 1857, 2nd sec., 33.

88. Young to Haight, Aug. 4, 1857, Letterpress Copybook 3:742, YOF.

89. Smith, Sept. 13, 1857, in "Remarks."

90. HBM, Aug. 17, 1857.

91. HOJ, Aug. 15–17, 1857; JHM, Aug. 16–17, 1857, 132; Martineau, letter to the editor, Aug. 22, 1857, in "Trip to the Santa Clara"; PSHR, Aug. 15, 1857, 2nd sec., 33.

92. JHM, Aug. 14–15, 1857, 131–32; HOJ, Aug. 15, 1857; PSHR, Aug. 15, 1857, 2nd sec., 33.

93. Douglas D. Alder and Karl F. Brooks, *A History of Washington County: From Isolation to Destination* (Salt Lake City: Utah State Historical Society/Washington County Commission, 1996), xvi.

94. Smith, Sept. 13, 1857, in "Remarks."

95. Smith, "History of the Settling of Southern Utah," Oct. 17, 1861, Smith Papers.

96. JHM, Aug. 17, 1857, 132; Martineau, letter to the editor, Aug. 22, 1857, in "Trip to the Santa Clara."

97. SAJ, Aug. 18, 1857, CHL; PSHR, Aug. 15, 1857, 2nd sec., 33; HOJ, Aug. 18, 1857; Daniel H. Wells to A. Johnson, Aug. 13, 1857, Letterpress Copybook, 97, Nauvoo Legion (UT) Adj. Gen. Records, 1851–70, CHL. Copies were also sent to other military leaders in the south, including Dame and Haight.

98. Elias Smith, Journal, Aug. 11, 1857, CHL; JHM, Aug. 24, Sept. 4, 1857, 133; Fish, 53; James C. Snow, remarks, in PGM, Aug. 30, 1857.

99. Chatterley.

100. Elias Morris, statement to Andrew Jenson, Feb. 2, 1892, CM.

101. Elias Smith, Journal, Aug. 11, 1857; JHM, Aug. 24, Sept. 4, 1857, 133; Fish, 53; Chatterley.

102. Daniel H. Wells to A. Johnson, Aug. 13, 1857, Letterpress Copybook, 97, Nauvoo Legion (UT) Adj. Gen. Records; Daniel H. Wells to William H. Dame, Aug. 13, 1857, William R. Palmer, Collection, Special Collections, Gerald R. Sheratt Library, Southern Utah University, Cedar City, UT. See also SAJ, Aug. 18, 1857.

103. HOJ, Aug. 18–20, 1857; Fish, 55; JHM, Aug. 21, 1857, Sept. 4, 1857, 133.

104. G. A. Smith, Sept. 13, 1857, in "Remarks."

105. Martineau, letter to the editor, Aug. 22, 1857, in "Trip to the Santa Clara"; Smith, Sept. 13, 1857, in "Remarks."

106. "Sketch of the Life of Mary Minerva Dart Judd," typescript, 20, BYU.

107. Martineau, letter to the editor, Aug. 22, 1857, in "Trip to the Santa Clara"; John R. Young, *Memoirs of John R. Young: Utah Pioneer, 1847* (Salt Lake City: Deseret News, 1920), 112–13; Hoth, Oct. 13–15, 1856. Jackson's village was near the bend of the Santa Clara River where the California road veered off to the southwest. It lay twenty-five miles south of the Mountain Meadows and close to the present-day reservation town of Shivwits. Melvin Bashore, "Where Did Chief Jackson's Band Live," copy in possession of authors.

108. G. A. Smith, Sept. 13, 1857, in "Remarks"; Martineau, letter to the editor, Aug. 22, 1857, in "Trip to the Santa Clara."

109. HOJ, Aug. 20, 1857; Martineau, letter to the editor, Aug. 22, 1857, in "Trip to the Santa Clara"; PSHR, Aug. 15, 1857, 2nd sec., 33.

110. G. A. Smith, Remarks, Aug. 23, 1857, in PSHR, Aug. 15, 1857, 1st sec., 31; HOJ, Aug. 20–21, 1857; Martineau, letter to the editor, Aug. 22, 1857, in "Trip to the Santa Clara"; PSHR, Aug. 15, 1857, 2nd sec., 33. On Hamblin's appointment, see Brigham Young to Jacob Hamblin, Aug. 4, 1857, Jacob Hamblin, Papers, BYU; Brigham Young to Jacob Hamblin, Aug. 4, 1857, Letterpress Copybook 3:737, YOF; Brigham Young to I. C. Haight, Aug. 4, 1857, Letterpress Copybook 3:742, YOF.

111. "LC"; "LLC."

112. "LC"; "LLC." Cf. the later *MU*, 223–24, which gives an even more elaborate version of this purported conversation.

113. *MU*, 225.

114. See, e.g., Bagley, 83–87, 376–82; Sally Denton, *American Massacre: The Tragedy at Mountain Meadows, September 11, 1857* (New York: Alfred A. Knopf, 2003), 114–17.

115. Richard E. Turley Jr., "Problems with Mountain Meadows Massacre Sources" (paper presented at annual Mormon History Association Conference, Provo, Utah, May 22, 2004); Wm. W. Bishop to John D. Lee, Feb. 23, 1877, HM 31234, JDLC; John D. Lee to Joseph H. Lee, Feb. 24, 1877, HM 31217, JDLC; Wm W. Bishop to John D. Lee, Mar. 9, 1877, HM 31235, JDLC. "LC"; "LLC," omit the explicit statement about Smith cited in the text accompanying note 113 above.

116. C. J. S. to Salt Lake Tribune, Mar. 25, 1877, in "Shooting of Lee," *Salt Lake Tribune*, Mar. 30, 1877.

117. See Lee's journal entries for the dates Sept. 20, 23, 24; Oct. 16, 31, 1875, in *MC*, 2:364–65, 368, 369, 369n14, 378, 382; LeGrand Young to Brigham Young, Mar. 23, 1877, Incoming Correspondence, YOF. See also the journal entries for Aug. 25 and Sept. 11, 1875 in *MC*, 2:350, 361.

118. McGlashan. McGlashan's informant was Hamblin.

119. Fish, 55; Daniel H. Wells to A. Johnson, Aug. 13, 1857, Letterpress Copybook, 97, Nauvoo Legion (Utah) Adj. Gen. Records.

120. Lee said that Smith had made just such a point during his preaching tour. "*Our greatest danger* lies in the people of California—a class of reckless miners who are strangers to God and his righteousness," Smith supposedly said. "They are likely to come upon us from the south and destroy the small settlements." *MU*, 222, emphasis in original.

121. Juanita Brooks's 1950 book, *Mountain Meadows Massacre*, which began modern historical interpretation of the event, dismissed the charge that Smith had brought secret orders from Brigham Young for the killing of the Arkansas emigrants. "No real evidence…has been found" to link Smith to the "ultimate destruction" of the emigrant party, she wrote, though crediting Smith with inflaming settlers' emotions. Brooks2, 35, 61. However, in her 1972 version of *John Doyle Lee: Zealot, Pioneer Builder, Scapegoat*, Brooks mentioned a "folk-tale that at [a Mormon investigation of the massacre] Dame declared: 'You can NOT lay this onto me! I will not take it! If you dare try, I'll just put the saddle onto the right horse, and you all know well who that is!'" Brooks concluded, "It could be no other than George A. Smith himself, sitting at the head of the table." Yet one might just as easily conclude that, if this "folk-tale" is true, Dame was referring to "Isaac C. Haight," who was also "sitting in the circle" at the investigation. Brooks1, 255. More recently, Bagley, 83–87, 376–82, and Denton, *American Massacre*, 114–17, rejected Brooks's initial conclusion with circumstantial arguments. For both Bagley and Denton, a crucial piece of "circumstance" was Lee's supposed statement in the flawed *Mormonism Unveiled*. Because no piece of substantive evidence links Smith to ordering the massacre, Brooks's cautious initial judgment remains the best.

122. G. A. Smith, Sept. 13, 1857, in "Remarks."

123. HOJ, Aug. 21–25, 1857.

124. G. A. Smith, Aug. 23, 1857, PSHR, Aug. 23, 1857, 1st sec., 24–26.

125. William H. Dame to Daniel H. Wells, Aug. 23, 1857, in Utah Territorial Militia Correspondence, Nauvoo Legion (Utah) Records.

126. Knight.

127. Smith, Sept. 13, 1857, in "Remarks."

128. Emily Hoyt, Reminiscences and Diary, Aug. 19, 26, 27, 1857, CHL.

129. Smith, Sept. 13, 1857, in "Remarks."

130. Smith, Aug. 23, 1857, PSHR, Aug. 23, 1857, 1st sec., 25. See also Smith, Sept. 13, 1857, in "Remarks."

131. Smith, Sept. 13, 1857, in "Remarks." See also Smith, Aug. 23, 1857, PSHR, Aug. 23, 1857, 1st sec., 25.

Chapter 6

1. "News from the Plains," *Leavenworth Kansas Weekly Herald*, May 30, 1857; "Arrival of the Utah Mails," *St. Louis Daily Missouri Republican*, May 17, 1857; "St. Joseph Correspondence," *Daily Missouri Republican*, Apr. 17, 1857; "News from the Plains," *Daily Missouri Republican*, May 5, 1857;

Daily Missouri Republican, May 22, 1857; "The Indians in Utah," *Kansas City Enterprise*, Aug. 22, 1857; D. C. Hail, letter to the editor, Oct. 20, 1857, in "Horrible Massacre of Emigrants upon the Plains," *Daily Missouri Republican*, Dec. 9, 1857, from correspondence of *Little Rock True Democrat;* "From Utah Territory," *Missouri Republican*, July 26, 1857. See also "Famine at the West," *San Francisco Globe*, July 17, 1857; "Later from Carson Valley," *San Francisco Globe*, Aug. 4, 1857; "By Magnetic Telegraph!" *San Francisco Globe*, Aug. 6, 1857.

2. Editorial, *Kansas Weekly Herald*, May 23, 1857.

3. "Overland Emigration to California," *Daily Missouri Republican*, Nov. 24, 1857; "News from the Plains," *Kansas Weekly Herald*, Aug. 22, 1857. On the size of the 1857 emigration, see Letter, June 10, 1857, in "The Great City of the Plains," *Daily Missouri Republican*, June 27, 1857 ("the emigration of this season is immense"); "Overland Emigration to California," *Daily Missouri Republican*, Nov. 24, 1857 ("the largest overland emigration to California that has been known for years"); "The Overland Immigration," *Stockton (CA) San Joaquin Republican*, Aug. 27, 1857, taken from the *Sacramento Union* ("the immigration ... will be larger this year than it has been since 1852"); "Arrival of Immigrants," *San Joaquin Republican*, Aug. 16, 1857 ("a very heavy immigration"); "Arrival of the Advance Immigration," *San Joaquin Republican*, Aug. 4, 1857, taken from *San Francisco Bulletin* ("very large overland immigration is reported"); "Crossing the Plains," *San Joaquin Republican*, July 28, 1857 ("emigration to California is greatly on the increase in that part of the State, never before having been greater, if equalled, unless in the years 1851 and 1852"); "News from the Plains," *Kansas Weekly Herald*, Aug. 22, 1857, taken from *Westport (MO) Star of Empire* ("emigration to Utah and California by this road had been large"); "Later from Carson Valley and the Plains," *San Joaquin Republican*, Aug. 8, 1857, taken from *Sacramento Union*, Aug. 5, 1857 ("the largest emigration ever out for California since '53"); "Latest News from Carson Valley and the Plains," *San Francisco Daily Evening Bulletin*, Aug. 13, 1857 ("the accounts of the immense immigration are fully confirmed"); "The Advancing Immigration," *San Francisco Daily Evening Bulletin*, Aug. 13, 1857 ("an immense immigration will certainly arrive this season"); "This Year's Immigration to California," *San Francisco Daily Evening Bulletin*, July 29, 1857, taken from *Shasta (CA) Republican* ("the immigration to California across the Plains is much larger this year than we have supposed it would be"). Cf. "Carson Valley," *San Francisco Daily Evening Bulletin*, Sept. 24, 1857. John D. Unruh's statistics show 1857 to be the third smallest emigrating year for the period 1849–60; the contemporary newspaper accounts, however, suggest otherwise. See Unruh, 120, 442n8.

4. For information on the Cherokee Trail, see Patricia K. A. Fletcher, Jack Earl Fletcher, and Lee Whiteley, *Cherokee Trail Diaries* (Caldwell, ID: Caxton Printers, [1999]–ca. 2001), 1:8–15, 31–33; Patricia K. A. Fletcher and Jack Earl Fletcher, "Pioneering the Trail," http://www.olympus.net/personal/jpfletcher/pioneering/pioneering.html (accessed Mar. 28, 2007).

5. "The Overland Immigration" *San Joaquin Republican*, Aug. 27, 1857, reprinted from the *Sacramento Union*; "Later from Carson Valley," *San Francisco Daily Alta California*, Aug. 25, 1857.

6. Letter, June 22, 1857, in "Life on the Plains," *New York Tribune*, July 29, 1857.

7. Richard H. Dillon, ed., *California Trail Herd: The 1850 Missouri-to-California Journal of Cyrus C. Loveland* (Los Gatos, CA: Talisman Press, 1961), 18–19; Siegfried G. Demke, *The Cattle Drives of Early California* (San Gabriel, CA: By the author, 1985), 14.

8. Frank S. Popplewell, "St. Joseph, Missouri as a Center of the Cattle Trade" (master's thesis, University of Missouri, 1937), 11–12; Demke, *Cattle Drives of Early California*, 9–11, 15; Thomas J. Linton, as cited in J. H. Atkinson, "Cattle Drives from Arkansas to California Prior to the Civil War," *Arkansas Historical Quarterly* 28 (Autumn 1969): 280.

9. For general details of the California cattle industry, see Terry G. Jordan, *North American Cattle-Ranching Frontiers: Origins, Diffusion, and Differentiation* (Albuquerque: University of New Mexico Press, 1993), 246–49, 279–80; Demke, *Cattle Drives of Early California*, 7–24; Dillon, *California Trail Herd*, 16–37; Louis Pelzer, *The Cattlemen's Frontier: A Record of the Trans-Mississippi Cattle Industry from Oxen Trains to Pooling Companies, 1850–1890* (New York: Russell & Russell, 1969), 26.

10. Demke, *Cattle Drives of Early California*, 13–14; Robert Glass Cleland, *The Cattle on a Thousand Hills: Southern California, 1850–1880* (San Marino, CA: Huntington Library, 1964), 109–10; Popplewell, "St. Joseph, Missouri," 13–14. The *Los Angeles Star*, Apr. 26, 1856, "quoted best cattle prices in the north as $16 to $18, with young stock as low as $7 to $8 a head." Cited in Demke, *Cattle Drives of Early California*, 13.

11. Linton, as cited in Atkinson, "Cattle Drives from Arkansas to California," 280–81; Cleland, *Cattle on a Thousand Hills*, 109–10.

12. See "Later from Carson Valley," *Daily Alta California*, Aug. 25, 1857.

13. "Overland Emigration to California," *Daily Missouri Republican*, Nov. 24, 1857.

14. See Unruh, 187.

15. "Letter." See also Ima Jean Baker Young, "William and Hannah (Edwards) Baker," in *The Heritage of Madison County, Alabama*, comp. Madison County Heritage Book Committee (Clanton, AL: Heritage Publishing Consultants, ca. 1998), 77.

16. Barbara Lasater Toney, "Baker-Pennington-Jones," in *The Heritage of Jackson County, Alabama* (Clanton, AL: Heritage Publishing, 1998), 75; "OBF" 160; Alabama, Madison County, 1850 U.S. Census, slave schedule; Alabama, Madison County, 1850 U.S. Census, population schedule, 346.

17. Alabama, Madison County, District No. 1, 1860 U.S. Census, population schedule, 262; Young, "William and Hannah (Edwards) Baker," 77.

18. Toney, "Baker-Pennington-Jones," 75; Charles Rodney Baker, "Baker," in *History of Boone County, Arkansas*, comp. Boone County Historical & Railroad Society (Paducah, KY: Turner Publishing, 1998), 159; Young, "William and Hannah (Edwards) Baker," 77; "OBF," 160.

19. Toney, "Baker-Pennington-Jones," 75; Young, "William and Hannah (Edwards) Baker," 77; "OBF," 161; Baker, "Baker," 159; Arkansas, Carroll County, Crooked Creek Township, 1850 U.S. Census, population schedule, 163B. Some sources list Mary's maiden name as Beller or Ashby, although circumstantial evidence based on collateral census and marriage records links her to the Williams family. Jack Stemmons, "Report concerning the Maiden Name of Mary Baker," copy in MMMRF.

20. W. W. Thompson, "A History of Paint Rock Valley and Its Early Settlers," Aug. 23, 1933, in *Jackson County Chronicles* 43 (Jan. 1986): 8, reproduced in Wendell Page, comp., *Jackson County Chronicles*, vol. 1, pt. 4 (Scottsboro, AL: Jackson County Historical Association and Scottsboro-Jackson Heritage Center, 1992).

21. "OBF," 161; Baker, "Baker," 159; Young, "William and Hannah (Edwards) Baker," 77. For a study on violence as part of southern culture, see Dov Cohen, Richard E. Nisbett, Brian F. Bowdle, and Norbert Schwarz, "Insult, Aggression, and the Southern Culture of Honor: An 'Experimental Ethnography,'" *Journal of Personality and Social Psychology* 70, no. 5 (1996): 945–60.

22. "OBF," 161–62; Arkansas, Carroll County, Crooked Creek Township, 1850 U.S. Census, population schedule, 163B; Mary Baker, deposition, Oct. 22, 1860, PPU. See also Parker2, 4, which claims, "Captain Jack Baker was born in Alabama and come to Arkansas Territory with his family in 1835."

23. Arkansas, Carroll County, Crooked Creek Township, 1850 U.S. Census, population schedule, 163B; Lawrence G. Coates, "The Fancher Party before Mountain Meadows" (paper presented at the Mormon History Conference in St. George, UT, May 1992), 33, copy in authors' possession.

24. Roger Logan Jr., "Slave Holders in Pre-War Days," *Boone County Historian* 1, no. 1 (Dec. 1978). For information on slavery in northern Arkansas, see Roger V. Logan Jr., "A Short History of Boone County, Arkansas," in *History of Boone County, Arkansas*, comp. Boone County Historical & Railroad Society (Paducah, KY: Turner Publishing, 1998), 16.

25. "Extract."

26. Logan1, 26.

27. "Letter"; John H. Baker, deposition, Oct. 22, 1860, PPU; "OBF," 163.

28. Mitchell, 10. Given her age at the time her family left Arkansas in 1857, Sarah's recollections of her father's motivations might well be called into question, except that she returned later to live with family members who undoubtedly knew and communicated to her why her father had started for California.

29. Parker2, 4; Parker1, 19, 57.

30. Mary Baker, John H. Baker, and John Crabtree, depositions, Oct. 22, 1860, PPU. Because of the depressed markets in California, however, the value of cattle in California in 1857 was approximately the same as it was in Arkansas. "Our Monthly Live Stock Report," *San Francisco Herald*, June 5, 1857, recorded: "Sales have been made in Santa Barbara of 600 two-year old and upwards, at $19....In Monterey, 500 head of cattle, large and small, at $16;

35 one to two year-old heifers at $15; 200 head cows and steers, large and fat, at $28. Tame cows are held at $38 a $45; wild cattle, grown, $20 a $25, two-year-old, $15 a $18."

31. Arkansas, Carroll County, Crooked Creek Township, 1850 U.S. Census, population schedule, 163B; Wm. C. Mitchell to A. B. Greenwood, Apr. 27, 1860, in USBIA; "Meeting"; "Letter."

32. Arkansas, Carroll County, Crooked Creek Township, 1850 U.S. Census, population schedule, 163B; Joseph B. Baines and John H. Baker, depositions, Oct. 23, 1860, PPU.

33. Logan2; "Meeting"; William C. Beller, deposition, Oct. 23, 1860, PPU; Logan, "Short History of Boone County," 12; Appendix A.

34. Roger V. Logan Jr., "Mitchell," in *History of Boone County, Arkansas* (Paducah, KY: Turner Publishing, 1998), 307; Logan2; William C. Mitchell, deposition, Oct. 22, 1860, PPU; "Meeting"; "Letter"; Appendix A.

35. William C. Mitchell and Samuel Mitchell, depositions, Oct. 22, 1860, PPU.

36. William C. Mitchell, deposition, Oct. 22, 1860, PPU.

37. "OBF," 162, 164; Logan, "Short History of Boone County," 12; Logan2; "Victims"; "Meeting"; Logan1, 26.

38. Information on the traditional starting point of the train comes from Roger V. Logan Jr., "A Pilgrimage to Some Local Places Connected to the History of the Mountain Meadows Massacre in Boone and Carroll Counties," *Boone County Historian* 24 (Apr.–June 2001): 31, 36–37; Greenhaw. The traditional gathering spot, designated Caravan Spring, is memorialized by Arkansas State Centennial Marker No. 021 on Highway 7. Logan, "Pilgrimage to Local Places," 37, 40; Greenhaw.

39. Parker2, 5–6; "Children"; Fielding Wilburn and Francis M. Rowan, depositions, Oct. 24, 1860, PPU.

40. Logan1, 26; Baker, "Baker," 160; Young, "William and Hannah (Edwards) Baker," 77–78; Arkansas, Carroll County, Crooked Creek Township, 1850 U.S. Census, population schedule, 163B; Mountain Meadows Association, "Mountain Meadows Massacre Genealogy," http://www.mtn-meadows-assoc.com/Genealogy/genealog.html (accessed Aug. 7, 2006).

41. Mitchell, 10, 15; " Letter." See also Terry, 44. Ralph R. Rea recorded Terry's account without the edits of the "professional writer," and did not include the portion about Mary Baker's premonition. See Rea. Logan1, 26, explains that Mary planned to go to California "after a home was established." Baker, "Baker," 160, says, "Most of his family remained in Arkansas planning to move west later." According to an early California source, Jack "intended, as soon as he could settle here, to return by water and bring the remainder of his family." " Letter." But Mary's 1860 deposition merely says, "The object my husband, the said John T. Baker had in going to California was to sell a large lot of cattle with which he started. . . . The stock cattle had been bought with the view to make quick sales on arriving at California." Mary Baker, deposition, Oct. 22, 1860, PPU.

42. "Last Will and Testament of John T. Baker," Apr. 1, 1857, typescript, Chancery Court Record Book A, 75–76, copy in family information and research materials of Cheri Baker Walker, Boone County Historical and Genealogical Society, Boone County, Arkansas.

43. Arkansas, Johnson County, Mulberry Township, 1850 U.S. Census, population schedule, 129B; 1855 Marion County Arkansas, tax records, 6, film no. 1955429, FHL; Logan1, 25; Logan, "Mitchell," 307; Logan, "Short History of Boone County," 12; Isabell Minnie Evins Kratz, "The Mountain Meadow Massacre," in *The Klingensmith Scrapbook*, comp. Anna Jean Duncan Backus (Provo, UT: Brigham Young University Press, 1996), 161; W. K. Sebastian to C. E. Mix, Sept. 11, 1858, in SDoc42, 47; Parker2, 5; William C. Mitchell, deposition regarding the property of Lorenzo Dunlap, Oct. 26, 1860, PPU; Samuel Mitchell, James D. Dunlap, and Adam P. Dunlap, joint deposition, Oct. 26, 1860, PPU; Robert H. Mitchell and William C. Dunlap, joint deposition regarding the property of Lorenzo Dunlap, Oct. 26, 1860, PPU; James D. Dunlap, deposition, Oct. 26, 1860, PPU; William C. Mitchell, deposition regarding the property of Jesse Dunlap, Oct. 26, 1860, PPU; William C. Dunlap and Robert H. Mitchell, joint deposition regarding the property of Jesse Dunlap, Oct. 26, 1860, PPU; Adam P. Dunlap and Samuel Mitchell, joint deposition, Oct. 26, 1860, PPU; Appendix A.

44. "Victims," citing emigrant P. K. Jacoby.

45. Mary Baker, deposition, Oct. 22, 1860, PPU.

46. See Appendix A.

47. Arkansas, Carroll County, Jefferson, 1850 U.S. Census, slave schedule; Arkansas, Carroll County, Jackson and Osage, 1860 U.S. Census, slave schedule; "Last Will and Testament of John T. Baker"; Kratz, "Mountain Meadow Massacre," 161; Logan1, 25–26.

48. No slaves were listed in post-massacre, pre–Civil War property claims made by the families. On the other hand, the families may have thought their claims for damages stood a better chance in Washington by not delving into the heated subject of slavery. See Depositions, PPU. Still, no one who saw the bodies of massacre victims reported black people among them. Shannon Novak and Derinna Kopp's study of the bones of some massacre victims did not identify any as coming from people of African ancestry. Shannon A. Novak, *House of Mourning: A Biocultural History of the Mountain Meadows Massacre* (Salt Lake City: University of Utah Press, 2008), 159; Shannon A. Novak and Derinna Kopp, "Osteological Analysis of Human Remains from the Mountain Meadows Massacre" (report prepared for the Office of Public Archaeology, Brigham Young University, Provo, UT, and Antiquities Section Division of State History, State of Utah, Salt Lake City, UT, 2002), 12–13.

49. California, San Diego County, 1850 U.S. Census, population schedule, 280; Jesse Lewis Russell, *Behind These Ozark Hills* (New York: Hobson Book Press, 1947), 98; Lair, 12; Appendix A.

50. Lair, 12; Russell, *Behind These Ozark Hills*, 98; Arkansas, Carroll County, Carrollton, 1850 U.S. Census, population schedule, 128A; Arkansas, Carroll

County, Osage, 1850 U.S. Census, population schedule, 138A; Arkansas, Carroll County, Osage, 1850 U.S. Census, slave schedule; "Uncle Dick Fancher Dies," *North Arkansas Star,* May 5, 1911, reprinted in *Carroll County Historical Quarterly* 15 (Sept. 1970): 23; Beverley Githens, "The Fancher Family—A Part of Our History," *White River Valley Historical Quarterly* 1 (Winter 1963): 15, also available at Springfield-Greene County Library website, http://thelibrary.springfield.missouri.org/lochist/periodicals/wrv/V1/N10/W63f.htm (accessed Oct. 9, 2006).

51. W. B. Flippin, in "The Tutt-Everett War," in Earl Berry, ed., *The History of Marion County* (Marion County Historical Association, ca. 1977), 65–70; Alexander Fancher, affidavit, Sept. 30, 1849, Thomas H. Fancher Family Files, Carroll County Historical and Genealogical Society, Berryville, AR.

52. William Bedford Temple to Wife and Children, May 11, June 2, 1850, Oregon Historical Society, Portland, OR. A Dec. 5, 1850, entry in the journal of Washington Peck—who went through Utah—mentions a Fancher without giving a first name. Washington Peck, Diary, typescript, National Frontier Trails Center, Independence, Missouri. Bagley, 60, gives a colorful account of the journey based on his tacit assumption that Alexander and John Fancher and their families accompanied Peck through Utah. Larry Coates, "The Fancher Name in the Washington Peck Diary," copy in authors' possession, questions the assumption. For the Fanchers' short stay in southern California, see California, San Diego County, 1850 U.S. Census, population schedule, 280. The portion of the census listing the Fanchers was not taken until Mar. 1851.

53. Brand Reservation Certificate, Dec. 19, 1852, reproduced in *Los Tulares,* no. 13 (Dec. 1952); Annie R. Mitchell, *Land of the Tules* (Fresno, CA: Valley Publishers, [1972]); Annie R. Mitchell, "Stock Industry of Early Days Led to Development of Visalia Saddle," *Visalia Times-Delta,* Mar. 29, 1952; Mariposa County Recorder, Stock Brands, Index to vols. 1 and 2, Mariposa Museum and History Center, Mariposa, CA.

54. No contemporaneous evidence of this trip has survived, though family tradition for the trip is strong. See, e.g., Paul Buford Fancher, *Richard Fancher (1700–1764) of Morris County, New Jersey* (Atlanta, GA: Paul B. Fancher, 1993), 182. For an indirect reference that may point to Alexander Fancher's trip, see Parker2, 1–2.

55. Sherida K. Eddlemon, *Index to the Arkansas General Land Office, 1820–1907* (Bowie, MD: Heritage Books, 1999), 4:79; Deed records, 1837–86, Index, 1837–1929, Benton County, Arkansas, film no. 1035046, FHL; Deed records, 1837–86, Benton County, Arkansas, vol. C, 249–50, film no. 1034925, FHL.

56. Russell, *Behind These Ozark Hills,* 98.

57. Lair, 12; Hill, 95–96; Russell, *Behind These Ozark Hills,* 98.

58. "Children."

59. H. B. Fancher to James C. Wilson, Aug. 2, 1885, enclosed in J. C. Wilson to J. P. Dunn, Aug. 11, 1885, JPDC; Mitchell to Greenwood, Apr. 27, 1860, in USBIA.

60. Appendix A; Lair, 12; Mitchell to Greenwood, Apr. 27, 1860, in USBIA.

61. Missouri, Dallas County, District 26, 1850 U.S. Census, population schedule, 347B; "Meeting"; Mitchell to Greenwood, Apr. 27, 1860, in USBIA; "Cates"; Logan, "Short History of Boone County," 13; Appendix A.

62. Francis M. Rowan, deposition, Oct. 24, 1860, PPU; "Meeting"; Mitchell to Greenwood, Apr. 27, 1860, in USBIA; Parker2, 5; "Letter"; Logan, "Short History of Boone County," 13; Appendix A. Felix Jones, a brother to John and Newton, thought their property worth only five to six hundred dollars. Felix W. Jones, deposition, Oct. 24, 1860, PPU; Coates, "Fancher Party before Mountain Meadows," 47.

63. Fielding Wilburn and Francis M. Rowan, depositions, Oct. 24, 1860, PPU.

64. Arkansas, Carroll County, Crooked Creek, 1850 U.S. Census, population schedule, 159; M1911.

65. M1911; Logan, "Short History of Boone County," 13; Joel Scott, deposition, May 2, 1911, Thurston; M1877-10; M1877-12; John P. Shaver, affidavit in support of H.R. 3945, Dec. 19, 1877, 45th Cong., 1st sess., National Archives, Washington, D.C., copy of transcript in CHL; Appendix A.

66. "Victims." P. K. Jacoby, who supplied the newspaper with its information, said that by the time the members of his group reached Fort Bridger, they and the others had experienced "months of weary journeying together and common peril."

67. S. Charles Bolton, *Arkansas, 1800–1860: Remote and Restless* (Fayetteville: University of Arkansas Press, 1998), 155–57. See also Priscilla McArthur, *Arkansas in the Gold Rush* (Little Rock: August House, 1986), 24–26, 33–37; Fletcher, Fletcher, and Whiteley, *Cherokee Trail Diaries*, 2:196.

68. Ruth Peterson, comp., *Across the Plains in '57: The Story of the Family of Peter Campbell and a Train of Immigrants As Told by Nancy Campbell Lowell, a Member of the Party*, pamphlet, June 1936, 1, conveniently republished in *Carroll County Historical Quarterly* 43 (June 1998): 60–62; Fletcher, Fletcher, and Whiteley, *Cherokee Trail Diaries*, 1:39, 3:170; Francis M. Rowan, affidavit, Oct. 24, 1860, PPU. P. K. Jacoby of the Duck company said, "Several families joined the train at a station in the Indian Territory, which was the last point of departure from civilization." "Victims."

69. "Victims." On rumors of Missourians joining the Arkansans, see Stenhouse, 427–28; JHM, Sept. 12, 1857, 136; "News of the Week," *Weaverville (CA) Trinity Journal*, Oct. 17, 1857; "For the East," *San Francisco Daily Alta California*, Oct. 20, 1857.

70. See Parker2, 6; Fletcher, Fletcher, and Whiteley, *Cherokee Trail Diaries*, 1:32.

71. "Children"; Lair, 12; Mitchell, 10; "Meeting"; "Letter"; "Victims." For historians calling the emigrant group the Fancher company, see Roger V. Logan Jr., "New Light on the Mountain Meadows Caravan," *Utah Historical Quarterly* 60 (Summer 1992): 227, 227n3; Gibbs, 12, 16, 38, 48; Andrew Love Neff, *History of Utah: 1847 to 1869* (Salt Lake City: Deseret News Press, 1940), 411–12; Brooks2, 44, 49, 52, 69, 142, 151; Fletcher, Fletcher, and Whiteley, *Cherokee Trail Diaries*, 3:170.

72. Parker2, 1, 5, 15–16. Parker actually spelled "Fancher" as "Francher." See also Logan, "New Light on the Mountain Meadows Caravan," 227; Parker1, 62.

73. Parker2, 6, 12; John P. Shaver, affidavit in support of H.R. 3945, Dec. 19, 1877. See also M1911.

74. Peterson, *Across the Plains*, 1–2.

75. M1911.

76. See Marcy, 45–46.

77. Peterson, *Across the Plains*, 2–3; George R. Stewart, *The California Trail: An Epic with Many Heroes* (New York: McGraw-Hill, 1962), 108, 111; William E. Lass, *From the Missouri to the Great Salt Lake: An Account of Overland Freighting* (Nebraska State Historical Society, 1972), 32.

78. Parker1, 58.

79. M1911.

80. Unruh, 176–86.

81. "Indian Hostilities on the Plains," *Springfield (MO) Mirror,* June 25, 1857; "News from the Plains," *Kansas Weekly Herald,* Aug. 22, 1857; "Overland Emigration for Oregon," *Hornellsville (NY) Tribune,* Dec. 3, 1857; LeRoy R. Hafen and Anne W. Hafen, *Relations with the Indians of the Plains, 1857–1861: A Documentary Account of the Military Campaigns, and Negotiations of Indian Agents—with Reports and Journals of P. G. Lowe, R. M. Peck, J. E. B. Stuart, S. D. Sturgis, and Other Official Papers,* The Far West and the Rockies Historical, Series, 1820–1875, vol. 9 (Glendale, CA: Arthur H. Clark, 1959), 24n5.

82. See "R. M. Peck's Account of the Sedgwick Division," in Hafen and Hafen, *Relations with the Indians,* 112–22; William S. Harney to L. Thomas, Aug. 22, 1857 (ibid., 146–47); E. G. Marshall to S. Cooper, Sept. 12, 1857 (ibid., 152); E. G. Marshall to Adj. Gen., Sept. 15, 1857 (ibid., 153).

83. Unruh, 186. See also Unruh, 176–79, 186–89; Michael L. Tate, "From Cooperation to Conflict: Sioux Relations with the Overland Emigrants, 1845–1865," *Overland Journal* 18 (Winter 2000–1): 18, 22.

84. Parker1, 59.

85. Ibid., 60.

86. Ibid., 47–48, 51–52.

87. Peterson, *Across the Plains*, 3. Page 7 of the pamphlet explains, "Concerning all these adventures, Mrs. Lowell, the little Nancy of the wagon train, though only four years old at that time, remembers many incidents very distinctly. The experience of the three Indians grabbing at her made an impression very clear."

88. Ibid., 3–4.

89. Ibid., 2.

90. "Victims." P. K. Jacoby, one of the emigrants, said this incident occurred "shortly before reaching Fort Bridger." Later on the trail near a tributary of the Humboldt, Indians ran off sixty head of the Thomas D. Harp company's cattle, and a posse again took an Indian prisoner, promising to free him and

give him a gun if he took the posse to the cattle. The Indian kept his end of the bargain and the whites eventually did too, but not until "Harp's company whipped the Indian with ramrods raising great welts on his back." Helen Carpenter, "A Trip Across the Plains in an Ox Wagon, 1857," in *Ho for California! Women's Overland Diaries from the Huntington Library*, ed. Sandra L. Myres (San Marino, CA: Huntington Library, 1980), 165–68. Parker had four men in the posse and wrote, "I think the indians were killed." Parker1, 67.

91. S. B. Honea, in "Outrages"; "Letter."
92. The excitement at Fort Bridger was reported by D. C. Hail, another Arkansan, who was in the area about the same time as the Baker and Fancher parties. See Hail, letter to the editor, Oct. 20, 1857, in "Horrible Massacre of Emigrants." See also Welch; "Victims"; Brigham Young to Lewis Robison, Aug. 4, 1857, Letterpress Copybook 3:757–58, YOF.
93. "Victims."
94. Frank King, JDL1-BT 4:116–17, JDL1-PS 7:2–4; Gibbs, 12–13; Linda King Newell, "A Web of Trails: Bringing History Home," *Journal of Mormon History* 24 (Spring 1998): 14–27.
95. HOJ, July 20, 25, 27, 1857; Heber C. Kimball to William Kimball, Dec. 21, 1854, in "Foreign Correspondence," *Latter-day Saints' Millennial Star* 17, no. 16 (1855): 251.
96. "Massacre."
97. Stenhouse, 427–28; Ronald W. Walker, *Wayward Saints: The Godbeites and Brigham Young* (Urbana: University of Illinois Press, 1998), 129–30, 299–300. While Stenhouse did not give the name of his informant, his wife did. Fanny Warn Stenhouse, *"Tell It All": The Story of a Life's Experience in Mormonism* (Hartford, CT: A. D. Worthington, 1874), 325. On July 26 Kelsey preached a sermon to his fellow missionaries before leaving for Salt Lake City with the westward-bound Arkansas trains. Shoshone Mission, Journal, July 26, 1857, CHL.
98. Stenhouse, 427–29. See also "Massacre."
99. See, e.g., Brooks2, 47–48, 219.
100. Carpenter, "Trip Across the Plains," 165–69; Parker1, 65–67.
101. M1877-10; M1911, both give the company's arrival as Aug. 3. M1877-12 says they arrived "on or about the first of Aug."
102. "Massacre."
103. "Massacre."

Chapter 7

1. See "Overland Emigration to California," *St. Louis Daily Missouri Republican*, Nov. 24, 1857; Ashel T. Barrett to his brother, July 3, 1853, in *Kanesville Western Bugle*, Sept. 21, 1853, cited with other emigrant comments in Unruh, 333; Radnor, letter to the editor, Apr. 30, 1855, "Salt Lake Correspondence," *Deseret News*, Aug. 1, 1855.

2. Fred E. Woods, "'Surely This City Is Bound to Shine': Descriptions of Salt Lake City by Western-Bound Emigrants, 1849–1868," *Utah Historical Quarterly* 74 (Fall 2006): 334–48.

3. Theophilus F. Rodenbough, comp., *From Everglade to Canyon with the Second United States Cavalry*, 2nd ed. (Norman: University of Oklahoma Press, 2000), 230; Virginia Wilcox Ivins, *Pen Pictures of Early Western Days* (1905), 90–91. Summed up another visitor, "We are surprised and refreshed with its general appearance of neatness and order." "Journal of Captain Albert Tracy, 1858–1860," *Utah Historical Quarterly* 13, nos. 1–4 (1945): 26.

4. Barrett to his brother, July 3, 1853, in *Kanesville Western Bugle*, Sept. 21, 1853, in Unruh, 333.

5. T. S. Hawkins, *Some Recollections on a Busy Life* (San Francisco: Paul Elder, [1913]), 102; Arrington2, 68–71; Brigham D. Madsen, *Gold Rush Sojourners in Great Salt Lake City 1849 and 1850*, Publications in the American West 18 (Salt Lake City: University of Utah Press, 1983), 51–80; Brigham Young, Heber C. Kimball, and Willard Richards, Apr. 7, 1851, in "Fifth General Epistle," *Deseret News*, Apr. 8, 1851. Fear of disease prompted a quarantine law, approved Jan. 14, 1857. See *Acts, Resolutions and Memorials, Passed at the Several Annual Sessions, of the Legislative Assembly of the Territory of Utah, from 1851 to 1870 Inclusive* (Salt Lake City: Joseph Bull, 1870), 78. See also Harriet Sherrill Ward, *Prairie Schooner Lady: The Journal of Harriet Sherrill Ward, 1853*, ed. Ward G. DeWitt and Florence Stark DeWitt (Los Angeles: Westernlore Press, 1959), 119.

6. Wilford Woodruff to editor of the *Western Standard*, Aug. 4, 1857, Historian's Office Letterpress Copybook 1:476–77, CHL; HOJ, Aug. 3, 4, 5, 8, 10, 11, 12, 28, 1857. Sources on emigrant companies passing through Salt Lake City in 1857 include "Over the Plains," *San Francisco Daily Alta California*, July 8, 1857; "Later from Salt Lake," *Stockton (CA) San Joaquin Republican*, July 15, 1857; "Later from Carson Valley and the Plains," *San Joaquin Republican*, Aug. 8, 1857; "One Month Later from Salt Lake City," *San Joaquin Republican*, Aug. 11, 1857; "Eastern Bound Emigrants by Overland Route," *Daily Alta California*, Sept. 13, 1857; "Gathering Them In," *Sacramento Daily Bee*, Sept. 14, 1857; "From the Plains," *Daily Alta California*, Oct. 21, 1857; Parker2, 6; James Miller Guinn, *Historical and Biographical Record of Southern California: Containing a History of Southern California from Its Earliest Settlement to the Opening Year of the Twentieth Century* (Chicago: Chapman Publishing, 1902), 135–37; Eugene L. Menefee and Fred A. Dodge, *History of Tulare and Kings Counties, California, with Biographical Sketches of the Leading Men and Women of the Counties Who Have Been Identified with Their Growth and Development from the Early Days to the Present* (Los Angeles: Historic Record, 1913), 768; Martha Ann Freeman Davis Wootten, "Reminiscences: Coming to California in 1857," *Yolo County Historical Society* 8, no. 5 (Jan. 1975); *Napa County (CA) Reporter*, Aug. 29, 1857; Eunice Bradbury, "Bloody Road to California," *Carroll County Historical Society Quarterly* 26 (Autumn 1981): 1–3; Myron W. Wood, *History of Alameda County, California: Including Its Geology, Topography, Soil, and*

Productions, Together with a Full and Particular Record of the Spanish Grants (Oakland, CA: M. W. Wood, 1883), 985; "More of the Mormons," *San Francisco Daily Evening Bulletin*, May 20, 1858.

7. For numbers of stock in the company massacred at Mountain Meadows, see Appendix B. For the number of stock from other companies passing through Salt Lake City, see "Important News from Salt Lake," *San Francisco Daily Evening Bulletin*, Aug. 22, 1857; "Later and Important from Carson Valley," *San Joaquin Republican*, Oct. 7, 1857, quoting letters to the *Sacramento Union*; Letter to the editor, Aug. 26, 1857, in "Arrival Across the Plains," *San Joaquin Republican*, Sept. 6, 1857; Information on the Homer Duncan Company, "Mormon Pioneer Overland Trail, 1847–1868," http://www.lds.org/churchhistory/library/pioneercompany/0,15797,4017-1-46,00.html (accessed Oct. 17, 2007); Helen Carpenter, "A Trip Across the Plains in an Ox Wagon, 1857," in *Ho for California! Women's Overland Diaries from the Huntington Library*, ed. Sandra L. Myres (San Marino, CA: Huntington Library, 1980), 165; Parker1, 65–66; J. W. Dunn, Diary, May, 9–12, Aug. 24, Sept. 4–5, 1857, typescript, Center for American History, University of Texas, Austin, Texas; William Audley Maxwell, *Crossing the Plains, Days of '57: A Narrative of Early Emigrant Travel to California by the Ox-Team Method* (San Francisco: Sunset Publishing House, 1915), 2; Wood, *History of Alameda County*, 985; Welch; "Later from Carson Valley," *San Joaquin Republican*, Oct. 30, 1857; Menefee and Dodge, *History of Tulare and Kings Counties*, 768; "More Mormon Murders," *San Francisco Herald*, Nov. 2, 1857.

8. Brigham Young, Heber C. Kimball, and Willard Richards, Apr. 7, 1851, in "Fifth General Epistle," *Deseret News*, Apr. 8, 1851.

9. Hawkins, *Some Recollections*, 80, 101; Young, Kimball, and Richards, Apr. 7, 1851, in "Fifth General Epistle"; Alonzo Hazelton Raleigh, Journal, May 30, 185[4], CHL.

10. See Chandless, 141; Pitchforth, Aug. 15, 1857; Hawley, 15.

11. See Parker2, 11. For Wells's and Young's letters, see Daniel H. Wells, General Orders, Aug. 1, 1857, Letter Book, 93, Nauvoo Legion (Utah) Adj. Gen., Records, 1851–70, CHL; Brigham Young to Bishop Br[u]nson, Aug. 2, 1857, Letterpress Copybook 3:732, YOF.

12. James Pearce, JDL1-RT 2:285–86; Maxwell, *Crossing the Plains, Days of '57*, 5–6. On needing grain for mules and horses, see *The Encyclopedia Americana International Edition* (Danbury, CT: Grolier, 1995), 14:397; Kyle D. Kauffman and Johnathan J. Liebowitz, "Draft Animals on the United States Frontier," *Overland Journal* 15 (Summer 1997): 22.

13. Parker2, 12.

14. David O. Calder to John, Aug. 11, 1857, in David O. Calder, Letterpress Copybook, 1855–1867, CHL.

15. D. C. Hail, letter to the editor, Oct. 20, 1857, in "Horrible Massacre of Emigrants upon the Plains," *Daily Missouri Republican*, Dec. 9, 1857, from correspondence of *Little Rock True Democrat*.

16. William Strong, statement, n.d., in John Steele letter, John Steele Papers, BYU.

17. George Armstrong Hicks, "Family Record and History of Geo. A. Hicks," typescript, 25, CHL.

18. This was the account of the firm's clerk. See *History of Montana, 1739–1885* (Chicago: Warner, Beers, & Company, 1885), 1145, cited in William P. MacKinnon, "'Unquestionably Authentic and Correct in Every Detail': Probing John I. Ginn and His Remarkable Utah War Story," *Utah Historical Quarterly* 72 (Fall 2004): 336–37.

19. "Later from Salt Lake—War Certain," *Daily Alta California*, Dec. 11, 1857.

20. S. B. Honea, in "Outrages."

21. Sarah Killion to George A. Smith, Dec. 9, 1858, Historian's Office, Obituary Notices of Distinguished Persons, CHL; Clark V. Johnson, ed., *Mormon Redress Petitions: Documents of the 1833–1838 Missouri Conflict* (Provo, UT: Religious Studies Center, Brigham Young University, 1992), 78, 257, 665, 672–73; "Died," *Deseret News*, Dec. 15, 1858. In Mormon records, the surname is spelled "Killian," "Killien," and "Killion."

22. Jeffrey Carlstrom and Cynthia Furse, *The History of Emigration Canyon, Gateway to Salt Lake Valley* (Logan: Utah State University Press, 2003), 59–61, citing Minutes, Salt Lake County Court, Oct. 25, 1852; "Died."

23. Muster Rolls, Mormon War Papers, 1838, Special Collections, Secretary of State RG, Missouri State Archives, Jefferson City, MO; Craig L. Foster, "Report on the Turner-Hopper-Helm-Killian Connections," MMMRF; "Died"; Killion to Smith, Dec. 9, 1858, Historian's Office Obituary Notices. On Turner, see Turner Surname File, Johnson County Historical Society, Warrensburg, MO; Craig Foster, "Report on the Turner-Hopper-Helm-Killian Connections" MMMRF; Tom Sutak, "Nicholas Turner—Preliminary Findings," MMMRF; Sharon White, genealogical file, MMMRF; Dorothy J. O'Brien correspondence, MMMRF; Capt. Nicholas Turner Co., Mounted Volunteers, 4th Div., Missouri Militia Card Index, Mormon War Papers; Pay Accounts, Supplies, 3rd Div., Officers and Supplies, 4th Div., Mormon War Papers; Payroll account for Nicholas Turner, 1st Lt., 2nd Co., 2nd Reg., 2nd Brig., 4th Div., Missouri Mounted volunteers, Osage War, RG 133 Adj. Gen., Missouri National Guard, Indian Wars, Missouri State Archives, Jefferson City, MO.

24. "Overland Emigration."

25. Calvin Pierce, report, in "Interesting from Salt Lake," *Daily Alta California*, Oct. 21, 1857. See also George Powers, in "Horrible"; Milton D. Hammond, Autobiography and Journal, Aug. 17, 1857, typescript, CHL; James Leach, Reminiscence and Diary, Aug. 13, 1857, CHL; Raleigh Journal, Aug. 14, 1857.

26. Hail, letter to the editor, Oct. 20, 1857, in "Horrible Massacre of Emigrants."

27. William H. Cureton, "Trekking to California," undated, typescript, Bancroft Library, Berkeley, CA, copy in MMMRF; HOJ, July 25, 1857. Cureton's reminiscent account gives the time of his arrival in Salt Lake City as June

1857, almost certainly misdated a month early since he notes the July 24 anniversary event in Utah.

28. Hamilton Gray Park, statement, ca. 1910, CHL. Park's statement may have been part of his sworn statement, also regarding Mountain Meadows Massacre events, given in 1907.

29. Parker2, 6–7; Suzanne D. Rogers, "Hickman Farmstead, Buffalo National River, Arkansas," May 1987, typescript in possession of Ron Loving, copy at CHL.

30. Strong, statement, n.d., in John Steele letter, Steele Papers.

31. Ibid.; Harriet Strong Speirs, "A Biography of William Strong: A Member of the Mormon Battalion," typescript, June–July 1927, 1–3, CHL; Ronald Vern Jackson and David L. Grundvig, *Early Mormon Series, vol. 1: Directory of Individuals Residing in Salt Lake City Wards, 1854–1861* (Bountiful, UT: Accelerated Indexing Systems, n.d.), 50, 82; "Hamilton G. Park," *Deseret News*, Apr. 6, 1918; Jenson, 1:684–85.

32. Lorenzo Snow to Brigham Young, Aug. 7, 1857, Incoming Correspondence, YOF; Lorenzo Snow to Brigham Young, Aug. [13], 1857, Incoming Correspondence, YOF; Verulam Dive to Brigham Young, Aug. 8, 1857, Incoming Correspondence, YOF.

33. The James Luttrell train was attacked on Aug. 19 at Box Elder Creek, where Brigham City is located. "The Overland Immigration," *Daily Alta California*, Oct. 13, 1857; John W. Van Cott, *Utah Place Names* (Salt Lake City: University of Utah Press, 1990), 48, 50. The Dan Abbott and Henry Obarr trains were attacked at the City of Rocks on Aug. 24. Menefee and Dodge, *History of Tulare and Kings Counties*, 534–35; "More Mormon Murders." The John Fine train was attacked three times, once in late Aug. between Salt Lake City and the Bear River ford, where Fine's train joined with the Linton-McCune train; again on Sept. 9 at Pilot Spring on the Salt Lake Cutoff; and the third time on Sept. 12 at the City of Rocks. "More Testimony against the Mormons," *Daily Alta California*, Nov. 9, 1857; Menefee and Dodge, *History of Tulare and Kings Counties*, 768; Dunn Diary, Sept. 1–12, 1857; Angus McLeod, statement, in "More Mormon Atrocities," *San Francisco Herald*, Nov. 12, 1857.

34. Dive to Young, Aug. 8, 1857, Incoming Correspondence, YOF; Snow to Young, Aug. 7, 1857, Incoming Correspondence, YOF.

35. Dive to Young, Aug. 8, 1857, Incoming Correspondence, YOF.

36. Snow to Young, Aug. 7, 1857, Incoming Correspondence, YOF.

37. Hail, letter to the editor, Oct. 20, 1857, in "Horrible Massacre of Emigrants." See also "Overland Immigration"; "More Mormon Massacres," *Daily Alta California*, Nov. 1, 1857.

38. Brigham Young, Discourse, Aug. 16, 1857, reported by George D. Watt, in Historian's Office, Reports of Speeches, ca. 1845–85, CHL.

39. Snow to Young, Aug. 7, 1857, Incoming Correspondence, YOF. See also Geo. W. Armstrong to Brigham Young, Sept. 30, 1857, USBIA.

40. Snow to Young, Aug. [13], 1857, Incoming Correspondence, YOF.

41. For examples of subsequent emigrant outrage, see "More Outrages," *Los Angeles Star*, Nov. 7, 1857; "The Mormons in the Capacity of Savages," *San Joaquin Republican*, Oct. 28, 1857.

42. Snow to Young, Aug. [13], 1857, Incoming Correspondence, YOF.

43. Young, Discourse, Aug. 16, 1857, in Historian's Office, Reports of Speeches. See also Wilford Woodruff to editor of the *Millennial Star*, Sept. 12, 1857, Historian's Office Letterpress Copybook 1:489.

44. Letter, Aug. 23, 1857, in "Murder of a Providence Man in Utah," *New York Herald*, Nov. 8, 1857; "Arrival from the Plains—Indian Attack—Eighteen Killed," *San Francisco Daily Globe*, Aug. 21, 1857; "Later from Carson Valley," *San Francisco Daily Globe*, Aug. 18, 1857; *Sacramento Daily Bee*, Aug. 19, 1857. See also "The Mormons," *New York Times*, Nov. 9, 1857.

45. Unruh, 185, 197, 395.

46. Huntington, Aug. 10, 1857.

47. Robert T. Burton, Vouchers 9–16, filed Feb. 12, 1861, in U.S. Congress, House, *Accounts of Brigham Young, Superintendent of Indian Affairs in Utah Territory*, 37th Cong., 2nd sess., 1862, H. Doc. 29, 21.

48. Wm. H. Hooper, H. S. Beatie, and Edward Hunter, Vouchers 6, 7, and 8, filed Aug. 8, 9, 1857, in House, *Accounts of Brigham Young*, Doc. 29, 80–81. On Young's Indian policy, see Brigham Young to James W. Denver, Sept. 12, 1857, Governor's Letterbook, 2:651, YOF; John Alton Peterson, *Utah's Black Hawk War* (Salt Lake City: University of Utah Press, 1998); Howard A. Christy, "The Walker War: Defense and Conciliation as Strategy," *Utah Historical Quarterly* 47, no. 4 (Fall 1979): 395–420; Howard A. Christy, "Open Hand and Mailed Fist: Mormon Indian Relations in Utah, 1847–52," *Utah Historical Quarterly* 46 (Summer 1978): 216–35; Lawrence G. Coates, "Brigham Young and Mormon Indian Policies: The Formative Period, 1836–1851," *BYU Studies* 18 (1977–78): 428–51.

49. Oliver Boardman Huntington, Diary and Reminiscences, 129, typescript, CHL; Whitney, 4:209–10; Jenson, 4:748–49. On Huntington's position as chief interpreter, see House, *Accounts of Brigham Young*, Doc. 29, 8.

50. Huntington, Aug. 10, 11, 31, 1857. On Little Soldier's relations with the Mormons, see Scott R. Christensen, "Chief Little Soldier," *Pioneer* 42 (Winter 1995): 16–19.

51. "Interesting from Utah," *New York Herald*, Feb. 23, 1858.

52. Huntington, Aug. 1857.

53. Woodruff, Aug. 13, 1857.

54. Daniel H. Wells to A. Johnson, Aug. 13, 1857, Letter Book, 97, Nauvoo Legion (Utah) Adj. Gen. Records.

55. Young, Discourse, Aug. 16, 1857, in Historian's Office, Reports of Speeches.

56. On Mormon apprehensions of attacks by Indians, see "The Mormons," *New York Weekly Times*, Sept. 19, 1857; "Later and Important from Carson Valley," *San Joaquin Republican*, Oct. 7, 1857.

57. Brigham Young to Franklin D. Richards, Mar. 30, 1855, Letterpress Copy-book 2:42–43, YOF; Brigham Young to James W. Denver, Sept. 12, 1857, Governor's Letterbook, 2:651–52, YOF; J. W. Denver to Brigham Young, Nov. 11, 1857, in *Report of the Commissioner of Indian Affairs, Accompanying the Annual Report of the Secretary of the Interior for the Year 1857* (Washington: William A. Harris, 1858), 312–14.
58. Woodruff, Aug. 16, 1857; Young, Discourse, Aug. 16, 1857, in Historian's Office, Reports of Speeches.
59. Young, Discourse, Aug. 16, 1857, in Historian's Office, Reports of Speeches.
60. Raleigh Journal, Aug. 16, 1857; Young, Discourse, Aug. 16, 1857, in Historian's Office, Reports of Speeches.
61. Young, Discourse, Aug. 16, 1857, in Historian's Office, Reports of Speeches. According to Harriet Thatcher, gentile merchants didn't raise their hands in assent. [Harriet Thatcher] to William Preston, Aug. 5, 1857, William Preston, Papers, Special Collections, Utah State University, Logan, UT. The content of Thatcher's letter suggests she was present at Young's mid-Aug. address, though the opening of her letter was dated nine days before the address was given.
62. President's Office Journal, Aug. 19, 1857, YOF; *DBY,* 62, Aug. 19, 1857; Young, Discourse, Aug. 16, 1857, in Historian's Office, Reports of Speeches.
63. Young, Discourse, Aug. 16, 1857, in Historian's Office, Reports of Speeches.
64. *DBY,* 62, Aug. 19, 1857.
65. Woodruff, Aug. 26, 1857.

Chapter 8

1. Jacob Hamblin, statement, in Carleton, 6.
2. "Immigrant Massacre."
3. "Letter."
4. Silas Smith, JDL1-RS 7:32, JDL1-BT 5:222; *MU,* 242–43; NJ1908. Relying on southern Utah tradition, Juanita Brooks consistently called it the Fancher train. Brooks2, 44–49, 52, 69, 142, 151.
5. "Report of J. Hamblin," June 22, 1858, Jacob Forney, Letter Book 1857–59, 292, CHL; George A. Smith, statement, [Nov. 1869], George A. Smith, Papers, CHL; Jacob Hamblin, statement, in Carleton, 6.
6. Jacob Hamblin, statement, in Carleton, 6; Appendix A.
7. "BY."
8. "Massacre."
9. "Outrages"; "Later from Salt Lake—War Certain," *San Francisco Daily Alta California,* Dec. 11, 1857; "Later from Great Salt Lake," *San Francisco Daily Evening Bulletin,* Dec. 11, 1857.
10. Brigham Young, deposition, Aug. 2, 1875, CCF 31; "BY."
11. Hamilton Gray Park, statement, ca. 1910, CHL.
12. Welch.

13. See Parker2, 6–9; James Leach, Reminiscence and Diary, Aug. 13, 1857, CHL; Alonzo Hazelton Raleigh, Journal, Aug. 16, 1857, CHL.

14. See Appendix A and mountainmeadowsmassacre.org.

15. The numerous examples of such claims include Frances Fawcett Haynes to the Bancroft Library, July 19, 1932, Hubert Howe Bancroft Library, University of California, Berkeley, CA; Frances Fawcett Haynes to Mrs. E. A. Brush, Oct. 2, 1935, CHL; Douglas McEuen, *The Legend of Francis Marion Poteet and the Mountain Meadows Massacre* (Pleasanton, TX: Zabava Printing, 1996), 45, 58, 62, 74; California, Los Angeles County, Los Angeles, 1860 U.S. Census, population schedule, 377; Douglas McEuen, "Francis Marion Poteet," *Branches & Acorns* 14 (June 1999): 12.

16. M1911; M1877-10; M1877-12.

17. Appendix A.

18. Ibid.

19. "Journal for August, 1857," *Deseret News*, Sept. 9, 1857.

20. Appendix B.

21. Ibid.; Depositions in PPU. Some longhorns were reported in southern Utah as early as 1853, coming via Texas and southern Colorado over the Old Spanish Trail. Archibald F. Bennett, Ella M. Bennett, and Barbara Bennett Roach, *Valiant in the Faith: Gardner and Sarah Snow and Their Family* (Murray, UT: Roylance Publishing, 1990), 241; Don D. Walker, "Longhorns Come to Utah," *Utah Historical Quarterly* 30 (1962): 137. Nephi Johnson said many of the massacred emigrants' cattle were Texas longhorns. JDL2-BT 1:66–67.

22. Appendix B; The Inflation Calculator, http://www.westegg.com/inflation/.

23. William Carey, JDL1-BT 2:1. Several 1857 trains had property that rivaled or exceeded that of the Arkansas company. A few examples are the J. J. Bush company with eight hundred head of cattle and five hundred mules; the John Fine company with ninety wagons and an unknown number of loose stock; Daniel Teeter's Pope County, Arkansas, train with fourteen hundred head of cattle; the Jackson company with seventy-five wagons and a large number of loose stock; and the Rawson company that started with seven thousand sheep of which four thousand actually made it to California. "Important News from Salt Lake," *San Francisco Daily Evening Bulletin*, Aug. 22, 1857; Eugene L. Menefee and Fred A. Dodge, *History of Tulare and Kings Counties, California with Biographical Sketches of the Leading Men and Women of the Counties Who Have Been Identified with Their Growth and Development from the Early Days to the Present* (Los Angeles: Historic Record, 1913), 768; Myron W. Wood, *History of Alameda County, California: Including its Geology, Topography, Soil, and Productions, together with a Full and Particular Record of the Spanish Grants* (Oakland, CA: M. W. Wood, 1883), 985; Mary Elizabeth Jackson Brayton, "Recollections of Crossing the Plains," Merrill Mattes Library, National Frontier Trails Center, Independence, MO, quoted in Patricia K. A. Fletcher, Jack Earl Fletcher, and Lee Whiteley, *Cherokee*

Trail Diaries (Caldwell, ID: Caxton Printers, [1999]–ca. 2001), 3:180–81; E. J. Lewis, *Tehama County, California . . .* (San Francisco: Elliott & Moore, 1880), 151.

24. *CHC*, 4:140.

25. W. T. B. Sanford, in "The Route to Salt Lake City," *Los Angeles Star,* Dec. 19, 1857; Brigham Young to E. J. Steptoe, Jan. 2, 1855, Letterpress Copybook 1:813–16, YOF.

26. Hoth, Sept. 21–29, 1856.

27. Ibid., Sept. 26–30, 1856.

28. Welch; "The Late Outrages on the Plains—Further Particulars," *Los Angeles Star,* Nov. 7, 1857; Petition for Payment of Losses, Sept. 20, 1857, HR 35A-G7.1, RG 223, National Archives, Washington, D. C.; Willson Nowers, note to Andrew Jenson, AJ1. Collins's train was known as the Crook & Collins company when it left Arkansas. S. B. Honea, in "Outrages."

29. S. B. Honea, in "Outrages"; Welch; "Horrible"; William Mathews, JDL1-BT 4:45–46.

30. Volney Leroy King, statement, ca. 1875, 73, Volney Leroy King Papers, UofU.

31. Appendix B; "The Late Outrages on the Plains—Another Account," *Los Angeles Star,* Oct. 31, 1857; "Outrages"; Welch.

32. George Armstrong Hicks, "Family Record and History of Geo. A. Hicks," typescript, 25, CHL; Davis Bitton, "I'd Rather Have Some Roasting Ears: The Peregrinations of George Armstrong Hicks," *Utah Historical Quarterly* 68 (Summer 2000): 211.

33. Welch.

34. PGM, Aug. 2, 1857; Jenson, 4:750.

35. [John G. McQuarrie] to [A.] Will Lund, undated and untitled typescript, [6–7], CM; Hawley, 15.

36. Lawrence L. Linford, "Establishing and Maintaining Land Ownership in Utah Prior to 1869," *Utah Historical Quarterly* 42 (Spring 1974): 126–43; Paul W. Gates, *History of Public Land Law Development* (Washington, D.C., 1968), 219–47.

37. Arrington2, 148–51; Pitchforth, June 14, 1857.

38. [McQuarrie] to Lund, [6–7], CM.

39. PGM, Aug. 9, 1857.

40. Ibid., Aug. 9, 1857.

41. Ibid., Aug. 16, 1857.

42. Alvira L. Parish, Orrin E. Parrish, Joseph Bartholomew, Zephaniah J. War-ren, Alva A. Warren, James W. Webb, Abraham Durfee, Thomas O'Bannion, Nathaniel Case, Andrew J. Moore, Thomas Hollingshead, Abner M. Hollingshead, Amos B. Moore, and Alice Lamb, affidavits, in Cradlebaugh, 43–67.

43. Zephaniah J. Warren, Mar. 26, 1859, in Cradlebaugh, 54; Polly Aird, "'You Nasty Apostates, Clear Out': Reasons for Disaffection in the Late 1850s," *Journal of Mormon History* 30 (Fall 2004): 173–91.

44. James Pearce, JDL1-RT 2:285–86. James Pearce testified in John D. Lee's first trial that he was fourteen at the time of the massacre. Born in 1839, he was actually eighteen. James Pearce, JDL1-BT 4:105.

45. Charles B. Hancock, Biographical Sketch, Collection of Mormon Diaries, 46, Library of Congress, Washington, D.C., microfilm copy at CHL. See also "The Mountain Meadow Massacre," *New York Herald*, Aug. 3, 1875. For other violent incidents in Payson, see Franklin Wheeler Young, Journal, 1858, CHL, which describes the castration of Henry Jones—a Payson man accused of adultery as well as of incest with his mother—and the later killing of both son and mother when they were suspected of planning to steal local horses. The Jones murders would later be heralded as evidence of extralegal violence in the territory. Franklin Wheeler Young did "not pretend to justify" the murders, acknowledging that whatever wrongs the victims committed could have been handled in a different way.

46. Ann Eliza Webb, interview, Aug. 2, 1875, in "The Mountain Meadow Massacre," *New York Herald*, Aug. 3, 1875.

47. PGM, Sept. 27, 1857; Maryette Parrish Keir, "San Bernardino Pioneers: Frank Hinckley Keir Family," Manuscripts and Documents, George William and Helen Pruitt Beattie Collection, Huntington Library, San Marino, CA; *The Story of Oak Glen and the Yucaipa Valley* (O. W. Willits, 1971), 24–25.

48. Myrtilla Nebeker Frey, Memoir, original in possession of Carolyn King Fillmore, Kaysville, UT, photocopy of manuscript at CHL.

49. Pitchforth, Aug. 15, 1857.

50. Ibid., Aug. 17, 1857.

51. Hawley, 15.

52. "BY"; Mary S. Campbell, AJ1; Elias Morris, statement, Feb. 2, 1892, in CM; Hawley, 15; "LC"; "LLC."

53. J. D. Borthwick, *Three Years in California* (Edinburgh: William Blackwood and Sons, 1857), 329; Chandless, 20; Mitford M. Mathews, ed., *A Dictionary of Americanisms on Historical Principles* (Chicago: University of Chicago Press, 1951), 536, s.v. "Dutchman"; *The Oxford English Dictionary*, 2nd ed. (Oxford: Clarendon Press, 1989), 4:1141–42, s.v. "Dutchman." Borthwick reported that all Europeans except the French, English, and Italians "are in California classed under the general denomination of Dutchmen."

54. *The Oxford Companion to United States History* (Oxford: Oxford University Press, 2001), 423; Tyler Anbinder, *Nativism and Slavery: The Northern Know Nothings and the Politics of the 1850s* (New York: Oxford University Press, 1992).

55. John Gibson, ed., *History of York County, Pennsylvania* (Chicago: F. A. Battey Publishing, 1886), pt. 2, 20; Pennsylvania, York County, Borough of York, North Ward, 1850 U.S. Census, population schedule, 2. The sources on the Greslys give various spellings of the surname. We have standardized them to *Gresly*, the spelling that appears on family grave markers at the Prospect Hill Cemetery in York, Pennsylvania.

56. York County Quarter Sessions, Nov. 1842, Book C, 262, Apr. 1851, Book G, 137, 141, Aug. 1863, Book J, 450, Apr. 1858, Book K, 515, York County Archives, York, Pennsylvania.

57. "The Late Outrages on the Plains—Further Particulars"; Hawley, 15.

58. Powers, in "Horrible."

59. Ibid.

60. "The Late Outrages on the Plains—Further Particulars"; "Statement of G. W. Davis," *Daily Alta California*, Nov. 13, 1857; Arkansas, Pope County, 1850 U.S. Census, population schedule, 243B.

61. Thomas Waters Cropper, Autobiography, Jan. 15, 1926, CHL. The earliest known use of the term "Missouri Wildcats" is in Stenhouse, 424, 427, 428. Whether Cropper actually heard the Missourians call themselves "Missouri Wildcats" or simply borrowed the phrase from Stenhouse cannot be determined.

62. Cropper Autobiography.

63. Ray. The emigrants were probably not far off in their description of Fillmore. To Hans Hoth, the Mormon dissenter who passed through the new village the previous year, the Fillmore courthouse, or territorial capital, was "large and nicely built," but the rest of the buildings were "practically all log cabins," making "the whole place…not look like a city at all." Hoth, Sept. 24, 1856.

64. Warn, in "Horrible"; Warn, in "Our Los Angeles Corresondence," *Daily Alta California*, Oct. 27, 1857; Ethan Pettit, Diary, Aug. 12, 13, 16, 21, 23, 26, 1857, CHL.

65. "BY."

66. Ibid.

67. L. H. McCullough to Daniel H. Wells, Aug. 27, 1857, Nauvoo Legion (UT) Adj. Gen. Records, 1851–70, CHL; Samuel P. Hoyt, for Lewis Brunson, to Brigham Young, Aug. 29, 1857, Incoming Correspondence, YOF.

68. Maurice Halbwachs, *The Collective Memory*, trans. Francis J. Ditter Jr. and Vida Yazdi Ditter (New York: Harper & Row, 1980); Michael Kammen, *Mystic Chords of Memory: The Transformation of Tradition in American Culture* (New York: Knopf, 1991); Michael Kammen, "Some Patterns and Meanings of Memory Distortion in American History," chap. 8, in *In the Past Lane: Historical Perspectives on American Culture* (New York: Oxford University Press, 1997), 199–212.

69. The argument that historians too often create an artificial and misleading chain of causes to explain events has been made most recently by Nassim Nicholas Taleb, *The Black Swan: The Impact of the Highly Improbable* (New York: Random House, 2007).

Chapter 9

1. Addison Pratt, Journal, 1843–1852, Oct. 15, 1849, CHL, published in *The Journals of Addison Pratt*, ed. S. George Ellsworth (Salt Lake City: University of Utah Press, 1990), 382, Oct. 15, 1849; "History of the Iron County

Mission," Jan. 2, 1851, in JH. The grasses, like the stream, could be intermittent. In spring 1855 George Washington Bean found "not much grass" at Corn Creek. George Washington Bean, Journal, May 10, 1855, microfilm of typescript, CHL. However, Amasa M. Lyman found "good Grass" there in late fall 1855. Amasa Lyman, Diary, Nov. 25, 1855, Amasa M. Lyman, Collection, CHL. See also Amos Milton Musser, Diary, Oct. 28, 1852, CHL; Silas Smith, Journal, May 15, 1854, CHL. A present-day investigation of the banks of Corn Creek, now virtually dried up, shows a stream bed, from high bank to high bank, of sixty feet, stretching out to the west in its fan to several hundred feet.

2. William R. Palmer, "Utah Indians Past and Present," *Utah Historical Quarterly* 1 (Apr. 1928): 35–52; J. H. Simpson, *Report of Explorations Across the Great Basin of the Territory of Utah* (Washington, D.C.: Government Printing Office [hereafter GPO], 1876), 117; Knack, 31–32, 143–44.

3. "Sketch of a Trip to Pauvan Valley," *Deseret News*, Dec. 13, 1851; John D. Lee to George A. Smith, June 8, 1851, George A. Smith, Papers, CHL; Omer C. Stewart, "Culture Element Distributions, XVIII: Ute—Southern Paiute," *University of California Anthropological Records* 6, no. 4 (1941): 250–51.

4. E. L. Black, "Life Story of Indian Chief Kanosh," manuscript, UofU.

5. "Sketch of a Trip to Pauvan Valley"; Anson Call, letter to the editor, Mar. 7, 1852, in *Deseret News*, Apr. 17, 1852.

6. Garland Hurt to Brigham Young, June 30, 1855, USBIA.

7. Hurt to Denver, June 30, 1857, USBIA.

8. John Richard Alley Jr., "The Fur Trapper and the Great Basin Indian" (master's thesis, University of Utah, 1978), 60. For conditions after the Mormon settlement, see Samuel L. Sprague, letter to the editor, Dec. 29, 1855, in *Deseret News*, Jan. 9, 1856.

9. J. McKnight, letter to the editor, Oct. 20, 1858, in "The Storms of Utah, Corn Creek—Scanty Harvest," *Milwaukee Weekly Wisconsin*, Dec. 29, 1858, copy in Historian's Office, Historical Scrapbooks, 1840–1904, 11:34, CHL; "Excursion to Fillmore," *Deseret News*, Aug. 29, 1855; "Indians," *Deseret News*, Nov. 16, 1854; Orson K. Whitney, Journal, May 15, 1854, in Newel Kimball Whitney, Papers, CHL; Daniel H. Wells, "Narrative," Utah and the Mormons Manuscript Collection, [17–19], Bancroft Library, University of California, Berkeley, CA, microfilm copy at CHL; Henry Standage to George A. Smith, Sept. 29, 1853, Smith Papers; Ronald W. Walker, ed., "President Young Writes Jefferson Davis about the Gunnison Massacre Affair," *BYU Studies* 35 (1995): 146–70.

10. George A. Smith to Mr. St. Clair, Nov. 25, 1869, Historian's Office, Letterpress Copybook 2:941–49, CHL; George A. Smith, statement, [Nov. 1869], Smith Papers; Philo T. Farnsworth, JDL1-BT 5:277–78, 303, JDL1-RS 8:24; Silas S. Smith, JDL1-BT 5:220, JDL1-RS 7:31; Elisha Hoopes, JDL1-BT 5:246; George A. Smith, deposition, July 30, 1875, CCF 31.

11. HOJ, Aug. 25, 1857; Jacob Hamblin, Journal, 1854–57, 81–82, in Jacob Hamblin, Papers, CHL; Silas Smith, JDL1-BT 5:218–22; Smith to St. Clair, Nov. 25, 1869, Historian's Office, Letterpress Copybook 2:941–49; Smith, statement, [Nov. 1869], Smith Papers; Huntington, Sept. 1, 1857; Silas Smith, JDL1-BT 5:229; Elisha Hoopes, JDL1-RS 8:4, JDL1-BT 5:246. See also Philo T. Farnsworth, JDL1-BT 5:299.

12. Smith to St. Clair, Nov. 25, 1869, Historian's Office, Letterpress Copybook 2:941–49, CHL; Smith, statement, [Nov. 1869], Smith Papers; HOJ, Aug., 25, 1857; Jacob Hamblin, statement, in Carleton, 6.

13. Smith to St. Clair, Nov. 25, 1869, Historian's Office, Letterpress Copybook 2:941–49, CHL; Smith, statement, [Nov. 1869], Smith Papers; Silas Smith, JDL1-BT 5:222, 239; Jacob Hamblin, statement, in Carleton, 6.

14. Elisha Hoopes, JDL1-RS 8:4, JDL1-BT 5:246; Jacob Hamblin, statement, in Carleton, 6; Silas Smith, JDL1-BT 5:229. In 1849 George Q. Cannon noted that a fifty-mile desert lay ahead of him on the Spanish Trail from the Muddy to Vegas. Michael N. Landon, ed., *To California in '49*, vol. 1, *The Journals of George Q. Cannon*, ed. Adrian W. Cannon and Richard E. Turley Jr. (Salt Lake City: Deseret Book, 1999), 55, 59–60.

15. William Bedford Temple to Wife and Children, May 11, June 2, 1850, Oregon Historical Society, Portland, OR; Washington Peck, Diary, Oct. 27–Dec. 27, 1857 typescript, National Frontier Trails Center, Independence, MO; Silas Smith, JDL1-BT 5:229; Jacob Hamblin, JDL2-BT 1:92.

16. Jacob Hamblin, statement, in Carleton, 6.

17. Ibid.; Hawley, 15.

18. Silas Smith, JDL1-BT 5:221, 237–39; Hamblin Journal, 81–82, in Hamblin Papers; Smith to St. Clair, Nov. 25, 1869, Historian's Office, Letterpress Copybook 2:941–49, CHL; Smith, statement, [Nov. 1869], Smith Papers; Elisha Hoopes, JDL1-BT 5:245–73, JDL1-RS 8:12–21; Philo T. Farnsworth, JDL1-BT 5:278–79, 303; HOJ, Aug. 25, 1857.

19. Smith to St. Clair, Nov. 25, 1869, Historian's Office, Letterpress Copybook 2:941–49, CHL; Smith, statement, [Nov. 1869], Smith Papers; Elisha Hoopes, JDL1-BT 5:245–73, JDL1-RS 8:12–21; Silas Smith, JDL1-BT 5:221; Philo T. Farnsworth, JDL1-RS 4:24, JDL1-BT 5:278–79, 303.

20. Powers, in "Horrible"; George W. Davis, in "Letter from San Bernardino," *San Francisco Daily Evening Bulletin*, Nov. 12, 1857.

21. Welch; *An Illustrated History of Los Angeles County, California* (Chicago: Lewis Publishing, 1889), 676–77.

22. Welch.

23. Honea, in "Outrages."

24. Peter Bo[y]ce, letter to the editor, Jan. 31, 1875, in "Correspondence," *Ogden Junction*, Feb. 5, 1875. The general outline of these events can also be found in T. S. W., "Mountain Me[a]dow Massacre," 16–17, Articles Pertaining to the Mormons in Utah, ca. 1860, CHL.

25. Warn, in "Horrible."

26. Ray; Joleen Ashman Robison, *Almon Robison, Utah Pioneer, Man of Mystique and Tragedy* (Lawrence, KS: Richard A. Robison, 1995), 83.

27. Eleanor F. Knowlton, reminiscence, 1:75, typed excerpts, California Historical Society, San Francisco, CA.

28. Woodruff, Jan. 13, 1856; Elisha Hoopes, JDL1-BT 5:245–73; Honea, in "Outrages"; Powers, in "Horrible."

29. Honea, in "Outrages." Hoopes's florid retelling of the Corn Creek episode during the John D. Lee prosecution almost two decades later earned him a withering cross-examination. Elisha Hoopes, JDL1-BT 5:245–73.

30. Forney, 370.

31. Carleton, 17; Rogers. Rogers examined Corn Creek during the spring runoff.

32. See, e.g., *Covered Wagon Women: Diaries & Letters from the Western Trails, 1840–1890*, eds. Kenneth L. Holmes and David C. Duniway (Glendale, CA: Arthur H. Clark, 1986), 14; Karen M. Offen and David C. Duniway, eds. "William Cornell's Journal, 1852, with His Overland Guide to Oregon," *Oregon Historical Quarterly* 79 (Winter 1978): 388.

33. Richard H. Dillon, ed., *California Trail Herd: The 1850 Missouri-to-California Journal of Cyrus C. Loveland* (Los Gatos, CA: Talisman Press, 1961), 19; Tamara Miner Haygood, "Texas Fever," The Handbook of Texas, http://www.tsha.utexas.edu/handbook/online/articles/TT/awt1.html (accessed Nov. 6, 2007). For Texas longhorns in Utah, see Nephi Johnson, JDL2-BT 1:66–67; Jacob Hamblin, JDL2-BT 1:93. The longhorns of 1857 were not the first in Utah. The Preston Thomas company of 1853 included a thousand head. Archibald F. Bennett, Ella M. Bennett, and Barbara Bennett Roach, *Valiant in the Faith: Gardner and Sarah Snow and Their Family* (Murray, UT: Roylance Publishing, 1990), 241. See also Don D. Walker, "Longhorns Come to Utah," *Utah Historical Quarterly* 30 (1962): 137.

34. Dillon, *California Trail Herd*, 19.

35. Eleftherios Mylonakis, "When to Suspect and How to Monitor Babesiosis," *American Family Physician* 63 (May 2001): 1969–74. Texas Fever was the nineteenth-century term for babesiosis.

36. H. B. Rees Jr., M. A. Smith, J. C. Spendlove, R. S. Fraser, T. Fukushima, A. G. Barbour Jr., and F. J. Schoenfeld, "Epidemiologic and Laboratory Investigations of Bovine Anthrax in Two Utah Counties in 1975," *Public Health Reports* 92 (Mar.–Apr. 1977): 176–86.

37. See, e.g., Woodruff, Apr. 25–May 18, 1856; "Disease Among Cattle," *Stockton (CA) San Joaquin Republican*, Nov. 10, 1857; Patty Bartlett Sessions, Diary, Aug. 6, 1858, CHL; "Beware of Dead Cattle," *Mountaineer*, Sept. 3, 1859; Ray; Thomas Cropper, Autobiography, 1926, photocopy, CHL.

38. The authors thank Drs. Edmund C. Evans, DeVon C. Hale, Quinton S. Harris, John H. Holbrook, and George F. Snell for their 2007 evaluation of the evidence. Drs. Robert K. Maddock Jr. and John M. Matsen joined them in a preliminary evaluation of the evidence in 2002.

39. Arthur M. Friedlander, "Anthrax," *Medical Aspects of Chemical and Biological Warfare*, pt. 1, *Warfare Weaponry and the Casualty*, vol. 3, *Textbook of Military Medicine*, ed. Frederick R. Sidell, Ernest T. Takafuji, and David R. Franz (Washington, D.C.: Borden Institute, 1997), 468; William Arthur Hagan and Dorsey William Bruner, *The Infectious Diseases of Domestic Animals*, 4th ed. (Ithaca: Comstock Publishing Associates, Cornell University, 1961), 185; *Taber's Cyclopedic Medical Dictionary*, 19th ed. (Philadelphia: F. A. Davis, 2001), 131, s.v. "anthrax"; Gregory B. Knudson, "Treatment of Anthrax in Man: History and Current Concepts," *Military Medicine* 151 (Feb. 1986): 71.

40. Friedlander, "Anthrax," 467–75; *Taber's Cyclopedic Medical Dictionary*, 131, s.v. "anthrax"; E. Mallon and P. H. McKee, "Extraordinary Case Report: Cutaneous Anthrax," *American Journal of Dermatopathology* 19, no. 1 (1997): 82.

41. "Disease Among Cattle."

42. P. K. Jacoby, in "Victims"; "Meeting."

43. Elias Smith, Diary, July 31, 1857, CHL.

44. Parker2, 7.

45. Jacob Hamblin, statement, in Carleton, 6; Appendix B.

46. Ray. In an 1872 interview, John D. Lee told journalist J. H. Beadle that a "Widow Tomlinson" got "poison" from an ox carcass in her eyes while trying "to save the hide and taller." Her face swelled before she reportedly perished. Beadle1. We have been unable to confirm the death of a woman surnamed Tomlinson and believe Lee may have conflated the cases of John Ray's wife and Proctor Robison.

47. Cropper Autobiography, Jan. 15, 1926; Ray; Elisha Hoopes, JDL1-BT 5:270–71. For additional sources on Robison's death, see Robison, *Almon Robison*, 79–82.

48. Robison, *Almon Robison*, 83.

49. Ray; Cropper Autobiography, Jan. 15, 1926.

50. Lois Inman Baker, "Joel C. Inman to Oregon in 1852," *Lane County Pioneer Historical Society* 8 (Nov. 1963), http://inman.surnameweb.org/documents/joelcinman.htm (accessed Nov. 6, 2007).

51. Claude Elliot, "Abolition," The Handbook of Texas, http://www.tsha.utexas.edu/handbook/online/articles/AA/vaa1.html (accessed Nov. 6, 2007).

52. Mark Regan Essig, "Science and Sensation: Poison Murder and Forensic Medicine in Nineteenth-Century America" (PhD diss., Cornell University, 2000), 4–5, 216–60.

53. Powers, in "Horrible"; Davis, in "Letter from San Bernardino"; Welch; Silas Smith, JDL1-BT 5:222; HOJ, Aug. 27, 1857.

54. Silas Smith, JDL1-BT 5:222.

55. Robert Kershaw, JDL1-BT 4:90–92.

56. Powers, in "Horrible."

57. Powers and Warn, in "Horrible."

58. Joel White, JDL1-BT 4:5; PSHR, Sept. 7, 1857, 2nd sec., 34; Mary S. Campbell, AJ1; Benjamin Platt, Reminiscences, 5, photocopy of typescript,

CHL; James Pearce, JDL1-BT 4:102; Rachel Hamblin, statement, May 20, 1859, in Carleton, 11; *MU*, 219; Joseph Sudweeks, "Concerning Myself: The Life of Laban Morrill," typescript, MMMRF; McGlashan.

59. PSHR, Sept. 7, 1857, 2nd sec., 34, provides the earliest evidence of the poisoning rumors' penetration to a town with links to the massacre. Internal evidence suggests, however, that the entry was not made until Sept. 12, at the earliest, which was after the massacre.

60. PSHR, Sept. 7, 1857, 2nd sec., 34; Woodruff, Sept. 29, 1857; *Los Angeles Star*, Oct. 10, 1857; John D. Lee to Brigham Young, Nov. 20, 1857, Incoming Correspondence, YOF.

61. J. Forney to A. B. Greenwood, Aug. 1859, in SDoc42, 76.

62. Willson Gates Nowers, note to Andrew Jenson, AJ1.

63. [John G. McQuarrie] to [A.] Will Lund, undated and untitled typescript, [9], CM.

64. Ellott Willden, AJ1; Beadle1; Elias Morris, statement, Feb. 2, 1892, CM; James Pearce, JDL1-BT 4:101–2.

65. William H. Dame to George A. Smith, quoted in HOJ, Aug. 31, 1857.

66. Argus, open letter to Brigham Young, July 20, 18[71], in "History of Mormonism," *Corrinne (UT) Reporter*, July 22, 1871; Dame to Smith, in HOJ, Aug. 31, 1857; William Carey, JDL1-BT 2:2–3, JDL1-PS 2:17.

67. See, e.g., Cedar City leader Isaac Haight's counsel in CSM, Aug. 19, 1855, May 4, 1856.

68. Hoth, Oct. 6, 1856, described those who disobeyed local directives in order to make money. Nowers in Beaver thought local leaders "misconstrued or misunderstood" instructions "to mean that the people were not to sell the emigrants anything." Willson Gates Nowers, note to Andrew Jenson, AJ1.

69. Silas Smith, JDL1-BT 5:222; SAJ, Sept. 3, 1857; Jesse N. Smith, JDL1-BT 5:214–15;"Parowan," undated notes, AJ1.

70. William Leany, Reminiscence, 1888, 21–22, CHL.

71. S. B. Aden to Brigham Young, Mar. 14, 1859, Incoming Correspondence, YOF; "$1,000 Reward! William A. Aden," *Salt Lake City Valley Tan*, July 6, 1859; "Supposed to be Murdered in Mormondom," *San Francisco Daily Evening Bulletin*, Aug. 8, 1859; S. B. Aden, Dec. 14, 1874, in "Lingering Hope," *Salt Lake Daily Tribune*, Dec. 24, 1874.

72. Gibbs, 8; Leany, Reminiscence, 22.

73. S. B. Aden to Alfred Cumming, Jan. 27, 1859, Alfred Cumming, Papers, Duke University, Durham, NC; "William D. Roberts," in *Utah Since Statehood: Historical and Biographical* (Chicago: S. J. Clarke, 1919), 566–70; "$1,000 Reward!"; Aden, Dec. 14, 1874, in "Lingering Hope"; Jenson, 1:499–502; Daniel W. Jones, *Forty Years Among the Indians* (Salt Lake City: Juvenile Instructor Office, 1890), 115–16.

74. Aden to Young, Mar. 14, 1859, Incoming Correspondence, YOF; "$1,000 Reward!"; "Information Wanted," *Valley Tan*, May 17, 1859; Aden to Cumming, Jan. 27, 1859, Cumming Papers; Jones, *Forty Years Among the Indians*, 115–16.

75. Leany Reminiscence, 22; "Notes from the 'Life of John D. Lee,'" *Pioche (NV) Weekly Record*, Mar. 31, 1877; "LC"; "LLC"; *MU*, 280–81; Gibbs, 2, 16–18; R. N. Baskin, *Reminiscences of Early Utah* (Salt Lake City: Tribune-Reporter Printing, 1914), 112.

76. PSHR, Aug. 28, 1857, 2nd sec., 34.

77. James Pearce, JDL1-BT 4:105; JDL1-RT 2:286; Leany Reminiscence, 22.

78. Gibbs, 17, 48–49.

79. Brooks2, 59.

80. Regina M. Schwartz, *The Curse of Cain: The Violent Legacy of Monotheism* (Chicago: University of Chicago Press, 1997), 5.

81. Two impulses lead to the final outburst of violence. "These are, simultaneously, rage and anger at the enemy's alleged attack on the integrity, values, or well-being of the community in question, on the one hand, and successively, or in oscillation, fear and mounting panic that the ethnic enemy is violent, dangerous by nature, and has the capacities and resources to launch an attack and do great harm, on the other.... The two states of collective perception and emotion dialectically act on each other and produce a mounting tension and a heightened mood, which when it explodes may lead to terrible brutalities and acts of destruction." Tambiah, 284.

82. Rosa Brooks, "Good People, Evil Deeds," *Los Angeles Times*, June 9, 2006, also reprinted in "Killings in Iraq by 'Bad Apples'? Probably Not," *Deseret Morning News*, June 18, 2006. These perspectives are those of Yale University psychologist Stanley Milgram, whose famous experiments, conducted in 1961, have been repeatedly confirmed in many cultures.

83. Cited in Lauren Green, "The Problem of Evil: Why Do 'Good' People Do Bad Things," Apr. 11, 2007, Fox News, http://www.foxnews.com/story/o,2933,265314,oo.html (accessed Nov. 7, 2007). See also Philip Zimbardo, *The Lucifer Effect: Understanding How Good People Turn Evil* (New York: Random House, 2007); Staub; Peck.

Chapter 10

1. See Brigham Young and Heber C. Kimball to "the Saints in Parowan and Cedar Cities," [May 1852], Outgoing Correspondence, YOF.

2. Erastus Snow, letter to the editor, Dec. 21, 1852, in *Deseret News*, Dec. 25, 1852.

3. Janet Burton Seegmiller, *A History of Iron County: Community above Self* (Salt Lake City: Utah State Historical Society/Iron County Commission, 1998), 64; TF, 373–81, 409.

4. Christopher J. Arthur, "Records of Christopher J. Arthur, 1860–1900," typescript, 1937, pt. 1, 16, copy at BYU.

5. Hoth, Oct. 2–7, 1856; Cedar Stake Journal, July 29, Aug. 19, 1855, Jan. 13, 27, Feb. 10, Mar. 16, May 4, 1856, William R. Palmer, Collection, Special Collections, Gerald R. Sherratt Library, Southern Utah University, Cedar City, UT. On counsel not to sell grain, see chap. 4, n. 53.

6. Kim S. Whitehead, "William and Elizabeth Tait: A History of Their Life," [18], unpublished family history, copy in MMMRF; *TF*, 317, 325–26, 328, 372, 377, 397; Isaac Chauncey Haight, Journal, 1852–62, May 1, Dec. 1, 1857, photocopy of manuscript, CHL. For the use of the terms "Old Town" and "New Town," see Christopher J. Arthur, AJ2; Daniel S. Macfarlane, AJ2; Elias Morris, statement, Feb. 2, 1892, CM; Clewes; John Henry Willis, JDL1-BT 4:39.

7. Martin Slack and George K. Bowering, dispatch, in "Celebrations of the 24th of July," *Deseret News*, Aug. 19, 1857; Cedar Stake Journal, July 24, 1857, Palmer Collection; John D. Lee to Brigham Young, Nov. 4, 1856, Incoming Correspondence, YOF. For examples of using the slogan "terror to evil doers," see "More of the Doings on the 24th," *Deseret News*, Aug. 8, 1860; Fancher, 136. The biblical reference is Romans 13:3. Young men in Ogden, Utah, carried the slogan on their banner on July 24, 1855. "Anniversaries," *Deseret News*, Aug. 1, 1855.

8. Palmer, 3; JHM, Aug. 2, 1857, 130. Brooks2, 52, has Haight making the statement on Sept. 6, 1857, after the Arkansas company passed through Cedar City. She cites "'Cedar City Ward Records,' now reported to be in the archives of the Latter-day Saints church historian." Bagley, 120, 407, follows Brooks. The record in question, however, was never sent to "the archives of the Latter-day Saints church historian." A set of minutes from the Cedar City Ward for 1857 is in the William R. Palmer collection at Southern Utah University but lacks the quote in question. Palmer reported that Brooks got her information on Haight's speech from him but misdated it:

> Mrs. Brooks...has her meetings mixed. Perhaps I am partly to blame for that for I think it was I who gave her the substance of Haight's speech. The time element was not important to me then, but his speech was. She assumes that this speech was directed at the Fancher party. This is a mistake. The speech was made before the Fanchers were ever heard of. It was not aimed at any traveling party but rather at the coming Johnston's Army.

In the lefthand margin, Palmer wrote that his source was a "Cedar City lost minute Book." William R. Palmer to Dabney Otis Collins, Dec. 16, 1958, Palmer Material, First Presidency General Administration Files. The "lost" minute book may be one burned by Kate Carter, longtime head of the Daughters of Utah Pioneers. See Russell R. Rich, "The Mountain Meadows Massacre," in Russell R. Rich, Collection, BYU; Peter M. Hansen, "The Mountain Meadows Massacre," Feb. 1974, 5, Rich Collection.

9. Smith, Sept. 13, 1857, in "Remarks"; Wells to Johnson, Aug. 13, 1857, Letter Book, p. 97, Nauvoo Legion (Utah) Adj. Gen. Records, 1851–70, CHL.

10. William R. Palmer to Joseph Anderson, Oct. 16, 1959, Palmer Material.

11. See *Acts and Resolutions Passed by the Legislative Assembly of the Territory of Utah, during the Sixth Annual Session, 1856–57* (Salt Lake City: James McKnight, 1857), 19; Gardner, 318–24; George A. Smith, Sept. 13, 1857, in "Remarks," *Deseret News*, Sept. 23, 1857.

12. Higbee, deposition, June 15, 1896, 2, in CM; OIMD; MRIMD; Morris, statement, Feb. 2, 1892, CM; Cedar City Utah Stake, General Minutes, Nov. 6, 1856, CHL.

13. Philip Klingensmith, JDL1-BT 3:41, 45; John W. Bradshaw, JDL1-BT 4:74; Hawley, 15; PSHR, Aug. 28, 1857, 2nd sec., 34.

14. George Powers and P. M. Warn, in "Horrible"; S. B. Honea, in "Outrages"; George B. Davis, in "Letter from San Bernardino," *San Francisco Daily Evening Bulletin*, Nov. 12, 1857; James Pearce, JDL1-BT 4:100–2; *MU*, 219.

15. Joel White, JDL1-BT 4:5, JDL1-PS 4:29–30; Mary S. Campbell, AJ1. According to Harmony resident Benjamin Platt, word of the poisoning had also reached John D. Lee. Benjamin Platt, Reminiscences, 5, typescript, CHL. Rumors, including false rumors of poisoning, have contributed to group violence throughout history. See, e.g., Donald L. Horowitz, *The Deadly Ethnic Riot* (Berkeley: University of California Press, 2001), 74–88; Baumeister, 86–87, 259. Rumors can taint perceptions and become self-fulfilling prophecies. "The bad report that reached Cedar in advance of the company naturally stirred up the anger of the citizens," Mary Campbell claimed. "And when finally the company came along, they behaved every bit as badly as they were reported to have acted in the other settlements through which they had previously passed." Campbell, AJ2; Campbell, AJ1.

16. Campbell, AJ1; Campbell, AJ2. Campbell may have misremembered the sequence of events. Philip Klingensmith, a perpetrator who turned state's evidence, was asked under oath, "Did you have any counsel in which this emigrant train was referred to previous to the arrival of the emigrant train, or previous to their passing through Cedar City?" He replied, "No, sir." JDL1-BT 3:48, JDL1-PS 3:21–22. If Klingensmith was correct, then Haight's statement may have been made not long after the emigrants passed through the city.

17. "Horrible."

18. "BY." Another man later claimed he overheard an early 1870s conversation of John M. Higbee, full of formulaic phrases, in which Higbee admitted a conspiracy between himself, Klingensmith, and Haight to "make some money easily and quickly." Sam Gould, statement, undated, typescript, Juanita Brooks Collection, USHS.

19. Bowering, 230. Evidence on the date of their arrival is conflicting. Mormons situated at Mountain Meadows uniformly recalled that the emigrants arrived there by Saturday evening at the latest. See D. W. Tullis, AJ1; Rachel Hamblin, statement, May 20, 1859, in Carleton, 10; Ellott Willden, AJ2; Corr2. Because the emigrants spent two nights camped between Cedar City and the Meadows, they must have passed through the city no later than Thursday. Lee placed the emigrants' arrival on Wednesday or Thursday. "LC"; "LLC." SAJ puts the emigrants at or near Parowan on Thursday, Sept. 3, meaning they would have arrived in Cedar on Friday. Smith may have kept a daybook in fall 1857 and used it to record dates to which he later added details and

additional comments, but internal evidence indicates that the extant diary was penned after 1861. Also supporting a Friday passage is Philip Klingensmith, JDL1-BT 3:47–48.

20. Bowering, 230; Charles Willden Sr., deposition, Feb. 18, 1882, CM; Chatterley; Fish, 57; Map of Cedar City, AJ1. Bowering's journal recorded that the Arkansas company had between twelve and fourteen wagons. Willden remembered the emigrants having twenty.

21. Philip Klingensmith, JDL1-BT 3:2, 58–59, JDL1-RS 2:19; Argus, open letter to Brigham Young, July 20, 18[71], in "History of Mormonism," *Corinne (UT) Reporter*, July 22, 1871. On the location of Samuel Jackson's farm, see Iron County Recorder, Deeds, 1851–1961, Book A, 138, Series 6205, Utah State Archives, Salt Lake City, UT. At Lee's first trial in 1875, Jackson could not recall the transaction. Samuel Jackson Sr., JDL1-BT 5:327, JDL1-PS 11:2, JDL1-RS 9:27.

22. Fish, 57–58. Fish was reporting what he heard from Stephen Barton in Paragonah on Sept. 11, 1857. See also T. S. W., "Mountain Me[a]dow Massacre," 17, Articles Pertaining to the Mormons in Utah, ca. 1860, CHL.

23. Bowering, 230. Parker2, 11, confirms that the grain was ground by a local miller. See also Argus, open letter to Brigham Young, July 20, 18[71], in "History of Mormonism"; Willden, deposition, Feb. 18, 1882, CM.

24. Bowering, 230; Willden, deposition, Feb. 18, 1882, CM; Pitchforth, Sept. 9, 1857. Additional Mormon reminiscences—most of them hearsay—recount taunts, threats, and near-fights when the emigrants passed through Cedar City. Morris, statement, Feb. 2, 1892, CM; JHM1907; James H. Martineau to Susan [Martineau], May 3, 1876, James Henry Martineau, Collection, CHL; "LC"; "LLC"; *MU*, 218–19; Laban Morrill, JDL2-BT 1:6, 9; Christopher J. Arthur, AJ1; Fish, 57–58.

25. NJ1908; Bowering, 230; Fish, 57–58.

26. Christopher J. Arthur, AJ1. On the location of the store, see Map of Cedar City, AJ1.

27. Annie Elizabeth Hoag, JDL1-BT 4:26–27, JDL1-PS 5:16–17, JDL1-RS 4:12.

28. Annie Elizabeth Hoag, JDL1-BT 4:26, JDL1-PS 5:17, JDL1-RS 4:12; Philip Klingensmith, JDL1-BT 3:3, JDL1-PS 2:34, JDL1-RS 2:19.

29. Ordinance enacted on Jan. 8, 1856, noted in *Acts, Resolutions, and Memorials, Passed by the First Annual, and Special Sessions, of the Legislative Assembly of the Territory of Utah, Begun and Held at Great Salt Lake City, on the 22nd Day of September, A. D., 1851* (Salt Lake City: Brigham H. Young, 1852), 89; "Bill for an Ordinance in Relation to Profanity & Drunkenness," Cedar City Council Ordinance Book, 1853–56, 1900–21, film 497772, FHL; Evelyn K. Jones and York F. Jones, *Mayors of Cedar City* (Cedar City: Southern Utah State College, 1986), 17. Profanity laws originated in early America and continue in some parts of the country today. See, e.g., *The Code of 1650, Being a Compilation of the Earliest Laws and Orders of the General Court of Connecticut . . .* (Hartford: Silas Andrus, 1822), 32; *Laws of the State of New York,*

Passed at the First Meeting of the Eleventh Session of the Legislature of the Said State, 681; Statutes of the State of Ohio...(Columbus: Samuel Medary, 1841), 257, paragraph 128; The Revised Statutes of the State of Missouri...(Jefferson: James Lusk, 1856), 630, sec. 30. On the Mormon practice of fining emigrants for perceived offenses, see Unruh, 326; J. W. Goodell, letter to the editor, in Portland Oregonian, Apr. 3, 1852, published in David L. Bigler, ed., A Winter with the Mormons: The 1852 Letters of Jotham Goodell (Salt Lake City: Tanner Trust Fund, J. Willard Marriott Library, University of Utah, 2001), 70–71; Diary of Dr. Thomas Flint: California to Maine and Return in 1851–1855, 2nd ed. (Hollister, CA: Evening Free Lance, n.d.), 79.

30. "LC"; "LLC."

31. Morris, statement, Feb. 2, 1892, CM; Notes regarding Mountain Meadows Massacre, undated, AJ1.

32. Campbell, AJ1; Morris, statement, Feb. 2, 1892, in CM. Elias Morris and Daniel Macfarlane later claimed the emigrants also insulted children and other women in Cedar City. Morris, statement, Feb. 2, 1892, in CM; Daniel S. Macfarlane, AJ2.

33. Richard E. Nisbett and Dov Cohen, Culture of Honor: The Psychology of Violence in the South (Boulder, CO: Westview Press, 1996), 5; Bertram Wyatt-Brown, Southern Honor: Ethics and Behavior in the Old South (New York: Oxford University Press, 1982), 53–54. In an 1872 interview about the massacre, John D. Lee said that an emigrant man insulted "the widow Evans, this side o' Corn Creek," and that "her folks got out with guns and swore revenge on the whole outfit." Beadle1. "The widow Evans" appears to be a pseudonym for Barbara Morris. That the published interview employs pseudonyms becomes obvious from its use of "the widow Tomlinson" for a wife of John A. Ray whose arm became infected and crippled after skinning cattle. See Ray.

34. Morris, statement, Feb. 2, 1892, CM; Christopher J. Arthur, AJ1; Annie Elizabeth Hoag, JDL1-BT 4:26, JDL1-PS 5:16–17, JDL1-RS 4:12; "LC"; "LLC"; PSHR, Sept. 7, 1857, 2nd sec., 34; Philip Klingensmith, JDL1-BT 3:3, JDL1-PS 2:34, JDL1-RS 2:19; Notes regarding the Mountain Meadows Massacre, undated, AJ1; MU, 219.

35. See Mary H. White, AJ1; John Hamilton Jr., JDL1-BT 5:313–14, JDL1-RS 9:15–18. MU, 219, said that "after leaving Cedar City the emigrants camped by the company, or cooperative field, just below Cedar City, and burned a large portion of the fencing, leaving the crops open to the large herds of stock in the surrounding country." According to TF, 169, the cooperative fields were west of the city.

36. Pitchforth, Sept. 9, 1857. Pitchforth was recording news conveyed by Mormon expressman James Haslam, who was riding north to Salt Lake City. For testimony that Bishop Klingensmith was in Cedar City and saw the emigrants, see Philip Klingensmith, JDL1-BT 3:2, 47–48, JDL1-PS 2:34, JDL1-RS 2:19; Joel White, JDL1-BT 3:120–21.

37. Cedar City Ward, Parowan Stake, Relief Society Minute Book, Sept. 10, 1857, CHL.

38. "Church History," *Times and Seasons* 3, no. 9 (1842): 709; Revelation recorded July 12, 1843, published in *Doctrine and Covenants of the Church of Jesus Christ of Latter-day Saints* (Salt Lake City: Deseret News, 1876), 425–27 (current D&C 132:19–27).

39. Woodruff, Mar. 15, 1856.

40. On the role of rumors in sparking violence, see Donald L. Horowitz, *The Deadly Ethnic Riot* (Berkeley: University of California Press, 2001), 74–88; Tambiah, 281–82.

41. Martineau to Susan, May 3, 1876, Martineau Collection; JHM1907; Ordinance for creating a police force for Cedar City, Aug. 4, 1855, Ordinance Book No. 1, Cedar City, quoted in Jones and Jones, *Mayors of Cedar City*, 16.

42. Chatterley.

43. JHM1907; Martineau to Susan, May 3, 1876, Martineau Collection. Martineau left Parowan to scout for U.S. troops on Friday, Sept. 4, after the council meeting had taken place. JHM, Sept. 4, 1857; Joseph Fish, Reminiscence and Journal, Aug. 26–Sept. 8, 1857, Joseph Fish, Collection, CHL; Fish, 55–57.

44. George A. Smith to Geo. C. Bates, November 22, 1874, Letterpress Copybook, Bleak Papers, 1861–1989, CHL. Smith said John D. Lee shared Haight's contempt for Dame.

45. Staub, 237.

46. Baumeister, 254.

47. Brigham Young, Discourse, Aug. 16, 1857, reported by George D. Watt, in Historian's Office, Reports of Speeches, CHL.

48. E. H. Blackburn, in PGM, Aug. 30, 1857; Elias Smith, Journal, Aug. 11, 1857, CHL; JHM, Aug. 24, Sept. 4, 1857, 133; Fish, 53; James C. Snow, remarks, in PGM, Aug. 30, 1857.

49. Diarist Samuel Pitchforth recorded that news of the speech had reached Nephi by Aug. 19, 1857. Pitchforth, Aug. 19, 22, 1857.

50. *MU*, 219; Ellott Willden, AJ2; Ellott Willlden2, AJ2; Ellott Willden, AJ1. *The Oxford English Dictionary*, 2nd ed., defines *brush* as "a forcible rush, a hostile collision or encounter."

51. Thomas T. Willis, JDL1-BT 4:32, JDL1-PS 5:21–22, JDL1-RS 4:15. For William Willis's status as a veteran, see Norma Baldwin Ricketts, *The Mormon Battalion: U.S. Army of the West, 1846–1848* (Logan: Utah State University Press, 1996), 21, 48, 70, 79, 240–44, 249. As a member of the Mormon Battalion in the Mexican War, Willis trained for battle but never saw any real action.

52. Conversation with Samuel Knight, recorded in Cannon, June 13, 1895; Ellott Willden, AJ1.

53. Hoth, Oct. 13–15, 1856.

54. Holt, 19–22, 39–42, 48–51, 70–71; Knack, 34–36, 39–47; *Nuwuvi*, 39–42, 48–51, 70–71; Ned Blackhawk, *Violence over the Land: Indian Empires in the*

Early American West (Cambridge, MA: Harvard University Press, 2006), 7, 57–58, 84–86, 108–11, 120, 136, 141–43, 148; Carling I. Malouf and John M. Findlay, "Euro-American Impact Before 1870," in William C. Sturtevant, ed., *Handbook of North American Indians*, vol. 11, *Great Basin* (Washington, D.C.: Smithsonian Institution, 1986), 506; George Q. Cannon, Journal, Nov. 3, 1849, in Michael N. Landon, ed., *To California in '49*, vol. 1, *The Journals of George Q. Cannon*, ed. Adrian W. Cannon and Richard E. Turley Jr. (Salt Lake City: Deseret Book, 1999), 41; George A. Smith to Franklin D. Richards, Apr. 19, 1854, reprinted in "Foreign Intelligence—Deseret," *Millennial Star* 16 (1854): 584.

55. Ardis E. Parshall, "'Pursue, Retake & Punish': The 1857 Santa Clara Ambush," *Utah Historical Quarterly* 73 (Winter 2005): 64–86; [Brigham Young] to Aaron Johnson, Feb. 3, 1857, Letterpress Copybook 3:352, YOF; Brigham Young to Bishops & Presidents South, Feb. 6, 1857, Letterpress Copybook 3:387, YOF; Wayne Gard, *Frontier Justice* (Norman: University of Oklahoma Press, 1949), 190, 192.

56. Parshall, "'Pursue, Retake & Punish,'" 74–75, 74–75n24, 79.

57. Chad Foulger and Chad M. Orton, "February 1857, Attack on John Tobin," Oct. 18, 2007, MMMRF.

58. Ellott Willden, AJ1.

59. Ellott Willden, AJ2; Ellott Willden2, AJ2; Unattributed notes, likely from discussion with Ellott Willden, AJ1.

60. "LC"; "LLC"; OIMD; MRIMD. Lee dated his visit with Haight as Saturday, Sept. 5.

61. Rachel Lee, interview, Dec. 27, 1874, in "Mountain Meadow Massacre: The Herald's Special Correspondent Interviews the Noted Rachel, Wife of John D. Lee," *Salt Lake Daily Herald*, Jan. 1, 1875.

62. After Lee's arrest in 1874, Rachel Lee claimed that Haight had Lee "thrown out of all offices—church, territory, county and militia." Lee, interview, Dec. 27, 1874, in "Correspondent Interviews the Noted Rachel." Though the people at Harmony had voted to remove Lee as their presiding elder in 1856, in Sept. 1857 Lee was still a militia major and a government-appointed farmer to the Indians. Documents of the period also show Haight defending Lee and interacting amicably with him. John D. Lee to Brigham Young, Aug. 22, 1856, Incoming Correspondence, YOF; Isaac C. Haight to Heber C. Kimball, Aug. 20, 1856, Divorce and Family Difficulties Files, YOF; HBM, July 4–5, 24, 1857; JHM, Aug. 16, 1857, 132.

63. Haight Journal, 1852–62, Mar. 4–8, 1856.

64. Ellott Willden, AJ2; Mary S. Campbell, AJ1; Mary S. Campbell, AJ2; D. W. Tullis, AJ1; Ellott Willden, AJ1; McGlashan; Whitney, 1:699.

65. Ellott Willden, AJ1. Jenson routinely omits the "e" in "the" in his field notes. We have supplied them throughout the book for readability.

66. Ibid.

67. Mary S. Campbell, AJ2; Mary S. Campbell, AJ1.

68. Conversation with Samuel Knight, in Cannon, June 13, 1895; Samuel Knight, AJ1. On Knight's position as counselor, see Santa Clara Ward, St. George Stake, Manuscript History and Historical Reports, 1857, CHL.

69. Knack, 2, 10–17.

70. PKS; Philip Klingensmith, JDL1-BT 3:5–6, JDL1-PS 2:35–36, JDL1-RS 3:20–21; OIMD; MRIMD. On Klingensmith's zealousness, see Laban Morrill, JDL2-BT 1:9; Ellott Willden, AJ1. White testified that he and Klingensmith left the day after the emigrants passed through Cedar City. See Joel White, JDL1-BT 3:120–21, 4:3.

71. Joel White, JDL2-BT 1:15. Compare similar words in White, JDL1-BT 3:120–21; Philip Klingensmith, JDL1-BT 3:5, 69. Under close questioning at Lee's trial, Klingensmith virtually conceded that the Indians did not need to be pacified because they were not stirred up in the first place. Philip Klingensmith, JDL1-BT 3:50–51.

72. Joel White, JDL2-BT 1:15–16; Joel White, JDL1-BT 3:121–22; Philip Klingensmith, JDL1-BT 3:5–6. See also PKS.

73. *MU*, 217–18.

74. "LC"; "LLC"; *MU*, 226.

75. Joel White, JDL1-BT 4:3–4; Joel White, JDL2-BT 1:16, 28; Philip Klingensmith, JDL1-BT 3:6.

76. Joel White, JDL1-BT 3:122.

77. Richard S. Robinson, JDL1-BT 5:320. Robinson did acknowledge receiving a letter that had been delivered to Amos Thornton, but it was the letter delivered the following week by Joseph Clewes. See Richard S. Robinson, JDL1-BT 5:320, 324; Clewes; Richard S. Robinson, AJ1.

78. Joel White, JDL1-BT 3:122–23; Philip Klingensmith, JDL1-BT 3:54.

79. Joel White, JDL2-BT 1:16, 18; Joel White, JDL1-BT 4:4; Philip Klingensmith, JDL1-BT 3:6; PKS.

80. Joel White, JDL1-BT 3:120.

81. PKS; Klingensmith, JDL1-BT 3:6–7.

82. White, JDL1-BT 4:5–6.

83. *MU*, 218.

84. "LC"; "LLC"; *MU*, 218–19. In *MU*, 218, the location of the meeting is changed to the iron works. On the location of Haight's house, see Philip Klingensmith, JDL1-BT 3:7, 40.

85. *MU*, 219–20; "LC"; "LLC."

86. Staub, xi, xiv, 5.

87. *MU*, 220. See also "LC"; "LLC."

88. See John D. Lee, in PGM, Sept. 27, 1857; Woodruff, Sept. 29, 1857; John D. Lee to Brigham Young, Nov. 20, 1857, Incoming Correspondence, YOF; David Tullis and [Albert] Hamblin, interviews, Apr. 1859, in J. Forney to A. B. Greenwood, Aug. 1859, in SDoc42, 76–78; Carleton, 8–15.

89. Morris, statement, Feb. 2, 1892, CM. See also NJ1908; NJ1910.

90. *MU*, 218–20. However, "LC" merely says that he "did just as [he] was ordered."

91. OIMD; MRIMD; *Acts and Resolutions Passed by the Legislative Assembly of the Territory of Utah, during the Sixth Annual Session, 1856–7* (Salt Lake City: James McKnight, 1857), 32, sec. 14.

92. See, e.g., *MC*, 1:181–82, Sept. 15, 1858. Haight and Lee "were both like bull dogs, too proud to yield." *Journals*, 216, June 12, 1859.

93. *MU*, 221.

94. Extracts from Jacob Hamblin's journal, in Jacob Hamblin to Brigham Young, Nov. 13, 1871, General Office Files, President's Office Files, YOF; Jacob Hamblin, statement, Nov. 28, 1871, General Office Files, President's Office Files, YOF.

95. Annie Elizabeth Hoag, JDL1-PS 5:16–17, JDL1-RS 4:12, JDL1-BT 4:26–27; *MU*, 220. See also "LC"; "LLC."

96. Annie Elizabeth Hoag, JDL1-BT 4:26, JDL1-PS 5:16, JDL1-RS 4:11–12; Mary S. Campbell, AJ1.

97. Baumeister, 254.

98. John D. Lee to Brigham Young, Sept. 24, 1853, Incoming Correspondence, YOF.

99. Smith, Sept. 13, 1857, in "Remarks."

100. "LC"; "LLC"; *MU*, 219–20.

101. *MU*, 226; Mary S. Campbell, AJ1.

102. Wells to Johnson, Aug. 13, 1857, Letter Book, 97, Nauvoo Legion (Utah) Adj. Gen. Records.

103. Woodruff, Sept. 1, 1857; Brigham Young, President's Office Journal, Sept. 1, 1857, YOF; *DBY*, 71, Sept. 1, 1857; Huntington, Sept. 1, 1857.

104. HOJ, Aug. 25, Sept. 1, 1857; Huntington, Sept. 1, 1857.

105. Huntington, [Aug. 31], 1857.

106. Ibid., Sept. 1, 1857.

107. Bagley, 112–14.

108. Ibid., 379. See also Brooks2, 41–42. Bagley also places into his narrative the report that James Gemmell, a frontier adventurer and Mormon convert, was in Young's office on Sept. 1 and overheard Hamblin tell Young of the misconduct of members of the Arkansas party, whom he had met at Corn Creek while traveling with George A. Smith. "If he (Brigham) were in command of the Legion he would wipe them out," Young supposedly said. See Bagley, 285. To give credibility to the incident, Bagley suggests Gemmell may have tried to blackmail Young and was forced to flee from Utah in order to save his life. The details in the sources he gives, however, are contradictory, and some appear to be anachronistic. See Richard E. Turley Jr., "Parley P. Pratt and the Mountain Meadows Massacre," symposium paper, Religion & Reaction: The Life, Times, and Legacy of Parley P. Pratt, Fort Smith, AR, Apr. 21, 2007.

109. See, e.g., Furniss, 139, 142–44.

110. Huntington, Sept. 1, 1857.

111. D. B. Huntington, Voucher No. 17, Sept. 11, 1857, Superintendent's Vouchers, Superintendent of Indian Affairs Files, YOF; U.S. Congress,

House, *Accounts of Brigham Young, Superintendent of Indian Affairs in Utah Territory*, 37th Cong., 2nd sess., 1862, H. Doc. 29, 85.

112. William H. Hooper, Voucher No. 27, Sept. 12, 1857, Superintendent's Vouchers, Superintendent of Indian Affairs Files, YOF; House, *Accounts of Brigham Young*, Doc. 29, 90.

113. Both Dimick Huntington (Huntington, Sept. 10, 1857) and Wilford Woodruff (Woodruff, Sept. 16, 1857) mention Tutsegavits's ordination, but George A. Smith wrote in a letter on "Sunday evening," Sept. 13, "We ordained Tutsegabbotts an Elder this Evening." George A. Smith to William H. Dame, Aug. [Sept.] 12[–13], William H. Dame, Papers, CHL.

114. Jacob Hamblin, Journal, 1854–58, 82, Jacob Hamblin, Papers, CHL.

115. Woodruff, Sept. 16, 1857.

116. "Lee Trial."

117. Hurt, 203.

118. *MU*, 220; "LC"; "LLC"; Annie Elizabeth Hoag, JDL1-RS 4:12, JDL1-PS 5:16, JDL1-BT 4:26.

119. *MU*, 226; "Execution of Lee!" *Pioche Weekly Record*, Mar. 24, 1877.

120. *MU*, 226; "Execution of Lee!"

Chapter 11

1. Washington County Court Records, Book A, 1854–72, 7, June 2, 1856, film 484840, FHL; Knack, 10–11.

2. D. W. Tullis, AJ1.

3. Ellott Willden, AJ1; Mary S. Campbell, AJ2; McGlashan.

4. Tullis, interview with Jacob Forney, Apr. 13, 1859, in Jacob Forney to A. B. Greenwood, Aug. 1859, SDoc42, 76; Tullis, AJ1; McGlashan; Rogers. Rogers mistakenly identifies Tullis as Carl Shirts.

5. Rachel Hamblin, statement, May 20, 1859, in Carleton, 10.

6. Samuel Knight, JDL2-BT 1:32.

7. Samuel Knight, JDL2-BT 1:19; William Hartley, *Stand by My Servant Joseph: The Story of the Joseph Knight Family and the Restoration* (Salt Lake City: Deseret Book and Joseph Fielding Smith Institute, 2003), 198–99, 424–25; Arthur Knight Hafen, "Samuel Knight, 1832–1910: Frontiersman, Indian Missionary, Early Southern Utah Pioneerman and Churchman," in Joyce Wittwer Whittaker, *History of Santa Clara Utah: "A Blossom in the Desert"* (St. George, UT: Santa Clara Historical Society, 2003), 133–39; Robert Hafen Briggs, "Samuel Knight and Events Incident to the Utah War, 1857–1858: A Preliminary Study" (unpublished paper written for the Swiss Days Celebration and Samuel Knight Reunion, Sept. 21–23, 2001, Santa Clara, UT), 3, copy in MMMRF; Robert Hafen Briggs, "Researching Samuel Knight: A Preliminary Study" (unpublished paper written for the Swiss Days Celebration and Samuel Knight Reunion, Sept. 21–23, 2001, Santa Clara, UT), 7, 10, copy in MMMRF; Robert Hafen Briggs, "The Missing Memoir of Samuel Knight: A Preliminary Study" (unpublished

paper written for the Swiss Days Celebration and Samuel Knight Reunion, Sept. 21–23, 2001, Santa Clara, Utah), 5, copy in MMMRF. On the cool climate of the Meadows and surrounding area, see Pearson H. Corbett, *Jacob Hamblin: The Peacemaker* (Salt Lake City: Deseret Book, 1952), 95–96.

8. Conversation with Samuel Knight, recorded in Cannon, June 13, 1895; Samuel Knight, JDL2-BT 1:19, 32; Samuel Knight, AJ1. According to Cannon's account of his interview with Knight, "some of the emigrants were very boastful and seemed to be filled with a wicked spirit."

9. Albert Hamblin, statement, May 20, 1859, in Carleton, 12–13.

10. Marcy, 57, 61–62, 67–68, 133.

11. Forney to Greenwood, Aug. 1859, SDoc42, 78; McGlashan; Jacob Hamblin, statement, in Carleton, 6. Overlooking the area of the emigrants' campsite on Sept. 11, 2007, Richard Wilson, a cattle rancher and third-great grandson of Alexander Fancher, observed that the draw would be the ideal place to keep cattle for the night. Richard Wilson to Barbara Jones Brown, Oct. 18, 2007, email.

12. Forney to Greenwood, Aug. 1859, SDoc42, 78; J. Forney to Elias Smith, May 5, 1859, in "Visit of the Superintendent of Indian Affairs to Southern Utah," *Salt Lake City Deseret News*, May 11, 1859; J. Forney to Kirk Anderson, May 5, 1859, in *Salt Lake City Valley Tan*, May 10, 1859; Shirts.

13. McGlashan; Parker2, 12; Stenhouse, 427.

14. Rachel Hamblin, statement, May 20, 1859, in Carleton, 10.

15. Ellott Willden, AJ2; Ellott Willden, AJ1; Mary S. Campbell, AJ2.

16. Ellott Willden, AJ2; Whitney, 1:699; "Mountain Meadows," notes of discussion with an unnamed informant, undated, AJ1.

17. Ellott Willden, AJ2.

18. D. W. Tullis, AJ1.

19. Conversation with Knight, in Cannon, June 13, 1895; Samuel Knight, AJ1.

20. Conversation with Knight, in Cannon, June 13, 1895; Knight; Samuel Knight, AJ1; Samuel Knight, JDL2-BT 1:23.

21. "Gilbert Morse," *Salt Lake Daily Tribune*, Sept. 28, 1876; Benjamin Platt, Reminiscences, 1899–1905, typescript, 5–6, CHL; Annie Elizabeth Hoag, JDL1-PS 5:16.

22. Annie Elizabeth Hoag, JDL1-BT 4:25–27, JDL1-PS 5:15–17, JDL1-RS 4:11–12; HBM, [Sept. 6], 1857; *MU*, 219.

23. Annie Elizabeth Hoag, JDL1-RS 4:12, JDL1-PS 5:17, JDL1-BT 4:25–27. On Hoag's relationship to Peter Shirts see, "The Lee Trial," *Pioche (NV) Daily Record*, July 29, 1875; "Chronology of Peter Shirts," Nov. 1856, in Mary Elizabeth Robinson Adams, Compiled information on Peter Shirts, ca. 1950–60, CHL; William W. Bishop, Closing argument, JDL1-PS 12:39.

24. Chatterley; "Gilbert Morse."

25. Shirts.

26. Chatterley.

27. Gibbs, 53–54. Comanche, born around 1830, was living in the "Indian Village located in the Suburbs of Cedar City" when the census taker came

through in June 1880. Utah, Iron County, Cedar City, 1880 U.S. Census, Population Schedule, 375.

28. George W. Armstrong to Brigham Young, Aug. 29, 1857, Incoming Correspondence, YOF; Huntington, Sept. 1, 1857, CHL; Jacob Hamblin, Journal, 1854–57, 81–82, in Jacob Hamblin, Papers, CHL; JH, Sept. 1, 1857. Cf. James Lynch, affidavit, July 27, 1859, enclosed in S. H. Montgomery to A. B. Greenwood, Aug. 17, 1859, USBIA.

29. HBM, [Sept.] 6, 1857.

30. "Gilbert Morse"; Platt Reminiscences.

31. Hoag said she believed most of the men from Harmony accompanied "John D. Lee and the Indians" as they left the fort. Annie Elizabeth Hoag, JDL1-BT 4:27. Other witnesses identify only Lee and Shirts as leaving with the Indians. In addition, men who were at the Meadows during the week of the massacre gave the names of more than fifty participants, but the only three Harmony residents identified were Shirts, Lee, and his Indian ward, Lemuel.

32. "LC"; "LLC."

33. D. W. Tullis, AJ1; Whitney, 1:699–700.

34. James Pearce, JDL1-BT 4:100.

35. William Young, JDL1-RS 4:30–32, JDL1-BT 4:56–57, JDL1-PS 5:41; "Gilbert Morse."

36. Hawley, 15. Hawley arrived in Parowan no later than Aug. 28 when the PSHR, 2nd sec., 34, records a piece of news that he brought from Salt Lake City. Given his speed, it is unlikely he knew about events at Corn Creek.

37. William Young, JDL1-BT 4:56–57.

38. Elias Morris, statement, Feb. 2, 1892, CM; Laban Morrill, JDL2-BT 1:3–4, 6–9; Philip Klingensmith, JDL1-BT 3:4–5; Joseph Sudweeks, "Concerning Myself: The Life of Laban Morrill," typescript, 10, in MMMRF; NJ1917; Mary H. White, AJ1. Sudweeks includes a parenthetical statement about Indians being present, which may be an editorial addition to Morrill's original statement. On the composition of the Cedar City high council, see CSM; Isaac C. Haight to Erastus Snow, June 9, 1855, in *St. Louis Luminary*, Aug. 18, 1855. Elias Morris places the meeting on "Sunday morning." Morris also incorrectly identifies Samuel McMurdy as one of Klingensmith's counselors. McMurdy had been released in Oct. 1856, and Whittaker, his replacement, was serving as Klingensmith's counselor in Sept. 1857. Philip Klingensmith, JDL1-BT 3:40; Cedar City Stake, General Minutes 1856, Oct. 19, 1856, CHL.

39. Gibbs, 22; Sudweeks, "Life of Laban Morrill," 10, 16–17, MMMRF.

40. CSM, 61.

41. Laban Morrill, JDL2-BT 1:4, 9, 15.

42. Ibid., JDL2-BT 1:3–4, 6; Sudweeks, "Life of Laban Morrill," 10, MMMRF.

43. Morris, statement, Feb. 2, 1892, CM; Philip Klingensmith, JDL1-BT 3:4–5, JDL1-PS 2:35; Laban Morrill, JDL2-PS 2:15–17, 18–19, JDL2-BT 1:6, 8–9; NJ1917.

44. Sudweeks, "Life of Laban Morrill," 10, MMMRF; Laban Morrill, JDL2-BT 1:3–4, 6.

45. Laban Morrill, JDL2-BT 1:10–11, JDL2-PS 2:20–21.

46. JHM1907.

47. Morris, statement, Feb. 2, 1892, CM; Laban Morrill, JDL2-BT 1:6–7, 9–11, JDL2-PS 2:15–17, 19–21; Philip Klingensmith, JDL1-BT 3:4–5; NJ1917.

48. Morris, statement, Feb. 2, 1892, CM; Philip Klingensmith, JDL1-BT 3:4–5.

49. See Mary S. Campbell, AJ1; *MU*, 226; Daniel S. Macfarlane, AJ2; William C. Stewart to Wilford Woodruff and Council, Nov. 1, 1890, in Wilford Woodruff, General Correspondence Files, 1887–98, CHL; William Barton, AJ1; Morris, statement, Feb. 2, 1892, CM.

50. Laban Morrill, JDL2-BT 1:9.

51. Philip Klingensmith, JDL1-BT 3:4.

52. Laban Morrill, JDL2-PS 2:16–18, JDL2-BT 1:6–8. Morrill probably had similar feelings to those of his neighbor, Nephi Johnson, who was not at the meeting but told Haight to put off attacking the train "until He Rec[eived] Word from President Young for I was satisfied What His Answer Would Be." NJ1910.

53. Laban Morrill, JDL2-BT 1:6–8.

54. The telegraph would not reach southern Utah for another decade. John C. Clowes to Brigham Young, Feb. 18, 1867, in Historian's Office, History of the Church, manuscript, 1867, 175–78, CHL.

55. Sudweeks, "Life of Laban Morrill," 12, MMMRF. In another version of Sudweeks, "Life of Laban Morrill," Daniel Macfarlane and Joseph H. Smith are the names given of the men who left early. Liston, another high council member who later claimed to oppose Haight, reported that he felt the same danger. "But the Lord showed me my way and I walked in it, and he preserved me," Liston said, without giving details. Commodore Perry Liston, Autobiography, photocopy of typescript, 6, 7, BYU.

56. Laban Morrill, JDL2-BT 1:6.

57. Willden saw the two men early Monday morning at the Meadows. Ellott Willden, AJ2. See also Clewes. White would later conflate this mission with his earlier mission to stir up the Indians. Joel White, JDL1-BT 3:120–23, 4:3–6, JDL2-BT 1:15–18, JDL1-PS 4:18–21, JDL1-RS 3:26–29.

58. John M. Higbee, affidavit, June 15, 1896, 4, CM.

59. Whitney, 1:699–700; Ellott Willden, AJ2; Gibbs, 53–54.

60. Unattributed notes, likely from discussion with Ellott Willden, AJ1.

61. Gibbs, 53–54. Lee's journals are full of his dreams and interpretations. See, for example, *MC*, 1:61, 148, 151–53, 205, July 18, 1848, Feb. 5, 19, 1858, Mar. 30, 1859.

62. See, for example, Bull Valley Snort, statement, Feb. 1894, CM; *CHC*, 4:152; Leland H. Creer, *Utah and the Nation* (Seattle: University of Washington Press, 1929), 201–2; David S. King, *Mountain Meadows Massacre: A Search for Perspective* (Washington, D.C.: Potomac Corral of the Westerners, 1970),

13. "Bull Valley Snort" is a pseudonym for John M. Higbee, who wrote his account of the massacre in 1894 while evading prosecution.

63. *MU*, 226–27; "Lee's Confession," *New York Herald*, Mar. 22, 1877; "LC"; "LLC"; "Execution of Lee!" *Pioche Weekly Record*, Mar. 24, 1877; Beadle 1. Lee was probably also the person responsible for falsifying the county court minutes that showed him at Harmony doing judicial duties on the same day. Washington County Court Records, Book A, 1854–72, 23, Sept. 7, 1857, film 484840, FHL.

64. Shirts; Samuel Knight, AJ1; Samuel Knight, JDL2-BT 1:20–21. As early as 1853, one observer noted that the Paiutes at Harmony "appear to be perfectly under the control of Major J D Lee...They reverence Colonel J D Lee as the Mormon Chief & are willing to obey him." William Wall, Report "of a Detachment of the Nauvoo Legion Cavalry on the Expedition, to the extreme Southern Settlements of the Territory of Utah," Apr. 24–May 11, 1853, Utah Territorial Militia Records, Series 2210, Utah State Archives, Salt Lake City, UT. On the possible participation of other white men, see note 77 below.

65. Shirts; McGlashan. See also S. N. Carvalho, *Incidents of Travel and Adventure in the Far West; with Col. Fremont's Last Expedition* (New York: Derby & Jackson, 1857), 176.

66. Beadle 1; Hamblin, statement, in Carleton, 8. For Paiute use of skin paints, see William Bright, ed., *The Collected Works of Edward Sapir*, vol. 10 (Berlin: Mouton de Gruyter, 1992), 817; James G. Bleak, Annals of the Southern Utah Mission, ca. 1898–1907, 34, CHL. For the Indians at the massacre being painted, see John Hamilton Sr. and John Hamilton Jr., JDL1-BT 5:311, 318; William Young, JDL1-BT 4:60.

67. Beadle 1; Shirts; Jacob Hamblin, statement, in Carleton, 8; Terry, 48–49.

68. Shirts; Beadle 1; Jacob Hamblin, statement, in Carleton, 8.

69. Beadle 1; Jacob Hamblin, statement, in Carleton, 8; Shirts.

70. "Lee's Confession," *New York Herald*, Mar. 22, 1877; "Execution of Lee!"; *MU*, 226–27; Jacob Hamblin, statement, in Carleton, 8; McGlashan.

71. "Children"; McGlashan.

72. "LC"; "LLC"; NJ1909; Nephi Johnson, JDL2-BT 1:45; Philip Klingensmith, JDL1-BT 3:29, 98, JDL1-PS 3:9, JDL1-RS 2:37; James Pearce, JDL1-BT 4:114; Joel White, JDL1-BT 4:14; Jacob Hamblin, statement, in Carleton, 8; McGlashan; Palmer, 8. Klingensmith called the Indians Bill and Tom. Each man was hit in the thigh, "not an inch difference in the location of the wounds." McGlashan; Shirts.

73. Terry, 49. See also Rogers. Rea, 28–45, recorded Terry's account without the edits of the "professional writer," and did not include this language.

74. Jacob Hamblin, statement, in Carleton, 8; Carleton, 30; Rogers.

75. Rachel and Albert Hamblin, statements, May 20, 1859, in Carleton, 11, 13.

76. Elliott Willden, AJ1; Elliott Willden, AJ2; "LC"; "LLC."

77. The weight of evidence suggests Lee was the only white man among the attackers but is not conclusive. Lee's co-conspirators in the killings later in the week admitted their presence at the final massacre but said Lee was the

only white in the Monday assault. See, e.g., Corr1. In 1874, Lee's wife Rachel claimed that four friends of "nerve, courage and discretion" had secretly gone to the Meadows with her husband, and Lee reiterated this detail just before his death. Rachel Lee, interview, Dec. 27, 1874, in "Mountain Meadow Massacre: The Herald's Special Correspondent Interviews the Noted Rachel, Wife of John D. Lee," *Salt Lake Daily Herald*, Jan. 1, 1875; "The Lee Execution," *New York Herald*, Mar. 25, 1877. The identity of these four has been a matter of speculation but might include Willden and his fellows at Hamblin's ranch that morning, though Lee never said that they actually assisted in the attack. Another possibility is that men from Harmony were with Lee at the time of the first attack and returned to Harmony with some of the emigrants' best horses before the men from Washington and Cedar City arrived later in the week. JDL1-BT 4:12–13; NJ1908. Deputy William H. Rogers published an account in 1860 that purported to rely on a confession from an unidentified participant. It maintained that "a large number" of whites from Cedar City and other settlements were assigned to go to the Meadows for the Monday morning attack, where they painted and disguised themselves as Indians. See Rogers. Rogers's story may be a conflation of information in Carleton and Cradlebaugh that hinges on what Paiute headman Jackson told officers who confronted him in 1859. Jackson, however, was not present for the Monday attack, and his account conflicts with the earliest known Paiute testimony. Hurt, 203.

78. Elliott Willden, AJ2.

79. Ibid.; "LC"; "LLC"; Elliott Willden2, AJ2; Elliott Willden, AJ1; Philip Klingensmith, JDL1-BT 3:77; Beadle1.

80. Rogers; Jacob Hamblin, statement, in Carleton, 8; Forney to Greenwood, Aug. 1859, in SDoc42, 78; Forney, 371; Forney to Smith, May 5, 1859, in "Visit of the Superintendent of Indian Affairs"; Forney to Anderson, May 5, 1859, in *Valley Tan*, May 10, 1859; "LC"; "LLC"; "Execution of Lee!"; *MU*, 230; McGlashan; "Cates"; JHM1907.

81. Parker2, 12; Mitchell, 10–11, 15, 18; Whitney, 1:700–1; *MU*, 240.

82. Terry, 48, 94–95; "Children"; McGlashan.

83. Beadle1; Orson Welcome Huntsman, Diary, Jan. 20, 1898, 220, CHL; John W. Van Cott, *Utah Place Names* (Salt Lake City: University of Utah Press, 1990), 54–55; "Mountain Meadow Massacre," *Daily Union-Vedette*, July 27, 1866. See also Orson W. Huntsman, *A Brief History of Shoal Creek, Hebron and Enterprise* (St. George, UT: Dixie College, 1929), 3.

84. "LC"; "LLC."

85. *MU*, 227.

86. "LC"; "LLC"; Shirts. See also Nephi Johnson, JDL2-BT 1:45; Jacob Hamblin, JDL2-BT 1:87, JDL2-PS 3:3; Knight; Samuel Knight, AJ1; Clewes; *MU*, 229.

87. "Mountain Meadows," notes of discussion with an unnamed informant, undated, AJ1.

88. "Execution of Lee!"; *MU*, 226–27; "LC"; "LLC"; Conversation with Samuel Knight, in Cannon, June 13, 1895; Samuel Knight, AJ1.

89. Knight; Samuel Knight, AJ1; Conversation with Samuel Knight, in Cannon, June 13, 1895; "LC"; "LLC." In his 1904 affidavit, Knight recalled that the meeting occurred at 10:00 p.m. In earlier testimony at Lee's second trial, Knight remembered the encounter as near dusk. Samuel Knight, JDL2-BT 1:20–21. On Leavitt being a counselor in the Southern Indian Mission presidency, see Santa Clara Ward, St. George Stake, Manuscript History and Historical Reports, 1857, CHL.

90. Samuel Knight, AJ1.

91. "Mountain Meadows," notes of discussion with an unnamed informant, undated, AJ1; Samuel Knight, JDL2-BT 1:20–22; Samuel Knight, AJ1; Knight; Conversation with Samuel Knight, in Cannon, June 13, 1895. Albert Hamblin said, "Dudley Leavett came up from Santa Clara in the night, while the emigrants were camped here." Carleton, 13.

92. *MU*, 227–28; "LC"; "LLC"; "Lee's Confession," *New York Herald*, Mar. 22, 1877; "Execution of Lee!"; Samuel Knight, JDL2-BT 1:22.

93. James Haslam, JDL2-BT 1:11–12. Haslam, 3, said, "Word came up to Mr. Haight from John D. Lee, stating that the Indians had got the emigrants corralled, on the Mountain Meadows, and wanted to know what ~~they~~ he should do."

94. Clewes; Ronald W. Walker, "'Save the Emigrants': Joseph Clewes on the Mountain Meadows Massacre," *BYU Studies* 42, no. 1 (2003): 140–41.

95. "Made Gallant Ride to Prevent Massacre: Death of James H. Haslam, Who Carried Dispatches at Time of Mountain Meadow Horror," *Deseret Evening News*, Mar. 15, 1913; John Stewart to Brian Reeves, June 22, 2002, MMMRF; Dabney Otis Collins to William R. Palmer, Oct. 18, 1958, in William R. Palmer Material, First Presidency, General Administration Files, 1923, 1932, 1937–67, CHL; OIMD; MRIMD.

96. Collins to Palmer, Oct. 18, 1958, in Palmer Material.

97. Haslam, 4; Clewes.

98. Clewes; Extracts from Jacob Hamblin's journal, in Jacob Hamblin to Brigham Young, Nov. 13, 1871, General Office Files, President's Office Files, YOF; Pitchforth, Sept. 9, 1857; Jacob Hamblin, statement, Nov. 28, 1871, General Office Files, President's Office Files, YOF; Hurt, 202; Haslam, 4–5; Charles B. Hancock, Autobiography, ca. 1882, CHL.

99. Hurt, 202; Brooks2, 49, 62, 65.

100. See for instance the calculations of William Palmer, notes on back page of a copy of James Haslam, testimony, *United States v. John D. Lee*, Palmer Collection; Dabney Otis Collins, *Great Western Rides* (Denver, CO: Sage Books, 1961), 246–72.

101. Retained draft of William H. Dame, express, Sept. 7, 1857, William H. Dame, Papers, BYU; Haslam, 6. The retained draft shows that Dame either recycled an identical letter sent a month earlier or initially misdated it Aug. 7. "Aug" was subsequently crossed out in pencil and redated "Sept." Also, "Duplicate" was written across the page, suggesting that Dame retained the draft and sent the finished copy with Haslam.

102. Clewes; James H. Haslam, JDL2-BT 1:12–14. Haslam and Clewes differ on who left first, but the two left at nearly the same time.

103. Clewes.

104. Clewes; Richard S. Robinson, AJ1; Ellott Willden, AJ1; Richard Robinson, JDL1-BT 5:320, 324.

105. Lee later confirmed the critical role of Aden's killing in the decision making leading to the massacre. It was all "brought to a head by the killin' of the man at the spring," he said. Beadle1; "LC"; "LLC."

106. NJ1910. Paiute tradition was that those with plentiful harvests would share their crops "freely with relatives and friends." Based on Mormon professions of friendship, Paiute women may have assumed they could freely partake of the bountiful 1857 harvest. A year earlier in Las Vegas, Paiute women, "perhaps taking missionary protestations of friendship at face value," similarly "entered the missionaries' fields but were driven out, 'which miffed some of them very much.'" Knack, 88.

107. NJ1910. NJ1908 recites, "I…advised him to wait until he received the letter, or the answer, as it was a great responsibility to kill so many people." Nephi Johnson, JDL2-BT 1:59, does not mention this conversation but portrays Johnson as unwilling to speak boldly to superiors.

108. NJ1908; NJ1910.

Chapter 12

1. JHM1907; James H. Martineau to Susan [Martineau], May 3, 1876, James Henry Martineau, Collection, CHL; Retained draft of William H. Dame, express, Sept. 7, 1857, William H. Dame, Papers, BYU; Haslam, 6.

2. William Barton, AJ2; William Barton, AJ1.

3. Brigham Young, Discourse, Aug. 16, 1857, reported by George D. Watt, in Historian's Office, Reports of Speeches, ca. 1845–85, CHL; Daniel H. Wells to A. Johnson, Aug. 13, 1857, Letterpress Copybook, 97, Nauvoo Legion (UT) Adj. Gen. Records, 1851–70, CHL.

4. SAJ, Sept. 8, 1857; George Powers, in "Horrible"; George A. Smith to Brigham Young, Aug. 17, 1858, Incoming Correspondence, YOF, copy in Historian's Office, Letterpress Copybook 1:885–91, CHL; William Barton, AJ1.

5. SAJ, Sept. 8, 1857; Jesse N. Smith, JDL1-BT 5:216–17; "Parowan," notes regarding the Mountain Meadows Massacre, undated, AJ1. On Edward Dalton, see Jenson, 4:609; William C. McGregor, letter to the editor, Dec. 23, 1886, in "Slanders against the Dead and Living Refuted," *Deseret Evening News*, Dec. 27, 1886; Mark Ardath Dalton, *John Dalton Book of Genealogy* (Long Beach, CA: Dalton Family Organization, 1964), 51.

6. SAJ, Sept. 8, 1857; Jesse N. Smith, JDL1-BT 5:216–17.

7. Ellott Willden, AJ2; Clewes; James Haslam, JDL2-BT 1:11.

8. "LC"; "LLC"; Ellott Willden, AJ2; Clewes; *MU*, 230; Bull Valley Snort [John M. Higbee], statement, Feb. 1894, typescript, 2, CM. Lee could

remember only six of the men but suggested he met a slightly larger company. "Another Confession," *New York Herald*, Mar. 24, 1877; *MU*, 230. A young man in Cedar City remembered seeing eight or ten armed men leave the city early in the week. McGlashan. Information on Tait being a British army officer comes from Bowering, 227–28.

9. "LC"; "LLC."

10. Clewes.

11. Willden, AJ2; Willden2, AJ2; Ellott Willden, AJ1. Willden said he later saw the two emigrants' bodies "carried over a ridge" to conceal the killing. Lee said that on Tuesday evening two Paiutes told him "they had seen two men on horseback come out of the emigrants' camp under full speed, and that they went toward Cedar City." Lee did not specify whether these emigrants escaped Monday or Tuesday. "LC"; "LLC." The fact that the two emigrants did not stop at Hamblin's ranch or Pinto for help suggests that they had taken a different route to Leach's Springs.

12. Clewes.

13. Isaac C. Riddle, JDL1-BT 4:122.

14. Ellott Willden, AJ2; Whitney, 1:699; "Mountain Meadows," notes of discussion with an unnamed informant, undated, AJ1.

15. "LC"; "LLC"; William Young, JDL1-BT 4:59–60, JDL1-RS 3:33–35.

16. "LC"; "LLC"; Jacob Hamblin, JDL2-BT 1:100–1.

17. Rogers; Carleton, 19–21.

18. Jacob Hamblin, JDL2-PS 3:16; Annie Elizabeth Hoag, JDL1-RS 4:13, JDL1-PS 4:18.

19. "LC"; "LLC."

20. Philip Klingensmith, JDL1-RS1:36, JDL1-PS 3:8, JDL1-BT 3:101; Nels Anderson, *Desert Saints: The Mormon Frontier in Utah* (Chicago: University of Chicago Press, 1942), 192n31.

21. John A. Lee to L. W. Peterson, Aug. 4, 1938, CM.

22. M1877-10; M1877-12; M1911.

23. NJ1908.

24. Clewes; Jacob Hamblin, JDL2-BT 1:89; Clew/Will.

25. "LC"; "LLC"; *MU*, 229.

26. Ibid.

27. NJ1908; Samuel Knight, JDL2-BT 1:21–22; Jacob Hamblin, JDL2-BT 1:86–87, 99, JDL2-PS 3:2–3; Hoag, JDL1-BT 4:27–29, JDL1-PS 5:18, JDL1-RS 4:13; Clew/Will.

28. Hurt, 203.

29. Jacob Hamblin, JDL2-PS 3:16. In the original shorthand "getting them into the" is crossed out. Crossed-out phrases are common in the Patterson shorthand, but there is no way of knowing by whom or when they were crossed out.

30. Annie Elizabeth Hoag, JDL1-RS 4:13, JDL1-PS 4:18.

31. "LC"; "LLC"; *MU*, 229.

32. *MC*, 2:214, Oct. 7, 1872; *MU*, 229; Beckwith, 119–21. For another explanation of how Lee got his nickname, see Rogers.

33. "LC"; "LLC."

34. James M. Mangum, deposition, July 5, 1875, MBB.

35. NJ1910.

36. "LC"; "LLC."

37. *MU*, 229; "LC"; "LLC"; "Execution of Lee!" *Pioche (NV) Weekly Record*, Mar. 24, 1877. According to *MU*, the messenger "was either Edwards or Adair." In "LC," Lee says "I think his [the messenger's] name was Edwards." The only Edwards known to have gone to the Meadows was fifteen-year-old William Edwards of Cedar, who did not see Lee there until Wednesday afternoon at the earliest—after the time that Lee says he sent the message. Washington militiaman George Adair came to the Meadows on Monday night, later said he had seen messages at the Meadows, and was a mail carrier by profession. See David O. McKay, Diary, July 27, 1907, UofU.

38. "LC"; "LLC"; NJ1908; NJ1909; Jacob Hamblin, JDL2-BT 1:88.

39. "LC"; "LLC"; *MU*, 231.

40. "LC"; "LLC."

41. Mary S. Campbell, AJ1.

42. Ellott Willden, AJ2.

43. Clewes; Clew/Will.

44. Clew/Will; Clewes.

45. Ibid. Willden later identified himself as the "Wilson" in Clewes's account. Clew/Will.

46. Clewes.

47. Clew/Will; Clewes.

48. Clewes.

49. Bull Valley Snort [Higbee], statement, Feb. 1894, 2–3, CM.

50. James Pearce, JDL1-BT 4:105.

51. Bull Valley Snort [Higbee], statement, Feb. 1894, 3, CM; "LC"; "LLC"; *MU*, 229; Philip Klingensmith, JDL1-BT 3:82; Samuel McMurdy, JDL2-BT 1:33; Nephi Johnson, JDL2-BT 1:55.

52. "LC"; "LLC"; *MU*, 230; Joel White, JDL1-BT 3:124, 4:8–10, 14; James Pearce, JDL1-BT 4:105; Samuel Pollock, JDL1-BT 5:183–84.

53. Albert Hamblin, statement, May 20, 1859, in Carleton, 13.

54. James Pearce, JDL1-BT 4:106.

55. Joel White, JDL1-BT 3:124.

56. Rogers.

57. Joel White, JDL1-BT 4:10–11.

58. Ellott Willden, AJ2; "LC"; "LLC."

59. "LC"; "LLC."

60. Ibid.

61. Elias Morris, statement, Feb. 2, 1892, CM.

62. Jesse N. Smith, JDL1-BT 5:216–17; SAJ, Sept. 8–9, 1857.

63. Welch; J. Ward Christian, statement, Oct. 18 1857, in "The Late Outrages on the Plains—Another Account," *Los Angeles Star*, Oct. 31, 1857; S. B. Honea, in "Outrages"; Willson Gates Nowers, note to Andrew Jenson, AJ1. On Fillmore's bishop, see "Statement of G. W. Davis," *Daily Alta California*, Nov. 13, 1857.

64. Farnsworth; Honea, in "Outrages"; Christian, Oct. 18, 1857, in "Late Outrages on the Plains"; Welch; Willson G. Nowers, AJ1; Philo T. Farnsworth, JDL1-BT 5:279–80. See also "How Indian Creek Came by Its Name," in *Monuments to Courage: A History of Beaver County*, ed. Aird G. Merkley (Beaver County, UT: Daughters of Utah Pioneers, 1948), 17–18.

65. Farnsworth; Christian, Oct. 18, 1857, in "Late Outrages on the Plains"; Welch.

66. Farnsworth; Honea, in "Outrages"; Welch; "William A. Wilson," in *An Illustrated History of Los Angeles County, California* (Chicago: Lewis Publishing, 1889), 676–77.

67. Honea, in "Outrages"; Farnsworth; Welch; Knack, 41–44.

68. Honea, in "Outrages"; Welch.

69. Welch; Honea, in "Outrages"; *Monuments to Courage*, 17–18, 22–25; Farnsworth.

70. Honea, in "Outrages"; Welch; PSHR, Sept. 10, 1857, 2nd sec., 34; Willson Gates Nowers, note to Andrew Jenson, AJ1.

71. Farnsworth.

72. Silas S. Smith, JDL1-BT 5:222–25; Farnsworth; Willson Gates Nowers, note to Andrew Jenson, AJ1; SAJ, Sept. 9, 1857; Willson G. Nowers, AJ1.

73. Powers, in "Horrible"; William Mathews, letter to the editor, Oct. 8, 1857, in *San Diego Herald*, Oct. 17, 1857; William Mathews, JDL1-BT 4:45–46; Dan L. Thrapp, *Encyclopedia of Frontier Biography* (Glendale, CA: Arthur H. Clark, 1988), 1401; John Ward Christian, Dictation, [1886], H. H. Bancroft Manuscript Collection, Bancroft Library, Berkeley, CA, microfilm copy located at CHL.

74. Powers, in "Horrible"; SAJ, Sept. 8–9, 1857; Mathews, letter to the editor, Oct. 8, 1857, in *San Diego Herald*, Oct. 17, 1857; William Mathews, JDL1-BT 4:45–47; E. C. Mathews, JDL1-BT 4:97–98; William Barton, AJ1; Christian Dictation, [1886]. Powers remembered the date as Sept. 18, but other events in his narrative show his dating was off.

75. Powers, in "Horrible."

76. William Barton, AJ2; William Barton, AJ1.

77. Powers, in "Horrible"; Willson Gates Nowers, note to Andrew Jenson, AJ1; Silas S. Smith, JDL1-BT 5:222–25; SAJ, Sept. 9, 1857; Willson G. Nowers, AJ1; William Barton, AJ1; PSHR, Sept. 10, 1857, 2nd sec., 34; Farnsworth.

78. Farnsworth; William Mathews, JDL1-BT 4:47, JDL1-PS 5:33, JDL1-RS 4:24; Huntington, Sept. 1, 1857.

79. Honea, in "Outrages."

80. Ronald W. Walker, "Wakara Meets the Mormons, 1848–52: A Case Study in Native American Accommodation," *Utah Historical Quarterly* 70 (Summer 2002): 215–37; Farnsworth.

81. Powers, in "Horrible."

82. William Barton, AJ2; William Barton, AJ1; SAJ, Sept. 8–9, 1857. Cf. Jesse N. Smith, JDL1-BT 5:216–17.

83. Barton, AJ2; Barton, AJ1; Morris, statement, Feb. 2, 1892, CM; "Parowan," notes regarding the Mountain Meadows Massacre, undated, AJ1.

84. Morris, statement, Feb. 2, 1892, CM.

85. Barton, AJ1; Morris, statement, Feb. 2, 1892, CM. In Higbee's self-serving account, which shifted blame for the massacre primarily to Lee, Higbee claimed that during the meeting Dame wrote out orders and that he, Higbee, delivered them to Lee at the Meadows. No council participants, however, mentioned written orders. According to Higbee, the orders read: "Compromise with [the] Indians If Possible by letting them take all the stock and go to their Homes and let [the] Company alone but on no Conditions you are not to Precipitate a war with Indians while there is an Army M[a]rching Against our People. As Indian Farmer and a Major in the Legion I trust you [Lee] will have Influence enough to restrain Indians and Save the Company. If not Possible Save Wimen and Children at all Hazards. Hoping you will be able to give a good account of the Important duty Entrusted to your Charge. I Call upon all good Citizens in That Part of the District to help you Cary out the above Orders. In helping to Make Peace between the two Parties." Bull Valley Snort [Higbee], statement, Feb. 1894, 4, CM. The double negative in Higbee's manuscript—"on no Conditions you are not"—is almost certainly an unintentional writing error.

86. Barton, AJ1. On Morris's involvement, see William C. Stewart to Wilford Woodruff and Council, Nov. 1, 1890, in Wilford Woodruff, General Correspondence Files, 1887–98, CHL. Dame said their conversation began again at a "Second Mound," four miles west of town. He claimed to follow Haight through the night, hoping to dispel any misunderstanding. [Josiah Rogerson], "Review of John D. Lee's Life and Confessions," typescript, 21–22, CM.

87. See [Rogerson], "Review of John D. Lee's Life and Confessions," 21, CM; "LC"; "LLC"; MU, 256; Beadle1.

88. Powers, in "Horrible"; William Mathews, JDL1-BT 4:46, JDL1-PS 5:31–32, JDL1-RS 4:23.

89. Willden, AJ1.

90. Extracts from Jacob Hamblin's journal, in Jacob Hamblin to Brigham Young, Nov. 13, 1871, General Office Files, President's Office Files, YOF. The same information, in a more formal statement, is in Jacob Hamblin, statement, Nov. 28, 1871, General Office Files, President's Office Files, YOF.

91. Macfarlane, AJ2.

92. William Mathews, JDL1-BT 4:47, JDL1-PS 5:32, JDL1-RS 4:24; John H. Henderson, AJ1.

93. Farnsworth.

94. Morris, statement, Feb. 2, 1892, CM.

95. Macfarlane, AJ2.

96. NJ1917; John W. Bradshaw, JDL1-BT 4:75, 84–85; Samuel Pollock, JDL1-BT 5:180; Samuel McMurdy, JDL2-BT 1:33; Nephi Johnson, JDL2-BT 1:44.

97. Corr2. Cedar City militiaman Samuel Pollock testified he was told to take a shovel or pick, as well as a gun, and that there were "spades, shovels and picks in the wagons" when he went to the Meadows. JDL1-BT 4:68, 5:182.

98. John W. Bradshaw, JDL1-BT 4:75, 82, 85–86.

99. NJ1910; NJ1908; Nephi Johnson, JDL2-BT 1:43–44, 54–55, 59–61, 76–77, JDL2-PS 2:66, 78–79.

100. NJ1909; NJ1908; NJ1917.

101. [Josiah Rogerson], "Excerpts—From Bishop's Confessions of John D. Lee," undated, 7, CM.

102. Hamilton Wallace, Reminiscence, undated, Collection of Mormon Diaries, Library of Congress, Washington, D.C., microfilm copy at CHL.

103. Jerrold J. Myrup to Brian Reeves, [June 2002], MMMRF.

104. The man said to have avoided the massacre by feigning fever was David Tullis. Verda Tullis, "David Wilson Tullis," ca. 1953, 4, copy in MMMRF; Leila Mangum Bradford, "David Wilson Tullis," May 30, 1988, 7, unpublished manuscript, MMMRF; Sharon M. Bliss, ed., "Autobiographies/ Biography of Tullis, Mangum, Pulsipher, Maughan, Davenport, Dahle, Griffin, etc.," typescript, [1995], copy at FHL; "David Wilson Tullis," entry submitted by Leilani Grange, in Sons of Utah Pioneers, *Conquerors of the West: Stalwart Mormon Pioneers* ([Sandy, UT]: Agreka Books, 1999), 4.2600–2602. Two witnesses, however, placed Tullis at the scene of the massacre. [James] Lynch, statement, in "The Mountain Meadows Massacre: Surviving Children of the Murdered Fix the Crime upon the Mormons," *San Francisco Daily Evening Bulletin*, May 31, 1859; Albert Hamblin, statement, May 20, 1859, in Carleton, 14; [Albert] Hamblin, interview with Jacob Forney, in J. Forney to A. B. Greenwood, Aug. 1859, in SDoc42, 78.

105. [Josiah Rogerson], untitled document, June 17, 1911, 30, CM.

106. OIMD; MRIMD.

107. NJ1917; PKS; NJ1908.

108. Cedar City Ward, Relief Society Minute Book, Sept. 10, 1857, CHL.

109. Charles B. Hancock, Autobiography, ca. 1882, CHL; Haslam, 6. Haslam said he changed horses and ate breakfast at Nephi, changed horses again at Payson—taking only a few minutes—and spent an hour at Provo.

110. Haslam, 8–9; HOJ, Sept. 10, 1857, CHL; James Haslam, JDL2-BT 1:12.

111. Dame, express, Sept. 7, 1857, Dame Papers; Haslam, 6; James Haslam, JDL2-BT 1:12.

112. Haslam, 9.

113. Extracts from Hamblin's journal, in Hamblin to Young, Nov. 13, 1871, General Office Files, President's Office Files, YOF; Hamblin, statement, Nov. 28, 1871, General Office Files, President's Office Files, YOF; Haslam, 9–12.

114. HOJ, Sept. 8–10, 1857; Brigham Young, Office Journal, Sept. 8–10, 1857, YOF; Brigham Young to Orson Pratt, Sept. 12, 1857, Letterpress Copybook 3:844–45, YOF; *DBY*, 76–79, Sept. 8–10, 1857; Editorial, *Deseret News*, Sept. 16, 1857. Brigham Young to Lewis Robinson, Sept. 7, 1857, Letterpress Copybook 3:822–23, YOF, mentions Van Vliet, but apparently was started on the 7th and not finished until a later date, as the second paragraph contradicts an earlier paragraph, showing a time lapse and a change of thought. Brigham Young to William I. Appleby, Sept. 12, 1857, Letterpress Copybook 3:834–35, YOF.

115. Extracts from Hamblin's journal, in Hamblin to Young, Nov. 13, 1871, General Office Files, President's Office Files, YOF; Hamblin, statement, Nov. 28, 1871, General Office Files, President's Office Files, YOF. The Nov. 13 letter shows editing marks, perhaps in preparation for the formal statement. The portion of the letter quoted in the text does not include the edits. The following is the cited portion of the letter including the edits: "While in S. L. City on business having accompanied Geo. A. Smith there, an express came from Iron Co, asking what should be done with a certain Company of Emigrants, that had behaved verry mean while passing through the differant Towns, the spirit of the Express, rather or the expressman asked the privilege to chastize them.... President Young answered them rather haistily, saying No, they have a perfect right to pass, when I want Marshal Law proclaimed, I will let you know or You will know it!"

116. *DBY*, 68–69, 80–81, Aug. 30, Sept. 1, 1857. Although scholars once debated whether Young issued two martial law proclamations—one in early Aug. 1857, the other in Sept.—the evidence shows that the purported Aug. document was actually a Sept. document with a typesetting error. See Will Bagley, "If the Document Is Authentic, How Can We Explain Weird Dates?" *Salt Lake Tribune*, Aug. 10, 2003.

117. Haslam, 9–12; James Haslam, JDL2-BT 1:11–14, JDL2-PS 2:22; HOJ, Sept. 10, 1857.

118. Brigham Young to Isaac C. Haight, Sept. 10, 1857, Letterpress Copybook 3:827–28, YOF. A clerk's draft of this letter also has been preserved in Incoming Correspondence, YOF.

119. Young to Haight, Sept. 10, 1857, Letterpress Copybook 3:827, YOF.

120. *DBY*, 62, Aug. 19, 1857.

121. Young to Haight, Sept. 10, 1857, Letterpress Copybook 3:827, YOF.

122. Ibid.

123. Carleton, 6.

124. Young to Haight, Sept. 10, 1857, Letterpress Copybook 3:827–28, YOF.

125. Hamilton G. Park, statement, Oct. 1907, typescript, CM; Hamilton G. Park, statement, ca. 1910, CHL; Haslam, 9–12; James Haslam, JDL2-BT 1:12.

126. Park, statement, Oct. 1907, CM.

Chapter 13

1. Philip Klingensmith, testimony, July 23, 1875, in "The Lee Trial," *Salt Lake Daily Tribune*, July 24, 1875; NJ1909; Philip Klingensmith, JDL1-BT 3:8–9; Samuel McMurdy, JDL2-BT 1:33.

2. NJ1909; NJ1908. Leadership among Paiutes was often situational. Knack, 22–24. The Paiute leaders best known to the whites had gone north to meet with Brigham Young, and Joel White said "there was no very high chief or noted chief among Indians there" at the Meadows. Joel White, JDL1-RS 4:3, JDL1-BT 4:12.

3. Philip Klingensmith, JDL1-BT 3:7–9, 72–87, JDL1-PS 2:37–39, JDL1-RS 3:2–3; "LC"; "LLC"; NJ1917; PKS.

4. NJ1909; NJ1908; Nephi Johnson, JDL2-BT 1:76–77. See also Daniel S. Macfarlane, affidavit, June 29, 1896, CM; William Tait, affidavit, June 30, 1896, CM.

5. Nephi Johnson, JDL2-BT 1:76–77; NJ1908. In his trial testimony, Johnson said Lee told him to tell the Paiutes that the militia "would get the emigrants out some way so they could have their guns and horses."

6. "Execution of Lee!" *Pioche (NV) Weekly Record*, Mar. 24, 1877; NJ1909; Philip Klingensmith, JDL1-BT 3:8–10, JDL1-PS 2:38–39, JDL1-RS 2:23; Clewes; "LC"; "LLC"; *MU*, 232–33; Nephi Johnson, JDL2-BT 1:56–57. Joseph Clewes said they were "sitting in something of a circle," going through "something sacred"—language that later interpreters claimed to be a prayer circle. Clewes. Ellott Willden said "it was no prayer circle; the men only happened to sit in a circle on the ground as they talked, for convenience sake." Clew/Will. On Mormon prayer circles, see George S. Tate, "Prayer Circle," in *Encyclopedia of Mormonism*, ed. Daniel H. Ludlow (New York: Macmillan, 1992), 3:1120–21.

7. See "LC"; "LLC."

8. "LC"; "LLC"; Jacob Hamblin, JDL2-BT 1:87–88, 107; *MU*, 233–34.

9. Staub, 83, 147. See also Baumeister, 29.

10. NJ1909; "LC"; "LLC"; "Execution of Lee!"; Nephi Johnson, JDL2-BT 1:76–77.

11. "LC"; "LLC"; Jacob Hamblin, JDL2-BT 1:87–88, 107; *MU*, 233–34; Philip Klingensmith, JDL1-BT 3:7, 9, 59, 72–73. Euphemistic language often plays a role in both the planning and carrying out of large-scale killings. "Euphemistic language serve[s] to deny reality and distance the self from violent actions and their victims. Denial of obvious reality, though it consumes much psychological energy, allows perpetrators to avoid feeling responsibility and guilt." Staub, 29.

12. "LC"; "LLC"; *MU*, 243. "How is it that a person who is not basically evil may participate in monstrous evil without the awareness of what he has done?" psychiatrist-author M. Scott Peck asked. He concluded that "whenever the roles of individuals within a group become specialized, it becomes

both possible and easy for the individual to pass the moral buck to some other part of the group." As a result, "not only does the individual forsake his conscience but the conscience of the group as a whole can become so fragmented and diluted as to be nonexistent." Peck, 118, 218–20. Staub writes, "Even in a society that fosters individual moral responsibility, there is no guarantee that individuals will oppose the group. Resisting is extremely difficult." Staub, 149.

13. *MU*, 243.

14. Beadle1. Roy F. Baumeister explains how people fail to express reservations during this rationalization process: "It may often happen that the members harbor private doubts about what the group is doing, but they refuse to say them, and the group proceeds on its course of action as if the doubts did not exist." Baumeister, 303.

15. *MU*, 290–91; Josiah Rogerson, "Speech of John D. Lee at Mountain Meadows," CM; C. J. S., Mar. 25, 1877, in "Shooting of Lee!" *Salt Lake Daily Tribune*, Mar. 30, 1877.

16. *MU*, 237; NJ1908; Carleton, 21; Nephi Johnson, JDL2-BT 1:76–77.

17. Philip Klingensmith, JDL1-BT 3:9–10, JDL1-PS 2:38–39, JDL1-RS 2:23.

18. Philip Klingensmith, JDL1-BT 3:10–11, JDL1-PS 2:39–40, JDL1-RS 2:23–24; Clewes. Klingensmith alone testified of the hollow square. In reality the formation may have been informal.

19. OIMD; MRIMD; James Pearce, JDL1-BT 4:114; Laban Morrill, JDL2-BT 1:9.

20. See Appendix C.

21. Gardner, 314. For the local organization, see OIMD; MRIMD.

22. OIMD; MRIMD; Appendix C.

23. See, for instance, NJ1908; Nephi Johnson, JDL2-BT 1:53, 60; Petition to E. V. Higgins on behalf of John M. Higbee regarding *People of the United States v. John M. Higby*, Feb. 27, 1896, CM; John W. Judd to Jabez G. Sutherland, Feb. 4, 1896, and J. G. Sutherland to John W. Christian, Feb. 5, 1896, in Florence Spilsbury Higbee, John M. Higbee and Mountain Meadows Massacre Papers, CHL, also in CM; William Edwards, affidavit, May 14, 1924, USHS; Unattributed notes, likely from discussion with Ellott Willden, AJ1.

24. See Appendix C; Michael Shamo, "Militia Profiles," 2007, MMMRF. These statistics reflect those men designated as clearly participating in or witnessing the killing of emigrants at or near the Meadows. On respectable citizens participating in mob violence, see W. Fitzhugh Brundage, *Lynching in the New South: Georgia and Virginia, 1880–1930* (Urbana: University of Illinois Press, 1993), 38; Richard Maxwell Brown, *Strain of Violence: Historical Studies of American Violence and Vigilantism* (New York: Oxford University Press, 1975), 120; Dallin H. Oaks and Marvin S. Hill, *Carthage Conspiracy: The Trial of the Accused Assassins of Joseph Smith* (Urbana: University of Illinois Press, 1975), 6–29.

25. "LC"; "LLC"; *MU*, 236–37; Conversation with Samuel Knight, in Cannon, June 13, 1895; Clewes; PKS; Joel White, JDL1-BT 3:126; Philip Klingensmith, JDL1-BT 3:13, 74–76.

26. *MU*, 237.

27. James Pearce, JDL1-BT 4:101–5; NJ1908; Daniel S. Macfarlane, AJ2; Joel White, JDL1-PS 5:4, JDL1-BT 4:12; Philip Klingensmith, JDL1-BT 3:8; Samuel Pollock, JDL1-BT 4:64.

28. Nephi Johnson, JDL2-BT 1:75; Ellott Willden, AJ1; Whitney, 1:708–9; Clewes; Philip Klingensmith, JDL1-BT 3:11; Bull Valley Snort [John M. Higbee], statement, Feb. 1894, typescript, 5, CM.

29. NJ1908.

30. Clewes.

31. NJ1908; "LC"; "LLC"; Philip Klingensmith, JDL1-BT 3:10–11, 28, 31, JDL1-PS 3:11, JDL1-RS 2:38; *MU*, 237; Jacob Forney to A. B. Greenwood, Sept. 22, 1859, in SDoc42, 79; Carleton, 9, 14, 21; Knight; Conversation with Samuel Knight, in Cannon, June 13, 1895.

32. *MU*, 237; "LC"; "LLC"; Philip Klingensmith, JDL1-BT 3:72–74; Wilford Woodruff, Sept. 29, 1857; Wilford Woodruff, statement, manuscript, 1882, CM.

33. NJ1909; NJ1908; Nephi Johnson, JDL2-BT 1:47–49.

34. Juanita Brooks, "Speech Given at the Dedication of a Monument Honoring the Victims of the Massacre at the Mountain Meadows," reprinted in "An Historical Epilogue," *Utah Historical Quarterly* 24 (Jan. 1956): 72–73, also printed in *Carroll County Historical Quarterly* 10 (June 1965): 8–9; Brooks1, 12–15.

35. See Knack, 28–29; James McKnight, letter to the *Daily Wisconsin*, Aug. 10, 1858, printed in "Interesting Letter from Utah: The Mormon Exodus—The Indians," *Weekly Wisconsin*, Sept. 24, 1858, Historian's Office, Historical Scrapbook, 10:126, CHL.

36. See Appendix D; Applied Urban Field School, University of Wisconsin–Parkside, *Nungwu-uakapi: Southern Paiute Indians Comment on the Intermountain Power Project, Intermountain-Adelanto Biopole I Transmission Line* (Kenosha, WI: University of Wisconsin–Parkside, 1983), 57.

37. "Lee Trial."

38. Joel White, JDL1-BT 3:124, 127–28, 4:15, JDL1-PS 5:6–7, JDL1-RS 4:5; Bull Valley Snort [Higbee], Feb. 1894, 3, CM; John M. Higbee, affidavit, June 15, 1896, CM; Samuel Pollock, JDL1-BT 4:67–68.

39. NJ1909; Nephi Johnson, JDL2-BT 1:72.

40. Clewes.

41. Philip Klingensmith, JDL1-BT 3:28, 97, 116.

42. Carleton, 19–20.

43. Hurt, 203.

44. *Nuwuvi*, 80.

45. Samuel Pollock, JDL1-BT 5:191; Philip Klingensmith, JDL1-BT 3:10–11, 15–16, 19, JDL1-PS 2:39–40, JDL1-RS 2:23–24, 28; Samuel McMurdy, JDL2-BT 1:33–34; Samuel Knight, JDL2-BT 1:25–26, JDL2-PS 2:36–37; Samuel Knight, AJ1; *MU*, 240. Timing deduced from Clewes; "LC"; "LLC." Gibbs, 35, puts Higbee on horseback. *MU*, 237, mentions three men on

horseback, but does not specifically name Higbee. Klingensmith saw Higbee
during the massacre, but did not mention his being on a horse. Philip
Klingensmith, JDL1-BT 3:7, 17, 81.

46. Samuel McMurdy, JDL2-BT 1:33–34; Samuel Knight, JDL2-BT 1:23–24;
Samuel Knight, AJ1.

47. McGlashan; Philip Klingensmith, JDL1-BT 3:15, JDL1-PS 3:1, JDL1-RS 2:26.

48. James Pearce, JDL1-BT 4:105–6; William Young, JDL1-BT 4:51–52;
Samuel Pollock, JDL1-BT 4:64–65.

49. NJ1908; James Pearce, JDL1-BT 4:100; Joel White, JDL1-BT 3:124–25;
"LC"; "LLC."

50. "Cates"; Samuel Pollock, JDL1-BT 4:64–65, 5:192–93; James Pearce, JDL1-
BT 4:107.

51. Samuel Knight, JDL2-BT 1:25; "LC"; "LLC"; Samuel McMurdy, JDL2-BT
1:34–35; William Young, JDL1-BT 4:50–51, 5:205–6, JDL1-PS 5:36, JDL1-
RS 4:27–28; Philip Klingensmith, JDL1-BT 3:78; NJ1908; NJ1909; NJ1917;
Nephi Johnson, JDL2-BT 1:46; *MU*, 238; OIMD; MRIMD; Henry Lunt,
Diary, Aug. 1, 1852, microfilm, CHL.

52. "LC"; "LLC"; Samuel McMurdy, JDL2-BT 1:34–35; William Young, JDL1-
BT 4:50–51, 5:205–6, JDL1-PS 5:36, JDL1-RS 4:27–28; Samuel Pollock,
JDL1-BT 4:64–65, 5:192–93, JDL1-RS 4:38–39; Samuel Knight, JDL2-BT
1:24–25, JDL2-PS 2:36–37; *MU*, 238–39.

53. NJ1908 ("Captain F[a]ncher was killed in the third attack"); "Cates"; Mitchell. Though Nephi Johnson said there were two or three emigrant representatives who came out of the corral, he was not an eyewitness of the event.
Eyewitnesses, including Lee, uniformly reported that one emigrant man
came out of the corral. NJ1909; NJ1917; Nephi Johnson, JDL2-BT 1:46.

54. *MU*, 238; Gibbs, 13, 32; Appendix A.

55. Bagley, 145.

56. *MU*, 238–39; "LC"; "LLC"; Samuel McMurdy, JDL2-BT 1:34–35; Samuel
Pollock, JDL1-BT 4:64–65, 5:192–93, JDL1-RS 4:38–39; Samuel Knight,
JDL2-BT 1:24–25; William Young, JDL1-BT 4:50–51, 5:205–6, JDL1-PS
5:36, JDL1-RS 4:27–28.

57. *MU*, 239; Samuel Knight, JDL2-BT 1:23; Philip Klingensmith, JDL1-BT 3:79.

58. *MU*, 239–40; "LC"; "LLC."

59. *MU*, 239–40.

60. Rogers; Forney, 371.

61. [James] Lynch, statement, in "The Mountain Meadows Massacre: Surviving
Children of the Murdered Fix the Crime upon the Mormons," *San Francisco
Daily Evening Bulletin*, May 31, 1859; "Cates"; Rogers. Lynch incorrectly
identified the negotiator as "Bishop H[a]ight of Cedar City."

62. "LC"; "LLC"; NJ1909; *MU*, 240.

63. *MU*, 236; Carleton, 21; Albert Hamblin, statement, May 20, 1859, in
Carleton, 14; NJ1909; McGlashan; PKS.

64. "LC"; "LLC"; Beadle1; Elliott Willden, AJ2; Elliott Willden2, AJ2.

65. NJ1909; NJ1908; NJ1917; "LC"; "LLC"; *MU*, 235.

66. NJ1908; NJ1909.

67. Annie Elizabeth Hoag, JDL1-BT 4:28, JDL1-PS 5:18, JDL1-RS 4:13.

68. Although some sources say that the emigrants were able to get water safely during the siege, more reliable sources suggest they endangered their lives by doing so. "Horrible Massacre of Emigrants!" *Los Angeles Star,* Oct. 10, 1857; "Massacre of One Hundred Emigrants!" *Sacramento Daily Union,* Oct. 13, 1857; Hamilton Wallace, Reminiscence, undated, 1, Collection of Mormon Diaries, Library of Congress, microfilm copy at CHL; Carleton, 20; McGlashan; "Butchery"; "Surviving Children of the Murdered Fix the Crime"; Rogers.

69. *MU*, 240; McGlashan; Rea, 34.

70. NJ1908; NJ1909; "Butchery"; Mitchell, 15.

71. "LC", "LLC"; *MU*, 239.

72. "LC"; "LLC."

73. Samuel Knight, JDL2-BT 1:25–26, JDL2-PS 2:37–38; Samuel McMurdy, JDL2-BT 1:35.

74. Conversation with Samuel Knight, in Cannon, June 13, 1895; Samuel Knight, AJ1; Samuel Knight, JDL2-BT 1:25–26, JDL1-PS 2:37–38; Collins R. Hakes, statement, Apr. 24, 1916, CM.

75. Samuel McMurdy, JDL2-BT 1:35, JDL1-PS 2:45–46; William Young, JDL1-BT 4:51, 5:206, JDL1-PS 5:36; Nephi Johnson, JDL2-BT 1:46–47; Mitchell; "LC"; "LLC."

76. Samuel Knight, JDL2-BT 1:26.

77. Samuel McMurdy, JDL2-BT 1:36, JDL2-PS 2:46–47.

78. William Young, JDL1-BT 4:51; Forney, 371; NJ1908.

79. Carleton, 21; Joel White, JDL1-BT 3:125–26, JDL1-PS 4:22. Other estimates would vary on the length of the meeting. Samuel Knight, JDL2-BT 1:25; Samuel Pollock, JDL1-BT 4:65, JDL1-RS 4:39; Philip Klingensmith, JDL1-BT 3:12, 79.

80. Corr1; Whitney, 1:706, 706n†.

81. For the pressure the men felt under orders, see Nephi Johnson, JDL2-BT 1:75. On killing quickly, Baumeister, 257, writes: "Another way of helping people cross the line into committing violence is to keep them in ignorance of what they are doing for as long as possible.... If the instructions become clear only moments before the deed is to be done, then there is minimal time or opportunity for protest."

82. "LC"; "LLC"; *MU*, 240; L. W. Macfarlane, *Yours Sincerely, John M. Macfarlane* (Salt Lake City: By the author, 1980), 37, 49–50, 55–56.

83. "LC"; "LLC"; *MU*, 240; Samuel Knight, JDL2-BT 1:26; Samuel McMurdy, JDL2-BT 1:35–36; Nephi Johnson, JDL2-BT 1:47; Samuel Pollock, JDL1-BT 4:66; William Young, JDL1-BT 4:51–52, JDL1-PS 5:36–37. Cf. Philip Klingensmith, JDL1-BT 3:12–13.

84. Corr1; Joel White, JDL1-BT 3:126, 4:16–17, JDL1-PS 4:23, JDL1-RS 3:30; *MU*, 240–41; William Young, JDL1-BT 4:51, JDL1-PS 5:36–37; Nephi

Johnson, JDL2-BT 1:47–48, JDL2-PS 3:56; Daniel S. Macfarlane, AJ2; Samuel Pollock, JDL1-BT 5:194.

85. *MU*, 240; Joel White, JDL1-BT 3:126, 4:16–17, JDL1-PS 4:23, JDL1-RS 3:31.

86. "LC"; "LLC"; *MU*, 239. The number wounded is given as an improbable forty-six in "LC." *MU* placed the number at seventeen, of which three had died. *MU*, 239. Cradlebaugh said "ten or twelve of the emigrants were killed or wounded." Cradlebaugh, 18. Jacob Hamblin said the Indians told him of "killing and wounding fifteen at the first discharge." Jacob Hamblin, statement, in Carleton, 8.

87. Ellott Willden, AJ2; Ellott Willden2, AJ2; "Mountain Meadows," undated notes, AJ1; Whitney, 1:699, 704; "LC"; "LLC"; Jacob Hamblin, JDL2-BT 1:107–8, JDL2-PS 3:23; McGlashan; Carleton, 24–25. Nephi Johnson and Joel White estimated the number of emigrant men killed in Friday's massacre was twenty-five to thirty. Philip Klingensmith and William Young placed the number at twenty to thirty men. Nephi Johnson, JDL2-BT 1:48; Joel White, JDL1-BT 3:129; Philip Klingensmith, JDL1-BT 3:79; William Young, JDL1-BT 4:53.

88. For various estimates of the numbers of militiamen, see Nephi Johnson, JDL2-BT 1:55, 70, 74–75; Philip Klingensmith, JDL1-BT 3:10; *MU*, 379–80; Carleton, 19–20; Samuel Pollock, JDL1-BT 4:63; Appendix C. For men who stayed behind at the militia camp, see William Young, JDL1-BT 4:52, 5:210, JDL1-PS 5:38, JDL1-RS 4:28; James Pearce, JDL1-BT 4:105–6; Samuel Pollock, JDL1-BT 5:182, 185. In addition to the fifty to sixty members of the militia at the Meadows, the Mormons had some herdsmen and Indian wards there, too. "There were more militia men than emigrant men." Corr2; Corr1.

89. NJ1909; Philip Klingensmith, JDL1-BT 3:17, JDL1-PS 3:2, JDL1-RS 2:27; "Execution of Lee!"

90. Daniel S. Macfarlane, AJ2; Whitney, 1:706n*.

91. Corr2; Corr1; Philip Klingensmith, JDL1-RT 1:108, JDL1-RS 3:7, JDL1-PS 3:43.

92. *MU*, 240; Philip Klingensmith, JDL1-BT 3:17, JDL1-PS 3:2, JDL1-RS 2:27.

93. *MU*, 240; Joel White, JDL1-BT 3:126, 4:12; Philip Klingensmith, JDL1-BT 3:17; Corr1.

94. *MU*, 240; PKS; Philip Klingensmith, JDL1-BT 3:81; Joel White, JDL1-BT 3:128.

95. Joel White, JDL1-BT 3:126.

96. Samuel McMurdy, JDL2-BT 1:36; Samuel Knight, JDL2-BT 1:23, 27; "LC"; Joel White, JDL1-BT 4:18–19; Nephi Johnson, JDL2-BT 1:47.

97. "LC"; "LLC." Klingensmith said the final distance between Lee at the head of the line with the wagons and his own position with the men was two to three hundred yards. Philip Klingensmith, JDL1-BT 3:81.

98. Samuel McMurdy, JDL2-BT 1:36.

99. Albert Hamblin, statement, May 20, 1859, in Carleton, 13–14; "LC";
"LLC"; [Albert] Hamblin, interview with Jacob Forney, in Jacob Forney
to A. B. Greenwood, Aug. 1859, in SDoc42, 78; *MU*, 240; Samuel Knight,
JDL2-BT 1:27. For descriptions of where the Indians hid, see Forney, 371;
Carleton, 21; Knight.

100. Clues on the timing of the massacre come from Clewes; Elias Morris, statement, given to Andrew Jenson, Feb. 2, 1892, CM; Christopher J. Arthur,
AJ1; Albert Hamblin, statement, May 20, 1859, in Carleton, 13.

101. See Daniel S. Macfarlane, AJ2; NJ1908; "LC"; "LLC"; Knight. What
early settlers called the Rim of the Basin was likely the point at which the
California road crested the hill and dropped down into the northern part
of the Meadows. This point was east of the headwaters of the Magotsu and
therefore technically south of what some modern cartographers designate as
the Rim of the Basin.

102. Corr2; Corr1; Whitney, 1:706n†; Gibbs, 35.

103. Corr2; Corr1; Whitney, 1:706; Jacob Hamblin and Albert Hamblin, statements, in Carleton, 9, 14; Forney to Greenwood, Aug. 1859, in SDoc42, 79.

104. Corr2; Corr1.

105. Corr2; Corr1; Whitney, 1:706n†; NJ1908; Philip Klingensmith, JDL1-BT
3:81; Joel White, JDL1-BT 3:126–27, JDL1-PS 4:23–24, JDL1-RS 3:30–31;
Chatterley. Others who confirmed that Higbee spoke the order include
George Washington Adair, in David O. McKay, Diary, July 27, 1907, UofU;
NJ1917; Rogers; Carleton, 21. "The fatal signal...consisted of calling out in
a loud tone the word, 'halt' (not 'do your duty')." Corr2.

106. Samuel Pollock, JDL1-BT 5:196.

107. Jacob Hamblin, statement, in Carleton, 9; Charles Brewer to R. P. Campbell,
May 6, 1859, in SDoc42, 17; Shannon A. Novak and Derinna Kopp, *Osteo-
logical Analysis of Human Remains from the Mountain Meadows Massacre* (Salt
Lake City: Department of Anthropology, University of Utah, 2002), 32–33.

108. Ellott Willden, AJ2; Ellott Willden, AJ1; NJ1909; William Edwards, affidavit, May 14, 1924, USHS; Bull Valley Snort [Higbee], statement, Feb. 1894,
5, CM. Ellott Willden said, "The supposed reason why the three or four
men escaped was that som[e] of the militia men fired in the air, unwilling
to do the part assigned them." Corr1. John M. Higbee later asserted that
Lee had given a back-handed approval for the men to drop down instead
of shoot. Those who chose to do so, Lee reportedly said, were cowards.
Bull Valley Snort [Higbee], statement, Feb. 1894, 5, CM. Baumeister, 206,
points out that even some trained soldiers in combat settings find it difficult
"to aim and shoot...during a battle."

109. Corr2; Corr1; McGlashan; Philip Klingensmith, JDL1-BT 3:15–16.

110. Ellott Willden, AJ1; Corr2; "Lee's Confession," *New York Herald*, Mar.
22, 1877; Conversation with Samuel Knight, in Cannon, June 13, 1895.
White repeatedly feigned innocence in his testimony. Joel White, JDL1-BT
4:6, 19, 21.

111. Corr2; *MU*, 236–237; Daniel S. Macfarlane, AJ2; "Execution of Lee!"; Philip Klingensmith, JDL1-BT 3:15–16, JDL1-PS 3:1, JDL1-RS 2:26.

112. Joel White, JDL1-BT 3:129–30, JDL1-PS 4:24–25, JDL1-RS 3:32.

113. Philip Klingensmith, JDL1-BT 3: 82–83.

114. Philip Klingensmith, JDL1-BT 3:17–18, JDL1-RS 2:27, JDL1-PS 3:2–3.

115. Lyman, Sept. 21, 1895. On the Indians having guns, see Samuel Pollock, JDL1-BT 4:70–71, JDL1-RS 5:5; Jimmie Pete, interview with Alva Matheson, Jan. 15, 1968, in American Indian Oral History, Duke Collection, UofU.

116. Albert Hamblin, statement, May 20, 1859, in Carleton, 14; William Young, JDL1-BT 5:210–11, JDL1-PS 5:38–39; Corr2; "Cates."

117. Shirts. Other mentions of varied Indian weapons are in Jacob Hamblin and Albert Hamblin, statements, in Carleton, 9, 14; [Albert] Hamblin, interview with Jacob Forney, in Forney to Greenwood, Aug. 1859, in SDoc42, 78; Samuel Pollock, JDL1-BT 4:69, 70–71, 5:195–96, 201; Parker2, 18.

118. William Young, JDL1-BT 4:53–54, 5:211, JDL1-PS 5:39.

119. Philip Klingensmith, JDL1-BT 3:18.

120. Albert Hamblin, statement, May 20, 1859, in Carleton, 14; Corr2; *MU*, 242.

121. "LC"; "LLC."

122. "Cates"; Albert Hamblin, statement, May 20, 1859, in Carleton, 14; Corr2.

123. William Young, JDL1-BT 4:53, 5:211.

124. "Butchery." Rebecca Dunlap later insisted the rescuer was Jacob Hamblin, but Hamblin was in Salt Lake City on Sept. 11, 1857.

125. Kearny; Carleton, 26. Cf. Cradlebaugh, 20.

126. Samuel Pollock, JDL1-RS 5:5.

127. *Congressional Record Containing the Proceedings and Debates of the Fifty-Ninth Congress, Second Session* (Washington, D.C.: GPO, 1907), 91:2687, Feb. 11, 1907.

128. "Cates."

129. Samuel McMurdy, JDL2-BT 1:37; Nephi Johnson, JDL2-BT 1:48–50, 67.

130. Samuel Knight, JDL2-BT 1:28; Samuel McMurdy, JDL2-BT 1:37.

131. Samuel McMurdy, JDL2-BT 1:37; Samuel Knight, JDL-BT 1:28; *MU*, 242; "LC"; "LLC." These posthumously published accounts have Lee saying that he killed no one during the massacre because his pistol jammed, though he begrudged, "I fully intended to do my part of the killing." *MU*, 242.

132. Mitchell.

133. Nephi Johnson, JDL2-BT 1:49–50, 67.

134. C. J. S., Mar. 25, 1877, in "Shooting of Lee!"; Hakes, statement, Apr. 24, 1916, CM; Dispatch, Mar. 23, 1877, in "Territorial Dispatches," *Deseret Evening News*, Mar. 24, 1877; "The Last of Lee," *San Francisco Daily Evening Post*, Mar. 24, 1877; Jacob Hamblin to Brigham Young, Nov. 13, 1871, YOF; Annie Elizabeth Hoag, JDL1-BT 4:27–29, JDL1-PS 5:18–19, JDL1-RS 4:13–14; Jacob Hamblin JDL2-BT 1:86–108; Shirts.

135. "Lee's Confession," *New York Herald,* Mar. 22, 1877; Samuel Knight, JDL2-BT 1:28; Samuel McMurdy, JDL2-BT 1:37.

136. *MU*, 241–42; "LC"; "LLC."

137. Samuel McMurdy, JDL2-BT 1:42.

138. Samuel Knight, AJ1; Samuel Knight, JDL2-BT 1:23, 26, 28.

139. John D. Lee to Emma B. Lee, Sept. 21, 1876, HM 31211, JDLC.

140. Nephi Johnson, JDL2-BT 1:63; Samuel Knight, JDL2-BT 1:29–31. The man may have possibly been Daniel Macfarlane or David Tullis. "Mormon Assassins: Another List of Men Who Were at Mountain Meadows," *New York Herald*, June 26, 1877; *MU*, 254; "Surviving Children of the Murdered Fix the Crime"; Albert Hamblin, statement, May 20, 1859, in Carleton, 14; Carleton, 10, 12; [Albert] Hamblin, interview with Jacob Forney, in Forney to Greenwood, Aug. 1859, in SDoc42, 78.

141. Nephi Johnson, JDL2-BT 1:30; "LC"; "LLC"; Samuel Knight, JDL2-BT 1:50, 67.

142. *MU*, 242; Annie Elizabeth Hoag, JDL1-BT 4:29–30, JDL1-PS 5:20, JDL1-RS 4:14.

143. Nephi Johnson, JDL2-BT 1:50; NJ1909.

144. NJ1908.

145. Lyman, Sept. 21, 1895. Johnson's statement was in response to one from George Adair, who said that very few people were killed by whites. Lyman, Sept. 19, 1895. Adair did not have the perspective of viewing the entire scene during the massacre, as Johnson did. Johnson, who directed the Indians in the Friday attack, may have answered as he did to downplay his own role.

146. Samuel Pollock, JDL1-BT 4:67.

147. Philip Klingensmith, JDL1-BT 3:14.

148. Sources differ on this issue, ranging from no scalps taken to only a few. Robert Keyes, JDL1-BT 3:2–3; Joel White, JDL1-BT 3:130; Corr1. In her examination of the bones of some massacre victims, Shannon A. Novak reported, "There was no evidence for the use of knives to scalp, behead, or cut the throats of the victims." Shannon A. Novak, *House of Mourning: A Biocultural History of the Mountain Meadows Massacre* (Salt Lake City: University of Utah Press, 2008), 173.

149. Jacob Hamblin, statement, in Carleton, 9. See also Brewer to Campbell, May 6, 1859, in SDoc42, 16–17.

150. "LC"; "LLC"; Robert Keyes, JDL1-BT 3:1–2, JDL1-PS 2:29; Asahel Bennett, JDL1-BT 3:4; Philip Klingensmith, JDL1-BT 3:14, 20, JDL1-PS 3:4; Appendix A.

151. William Young, JDL1-BT 4:54.

152. Pete, interview, Jan. 15, 1968, in American Indian Oral History, Duke Collection; "LC"; "LLC."

153. Annie Elizabeth Hoag, JDL1-PS 5:19, JDL1-BT 4:29, JDL1-RS 3:13–14; Corr1; *MU*, 241. Other versions of the story include slight variations in details. Hubert Howe Bancroft, *History of Utah, 1540–1886* (San Francisco: History Company, 1889), 26:554; Shirts.

154. Annie Elizabeth Hoag, JDL1-BT 4:28–29, JDL1-PS 5:19, JDL1-RS 4:13–14. On Lee's calling his experience a dream, see Shirts.
155. Shirts.
156. Corr1; Corr2.
157. Albert Hamblin, statement, May 20, 1859, in Carleton, 14; Shirts; Jacob Hamblin, JDL2-BT 1:94–98.
158. William Young, JDL1-PS 5:38, JDL1-BT 4:53.
159. Jacob Hamblin, JDL2-BT 1:94–98; Jacob Hamblin, statement, in Carleton, 8; Albert Hamblin, statement, May 20, 1859, in Carleton, 14; Shirts. Albert's role may have been larger than he later admitted. Two surviving children told Jacob Forney that Albert was "an Indian whom they saw kill their two sisters." Carleton, 15; "Surviving Children of the Murdered Fix the Crime."
160. Shirts. See also Gibbs, 36–37. Another lurid story suggested the girls had been forced to dance nude before they died. Joseph C. Walker, "History of the Mormons in the Early Days of Utah," Joseph C. Walker Papers, BYU.
161. Beadle1. Lee again denied the rapes the morning of his execution. Dispatch, Mar. 23, 1877, "Territorial Dispatches," *Deseret Evening News*, Mar. 24, 1877.
162. McKay Diary, July 27, 1907.
163. "LC"; "LLC"; *MU*, 244; Hurt, 203; Carleton, 18, 22.
164. "Gilbert Morse," *Salt Lake Daily Tribune*, Sept. 28, 1876.
165. Martineau, 62; *Kaibab*; "Paiute," 136.
166. Pete, interview, Jan. 15, 1968, in American Indian Oral History, Duke Collection.
167. Jacob Hamblin, statement, in Carleton, 8; "LC"; "LLC"; Albert Hamblin, statement, May 20, 1859, in Carleton, 15; [Albert] Hamblin, interview with Jacob Forney, in Forney to Greenwood, Aug. 1859, SDoc42, 78; E. C. Mathews, JDL1-BT 4:99.
168. Nephi Johnson, JDL2-BT 1:68.
169. Ibid., JDL2-BT 1:70–72; NJ1908. Cf. NJ1909.
170. See "S.," June 12, 1858, in "Interesting from Utah," *New York Times*, July 8, 1858; Carleton, 23; Rogers.
171. PKS. Sources vary on who drove the wagons with the children to Hamblin's Ranch. Philip Klingensmith, JDL1-BT 3:16–18, 20, 85–86, JDL1-PS 3:1–4, JDL1-RS 2:26–28; "LC"; "LLC"; *MU*, 243; Rachel and Albert Hamblin, statements, in Carleton, 11, 14; [Albert] Hamblin, interview by Jacob Forney, in Forney to Greenwood, Aug. 1859, in SDoc42, 78; "Reminiscences of John R. Young," *Utah Historical Quarterly* 3 (July 1930): 85.
172. NJ1908. Cf. Philip Klingensmith, JDL1-BT 3:102–3.
173. "Cates."
174. Rachel Hamblin, statement, May 20, 1859, in Carleton, 11–12; William C. Mitchell to A. B. Greenwood, Apr. 27, 1860, USBIA; "Children"; Samuel Knight, JDL2-BT 1:19; Bowering, 230; Philip Klingensmith, JDL1-BT 3:20–21; Rogers; "Butchery."
175. Albert Hamblin, statement, May 20, 1859, in Carleton, 14; Rachel Hamblin, statement, May 20, 1859, in Carleton, 11.

176. Albert R. Lyman, *Biography of Francis Marion Lyman, 1840–1916* (Delta, UT: Melvin A. Lyman, 1958), 37. In her biography of Lee, Juanita Brooks created a similar setting, mentioning the moon and coyotes. Brooks1, 217.

177. "LC"; "LLC."

178. Lee's mantra much of the rest of his life was that he had done nothing designedly wrong. See, e.g., *MU*, 290; Josiah Rogerson, "Speech of John D. Lee at Mountain Meadows," CM; C. J. S., Mar. 25, 1877, in "Shooting of Lee!" "Tragically human beings have the capacity to come to experience killing other people as nothing extraordinary. Some perpetrators may feel sick and disgusted when killing large numbers of people, as they might feel in slaughtering animals, but even they will proceed to kill for a 'good' reason, for a 'higher' cause." Staub, 13.

179. Baumeister, 11, writes that "sensitive perpetrators often suffer nightmares, anxiety attacks, debilitating guilt, gastrointestinal problems, and many other signs of stress." Some of the Mountain Meadows Massacre participants fit well the description found in Peck, 67: "Forever fleeing the light of self-exposure and the voice of their own conscience, they are the most frightened of human beings. They live their lives in sheer terror. They need not be consigned to any hell; they are already in it."

Chapter 14

1. Elias Morris, statement, Feb. 2, 1892, communicated to Andrew Jenson, CM; Clewes; Christopher J. Arthur, AJ1.

2. Clewes. Morris said the message was not written. Arthur said they carried Brigham Young's express that James Haslam had brought, but that was impossible because Haslam did not return to Cedar City until Sept. 13. See Morris, statement, Feb. 2, 1892, CM; Christopher J. Arthur, AJ2; Christopher J. Arthur, AJ1.

3. See Morris, statement, Feb. 2, 1892, CM; William Barton, AJ1; Daniel S. Macfarlane, AJ2; Christopher J. Arthur, AJ1.

4. George W. Powers, in "Horrible"; William Mathews, JDL1-BT 4:45–46; E. C. Mathews, JDL1-BT 4:97; Clewes.

5. William Mathews, JDL1-BT 4:46–47; JDL1-PS 5:32–33, JDL1-RS 4:24.

6. William Barton, AJ1; William Mathews, JDL1-BT 4:47, JDL1-PS 5:32–33, JDL1-RS 4:24; John H. Henderson, AJ1; PSHR, Sept. 10, 1857, 2nd sec., 34.

7. William Mathews, JDL1-BT 4:46–47, JDL1-PS 5:32–33, JDL1-RS 4:24; E. C. Mathews, JDL1-BT 4:97; *MU*, 245; Powers and P. M. Warn, in "Horrible"; Gardner, 329; William Barton, AJ1; OIMD. Parowan militia privates Beason Lewis and Barney Carter were the other two men who accompanied Dame from Parowan to Cedar City. William Barton, AJ1; OIMD.

8. William Mathews, JDL1-BT 4:47–48, JDL1-PS 5:32–33, JDL1-RS 4:24. See also E. C. Mathews, JDL1-BT 4:97–98, JDL1-RS 5:38; Warn, in "Horrible."

9. Powers, in "Horrible." Although the Indian runner reported only five or six emigrants dead by Friday morning, Mathews was also present at the arrival

of Joseph Clewes. Mathews conflated the two messages in his Oct. 8, 1857, letter to a California newspaper editor: "On our arrival at Cedar City we ascertained, from reports brought by friendly Indians, of the utter destruction of the train ahead." *San Diego Herald*, Oct. 17, 1857. For evidence that Lee and Haight were reporting most of the emigrants dead by Tuesday evening, see "LC"; "LLC."

10. Clewes; William Mathews, JDL1-BT 4:47–48, JDL-PS 5:33, JDL1-RS 4:24.

11. Ronald W. Walker, " 'Save the Emigrants': Joseph Clewes on the Mountain Meadows Massacre." *BYU Studies* 42 (2003): 142.

12. William Mathews, JDL1-PS 5:33, DL1-BT 4:47–48, JDL1-RS 4:24.

13. William Mathews, JDL1-BT 4:47, JDL1-PS 5:33, JDL1-RS 4:24; Powers and Warn, in "Horrible"; *MU*, 245; William Barton, AJ1.

14. Warn, in "Horrible"; William Mathews, JDL1-BT 4:47, JDL1-PS 5:33, JDL1-RS 4:24; E. C. Mathews, JDL1-BT 4:98, JDL1-RS 5:38.

15. E. C. Mathews, JDL1-BT 4:98. George A. Smith and James McKnight reported that Dame and Haight went out "to endeavor to put a stop to the fight." Smith and McKnight, "The Emigrant and Indian War at Mountain Meadows, Sept. 21, 22, 23, 24 and 25, 1857," Aug. 6, 1858, in Historian's Office, Collected Historical Documents, CHL.

16. Laban Morrill, JDL2-BT 1:6–7; William Mathews, JDL1-BT 4:47.

17. John H. Henderson, AJ1; Corr1; Smith and McKnight, "Emigrant and Indian War." Klingensmith said he saw Haight "the evening of" the massacre "at Hamblins ranch." JDL1-BT 3:66–67.

18. PKS. On the smoldering resentment, see Clewes.

19. "LC"; "LLC." Cf. *MU*, 245, which says Lee "was unable to hear what they were quarreling about."

20. Conversation with Samuel Knight, in Cannon, June 13, 1895.

21. NJ1909; Nephi Johnson, JDL2-BT 1:68–70, JDL2-PS 2:72–74; NJ1908.

22. *MU*, 245–46; "LC"; "LLC"; William Young, JDL1-BT 4:55–56; Samuel Pollock, JDL1-BT 5:185; Nephi Johnson, JDL2-BT 1:68–72, JDL2-PS 2:72–75; Cannon, June 11, 1895. See also Bull Valley Snort [John M. Higbee], Feb. 1894, typescript, 6, CM, also published in Brooks2, 231; Albert Hamblin, statement, May 20, 1859, in Carleton, 15.

23. "LC"; "LLC"; *MU*, 246–47; Cannon, June 11, 1895.

24. William Young, JDL1-PS 5:40, JDL1-BT 4:55–56 ("Haight made the lamantation."); Bull Valley Snort [Higbee], Feb. 1894, 6, CM; "LC"; "LLC"; *MU*, 246–47.

25. NJ1908; Corr2; Corr1; Joel White, JDL1-BT 3:130, 134; Nephi Johnson, JDL2-BT 1:44, 73; "LC"; "LLC"; *MU*, 247; William Young, JDL1-BT 4:55; James Pearce, JDL1-BT 4:107.

26. Samuel Pollock, JDL1-BT 4:67, 71, 5:182, JDL1-RS 4:40; *MU*, 247; Smith and McKnight, "Emigrant and Indian War"; Corr1. An excellent early description of the three groupings is Charles Brewer to R. P. Campbell, May 6, 1859, in SDoc42, 16–17; also in Cradlebaugh, 32–33. See also McGlashan; Jacob Forney to Kirk Anderson, May 5, 1859, in *Salt Lake City Valley Tan*,

May 10, 1859; Jacob Forney to Elias Smith, May 5, 1859, in "Visit of the Superintendent of Indian Affairs to Southern Utah," *Deseret News*, May 11, 1859; Jacob Hamblin, JDL2-BT 1:98.

27. NJ1908. Despite the fiery rhetoric that preceded the massacre, the atrocity was almost universally a matter of deep regret. Investigative reporter C. F. McGlashan interviewed sources ranging from the Latter-day Saint "'First Presidency' down to the humblest farmer" and concluded: "While they all attempt to soften the wiry edge of public opinion by mentioning the provocation which brought on the deed, I must bear witness that the Mormons repudiate the crime. From no one have I obtained a single word of approval, or aught that could be construed into a sanction of the massacre." McGlashan.

28. "LC"; "LLC." Baumeister, 212–13, writes: "Humor is one defense against a shocking or disgusting task....Laughter may also arise from nervousness or uncertainty about how to react."

29. Samuel McMurdy, JDL2-BT 1:38.

30. Hamilton Wallace, Reminiscence, undated, Collection of Mormon Diaries, Library of Congress, Washington, D.C., microfilm copy in CHL.

31. Conversation with Samuel Knight, in Cannon, June 13, 1895; Jacob Hamblin, statement, in Carleton, 8; Corr2; Corr1; Whitney, 1:707; "LC"; "LLC"; *MU*, 247. Lee later supposed that some corpses were unearthed by rains that washed out the soft soil of the ravines. Other sources, however, refute this claim. Corr2; Whitney, 1:707; Corr1. Powers went through the Meadows at night under wagon cover and did not see the bodies. "From what I heard," he said, "I believe the bodies were left lying naked upon the ground, having been stripped of their clothing by the Indians." "Horrible." The Turner-Dukes company did not rebury the dead because Dame routed them around the Meadows. "Outrages." U.S. Army surgeon Charles Brewer reported seeing scattered remains even at the corral where the emigrants buried their own dead. Brewer to Campbell, May 6, 1859, in SDoc42, 16–17; Cradlebaugh, 32–33. Brewer's report seems to confirm Ellott Willden's supposition "that all the bodies were exhumed by wolves even those the emigrants themselves buried in their corral." Corr2. Emigrants frequently encountered bodies exhumed by wild animals on overland trails. Merrill J. Mattes, *The Great Platte River Road: The Covered Wagon Mainline Via Fort Kearny to Fort Laramie* (Nebraska State Historical Society, 1969), 88, notes: "Succeeding emigrants were greeted, not only with scattered bones, buttons, and bits of clothing, but hands, feet, and various other parts of the human anatomy in varying stages of decomposition, with 'prairie wolves howling over their loathsome repast.'"

32. Nephi Johnson, JDL2-BT 1:77–79, JDL2-PS 2:80–81. In Lee's posthumously published memoirs, edited by his attorney, the following passage appears:

> After the dead were covered up or buried (but it was not much of a burial,) the brethren were called together, and a council was held at the emigrant camp. All the leading men made speeches; Colonel Dame, President Haight, Klingensmith,

John M. Higbee, Hopkins and myself. The speeches were first—Thanks to
God for delivering our enemies into our hands; next, thanking the brethren for
their zeal in God's cause; and then the necessity of always saying the Indians
did it alone, and that the Mormons had nothing to do with it. The most of the
speeches, however, were in the shape of exhortations and commands to keep the
whole matter secret from every one but Brigham Young. It was voted unani-
mously that any man who should divulge the secret, or tell who was present, or
do anything that would lead to a discovery of truth, should suffer death.

The brethren then all took a most solemn oath, binding themselves under
the most dreadful and awful penalties, to keep the whole matter secret from
every human being, as long as they should live. No man was to know the facts.
The brethren were sworn not to talk of it among themselves, and each one
swore to help kill all who proved to be traitors to the Church or people in this
matter. (*MU*, 247–48.)

This passage, however, does not comport with other sources. Despite
purportedly swearing not to discuss the massacre even among themselves,
many of the participants discussed it with others and never came to harm
for breaking the supposed death oath. See Annie Elizabeth Hoag, JDL1-BT
4:27–29, JDL1-PS 5:17–19, JDL1-RS 4:13–14; Shirts; Hawley, 16; Wallace
Reminiscence; Thomas T. Willis, JDL1-BT 4:33; Jacob Hamblin, JDL2-BT
1:85–114.

33. Joel White, JDL1-BT 4:15–16, JDL1-PS 4:7–8, JDL1-RS 4:5–6. See
also PKS.

34. NJ1909; Nephi Johnson, affidavit, Nov. 30, 1909, edited version, in Brooks2,
224–26; NJ1917. See also NJ1908. In all these documents except his trial
testimony, Johnson places this conversation on Friday afternoon, "about one
half hour after" Johnson arrived at the wagons to prevent the looting; but
in trial testimony, Johnson stated that Lee and Haight reached the emigrant
wagons Saturday morning. Nephi Johnson, JDL2-BT 1:68–71.

35. At Lee's second trial, Johnson portrayed himself as "a boy" who hesitated to
speak boldly to his superior officers. JDL2-BT 1:59.

36. See, for example, "LC"; "LLC"; Carleton, 22–23.

37. For accounts of the supposed offspring of emigrant cattle, see Orson
Welcome Huntsman, Diary, Jan. 20, 1898, CHL; John W. Van Cott, *Utah
Place Names* (Salt Lake City: University of Utah Press, 1990), 55; Beadle1;
"Mountain Meadow Massacre," *Daily Union-Vedette*, July 27, 1866; Juanita
Brooks, "The Cotton Mission," *Utah Historical Quarterly* 29 (July 1961): 214.
On animals dying during early assaults or being taken away before the final
massacre, see Bull Valley Snort [Higbee], February 1894, in CM; Smith and
McKnight, "Emigrant and Indian War"; George A. Smith to Brigham Young,
Aug. 17, 1858, Incoming Correspondence, YOF, copy in Historian's Office
Letter Book 1:885–91, CHL; "LC"; "LLC"; Albert Hamblin, statement, May
20, 1859, in Carleton, 15; James Pearce, JDL1-BT 4:105; Carleton, 21.

38. Daniel S. Macfarlane, AJ2; Samuel Pollock, JDL1-BT 4:69–70. Pollock said he understood that the driving of the stock and wagons was under Klingensmith's supervision, but he apparently conflated two legs of the trip, the first one from Mountain Meadows to Iron Springs, and the second one a few days later from Iron Springs to Cedar City.

39. Daniel S. Macfarlane, AJ2.

40. Nephi Johnson, JDL2-BT 1:51, 69–73, 77–78; Albert Hamblin, statement, May 20, 1859, in Carleton, 14–15. As he approached his home at the Mountain Meadows two and a half weeks after the massacre, Hamblin encountered young herdsmen "driving two or three hundred head of cattle, going to the Iron Springs." Later, he "saw them on the Harmony Range" and "learned that Mr. Lee took them." Jacob Hamblin, JDL2-BT 1:93, 111–12. Klingensmith described Iron Springs as being "seven miles from Cedar City on the old emigrant road" that was used "in the early days." Philip Klingensmith, JDL1-BT 3:24.

41. Rachel Hamblin, statement, May 20, 1859, in Carleton, 11–12.

42. Rogers. See also Rachel Hamblin, statement, May 20, 1859, in Carleton, 11–12. On the practice of Mormons buying children from Indians, see Robert M. Muhlestein, "Utah Indians and the Indian Slave Trade: The Mormon Adoption Program and Its Effect on the Indian Slaves" (master's thesis, Brigham Young University, 1991); Juanita Brooks, "Indian Relations on the Mormon Frontier," *Utah Historical Quarterly* 12 (Jan.–Apr. 1944): 1–48. In the Howard version of his "Confessions," Lee portrays himself during the massacre as having no part in the killing but instead rushing about saving children. At one point, he claims that he saved a little girl. "I rescued her as soon as I could speak," he wrote. "I told the Indians that they must not hurt the children—that I would die before they should be hurt; that we would buy the children of them." "LC."

43. Rogers. Lee's version became the accepted account for some time. Smith and McKnight, "Emigrant and Indian War," reported, "The Indians had killed the entire company, with the exception of a few small children, which were with difficulty obtained from them." Nearly fifteen years after the massacre, Lee was still telling the same story. Though admitting limited white involvement, he attributed the killing largely or entirely to Indians and claimed, "I told them I would buy the children of them, and seventeen children were saved." Beadle1.

44. Rachel Hamblin, statement, May 20, 1859, in Carleton, 12; Rogers; "Butchery"; Jacob Forney to C. E. Mix, May 4, 1859, in SDoc42, 58; Kearny; Carleton, 27; Wm. C. Mitchell to Elias N. Conway, Oct. 11, 1860, in Carleton, 32. For the full names and ages of the emigrant children, see Appendix A.

45. PKS.

46. See Appendix A.

47. Philip Klingensmith, JDL1-BT 3:21–22, 88–89; Kearny; Mitchell to Conway, Oct. 11, 1860, in Carleton, 32; Wallace Reminiscence; Carleton, 27.

One child was still at Pinto when Forney picked up the surviving children in 1859. According to James Lynch, who accompanied him, Forney picked up ten children in Santa Clara and then went on "to Cedar City, there obtained two more, and another at Painter Creek [Pinto]." [James] Lynch, statement, in "The Mountain Meadows Massacre: Surviving Children of the Murdered Fix the Crime upon the Mormons," *San Francisco Daily Evening Bulletin*, May 31, 1859; Marion Jackson Shelton, Diary, Apr. 21, 1859, CHL, transcription by LaJean Carruth in MMMRF.

48. "The Emigrant Children Were Brought First to My Parents' Home," typescript, Caroline Parry Woolley Collection, Special Collections, Gerald R. Sherratt Library, Southern Utah University, Cedar City, UT; Philip Klingensmith, JDL1-BT 3:22, JDL1-PS 3:5, JDL1-RS 2:29; PKS. On the location of Hopkins's home, see Plat A of Cedar City, in Lehi Hintze, *My Jones Ancestors: A History of My Mother's Welsh, and English Mormon Ancestors* (Provo, UT: By the author, 2001), 4. On Lydia Hopkins's role as president of the society, see Cedar City Ward, Relief Society Minute Book, 1856–75, CHL. Evidence suggests strongly that at least some leaders among the Cedar City women knew the truth. Klingensmith testified that when he brought surviving children to Lydia Hopkins's home, "I told her I had so many children got from that place [the Meadows]. I didn't tell her any particulars about it; though she perfectly well understood that because her husband [massacre participant Charles Hopkins] was in and out." Philip Klingensmith, JDL1-BT 3:22.

49. "Emigrant Children Were Brought First," Woolley Collection; Philip Klingensmith, JDL1-BT 3:21–22, 89, JDL1-PS 3:5, 47–48, JDL1-RS 2:29, 3:10–11; Samuel McMurdy, JDL2-BT 1:42–43, JDL2-PS 2:52–53; Mary S. Campbell, AJ1.

50. "Emigrant Children Were Brought First," Woolley Collection.

51. Ibid.

52. Ibid.

53. "Mary Ann and Ann Marie," Woolley Collection. See also "The Emigrant Children Were Brought First," Woolley Collection.

54. Kearny; Carleton, 26–27. Kearny and Carleton both report that Mary was obtained from John Morris. At the time, Isaac Haight was in hiding to avoid arrest and may have shifted the child to Morris in order to divert attention away from himself and his family. Additional evidence that the child kept by the Haights was Mary Miller comes from Haight family tradition. Mary Miller went to live in Tennessee. Haight's grandson, Isaac Parry, went on a mission to Tennessee and saw her there. "Mary Ann and Ann Marie," Woolley Collection.

55. "Cates"; Forney to Mix, May 4, 1859, in SDoc42, 58; Mitchell to Conway, Oct. 11, 1860, in Carleton, 32; Carleton, 27; Thomas T. Willis, JDL1-BT 4:34–35. Huff later moved with the Willises to Toquerville. Kearny.

56. Philip Klingensmith, JDL1-BT 3:22.

57. Kearny; Mitchell to Conway, Oct. 11, 1860, in Carleton, 32; John
    W. Bradshaw, JDL1-BT 4:79–80, JDL1-RS 4:27.

58. Kearny; Forney to Mix, May 4, 1859, in SDoc42, 58; Mitchell to Conway,
    Oct. 11, 1860, in Carleton, 32; Carleton, 27.

59. Kearny; Forney to Mix, May 4, 1859, in SDoc42, 58; Carleton, 26; Mitchell
    to Conway, Oct. 11, 1860, in Carleton, 32; Philip Klingensmith, JDL1-BT
    3:89; Thomas T. Willis, JDL1-BT 4:34–35; John W. Bradshaw, JDL1-BT
    4:79–80. Kearny, Forney, and Carleton call the boy Ambrose Miram Taget.

60. Kearny; John W. Bradshaw, JDL1-BT 4:81.

61. Kearny; Forney to Mix, May 4, 1859, in SDoc42, 58; Mitchell to Conway,
    Oct. 11, 1860, in Carleton, 32; Carleton, 27. Kearny and Forney both list the
    boy's name as Elisha Huff. Carleton called him William W. Huff.

62. Kearny; Mitchell to Conway, Oct. 11, 1860, in Carleton, 32; Carleton,
    26. Kearny reports that some of the other children called her Demars;
    Carleton says Demurr. Curiously, the Smiths' firstborn child was a baby girl
    named Tryphenia who died as an infant in 1846. Tryphenia Fancher later
    remembered that the Mormons called her Annie. James C. Wilson to Jacob
    P. Dunn, Mar. 13, 1885, JPDC.

63. Kearny; Forney to Mix, May 4, 1859, in SDoc42, 58; Mitchell to Conway,
    Oct. 11, 1860, in Carleton, 32; Carleton, 27; Mary S. Campbell, AJ1; Names
    of Participants, AJ1. In a church service on Apr. 28, 1858, the child was
    blessed as "Angeline Jewkes." Cedar City Stake, Record of Children Blessed,
    1856–63, CHL.

64. Kearny; Forney to Mix, May 4, 1859, in SDoc42, 58; Mitchell to Con-
    way, Oct. 11, 1860, in Carleton, 32; Philip Klingensmith, JDL1-BT 3:22.
    See also Thomas T. Willis, JDL1-BT 4:34–35; John W. Bradshaw,
    JDL1-BT 4:80.

65. Bowering, 230.

66. MC, 1:199, Mar. 2, 1859; MU, 242–43; Kearny; "LC"; "LLC"; Forney to
    Mix, May 4, 1859, in SDoc42, 58; Mitchell to Conway, Oct. 11, 1860, in
    Carleton, 32; Carleton, 27. "LC" and "LLC" call the boy William. In report-
    ing the "Indian" massacre to Brigham Young on Sept. 29, 1857, Lee claimed
    he had taken in an emigrant boy and girl. Attempting to justify the massacre,
    Lee vilified the emigrants and their children, claiming that "Charley" refused
    to kneel at the family's prayers and ridiculed the emigrant girl when she did.
    "They would sware like pirat[e]s," he claimed. Woodruff, Sept. 29, 1857.
    Other accounts, including those of Lee, say that he only had one emigrant
    child, Kit Carson Fancher. Annie Elizabeth Hoag, JDL1-BT 4:29, JDL1-PS
    5:20, JDL1-RS 4:14; MC, 1:199, Mar. 2, 1859; MU, 243.

67. Kearny; Forney to Mix, May 4, 1859, in SDoc42, 57; Mitchell to Conway,
    Oct. 11, 1860, in Carleton, 32; Annie Elizabeth Hoag, JDL1-BT 4:29–30;
    Carleton, 26, 27.

68. Kearny; Jacob Forney to C. E. Mix, May 30, 1859, in SDoc42, 59–60; Jacob
    Forney to Hon. Commissioner of Indian Affairs, June 16, 1859, in SDoc42,

60; Mitchell to Conway, Oct. 11, 1860, in Carleton, 32; Rogers; Mary S. Campbell, AJ1.

69. Philip Klingensmith, JDL1-BT 3:89.

70. Elizabeth Ann [Shirts] McDonald, "Story of John D. Lee and Mountain Meadows Massacre," oral history, Feb. 26, 1936, in Kimball Young, Research Notes, photocopy of typescript at BYU.

71. Annie Elizabeth Hoag, JDL1-BT 4:29–30, JDL1-PS 5:20, JDL1-RS 4:14; John W. Bradshaw, JDL1-BT 4:81; Mary S. Campbell, AJ1; Argus, open letter to Brigham Young, Aug. 3, 1871, in "History of Mormonism," *Corinne (UT) Reporter,* Aug. 5, 1871, which asserts that two children who made dangerous remarks were killed. See also "The Mountain Meadow Massacre," *Visalia Weekly Delta,* Oct. 22, 1874; "The Massacre," *Salt Lake Daily Tribune,* Aug. 10, 1875, quoting *Helena Independent.*

72. "Massacre." See also Annie Elizabeth Hoag, JDL1-BT 4:29–30, JDL1-PS 5:20, JDL1-RS 4:14.

73. Mary S. Campbell, AJ1.

74. PGM, Sept. 27, 1857. See also Rachel Hamblin, statement, May 20, 1859, in Carleton, 11; Philip Klingensmith, JDL1-BT 3:85; "The Lee Trial: Klingensmith Takes the Witness Stand and Tells It All," *Salt Lake Daily Tribune,* July 24, 1875.

75. Kearny; Forney to Anderson, May 5, 1859, in *Valley Tan,* May 10, 1859; Forney to Smith, May 5, 1859, in "Visit of the Superintendent of Indian Affairs"; Carleton, 26–27; Rogers; Forney to Mix, May 4, 30, 1859, in SDoc42, 57–58, 59–60; Forney to Hon. Commissioner of Indian Affairs, June 16, 1859, in SDoc42, 60; Jacob Hamblin, JDL2-BT 1:98. Some of these sources report finding only sixteen children, but they were made before Joseph Miller was found. See Rogers.

76. Joel White, JDL1-BT 4:15–16, JDL1-PS 5:8, JDL1-RS 4:6. See also PKS.

77. Annie Elizabeth Hoag, JDL1-BT 4:27, JDL1-PS 5:17–18, JDL1-RS 4:12–13; HBM, Sept. 13, 1857.

78. McDonald, "Story of John D. Lee and Mountain Meadows Massacre."

79. John Hamilton Sr., JDL1-BT 5:308–12, JDL1-RS 9:13–15. John Hamilton Jr. gave similar testimony. JDL1-BT 5:313–19.

80. Thomas T. Willis, JDL1-BT 4:33–34, 38, JDL1-PS 5:22–23, 26, JDL1-RS 4:17, 19. Thomas's elder brother, John Willis, testified, "I saw the Indians have some stock that I supposed came from there; that was the report around town, both horses and cattle." John Henry Willis, JDL1-BT 4:41, JDL1-PS 5:28, JDL1-RS 4:21. For information regarding relations between the settlers and local Paiutes, see TF, 286, 321; Knack, 93–94.

81. Powers, in "Horrible"; John Ward Christian, Dictation, [1886], H. H. Bancroft Manuscript Collection, Bancroft Library, Berkeley, CA, microfilm copy located at CHL.

82. "Horrible"; Mathews, letter to the editor, Oct. 8, 1857, in *San Diego Herald,* Oct. 17, 1857. Mathews said the meeting took place "some few miles from the place of massacre."

83. Powers, in "Horrible"; Mathews, letter to the editor, Oct. 8, 1857, in *San Diego Herald*, Oct. 17, 1857; William Mathews, JDL1-BT 4:47; E. C. Mathews, JDL1-BT 4:98, JDL1-RS 5:38–39. One newspaper reported that William Mathews told Powers not to "grieve or take on" as the emigrant "women were all prostitutes." Mathews reportedly said that Dame had seen their bodies, which supposedly showed signs of sexual disease. For Mathews, the massacre was "the beginning of long delayed vengeance" on the wicked. "Horrible." Lee later told Brigham Young that members of the company were rotten with "the pox," the nineteenth-century term for syphilis. Woodruff, Sept. 29, 1857. Forensic anthropologist Shannon Novak, who examined the bones of some of the victims in 1999, concluded that none showed signs of the disease. Shannon A. Novak, *House of Mourning: A Biocultural History of the Mountain Meadows Massacre* (Salt Lake City: University of Utah Press, 2008), 106–9; Richard E. Turley Jr. to Shannon Novak, email, February 10, 2004; Shannon Novak to Richard E. Turley Jr., email, Feb. 12, 2004. The impugning of the female victims' virtue would offend victims' relatives for generations.
84. Philip Klingensmith, JDL1-PS 3:4–5, JDL1-BT 3:21–22, 86–87, JDL1-RS 2:29.
85. E. C. Mathews, JDL1-BT 4:97–99. Also testifying at trial, William Mathews claimed he did not remember seeing much of anything at all. See William Mathews, JDL1-BT 4:48, JDL1-PS 5:33–34, JDL1-RS 4:24–25.
86. Albert R. Lyman, *Biography, Francis Marion Lyman: 1840–1916, Apostle, 1880–1916* (Delta, UT: Melvin A. Lyman, 1958), 37; E. C. Mathews, JDL1-BT 4:96.
87. Powers, in "Horrible"; Carleton, 19; William Mathews, JDL1-BT 4:48, JDL1-PS 5:33, JDL1-RS 4:24–25; E. C. Mathews, JDL1-BT 4:99.
88. Powers, in "Horrible"; Carleton, 19.
89. Powers, in "Horrible."
90. Beadle2, 500–501; PGM, Sept. 27, 1857. In 1859, Carleton, 24, reported: "Hamblin says three men escaped. They were doubtless herding when the attack was made, or crept out of the *corral* by night." After interviewing Willden and others, Andrew Jenson recorded, "Two or three had escaped during the siege som[e] time and had started for California." Corr1. The most detailed account of what happened to the three messengers appears in McGlashan. Sent to Utah by an editor who had sworn to avenge the massacred emigrants' deaths, McGlashan had access to a wide variety of sources while writing his story, which earned him a national reputation for news reporting. Both McGlashan and Beadle give the time of the escape as Thursday night. McGlashan; Beadle2, 500. These three who escaped should not be confused with (1) William Aden and his companion, who were northeast of the Mountain Meadows gathering stray cattle when the first attack occurred on Monday, (2) the emigrants who went to make pine tar before Monday's attack, or (3) or with two others who left the encampment on Tuesday and went toward Cedar City for help. See Jacob Hamblin, JDL2-BT 1:88–89, 107–8, JDL2-PS 3:23–24, Ellott Willden, AJ2.
91. McGlashan; Beadle2, 500.

92. Mormon scout Ira Hatch, who helped track down the men, identified one of them as "young Baker." S. B. Honea, in "Outrages." Abel, age nineteen, best fits this description.

93. Bagley, 142, reasons that the other two were "perhaps" either Jesse or Lorenzo Dunlap and John Milum Jones. Paiute leader Jackson reportedly had a journal in his possession with the inscription "Wm. B. Jones, Caldwell county, Missouri." Yo Mismo, Oct. 24, 1857, in "Our Los Angeles Correspondence," *San Francisco Daily Alta California*, Oct. 27, 1857. Bagley reads the name as "a garbled reference to Milum Jones of Carroll County." It is also possible, however, that there really was a William Jones from Missouri traveling with the Arkansas company. Other Arkansas emigrants saw Missourians camped with the Fanchers, Camerons, and Dunlaps in Salt Lake City before the doomed company started south. "Massacre." Another possibility is an otherwise unidentified emigrant named Williams. "Mountain Meadow Massacre," *Daily Union-Vedette*, July 27, 1866, reports that in the "valley of the Muddy...was killed the only adult, a man by the name of Williams, who escaped from Mountain Meadows." George Calvin Williams, who was probably related to the Bakers, said he had relatives killed in the massacre. See G. C. Williams to J. N. Smith, Jan. 28, 1895, enclosed in Jesse N. Smith to President Woodruff and Counselors, Feb. 19, 1895, in First Presidency, Court Cases and Related Matters, 1887–1915, CHL, photocopy in MMMRF. Beadle reported that an old man from one of the wagons carrying the wounded escaped and was never found, though it is unlikely anyone escaped in daylight on the final day of the massacre. Beadle2, 500; J. H. Beadle, *Polygamy: or, the Mysteries and Crimes of Mormonism* (Philadelphia: National Publishing, 1882), 172–73.

94. PGM, Sept. 27, 1857.

95. McGlashan. The informant was most likely Hamblin, since McGlashan says that this man later buried the unearthed skeletons of the emigrants, which Hamblin reported doing. Jacob Hamblin, JDL2-BT 1:85–86. If Hamblin was the informant, he was either unaware of the incident in 1859 when talking to Brevet Major James Henry Carleton or chose not to disclose it. See Carleton, 24.

96. McGlashan. If Hamblin was the source of this information, he either learned about it after his interview with Carleton in 1859 or chose to withhold the information from him, likely the former since he reported the deaths of the two other messengers in some detail. Regarding this messenger, however, Carleton reports that Hamblin told him: "The fate of one of those he had never learned. He must have been murdered off the road, or perished of hunger and thirst in the mountains. At all events, he never went through to California, or he would have been heard from." Carleton, 24. On Paiute cremation practices, see Isabel T. Kelly and Catherine S. Fowler, "Southern Paiute," in William C. Sturtevant, ed., *Handbook of North American Indians*, vol. 11, *Great Basin*, ed. William L. D'Azevedo (Washington, D.C.: Smithsonian

Institution, 1986), 380; Edward Sapir, *The Collected Works of Edward Sapir*, vol. 10, *Southern Paiute and Ute Linguistics and Ethnography*, ed. William Bright (Berlin: Walter de Gruyter, 1992), 910.

97. Beadle2, 501; Beadle, *Polygamy*, 172; McGlashan.

98. McGlashan; Beadle2, 500; Honea, in "Outrages." J. H. Beadle wrote that Hatch and the Indians found the emigrants "asleep on the Santa Clara Mountain, and killed two as they slept." Beadle2, 500.

99. McGlashan; Beadle2, 500. Cf. Carleton, 24. McGlashan says the man traveled fifty-four miles, Carleton says he traveled forty-five miles.

100. Carleton, 25; McGlashan; Beadle2, 500–501; Lynch, in "Surviving Children of the Murdered Fix the Crime." See also Powers, in "Horrible"; Honea, in "Outrages"; J. H. Beadle, *Life in Utah; or The Mysteries and Crimes of Mormonism* (Philadelphia: National Publishing, 1870), 184; David Tullis, statement, in Jacob Forney to A. B. Greenwood, Aug. 1859, in SDoc42, 77; Forney to Anderson, May 5, 1859, in *Valley Tan*, May 10, 1859; Forney to Smith, May 5, 1859, in "Visit of the Superintendent of Indian Affairs." Beadle calls the boys "John M. Young and another." A letter published years later in the *Corinne Weekly Reporter* claimed that "a man named Boyle was sent on a mission to the Mojave crossing well armed, and with a key to prevent any suspicious mail matter from reaching San Bernardino, and to pick off any one who by any possibility might have escaped and got along that far." Argus, open letter to Brigham Young, Aug. 10, 1871, in "History of Mormonism," *Corinne Reporter*, Aug. 12, 1871. Henry and McCan Young were no relation to Brigham Young or to massacre witness William Young.

101. [Josiah Rogerson], "Excerpts—From Bishop's Confessions of John. D Lee," undated, 6, CM; Hamilton G. Park, statement, ca. 1910, CHL; JHM, Sept. 12, 1857, 136; Haslam, 4, 12–14; James Haslam, JDL2-BT 1:11–14.

102. Brigham Young to Isaac C. Haight, Sept. 10, 1857, Letterpress Copybook 3:827–28, YOF; James Haslam, JDL2-BT 1:11–14; Haslam, 4, 12–14; Charles W. Penrose, *Supplement to the Lecture on the Mountain Meadows Massacre: Important Additional Testimony Recently Received* (Salt Lake City: Juvenile Instructor Office, 1885), 83–104; NJ1908; CSM, Sept. 13, 185[7].

Epilogue

1. Instructions of H. Douglas to George T. T. Patterson, Mar. 20, 1877, as cited in George T. T. Patterson to H. Douglas, Mar. 26, 1877, enclosed in H. Douglas to E. D. Townsend, Mar. 28, 1877, RG 94, file 1013 AGO 1877, U.S. Department of War, National Archives, Washington, D.C.

2. C. J. S., Mar. 25, 1877, in "Shooting of Lee!" *Salt Lake Daily Tribune*, Mar. 30, 1877; "Through the Heart," *Salt Lake Daily Herald*, Mar. 24, 1877; George T. T. Patterson to H. Douglas, Mar. 26, 1877, enclosed in H. Douglas to E. D. Townsend, Mar. 28, 1877, RG 94, file 1013 AGO 1877, U.S. Department of War, National Archives.

3. Patterson to Douglas, Mar. 26, 1877.

4. Ibid.

5. "Miscellaneous: John D. Lee to Be Shot on Friday, Mar. 23d," *Salt Lake Daily Tribune*, Mar. 8, 1877; Patterson to Douglas, Mar. 26, 1877; C. J. S., Mar. 25, 1877, in "Shooting of Lee!"; "Through the Heart."

6. "Mountain Meadow Massacre: The Jury Cannot Agree and Are Discharged," *Salt Lake Daily Herald*, Aug. 8, 1875; "The Verdict," *Salt Lake Daily Tribune*, Aug. 8, 1875; Dispatch, Sept. 20, 1876, in "The Lee Trial," *Salt Lake Daily Tribune*, Sept. 21, 1876.

7. "Lee and Young," *New York Herald*, Mar. 23, 1877. See also "Territorial Dispatches: Execution of John D. Lee," *Deseret Evening News*, Mar. 23, 1877; Dispatch, Mar. 22, 1877, in "Lee's Last Moments," *San Francisco Daily Evening Bulletin*, Mar. 23, 1877; "Through the Heart"; "The Last of Lee," *Salt Lake Daily Tribune*, Mar. 24, 1877; "M. M. M.," *Salt Lake Daily Herald*, Mar. 25, 1877; "Sight-Seeing," *Provo Enquirer*, Mar. 21, 1877.

8. C. J. S., Mar. 25, 1877, in "Shooting of Lee!" On the Stokes relationship, see Josiah Rogerson, "Speech of John D. Lee at the Mountain Meadows," CM; Collins R. Hakes, statement, Apr. 24, 1916, CM.

9. "LC"; "LLC."

10. Woodruff, Sept. 29, 1857; *MC*, 2:151–52, Dec. 29, 1870.

11. See "The Place of Execution," *Deseret Evening News*, Mar. 24, 1877; "The Execution of John D. Lee," *Carson City Appeal*, Mar. 24, 1877.

12. See "John D. Lee," *Salt Lake Daily Tribune*, Feb. 21, 1877; "John D. Lee," *Salt Lake Daily Tribune*, Feb. 14, 1877; "John D. Lee Sentenced," *Salt Lake Daily Tribune*, Mar. 9, 1877.

13. Beadle1; *MC*, 2:164–65, 203, 369, 378, 382, 386, 452–53, 462, ca. July 20, 1871, July 4, 1872, Sept. 24, Oct. 16, 31, Nov. 7, 1875, Apr. 6–7, 1876.

14. "The Lee Execution," *New York Herald*, Mar. 25, 1877; "Territorial Dispatches," *Deseret News*, Mar. 24, 1877; "Retribution!" *Sacramento Daily Record-Union*, Mar. 24, 1877; "Shooting of Lee!" *Salt Lake Tribune*, Mar. 30, 1877.

15. See, e.g., Brigham Young, Mar. 8, 1863, in *JD*, 10:110; Woodruff, Dec. 23, 1866; Brigham Young, sermon, December 23, 1866, George D. Watt, Papers, CHL, transcription by LaJean Purcell Carruth; Brigham Young, in "The Celebration of the Twenty-Fourth," *Deseret Weekly News*, July 27, 1870; Brigham Young to Wm. W. Belknap, May 21, 1872, Letterpress Copybook 13:81–82, YOF; A. Karl Larson and Katharine Miles Larson, eds., *Diary of Charles Lowell Walker*, vol. 1 (Logan: Utah State University Press, 1980), 427, June 11, 1876.

16. Edna Lee Brimhall and Anthon H. Lee, interview with Anthony W. Ivins, July 28, 1931, in Edna Lee Brimhall, comp., "Gleanings of John D. Lee," 14–15, Arizona Historical Society, Library and Archives, Tucson, AZ, copy at CHL; A. W. Ivins to Mrs. G. T. Welch, Oct. 16, 1922, First Presidency Letterpress Copybook, vol. 64, CHL; "John D. Lee's Last Days of Life," *Daily Nevada State Journal*, Mar. 21, 1877. On the distance between St. George

and Mountain Meadows, see Jesse W. Fox, Table of distances, n.d., General Office Files, President's Office Files, YOF.

17. Rogerson, "Speech of John D. Lee at the Mountain Meadows," CM. Rogerson's shorthand record of Lee's final words is not extant. Rogerson did not report most of the second Lee trial, although a few pages in his hand are extant.

18. Hakes, statement, Apr. 24, 1916, CM; Patterson to Douglas, Mar. 26, 1877; Orson Welcome Huntsman, Diary, Mar. 23, 1877, CHL. For a lower estimate, see "Execution of John D. Lee," *Provo Semi-Weekly Enquirer*, Mar. 24, 1877. References to Mormons at Mountain Meadows on the day of Lee's execution include Anthony W. Ivins to Mrs. G. T. Welch, Oct. 16, 1922, First Presidency Letterpress Copybook, vol. 64; Henry D. Holt, biographical questionnaire, 1939, in "Utah Pioneer Biographies," 13:94, FHL; Sharon M. Bliss, ed., "Autobiographies/Biography of Tullis, Mangum, Pulsipher, Maughan, Davenport, Dahle, Griffin, etc.," typescript, 3, [1995], copy at FHL; Hamilton Wallace, Reminiscence, undated, 1, Collection of Mormon Diaries, Library of Congress, microfilm copy at CHL.

19. "Lee Execution"; "Execution of John D. Lee," transcript, CM; "Through the Heart"; "M. M. M."; Henry Inman and William F. Cody, *The Great Salt Lake Trail* (New York: MacMillan, 1898), 143.

20. Rogerson, "Speech of John D. Lee at the Mountain Meadows," CM; C. J. S., Mar. 25, 1877, in "Shooting of Lee!"; "Lee Execution."

21. District Court (2nd) Criminal Case Files, Series 24291, Utah State Archives, Salt Lake City, UT; MBB, 429, 438, 444, 452–53; Minute Book 1, 1874–77, 494–95, Utah Second District Court (Beaver County), Court Records, 1865–81, microfilm 485239, FHL, original at Beaver County Recorder's Office, Beaver, UT; "Territorial Dispatches," *Deseret News*, weekly edition, Nov. 25, 1874; "Territorial Dispatches," *Deseret News*, weekly edition, Nov. 10, 1875; "An Assassin Arrested," *Salt Lake Daily Tribune*, Aug. 29, 1876.

22. Sumner Howard to Charles Devens, Mar. 26, 1877, RG 60, National Archives, copy in CHL.

23. *MC*, 1:xxiii.

24. C. J. S., Mar. 25, 1877, in "Shooting of Lee!"; "Lee Execution"; Rogerson, "Speech of John D. Lee at the Mountain Meadows," CM.

25. "Lee Execution."

26. Rogerson, "Speech of John D. Lee at the Mountain Meadows," CM; "John D. Lee," *San Francisco Daily Bulletin*, Mar. 24, 1877.

27. Lorraine Richardson Manderscheid, *Some Descendants of John D. Lee* (Bellevue, WA: Family Research and Development, 2000); Brooks1, 378–84.

28. "Lee's Execution," *Wilkes-Barre (PA) Record of the Times*, Mar. 24, 1877; "Vengeance," *New York Herald*, Mar. 24, 1877; "John D. Lee's Full Speech," *Sacramento Daily Union*, Apr. 7, 1877.

29. Rogerson, "Speech of John D. Lee at the Mountain Meadows," CM; "John D. Lee's Full Speech."

30. Joseph F. Smith, Journal, Oct. 8, 1870, CHL; *MC*, 2:151–52, Dec. 29, 1870.
31. David John, Journal, May 6, 186[3], BYU, microfilm at CHL.
32. *MC*, 2:338, Apr. 8, 1874.
33. "Vengeance," *New York Herald*, Mar. 24, 1877.
34. "Lee Execution"; "John D. Lee's Full Speech."

Appendix A

1. Ages are approximated from federal census records and other available family history resources.
2. Sidney B. Aden to Brigham Young, Mar. 14, May 30, 1859, Incoming Correspondence, YOF; Brigham Young to S. B. Aden, Apr. 27, July 12, 1859, Letterpress Copybook 5:116, 185, YOF; "Information Wanted," *Salt Lake City Valley Tan*, June 22, 1859; Gibbs, 12; Tennessee, Henry County, District 1, 1850 U.S. Census, population schedule, 241. According to William Aden's father, Sidney B. Aden, William stood six feet tall, was between 160 and 175 pounds, and had a fair complexion, blue eyes, and dark, curly hair. "Supposed to be Murdered in Mormondom," *San Francisco Daily Evening Bulletin*, Aug. 8, 1859.
3. "Meeting"; Mitchell to Greenwood, Apr. 27, 1860, in USBIA; Joseph B. Baines, William C. Beller, John H. Baker, and Irvin T. Beller, depositions regarding the property of George W. Baker, Oct. 23, 1860, PPU; Greenhaw; "Letter"; Arkansas, Carroll County, Crooked Creek Township, 1850 U.S. Census, population schedule, 163B.
4. Mitchell, 11.
5. Mitchell to Greenwood, Apr. 27, 1860, in USBIA; Mitchell to Elias N. Conway, Oct. 11, 1860, in Carleton, 32; Kearny; Terry, 43–49, 94–96; Greenhaw; Arkansas, Boone County, Crooked Creek Township, 1900 U.S. Census, population schedule, E. D. 26, sheet 2, 154; "Lives 83 Years after Surviving Massacre, Mrs. Martha E. Terry," as published in *Boone County Historian* 11, no. 1 (1988): 58.
6. Mitchell to Greenwood, Apr. 27, 1860, in USBIA; Mitchell to Conway, Oct. 11, 1860, in Carleton, 32; Mitchell, 10–11, 15, 18; Kearny; Arkansas, Boone County, Jackson Township, 1900 U.S. Census, population schedule, E.D. 22, sheet 11, 11B; Oklahoma State Death Certificate for Sarah Frances Mitchell, #14766, Oct. 4, 1947, Muskogee, OK.
7. Mitchell to Greenwood, Apr. 27, 1860, in USBIA; Mitchell to Conway, Oct. 11, 1860, in Carleton, 32; Kearny; "W. T. Baker, Survivor of Famous Massacre, Dies at Leslie Home," *Marshall (AR) Mountain Wave*, Feb. 5, 1937.
8. "Butchery"; "Meeting"; "Extract"; S. B. Honea, in "Outrages"; Mitchell to Greenwood, Apr. 27, 1860, in USBIA; Mary Baker, John H. Baker, John Crabtree, and Hugh A. Torrance, depositions regarding the property of John T. Baker, Oct. 22, 23, 1860, PPU; "Letter"; "Cates"; Parker2, 4; Arkansas, Carroll County, Crooked Creek Township, 1850 U.S. Census, population schedule, 163B.

9. "Meeting"; "Extract"; Mitchell to Greenwood, Apr. 27, 1860, in USBIA; Logan1, 26, 29; Arkansas, Carroll County, Crooked Creek Township, 1850 U.S. Census, population schedule, 163B. Mormon scout Ira Hatch identified one of the three men as "young Baker," and Abel Baker seems the most likely candidate. "Outrages."

10. S. C. Turnbo, *Ozark Frontier Stories*, indexed by Mrs. Carrie Basch (n.p., 1979), 1:138–39. John Beach is identified as John Burch in Logan1, 26.

11. William C. Beller and John H. Baker, depositions regarding the property of George W. Baker, Oct. 23, 1860, PPU; Mitchell to Greenwood, Apr. 27, 1860, in USBIA; Arkansas, Carroll County, Crooked Creek Township, 1850 U.S. Census, population schedule, 162.

12. Joseph B. Baines, William C. Beller, and John H. Baker, depositions regarding the property of George W. Baker, Oct. 23, 1860, PPU; Mitchell to Greenwood, Apr. 27, 1860, in USBIA; Arkansas, Carroll County, Crooked Creek Township, 1850 U.S. Census, population schedule, 162.

13. "Meeting"; Mitchell to Greenwood, Apr. 27, 1860, in USBIA; M1877-10; M1877-12; M1911; "Mrs. M. Thurston Has Passed Away," *Stockton Daily Evening Record*, Dec. 15, 1921; Arkansas, Carroll County, Crooked Creek Township, 1850 U.S. Census, population schedule, 159. The 1955 Harrison, Arkansas, monument (based on William C. Mitchell's list of victims given in the Apr. 27, 1860, letter to Greenwood) indicates that five children of William Cameron and his wife were killed in the massacre but does not give their names.

14. M1877-10; M1877-12; M1911. The name Tillman was also spelled Tilghman.

15. James Knox Porter to Minnie Alma Porter Wright, Mar. 7, 1916, typescript in possession of Nell Porter Howle, Brownwood, TX; Texas, Shelby County, 1850 U.S. Census, population schedule, 34B.

16. A headstone inscription at Latimer Hill Cemetery, Bloomfield, CT reads, "Wm. E. Cooper, June 4 1828. He and wife were murdered in Mountain Meadow Massacre—Utah, Sept. 11, 1857"; Iowa, Scott County, Davenport Township, 1856 Iowa State Census (Iowa: Census Board, n.d.), 646.

17. "Meeting"; Mitchell to Greenwood, Apr. 27, 1860, in USBIA; James Deshazo, Hugh A. Torrance, and Lorenzo D. Rush, depositions regarding the property of Allen Deshazo, Oct. 23, 1860, PPU; Tennessee, Hickman County, 1850 U.S. Census, population schedule, 45.

18. Mitchell to Greenwood, Apr. 27, 1860, in USBIA; James D. Dunlap, deposition, Oct. 26, 1860, PPU; "Butchery"; Parker2, 5; Logan2; Arkansas, Johnson County, Mulberry Township, 1850 U.S. Census, population schedule, 129B. The Harrison monument indicates that six children of Jesse Dunlap and his wife were killed in the massacre but does not give their names. The three surviving children of Jesse Dunlap, however, are mentioned by name.

19. Jacob and Albert Hamblin, statements, May 20, 1859, in Carleton, 8–9, 14; Shirts; Jacob Hamblin, JDL2-BT 1:94–98; William Young, JDL1-PS 5:38, JDL-BT 4:53.

20. Mitchell to Greenwood, Apr. 27, 1860, in USBIA; Mitchell to Conway, Oct. 11, 1860, in Carleton, 32; Kearny; "Butchery"; Rebecca Evins, listed in Arkansas, Calhoun County, Polk Township, 1880 U.S. Census, population schedule, E. D. 21, 97; "Descendants of Joshua Wharton," http://us.geocities.com/schiebert/gen006.htm.

21. Mitchell to Greenwood, Apr. 27, 1860, in USBIA; Mitchell to Conway, Oct. 11, 1860, in Carleton, 32; Kearny; Census record for her married name, Eliza Linton, in Arkansas, Pope County, Liberty Township, 1880 U.S. Census, population schedule, E. D. 133, 17; "Children"; Robyn Chambers Carr, telephone interview with David Putnam, Jan. 16, 2002.

22. Mitchell to Greenwood, Apr. 27, 1860, in USBIA; Mitchell to Conway, Oct. 11, 1860, in Carleton, 32; Kearny; "A Romantic Marriage," *Southern Standard*, Jan. 4, 1894; Arkansas, Pulaski County, Big Rock Township, 1880 U.S. Census, population schedule, E. D. 148, 417; Arkansas, Calhoun County, Polk Township, 1900 U.S. Census, population schedule, E.D. 27, Sheet 9, 74; "Descendants of Joshua Wharton," http://us.geocities.com/schiebert/gen006.htm.

23. Mitchell to Greenwood, Apr. 27, 1860, in USBIA; William C. Mitchell, deposition regarding the property of Lorenzo Dunlap, Oct. 26, 1860, PPU; Parker2, 5; Logan2; Arkansas, Johnson County, Mulberry Township, 1850 U.S. Census, population schedule, 129B. The Harrison monument names L. D. Dunlap and five children as victims of the massacre without giving the children's names. L. D. Dunlap's wife is not identified as a victim on the same monument, even though she is mentioned in Mitchell's letter. The Harrison monument, as well as Frank E. King in Gibbs, 13, names a Rachel and Ruth Dunlap, though no other known records confirm persons with those names were traveling with the group.

24. Mitchell to Greenwood, Apr. 27, 1860, in USBIA; Mitchell to Conway, Oct. 11, 1860, in Carleton, 32; Kearny; "Koen Family Bible," *Austin Genealogical Society Quarterly* 5 (Dec. 1964): 141; Mary C. Moody, *1890 Hamilton County, Texas Census: Uniquely Reconstructed & Annotated* (Arlington, TX: Blackstone Publishing, 1996), 51.

25. Mitchell to Greenwood, Apr. 27, 1860, in USBIA; Mitchell to Conway, Oct. 11, 1860, in Carleton, 32; Kearny; Arkansas, Boone County, Sugar Loaf Township (Lead Hill), 1880 U.S. Census, population schedule, 608; "McWhirter," *Dallas Morning News*, Sept. 23, 1920.

26. Gibbs, 12.

27. Honea, in "Outrages"; Logan2.

28. Lair, 12; "Meeting"; Mitchell to Greenwood, Apr. 27, 1860, in USBIA; Parker2, 5; James C. Wilson to J. P. Dunn, Mar. 13, 1885, in JPDC; California, San Diego County, 1850 U.S. Census, population schedule, 280; Hill, 95–96; Fancher, xvi, 46.

29. Mitchell to Greenwood, Apr. 27, 1860, in USBIA; Mitchell to Conway, Oct. 11, 1860, in Carleton, 32; Kearny; Wilson to Dunn, Mar. 13, 1885, in JPDC;

Hill, 96; Arkansas, Carroll County, Osage Township, 1860 U.S. Census, population schedule, handwritten, 201.

30. Mitchell to Greenwood, Apr. 27, 1860, in USBIA; Mitchell to Conway, Oct. 11, 1860, in Carleton, 32; Kearny; Wilson to Dunn, Mar. 13, 1885, in JPDC; "Children"; Hill, 96; Arkansas, Carroll County, Osage Township, 1860 U.S. Census, population schedule, handwritten, 201.

31. "James Mathew, b. in 1832; killed in Mountain Meadow Massacre with his brother Robert and cousin Capt. Alexander Fancher." Hill, 53; Fancher, 94. See also Arkansas, Carroll County, Carrollton Township, 1850 U.S. Census, population schedule, 128. Both James Fancher and his wife Frances "Fanny" Fancher are notably absent from the 1860 and subsequent census records.

32. According to a family tradition passed down through the James Polk "Red Polk" Fancher family and published in Fancher, 94, Matt had "become entangled with a young lady named Fanny Fulfer. California seemed to be a safe distance from impending fatherhood." According to that branch of the Fancher family, James Matthew Fancher and Fanny Fulfer were not married previous to the journey west and she did not accompany him.

33. According to John Gibson, ed., *History of York County, Pennsylvania* (Chicago: F. A. Battey Publishing, 1886), pt. 2, 20, Henry J. Gresly "had a brother killed in the Mountain Meadow massacre in Utah." John Gresly was the most likely candidate of Henry Gresly's brothers. According to an entry for John "Gressley," York County, PA, Court of Quarter Sessions, Dockets, Book G, Apr. Session, 1851, 137, 141, he was indicted for "malicious mischief." Pennsylvania, York County, North Ward, York Borough, 1850 U.S. Census, population schedule, 2.

34. *MU*, 238–39; Gibbs, 13, 32. The 1990 Mountain Meadows monument has "(Thomas?) Hamilton" listed under "Other Names Associated with the Caravan."

35. "Victims"; "Meeting"; Mitchell to Greenwood, Apr. 27, 1860, in USBIA; "Cates"; "A Survivor of the Mountain Meadow Massacre," *Fort Smith Weekly New Era*, Feb. 24, 1875; Missouri, Dallas County, Dist. 26, 1850 U.S. Census, population schedule, 347B. The Harrison monument identifies the children of Peter Huff and his wife as Angeline, Annie, and Ephraim W. No verifiable record shows those to be the names of the Huff children.

36. Mitchell to Greenwood, Apr. 27, 1860, in USBIA; Mitchell to Conway, Oct. 11, 1860, in Carleton, 32; "Cates"; "Survivor of the Mountain Meadow Massacre"; Kearny; Arkansas, Yell County, Delaware Township, 1870 U.S. Census, population schedule, 547; Shirley Pyron, "Grave Found of Massacre Survivor," *Carroll County Historical Quarterly* 52 (Mar. 2007): 6–10.

37. In the article "Cates," Nancy Saphrona Huff stated that she "had a sis-ter…and four brothers that they killed." The 1990 monument at Mountain Meadows and the 1999 memorial service program identified William Huff, Elisha Huff, and two other sons as victims of the massacre. The 1850 census records for the Huff family possibly identify the two other sons as John and

James. See Missouri, Dallas County, Dist. 26, 1850 U.S. Census, population schedule, 347B. There is no known record of an Elisha Huff or a fourth Huff son, who is mentioned on the Mountain Meadows monument and in the 1999 memorial service program. Government agent Jacob Forney misidentified one of the surviving children, Felix Marion Jones, as Elisha W. Huff and later, Ephraim W. Huff. See J. Forney to C. E. Mix, May 4, 1859, in SDoc42, 58; J. Forney to A. B. Greenwood, Aug. 1859, in SDoc42, 79.

38. "Meeting"; Mitchell to Greenwood, Apr. 27, 1860, in USBIA; Francis M. Rowan, Fielding Wilburn, and Felix W. Jones, depositions, Oct. 24, 1860, PPU; Arkansas, Johnson County, Spadra Township, 1850 U.S. Census, population schedule, 161B.

39. The 1990 monument at Mountain Meadows and the 1999 memorial service program say that the Jones child who died in the massacre was a daughter.

40. Mitchell to Greenwood, Apr. 27, 1860, in USBIA; Mitchell to Conway, Oct. 11, 1860, in Carleton, 32; Kearny; "F. M. Jones Died Tuesday Afternoon," *Lampasas (TX) Record*, June 2, 1932; Forney to Mix, May 4, 1859, in SDoc42, 58; Forney to Greenwood, Aug. 1859, in SDoc42, 79.

41. Francis M. Rowan, Fielding Wilburn, and Felix W. Jones, depositions, Oct. 24, 1860, PPU; "Meeting"; Arkansas, Marion County, 1850 U.S. Census, population schedule, 328B.

42. Mitchell to Greenwood, Apr. 27, 1860, in USBIA; Vicki A. Roberts and Mysty T. McPherson, comps. and eds., *Genealogies of Marion County Families, 1811–1900* (Yellville, AR: Historic Genealogical Society of Marion County, Arkansas, 1997), 269; *A Reminiscent History of The Ozark Region* (Chicago: Goodspeed, 1894), 328; Floydene Sanders Gillihan, *Moody, Tippit, McEntire, Patton, Milam* (n.p., [1999]), 8; Arkansas, Marion County, 1850 U.S. Census, population schedule, 327. Lawson McEntire is likely the Lawson Mitchell identified on the Harrison monument.

43. Sandra K. Ogle, *The Miller Family in California: Being a History of Felix Grundy Miller, 1814–1892, and His Wife, Susanna Matilda Cisco, 1816–1875* (Baltimore: Gateway Press; Napa, CA: S. K. Ogle, 1985), 16–19; Mitchell to Greenwood, Apr. 27, 1860, in USBIA; M1877-10; M1911; Kearny; Arkansas, Crawford County, Mountain Township, 1850 U.S. Census, population schedule, 329. Malinda Cameron Thurston's depositions identified her brother-in-law's name as Joseph or Joe Miller, but census and other records show his name was Josiah. The Harrison monument indicates that three children of Josiah Miller and his wife were killed at the massacre but does not give their names. Most sources say the Millers had only four children, despite Lt. Kearny's statement that John Calvin had two brothers, Henry and James, and three sisters, Nancy, Mary, and Martha. See Kearny.

44. McGlashan.

45. Mitchell to Greenwood, Apr. 27, 1860, in USBIA; Mitchell to Conway, Oct. 11, 1860, in Carleton, 32; Kearny; Arkansas, Yell County, Galley Rock Township, 1860 U.S. Census, population schedule, handwritten 38; Caroline

Parry Woolley, Collection, bx. 4, fd. 8, item 25, Special Collections, Gerald R. Sherratt Library, Southern Utah University, Cedar City, UT.

46. Mitchell to Greenwood, Apr. 27, 1860, in USBIA; Nancy Malejko to Sidney Price, Aug. 29, 2003, email; Kearny; Mitchell to Conway, Oct. 11, 1860, in Carleton, 32; Arkansas, Mississippi County, Chickasawba Township, 1870 U.S. Census, population schedule, 538B; Stanislaus County, California, vital records, Certificate of Death for William Tillman Miller, May 10, 1940; "Last Survivor of Massacre is Called by Death," *Modesto Bee*, May 10, 1940; Annie Elizabeth Hoag, JDL1-BT 4:29–30; Cradlebaugh, 20; HBM, Nov. 1, 1857; Arkansas, Carroll County, Carrollton Township, 1860 U.S. Census, population schedule, handwritten 722. M1877-10 claimed that one of the Miller children who survived the massacre was named Alfred. From other statements in her account, it appears she was referring to John Calvin Miller. Young Joseph Miller was identified as Josiah Miller in Mitchell to Greenwood, Apr. 27, 1860.

47. "Meeting"; "Extract"; Mitchell to Greenwood, Apr. 27, 1860, in USBIA; William C. Mitchell to William K. Sebastian, Dec. 31, 1857, as quoted in Logan1, 31; William C. Mitchell and Samuel Mitchell, depositions regarding the property of Charles R. and Joel Mitchell, Oct. 22, 1860, PPU; Logan2; Arkansas, Carroll County, Crooked Creek Township, 1850 U.S. Census, population schedule, 162B, 163B.

48. Mitchell to Greenwood, Apr. 27, 1860, in USBIA; Arkansas, Marion County, 1850 U.S. Census, population schedule, 325.

49. Mitchell to Greenwood, Apr. 27, 1860, in USBIA; Lorenzo D. Rush and Hugh A. Torrance, depositions regarding the property of Milam Rush, Oct. 23, 1860, PPU; Arkansas, Carroll County, Carrollton Township, 1850 U.S. Census, population schedule, 126B.

50. "Meeting"; Mitchell to Greenwood, Apr. 27, 1860, in USBIA; Francis M. Rowan and Fielding Wilburn, depositions, Oct. 24, 1860, PPU; Parker2, 5; Arkansas, Johnson County, Spadra Township, 1850 U.S. Census, population schedule, 161B; "Letter." Although modern memorials of the massacre use the name "Cynthia Tackitt," original records from the 1850s refer to her as "Cyntha" or "Cintha." The Harrison monument indicates that three children of "Cintha Tackett" were killed at the massacre but does not give their names. A total of eight Tackitt children possibly traveled with the Arkansas company. Two of those children, Pleasant Tackitt and Eloah Tackitt Jones, were married and are identified with their own families. Sebron Tackitt appeared as Sebbyrn Tackitt in the 1850 census.

51. "Meeting"; Mitchell to Greenwood, Apr. 27, 1860, in USBIA; Francis M. Rowan and Fielding Wilburn, depositions, Oct. 24, 1860, PPU; Arkansas, Johnson County, Spadra Township, 1850 U.S. Census, population schedule, 161B. The Harrison monument indicates that two children of Pleasant Tackitt and his wife were victims of the massacre. However, the only known children of Pleasant and Armilda Tackitt were Emberson Milum and William Henry, both of whom survived the killings and returned to Arkansas.

52. Ogle, *Miller Family in California*, 16–19.

53. Mitchell to Greenwood, Apr. 27, 1860, in USBIA; Mitchell to Conway, Oct. 11, 1860, in Carleton, 32; Kearny; Arkansas, Carroll County, Osage Township, 1860 U.S. Census, population schedule, 866; Barbara Baldwin Salyer, comp., *Arizona 1890 Great Registers* (Mesa, AZ: Arizona Genealogical Advisory Board, 2001), 318; Arizona, Coconino County, Williams Precinct, 1910 U.S. Census, population schedule, ED 22, sheet 13A. The Harrison monument named an "Ambrose Tackett" as a victim of the massacre—probably a mistake for Emberson Milum Tackitt, who survived. He is identified as Miram Tackett in Mitchell to Greenwood, Apr. 27, 1860, in USBIA. E. M. Tackitt is believed to be the only survivor to revisit the Mountain Meadows after returning to Arkansas. "Children."

54. Mitchell to Greenwood, Apr. 27, 1860, in USBIA; Mitchell to Conway, Oct. 11, 1860, in Carleton, 32; Kearny; "Children"; Arkansas, Carroll County, Osage Township, 1860 U.S. Census, population schedule, 866.

55. Mitchell to Greenwood, Apr. 27, 1860, in USBIA; Arkansas, Marion County, 1850 U.S. Census, population schedule, 323B; Margaret A. Butler, "Mountain Meadows Massacre Discussion," http://www.rootsweb.com/~armarion/marioncoinfo/MMM.html (accessed Apr. 4, 2007); Margaret Butler to Craig L. Foster, Jan. 16, 18, 21, 2004, email; Arkansas, Marion County, Union Township, 1860 U.S. Census, population schedule, 539.

56. Mitchell to Greenwood, Apr. 27, 1860, in USBIA; Roberts and McPherson, *Genealogies of Marion County Families*, 468–69; Earl Berry, *History of Marion County* (Little Rock, AR: Marion County Historical Association, 1977), 273; Arkansas, Marion County, 1850 U.S. Census, population schedule, 320B. Because Solomon and William's first cousin, William "Prairie Bill" Coker married Alexander Fancher's first cousin, Arminta Fancher, they would be kith-laws.

Appendix B

1. Samuel Pitchforth of Nephi, UT, wrote that the wagon train had at least three hundred head of cattle. Pitchforth, Aug. 15, 1857. James Pearce passed the train on his way to southern Utah and recalled seeing thirty to forty wagons. Pearce, JDL1-BT 4:100. Jacob Hamblin, who camped near the emigrants at Corn Creek recalled four hundred to five hundred head of horned cattle, twenty-five horses, some mules, several tents, and "not over thirty wagons." Hamblin, in Carleton, 6. Robert Kershaw of Beaver, UT, remembered the train having thirty-one wagons. Kershaw, JDL1-BT 4:90. E. W. Thompson, also of Beaver, remembered between thirty and forty wagons. Thompson, JDL1-BT 4:109. Thomas Willis of Cedar City, saw the wagon train with fifteen to twenty wagons and four hundred to five hundred head of cattle. Willis, JDL1-BT 4:31. George K. Bowering of Cedar City, saw five hundred head of cattle—including oxen, cows, and young stock—and about twelve to fourteen wagons, in addition to horses and mules used in

teams. Bowering, 230. Philip Klingensmith and Joel White passed the train just east of Pinto and estimated that the emigrants had twenty-five to thirty wagons pulled by ox, mule, and horse teams. Klingensmith, JDL1-BT 3:6, 20–21; White, JDL1-BT 3:130–31. David Tullis told Jacob Forney and William Rogers in 1859 that when the wagon train arrived at Mountain Meadows, it had seven hundred to eight hundred head of cattle and oxen, "a considerable number of horses and mules," and "about forty wagons." Rogers (Rogers misidentifies Tullis as Carl Shirts). Nephi Johnson said there were fifteen emigrant wagons at the emigrant corral after the massacre. NJ1909. John D. Lee said that the wagon train had eighteen wagons and "over five hundred head of cattle." *MU*, 250.

2. Joseph B. Baines, John H. Baker, William C. Beller, and Irvin T. Beller, depositions regarding the property of George W. Baker, Oct. 23, 1860, PPU. In the 1857 tax roll, found in Arkansas Tax Records, 1821–84, Carroll County taxes for 1857, [1], film no. 1954591, FHL, George W. Baker had one hundred acres of land, six horses, and twelve head of cattle, all valued at $1,650.

3. Estimated at $55 per yoke.

4. Estimated at $15 to $20 per head.

5. Estimated at $100 to $125 each.

6. Joseph Baines gave George W. Baker $700 for the care of Melissa Ann Beller but said that amount may have been used to purchase stock. Joseph B. Baines, John H. Baker, William C. Beller, and Irvin T. Beller, depositions regarding the property of George W. Baker, Oct. 23, 1860, PPU.

7. Mary Baker, John H. Baker, John Crabtree, and Hugh A. Torrance, depositions, Oct. 22–23, 1860, PPU. According to the 1857 tax roll, Jack Baker had 112 acres, 7 slaves, 6 horses, and 32 head of cattle, valued at $6,567. Arkansas Tax records, Carroll County taxes for 1857, [1].

8. Estimated at $50 to $70 per yoke.

9. Estimated at $20 per head.

10. Horse estimated at $100 and mules at $125 to $150 each.

11. M1877-10; M1877-12; M1911; John P. Shaver, affidavit in support of H.R. 3945, Dec. 19, 1877, 45th Cong., 2nd sess., National Archives, Washington, D.C., copy of transcript in CHL; Joel Scott, deposition, May 2, 1911, *Thurston;* "Children"; Wm. C. Mitchell to Elias N. Conway, Oct. 11, 1860, in Carleton, 32.

12. A pure-blood racing mare known as "One-Eye Blaze."

13. M1877-10; M1877-12; Shaver, affidavit, Dec. 19, 1877; M1911; Scott, deposition, May 2, 1911, *Thurston.* See also Frederick Arnold and Andrew Wolf, depositions, May 2, 1911, *Thurston.* According to the Arkansas Tax Records, 1821–84, Johnson County taxes for 1856, and 1857, film no. 1955327, FHL, William Cameron's real property and livestock were valued at a high of $510 and a low of $140.

14. Malinda Cameron Scott Thurston said in her May 2, 1911, statement that the Camerons traveled with two large wagons and "a small wagon." Previous

statements mention only the two large wagons. M1911; M1877-10; M1877-12.

15. The stated value for William Cameron's wagons appears also to include all his family's miscellaneous property, such as camp equipment and provisions. However, the value may not take into account the "small wagon."

16. Estimated at $150 to $250 per yoke.

17. M1877-10; M1877-12; M1911; Scott, deposition, May 2, 1911, *Thurston*.

18. Estimated at $75 to $90 each.

19. Horses estimated at $80 to $150 each and mules at $200 each.

20. According to Malinda Cameron Scott Thurston's May 2, 1911, statement, her father told her he had $3,000 in gold coin, which she believed he kept in "a place mortised under the wagon." She said she never actually saw the gold to verify its existence. M1911. See also M1877-10; M1877-12. John Chatterley, who lived in Cedar City in 1857 but was not at the massacre, reported that $1,700 in gold coin was found in one of the emigrants' wagons. Chatterley.

21. James Deshazo, Hugh A. Torrance, and Lorenzo D. Rush, depositions regarding the property of Allen Deshazo, Oct. 23, 1860, PPU; Arkansas Tax records, Carroll County taxes for 1857, [7]. The 1857 tax roll lists him owning one horse valued at $50.

22. Deshazo's cattle was worth $15 per head. According to Hugh A. Torrence, Deshazo planned on selling it for $25 per head. Hugh A. Torrance, deposition regarding the property of Allen Deshazo, Oct. 23, 1860, PPU.

23. James D. Dunlap and William C. Mitchell, depositions regarding the property of Jesse Dunlap, Oct. 26, 1860, PPU. Arkansas Tax records, 1821–84, Carroll County taxes for 1855, 16, film no. 1954591, FHL. The 1855 tax roll lists Jesse Dunlap owning forty acres, six horses, and six cattle for a total value of $260.

24. Estimated at $60 per yoke.

25. Estimated at $12 per head.

26. Estimated at $100 each.

27. William C. Mitchell, Samuel Mitchell, James D. Dunlap, Adam P. Dunlap, Robert H. Mitchell, and Wm. C. Dunlap, depositions regarding the property of Lorenzo Dunlap, Oct. 26, 1860, PPU.

28. Estimated at $60 per yoke.

29. Estimated at $15 per head.

30. S. B. Honea, in "Outrages."

31. Stephen B. Honea, who passed through Cedar City shortly after the massacre, recalled Isaac Haight "riding a large bay horse which he recognized as having belonged to Mr. Silas Edwards." Honea, in "Outrages."

32. The value of Silas Edwards's horse is not given in the newspaper article. Horses belonging to other emigrants ranged in value from $40 to $150, with the exception of Tillman Cameron's racing mare. Depositions in PPU; M1877-10; M1877-12; Shaver affidavit, Dec. 19, 1877.

33. H. B. Fancher to James C. Wilson, Aug. 2, 1885, enclosed in James C. Wilson to Jacob P. Dunn, Aug. 11, 1885, JPDC; Arkansas Tax records, 1821–84,

Benton County taxes for 1856, 9, film no. 1954479, FHL. In the letter from H. B. Fancher, the amount of property for Alexander Fancher is given, but its value is not. The value was determined using tax records and value ranges for other property of the train.

34. Emigrants' wagon values ranged from $100 to $137.50 each. Depositions in PPU.
35. Work oxen ranged from $50 to $150 per yoke. Depositions in PPU.
36. Cattle ranged from $12 to $20 per head. Depositions in PPU.
37. The value of Alexander Fancher's three horses was $130, according to the 1856 tax records for Benton County. The mule he owned in 1856 was worth $75. The most valuable mules from other emigrants in the train were worth $200. Shaver, affidavit, Dec. 19, 1877. Therefore, $75 to $200 is the value range given for the eight mules.
38. Arkansas Tax records, 1821–84, Carroll County taxes for 1856, [8], film no. 1954591, FHL. James Fancher owned three horses valued at $120.
39. Arkansas Tax records, Benton County taxes for 1856, 12; Benton County, AR, Deed records, 1837–56, vol. D, 169, film no. 1034925, FHL. Peter Huff's total value of real property and livestock was $955. He died en route to Utah on the high plains of modern-day Wyoming. His wife and children continued to Mountain Meadows. "Victims."
40. Benton County tax records for 1856 list twenty cows valued at $250.
41. Huff's three horses were valued at a total of $150. His mule was valued at $75.
42. According to Benton County, AR, Deed records, 1837–56, vol. D, 169, in March 1857 Huff sold his 160 acres of land in Benton County for $1,200. Although this money was likely used to prepare for the western move, it is unknown exactly how the Huffs allocated this money. The 1856 value of his 160 acres was only $480.
43. Francis M. Rowan, Fielding Wilburn, and Felix W. Jones, depositions, Oct. 24, 1860, PPU. In 1856, John Milum Jones had three horses valued at $50. Arkansas Tax records, Johnson County taxes for 1856. The Jones brothers jointly owned the property.
44. Estimated at $65 per yoke.
45. Estimated at $20 per head.
46. William C. Mitchell and Samuel Mitchell, depositions regarding the property of Charles R. and Joel Mitchell, Oct. 22, 1860, PPU, 1849–70. In 1855, Charles R. Mitchell owned two hundred acres, two horses, and two cattle valued at $1,220. Arkansas Tax records, 1821–84, Marion County taxes for 1855, 15, film no. 1955429, FHL.
47. Estimated at $60 per yoke.
48. William C. Mitchell noted that his sons, Charles and Joel, left Arkansas with sixty-two head of cattle. When they reached Washington County, AR, they purchased ten more head of cattle and intended to buy two more.
49. Estimated at $12 per head.
50. The Mitchell brothers left their home with $275 in cash. In Washington County, AR, they used some of that money to purchase ten to twelve head of

cattle at $12 per head. William Mitchell's affidavit put his sons' cash amount at $275 but did not reduce that figure by the amount used to purchase additional cattle in Washington County, AR.

51. Their exchange of cash for cattle in Washington County, AR, merely changed the form in which they held their wealth but not the total value of their property. They either had seventy-two cattle worth $864 and $155 cash or they had seventy-four cattle worth $888 and $131 cash.

52. Lorenzo D. Rush and Hugh A. Torrance, affidavits regarding the property of Milum L. Rush, Oct. 23, 1860, PPU.

53. Estimated at $15 per head.

54. The Poteet and Tackitt families and at least one person named Basham left Arkansas with the Jones brothers. Francis Rowan and Fielding Wilburn noted the group's property when they camped at Washington County, AR.

55. Although Wilburn saw three wagons with this group, Rowan identified one of the wagons as Pleasant Tackitt's. Zero is given as a low-end property value for the Poteets and Basham to reflect the possibility that all the property, and perhaps Basham, went to California with the Poteets.

56. Wagon values for the rest of the emigrants ranged from $100 to $137.50 each. Depositions in PPU.

57. Estimated at $20 per head because that is the price of the cattle belonging to the Joneses, who traveled with the group.

58. Values of the rest of the emigrants' horses ranged from $40 to $150, with the exception of Tillman Cameron's racing mare. Depositions in PPU; M1877–10; M1877–12; Shaver, affidavit, Dec. 19, 1877.

59. Francis M. Rowan, deposition, Oct. 24, 1860, PPU. According to Arkansas Tax records, Johnson County taxes for 1856, Pleasant Tackitt owned two horses and two cattle for a total value of $140.

60. The value for Pleasant Tackitt's wagon was not provided. However, wagon values for the rest of the emigrants ranged from $100 to $137.50 each. Depositions in PPU.

61. Wm. C. Mitchell to Elias N. Conway, Oct. 11, 1860, in Carleton, 32.

62. "Letter"; John H. Baker, deposition, Oct. 22, 1860, PPU; "OBF," 163; William Bedford Temple to Wife and Children, May 11, June 2, 1850, Oregon Historical Society, Portland, Oregon; Washington Peck, Diary, Dec. 5, 1850, typescript, National Frontier Trails Center, Independence, MO; California, San Diego County, 1850 U.S. Census, population schedule, 280.

63. Robert Glass Cleland, *The Cattle on a Thousand Hills: Southern California, 1850–1880* (San Marino, CA: Huntington Library, 1964), 106.

64. W. S. J., June 1, 1857, in "Our Monthly Live Stock Report," *San Francisco Herald,* June 5, 1857; X. Y. Z., May 23, 1857, in "Our Los Angeles Correspondence," *San Francisco Daily Alta California,* May 28, 1857; Geo. F. Lamson, "Los Angeles Price Current," *Los Angeles Star,* Jan. 31, 1857.

65. Vouchers 1–8, in U.S. Congress, House, *Accounts of Brigham Young, Superintendent of Indian Affairs in Utah Territory,* 37th Cong., 2nd sess., 1862,

H. Doc. 29, 97–101; John D. Lee to Brigham Young, Nov. 20, 1857, Incoming Correspondence, YOF; John D. Lee, Account Book, May 1858–Oct. 1859, HM 31204, JDLC; JHM, Sept. 24, 1857.

66. John Sherrett, JDL1-BT 4:72; Thomas T. Willis, JDL1-BT 4:43–45; Bowering, 230; McGlashan; Mary S. Campbell, AJ1; Carleton, 21–22; Jacob Forney to A. B. Greenwood, Aug. 1859, in SDoc42, 79.

67. Utah Territory, Great Salt Lake County, 1850 U.S. Census, population schedule, 105B; Utah Territory, Iron County, 1850 U.S. Census, population schedule, 18 (commenced May 12, 1851); Utah Territory, Washington County, Harmony Township, 1860 U.S. Census, population schedule, handwritten 139. In 1850, while he was living in Salt Lake City, Lee's property was valued at $2,500. The next year, Lee moved to Iron County where his property value was stated at $3,000. In 1860 Lee's real estate was valued at $40,000, in addition to personal property value of $9,500. Within a few months after the massacre, Lee purchased a city lot and sixteen acres of land in Washington City with $150 worth of livestock. MC, 1:150, Feb. 12, 1858.

68. Honea, in "Outrages."

69. MU, 250; Philip Klingensmith, JDL1-BT 3:90–91, John W. Bradshaw, JDL1-BT 4:77–78.

70. Nephi Johnson, JDL2-BT 1:66; Frank F. Jorden, "A True Story," ca. 1871, MMMRF.

71. Philip Kingensmith, JDL1-BT 3:29; John Hamilton Sr., JDL1-BT 5:308–12; John Hamilton Jr., JDL1-BT 5:316–19; Thomas T. Willis, JDL1-BT 4:33–34, see also JDL1-PS 5:22–23; George Powers, statement, in "Horrible"; MU, 250.

Appendix C

1. The sources for the militia members' ranks and places of residence are OIMD; MRIMD; James H. Martineau report to Adj. Gen. James Ferguson, listing Iron Military District officers elected July 28, 1857, reproduced in Gardner, 328–29. See also 1856 Utah Territorial Census; Utah Territory, 1860 U.S. Federal Census; TF, 473–89. The birth and death dates were obtained from family records and census reports.

2. In 1859 Judge John Cradlebaugh issued thirty-eight arrest warrants for men tied to the massacre. William Rogers, who assisted Cradlebaugh, said one witness came forward to give the names of twenty-five to thirty participants. It is unclear how Cradlebaugh got the other eight to thirteen names. While most names from Cradlebaugh's arrest warrants have been identified as massacre participants by other sources, some cannot be verified, including William Riggs, [Alexander] Ingram, Ira Allen's son, Jabes Nomlen [Jabus Nowlin], John W. Adair, [Oscar?] Tyler, Samuel Lewis, Sims Matheny, and Samuel Adair. Two names, Joseph Elang and F. C. McDulange, cannot be identified as individuals living within the Iron Military District in 1857. Two other names, E. Welean and James Price, are likely references to Ellott Willden and James Pearce, respectively. Therefore, only the names that are

supported by other evidence are reflected in this appendix. Cradlebaugh 19–20; Rogers. Additionally, Jacob Forney listed a "Bishop Davis" among the "names of the persons the most guilty." Although likely a reference to William R. Davies, the bishop at Harmony, no eyewitnesses or other known sources place him at the massacre. J. Forney to A. B. Greenwood, Sept. 22, 1859, in SDoc42, 86.

3. Notes from meeting with George W. Adair, David O. McKay, Diary, July 27, 1907, UofU, photocopy at CHL; Frederick S. Dellenbaugh to Charles Kelly, Aug. 16, 1934, published in *Utah Historical Quarterly* 37 (Spring 1969): 242; *MU*, 228–29, 379; William Young, JDL1-PS 5:35; Lyman, Sept. 19, 21, 1895; Joel White, affidavit, Oct. 9, 1896, CM; Indictment for murder against George Adair, Sept. 24, 1874, in CCF 31 and MBB, 442–44; Arrest Warrant, Dec. 4, 1874, MBB, 444–45 (served Nov. 2, 1875); John R. Young, "Reminiscences of John R. Young," *Utah Historical Quarterly* 3 (July 1930): 85; Case dismissal, Sept. 1, 1879, *United States v. George Adair Jr.*, MBB, 452–53; Jabez Sutherland, JDL1-BT 8:4, JDL1-PS 11:23. Cradlebaugh issued a warrant for a John W. Adair in 1859. Although there was a John Wesley Adair, George W. Adair Jr.'s uncle, he was not present at the massacre, and Cradlebaugh's warrant was most likely meant for George W. Adair Jr. Cradlebaugh, 20.

4. Philip Klingensmith, JDL1-BT 3:4, 16, 24, 42–43, 90–91; PKS; John W. Bradshaw, JDL1-BT 4:77–78; Jabez Sutherland, JDL1-BT 8:4; *MU*, 232, 379. See also "LC"; "LLC." Cradlebaugh issued an arrest warrant for "Ira Allen and son" in 1859. Two of Ira Allen's sons are listed in the same platoon as their father: Andrew, age 20, and Simeon, age 18. However, it is unclear whether either went with Ira to the Meadows since they are not named by other known sources. Cradlebaugh 19; OIMD; MRIMD.

5. *MU*, 230, 235, 379; Ellott Willden, Mary S. Campbell, AJ2; Mary S. Campbell, D. W. Tullis, Ellott Willden, AJ1; McGlashan; Whitney, 1:699; Conversation with Samuel Knight, in Cannon, June 13, 1895; Corr1; Corr2.

6. Christopher J. Arthur, AJ1; Elias Morris, statement, Feb. 2, 1892, communicated to Andrew Jenson, CM; Clewes.

7. Philip Klingensmith, JDL1-BT 3:78; William Young, JDL1-BT 4:50, 5:205–6; Samuel Pollock, JDL1-BT 4:62, 5:180–81; Samuel McMurdy, JDL2-BT 1:34–35; "LC"; "LLC"; *MU*, 236, 379; "Lee's Confession," *New York Herald*, Mar. 22, 1877; Henry Higgins, affidavit, Apr. 20, 1859, printed in Cradlebaugh, 42; Jabez Sutherland, JDL1-BT 8:4. Judge John Cradlebaugh issued a warrant in 1859 for William Bateman's arrest. Cradlebaugh, 20.

8. Samuel Pollock, JDL1-BT 4:62, 5:180–81; *MU*, 232, 379; Jabez Sutherland, JDL1-BT 8:4.

9. William Young, JDL1-BT 4:49; James Pearce, JDL1-BT 4:103–4; *MU*, 228, 379; "LC"; "LLC." In his closing argument for the first John D. Lee trial, defense attorney Jabez Sutherland contended that Clark remained at the militia camp during the massacre; however, this assertion is not supported by the trial testimony of eyewitnesses. Two of those who did remain at the

camp during the massacre, William Young and James Pearce, saw Clark at the Meadows, but they did not say he stayed behind at the camp during the massacre. Sutherland, JDL1-BT 8:4; JDL1-PS 11:38–39.

10. Clewes; Clew/Will; Morris, statement, Feb. 2, 1892, CM; Christopher J. Arthur, AJ1; *MU*, 232, 379; James Haslam, JDL2-BT 1:13–14.

11. Carleton, 15, 17, 24–25.

12. Samuel Pollock, JDL1-BT 4:62, 5:180–81; *MU*, 232, 379; Higgins, affidavit, Apr. 20, 1859, printed in Cradlebaugh, 42; Jabez Sutherland, JDL1-BT 8:4. Cradlebaugh issued a warrant in 1859 for Curtis's arrest. Cradlebaugh, 20.

13. William Barton, AJ1; Chatterley; Morris, statement, Feb. 2, 1892, CM; PKS; JHM1907; William Mathews, JDL1-BT 4:47; Jabez Sutherland, JDL1-BT 8:4; "LC"; "LLC"; *MU*, 245–47, 380–81; Indictment for murder against William H. Dame, Sept. 24, 1874, in CCF 31 and CCF 34; Dispatch, Nov. 18, 1874, in "Miscellaneous: Colonel Dame, Another of the Mountain Meadows Veterans, Arrested," *Salt Lake Daily Tribune*, Nov. 19, 1874; Case dismissal, Sept. 14, 1876, *United States v. William H. Dame*, Minute Book 1, 1874–77, 466, Utah Second District Court (Beaver County), Court Records 1865–81, microfilm 485239, FHL, original at Beaver County Recorders Office, Beaver, UT; J. C. Y., Sept. 14, 1876, in "The Lee Case," *Salt Lake Daily Tribune*, Sept. 17, 1876.

14. Albert Hamblin, in Carleton, 15.

15. *MU*, 232, 379.

16. William Edwards, affidavit, May 14, 1924, USHS, copy also located in MMMRF; "LC"; "LLC"; *MU*, 229, 379. In *MU*, Lee could not remember whether a messenger he sent from the Meadows to Cedar City was Edwards or George Adair. Adair was the likely candidate since Edwards arrived at the lower end of the Meadows after Lee had sent the messenger. Additionally, Edwards himself never mentioned being a messenger for Lee. Edwards's name does not appear on the militia rosters. OIMD; MRIMD.

17. *MU*, 232, 379. Columbus's father, John Freeman, and older brothers William and John W. Freeman are listed on the June 1857 and Oct. 10, 1857, militia rosters for Company I, First and Third Platoons, Washington County. OIMD; MRIMD. Cradlebaugh issued a warrant for Columbus Freeman's arrest in 1859. Cradlebaugh, 19.

18. *MU*, 218–21, 245–47, 381; "LC"; "LLC"; "Lee's Confession," *New York Herald*, Mar. 22, 1877; PKS; Philip Klingensmith, JDL1-BT 3:4, 33; *TF*, 386; William Young, JDL1-BT 4:55–56; John W. Bradshaw, JDL1-BT 4:75; Nephi Johnson, JDL2-BT 1:43–44, 57, 60; Chatterley; JHM1907; NJ1908; NJ1909; William Barton, AJ1; Ellott Willden, AJ2; Mary S. Campbell, AJ1; Ellott Willden, AJ1; Laban Morrill, JDL2-BT 1:7–10; Morris, statement, Feb. 2, 1892, CM; James Haslam, JDL2-BT 1:11–14; Haslam, 3–5, 12–13; Clewes; Jabez Sutherland, JDL1-BT 8:4; Indictment for murder against Isaac C. Haight, Sept. 24, 1874, BYU. In 1859, Judge Cradlebaugh issued an arrest warrant for "Jacob Haight, President of the Cedar City stake." Cradlebaugh, 19. See also Forney to Greenwood, Sept. 22, 1859, in SDoc42, 86.

19. *MU*, 228–29, 379; "LC"; "LLC"; James M. Mangum, deposition, July 5, 1875, MBB, 324; William Young, JDL1-BT 5:203; Jacob Hamblin, JDL2-BT 1:100, see JDL2-PS 3:16. According to a family legend, Oscar's wife Mary Ann kept him from participating in the massacre. "Mary Ann, learning there was to be trouble the next day, gave Oscar a double dose of epicac which induced vomiting and rendered him too ill to be involved in any way." Shauna Brimhall, "History of Oscar Hamblin," typescript, 3, Daughters of Utah Pioneers.

20. Frank F. Jorden, "A True Story," ca. 1871, 87–88, typescript copy located in MMMRF; *MU*, 232, 379; J. G. Sutherland, JDL1-BT 8:4. According to family tradition, when Richard Harrison was approached about going to Mountain Meadows he ordered the men off his property. Telephone conversation of Nada Gardner, Aug. 19, 2002, recorded by Brian Reeves, MMMRF. A warrant for a Harrison was issued by Cradlebaugh in 1859. Cradlebaugh, 20. Although most family history records place his birth date at Mar. 8, 1808, the Pinto, UT, cemetery records give his date of birth as Apr. 30, 1807. See Pinto, UT, cemetery records, microfilm, FHL.

21. Carleton, 17, 24–25; McGlashan; Beadle2, 500; Corr1; James Lynch, affidavit, July 27, 1859, enclosed in S. H. Montgomery to A. B. Greenwood, Aug. 17, 1859, USBIA; [James] Lynch, statement, in "The Mountain Meadows Massacre: Surviving Children of the Murdered Fix the Crime upon the Mormons," *San Francisco Daily Evening Bulletin*, May 31, 1859; S. B. Honea, in "Outrages"; Forney to Greenwood, Sept. 22, 1859, in SDoc42, 86.

22. "The Mormon Massacre: Names of All the White Murderers," *New York Herald*, May 22, 1877, also reprinted in "The Massacre: The Names of All the Whites Who Participated in It," *Salt Lake Daily Tribune*, May 30, 1877. The name "George Hanley" that appears in this newspaper list is likely a reference to George Hawley. Even though it said George was dead, he had actually just left Utah. Iowa, Shelby County, Grove Township, 1880 U.S. Census, population schedule, 8. This list, which claimed to be published posthumously from a handwritten note by Lee, included several names not associated with other lists attributed to Lee, nor are the names verified by other sources. Those names, as listed in the article, are: J. [Jehiel] McConnel, "two men named Curtis," J. [Jonathon] Pugmire [Sr.], Sam Adair, Nate Adair, George Hanley [Hawley], Hairgraves, and William Hamblin. Ezra Curtis is known to have lived in southern Utah in 1857 and to have been identified as a massacre participant by eyewitness accounts. The name Hairgraves does not resemble the name of any known individual residing within the jurisdiction of the Iron Military District.

23. *MU*, 228, 379; "LC"; "LLC"; John Hawley to Joseph Smith III, June 12, 1884, in *Saints' Herald* 31, no. 26 (1884): 412; Hawley, 15–16.

24. *MU*, 228, 379; "Lee's Book, Names of Participants Corrections," undated, AJ1. Legend claimed that William Hawley was chained to a wagon wheel at the Meadows by fellow militiamen because he opposed the massacre. Frank Beckwith, "Was William Hawley Chained to a Wagon Wheel?" chap. 2, in

"Shameful Friday: A Critical Study of the Mountain Meadows Massacre," HBM 31255, Henry E. Huntington Library, San Marino, CA. None of the witness accounts mention such an occurrence. Cradlebaugh issued a warrant for Hawley's arrest in 1859. Cradlebaugh, 19–20.

25. Philip Klingensmith, JDL1-BT 3:3–4, 9–10, 15, 17–18, 72–76, 82; Higgins, affidavit, Apr. 20, 1859, printed in Cradlebaugh, 42; Clewes; Isaac C. Riddle, JDL1-BT 4:120; *MU*, 232–33, 236, 379; "LC"; "LLC"; Corr1; Mary Campbell, AJ1; D. W. Tullis, AJ1; Morris, statement, Feb. 2, 1892, CM; Whitney, 1:706n†; Notes from meeting George W. Adair, found in McKay Diary, July 27, 1907; Indictment for murder against John M. Higbee, Sept. 24, 1874, in CCF 31 and CCF 32. Cradlebaugh issued a warrant for Higbee's arrest in 1859. Cradlebaugh, 19; Forney to Greenwood, Sept. 22, 1859, in SDoc42, 86; Jabez Sutherland, JDL1-BT 8:4. While still in hiding Higbee released his account of the massacre under the pseudonym "Bull Valley Snort." Bull Valley Snort [John M. Higbee], statement, Feb. 1894, typescript, CM. After the charges against him were dismissed, Higbee and a few of his supporters released affidavits in his defense. Higbee, affidavit, June 15, 1896, CM; Daniel S. Macfarlane, affidavit, June 29, 1896, CM; William Tait, affidavit, June 30, 1896, CM; Joel W. White, affidavit, Oct. 9, 1896, CM. Tait's and Macfarlane's affidavits were almost identical.

26. *MU*, 230, 232–34, 247, 379; "LC"; "LLC"; Philip Klingensmith, JDL1-BT 3:7–8, 82; Samuel Pollock, JDL1-BT 4:62; Nephi Johnson, JDL2-BT 1:57; Samuel McMurdy, JDL2-BT 1:33. Judge John Cradlebaugh issued a warrant for Charles Hopkins's arrest in 1859. Cradlebaugh, 20; Jabez Sutherland, JDL1-BT 8:4.

27. *MU*, 379; "Mormon Massacre" (this source simply lists the surname, "Humphrey"); "Mormon Assassins: Another List of Men Who Were at Mountain Meadows," *New York Herald*, June 26, 1877 ("John Humphrey: lived with old man Woods at Cedar"); "Lee's Book, Names of Participants Corrections," undated, AJ1; Ann Richey, List of Mountain Meadow Participants, enclosed in Ernest Cook to Samuel W. Taylor, July 6, 1979, CHL. Ann Richey, born at Pinto on Aug. 24, 1866, prepared a handwritten list of massacre participants that was later found in a box of papers owned by Ernest Cook's wife, Helen, a descendant of Ann Richey. Cook believed the list was from first-hand knowledge but admitted he was unsure of its origin. The list contains names in alphabetical order from A to L. It is unclear whether the other half is in existence. All but two names on the list can be confirmed as massacre participants from other sources. The two exceptions are John Bateman, likely a reference to William Bateman, and Tom Edwards, who cannot be confirmed as a resident within the jurisdiction of the Iron Military District.

28. *MU*, 232, 379; Philip Klingensmith, JDL1-BT 3:24, 90–91.

29. *MU*, 232, 380; "Lee's Confession," *New York Herald*, Mar. 22, 1877; John Jacobs, "Not There," *Salt Lake Daily Herald*, Mar. 30, 1877; "Lee's Book, Names of Participants Corrections," undated, AJ1.

30. Philip Klingensmith, JDL1-BT 3:10–11; "Lee's Book, Names of Participants Corrections," undated, AJ1; *MU*, 232, 380; Jabez Sutherland, JDL1-BT 8:4. Swen is likely the "Irvin Jacobs" named by Lee in the "Confessions" section of *MU*. According to family tradition another of the Jacobs brothers, Christopher, was forced to join the company going to Mountain Meadows. "He told them they could force him to go but they could not force him to kill anyone after he got there. This he didn't do as he wouldn't fire a gun." However, John Chatterley said that at the time of the massacre Christopher Jacobs was accompanying him on a reconnaissance mission along the Sevier River, looking for signs of the approaching U.S. army, which was feared to have taken a southern mountain pass into Utah. See James W. Sorensen, "Christopher Jacobs: 1819–1907," MMMRF; Chatterley.

31. *MU*, 232, 379; "Lee's Book, Names of Participants Corrections," undated, AJ1; Indictment for murder against Samuel Jewkes, Sept. 24, 1874, in CCF 31 and CCF 33. In 1892, Cedar City resident Mary Campbell told historian Andrew Jenson that Jewkes was given two children from the massacre. One of those children, a girl between seven and nine years old, reportedly pointed out her father's killer and "afterwards disappeared." Campbell, AJ1; Campbell, AJ2. Contemporary records identify only one child given to Jewkes, Prudence Angeline Dunlap. Because she was five years old at the time of the massacre and seven when she returned to Arkansas, she was likely the one Campbell remembered and was not killed as rumored. Cedar City Stake, "Record of Children Blessed 1856–1863," CHL; Kearny. During the closing arguments of the first Lee trial, defense attorney Jabez Sutherland pointed out that none of the trial testimony placed Jewkes at the massacre. Jabez Sutherland, JDL1-PS 11:23, JDL1-BT 8:4.

32. Nephi Johnson, JDL2-BT 1:43–85; Lyman, Sept. 19, 21, 1895; NJ1908; NJ1909; NJ1910; Samuel Pollock, JDL1-BT 5:191, 199 (Pollock recalled seeing a white man on a hill above the massacre, who was likely Nephi Johnson); *MU*, 220, 232, 237, 243, 380; "LC"; "LLC." In his testimony at Lee's second trial, Johnson claimed he saw the massacre from the hill after he chased his horse, which had gotten loose after being tied to a tree. Nephi Johnson, JDL2-BT 1:47, 74, 81. Gibbs, 34, wrote, "Nephi Johnson's horse had learned the trick of untying his halter rope when it was carelessly fastened." Judge John Cradlebaugh issued a warrant for Johnson's arrest in 1859. Cradlebaugh, 20.

33. PKS; Philip Klingensmith, JDL1-BT 3:1–118; Joel White, JDL1-BT 4:9; Samuel Pollock, JDL1-BT 4:69; Laban Morrill, JDL2-BT 1:9; Nephi Johnson, JDL2-BT 1:47; Jacob Hamblin, JDL2-BT 1:102; "LC"; "LLC"; *MU*, 244–45; Mary S. Campbell, AJ1; Ellott Willden, AJ2; Ellott Willden2, AJ2; Ellott Willden, AJ1; Whitney, 1:704; NJ1908; Forney to Greenwood, Sept. 22, 1859, in SDoc42, 86; Jabez Sutherland, JDL1-BT 8:4. Klingensmith himself suggested that at least one of the children died at Hamblin's ranch, but from wounds. Philip Klingensmith, JDL1-BT 3:20. Nancy Huff, one of the children who survived the massacre, remembered, "At the close of the massacre there was 18 children still alive, one girl, some

ten or twelve years old they said was t[o]o big and could tell so they killed her, leaving 17." "Cates." Before Klingensmith was sworn in as a witness in John D. Lee's first trial, prosecuting attorney William Carey entered a motion of "nolle prosequi" in his behalf. Indictment for murder against Philip Klingensmith, Sept. 24, 1874, in CCF 31; William Carey, JDL1-PS 2:32.

34. Samuel Knight, JDL2-BT 1:18–32; Samuel Knight, AJ1; Conversation Samuel Knight, in Cannon, June 13, 1895; MU, 228, 238, 241–43, 380; Nephi Johnson, JDL2-BT 1: 62–63; "LC"; "LLC"; Knight; Jabez Sutherland, JDL1-BT 8:4.

35. Juanita Brooks, *Dudley Leavitt, Pioneer to Southern Utah* (n.p., 1942), 33; Juanita Brooks, *On the Ragged Edge: The Life and Times of Dudley Leavitt* (Salt Lake City: Utah State Historical Society, 1973), 76–78; Notes regarding the Mountain Meadows Massacre, undated, AJ1; Samuel Knight, AJ1; MU, 228, 380; "Lee's Book, Names of Participants Corrections," undated, AJ1.

36. "LC"; "LLC"; MU, 213–92, 380; NJ1908; Samuel Knight, JDL2-BT 1:20–22; Samuel Knight, AJ1; Corr1; Benjamin Platt, Reminiscences, 1899–1905, typescript, 5–6, CHL; Gibbs, 53–54; Philip Klingensmith, JDL1-BT 3:9–10, 72–76; Annie Elizabeth Hoag, JDL1-BT 4:29; Samuel Knight, JDL2-BT 1:28–31; Samuel McMurdy, JDL2-BT 1:34–35, 37, 42; Nephi Johnson, JDL2-BT 1:45–46, 49–51, 67, 76; Jacob Hamblin, JDL2-BT 1:86–87, 94–97; Knight; C. J. S., Mar. 25, 1877, in "Shooting of Lee!" *Salt Lake Daily Tribune*, Mar. 30, 1877; Indictment for murder against John D. Lee, Sept. 24, 1874, in CCF 31 and CCF 40; Collins R. Hakes, Apr. 24, 1916, CM; Jabez Sutherland, JDL1-BT 8:4. Cradlebaugh issued a warrant for Lee's arrest in 1859. Cradlebaugh, 19. See also Forney to Greenwood, Sept. 22, 1859, in SDoc42, 86.

37. Higgins, affidavit, Apr. 20, 1859, printed in Cradlebaugh, 42; MU, 232, 380. Cradlebaugh issued a warrant for Loveridge's arrest in 1859. Cradlebaugh, 20.

38. Macfarlane, affidavit, June 29, 1896, in CM; Daniel S. Macfarlane, AJ2; MU, 232, 237, 240, 380; "Mormon Assassins"; "LC"; "LLC." According to MU: "I remember a circumstance that Haight then related to me about Dan. McFarland. He said: 'Dan will make a bully warrior.' I said, 'Why do you think so?' 'Well,' said he, 'Dan came to me and said, "You must get me another knife, because the one I have got has no good stuff in it, for the edge turned when I cut a fellow's throat that day at the Meadows. I caught one of the devils that was trying to get away, and when I cut his throat it took all the edge off of my knife." I tell you that boy will make a *bully* warrior.'" MU, 254. Cradlebaugh issued a warrant for Daniel Macfarlane's arrest in 1859. Cradlebaugh, 19.

39. Cradlebaugh, 20; MU, 232, 380.

40. Samuel McMurdy, JDL2-BT 1:32–43; PKS; Philip Klingensmith, JDL1-BT 3:8, 21; Nephi Johnson, JDL2-BT 1:62–63; MU, 232, 238, 241–42, 380; "LC"; "LLC"; "Lee's Book, Names of Participants Corrections," undated, AJ1; Jabez Sutherland, JDL1-BT 8:4. When asked whether he participated in the killing of the wounded emigrants, Samuel McMurdy refused to answer, stating, "I believe I am not on trial." Samuel McMurdy, JDL2-BT 1:42.

41. Mangum, deposition, July 5, 1875, MBB, 324–25; William Young, JDL1-BT 4:49, 58; William Young, JDL1-PS 5:35, JDL1-BT 4:58. Cradlebaugh issued a warrant in 1859 for James Mangum. Cradlebaugh, 20.

42. *MU*, 229, 231, 380; Jabez Sutherland, JDL1-BT 8:4. Cradlebaugh issued a warrant for John Mangum's arrest in 1859. Cradlebaugh, 20.

43. *MU*, 228, 380.

44. Morris, statement, Feb. 2, 1892, CM; William Barton, AJ1. According to Andrew Jenson's original notes from his interview with William Barton, the tan bark council was a "consultation of three consisting of I. C. Haight Wm. H. Dame and Elias Morris." Morris's name was later erased and replaced with "another man." In an 1890 letter, William C. Stewart, impoverished and in hiding, recalled a conversation he had with Mormon apostle Erastus Snow: "He [Snow] asked me if Elias Morris sent me any money. I said no. He said if he would lend you $1000 it is nothing but what he aught to do." Stewart added, "To save [Morris] & others, I am an Exile. He was I. C. H[aight's] Councler & only for him & a few more I would not bee here." William C. Stewart to Wilford Woodruff and Council, Nov. 1, 1890, in Wilford Woodruff, General Correspondence Files, 1887–98, CHL.

45. William Young, JDL1-BT 4:56–57; Philip Klingensmith, JDL1-BT 3:10; *MU*, 228, 380; Washington Branch Manuscript History, CHL; Hawley, 16; Jabez Sutherland, JDL1-BT 8:4. Cradlebaugh issued a warrant for Harrison Pearce's arrest in 1859. Cradlebaugh, 20.

46. James Pearce, JDL1-BT 4:100–8, 114–15; *MU*, 228, 380; Philip Klingensmith, JDL1-BT 3:10; "Lee's Book, Names of Participants Corrections," undated, AJ1; Samuel Pollock, JDL1-BT 5:199; William Young, JDL1-BT 4:56; Jabez Sutherland, JDL1-BT 8:4. In 1859 Cradlebaugh issued a warrant for a Jim Price that was likely meant for James Pearce. Cradlebaugh, 20. Although eyewitnesses William Young and Samuel Pollock verify Pearce's claim that he was sick and remained at the militia camp during the massacre, one legend claimed James was shot at by his father, Harrison Pearce, for attempting to protect an emigrant girl from the slaughter. The bullet reportedly grazed the side of his face, creating a noticeable scar. McGlashan; Frank Beckwith, chap. 6, in "Shameful Friday." Another version of this legend that gives no names appears in a newspaper article. "Among the Mormons: An Interesting Journey to the Southern Settlements," *New York Herald*, June 27, 1877. Juanita Brooks claimed the legend referred to James Pearce's twelve-year-old brother, Thomas Jefferson Pearce. Brooks2, 90. No primary evidence confirms either of these legends. Klingensmith raised the possibility that multiple members of the Pearce family may have been at the massacre, stating he thought he saw "Jim Pearce and brother and his sons but I would not be positive." Klingensmith, JDL1-BT 3:10. Klingensmith likely confused James Pearce with his father Harrison Pearce, since James had no sons in 1857. The available sources do not confirm that James had any brothers at the massacre.

47. Samuel Pollock, JDL1-BT 4:62–72, 180–203; *MU*, 232, 380; Higgins, affidavit, Apr. 20, 1859, printed in Cradlebaugh, 42; Jabez Sutherland, JDL1-BT 8:4. Cradlebaugh issued a warrant for Pollock's arrest in 1859. Cradlebaugh, 20.

48. Ellott Willden, AJ2; Mary S. Campbell, AJ1; Mary S. Campbell, AJ2; D. W. Tullis, AJ1; Ellott Willden, AJ1; McGlashan; Whitney, 1:699; Samuel Pollock, JDL1-BT 5:181.

49. Isaac Riddle, JDL1-BT 4:118–21; Ellott Willden, AJ2.

50. Richard S. Robinson, JDL1-BT 5:319–24; Richard S. Robinson, AJ1; Albert Hamblin, statement, in Carleton, 15; Joel White, JDL1-BT 3:122; Joel W. White, JDL2-BT 1:15–17; Clewes.

51. *MU*, 220, 226–28, 380; "LC"; "LLC"; Mangum, deposition, July 5, 1875, MBB, 324; Philip Klingensmith, JDL1-BT 3:28, 31; "Lee's Book, Names of Participants Corrections," undated, AJ1; Jabez Sutherland, JDL1-BT 8:4. Although Shirts appeared to carry out his duty as Indian interpreter and leader, Lee referred to him as "cowardly" and "made him suffer for being a coward." *MU*, 226, 243. Shirts's son Ambrose said that was because Carl gave orders to Indians that were in direct contradiction to the orders given him by Lee. After the massacre, Mary Adoline Lee divorced Carl Shirts with her father's help. Ambrose Shurtz, *History of Peter Shirts and his Descendants*, 93–94, undated family history located in the FHL; *MC*, 1:258, June 4–6, 1860.

52. *MU*, 228, 380; William Young, JDL1-PS 5:35, 42, JDL1-BT 4:49, 58; James Pearce, JDL1-BT 4:103; PKS; Philip Klingensmith, JDL1-BT 3:10–11. In 1859 Judge Cradlebaugh issued an arrest warrant for William Slade. The warrant could have been intended for either William Rufus Slade Sr. or his son William Slade Jr. Cradlebaugh 19. In his closing argument for the first Lee trial, defense attorney Jabez Sutherland contended that Slade remained at the militia camp during the massacre; however, this assertion is not supported by the trial testimony of eyewitnesses. Two of those who stayed at the camp during the massacre, William Young and James Pearce, saw Slade at the Mountain Meadows but did not say he remained in the camp. Jabez Sutherland, JDL1-BT 8:4, JDL1-PS 11:38–39.

53. *MU*, 228, 380; Philip Klingensmith, JDL1-BT 3:10.

54. *MU*, 380; "Lee's Confession," *New York Herald*, Mar. 22, 1877; "Mormon Assassins"; Cradlebaugh, 20; Kearny. Cradlebaugh issued an arrest warrant for Smith in connection with the massacre in 1859, but he may have done so because a surviving child was recovered from his home shortly before. Alexander Ingram, who did not participate in the massacre, also had one of the surviving children in 1859, and shortly thereafter Cradlebaugh issued an arrest warrant for him. Cradlebaugh, 19; Kearny; Rogers. Ingram, a Harmony resident, spoke in a church meeting after Lee left Harmony for the Meadows and was not identified by any of the witnesses as being at the Meadows. HBM, Sept. 6, 1857.

55. George Spencer to Erastus Snow, Mar. 26, 1867, Incoming Correspondence, YOF; McGlashan.

56. Philip Klingensmith, JDL1-BT 3:15–16 (says Stewart was on horseback during massacre, though he was more likely on foot); William Young, JDL1-BT 4:49–50; Samuel Pollock, JDL1-BT 4:64; Thomas T. Willis, JDL1-BT 4:33; "Lee's Confession," *New York Herald*, Mar. 22, 1877; Corr1; Ellott Willden, AJ2; Ellott Willden, AJ1; *MU*, 230, 235, 380; "LC"; "LLC"; Conversation with Samuel Knight, in Cannon, June 13, 1895; McGlashan. See also Jacob Hamblin, JDL2-BT 1:107–8; Higgins, affidavit, Apr. 20, 1859, printed in Cradlebaugh, 42; Indictment for murder against William C. Stewart, Sept. 24, 1874, in CCF 31 and CCF 35. Judge John Cradlebaugh issued a warrant for William Stewart's arrest in 1859. Cradlebaugh, 19; Jabez Sutherland, JDL1-BT 8:4.

57. John W. Bradshaw, JDL1-BT 4:85.

58. *MU*, 232, 380; "Lee's Confession," *New York Herald*, Mar. 22, 1877; "Mormon Massacre"; "Mormon Assassins." In some sources he is listed as Arthur Stratton, but massacre participant Ellott Willden clarified that his name was Anthony Stratton. "Lee's Book, Names of Participants Corrections," undated, AJ1.

59. Tait, affidavit, June 30, 1896, CM; *MU*, 230, 380; "Lee's Book, Names of Participants Corrections," undated, AJ1; Kim S. Whitehead, "William and Elizabeth Tait, A History of Their Life," 2, unpublished family history, copy in MMMRF; Adonis Findlay Robinson, *History of Kane County* (Salt Lake City: Utah Printing, 1970), 535.

60. D. W. Tullis, AJ1; Ellott Willden, AJ1; Clewes; Albert Hamblin, statement, in Carleton, 15. Cradlebaugh issued a warrant for a Thornton's arrest in 1859. Cradlebaugh, 20.

61. David W. Tullis, interview with Jacob Forney and William Rodgers, Apr. 13, 1859, in J. Forney to A. B. Greenwood, Aug. 1859, in SDoc42, 76–77; D. W. Tullis, AJ1; James Lynch, affidavit, July 27, 1859, in SDoc42, 81–85. Although Lynch claimed that Rebecca Dunlap identified Tullis as her mother's killer, according to another account attributed to James Lynch, "A very intelligent little girl, named Becky Dunlap, pointed out to me at Santa Clara an Englishman named Tellus, whom she says *she saw murder her father.*" Lynch, statement, in "The Mountain Meadows Massacre: Surviving Children of the Murdered Fix the Crime"; Albert Hamblin, interview with Jacob Forney, in Forney to Greenwood, Aug. 1859, in SDoc42, 78; Albert Hamblin, statement, in Carleton, 14; Forney to Greenwood, Sept. 22, 1859, in SDoc42, 86. A family legend claimed three women from Pinto, knowing of the massacre plans, put makeup over Tullis's upper body, arms and face, and placed hot bricks around his bed to make him look as if he had a fever. When militia leaders came to get him, he groaned and acted terribly ill, thus escaping participation. Yet in the two known statements Tullis made regarding the massacre, he made no mention of feigning illness to avoid the

massacre. One of the women who supposedly helped Tullis was the wife of Richard Harrison. The Harrisons were living at Cedar City at the time of the massacre, and Richard was also implicated as a participant. Sharon M. Bliss, ed., "Autobiographies/Biography of Tullis, Mangum, Pulsipher, Maughan, Davenport, Dahle, Griffin, etc.," typescript, 2, [1995], copy at FHL; Leila Mangum Bradford, "David Wilson Tullis," May 30, 1988, unpublished manuscript, MMMRF; Verda Tullis, "David Wilson Tullis," ca. 1953, 4, copy in MMMRF; "David Wilson Tullis," entry submitted by Leilani Grange, in Sons of Utah Pioneers, *Conquerors of the West: Stalwart Mormon Pioneers* ([Sandy, UT]: Agreka Books, 1999), 4:2600–2602.

62. *MU*, 232, 380; "Lee's Book, Names of Participants Corrections," undated, AJ1; Nephi Johnson, JDL2-BT 1:70; Philip Klingensmith, JDL1-BT 3:90–91.

63. *MU*, 380; "Mormon Assassins." After interviewing several massacre participants, Andrew Jenson concluded there was no John Weston at the massacre. "Lee's Book, Names of Participants Corrections," undated AJ1.

64. Nephi Johnson, JDL2-PS 2:54, 62 (Josiah Rogerson wrote "Weyson" over shorthand "WSN" or "RSN"; the shorthand omits only vowels and cannot be read "Western" or "Weston" as appears in the longhand transcriptions); Nephi Johnson, JDL2-BT 1:44, 55 ("Weston"); Nephi Johnson, JDL2-RT 1:72 ("Weston"), 84 ("Western"); *MU*, 340, 346 ("Western").

65. According to a family member who interwove family history with fiction, John Western worked as a distiller in Cedar City, secretly sold five barrels of whiskey to the Fancher party shortly after it left town, and also provided whiskey to the militia going to Mountain Meadows as a gift for Paiutes but did not go to Mountain Meadows himself. Robert E. Jones, *From Malaga to the Mountain: The Story of Matilda* (Las Vegas: Jones & Holt, 1971), 271–74.

66. Philip Klingensmith, JDL1-BT 3:8; Thomas T. Willis, JDL1-BT 4:32–33.

67. Joel White, JDL1-BT 3:119–34, 4:3–24, JDL2-BT 1:15–18; Philip Klingensmith, JDL1-BT 3:5–6; *MU*, 230, 235, 380; "LC"; "LLC"; Corr1; Ellott Willden, AJ1; Jabez Sutherland, JDL1-BT 8:4. Cradlebaugh issued a warrant for Joel White's arrest in 1859. Cradlebaugh, 20.

68. *MU*, 380; "Mormon Massacre"; "Mormon Assassins;" Mary H. White, AJ1. Samuel White's name does not appear in the "confessions" Lee gave to Sumner Howard ("LC"; "LLC"), nor in the narrative portion of what he gave to Bishop (*MU*, 213–92).

69. Samuel Pollock, JDL1-BT 4:62, 5:180–82; Philip Klingensmith, JDL1-BT 3:8–9; *MU*, 232, 380; "LC"; "LLC"; Jabez Sutherland, JDL1-BT 8:4.

70. Indictment for murder against Ellott Willden, Sept. 24, 1874, in CCF 31 and MBB, 431–33; Ellott Willden, AJ2; Clew/Will; Clewes; Corr1; Ellott Willden, AJ1; Mary S. Campbell, AJ1; D. W. Tullis, AJ1; Conversation with Samuel Knight, recorded in Cannon, June 13, 1895; McGlashan; Whitney, 1:699; *MU*, 230, 380; "LC"; "LLC." Lee refers to Willden as "Alexander Wilden." However, Andrew Jenson, who interviewed Ellott, noted that

Alexander and Ellott Willden were the same person. "Lee's Book, Names of Participants Corrections," Mountain Meadows file, Jenson Collection. Judge John Cradlebaugh issued a warrant for E. Welean in 1859. This may have been Ellott Willden. Cradlebaugh, 19; Jabez Sutherland, JDL1-PS 11:23, JDL1-BT 8:4.

71. John W. Bradshaw, JDL1-BT 4:84–85; Joel White, JDL1-BT 3:124; Jabez Sutherland, JDL1-BT 8:4. Andrew Jenson speculated that Williamson may have been one who "divulged" information about the massacre to investigators. "Lee's Book, Names of Participants Corrections," undated AJ1.

72. John Henry Willis, JDL1-BT 4:39–45; Philip Klingensmith, JDL1-BT 3:8; Thomas T. Willis, JDL1-BT 4:32–33.

73. Philip Klingensmith, JDL1-BT 3:11.

74. "Cates." Cradlebaugh issued a warrant for Willis's arrest in 1859. Cradlebaugh, 19.

75. William Young, JDL1-BT 4:49–61, 5:203–14; Samuel Pollock, JDL1-BT 5:185, 199; James Pearce, JDL1-BT 4:103, 105; Nephi Johnson, JDL2-BT 1:57–58; Jabez Sutherland, JDL1-BT 8:4; *MU*, 228–29, 380; "LC"; "LLC"; "Gilbert Morse," *Salt Lake Daily Tribune*, Sept. 28, 1876; Annie Elizabeth Hoag, JDL1-BT 4:25. At least two people remember seeing William Young with other men from Harmony before Lee left with the Paiutes for Mountain Meadows. Although Young was among the original settlers of Harmony, by the late summer of 1857 he made his home in Washington. William Young and John D. Lee had a history of bad feeling toward each other dating to the time their church had its headquarters in Nauvoo. See *Times and Seasons* 3, no. 16 (1842): 820–21 and 4, no. 4 (1843): 80; Alfred Douglas Young, Autobiography, BYU; Brown, Dec. 3, 1854, Mar. 18, 1855.

Appendix D

1. See pp. 132–209 herein and Appendix C.

2. See pp. 137–209 herein. As anthropologist Martha Knack points out, "Southern Paiute culture, political structure, and economy could not have produced an action like the Mountain Meadows Massacre without Mormon stimulus and support." Knack, 79–80.

3. "The people who grew the *haweave* were the 'Nuwuvi' or as they are called today, the Southern Paiutes." *Nuwuvi*, 5. "The term 'Paiute' itself, unfortunately, has no clear ethnic or linguistic reference; nevertheless, the term 'Southern Paiute' is well established as referring to…Numic 'bands' or subgroups which share a geographical center in southern Utah." William Bright, ed., *The Collected Works of Edward Sapir*, vol. 10 (Berlin: Walter de Gruyter, 1992), 13.

4. The growing body of literature on Southern Paiutes includes *Nuwuvi*; Holt; Knack.

5. See pp. 141–42, 145, 147–48, 153–54, herein.

6. See pp. 152, 154, 161–62, herein; Carleton, 19–20; Cradlebaugh, 17.

7. Carleton, 19–20.

8. See, e.g., story attributed to Minnie Jake in Martineau, xiii, 62. For other examples of this tradition, see excerpts of 1998 interviews with Clifford Jake and Will Rogers in "Paiute," 134–36.

9. See, e.g., story attributed to Johnny Jake in Martineau, xiii, 62. See also account attributed to Joseph Pikyavit in Beckwith, xiii, 120–21.

10. John D. Lee to Brigham Young, Nov. 20, 1857, Incoming Correspondence, YOF.

11. Voucher No. 9, Sept. 30, 1857, Superintendent's Vouchers, Superintendent of Indian Affairs Files, YOF. The dates, Sept. 21–26, closely match those given in a massacre report compiled by George A. Smith and James McKnight in 1858. Smith and McKnight, "The Emigrant and Indian War at Mountain Meadows, Sept. 21, 22, 23, 24 and 25, 1857," Aug. 6, 1858, in Historian's Office, Collected Historical Documents, CHL. Lee's Nov. 20, 1857, report gave the date of the massacre as Sept. 22, eleven days after it actually happened.

12. See Donald R. Moorman and Gene A. Sessions, *Camp Floyd and the Mormons: The Utah War* (Salt Lake City: University of Utah Press, 1992), 133, 303n50; Bagley, 128, 410n36.

13. Calder notation at the top of Lee to Young, Nov. 20, 1857, Incoming Correspondence, YOF; Jacob Hamblin, Journal, 1854–57, Oct. 7, 1856, 77–78, in Jacob Hamblin, Papers, CHL; Jacob Hamblin, *Jacob Hamblin: A Narrative of His Personal Experience, as a Frontiersman, Missionary to the Indians, and Explorer* (Salt Lake City: Juvenile Instructor Office, 1881), 38–40; Jacob Hamblin, *Jacob Hamblin: His Life in His Own Words* (Provo, UT: Paramount Books with Stratford Press, 1995), 33–34.

14. MU, 226–27; "LC"; "LLC"; Philip Klingensmith, JDL1-BT 3:28–29, 98, 101–2, JDL1-RT 1:86, 125, 127, JDL1-PS, 3:10, 4:5, 7, JDL1-RS 2:37, 3:15, 17; Feargus O'Connor Willden, Autobiography, 4, CHL.

15. Willden Autobiography, 4.

16. Gibbs, 53–54. "Indian Comanch" was enumerated in Utah Territory, Iron County, Indian Inhabitants in Cedar City Precinct, 1880 U.S. Census, population schedule, 375C.

17. Calder notation at the top of Lee to Young, Nov. 20, 1857, Incoming Correspondence, YOF.

18. George W. Armstrong to Brigham Young, Aug. 29, 1857, Incoming Correspondence, YOF; Lynch, affidavit, July 27, 1859, enclosed in Montgomery to Greenwood, Aug. 17, 1859, USBIA; "City Jottings," *Salt Lake Daily Tribune*, Sept. 1, 1875.

19. Carleton, 8, 11–17; J. Forney to A. B. Greenwood, Aug. 1859, in SDoc42, 77–78; Jacob Hamblin, JDL2-BT 1:97–98; [James] Lynch, statement, ca. 1859, Records of the Adj. Gen. Office, RG 94, National Archives, copy in MMMRF.

20. Indian Peak informant #24 (identified as Johnny Jake on page xiii), Martineau, 62; Clifford Jake, interview, Nov. 18, 1998, in "Paiute," 134–35.

21. Carleton, 19–20; Cradlebaugh, 17; "Our Los Angeles Correspondence," *San Francisco Daily Alta California*, Oct. 27, 1857; Reuben P. Campbell to F. J. Porter, July 6, 1859, in SDoc42, 15–16; John R. Young, *Memoirs of John R. Young, Utah Pioneer 1847* (Salt Lake City: Deseret News, 1920), 111–13; James H. Martineau, letter to the editor, Aug. 22, 1857, in "Trip to the Santa Clara," *Deseret News*, Sept. 23, 1857; McGlashan; Beadle2, 500–501; Calder notation at top of Lee to Young, Nov. 20, 1857, Incoming Correspondence, YOF; Voucher No. 9, Sept. 30, 1857, Superintendent's Vouchers, Superintendent of Indian Affairs Files, YOF.

22. *MU*, 242; Annie Elizabeth Hoag, JDL1-BT 4:29–30, JDL1-PS, 5:19, JDL1-RS, 4:13–14; Brown, Dec. 10, 1854; Kearny.

23. Martineau, Aug. 22, 1857, in "Trip to the Santa Clara."

24. Calder notation at the top of Lee to Young, Nov. 20, 1857, Incoming Correspondence, YOF; Thomas L. Kane, Memorandum Book, 1857–58, 19–20, BYU; *Nuwuvi*, 8. Kane obtained information at the Spanish Fork Indian farm from George W. Armstrong, Kanosh, or both.

25. Carleton, 13–14; Robert Hafen Briggs, "Samuel Knight and Events Incident to the Utah War, 1857–1858: A Preliminary Study" (unpublished paper written for the Swiss Days Celebration and Samuel Knight Reunion, Sept. 21–23, 2001, Santa Clara, UT), 3, copy in MMMRF.

26. Brooks1, 221–22; "Paiute," 146. Brooks spelled Kwi-toos, "Queetuse."

27. "LLC"; *MU*, 226, 249. Referred to in *MU* as "Clem," Lemuel was the first Paiute child adopted by Lee in southern Utah. Brooks1, 164; James M. Mangum, deposition, July 5, 1875, MBB, 324; Nephi Johnson, JDL2-BT 1:58; NJ1908; NJ1910; S. F. Atwood, letter to the editor, June 1, 1856, in "Correspondence," *Deseret News*, July 16, 1856.

28. "Lee Trial"; "Eastern News: What the Indians Say," *Los Angeles Weekly Herald*, Aug. 7, 1875; "Mountain Meadows," *San Francisco Daily Call*, Mar. 24, 1877; *MU*, 226–27; "LC"; "LLC"; Willden Autobiography, 4; Chatterley; *Journals*, 211–12, May 28, 1859; McGlashan; Voucher No. 9, Sept. 30, 1857, Superintendent's Vouchers, Superintendent of Indian Affairs Files, YOF; Calder notation at the top of Lee to Young, Nov. 20, 1857, Incoming Correspondence, YOF; Shirts.

29. "Unveiled," *St. Louis Globe-Democrat*, July 24, 1875; "Mountain Meadow Massacre," *Cumberland (IL) Democrat*, Aug. 5, 1875; "A Tale of Horror," *Steubenville (OH) Daily Herald*, July 24, 1875. The transcripts of Klingensmith's testimony do not list the name Myack; Patterson's shorthand records that Klingensmith saw a man named "My" cut a boy's throat. Rogerson's shorthand identifies the man as an Indian but does not give his name. Philip Klingensmith, JDL1-BT 3:28, JDL1-PS 3:9, JDL1-RS 2:37.

30. Calder notation at the top of Lee to Young, Nov. 20, 1857, Incoming Correspondence, YOF.

31. Will Rogers, interview, Dec. 1998, in "Paiute," 135–36; Carleton, 12–14. According to Albert Hamblin, "John and I could see where the Indians were

hid in the oak bushes and sage right by the side of the road a mile or more on their route, and I said to John, I would like to know what the emigrants left their wagons for, as they were going into a 'worse fix than ever they saw.'"

32. Jimmie Pete, interview with Alva Matheson, Jan. 15, 1968, in American Indian Oral History, Duke Collection, UofU; *Nuwuvi*, 8, 86; LaVan Martineau, *Southern Paiute Indian Genealogy* (Globe, AZ: Martineau Pub., 1996), 39.

33. Willden Autobiography, 4.

34. Philip Klingensmith, JDL1-BT 3:29, 98; James H. Martineau to George A. Smith, May 30, 1855, in "Home Correspondence: Iron County," *Deseret News*, July 11, 1855.

35. Carleton, 19; Huntington, Sept. 1–20, 1857; Voucher No. 17, Sept. 11, 1857, Superintendent's Vouchers, Superintendent of Indian Affairs Files, YOF; Voucher No. 9, Sept. 30, 1857, Superintendent's Vouchers, Superintendent of Indian Affairs Files, YOF.

36. U.S. Army, George Montague Wheeler, Daniel W. Lockwood, Geographical Surveys West of the 100th Meridian (U.S.), *Preliminary Report upon a Reconnaissance through Southern and Southeastern Nevada, Made in 1869, by Geo. M. Wheeler, Corps of Engineers, U.S. Army, Assisted by D. W. Lockwood, Corps of Engineers, U.S. Army* (Washington: GPO, 1875), 37, 47.

37. Tunanita'a was apparently John Seaman's father. The information on Tunanita'a came from Dan Bullets, a Paiute. *Kaibab*, inside front cover.

38. Woodruff, Sept. 1, 1857; Huntington, Sept. 1, 1857; HOJ, Sept. 1, 1857; S. B. Honea, in "Outrages"; Farnsworth; "Horrible"; Hurt, 202–3. Hurt reported that a Spoods, a well-known Ute, said that Ammon went to Iron County to dissuade Paiutes from going to the Meadows, only to be warned away by one of the white leaders. This story closely resembles events at Beaver, where Sissix shot at emigrants and was ordered away by Bishop Philo Farnsworth. Ammon arrived in Beaver from Salt Lake City and helped resolve the situation.

39. George A. Smith to Brigham Young, Aug. 17, 1858, Incoming Correspondence, YOF, copy in Historian's Office, Letterpress Copybook 1:885–91, CHL; William R. Palmer, "Pahute Indian Homelands," *Utah Historical Quarterly* 6 (July 1933): 93; *Nuwuvi*, 8, 86.

40. Huntington, Sept. 1, 1857; HOJ, Sept. 1, 1857; Woodruff, Sept. 1, 1857; Hamblin Journal, 1854–57, 81, in Hamblin Papers; Dimick B. Huntington, Voucher No. 28, Sept. 11, 1857, Superintendent's Vouchers, Superintendent of Indian Affairs Files, YOF; Elisha Hoopes, JDL1-BT 5:245–73; Nephi Johnson, JDL2-BT 1:45; Forney to Greenwood, Aug. 1859, in SDoc42, 76; Joe Pickyavit, account, in Beckwith, [119]; Willson G. Nowers, AJ1; Willson Gates Nowers, note to Andrew Jenson, AJ1; Philo T. Farnsworth, JDL1-BT 5:293.

41. Woodruff, Sept. 1, 16, 1857; Huntington, Sept. 1, 10, 1857; HOJ, Sept. 1, 1857; Hamblin Journal, 1854–57, 81–82, in Hamblin Papers; *Nuwuvi*,

72; Calder notation at the top of Lee to Young, Nov. 20, 1857, Incoming Correspondence, YOF; *Nuwuvi*, 8, 72, 86; Kane, Memorandum Book, 19–20; James McKnight, letter to the *Daily Wisconsin*, Aug. 10, 1858, printed in "Interesting Letter from Utah: The Mormon Exodus—The Indians," *Weekly Wisconsin*, Sept. 24, 1858, Historian's Office, Historical Scrapbook, 10:130, CHL.

42. Huntington, Sept. 1, 10, 1857; Hamblin Journal, 1854–57, 81–82, in Hamblin Papers; JH, Sept. 1, 1857. Identified as "Young-quick" in Calder notation at the top of Lee to Young, Nov. 20, 1857, Incoming Correspondence, YOF; also in Voucher No. 9, Sept. 30, 1857, Superintendent's Vouchers, Superintendent of Indian Affairs Files, YOF.

Index

Note: In this index *MMM* refers to Mountain Meadows Massacre, *MM* for Mountain Meadows, *BY* for Brigham Young, *JDL* for John D. Lee, and *GAS* for George A. Smith. Page numbers in bold face indicate an illustration.

Caldwell County, Missouri, 10, 92
California
  Bakers lived in, 78
  cattle industry, 75–76
  emigration to, in 1857, 75–76
  Fanchers lived in, 80
Cameron, Henry, 245
Cameron, Isom, 245
Cameron, James, 245
Cameron, Larkin, 245
Cameron, Martha, 245
Cameron, Martha (wife of William),
      81–82, 104, 244
Cameron, Nancy, 245
Cameron, Tillman, 82, 169, 245, 252
Cameron, William, 81–82, 104, 244, 252
Camp Floyd, Utah, 3–4
Campbell, Mary, 132, 134, 145
Campbell, Nancy Ann, 82–83, 85
Campbell, Peter, 82
Caravan Spring, Arkansas, 79, 315n38
Carey, William, 105
Carleton, James Henry, 2–5, 193
Carpenter, Helen, 87
Carroll County, Arkansas, 83
Carruth, LaJean Purcell, xii, 234
Carruthers, Matthew, 63
Carter, Kate, 337n8
Carthage Jail, Illinois, 14–15
Cartwright, Thomas H., 256
Cass, Lewis, 23
cattle
  BY's directive concerning, 63
  California industry, 75–76
  diseases, 121–23
  disposition of emigrant, 216
  drives, 75–76
  emigrant herd, 104, 161, 254, 388–89n1
  Indians given right to take emigrant,
      146–47
  killing of, at MM, 169
  poisoning accusation, 93
  prices, 254

problems in Utah, 90–91
range, **86**
scarce feed, 91
value, 253
cattle drovers, 76, 79–80
cattle herders, 80
Cedar City, Utah
  conditions, 129–30
  council meeting, 155–57
  emigrant incidents, 132–34
  emigrants' fate discussed at, 135–36
  emigrants reached, 132
  excited by approaching army, 131
  Female Benevolent Society,
      134–35, 181
  founded, 54–55
  GAS questions Haight at, 72
  GAS visited, 67–68
  Indian policy news reached, 137
  Indians recruited at, 145
  iron industry, 129
  massacre perpetrators from, 190
  militia, 190
  militia departs from, for MM, 181
  minute book, 337n8
  news of approaching emigrants, 131
  Pioneer Day, 131
  poisoning rumors reached, 132
  rebelled against BY's directive, 63
  reformation, 25
  surviving children at, 218–19
Chatterley, John, 136, 153
Cherokee Trail, 74–75
Cheyenne Indians, 47
Chick-eroo (Indian), 267
children, surviving emigrant, 216–17
Church of Jesus Christ of Latter-day
      Saints. *See* Mormon Church
City of Rocks, 94
Clark, John Wesley, 256
Clarke, N. S. (General), 3, 5
Clarksville, Arkansas, 82
Clewes, Joseph

Clewes, Joseph (*continued*)
arrived at Cedar City, 211–12
biography, 256
express ride to Pinto, 163–64
met Morris and Arthur, 210
ordered back to Cedar City, 192, 198
ordered to return to MM, 167
recruited as express rider, 162
shot at, 171–72
Coal Creek John. *See* Tau-gu (Coal Creek John)
Coal Creek, Utah, 55
Coker, Charity Porter, 245
Coker, Edward, 245
Coleman, Prime T., 256–57
Collins, Wilson, 105–6, 176
See also Turner-Dukes-Collins company
Columbia, California, 78
Comanche (Paiute Indian), 154, 267, 346–47n27
conformity, 127–28
consecrations, 24
Cooper, Abbey, 245
Cooper, William E., 245
Corn Creek, Utah
camping place, 116
emigrants camp at, **117**–18
Indian farm, 117
poisoning story, 119–21
Cottonwood Spring, 225
Cove Creek, Utah, 139
Crooked Creek Township, Arkansas, 77, 80–82
Cropper, Thomas, 112–13
Cumming, Alfred, 36, 38
Cummins, R. W., 9, 38
Cureton, William, 93
Curtis, Ezra H., 257

Dalton, Edward, 136, 167, 174, 177
Dame, William H.
accompanied GAS on tour, 67
angry at Haight, 212

argued with Haight about reporting MMM, 212–13
attack
did not approve, 156
JDL said, approved, 153
learned about, 166–67
learned of Cedar City role in, 174–75
Monday night council, 176
no role in planning, 144
Wednesday night councils, 175, 177–79
Beaver requests help from, 176
biography, 55–56, 257
drilled militia, 70
express message to, 68
Indians seen with, 222
indicted, 230
massacre
ordered killing emigrants, 179
saddened at carnage, 214
tried to stop, 211
met with Haight in Cedar City, 211
moved to Parowan, 63
opposed trading with emigrants, 125–26
permission to punish emigrants denied, 136
recalls flood, 125
war preparation, 72
went to MM, 212
wives and, **57**
Danites, 11
Davies, William R., 394n2
Daviess County, Missouri, 11
Davis, George W., 112, 119–20
Deseret Iron Company, 58, 133
Deseret, term, 22
Deshazo, Allen P., 245, 252
Devil's Gate, 74
Dickson, Robert, 257
diseases, livestock, 121–23
Dive, Verulam, 94
Dixie, land in southern Utah, 68

documentation, use, xv-xvi
Dominguez-Escalante expedition, 54
Douglas, Stephen A., 23, 27
dreams, 157–58
droughts, 35, 74, 91
drovers. *See* cattle drovers
Drummond, W. W., 21, 28–30, 41
Duck, W. B., 82
duels, 8
Dukes party, 175–76
 See also Turner-Dukes-Collins company
Dukes, William, 105–6, 176
Dunklin, Daniel, 10
Dunlap, America Jane, 246
Dunlap, Ellender, 245
Dunlap, Georgia Ann, 217, 219, 246
Dunlap, James D., 245
Dunlap, Jesse, Jr., 79, 104, 245, 252
Dunlap, John H., 246
Dunlap, Lorenzo Dow, 79, 104,
 246, 252
Dunlap, Louisa, 217, 245
Dunlap, Lucinda, 206–7, 245
Dunlap, Margarette, 245
Dunlap, Mary Ann (daughter of
 Jesse), 245
Dunlap, Mary Ann (daughter of
 Lorenzo), 246
Dunlap, Mary Wharton, 79, 104, 245
Dunlap, Nancy, 246
Dunlap, Nancy M., 245
Dunlap, Nancy Wharton, 79, 104, 246
Dunlap, Prudence Angeline, 217,
 219, 246
Dunlap, Rachel, 384n23
Dunlap, Rebecca Jane, 202, 205,
 217, 245
Dunlap, Ruth, 384n23
Dunlap, Sarah Elizabeth, 202, 205,
 208–9, 217, 246
Dunlap, Susannah, 206–7, 245
Dunlap, Talitha Emaline, 246
Dunlap, Thomas J., 246
Durfee, Jabez, 257

Dutchman
 escape of, reported, 164
 escaped being killed, 160
 identity, 111
 killed, 205
 term, 111
 troublesome, 110–12
 See also Gresly, John

Eaton, William M., 246
ecclesiastical abuse, xiv
Echo Canyon, Utah, 69
Edgerly, Thomas, 56
Edwards, Silas, 246, 252
Edwards, William, 191, 257, 354n37
Elang, Joseph, 393n2
emigrants
 ages, 104
 ambush place for, selected, 137–38, 141
 ammunition, 161, 196
 apostates join, 109–10
 begin journey, 82
 bury dead, 196
 BY said not to meddle with, 183–84
 Cedar City incidents, 132–34
 conflicts en route, 114
 confused identities, 106, 112
 Corn Creek, 118–19
 damaged crops, 94
 escaped from corral, 198, 224–25
 errors made by, xiv
 fate of, discussed, 135–36
 formed united company, 101, 103
 from Arkansas, 101
 from Missouri, 87–88, 101–2
 from Ohio, 82
 grazing disputes, 108, 110
 in Beaver, 123–24
 in Fillmore, 113
 in Payson, 109–10
 Indians to ambush, 137
 Indian incidents before Utah, 84–85
 killed at Leach's Spring, 167–68, 197
 leaders, 83

conflict with JDL and missionaries at, 65–66

established, 55

GAS preached at, 68

Indian missionaries move from, 67

Indians recruited at, 153

JDL released as presiding elder, 67

JDL returned to, 221

massacre perpetrators from, 190

militia, 190

ruins, **55**

surviving children at, 220

Fort Johnson, Utah, 155, 190

Fort Smith, Arkansas, 82

Fort Tejon, California, 3

forts, Mormon, 65

Freeman, Columbus R., 191, 257

Frémont, John C., 3, 18

Gemmell, James, 344n108

George (Paiute Indian), 267

Gilbert and Gerrish (firm), 91–92

Goodale, Tim, 47

government, Mormon attitude about, 22

grain

 caches, 69

 livestock needs, 91

 policy, 47–49, 53, 71, 91

grazing disputes, 108, 110

Great Basin, 18

Great Britain, conversion success in, 18

greed, as MMM motive, 132

Gresly family, 111

Gresly, Henry J., 111

Gresly, John, 111, 247

Groves, Elisha H., 204, 220

Gunnison, John W., 20–22, 28, 97, 117

gunpowder, 91

Haight, Eliza Ann Snyder, 217

Haight, Isaac C.

 accompanied GAS on southern tour, 68

 angry at Dame, 212

argued with Dame about reporting MMM, 212–13

at Cedar City council meeting, 155

attack

 ambush place selected, 137–38

 ambush plan, 139

 claimed little knowledge about, 167

 decided to halt, 157

 enlisted help of Nephi Johnson, 164–65

 express letter sent to BY, 163

 faced two options, 174

 initial plan, 137

 learned of, 162, 164

 plan to, put in motion by, 140

 planned with JDL, 144

 recruited JDL to manage, 142–43

 regretted killing emigrants, 178

 sent dispatch to JDL, 164

 sent men to MM, 167

 sent Riddle home, 168

biography, 57–**59**, 257

conversation with GAS, 70–71

emigrants confronted, 133

fighting spirit, 72

home, 67, 130–31

hosted GAS, 67

Indians recruited by, 145, 265

Indians seen with, 222

indicted, 230

JDL implicated, 229–30

JDL rescued, 139–40

law enforcer, 131

massacre

 called out militia, 179

 enjoined, participants to secrecy, 216

 ordered Nephi Johnson to report to MM, 180–81

 possibly sent men to halt, 210–12

 received permission to use militia, 179

 saddened at carnage, 214

meets with Dame in late-night Parowan councils, 174–75, 178–79

militia officer, 190

Morris, John, 134, 155
Morse, Gilbert, 153, 207
Mountain Meadows
  description, 3
  emigrants arrived at, 149–51
  eroded land, 229
  execution party reached, 229
  GAS traveled through, 70
  Hamblin got herding rights at, 149
  Hamblin recommended, to emigrants,
    119
  map, **130**
  Rim of the Basin, 192, 199, 365n101
  selected as execution place, 228
  siege site, **150**
  spring, 70
  Tanner-Mathews company at, 222–23
Mountain Meadows Massacre
  approaches to writing about, xii-xiv
  attacks
    Aden killed, 160
    Dame got news of, 166–67
    Dame investigated, 167
    militia help requested, 173
    Monday morning, 158–59
    reported to Haight, 164
    siege site, **150**
    standoff, 172
    suspended after Tuesday, 170
    Tuesday morning, 168–69
    Tuesday night, 169–70
    wagons circled, 161
  bodies disinterred by scavengers,
    214–15
  burial areas, 214
  characteristics of participants, 191
  escape corral, 198, 224–25
  goal in writing book about, x
  histories, xv
  illustration, **215**
  impact and interest in, ix-x
  insights into why it happened, xiii-xiv
  killing
    buried bodies, 214–15

carnage, 205
command given to begin, 199
Dame's orders, 179, 187
Indian/white role in, 204
leaders strategize, 187, 189
line of procession, 197–99
long wait, 197
men killed before, 197–98
men leave corral, 197
men slaughtered, 200–201
militia approach corral, 193–94
militia informed about plans, 190
militia instructed, 191
militia mustered, 179–80
Mormon hesitance, 199
number of Indians, 192–93
number of Mormons, 193
number slain, ix
rescue terms, 194
sinister plan, 199
to destroy all but small children, 187
wagons leave corral, 197
wagons loaded, 196–97
women and children slaughtered,
  201–4
limitations in understanding, xiv-xv
looting, 207–8
map, aerial, **188**
memorials
  1859 Carleton monument, 4–5
  1990 commemoration, x
motives
  Daniel H. Wells mentioned, 114
  Haight-JDL meeting, 144
  Parley Pratt's murder, 32
  Philetus Warn listed, 114
  poisoning, 124
  plunder, 132
no justification for, xiii
perpetrators, 128
plans
  ambush site changed, 157
  attempt to halt attack, 157
  discussed in Parowan, 179

initial ambush, 137–39
responsibility for crime, 144
portrayed as Indian atrocity, 215–16
questions concerning, ix
rationalizations after, 115, 132
reporting, to authorities, 212–13
search for sources, x-xi
secrecy about, 216
siege site, **150**
skeletal remains, 3–5
survivors
children, 208–9, 216–21
descendants, x
tragic victims, 209
trial testimonies, xv
writings about, xv
The Mountain Meadows Massacre
(book), xiii
Muddy River, 119
mules, 91, 253
murder, innocent blood, 135
Myack (Paiute Indian), 268

Nauvoo Expositor (newspaper), 13, 57
Nauvoo, Illinois, 13–14, 16
Nauvoo Legion
Illinois, 13
Utah militia, 38
drills, 52, 68, 70
guard duty, 69
war preparation, 47–48, 131
See also Iron Military District
Nebeker, George, 110
Nelson, Peter, 180
Nelson, William, 227–29
Nephi, Utah, 110
newspapers
anti-Mormon campaign, 28–30, 41
public reading, 30
Non-cap-in (Indian), 268
non-Mormons, conflict with Mormons,
21–22
North Willow Creek, Utah, 94
northern route to California, 50, 120

Northwest Ordinance of 1787, 23
Nowers, Willson Gates, 125
Nowlin, Jabus, 393n2

Ogden Hole, Utah, 96
Ohio, emigrants from, 82
Oregon-California Trail, 74–75
overland travel
BY threatened to impede, 98–99
described, 83–85
ox poisoning story, 119–21
oxen, values, 254

Pacific Springs, 86
Pahvant Indians
Ammon's influence with, 177–78
angered, 175
at Corn Creek, 116
attacked Turner company, 175
kill Gunnison, 20, 22
trade with emigrants, 120
Paiute Indians
allied with Mormons, 64
attack
ambush place selected, 137–39, 141
angered at JDL, 169
initial plans for, 137
killed, 168–69
Monday morning, 158–59
plans for, 143–44
recruited for, 141, 145, 147–48, 152
standoff, 173
took emigrant cattle, 161
impoverished, 64
JDL farmer to, 66
massacre
agreed to kill emigrants, 187
blamed for, 173, 209, 215–16
felt cheated by Mormons, 208
killed emigrants, 204
looted bodies, 207–8
number of participants, 192–93
participant biographies, 265–69
prepared for, 190, 192

EMIGRANT TRAIL FROM ARKANSAS

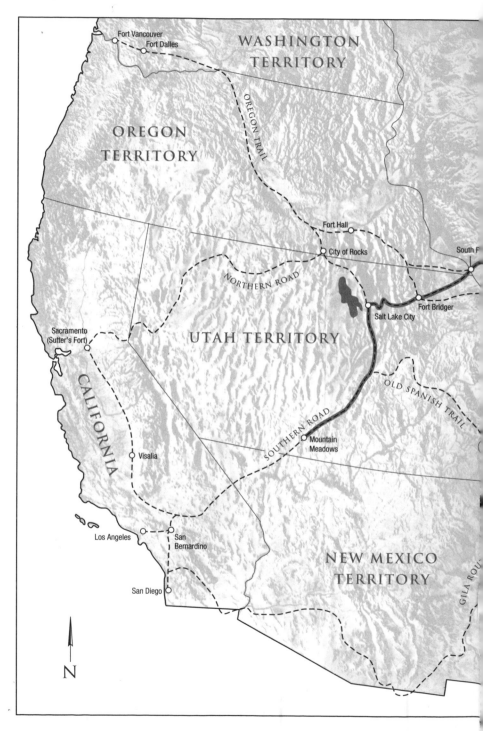

Fort Vancouver
Fort Dalles

WASHINGTON
TERRITORY

OREGON
TERRITORY

OREGON TRAIL

Fort Hall

City of Rocks

South P

NORTHERN ROAD

Sacramento
(Sutter's Fort)

UTAH TERRITORY

Salt Lake City

Fort Bridger

OLD SPANISH TRAIL

CALIFORNIA

SOUTHERN ROAD

Mountain
Meadows

Visalia

Los Angeles

San
Bernardino

San Diego

NEW MEXICO
TERRITORY

GILA ROU

N